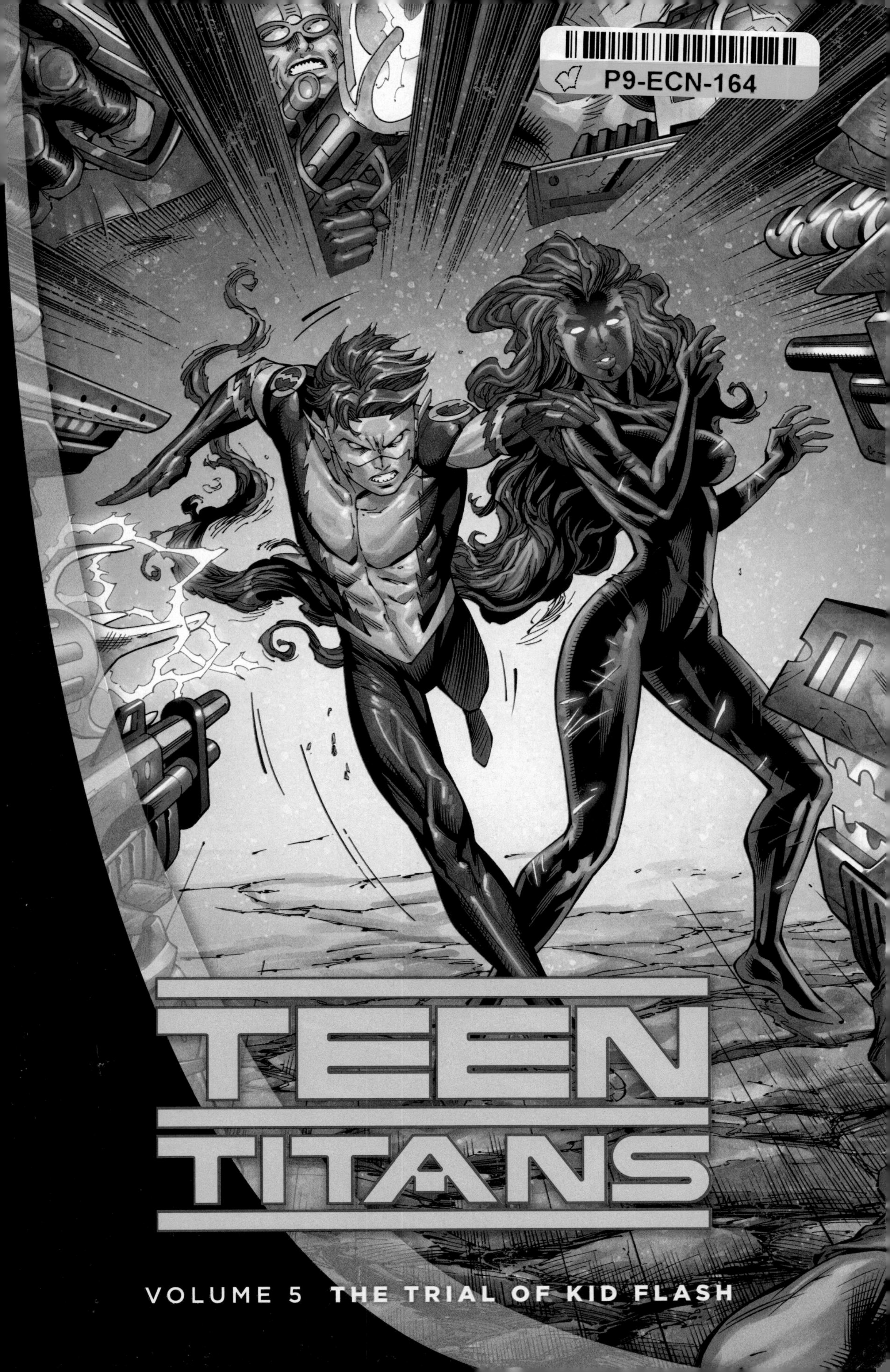

TEEN TITANS

VOLUME 5 **THE TRIAL OF KID FLASH**

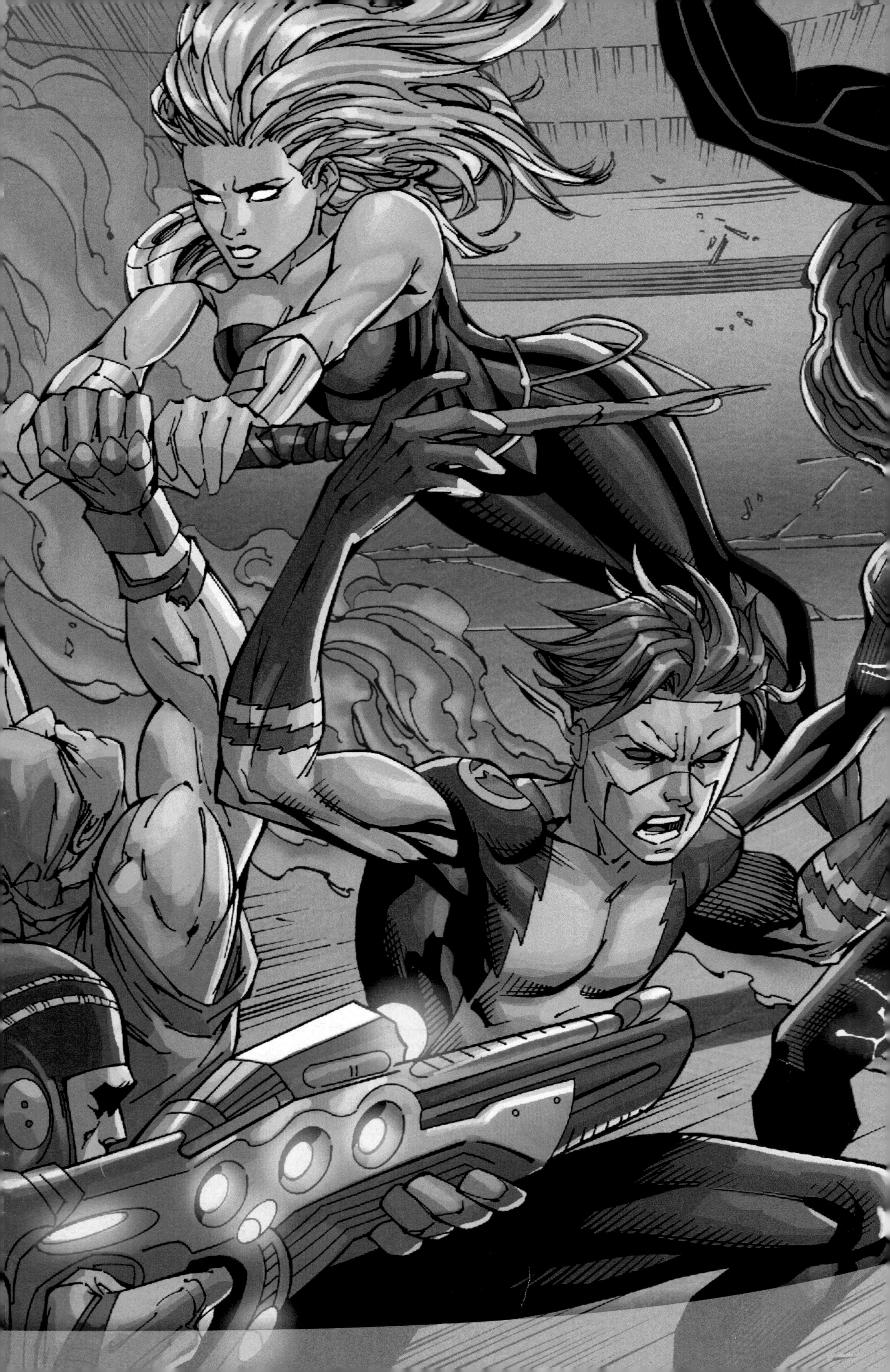

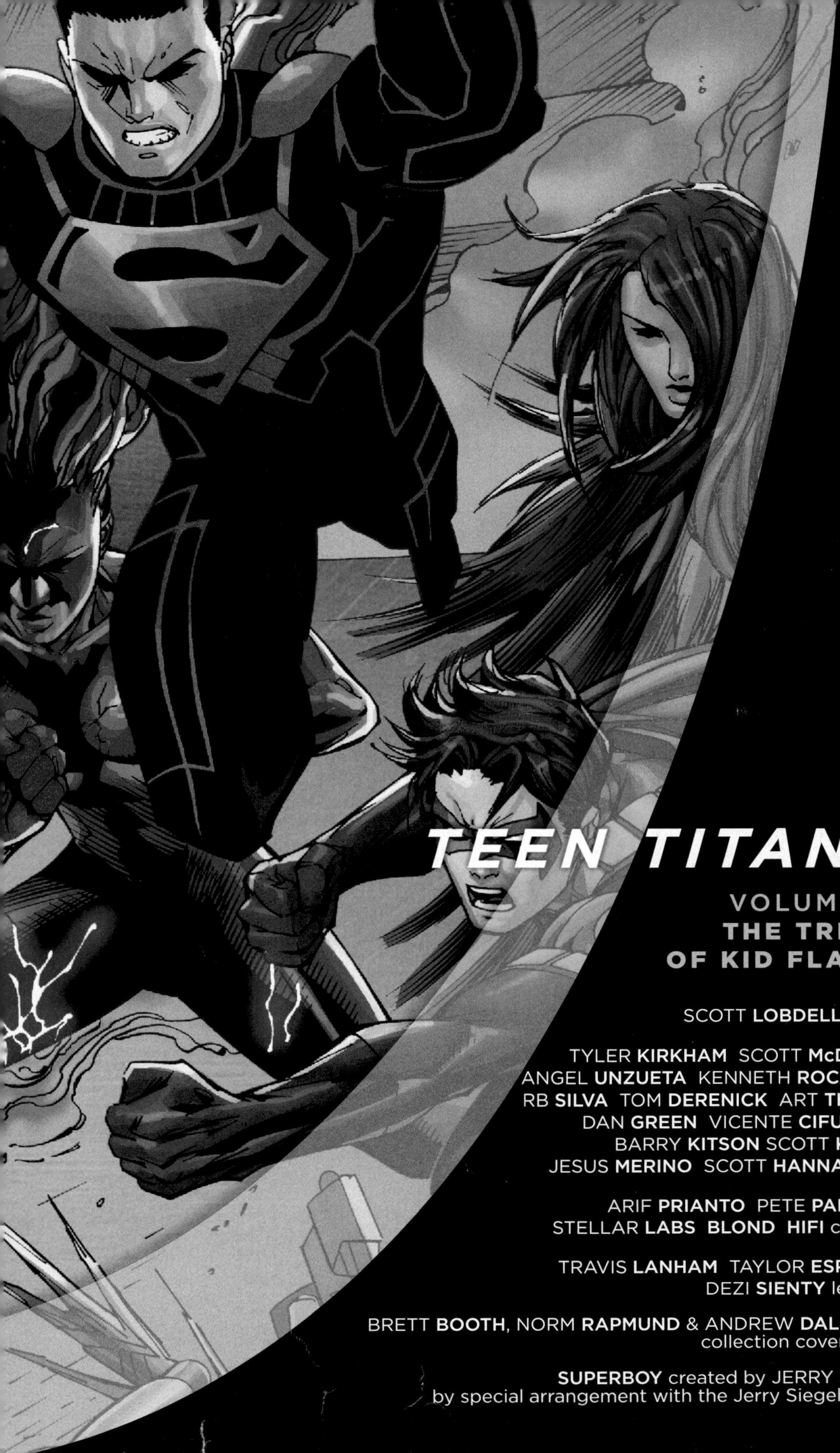

TEEN TITANS

VOLUME 5
THE TRIAL OF KID FLASH

SCOTT **LOBDELL** writer

TYLER **KIRKHAM** SCOTT **McDANIEL**
ANGEL **UNZUETA** KENNETH **ROCAFORT**
RB **SILVA** TOM **DERENICK** ART **THIBERT**
DAN **GREEN** VICENTE **CIFUENTES**
BARRY **KITSON** SCOTT **KOLINS**
JESUS **MERINO** SCOTT **HANNA** artists

ARIF **PRIANTO** PETE **PANTAZIS**
STELLAR **LABS** **BLOND** **HIFI** colorists

TRAVIS **LANHAM** TAYLOR **ESPOSITO**
DEZI **SIENTY** letterers

BRETT **BOOTH**, NORM **RAPMUND** & ANDREW **DALHOUSE**
collection cover artists

SUPERBOY created by JERRY **SIEGEL**
by special arrangement with the Jerry Siegel Family

MIKE COTTON Editor – Original Series
ANTHONY MARQUES Assistant Editor – Original Series JEREMY BENT Editor
ROBBIN BROSTERMAN Design Director – Books ROBBIE BIEDERMAN Publication Design

BOB HARRAS Senior VP – Editor-in-Chief, DC Comics

DIANE NELSON President DAN DIDIO and JIM LEE Co-Publishers GEOFF JOHNS Chief Creative Officer
AMIT DESAI Senior VP – Marketing and Franchise Management
AMY GENKINS Senior VP – Business and Legal Affairs NAIRI GARDINER Senior VP – Finance
JEFF BOISON VP – Publishing Planning MARK CHIARELLO VP – Art Direction and Design
JOHN CUNNINGHAM VP – Marketing TERRI CUNNINGHAM VP – Editorial Administration
LARRY GANEM VP – Talent Relations and Services ALISON GILL Senior VP – Manufacturing and Operations
HANK KANALZ Senior VP – Vertigo and Integrated Publishing JAY KOGAN VP – Business and Legal Affairs, Publishing
JACK MAHAN VP – Business Affairs, Talent NICK NAPOLITANO VP – Manufacturing Administration SUE POHJA VP – Book Sales
FRED RUIZ VP – Manufacturing Operations COURTNEY SIMMONS Senior VP – Publicity BOB WAYNE Senior VP – Sales

TEEN TITANS VOLUME 5: THE TRIAL OF KID FLASH

DC Comics, 1700 Broadway, New York, NY 10019
A Warner Bros. Entertainment Company.
Printed by RR Donnelley, Owensville, MO, USA. 1/2/15. First Printing.

ISBN: 978-1-4012-5053-9

Library of Congress Cataloging-in-Publication Data

Lobdell, Scott, author.
Teen Titans. Volume 5, The Trial of Kid Flash / Scott Lobdell, Tyler Kirkham.
pages cm. — (The New 52!)
ISBN 978-1-4012-5053-9 (paperback)
1. Graphic novels. I. Kirkham, Tyler illustrator. II. Title. III. Title: The Trial of Kid Flash.
PN6728.T34L66 2014
741.5'973—dc23
2014010812

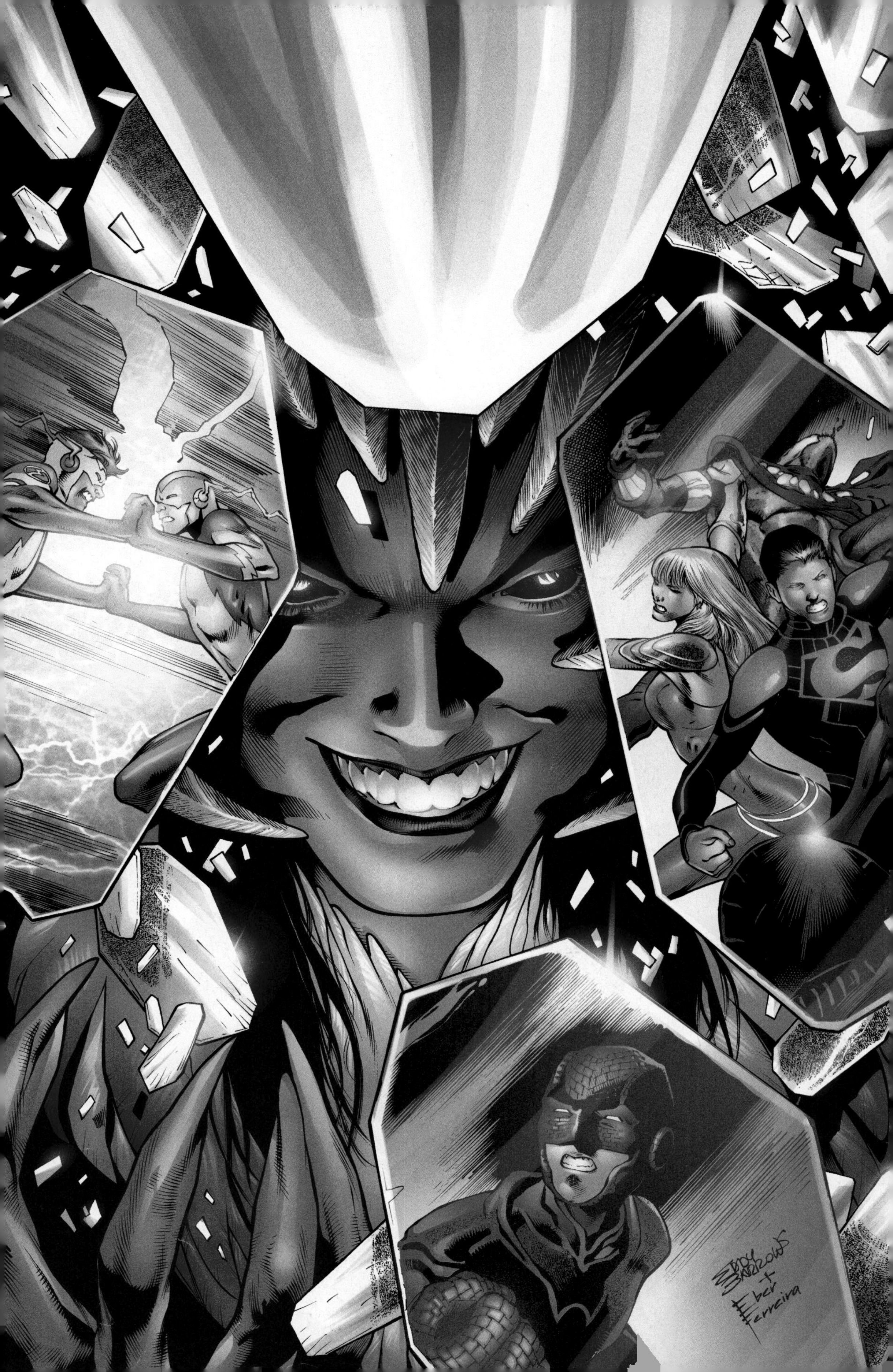

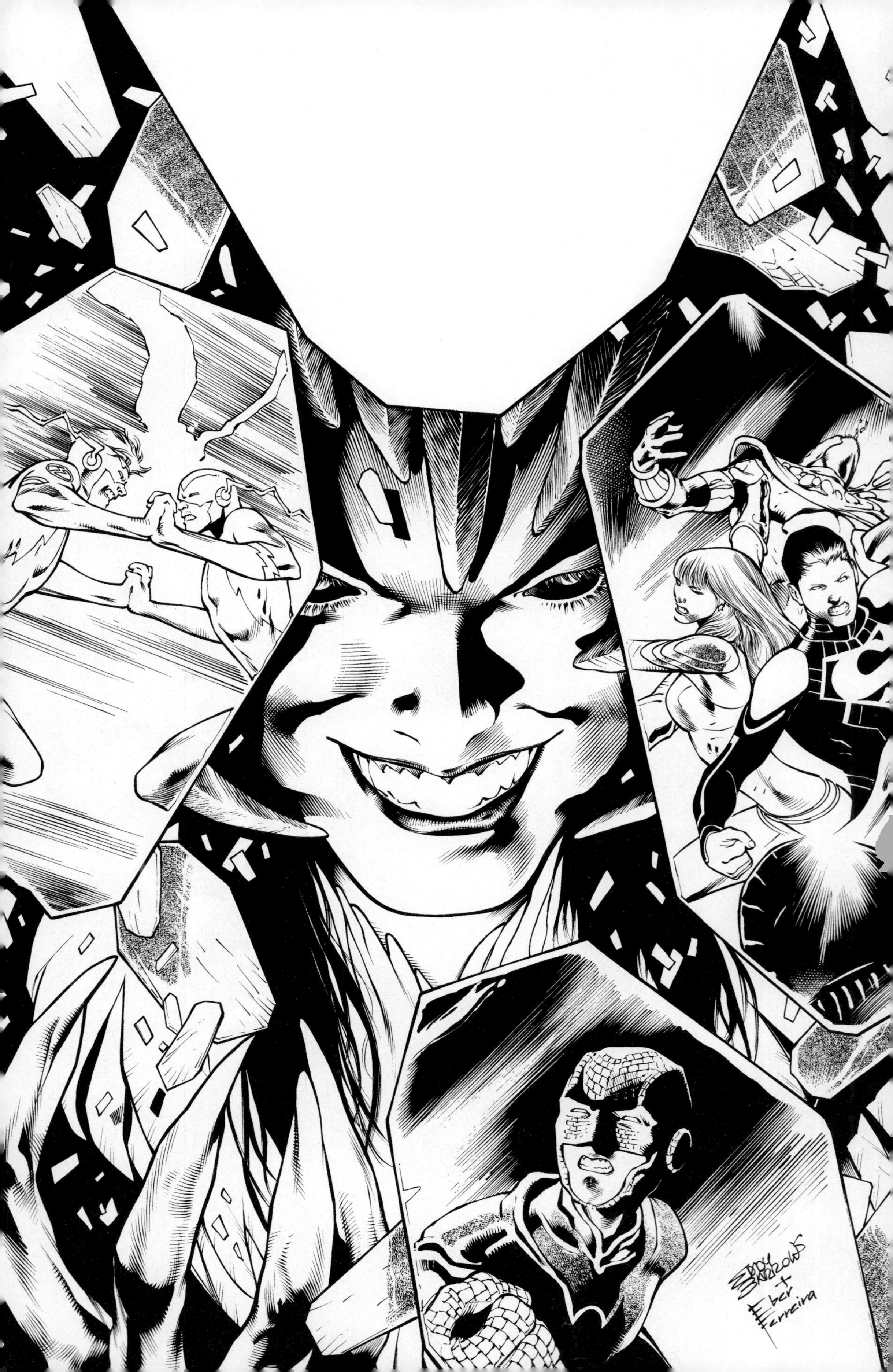
EDDY BARROWS
+
Eber Ferreira

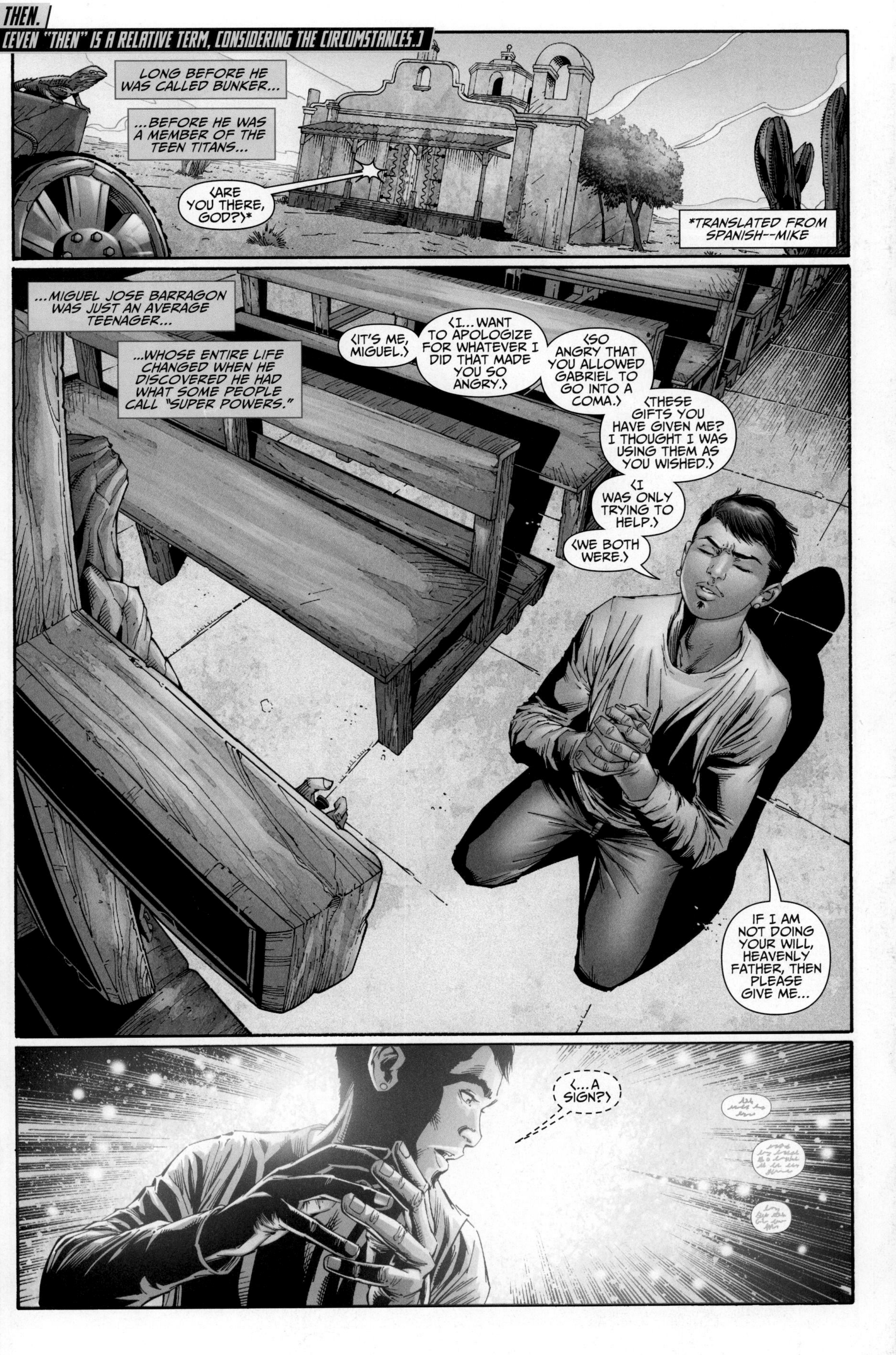
THEN.
(EVEN "THEN" IS A RELATIVE TERM, CONSIDERING THE CIRCUMSTANCES.)
LONG BEFORE HE WAS CALLED BUNKER...
...BEFORE HE WAS A MEMBER OF THE TEEN TITANS...
‹ARE YOU THERE, GOD?›*
*TRANSLATED FROM SPANISH--MIKE
...MIGUEL JOSE BARRAGON WAS JUST AN AVERAGE TEENAGER...
...WHOSE ENTIRE LIFE CHANGED WHEN HE DISCOVERED HE HAD WHAT SOME PEOPLE CALL "SUPER POWERS."
‹IT'S ME, MIGUEL.›
‹I...WANT TO APOLOGIZE FOR WHATEVER I DID THAT MADE YOU SO ANGRY.›
‹SO ANGRY THAT YOU ALLOWED GABRIEL TO GO INTO A COMA.›
‹THESE GIFTS YOU HAVE GIVEN ME? I THOUGHT I WAS USING THEM AS YOU WISHED.›
‹I WAS ONLY TRYING TO HELP.›
‹WE BOTH WERE.›
IF I AM NOT DOING YOUR WILL, HEAVENLY FATHER, THEN PLEASE GIVE ME...
‹...A SIGN?›

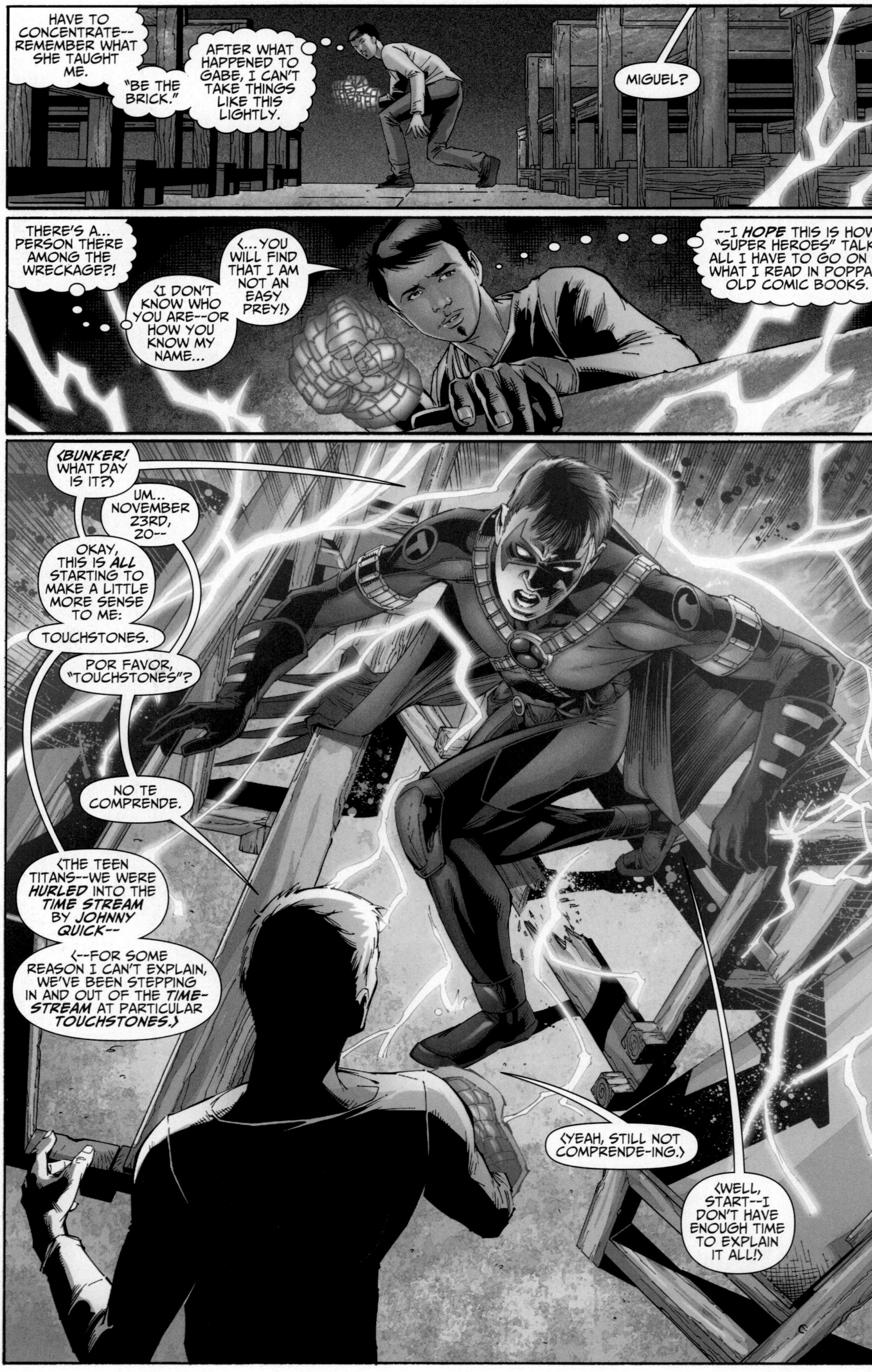
HAVE TO CONCENTRATE--REMEMBER WHAT SHE TAUGHT ME.
"BE THE BRICK."
AFTER WHAT HAPPENED TO GABE, I CAN'T TAKE THINGS LIKE THIS LIGHTLY.
MIGUEL?
THERE'S A... PERSON THERE AMONG THE WRECKAGE?!
‹I DON'T KNOW WHO YOU ARE--OR HOW YOU KNOW MY NAME...
‹...YOU WILL FIND THAT I AM NOT AN EASY PREY!›
--I HOPE THIS IS HOW "SUPER HEROES" TALK. ALL I HAVE TO GO ON IS WHAT I READ IN POPPA'S OLD COMIC BOOKS.
‹BUNKER! WHAT DAY IS IT?›
UM... NOVEMBER 23RD, 20--
OKAY, THIS IS ALL STARTING TO MAKE A LITTLE MORE SENSE TO ME:
TOUCHSTONES.
POR FAVOR, "TOUCHSTONES"?
NO TE COMPRENDE.
‹THE TEEN TITANS--WE WERE HURLED INTO THE TIME STREAM BY JOHNNY QUICK--
‹--FOR SOME REASON I CAN'T EXPLAIN, WE'VE BEEN STEPPING IN AND OUT OF THE TIME-STREAM AT PARTICULAR TOUCHSTONES.›
‹YEAH, STILL NOT COMPRENDE-ING.›
‹WELL, START--I DON'T HAVE ENOUGH TIME TO EXPLAIN IT ALL!›

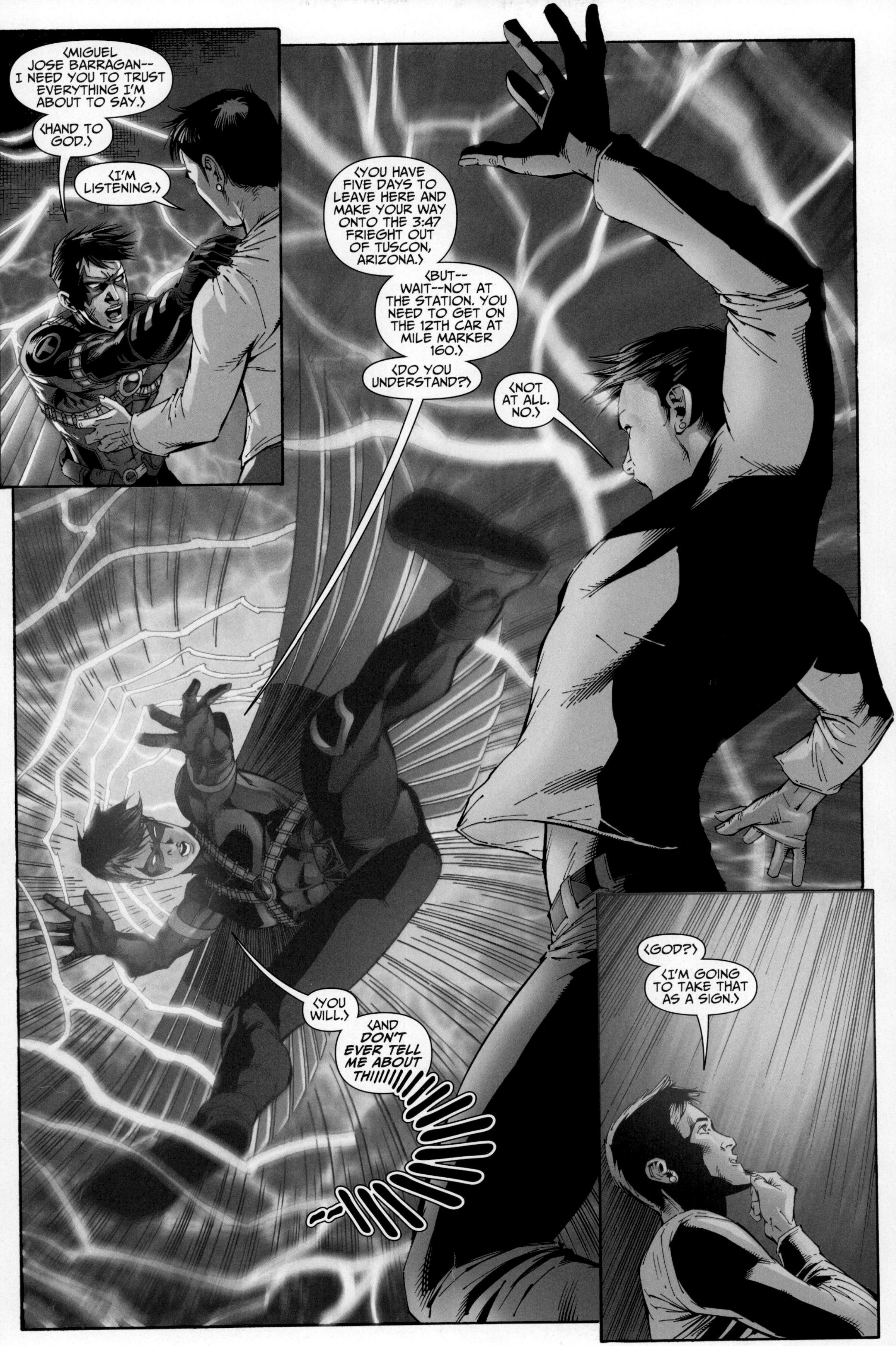

<MIGUEL JOSE BARRAGAN-- I NEED YOU TO TRUST EVERYTHING I'M ABOUT TO SAY.>
<HAND TO GOD.>
<I'M LISTENING.>
<YOU HAVE FIVE DAYS TO LEAVE HERE AND MAKE YOUR WAY ONTO THE 3:47 FRIEGHT OUT OF TUSCON, ARIZONA.>
<BUT-- WAIT--NOT AT THE STATION. YOU NEED TO GET ON THE 12TH CAR AT MILE MARKER 160.>
<DO YOU UNDERSTAND?>
<NOT AT ALL. NO.>
<YOU WILL.>
<AND DON'T EVER TELL ME ABOUT THI!!!!!!-->
<GOD?>
<I'M GOING TO TAKE THAT AS A SIGN.>

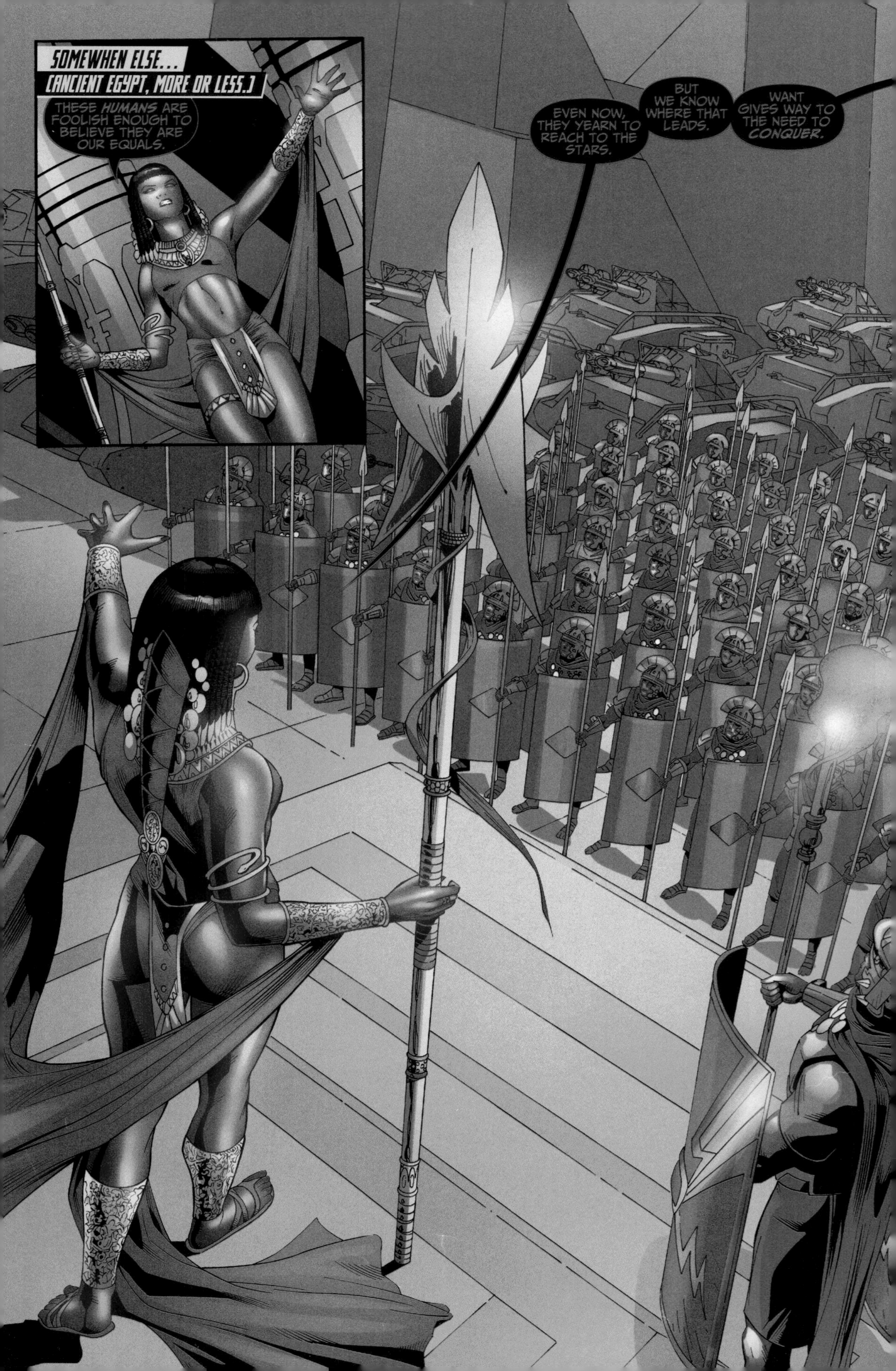
SOMEWHEN ELSE...
[ANCIENT EGYPT, MORE OR LESS.]
THESE *HUMANS* ARE FOOLISH ENOUGH TO BELIEVE THEY ARE OUR EQUALS.
EVEN NOW, THEY YEARN TO REACH TO THE STARS.
BUT WE KNOW WHERE THAT LEADS.
WANT GIVES WAY TO THE NEED TO *CONQUER*.

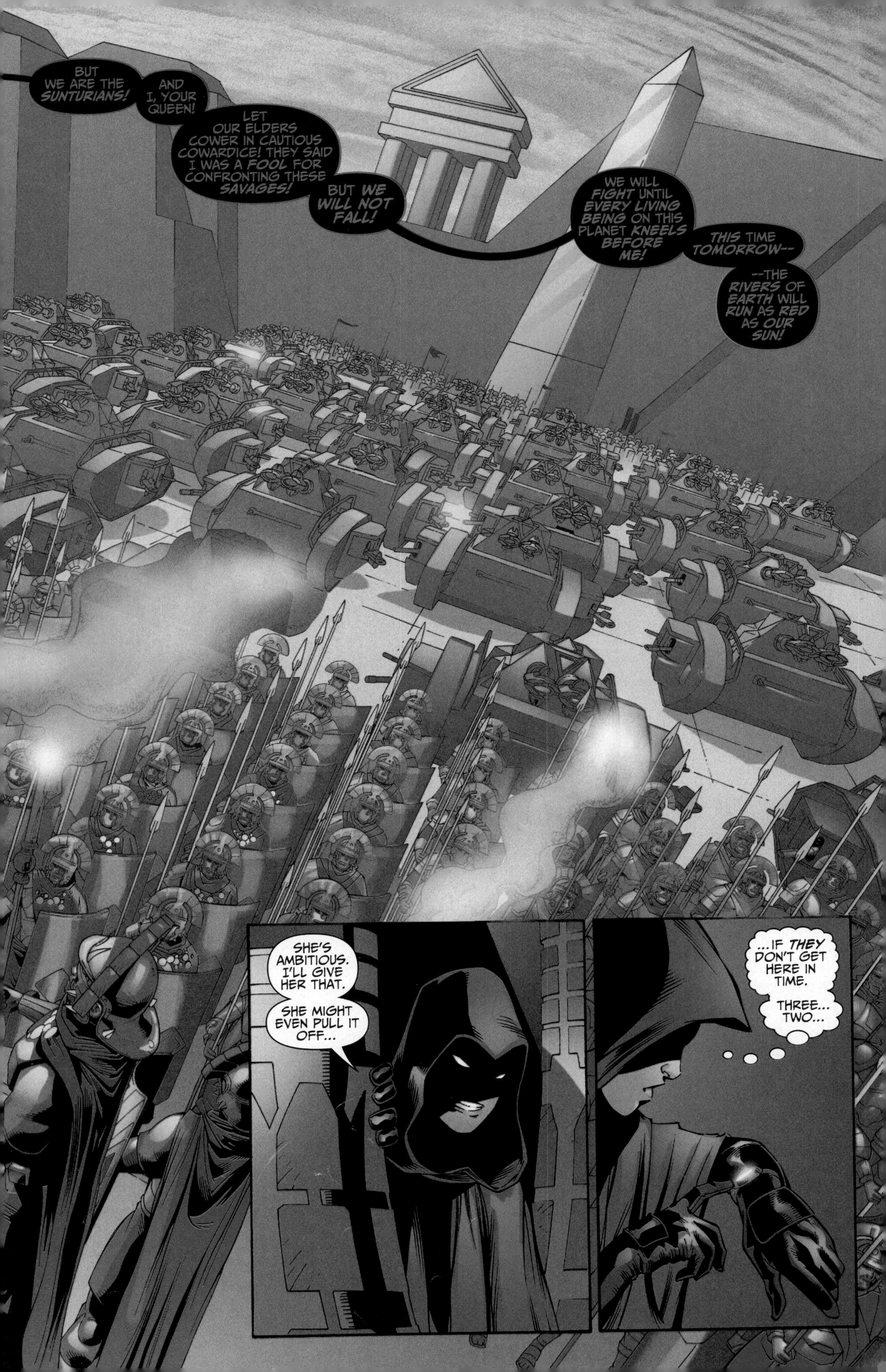

BUT WE ARE THE SUNTURIANS!
AND I, YOUR QUEEN!
LET OUR ELDERS COWER IN CAUTIOUS COWARDICE! THEY SAID I WAS A FOOL FOR CONFRONTING THESE SAVAGES!
BUT WE WILL NOT FALL!
WE WILL FIGHT UNTIL EVERY LIVING BEING ON THIS PLANET KNEELS BEFORE ME!
THIS TIME TOMORROW--
--THE RIVERS OF EARTH WILL RUN AS RED AS OUR SUN!
SHE'S AMBITIOUS. I'LL GIVE HER THAT.
SHE MIGHT EVEN PULL IT OFF...
...IF THEY DON'T GET HERE IN TIME.
THREE... TWO...

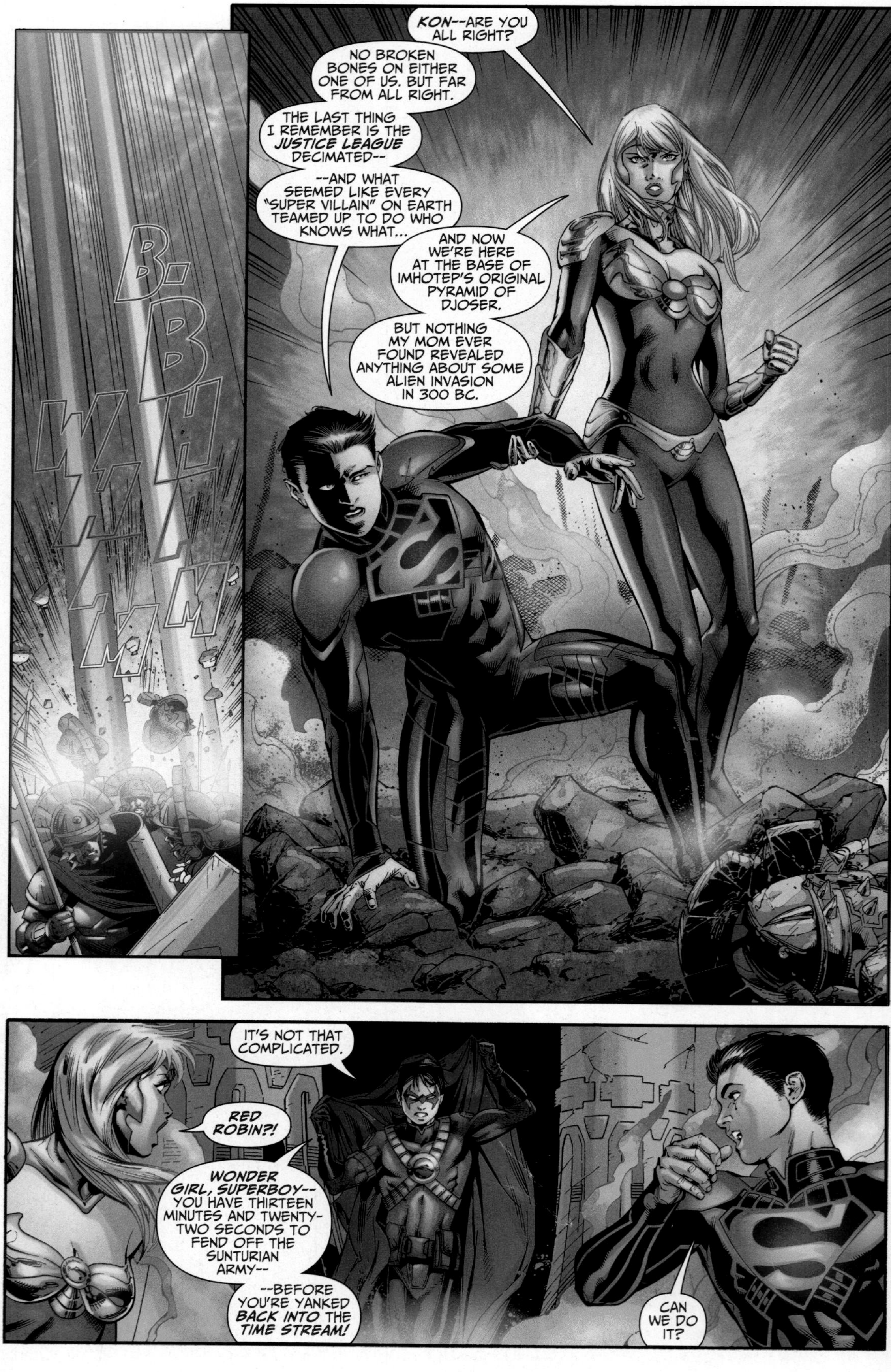
B-B-B-BHHM
WHHMMM
KON--ARE YOU ALL RIGHT?
NO BROKEN BONES ON EITHER ONE OF US. BUT FAR FROM ALL RIGHT.
THE LAST THING I REMEMBER IS THE JUSTICE LEAGUE DECIMATED--
--AND WHAT SEEMED LIKE EVERY "SUPER VILLAIN" ON EARTH TEAMED UP TO DO WHO KNOWS WHAT...
AND NOW WE'RE HERE AT THE BASE OF IMHOTEP'S ORIGINAL PYRAMID OF DJOSER.
BUT NOTHING MY MOM EVER FOUND REVEALED ANYTHING ABOUT SOME ALIEN INVASION IN 300 BC.
IT'S NOT THAT COMPLICATED.
RED ROBIN?!
WONDER GIRL, SUPERBOY-- YOU HAVE THIRTEEN MINUTES AND TWENTY-TWO SECONDS TO FEND OFF THE SUNTURIAN ARMY--
--BEFORE YOU'RE YANKED BACK INTO THE TIME STREAM!
CAN WE DO IT?

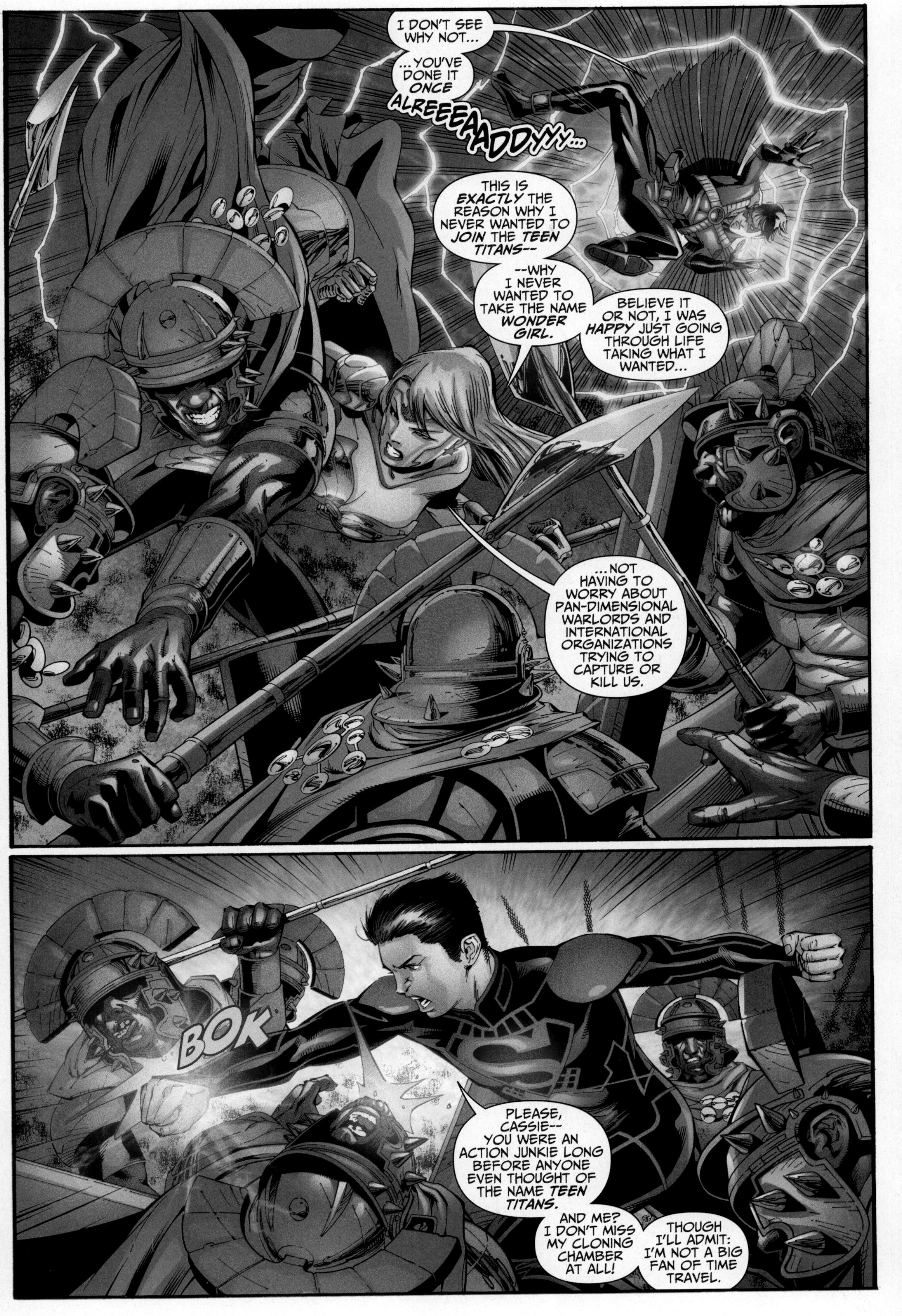
I DON'T SEE WHY NOT...
...YOU'VE DONE IT ONCE ALREEEEAADDYYY...
THIS IS EXACTLY THE REASON WHY I NEVER WANTED TO JOIN THE TEEN TITANS--
--WHY I NEVER WANTED TO TAKE THE NAME WONDER GIRL.
BELIEVE IT OR NOT, I WAS HAPPY JUST GOING THROUGH LIFE TAKING WHAT I WANTED...
...NOT HAVING TO WORRY ABOUT PAN-DIMENSIONAL WARLORDS AND INTERNATIONAL ORGANIZATIONS TRYING TO CAPTURE OR KILL US.
BOK
PLEASE, CASSIE-- YOU WERE AN ACTION JUNKIE LONG BEFORE ANYONE EVEN THOUGHT OF THE NAME TEEN TITANS.
AND ME? I DON'T MISS MY CLONING CHAMBER AT ALL!
THOUGH I'LL ADMIT: I'M NOT A BIG FAN OF TIME TRAVEL.

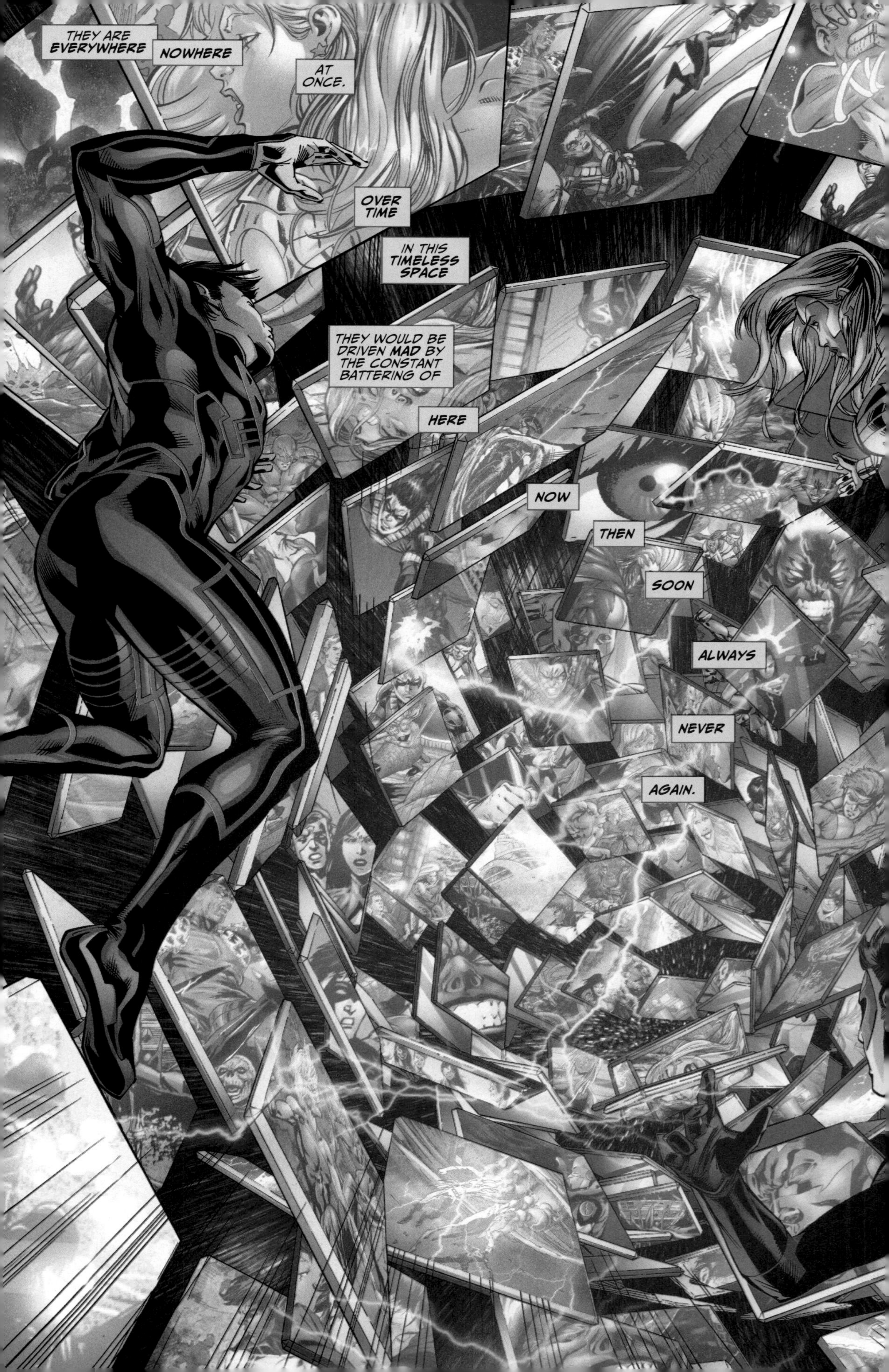
THEY ARE EVERYWHERE
NOWHERE
AT ONCE.
OVER TIME
IN THIS TIMELESS SPACE
THEY WOULD BE DRIVEN MAD BY THE CONSTANT BATTERING OF
HERE
NOW
THEN
SOON
ALWAYS
NEVER
AGAIN.

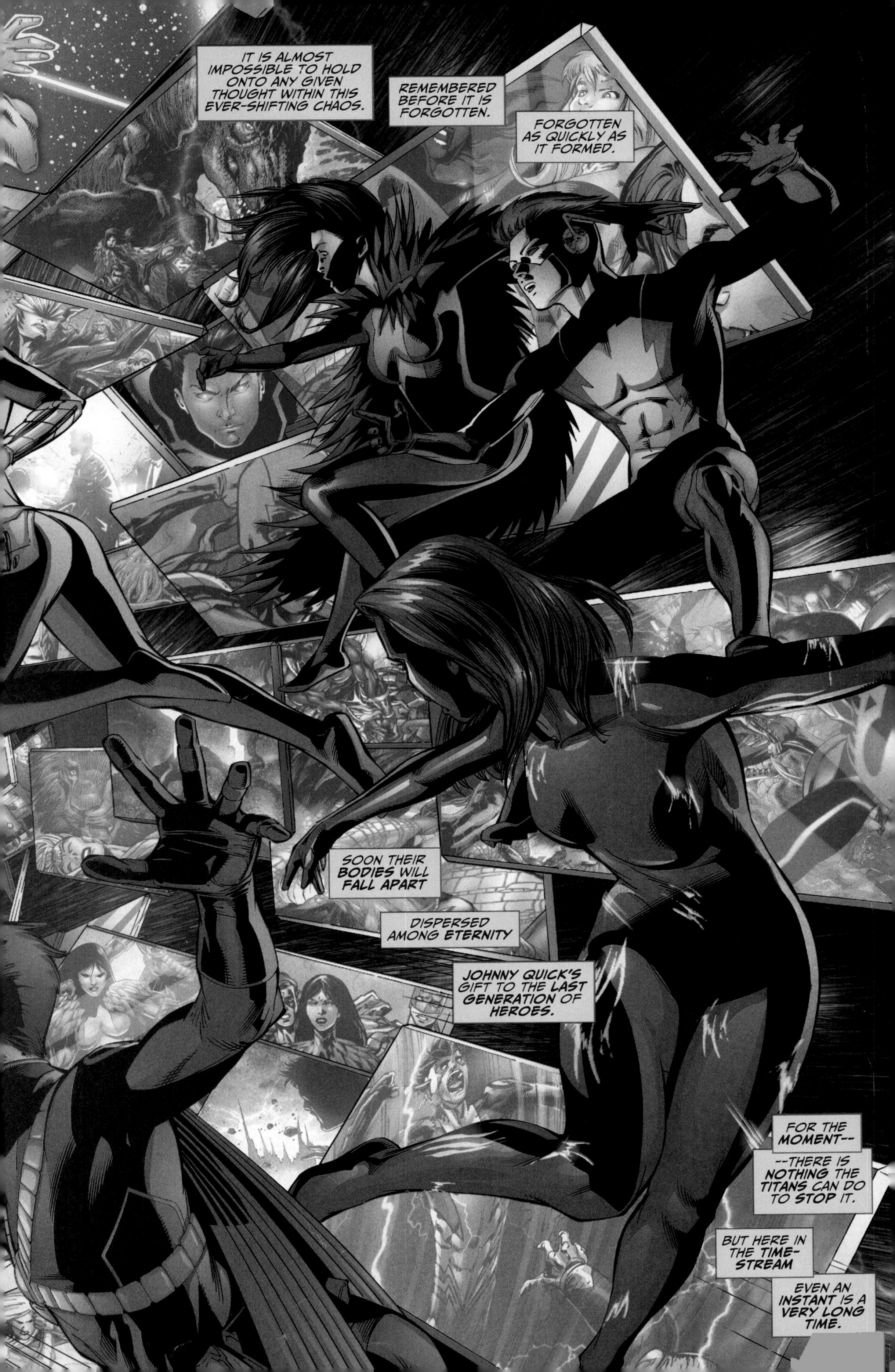
IT IS ALMOST IMPOSSIBLE TO HOLD ONTO ANY GIVEN THOUGHT WITHIN THIS EVER-SHIFTING CHAOS.
REMEMBERED BEFORE IT IS FORGOTTEN.
FORGOTTEN AS QUICKLY AS IT FORMED.
SOON THEIR BODIES WILL FALL APART
DISPERSED AMONG ETERNITY
JOHNNY QUICK'S GIFT TO THE LAST GENERATION OF HEROES.
FOR THE MOMENT--
--THERE IS NOTHING THE TITANS CAN DO TO STOP IT.
BUT HERE IN THE TIME-STREAM
EVEN AN INSTANT IS A VERY LONG TIME.

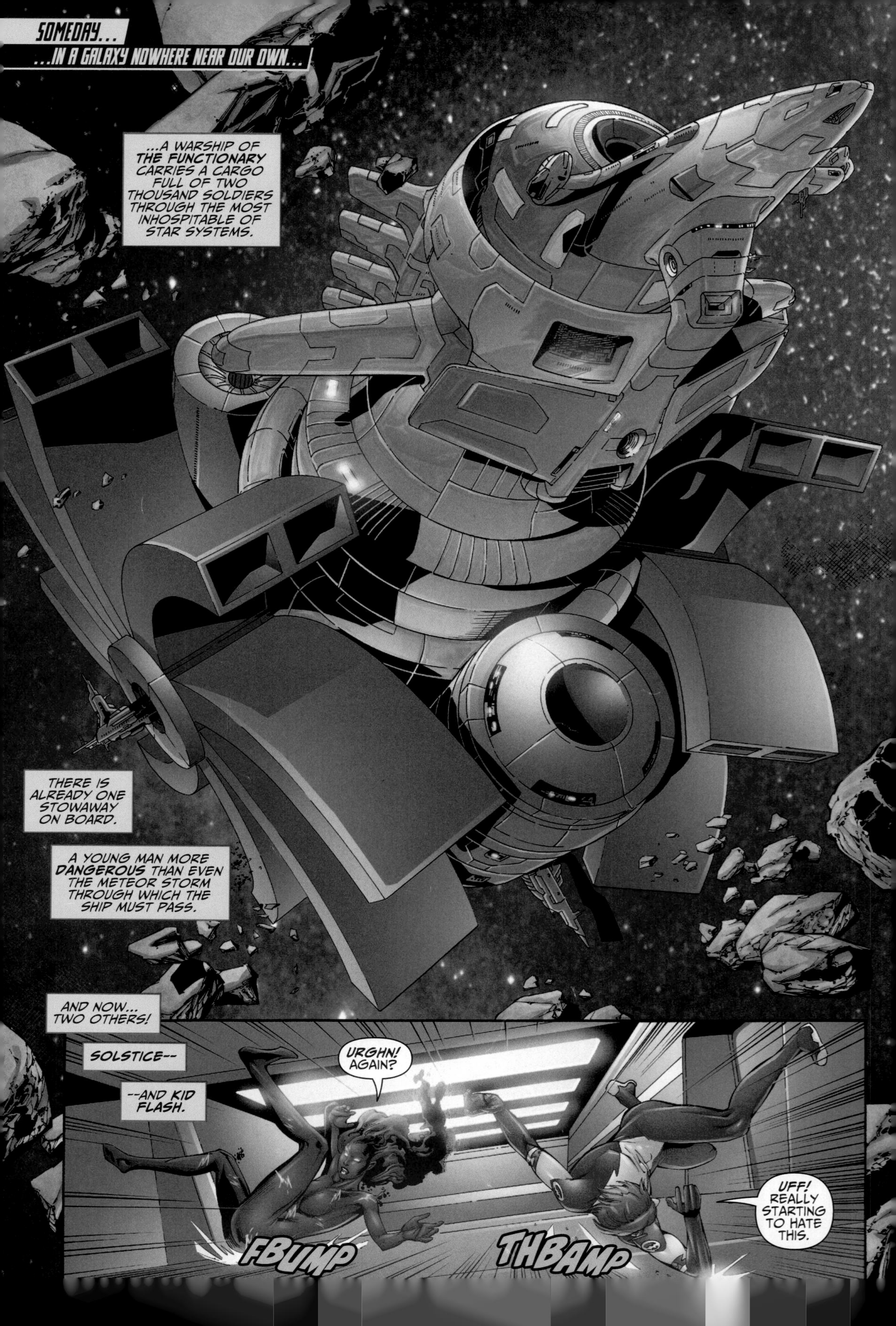
SOMEDAY...
...IN A GALAXY NOWHERE NEAR OUR OWN...
...A WARSHIP OF THE FUNCTIONARY CARRIES A CARGO FULL OF TWO THOUSAND SOLDIERS THROUGH THE MOST INHOSPITABLE OF STAR SYSTEMS.
THERE IS ALREADY ONE STOWAWAY ON BOARD.
A YOUNG MAN MORE DANGEROUS THAN EVEN THE METEOR STORM THROUGH WHICH THE SHIP MUST PASS.
AND NOW... TWO OTHERS!
SOLSTICE--
--AND KID FLASH.
URGHN! AGAIN?
UFF! REALLY STARTING TO HATE THIS.
FBUMP
THBAMP

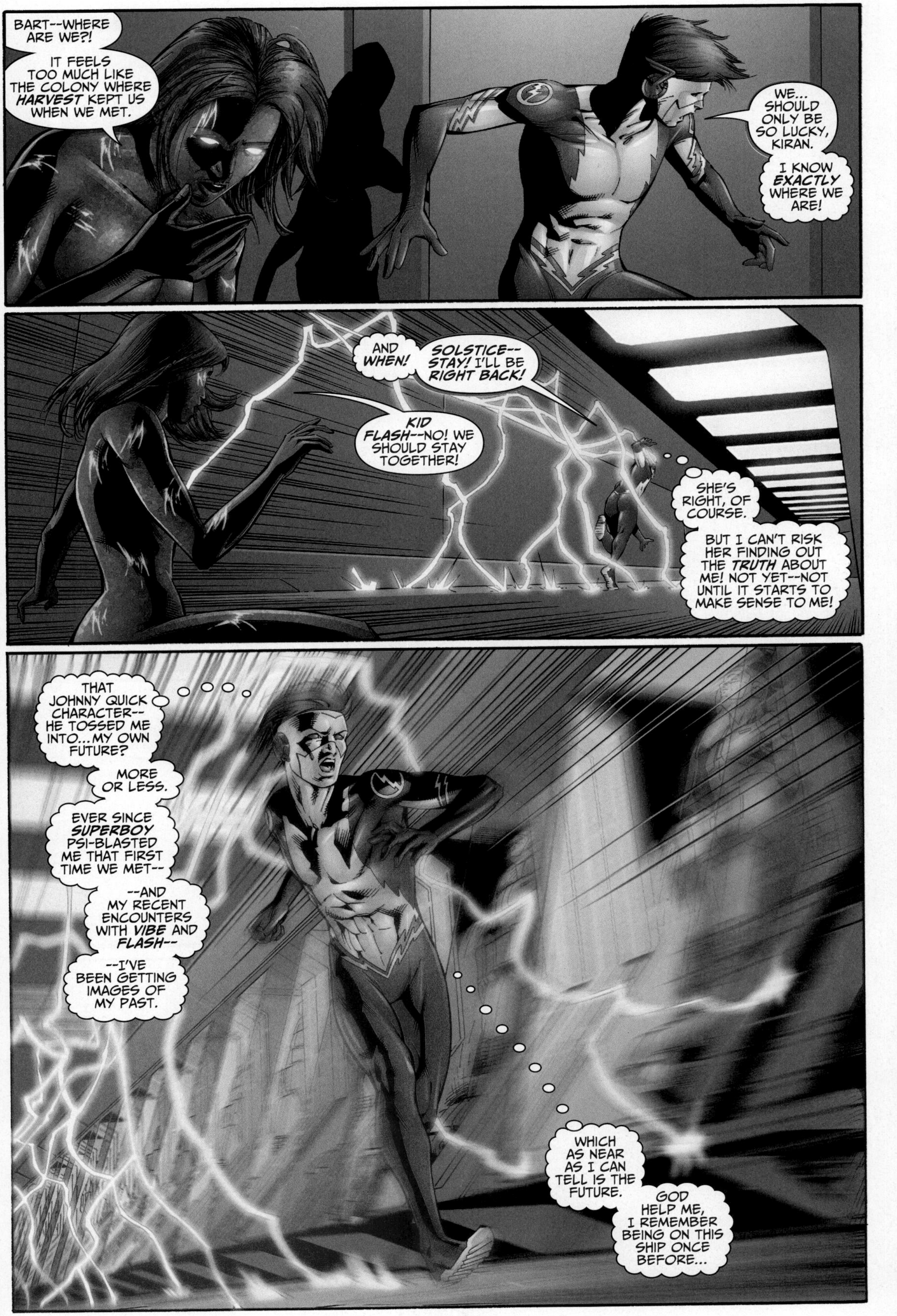
BART--WHERE ARE WE?!
IT FEELS TOO MUCH LIKE THE COLONY WHERE HARVEST KEPT US WHEN WE MET.
WE... SHOULD ONLY BE SO LUCKY, KIRAN.
I KNOW EXACTLY WHERE WE ARE!
AND WHEN!
SOLSTICE--STAY! I'LL BE RIGHT BACK!
KID FLASH--NO! WE SHOULD STAY TOGETHER!
SHE'S RIGHT, OF COURSE.
BUT I CAN'T RISK HER FINDING OUT THE TRUTH ABOUT ME! NOT YET--NOT UNTIL IT STARTS TO MAKE SENSE TO ME!
THAT JOHNNY QUICK CHARACTER--HE TOSSED ME INTO...MY OWN FUTURE?
MORE OR LESS.
EVER SINCE SUPERBOY PSI-BLASTED ME THAT FIRST TIME WE MET--
--AND MY RECENT ENCOUNTERS WITH VIBE AND FLASH--
--I'VE BEEN GETTING IMAGES OF MY PAST.
WHICH AS NEAR AS I CAN TELL IS THE FUTURE.
GOD HELP ME, I REMEMBER BEING ON THIS SHIP ONCE BEFORE...

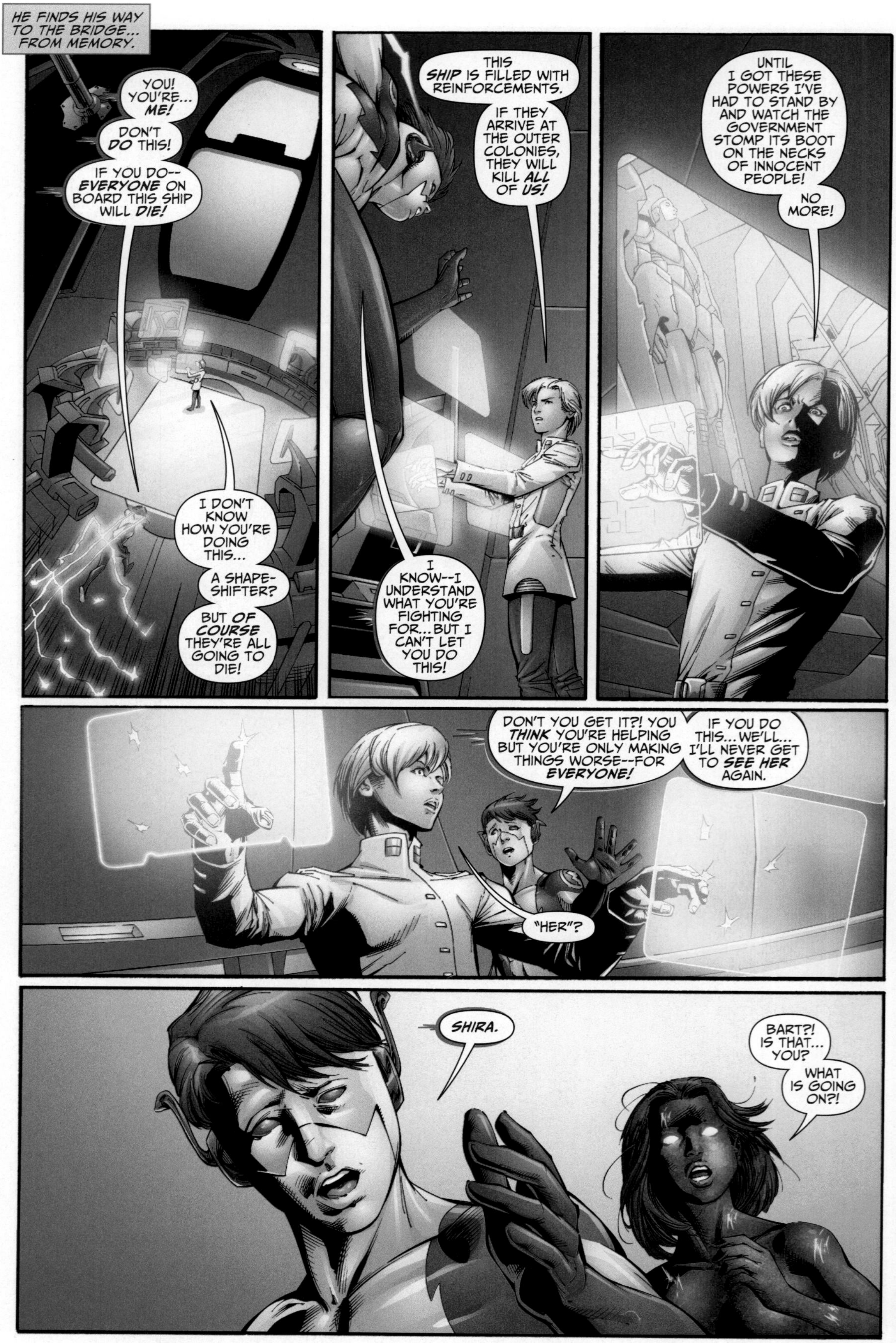
HE FINDS HIS WAY TO THE BRIDGE... FROM MEMORY.
YOU! YOU'RE... ME!
DON'T DO THIS!
IF YOU DO-- EVERYONE ON BOARD THIS SHIP WILL DIE!
I DON'T KNOW HOW YOU'RE DOING THIS...
A SHAPE-SHIFTER?
BUT OF COURSE THEY'RE ALL GOING TO DIE!
THIS SHIP IS FILLED WITH REINFORCEMENTS.
IF THEY ARRIVE AT THE OUTER COLONIES, THEY WILL KILL ALL OF US!
I KNOW--I UNDERSTAND WHAT YOU'RE FIGHTING FOR...BUT I CAN'T LET YOU DO THIS!
UNTIL I GOT THESE POWERS I'VE HAD TO STAND BY AND WATCH THE GOVERNMENT STOMP ITS BOOT ON THE NECKS OF INNOCENT PEOPLE!
NO MORE!
DON'T YOU GET IT?! YOU THINK YOU'RE HELPING BUT YOU'RE ONLY MAKING THINGS WORSE--FOR EVERYONE!
IF YOU DO THIS...WE'LL... I'LL NEVER GET TO SEE HER AGAIN.
"HER"?
SHIRA.
BART?! IS THAT... YOU?
WHAT IS GOING ON?!

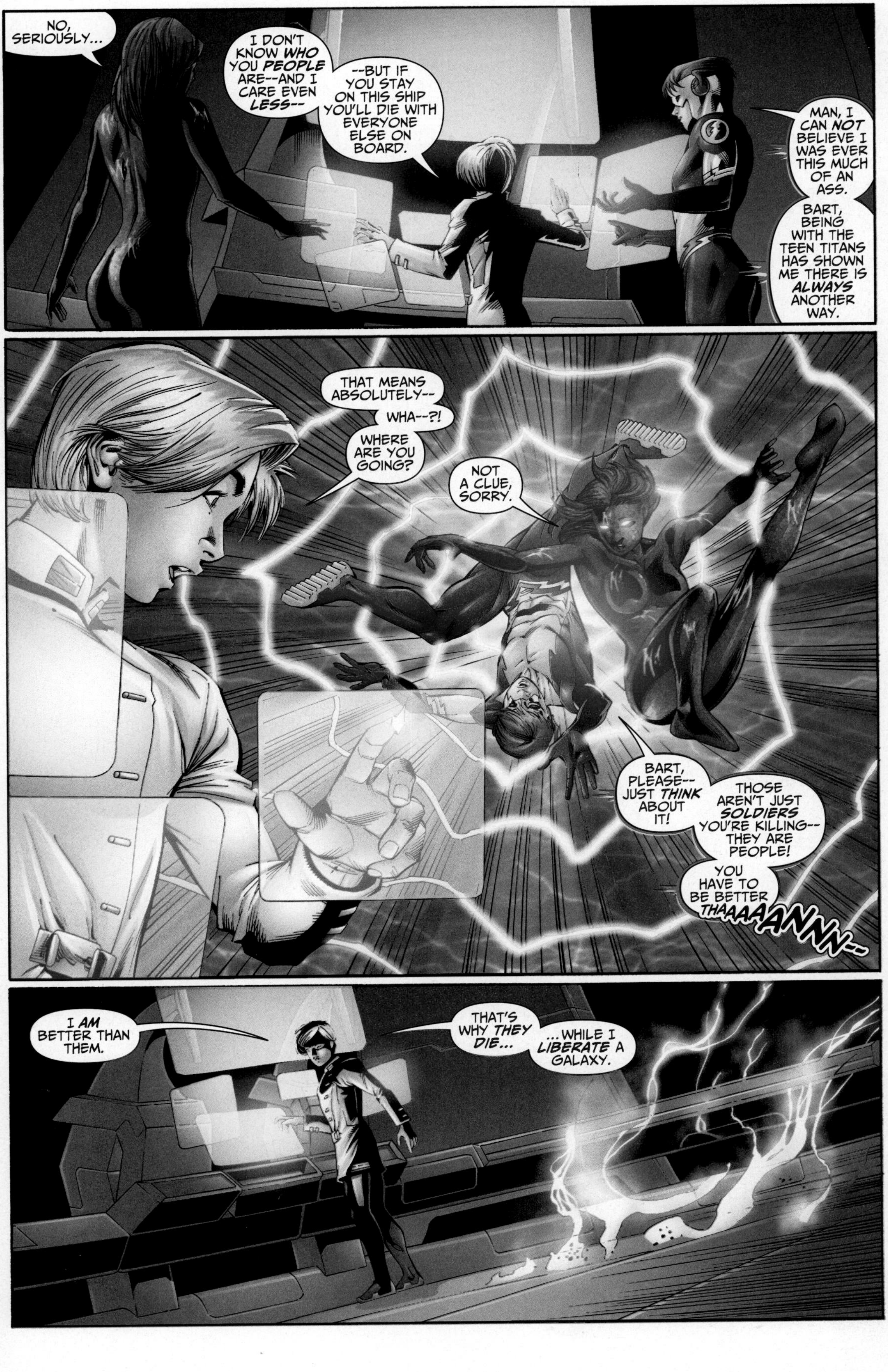
NO, SERIOUSLY...
I DON'T KNOW WHO YOU PEOPLE ARE--AND I CARE EVEN LESS--
--BUT IF YOU STAY ON THIS SHIP YOU'LL DIE WITH EVERYONE ELSE ON BOARD.
MAN, I CAN NOT BELIEVE I WAS EVER THIS MUCH OF AN ASS.
BART, BEING WITH THE TEEN TITANS HAS SHOWN ME THERE IS ALWAYS ANOTHER WAY.
THAT MEANS ABSOLUTELY--
WHA--?!
WHERE ARE YOU GOING?
NOT A CLUE, SORRY.
BART, PLEASE--JUST THINK ABOUT IT!
THOSE AREN'T JUST SOLDIERS YOU'RE KILLING--THEY ARE PEOPLE!
YOU HAVE TO BE BETTER THAAAAANNN--
I AM BETTER THAN THEM.
THAT'S WHY THEY DIE...
...WHILE I LIBERATE A GALAXY.

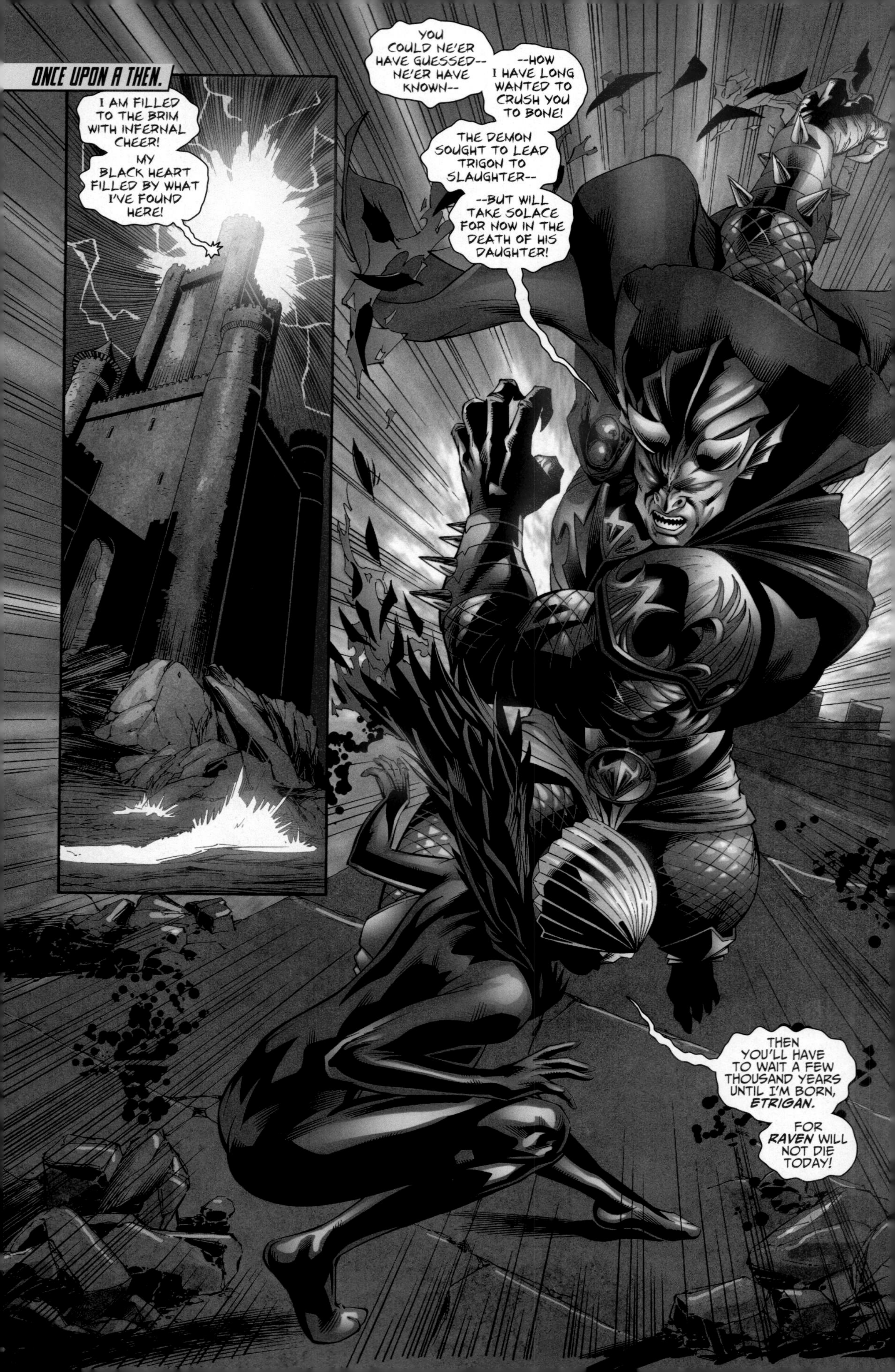
ONCE UPON A THEN.
I AM FILLED TO THE BRIM WITH INFERNAL CHEER!
MY BLACK HEART FILLED BY WHAT I'VE FOUND HERE!
YOU COULD NE'ER HAVE GUESSED-- NE'ER HAVE KNOWN--
--HOW I HAVE LONG WANTED TO CRUSH YOU TO BONE!
THE DEMON SOUGHT TO LEAD TRIGON TO SLAUGHTER--
--BUT WILL TAKE SOLACE FOR NOW IN THE DEATH OF HIS DAUGHTER!
THEN YOU'LL HAVE TO WAIT A FEW THOUSAND YEARS UNTIL I'M BORN, ETRIGAN.
FOR RAVEN WILL NOT DIE TODAY!

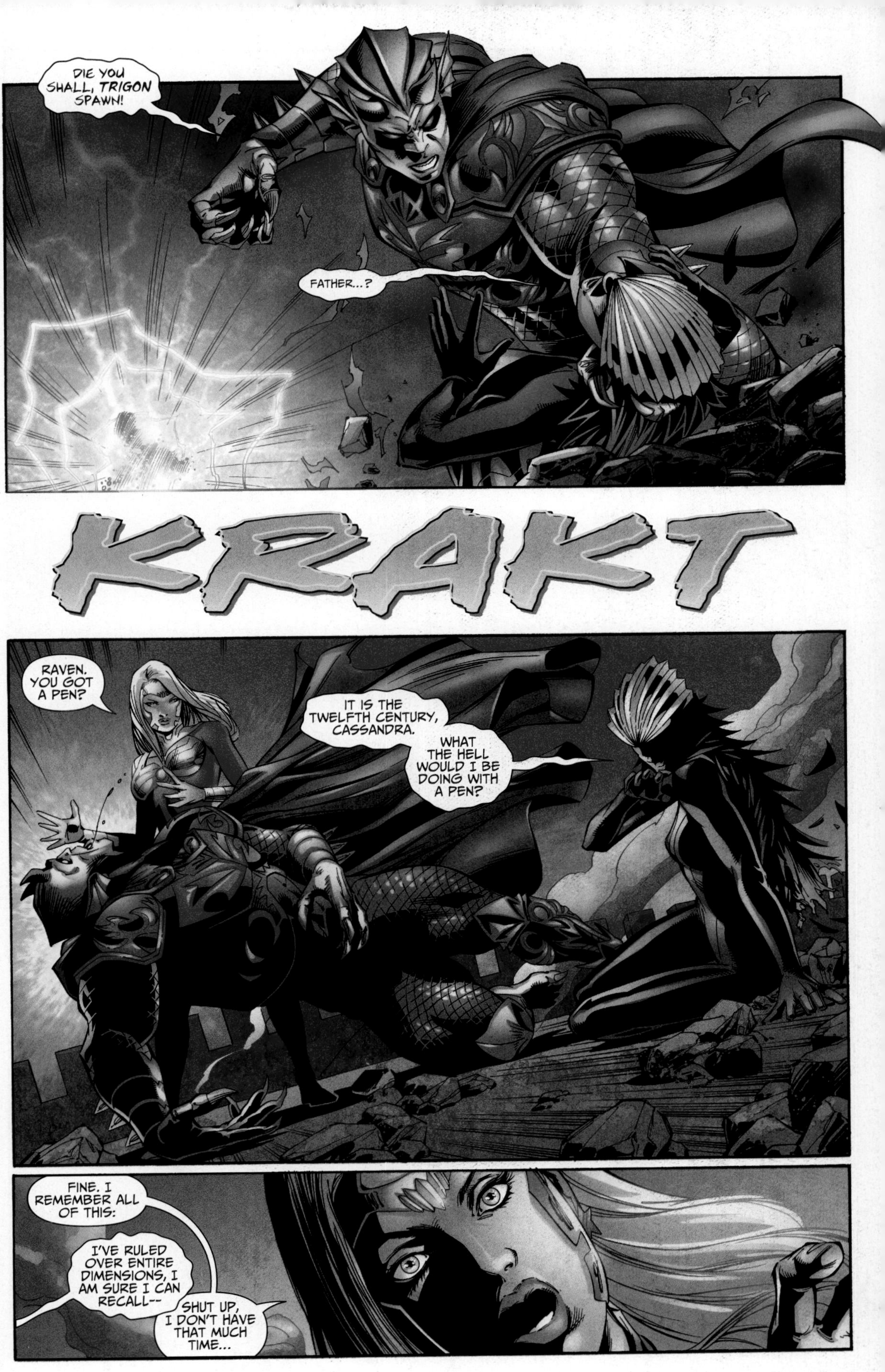
DIE YOU SHALL, TRIGON SPAWN!
FATHER...?
KRAKT
RAVEN. YOU GOT A PEN?
IT IS THE TWELFTH CENTURY, CASSANDRA.
WHAT THE HELL WOULD I BE DOING WITH A PEN?
FINE. I REMEMBER ALL OF THIS:
I'VE RULED OVER ENTIRE DIMENSIONS, I AM SURE I CAN RECALL--
SHUT UP, I DON'T HAVE THAT MUCH TIME...

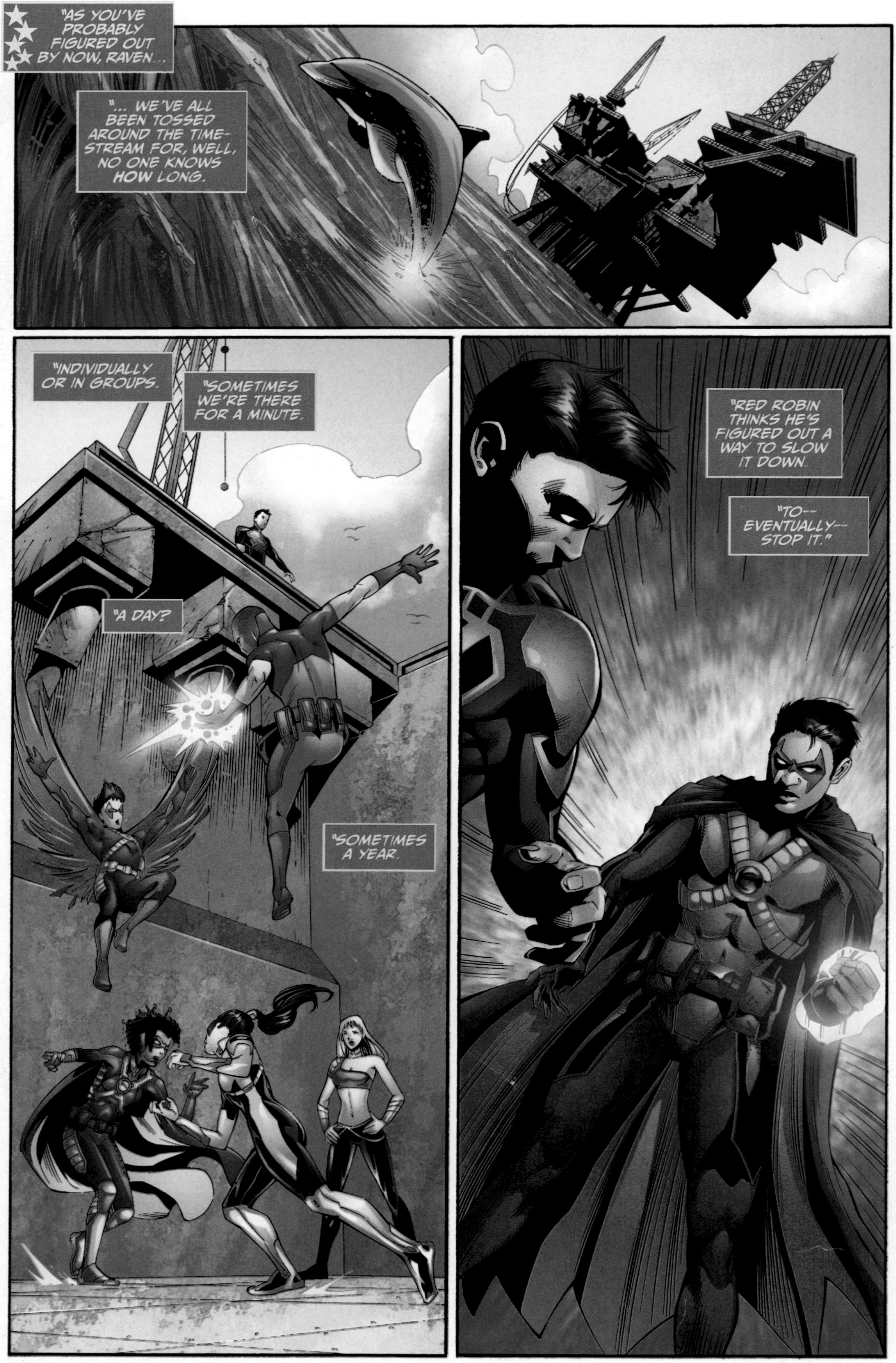
"AS YOU'VE PROBABLY FIGURED OUT BY NOW, RAVEN...
"... WE'VE ALL BEEN TOSSED AROUND THE TIME-STREAM FOR, WELL, NO ONE KNOWS HOW LONG.
"INDIVIDUALLY OR IN GROUPS.
"SOMETIMES WE'RE THERE FOR A MINUTE.
"A DAY?
"SOMETIMES A YEAR.
"RED ROBIN THINKS HE'S FIGURED OUT A WAY TO SLOW IT DOWN.
"TO--EVENTUALLY--STOP IT."

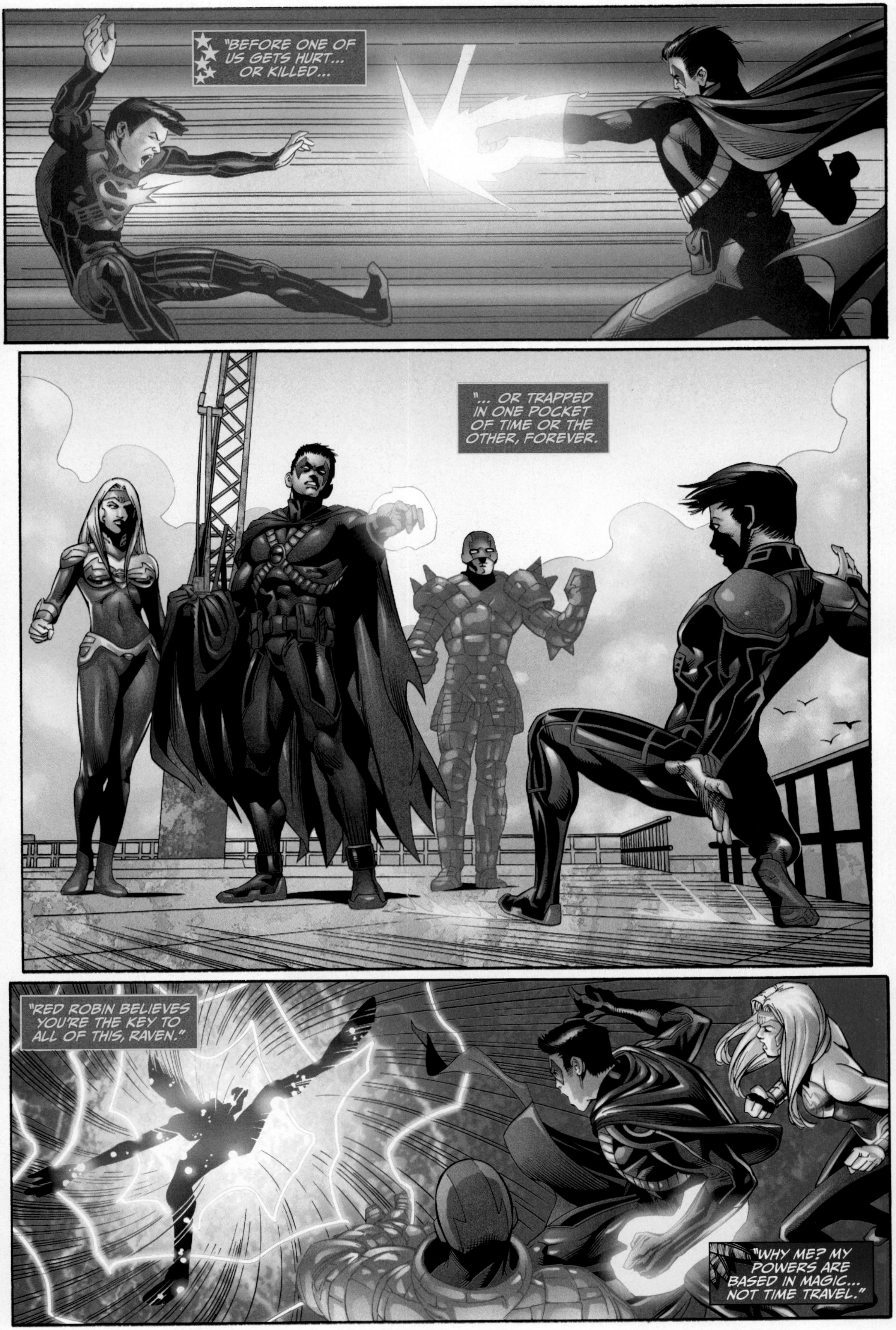
"BEFORE ONE OF US GETS HURT... OR KILLED...
"... OR TRAPPED IN ONE POCKET OF TIME OR THE OTHER, FOREVER.
"RED ROBIN BELIEVES YOU'RE THE KEY TO ALL OF THIS, RAVEN."
"WHY ME? MY POWERS ARE BASED IN MAGIC... NOT TIME TRAVEL."

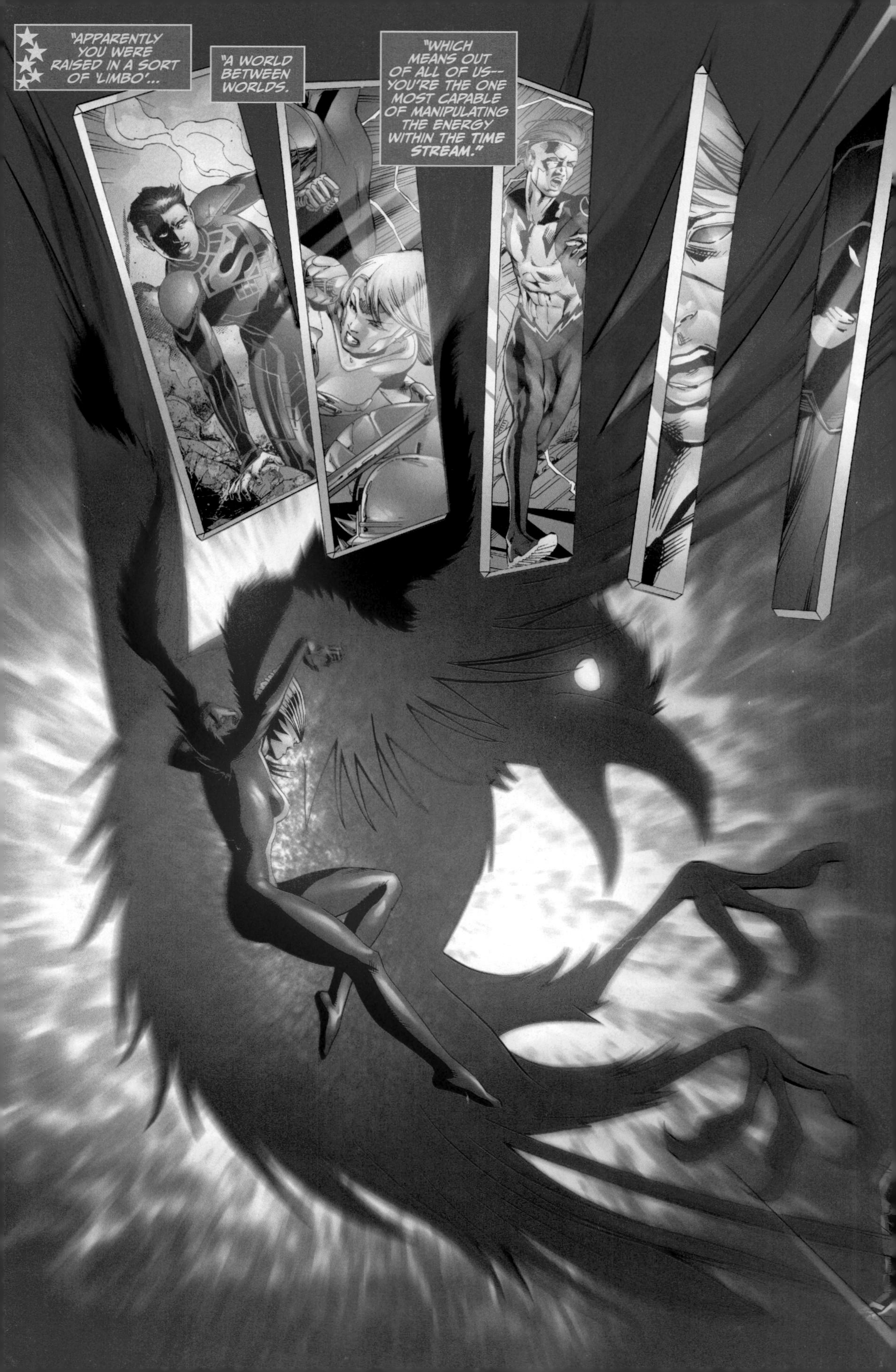
"APPARENTLY YOU WERE RAISED IN A SORT OF 'LIMBO'...
"A WORLD BETWEEN WORLDS.
"WHICH MEANS OUT OF ALL OF US-- YOU'RE THE ONE MOST CAPABLE OF MANIPULATING THE ENERGY WITHIN THE TIME STREAM."

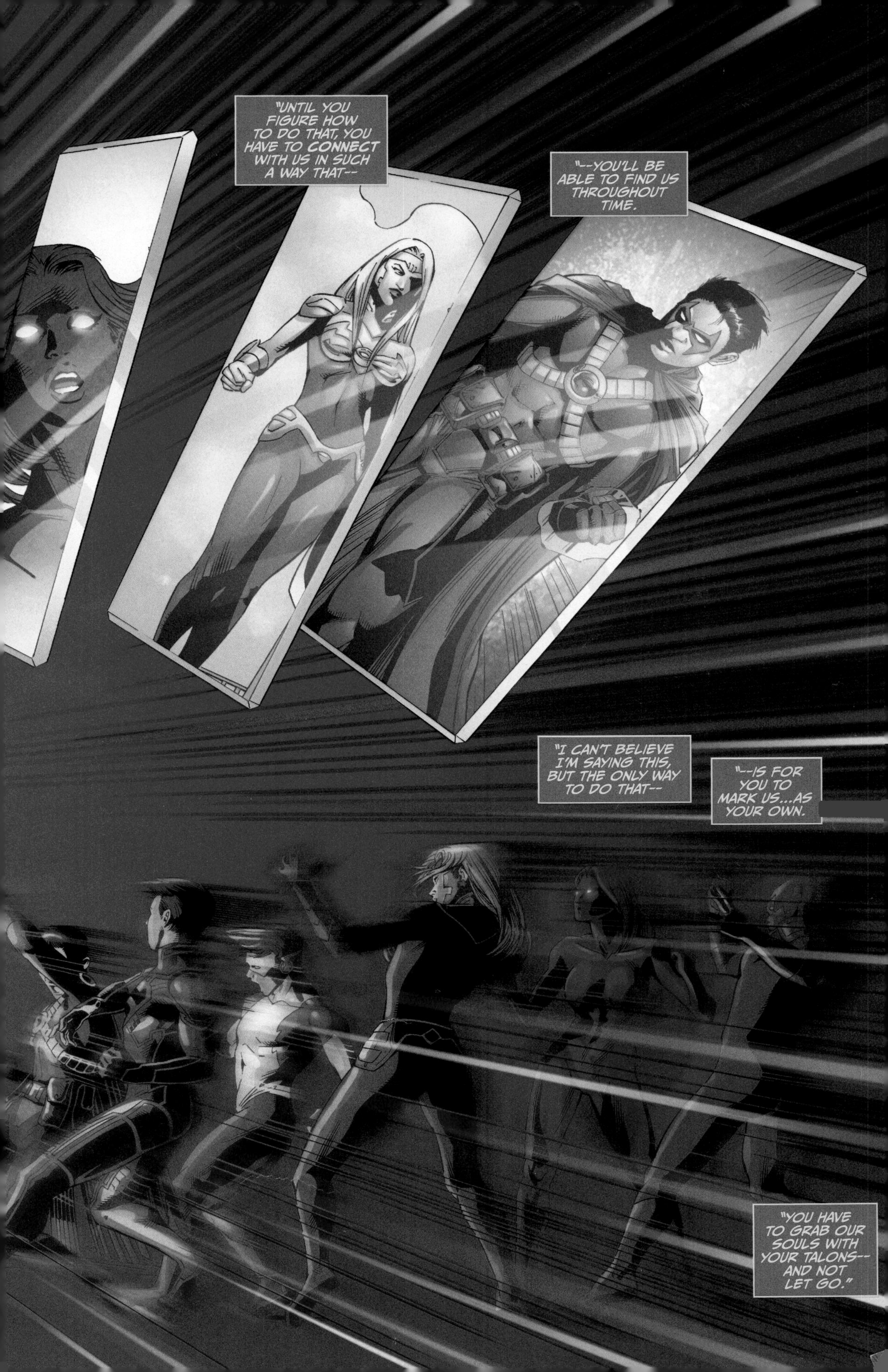
"UNTIL YOU FIGURE HOW TO DO THAT, YOU HAVE TO CONNECT WITH US IN SUCH A WAY THAT--
"--YOU'LL BE ABLE TO FIND US THROUGHOUT TIME.
"I CAN'T BELIEVE I'M SAYING THIS, BUT THE ONLY WAY TO DO THAT--
"--IS FOR YOU TO MARK US...AS YOUR OWN.
"YOU HAVE TO GRAB OUR SOULS WITH YOUR TALONS--AND NOT LET GO."

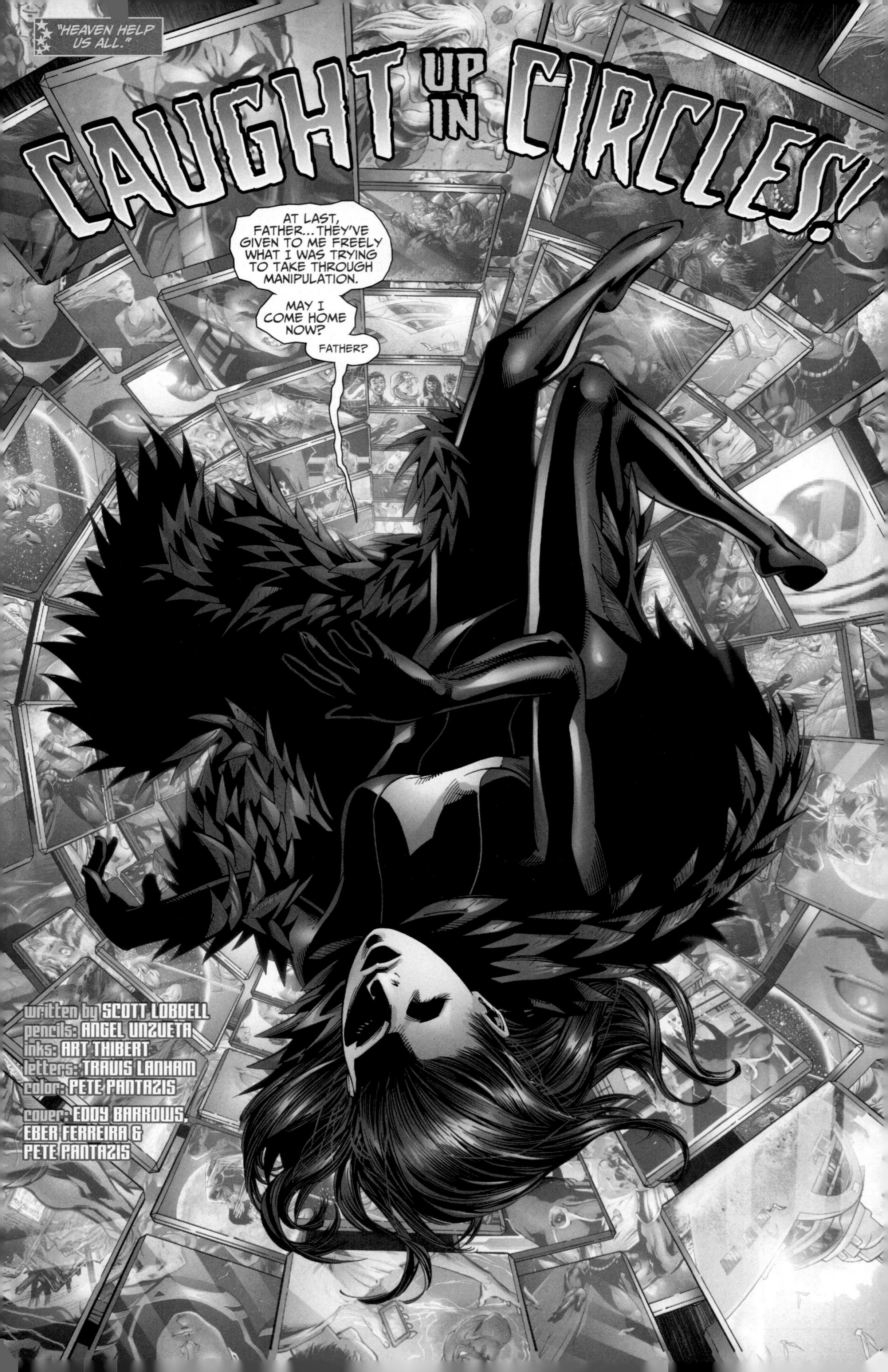
"HEAVEN HELP US ALL."
CAUGHT UP IN CIRCLES!
AT LAST, FATHER... THEY'VE GIVEN TO ME FREELY WHAT I WAS TRYING TO TAKE THROUGH MANIPULATION.
MAY I COME HOME NOW?
FATHER?
written by SCOTT LOBDELL
pencils: ANGEL UNZUETA
inks: ART THIBERT
letters: TRAVIS LANHAM
color: PETE PANTAZIS
cover: EDDY BARROWS, EBER FERREIRA & PETE PANTAZIS

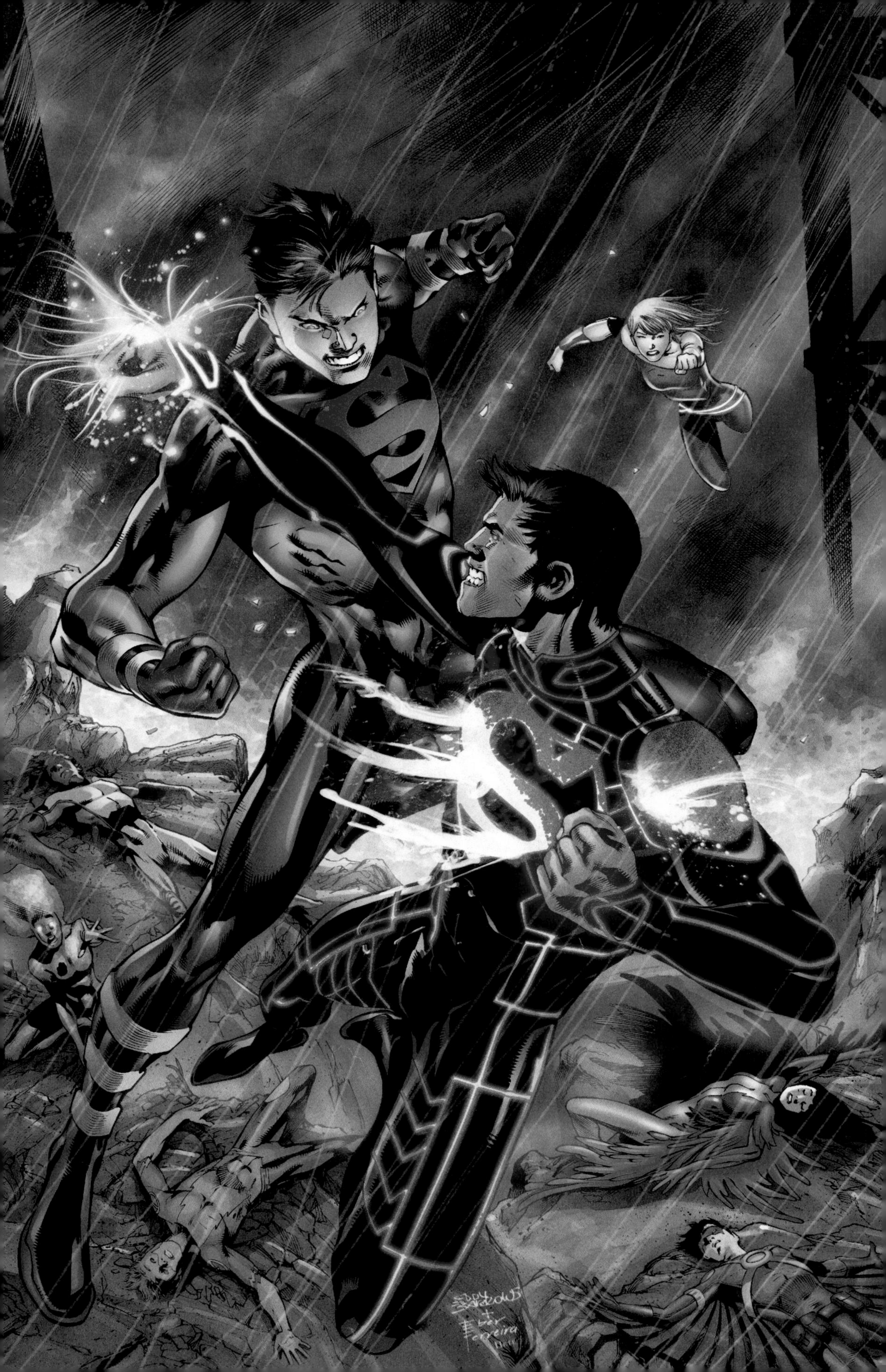

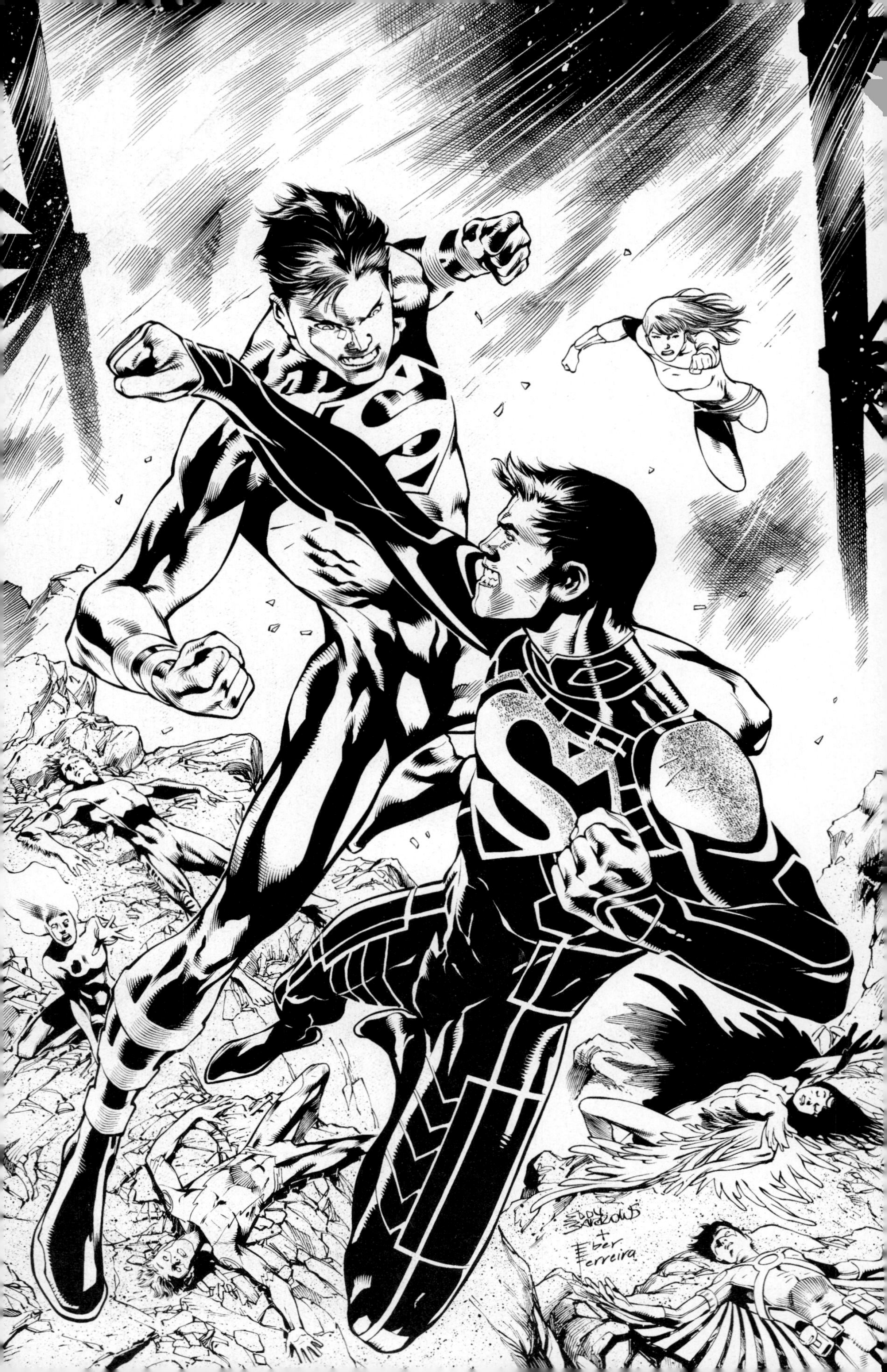
Eddy Barrows
+
Eber Ferreira

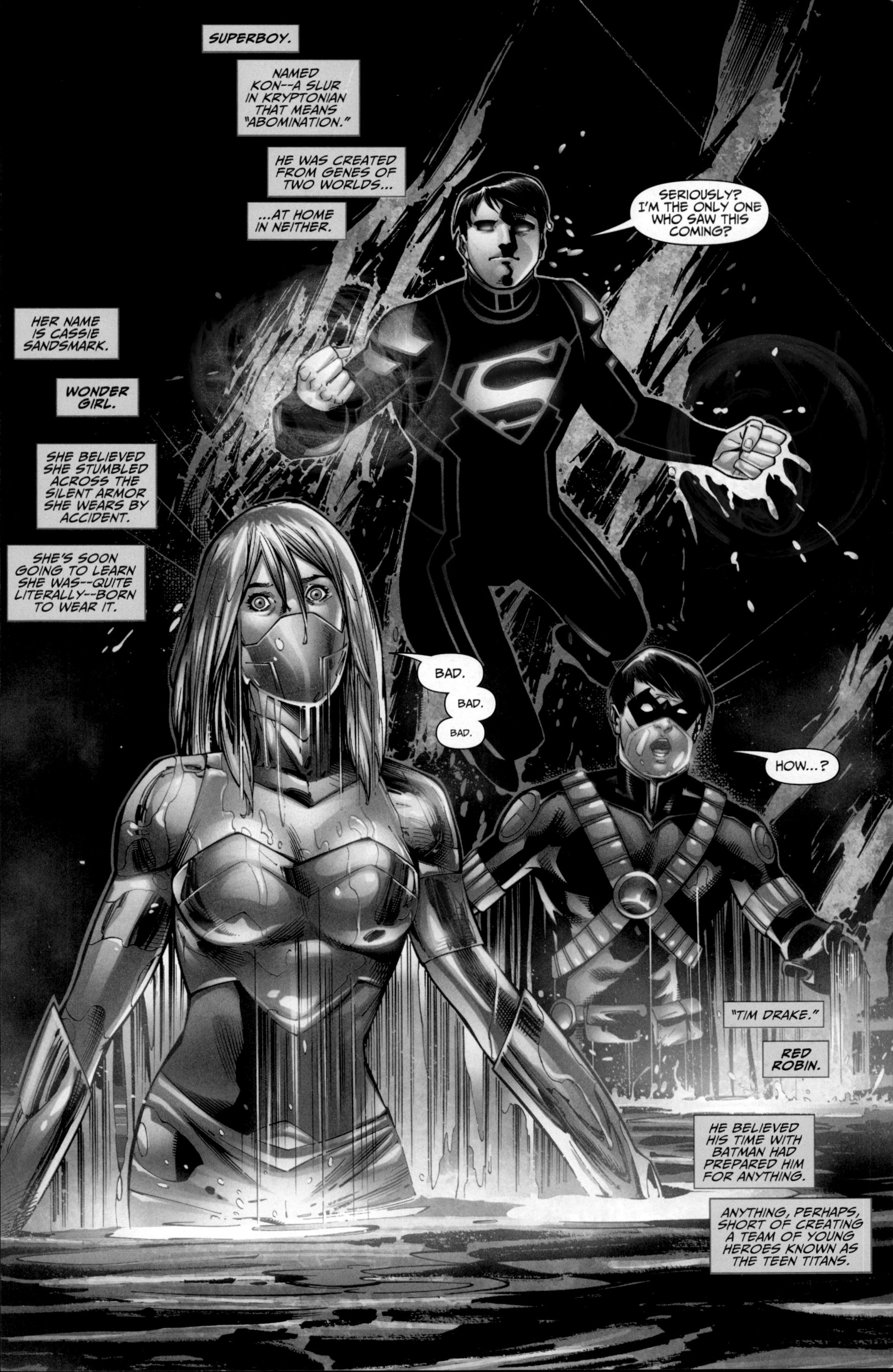
SUPERBOY.
NAMED KON--A SLUR IN KRYPTONIAN THAT MEANS "ABOMINATION."
HE WAS CREATED FROM GENES OF TWO WORLDS...
...AT HOME IN NEITHER.
SERIOUSLY? I'M THE ONLY ONE WHO SAW THIS COMING?
HER NAME IS CASSIE SANDSMARK.
WONDER GIRL.
SHE BELIEVED SHE STUMBLED ACROSS THE SILENT ARMOR SHE WEARS BY ACCIDENT.
SHE'S SOON GOING TO LEARN SHE WAS--QUITE LITERALLY--BORN TO WEAR IT.
BAD.
BAD.
BAD.
HOW...?
"TIM DRAKE."
RED ROBIN.
HE BELIEVED HIS TIME WITH BATMAN HAD PREPARED HIM FOR ANYTHING.
ANYTHING, PERHAPS, SHORT OF CREATING A TEAM OF YOUNG HEROES KNOWN AS THE TEEN TITANS.

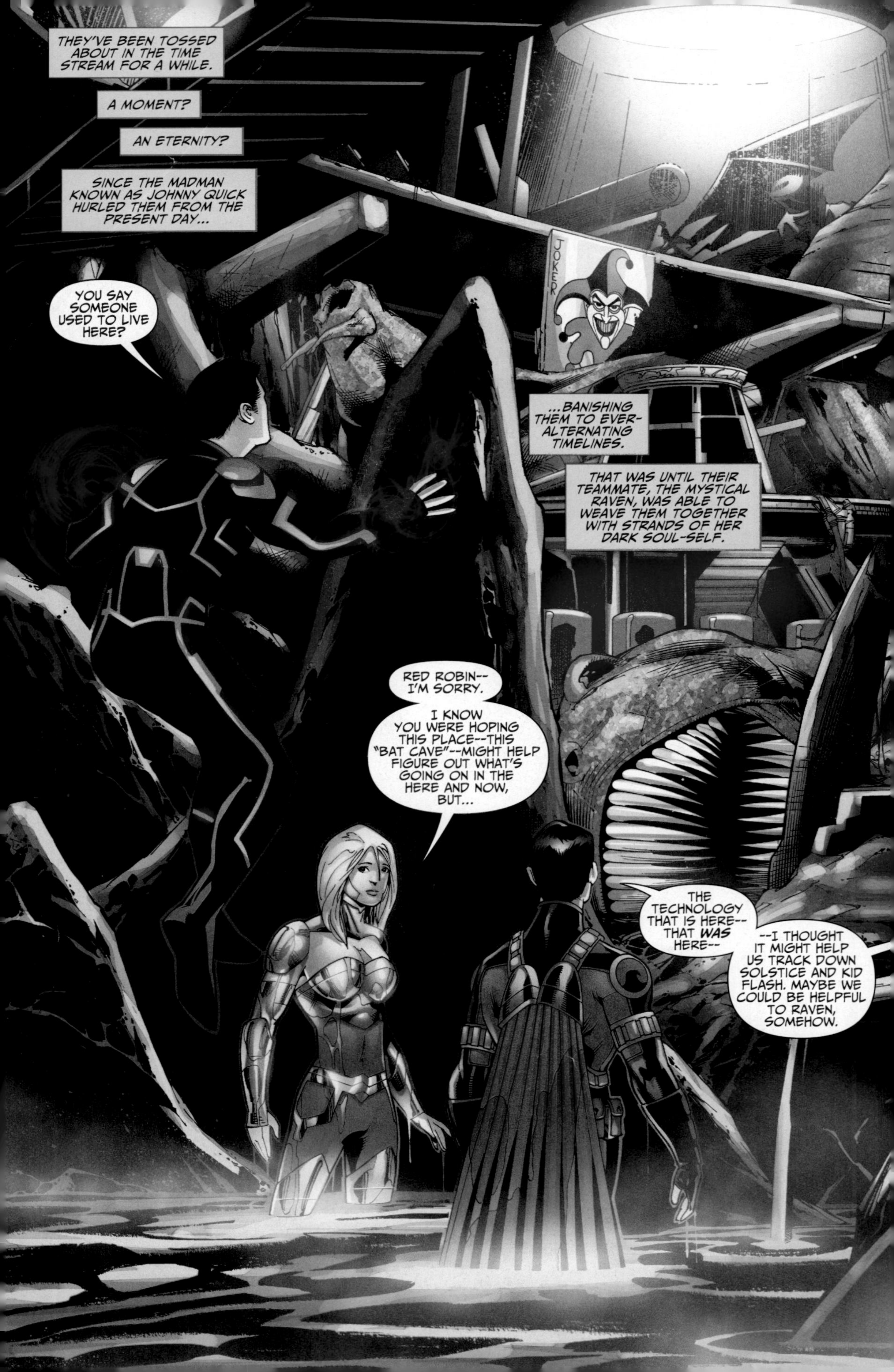
THEY'VE BEEN TOSSED ABOUT IN THE TIME STREAM FOR A WHILE.
A MOMENT?
AN ETERNITY?
SINCE THE MADMAN KNOWN AS JOHNNY QUICK HURLED THEM FROM THE PRESENT DAY...
YOU SAY SOMEONE USED TO LIVE HERE?
JOKER
...BANISHING THEM TO EVER-ALTERNATING TIMELINES.
THAT WAS UNTIL THEIR TEAMMATE, THE MYSTICAL RAVEN, WAS ABLE TO WEAVE THEM TOGETHER WITH STRANDS OF HER DARK SOUL-SELF.
RED ROBIN-- I'M SORRY.
I KNOW YOU WERE HOPING THIS PLACE--THIS "BAT CAVE"--MIGHT HELP FIGURE OUT WHAT'S GOING ON IN THE HERE AND NOW, BUT...
THE TECHNOLOGY THAT IS HERE-- THAT **WAS** HERE--
--I THOUGHT IT MIGHT HELP US TRACK DOWN SOLSTICE AND KID FLASH. MAYBE WE COULD BE HELPFUL TO RAVEN, SOMEHOW.

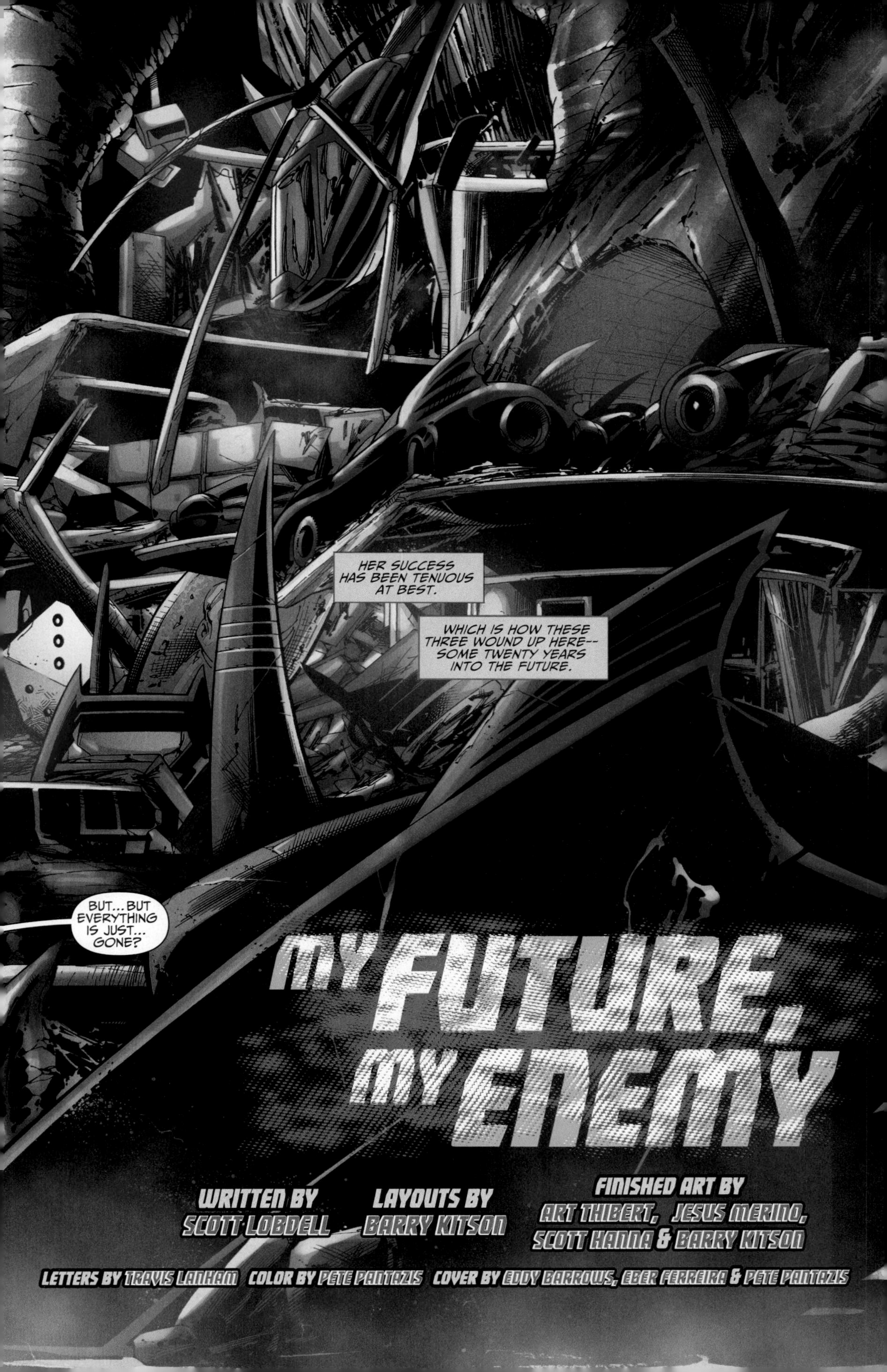
HER SUCCESS HAS BEEN TENUOUS AT BEST.
WHICH IS HOW THESE THREE WOUND UP HERE-- SOME TWENTY YEARS INTO THE FUTURE.
BUT...BUT EVERYTHING IS JUST... GONE?
MY FUTURE, MY ENEMY
WRITTEN BY SCOTT LOBDELL
LAYOUTS BY BARRY KITSON
FINISHED ART BY ART THIBERT, JESUS MERINO, SCOTT HANNA & BARRY KITSON
LETTERS BY TRAVIS LANHAM COLOR BY PETE PANTAZIS COVER BY EDDY BARROWS, EBER FERREIRA & PETE PANTAZIS

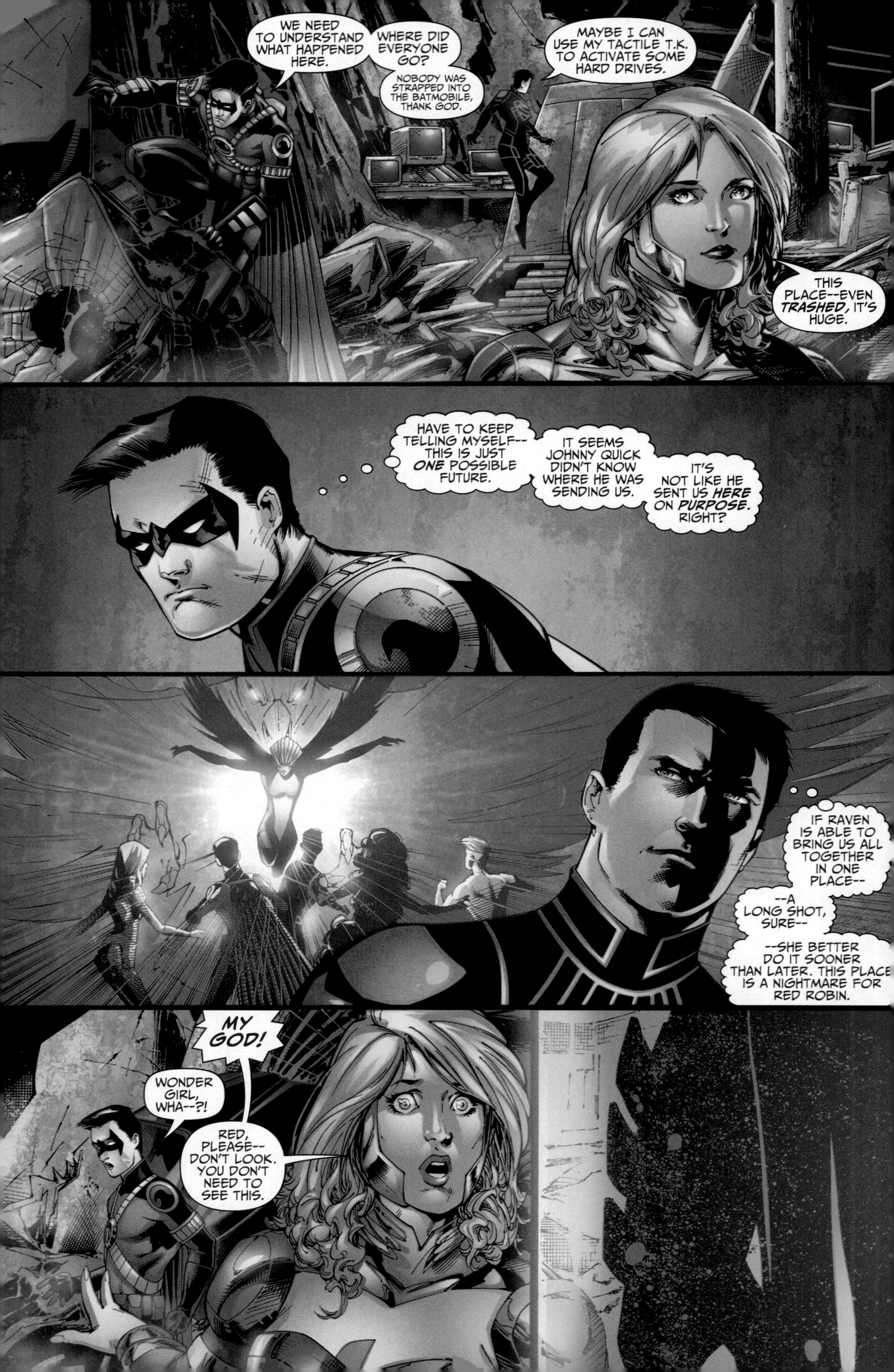
WE NEED TO UNDERSTAND WHAT HAPPENED HERE.
WHERE DID EVERYONE GO?
NOBODY WAS STRAPPED INTO THE BATMOBILE, THANK GOD.
MAYBE I CAN USE MY TACTILE T.K. TO ACTIVATE SOME HARD DRIVES.
THIS PLACE--EVEN TRASHED, IT'S HUGE.
HAVE TO KEEP TELLING MYSELF-- THIS IS JUST ONE POSSIBLE FUTURE.
IT SEEMS JOHNNY QUICK DIDN'T KNOW WHERE HE WAS SENDING US.
IT'S NOT LIKE HE SENT US HERE ON PURPOSE. RIGHT?
IF RAVEN IS ABLE TO BRING US ALL TOGETHER IN ONE PLACE--
--A LONG SHOT, SURE--
--SHE BETTER DO IT SOONER THAN LATER. THIS PLACE IS A NIGHTMARE FOR RED ROBIN.
MY GOD!
WONDER GIRL, WHA--?!
RED, PLEASE-- DON'T LOOK. YOU DON'T NEED TO SEE THIS.

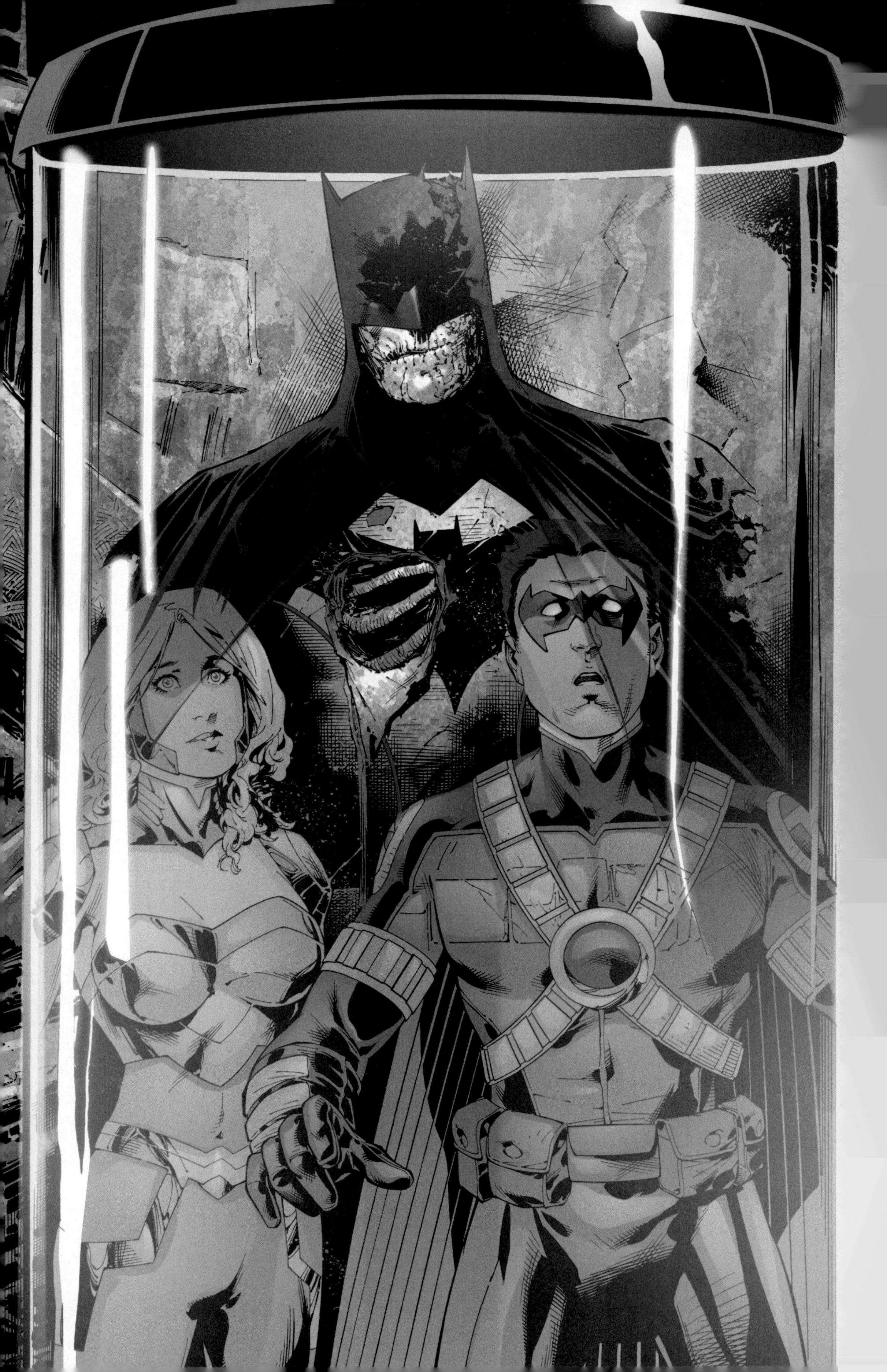

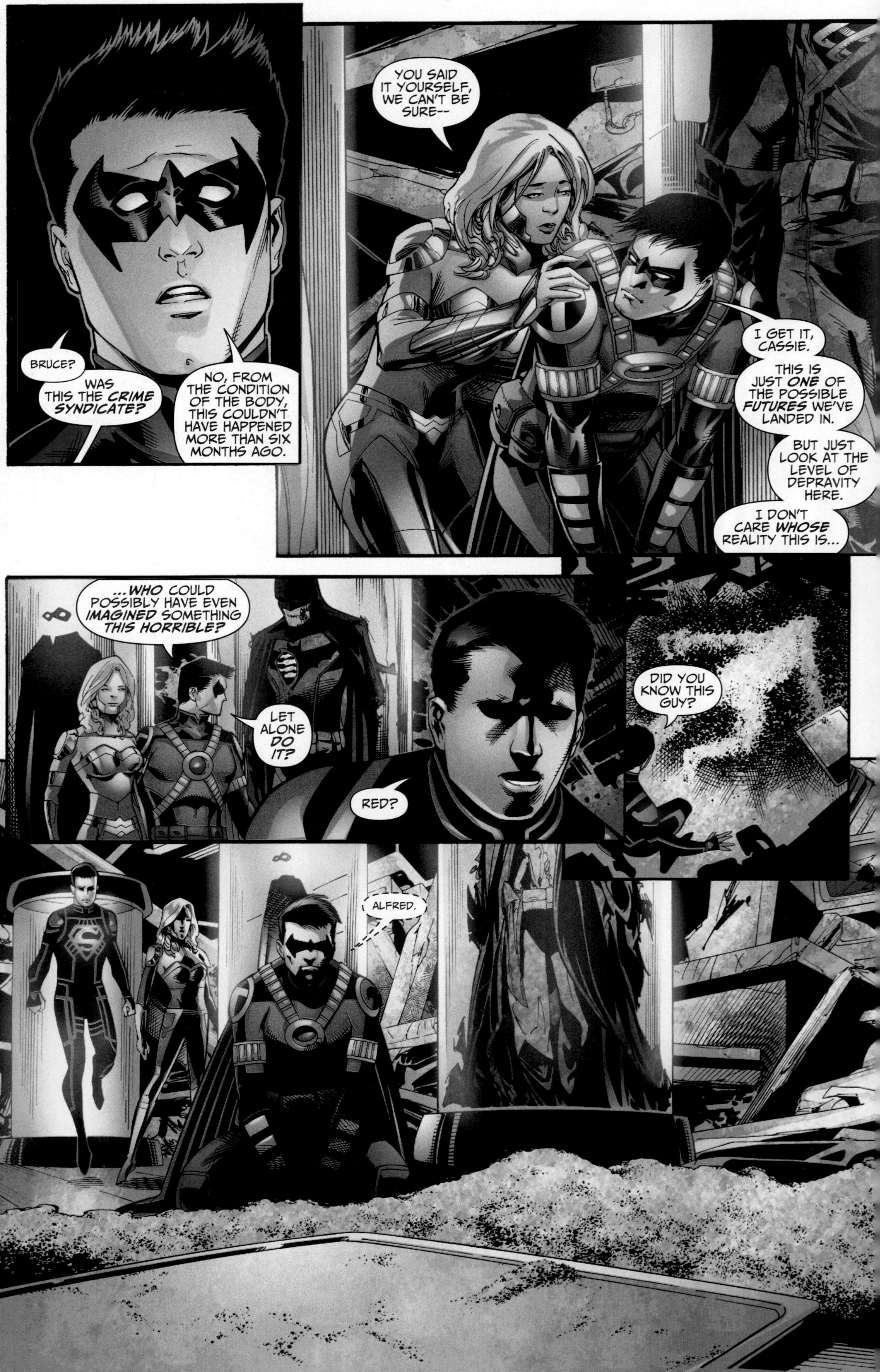
BRUCE?
WAS THIS THE CRIME SYNDICATE?
NO, FROM THE CONDITION OF THE BODY, THIS COULDN'T HAVE HAPPENED MORE THAN SIX MONTHS AGO.
YOU SAID IT YOURSELF, WE CAN'T BE SURE--
I GET IT, CASSIE.
THIS IS JUST ONE OF THE POSSIBLE FUTURES WE'VE LANDED IN.
BUT JUST LOOK AT THE LEVEL OF DEPRAVITY HERE.
I DON'T CARE WHOSE REALITY THIS IS...
...WHO COULD POSSIBLY HAVE EVEN IMAGINED SOMETHING THIS HORRIBLE?
LET ALONE DO IT?
RED?
DID YOU KNOW THIS GUY?
ALFRED.

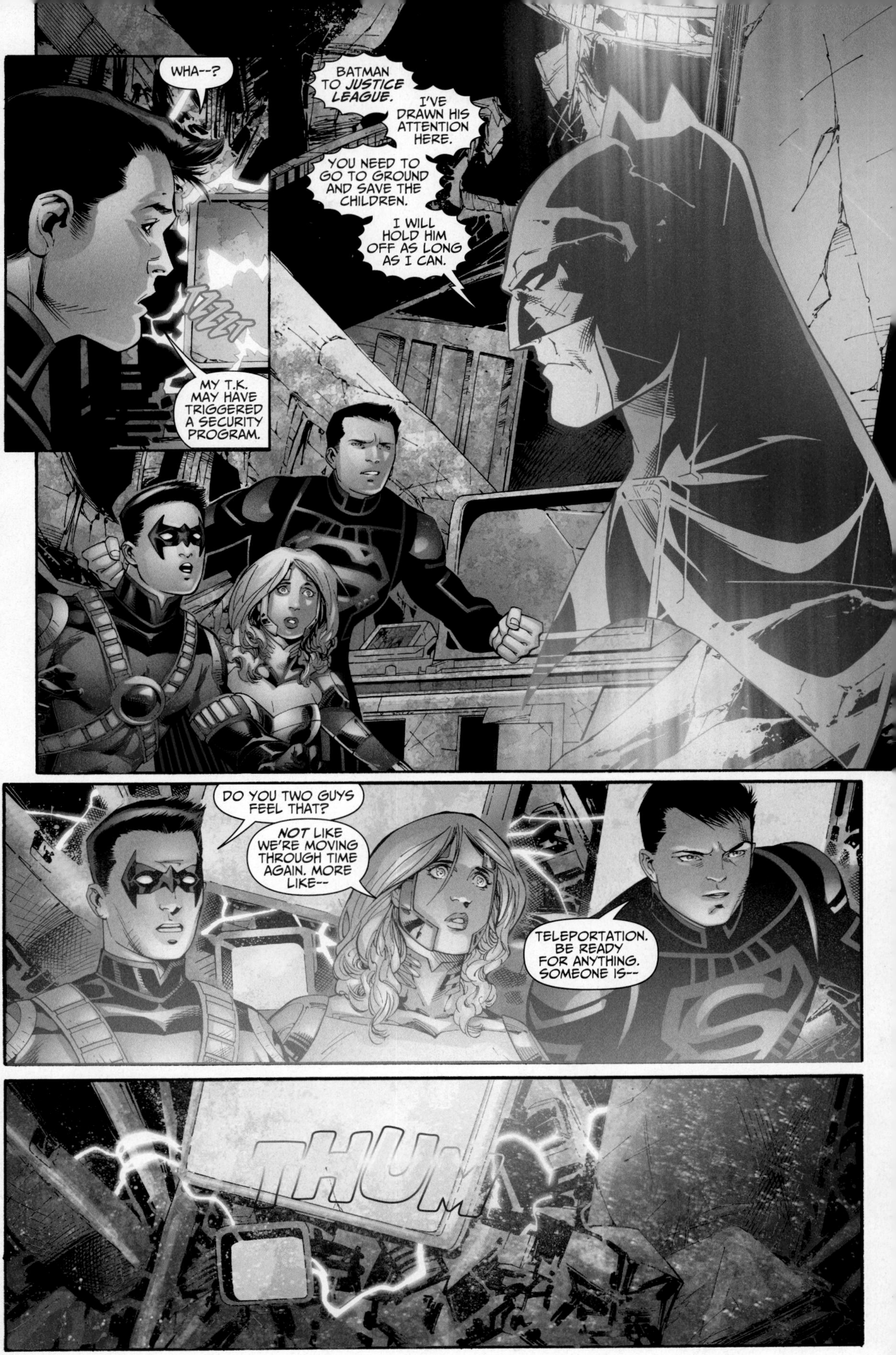
WHA--?
BATMAN TO JUSTICE LEAGUE.
I'VE DRAWN HIS ATTENTION HERE.
YOU NEED TO GO TO GROUND AND SAVE THE CHILDREN.
I WILL HOLD HIM OFF AS LONG AS I CAN.
TZZZT
MY T.K. MAY HAVE TRIGGERED A SECURITY PROGRAM.
DO YOU TWO GUYS FEEL THAT?
NOT LIKE WE'RE MOVING THROUGH TIME AGAIN. MORE LIKE--
TELEPORTATION. BE READY FOR ANYTHING. SOMEONE IS--
THUM

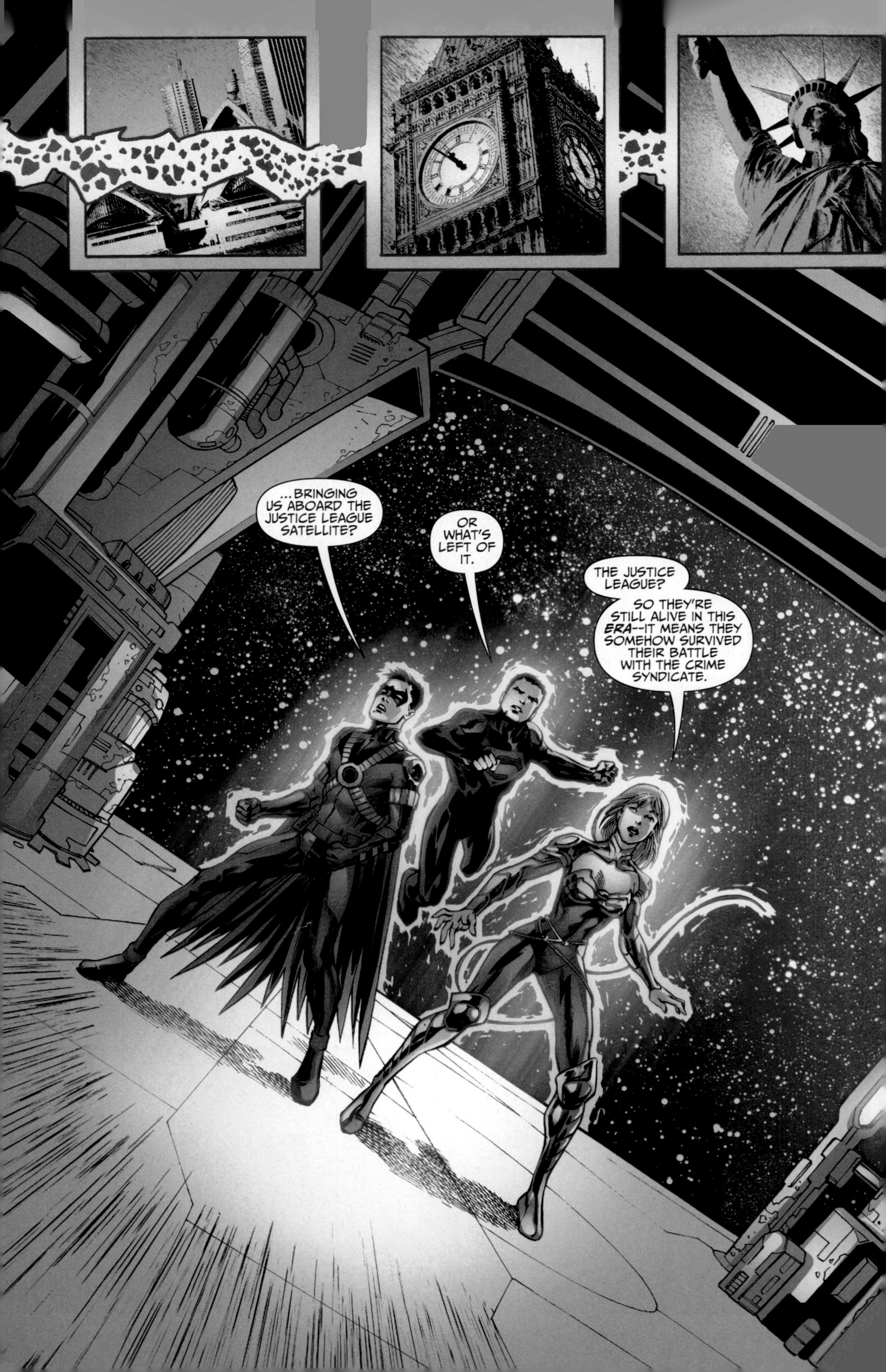
...BRINGING US ABOARD THE JUSTICE LEAGUE SATELLITE?
OR WHAT'S LEFT OF IT.
THE JUSTICE LEAGUE?
SO THEY'RE STILL ALIVE IN THIS ERA--IT MEANS THEY SOMEHOW SURVIVED THEIR BATTLE WITH THE CRIME SYNDICATE.

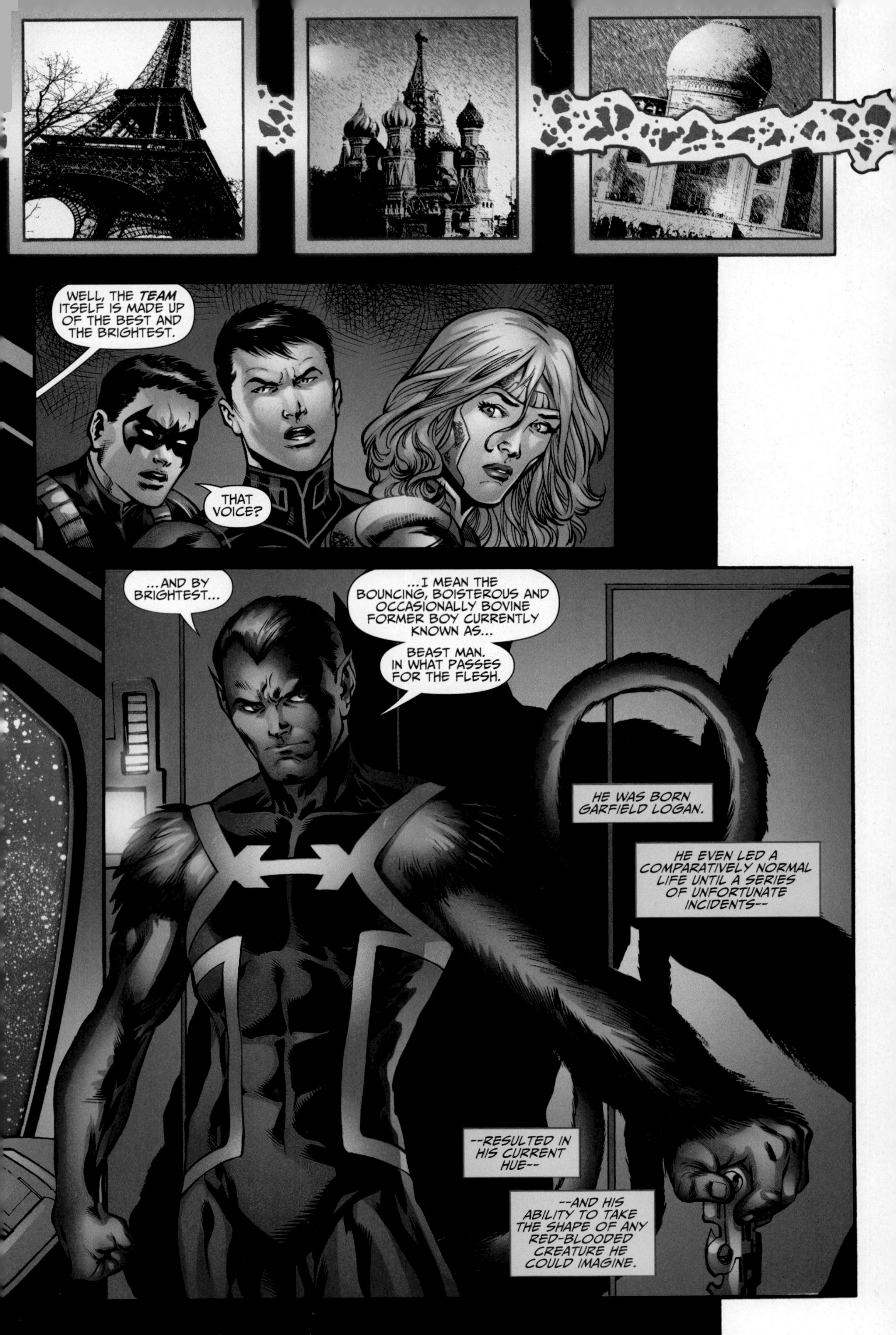

WELL, THE *TEAM* ITSELF IS MADE UP OF THE BEST AND THE BRIGHTEST.
THAT VOICE?
...AND BY BRIGHTEST...
...I MEAN THE BOUNCING, BOISTEROUS AND OCCASIONALLY BOVINE FORMER BOY CURRENTLY KNOWN AS...
BEAST MAN. IN WHAT PASSES FOR THE FLESH.
HE WAS BORN GARFIELD LOGAN.
HE EVEN LED A COMPARATIVELY NORMAL LIFE UNTIL A SERIES OF UNFORTUNATE INCIDENTS--
--RESULTED IN HIS CURRENT HUE--
--AND HIS ABILITY TO TAKE THE SHAPE OF ANY RED-BLOODED CREATURE HE COULD IMAGINE.

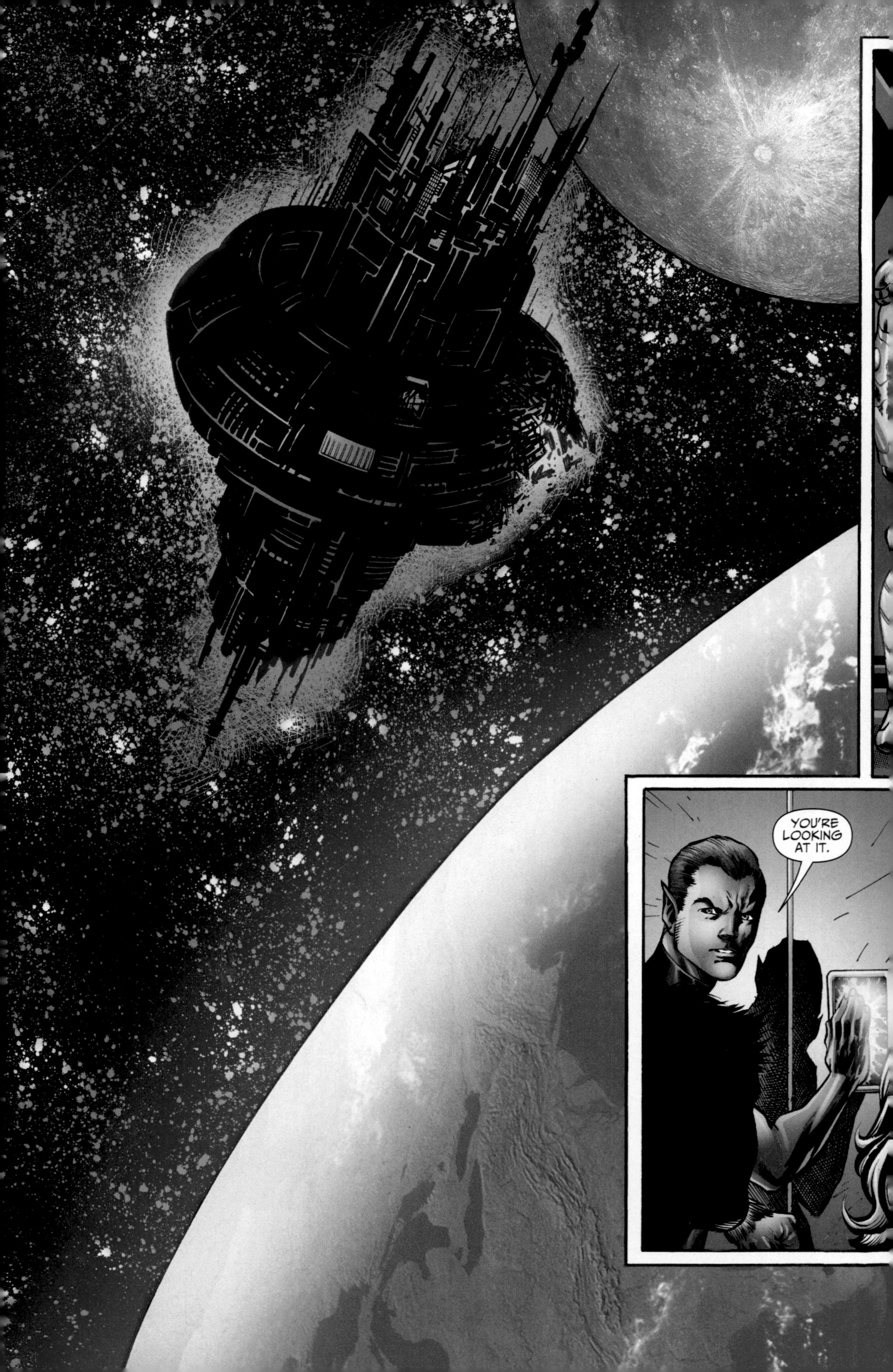
YOU'RE LOOKING AT IT.

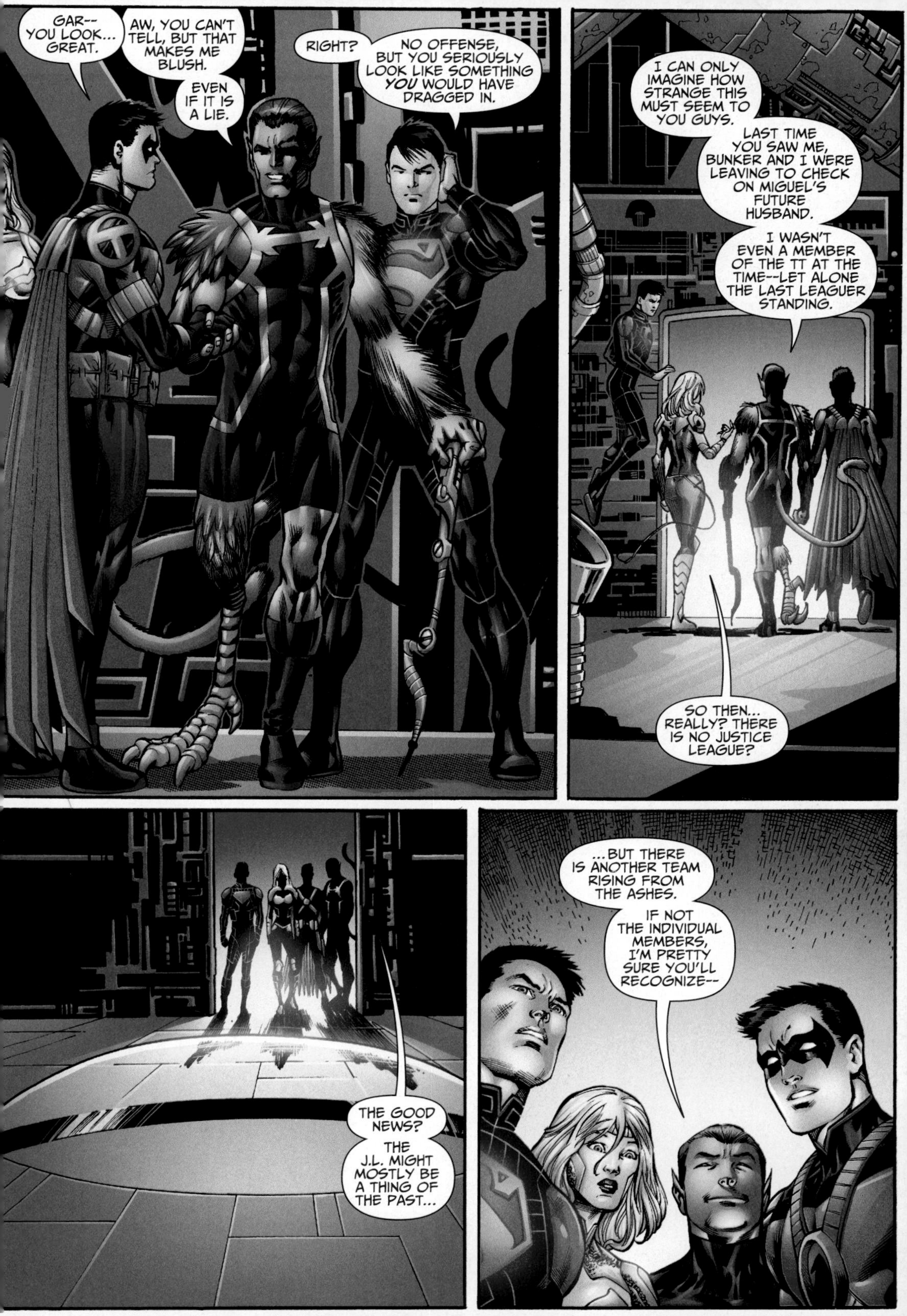
GAR-- YOU LOOK... GREAT.
AW, YOU CAN'T TELL, BUT THAT MAKES ME BLUSH.
EVEN IF IT IS A LIE.
RIGHT?
NO OFFENSE, BUT YOU SERIOUSLY LOOK LIKE SOMETHING *YOU* WOULD HAVE DRAGGED IN.
I CAN ONLY IMAGINE HOW STRANGE THIS MUST SEEM TO YOU GUYS.
LAST TIME YOU SAW ME, BUNKER AND I WERE LEAVING TO CHECK ON MIGUEL'S FUTURE HUSBAND.
I WASN'T EVEN A MEMBER OF THE TT AT THE TIME--LET ALONE THE LAST LEAGUER STANDING.
SO THEN... REALLY? THERE IS NO JUSTICE LEAGUE?
THE GOOD NEWS?
THE J.L. MIGHT MOSTLY BE A THING OF THE PAST...
...BUT THERE IS ANOTHER TEAM RISING FROM THE ASHES.
IF NOT THE INDIVIDUAL MEMBERS, I'M PRETTY SURE YOU'LL RECOGNIZE--

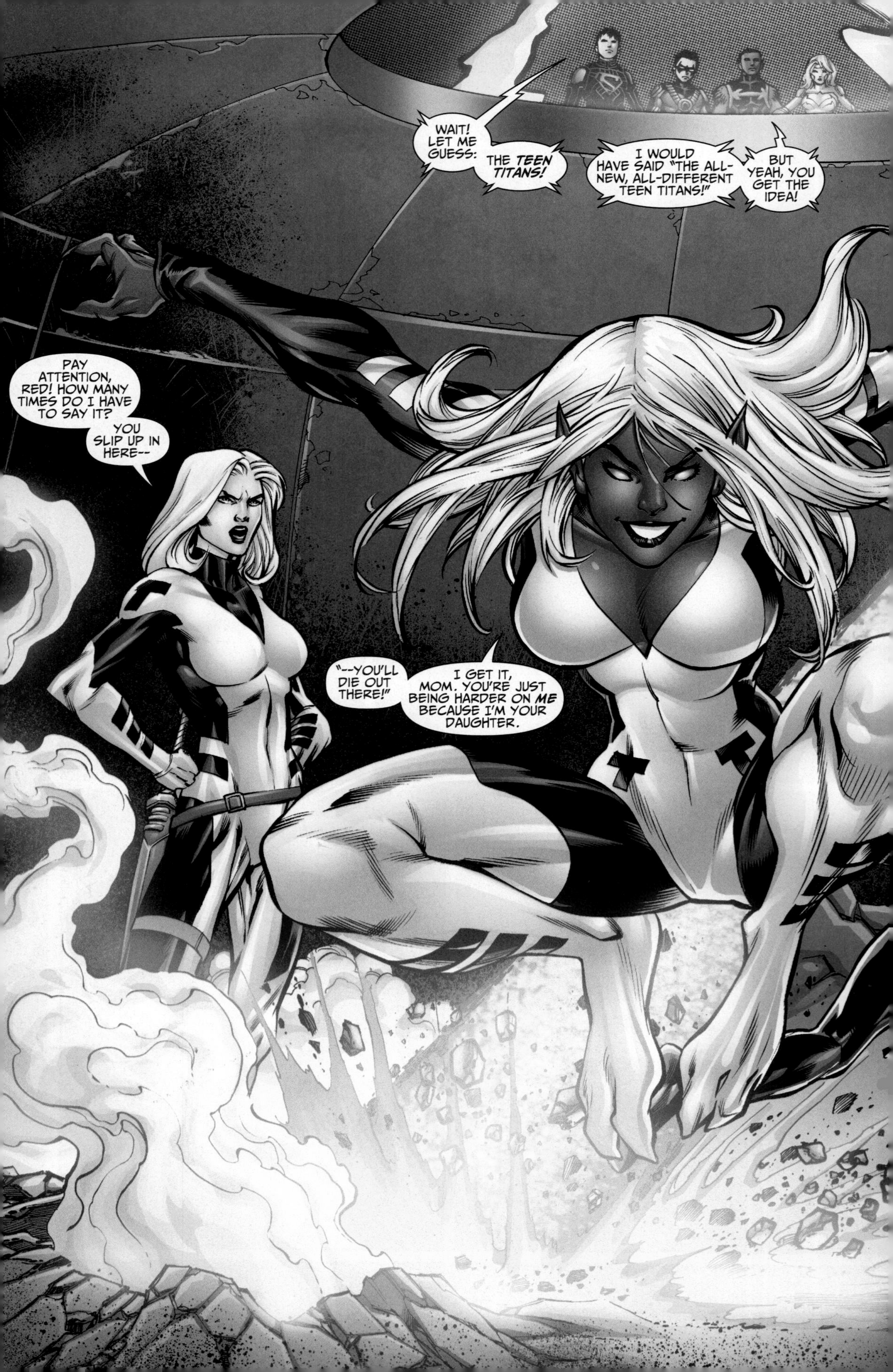
WAIT! LET ME GUESS:
THE TEEN TITANS!
I WOULD HAVE SAID "THE ALL-NEW, ALL-DIFFERENT TEEN TITANS!"
BUT YEAH, YOU GET THE IDEA!
PAY ATTENTION, RED! HOW MANY TIMES DO I HAVE TO SAY IT?
YOU SLIP UP IN HERE--
"--YOU'LL DIE OUT THERE!"
I GET IT, MOM. YOU'RE JUST BEING HARDER ON ME BECAUSE I'M YOUR DAUGHTER.

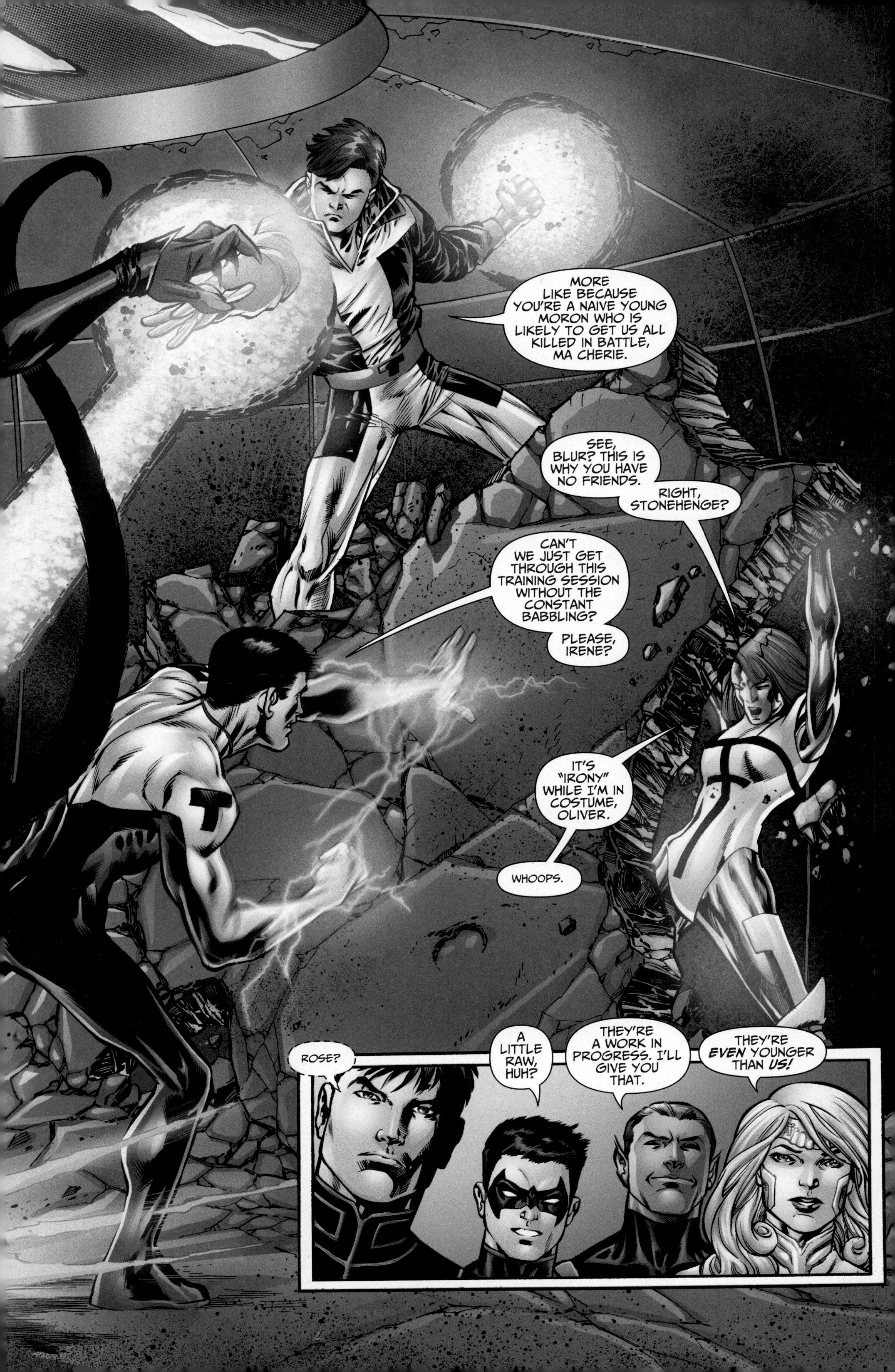
MORE LIKE BECAUSE YOU'RE A NAIVE YOUNG MORON WHO IS LIKELY TO GET US ALL KILLED IN BATTLE, MA CHERIE.
SEE, BLUR? THIS IS WHY YOU HAVE NO FRIENDS.
RIGHT, STONEHENGE?
CAN'T WE JUST GET THROUGH THIS TRAINING SESSION WITHOUT THE CONSTANT BABBLING?
PLEASE, IRENE?
IT'S "IRONY" WHILE I'M IN COSTUME, OLIVER.
WHOOPS.
ROSE?
A LITTLE RAW, HUH?
THEY'RE A WORK IN PROGRESS. I'LL GIVE YOU THAT.
THEY'RE EVEN YOUNGER THAN US!

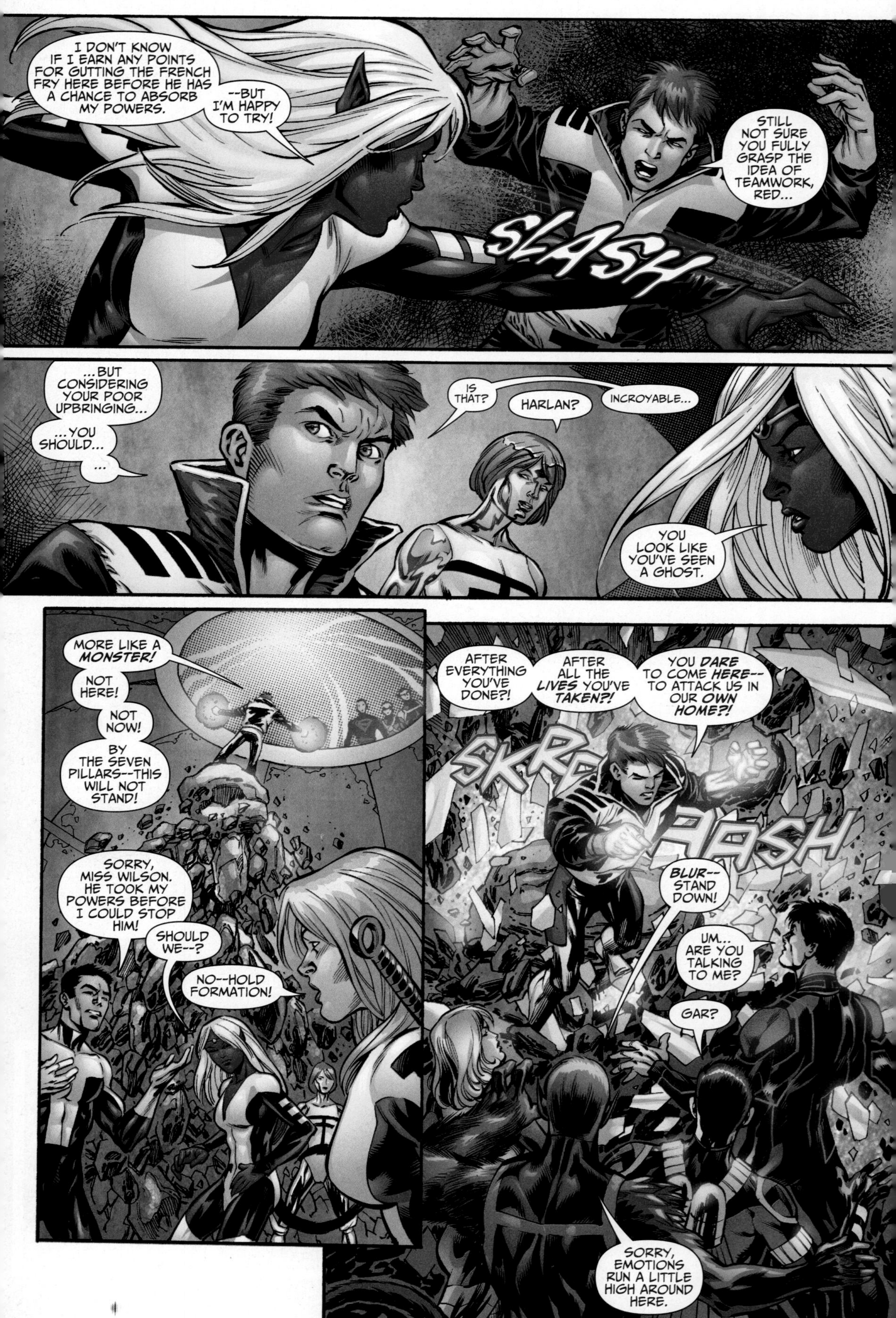
I DON'T KNOW IF I EARN ANY POINTS FOR GUTTING THE FRENCH FRY HERE BEFORE HE HAS A CHANCE TO ABSORB MY POWERS.
--BUT I'M HAPPY TO TRY!
STILL NOT SURE YOU FULLY GRASP THE IDEA OF TEAMWORK, RED...
SLASH
...BUT CONSIDERING YOUR POOR UPBRINGING...
...YOU SHOULD...
...
IS THAT?
HARLAN?
INCROYABLE...
YOU LOOK LIKE YOU'VE SEEN A GHOST.
MORE LIKE A MONSTER!
NOT HERE!
NOT NOW!
BY THE SEVEN PILLARS--THIS WILL NOT STAND!
SORRY, MISS WILSON. HE TOOK MY POWERS BEFORE I COULD STOP HIM!
SHOULD WE--?
NO--HOLD FORMATION!
AFTER EVERYTHING YOU'VE DONE?!
AFTER ALL THE LIVES YOU'VE TAKEN?!
YOU DARE TO COME HERE--TO ATTACK US IN OUR OWN HOME?!
SKRE
ASH
BLUR--STAND DOWN!
UM... ARE YOU TALKING TO ME?
GAR?
SORRY, EMOTIONS RUN A LITTLE HIGH AROUND HERE.

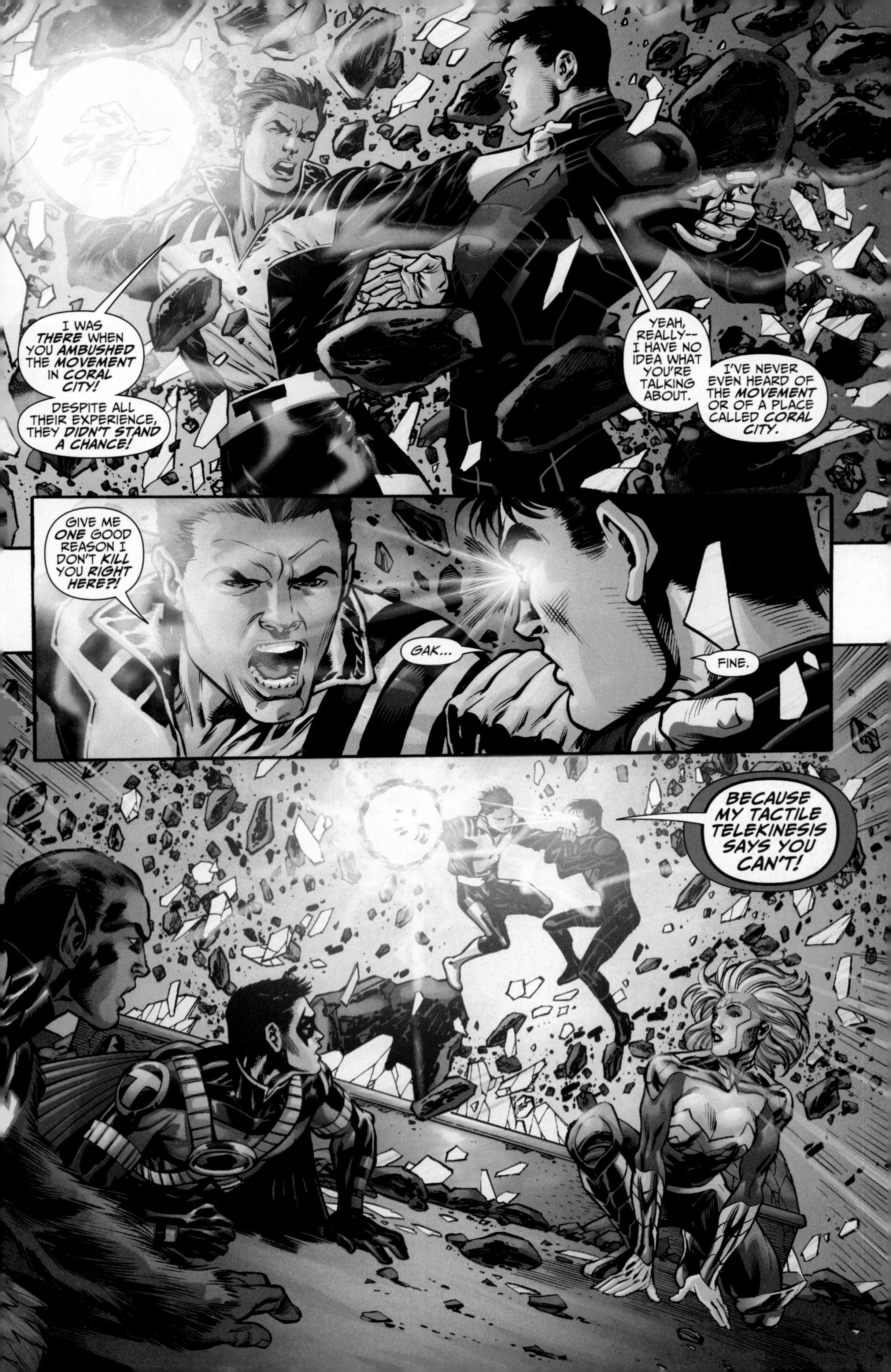
I WAS *THERE* WHEN YOU *AMBUSHED* THE *MOVEMENT* IN *CORAL CITY!*
DESPITE ALL THEIR EXPERIENCE, THEY *DIDN'T STAND A CHANCE!*
YEAH, REALLY-- I HAVE NO IDEA WHAT YOU'RE TALKING ABOUT.
I'VE NEVER EVEN HEARD OF THE *MOVEMENT* OR OF A PLACE CALLED *CORAL CITY.*
GIVE ME *ONE* GOOD REASON I DON'T *KILL* YOU *RIGHT HERE?!*
GAK...
FINE.
BECAUSE MY TACTILE TELEKINESIS SAYS YOU CAN'T!

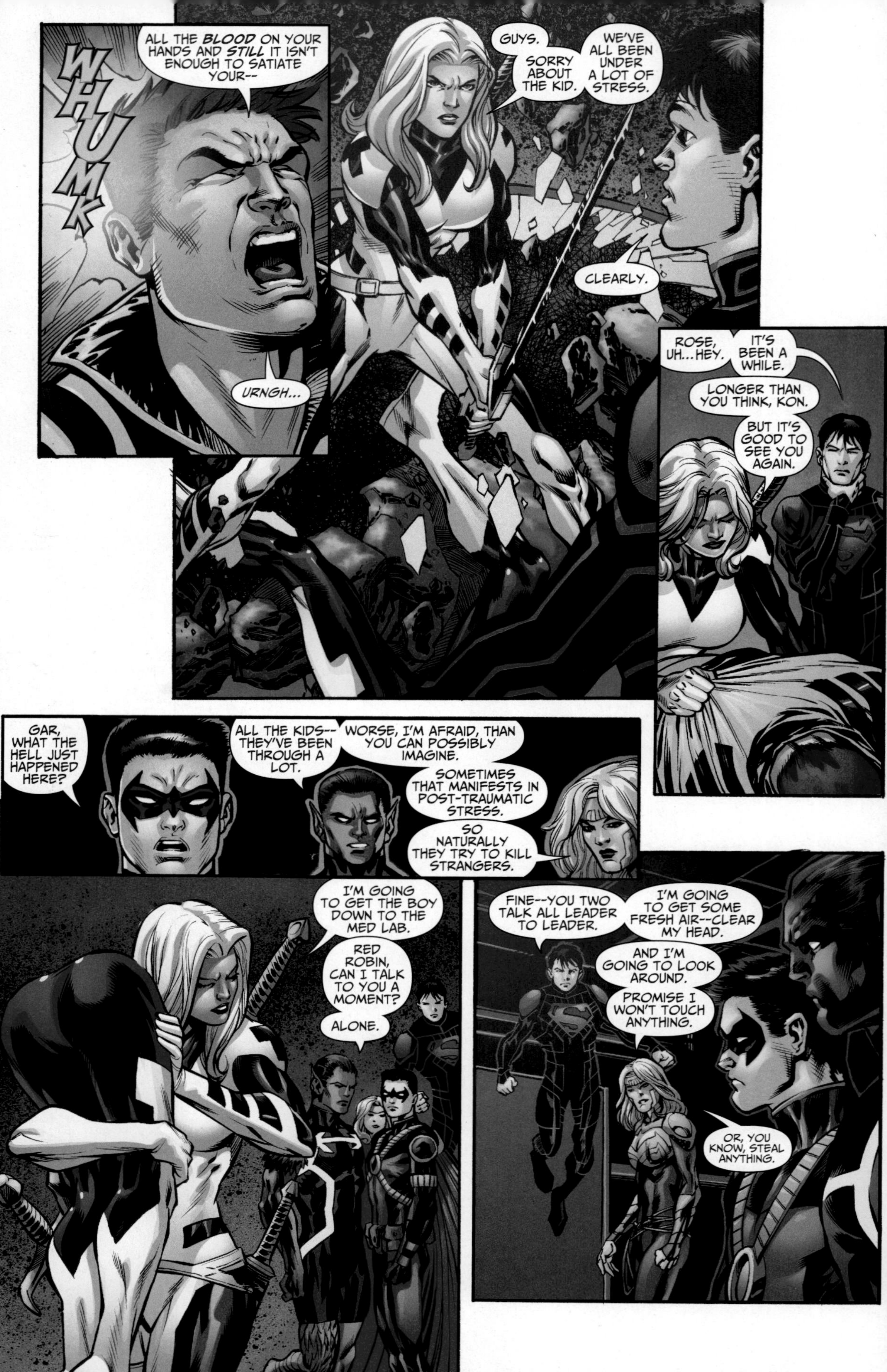
WHUMK
ALL THE BLOOD ON YOUR HANDS AND STILL IT ISN'T ENOUGH TO SATIATE YOUR--
URNGH...
GUYS.
SORRY ABOUT THE KID.
WE'VE ALL BEEN UNDER A LOT OF STRESS.
CLEARLY.
ROSE, UH...HEY.
IT'S BEEN A WHILE.
LONGER THAN YOU THINK, KON.
BUT IT'S GOOD TO SEE YOU AGAIN.
GAR, WHAT THE HELL JUST HAPPENED HERE?
ALL THE KIDS-- THEY'VE BEEN THROUGH A LOT.
WORSE, I'M AFRAID, THAN YOU CAN POSSIBLY IMAGINE.
SOMETIMES THAT MANIFESTS IN POST-TRAUMATIC STRESS.
SO NATURALLY THEY TRY TO KILL STRANGERS.
I'M GOING TO GET THE BOY DOWN TO THE MED LAB.
RED ROBIN, CAN I TALK TO YOU A MOMENT?
ALONE.
FINE--YOU TWO TALK ALL LEADER TO LEADER.
I'M GOING TO GET SOME FRESH AIR--CLEAR MY HEAD.
AND I'M GOING TO LOOK AROUND.
PROMISE I WON'T TOUCH ANYTHING.
OR, YOU KNOW, STEAL ANYTHING.

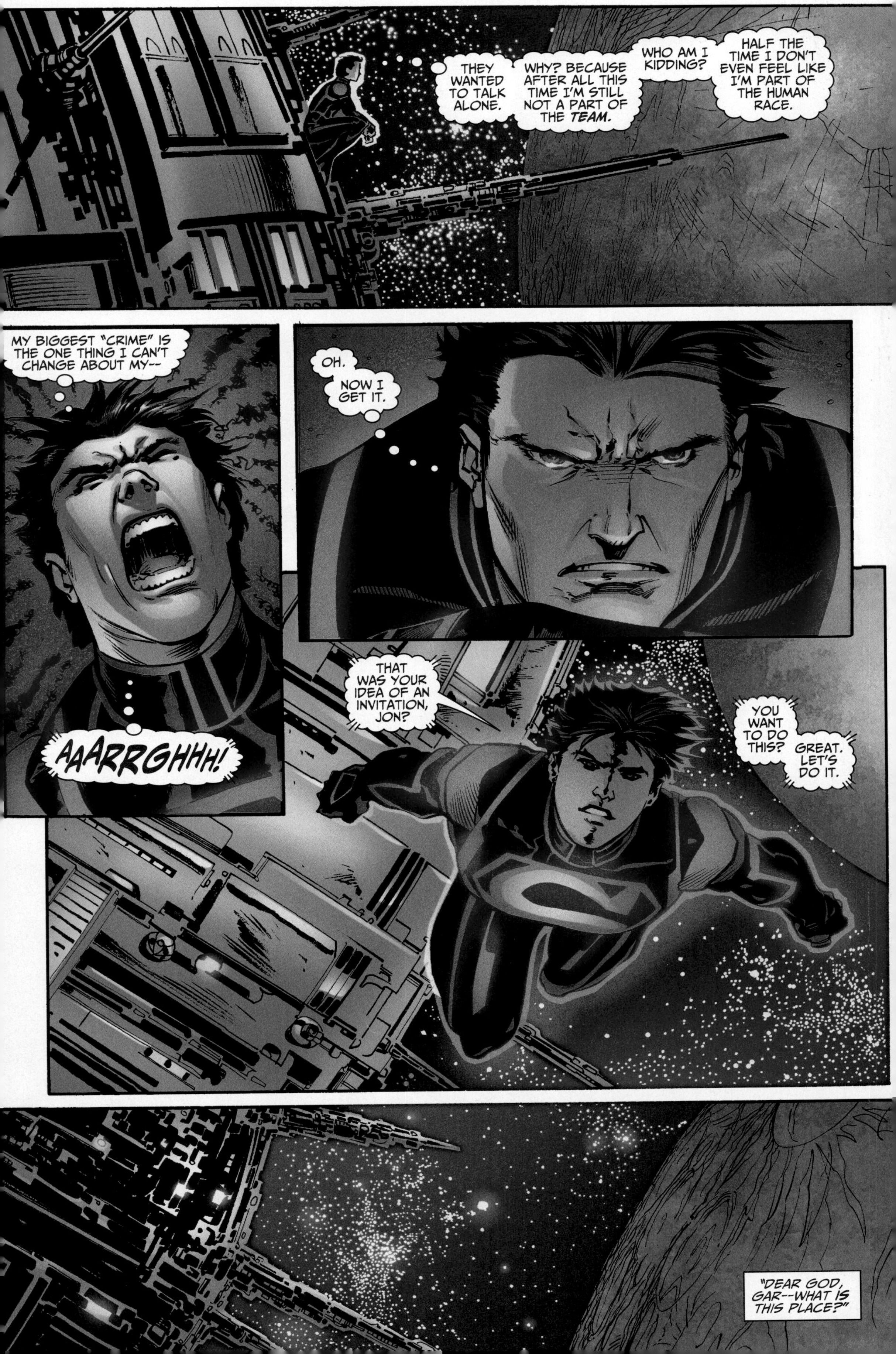
THEY WANTED TO TALK ALONE.
WHY? BECAUSE AFTER ALL THIS TIME I'M STILL NOT A PART OF THE *TEAM.*
WHO AM I KIDDING?
HALF THE TIME I DON'T EVEN FEEL LIKE I'M PART OF THE HUMAN RACE.
MY BIGGEST "CRIME" IS THE ONE THING I CAN'T CHANGE ABOUT MY--
AAARRGHHH!
OH.
NOW I GET IT.
THAT WAS YOUR IDEA OF AN INVITATION, JON?
YOU WANT TO DO THIS?
GREAT. LET'S DO IT.
"DEAR GOD, GAR--WHAT *IS* THIS PLACE?"

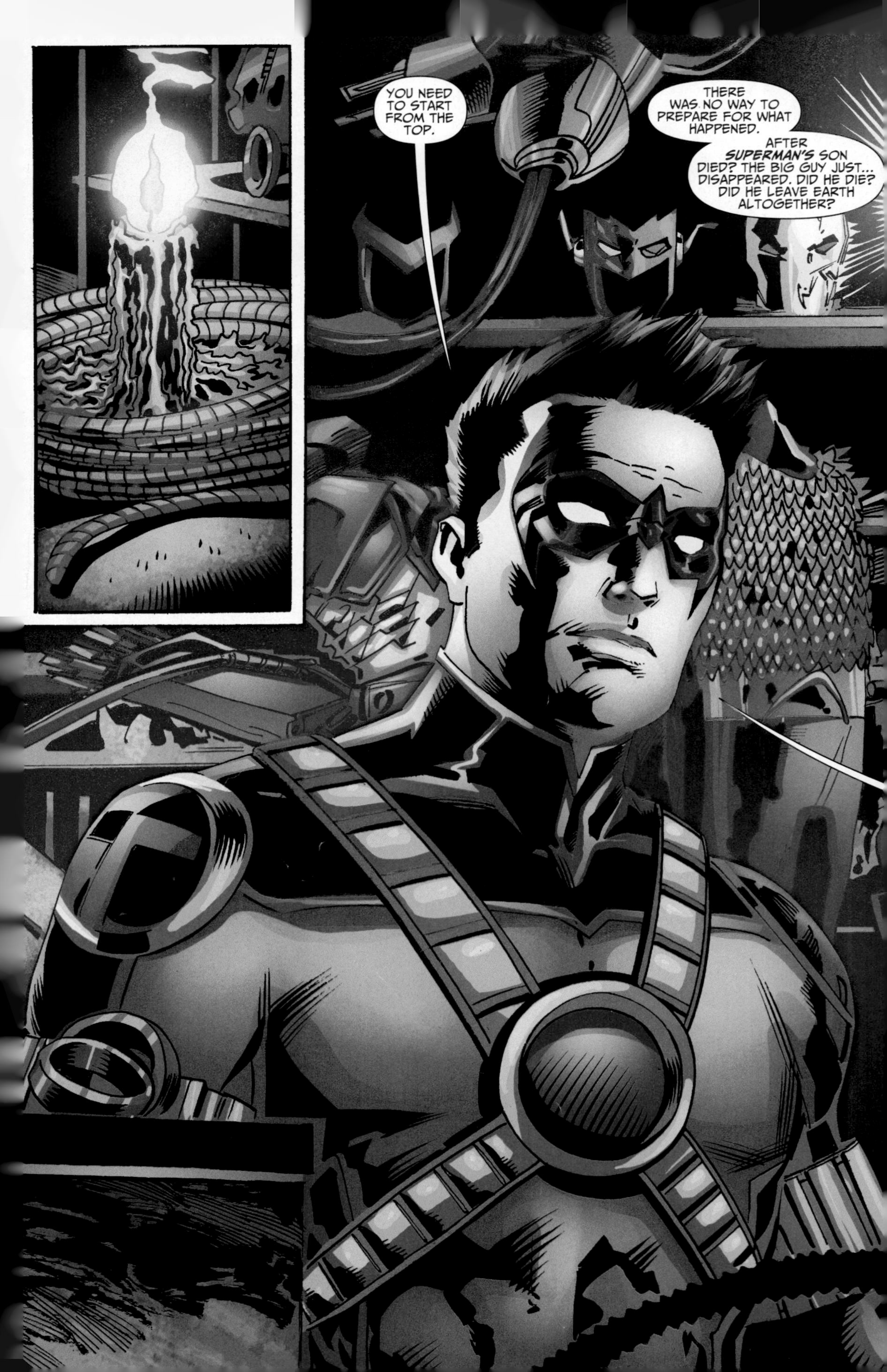

YOU NEED TO START FROM THE TOP.
THERE WAS NO WAY TO PREPARE FOR WHAT HAPPENED.
AFTER SUPERMAN'S SON DIED? THE BIG GUY JUST... DISAPPEARED. DID HE DIE? DID HE LEAVE EARTH ALTOGETHER?

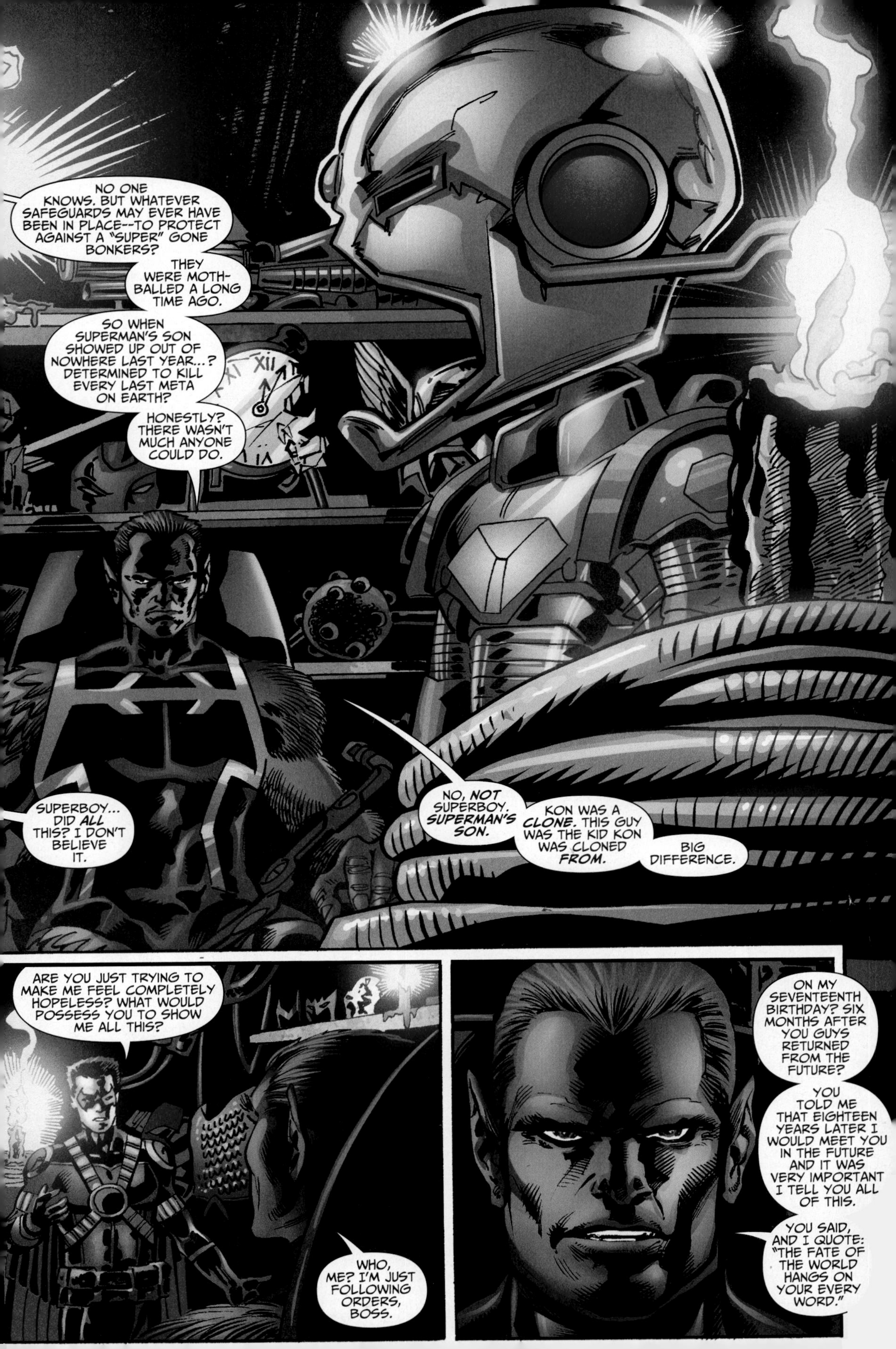
NO ONE KNOWS. BUT WHATEVER SAFEGUARDS MAY EVER HAVE BEEN IN PLACE--TO PROTECT AGAINST A "SUPER" GONE BONKERS?
THEY WERE MOTH-BALLED A LONG TIME AGO.
SO WHEN SUPERMAN'S SON SHOWED UP OUT OF NOWHERE LAST YEAR...? DETERMINED TO KILL EVERY LAST META ON EARTH?
HONESTLY? THERE WASN'T MUCH ANYONE COULD DO.
SUPERBOY... DID **ALL** THIS? I DON'T BELIEVE IT.
NO, **NOT** SUPERBOY. ***SUPERMAN'S SON.***
KON WAS A ***CLONE.*** THIS GUY WAS THE KID KON WAS CLONED ***FROM.***
BIG DIFFERENCE.
ARE YOU JUST TRYING TO MAKE ME FEEL COMPLETELY HOPELESS? WHAT WOULD POSSESS YOU TO SHOW ME ALL THIS?
WHO, ME? I'M JUST FOLLOWING ORDERS, BOSS.
ON MY SEVENTEENTH BIRTHDAY? SIX MONTHS AFTER YOU GUYS RETURNED FROM THE FUTURE?
YOU TOLD ME THAT EIGHTEEN YEARS LATER I WOULD MEET YOU IN THE FUTURE AND IT WAS VERY IMPORTANT I TELL YOU ALL OF THIS.
YOU SAID, AND I QUOTE: "THE FATE OF THE WORLD HANGS ON YOUR EVERY WORD."

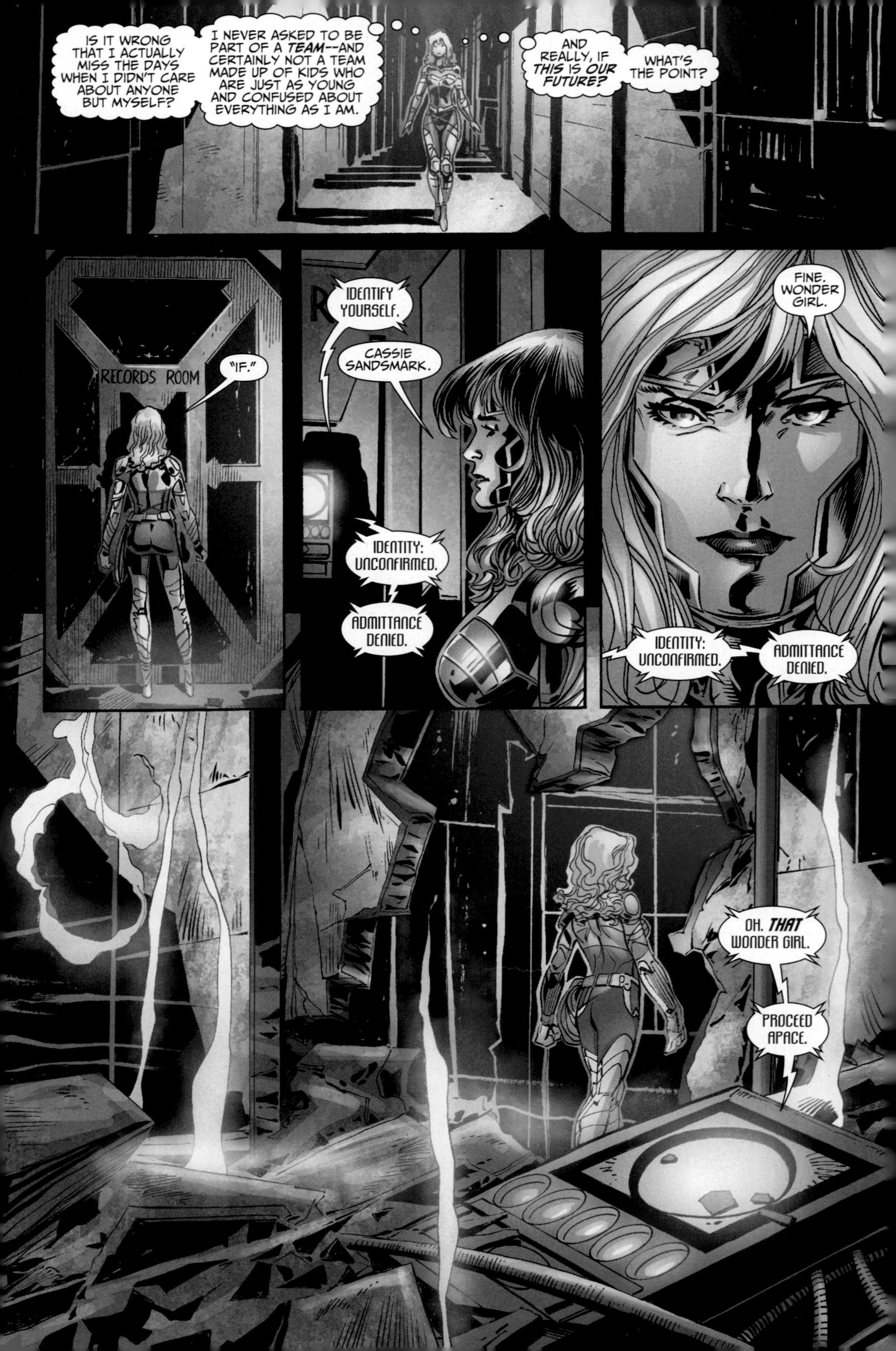
IS IT WRONG THAT I ACTUALLY MISS THE DAYS WHEN I DIDN'T CARE ABOUT ANYONE BUT MYSELF?
I NEVER ASKED TO BE PART OF A TEAM--AND CERTAINLY NOT A TEAM MADE UP OF KIDS WHO ARE JUST AS YOUNG AND CONFUSED ABOUT EVERYTHING AS I AM.
AND REALLY, IF THIS IS OUR FUTURE?
WHAT'S THE POINT?
RECORDS ROOM
"IF."
IDENTIFY YOURSELF.
CASSIE SANDSMARK.
IDENTITY: UNCONFIRMED.
ADMITTANCE DENIED.
FINE. WONDER GIRL.
IDENTITY: UNCONFIRMED.
ADMITTANCE DENIED.
OH. THAT WONDER GIRL.
PROCEED APACE.

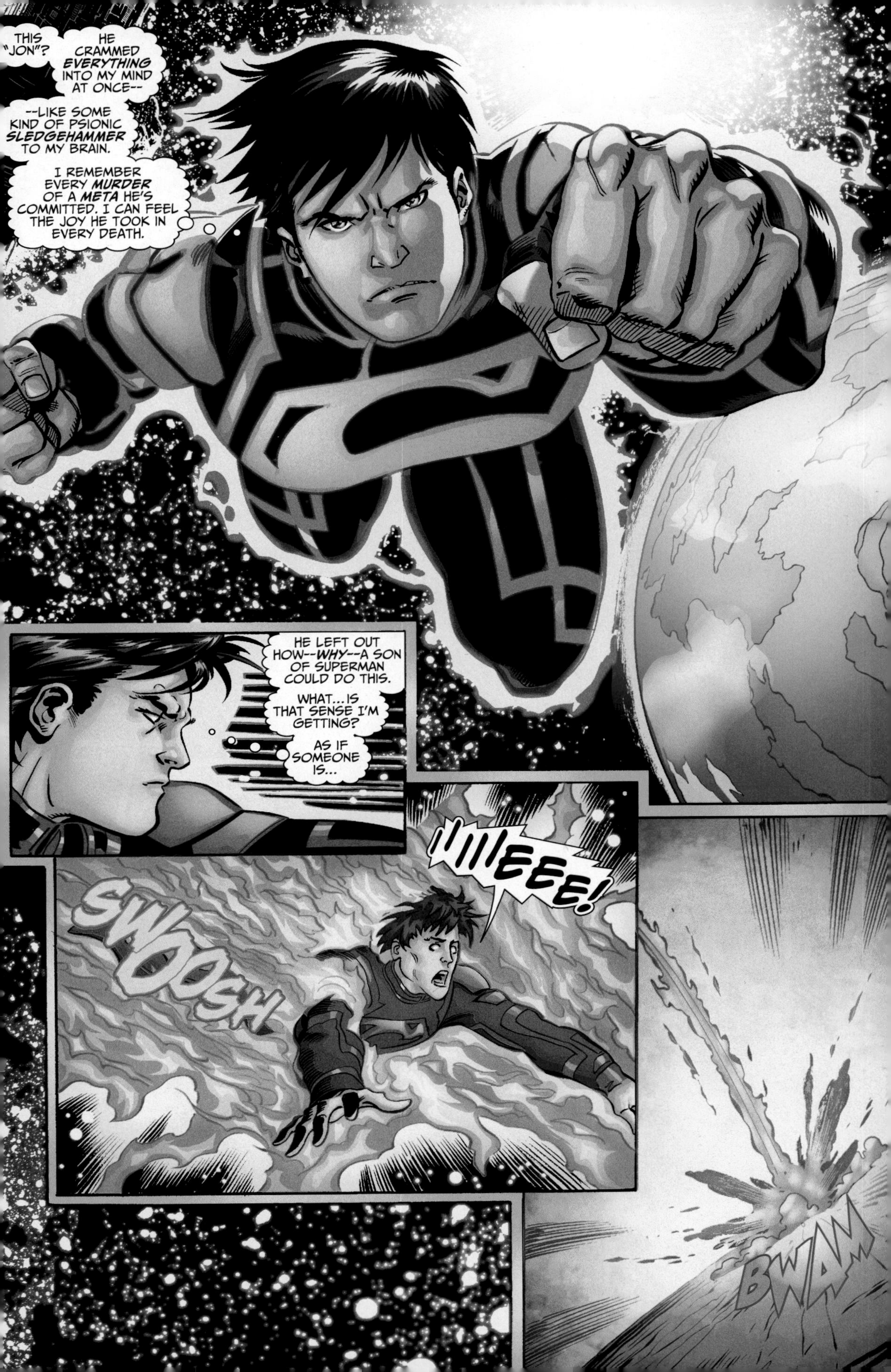
THIS "JON"?
HE CRAMMED EVERYTHING INTO MY MIND AT ONCE--
--LIKE SOME KIND OF PSIONIC SLEDGEHAMMER TO MY BRAIN.
I REMEMBER EVERY MURDER OF A META HE'S COMMITTED. I CAN FEEL THE JOY HE TOOK IN EVERY DEATH.
HE LEFT OUT HOW--WHY--A SON OF SUPERMAN COULD DO THIS.
WHAT...IS THAT SENSE I'M GETTING?
AS IF SOMEONE IS...
IIIIEEEE!
SWOOSH
BWAM

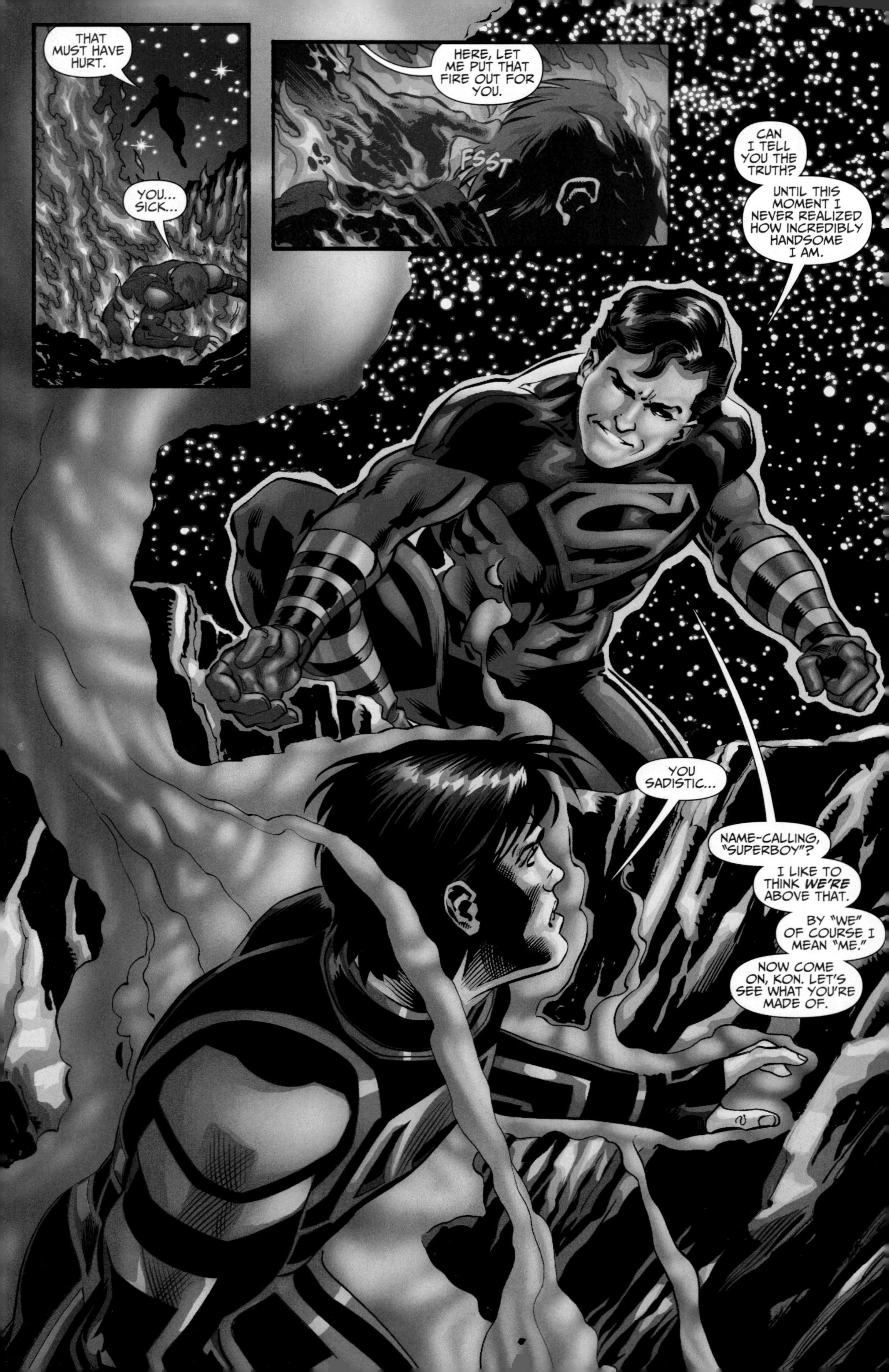
THAT MUST HAVE HURT.
YOU... SICK...
HERE, LET ME PUT THAT FIRE OUT FOR YOU.
FSST
CAN I TELL YOU THE TRUTH?
UNTIL THIS MOMENT I NEVER REALIZED HOW INCREDIBLY HANDSOME I AM.
YOU SADISTIC...
NAME-CALLING, "SUPERBOY"?
I LIKE TO THINK *WE'RE* ABOVE THAT.
BY "WE" OF COURSE I MEAN "ME."
NOW COME ON, KON. LET'S SEE WHAT YOU'RE MADE OF.

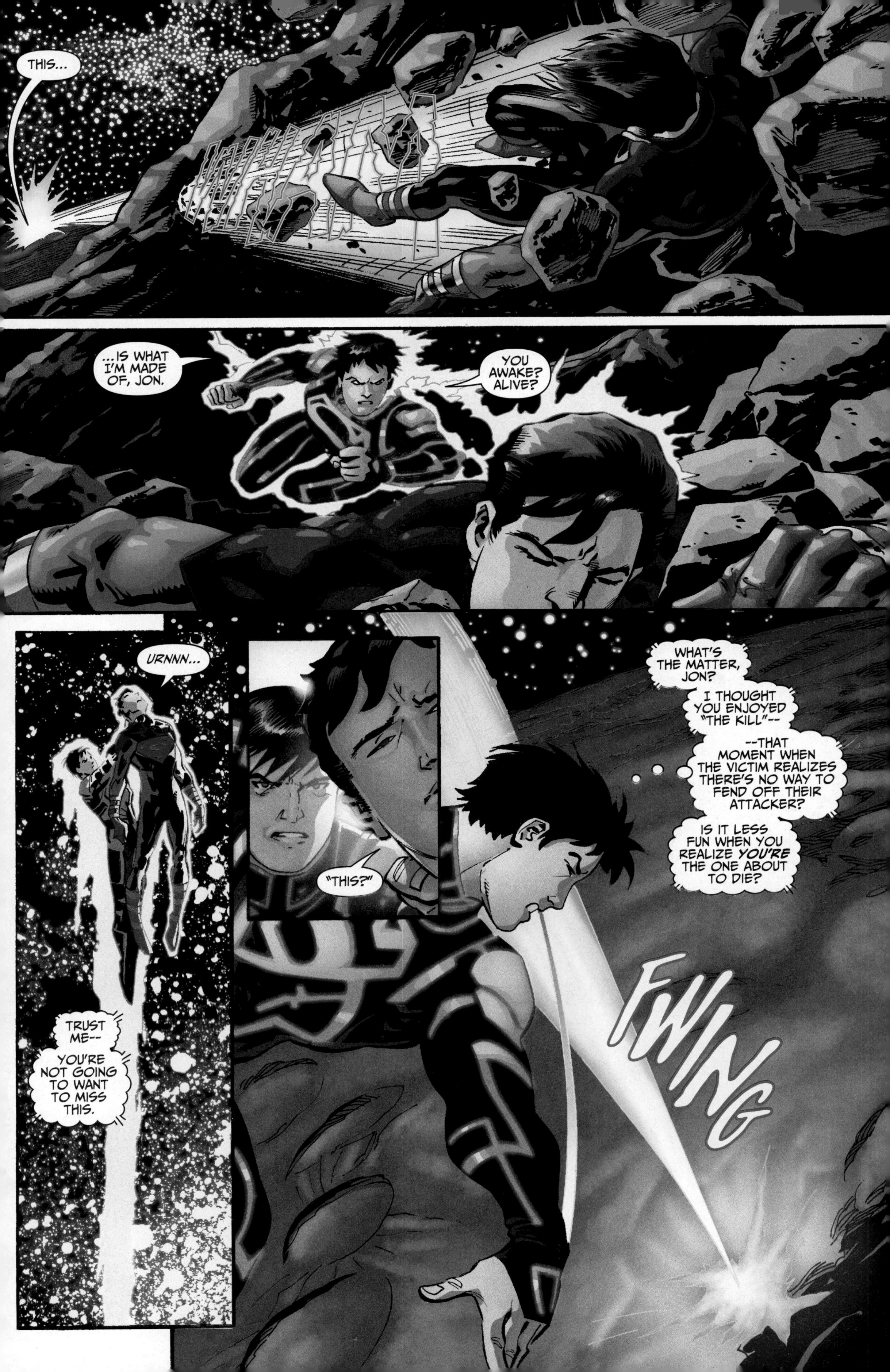
THIS...
...IS WHAT I'M MADE OF, JON.
YOU AWAKE? ALIVE?
URNNN...
TRUST ME--
YOU'RE NOT GOING TO WANT TO MISS THIS.
"THIS?"
WHAT'S THE MATTER, JON?
I THOUGHT YOU ENJOYED "THE KILL"--
--THAT MOMENT WHEN THE VICTIM REALIZES THERE'S NO WAY TO FEND OFF THEIR ATTACKER?
IS IT LESS FUN WHEN YOU REALIZE *YOU'RE* THE ONE ABOUT TO DIE?
FWING

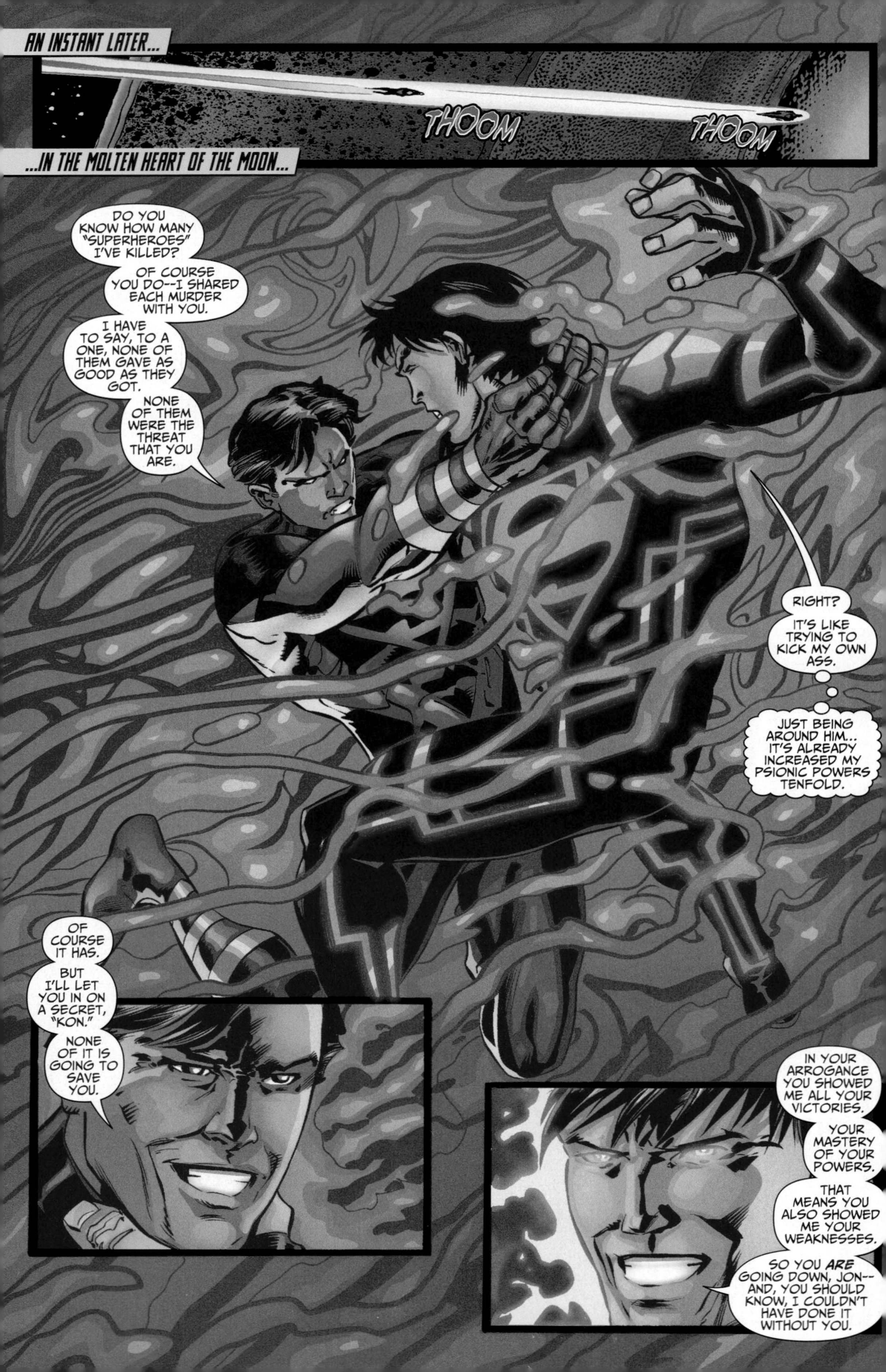
AN INSTANT LATER...
THOOM
THOOM
...IN THE MOLTEN HEART OF THE MOON...
DO YOU KNOW HOW MANY "SUPERHEROES" I'VE KILLED?
OF COURSE YOU DO--I SHARED EACH MURDER WITH YOU.
I HAVE TO SAY, TO A ONE, NONE OF THEM GAVE AS GOOD AS THEY GOT.
NONE OF THEM WERE THE THREAT THAT YOU ARE.
RIGHT?
IT'S LIKE TRYING TO KICK MY OWN ASS.
JUST BEING AROUND HIM... IT'S ALREADY INCREASED MY PSIONIC POWERS TENFOLD.
OF COURSE IT HAS.
BUT I'LL LET YOU IN ON A SECRET, "KON."
NONE OF IT IS GOING TO SAVE YOU.
IN YOUR ARROGANCE YOU SHOWED ME ALL YOUR VICTORIES.
YOUR MASTERY OF YOUR POWERS.
THAT MEANS YOU ALSO SHOWED ME YOUR WEAKNESSES.
SO YOU ARE GOING DOWN, JON-- AND, YOU SHOULD KNOW, I COULDN'T HAVE DONE IT WITHOUT YOU.

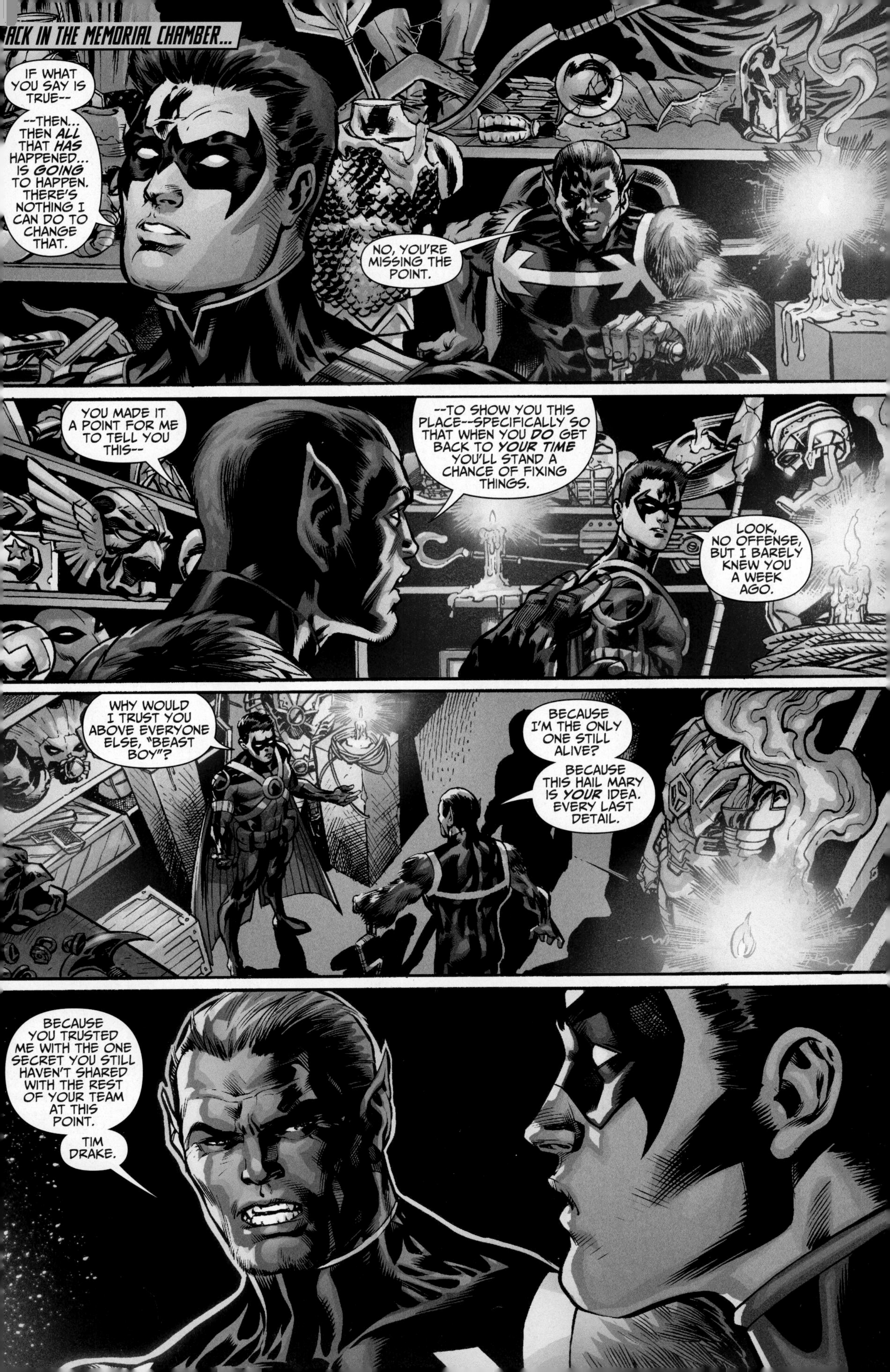

ACK IN THE MEMORIAL CHAMBER...
IF WHAT YOU SAY IS TRUE--
--THEN... THEN ALL THAT HAS HAPPENED... IS GOING TO HAPPEN. THERE'S NOTHING I CAN DO TO CHANGE THAT.
NO, YOU'RE MISSING THE POINT.
YOU MADE IT A POINT FOR ME TO TELL YOU THIS--
--TO SHOW YOU THIS PLACE--SPECIFICALLY SO THAT WHEN YOU DO GET BACK TO YOUR TIME YOU'LL STAND A CHANCE OF FIXING THINGS.
LOOK, NO OFFENSE, BUT I BARELY KNEW YOU A WEEK AGO.
WHY WOULD I TRUST YOU ABOVE EVERYONE ELSE, "BEAST BOY"?
BECAUSE I'M THE ONLY ONE STILL ALIVE?
BECAUSE THIS HAIL MARY IS YOUR IDEA. EVERY LAST DETAIL.
BECAUSE YOU TRUSTED ME WITH THE ONE SECRET YOU STILL HAVEN'T SHARED WITH THE REST OF YOUR TEAM AT THIS POINT.
TIM DRAKE.

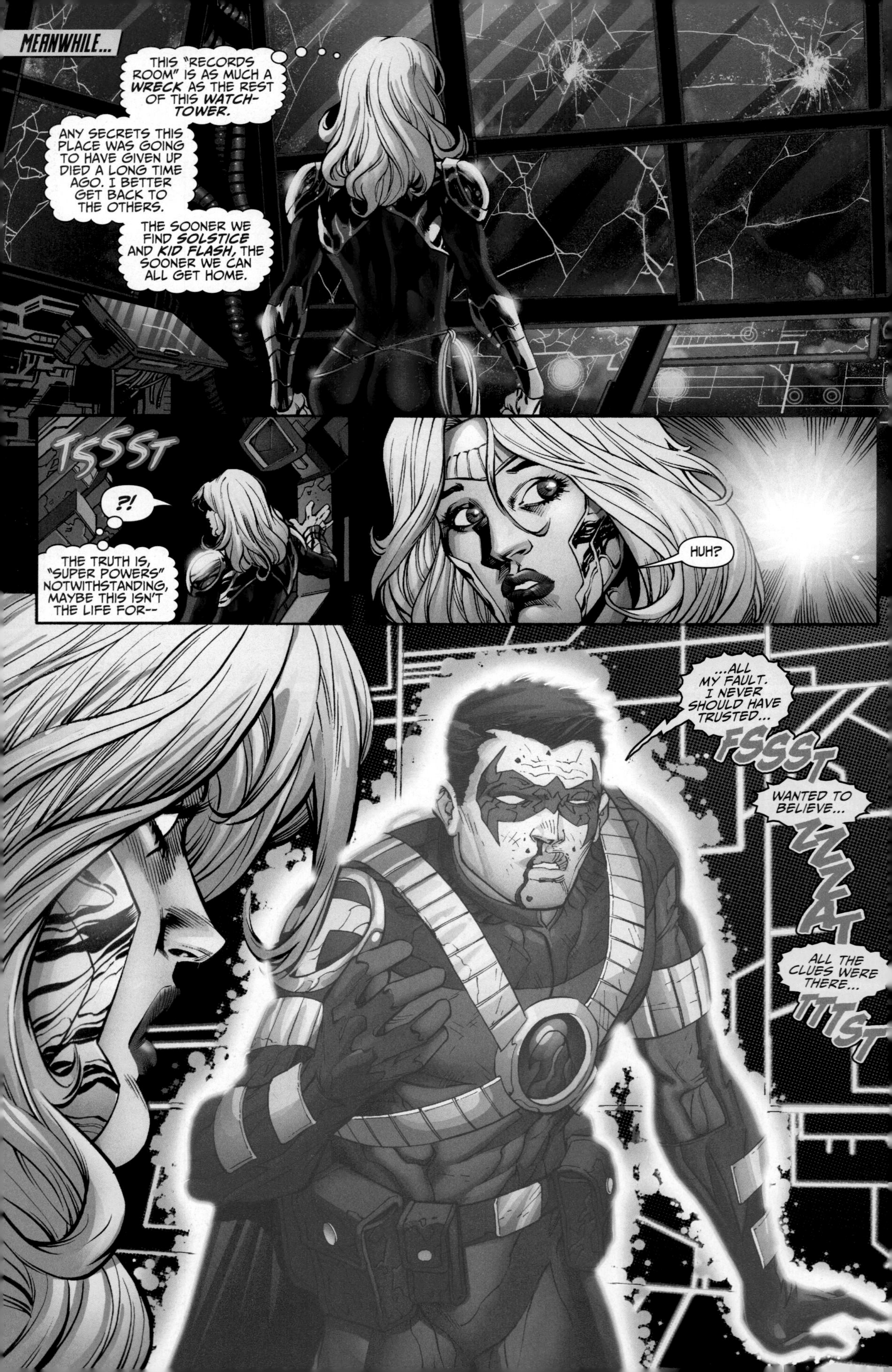
MEANWHILE...
THIS "RECORDS ROOM" IS AS MUCH A WRECK AS THE REST OF THIS WATCH-TOWER.
ANY SECRETS THIS PLACE WAS GOING TO HAVE GIVEN UP DIED A LONG TIME AGO. I BETTER GET BACK TO THE OTHERS.
THE SOONER WE FIND SOLSTICE AND KID FLASH, THE SOONER WE CAN ALL GET HOME.
TSSST
?!
THE TRUTH IS, "SUPER POWERS" NOTWITHSTANDING, MAYBE THIS ISN'T THE LIFE FOR--
HUH?
...ALL MY FAULT. I NEVER SHOULD HAVE TRUSTED...
FSSST
WANTED TO BELIEVE...
ZZZAT
ALL THE CLUES WERE THERE...
TTTST

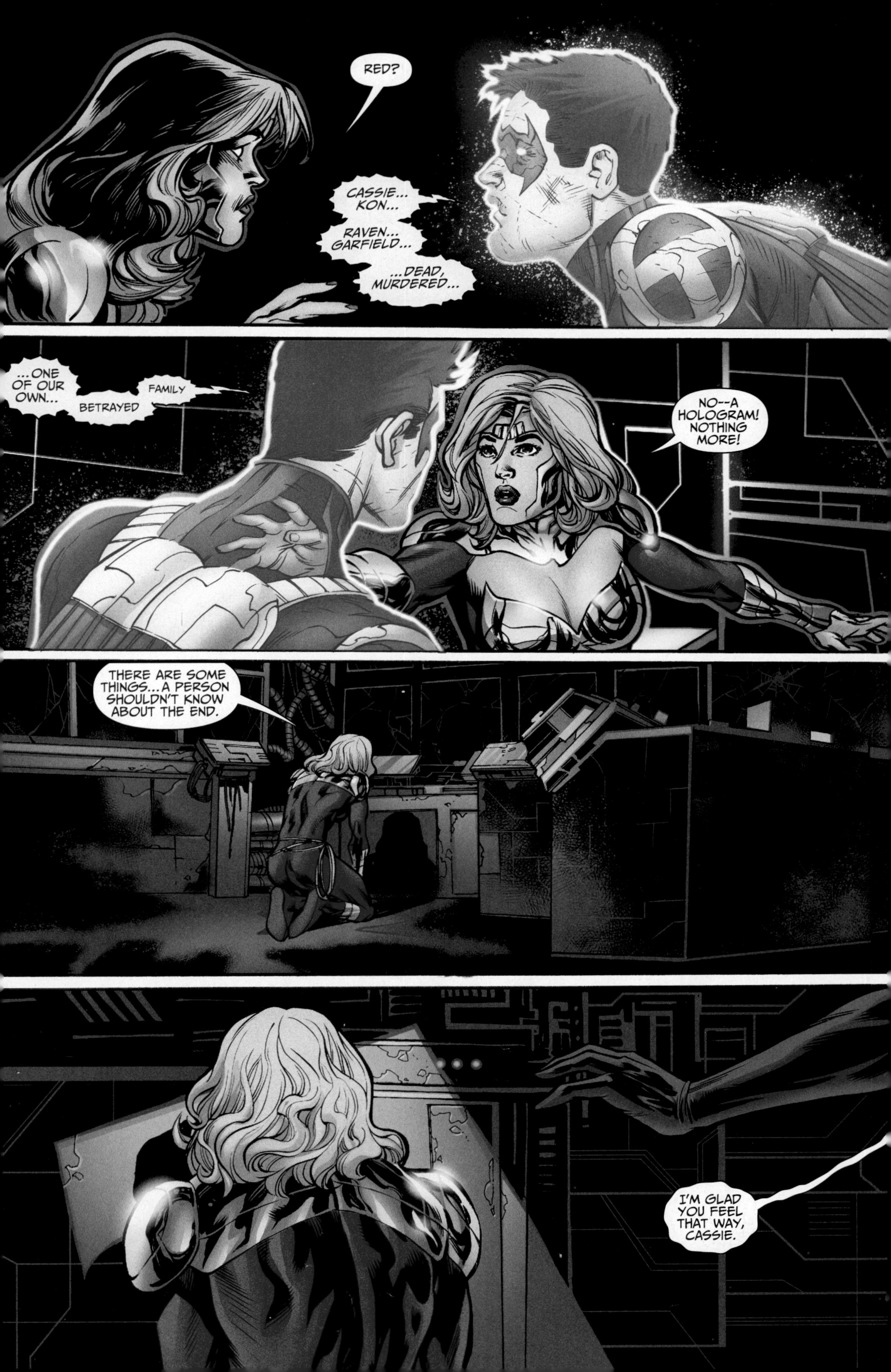
RED?
CASSIE... KON...
RAVEN... GARFIELD...
...DEAD, MURDERED...
...ONE OF OUR OWN...
BETRAYED
FAMILY
NO--A HOLOGRAM! NOTHING MORE!
THERE ARE SOME THINGS...A PERSON SHOULDN'T KNOW ABOUT THE END.
I'M GLAD YOU FEEL THAT WAY, CASSIE.

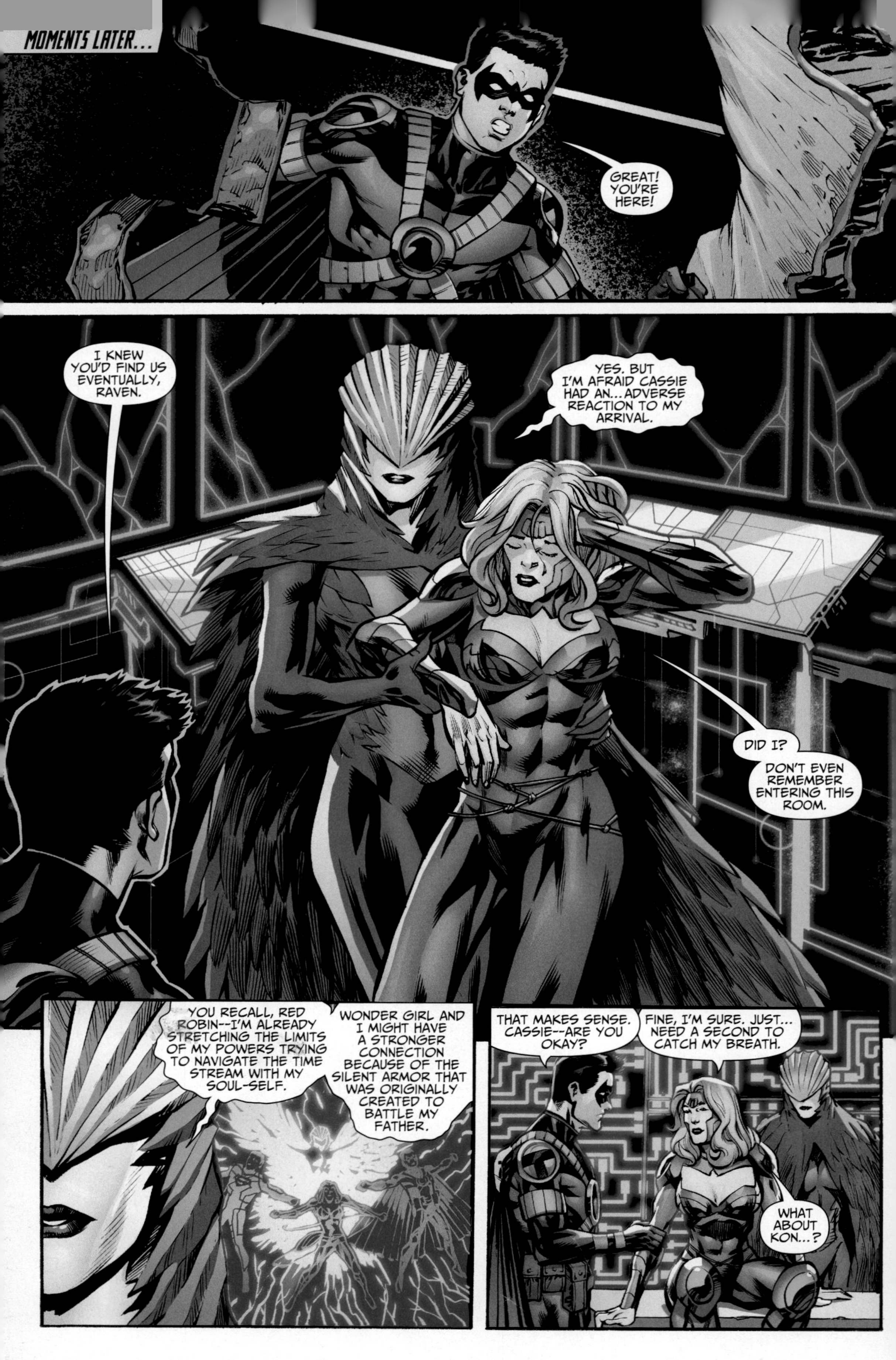
MOMENTS LATER...
GREAT! YOU'RE HERE!
I KNEW YOU'D FIND US EVENTUALLY, RAVEN.
YES. BUT I'M AFRAID CASSIE HAD AN...ADVERSE REACTION TO MY ARRIVAL.
DID I?
DON'T EVEN REMEMBER ENTERING THIS ROOM.
YOU RECALL, RED ROBIN--I'M ALREADY STRETCHING THE LIMITS OF MY POWERS TRYING TO NAVIGATE THE TIME STREAM WITH MY SOUL-SELF.
WONDER GIRL AND I MIGHT HAVE A STRONGER CONNECTION BECAUSE OF THE SILENT ARMOR THAT WAS ORIGINALLY CREATED TO BATTLE MY FATHER.
THAT MAKES SENSE. CASSIE--ARE YOU OKAY?
FINE, I'M SURE. JUST... NEED A SECOND TO CATCH MY BREATH.
WHAT ABOUT KON...?

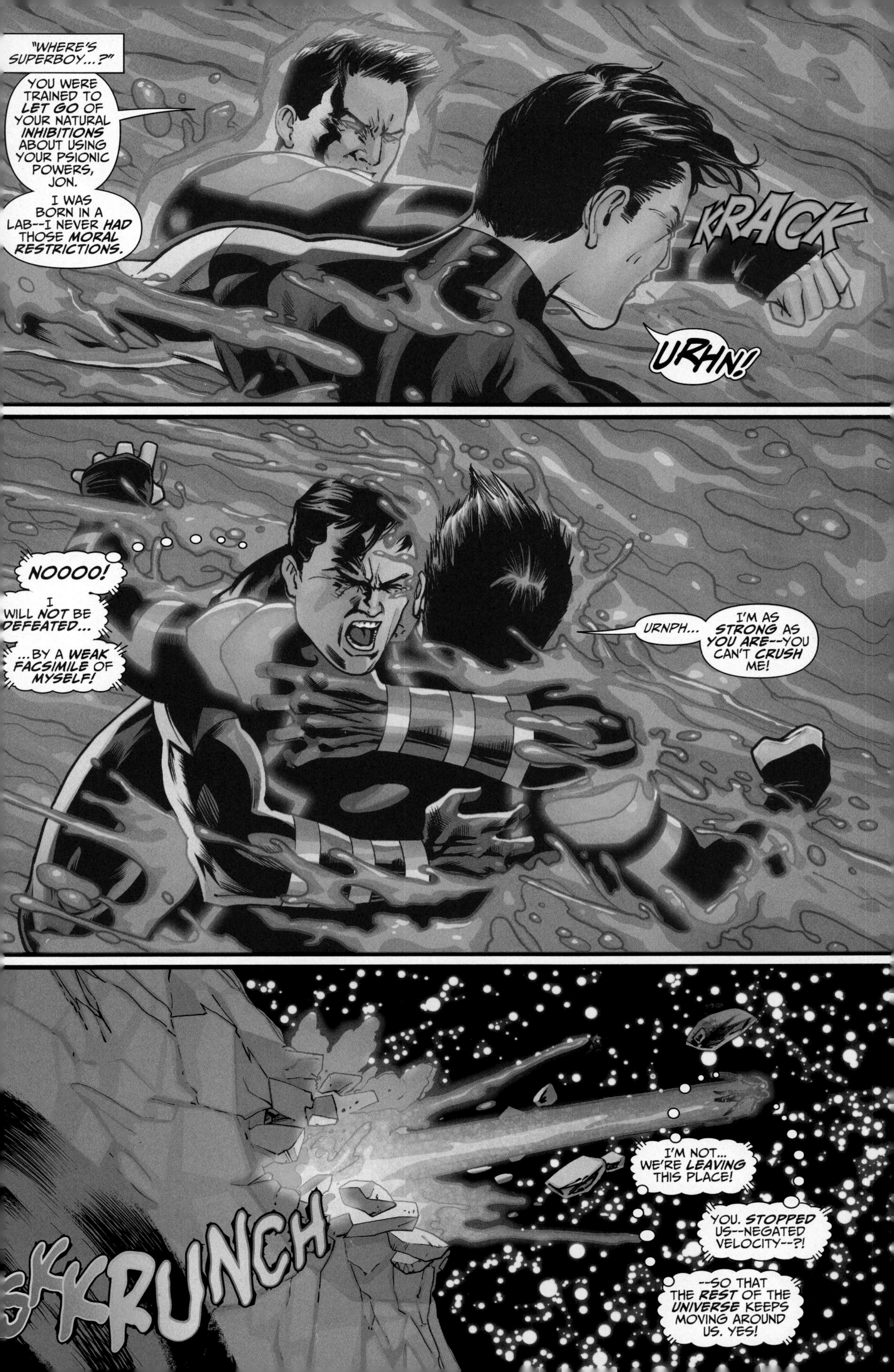
"WHERE'S SUPERBOY...?"
YOU WERE TRAINED TO LET GO OF YOUR NATURAL INHIBITIONS ABOUT USING YOUR PSIONIC POWERS, JON.
I WAS BORN IN A LAB--I NEVER HAD THOSE MORAL RESTRICTIONS.
KRACK
URHN!
NOOOO!
I WILL NOT BE DEFEATED...
...BY A WEAK FACSIMILE OF MYSELF!
URNPH...
I'M AS STRONG AS YOU ARE--YOU CAN'T CRUSH ME!
SKKRUNCH
I'M NOT... WE'RE LEAVING THIS PLACE!
YOU. STOPPED US--NEGATED VELOCITY--?!
--SO THAT THE REST OF THE UNIVERSE KEEPS MOVING AROUND US. YES!

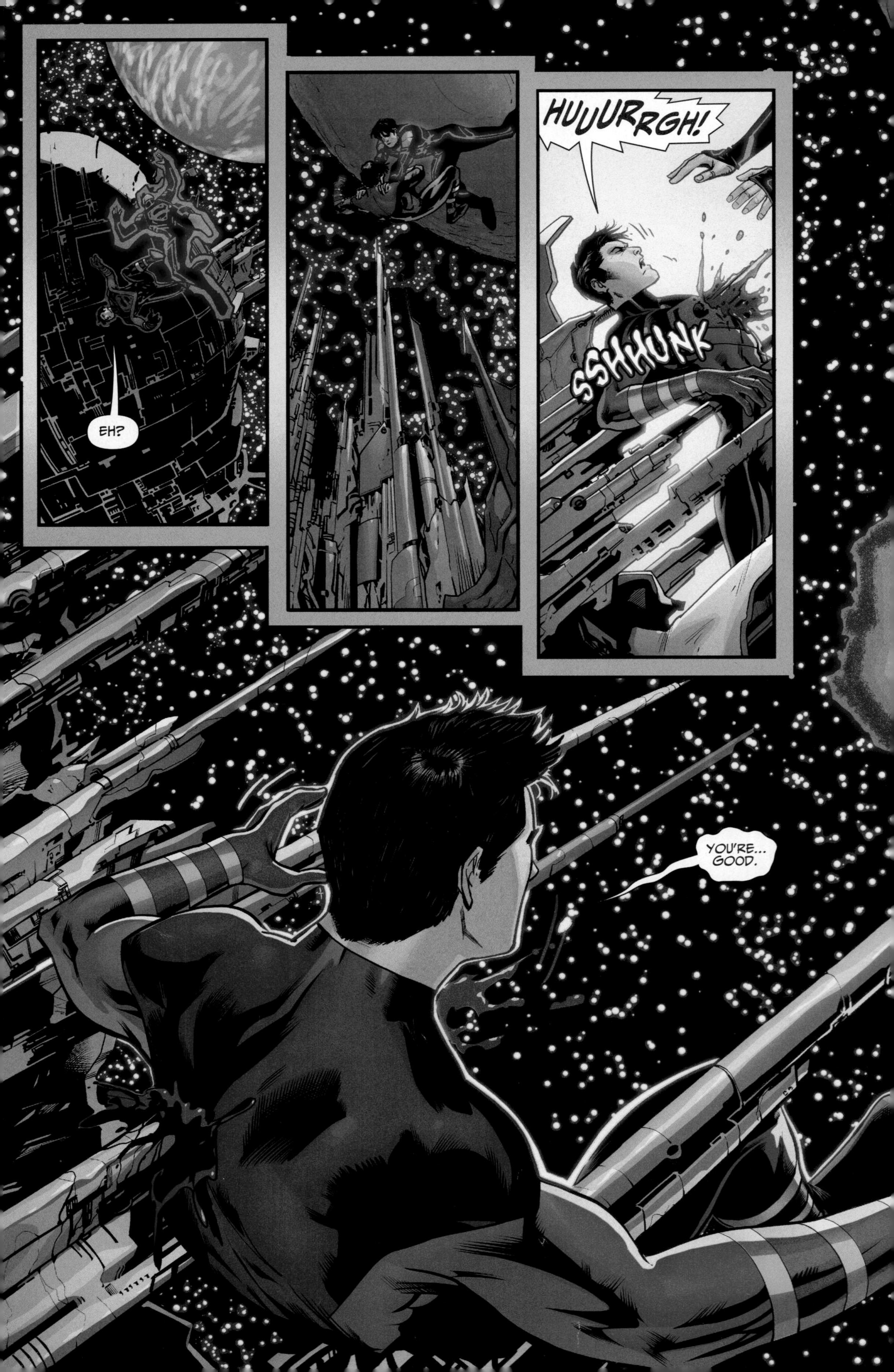
EH?
HUUURRGH!
SSHHUNK
YOU'RE... GOOD.

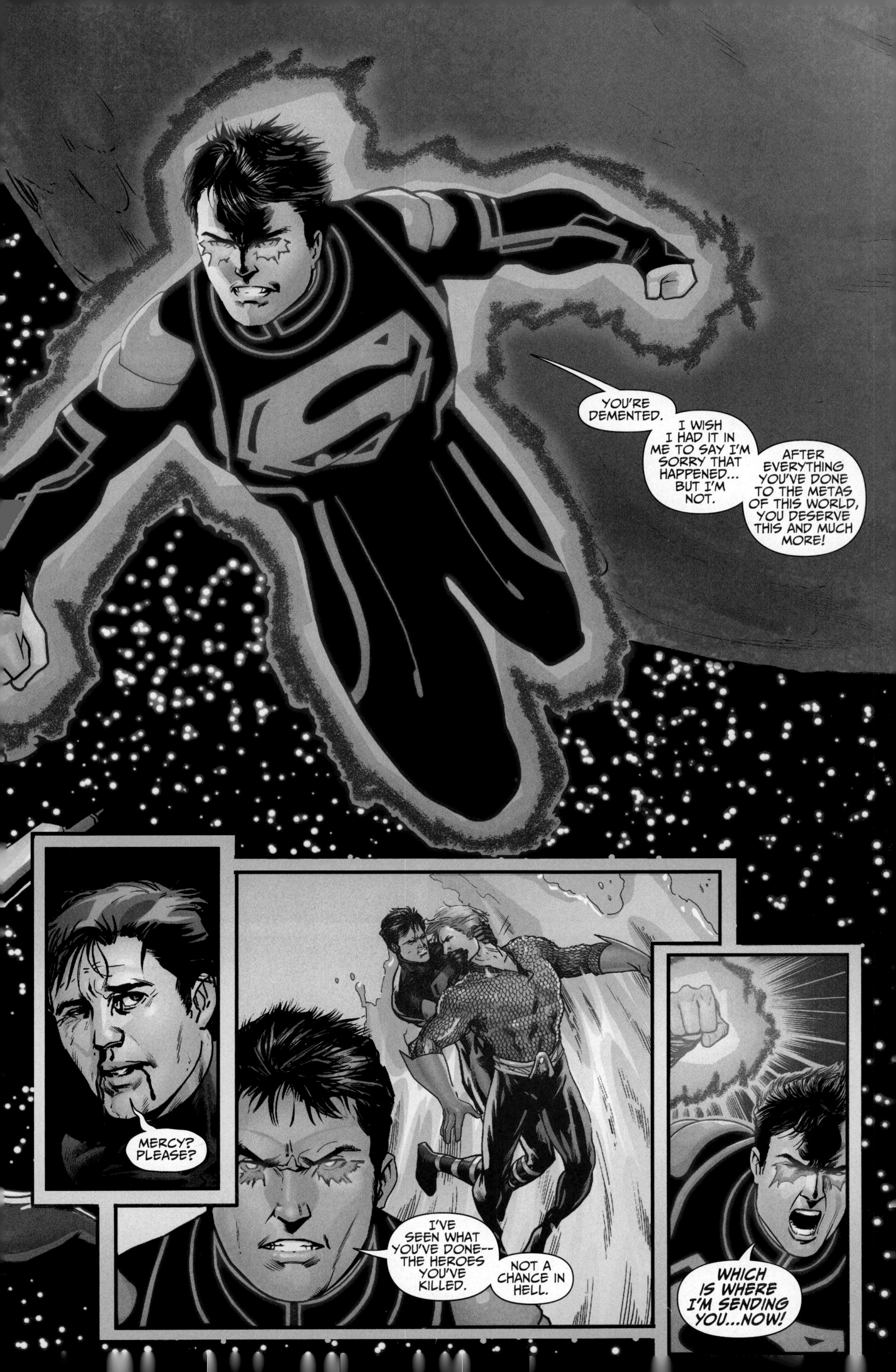
YOU'RE DEMENTED.
I WISH I HAD IT IN ME TO SAY I'M SORRY THAT HAPPENED... BUT I'M NOT.
AFTER EVERYTHING YOU'VE DONE TO THE METAS OF THIS WORLD, YOU DESERVE THIS AND MUCH MORE!
MERCY? PLEASE?
I'VE SEEN WHAT YOU'VE DONE-- THE HEROES YOU'VE KILLED.
NOT A CHANCE IN HELL.
WHICH IS WHERE I'M SENDING YOU...NOW!

WHA--?!

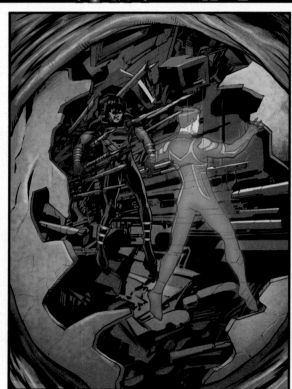

GONE...

...WHERE?

CHHSSST

DID YOU FIND HIM, GAR?

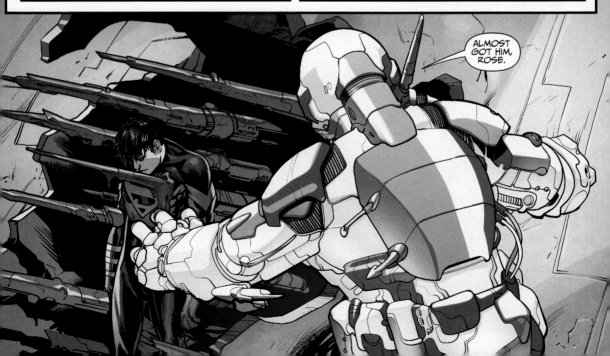

ALMOST GOT HIM, ROSE.

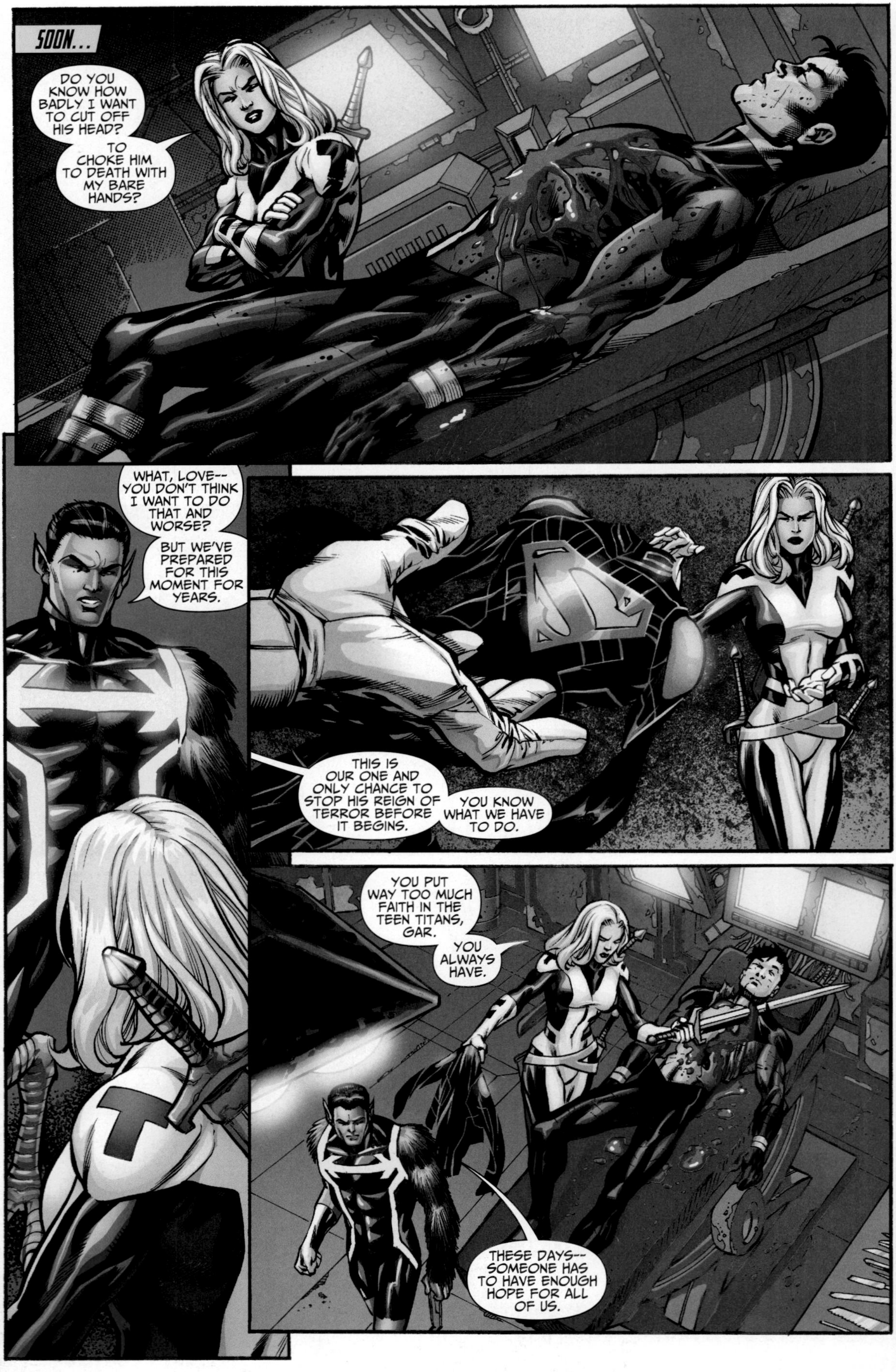
SOON...
DO YOU KNOW HOW BADLY I WANT TO CUT OFF HIS HEAD?
TO CHOKE HIM TO DEATH WITH MY BARE HANDS?
WHAT, LOVE-- YOU DON'T THINK I WANT TO DO THAT AND WORSE?
BUT WE'VE PREPARED FOR THIS MOMENT FOR YEARS.
THIS IS OUR ONE AND ONLY CHANCE TO STOP HIS REIGN OF TERROR BEFORE IT BEGINS.
YOU KNOW WHAT WE HAVE TO DO.
YOU PUT WAY TOO MUCH FAITH IN THE TEEN TITANS, GAR.
YOU ALWAYS HAVE.
THESE DAYS-- SOMEONE HAS TO HAVE ENOUGH HOPE FOR ALL OF US.

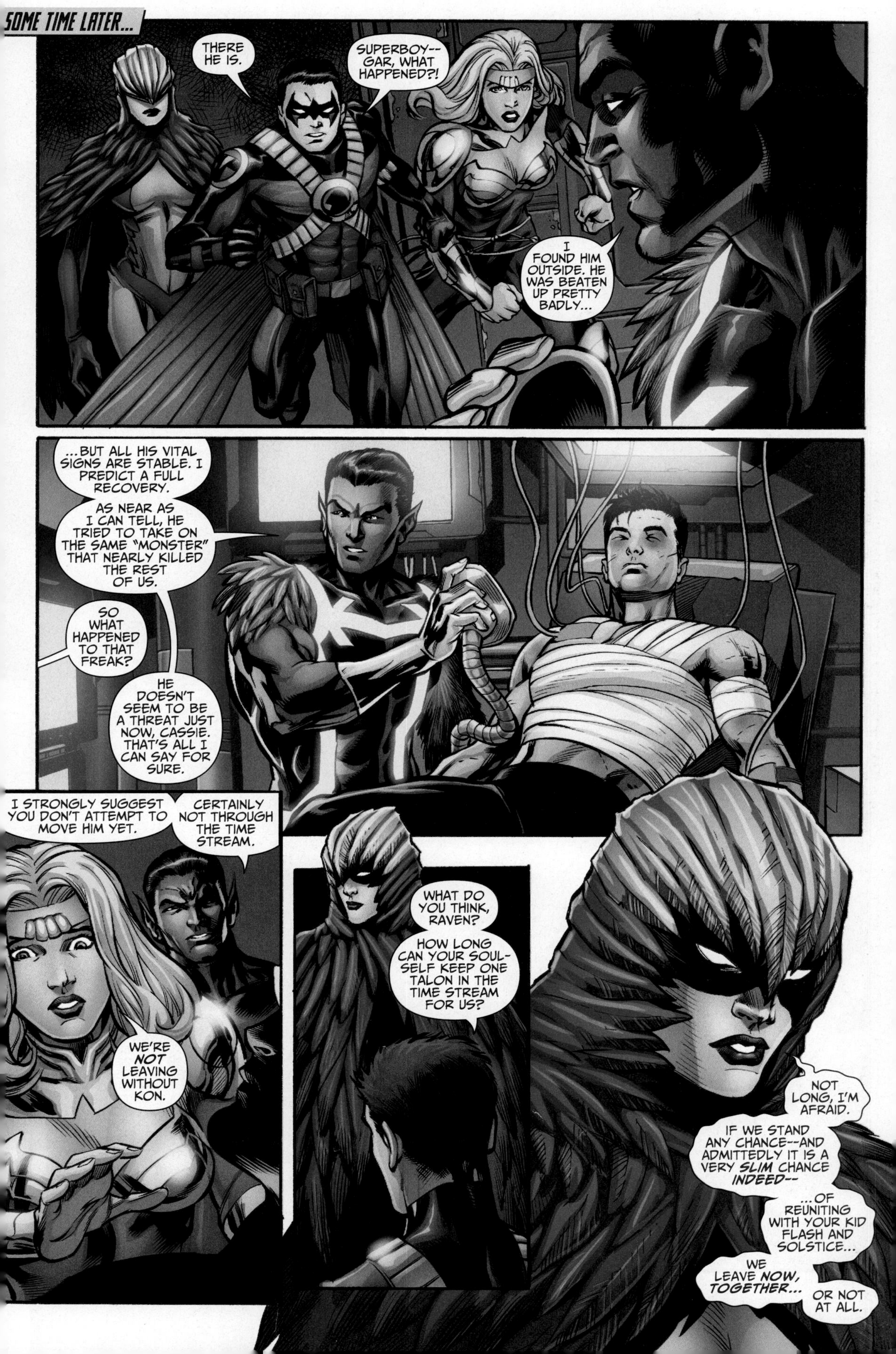
SOME TIME LATER...
THERE HE IS.
SUPERBOY--GAR, WHAT HAPPENED?!
I FOUND HIM OUTSIDE. HE WAS BEATEN UP PRETTY BADLY...
...BUT ALL HIS VITAL SIGNS ARE STABLE. I PREDICT A FULL RECOVERY.
AS NEAR AS I CAN TELL, HE TRIED TO TAKE ON THE SAME "MONSTER" THAT NEARLY KILLED THE REST OF US.
SO WHAT HAPPENED TO THAT FREAK?
HE DOESN'T SEEM TO BE A THREAT JUST NOW, CASSIE. THAT'S ALL I CAN SAY FOR SURE.
I STRONGLY SUGGEST YOU DON'T ATTEMPT TO MOVE HIM YET.
CERTAINLY NOT THROUGH THE TIME STREAM.
WE'RE NOT LEAVING WITHOUT KON.
WHAT DO YOU THINK, RAVEN?
HOW LONG CAN YOUR SOUL-SELF KEEP ONE TALON IN THE TIME STREAM FOR US?
NOT LONG, I'M AFRAID.
IF WE STAND ANY CHANCE--AND ADMITTEDLY IT IS A VERY SLIM CHANCE INDEED--
...OF REUNITING WITH YOUR KID FLASH AND SOLSTICE...
WE LEAVE NOW, TOGETHER...
OR NOT AT ALL.

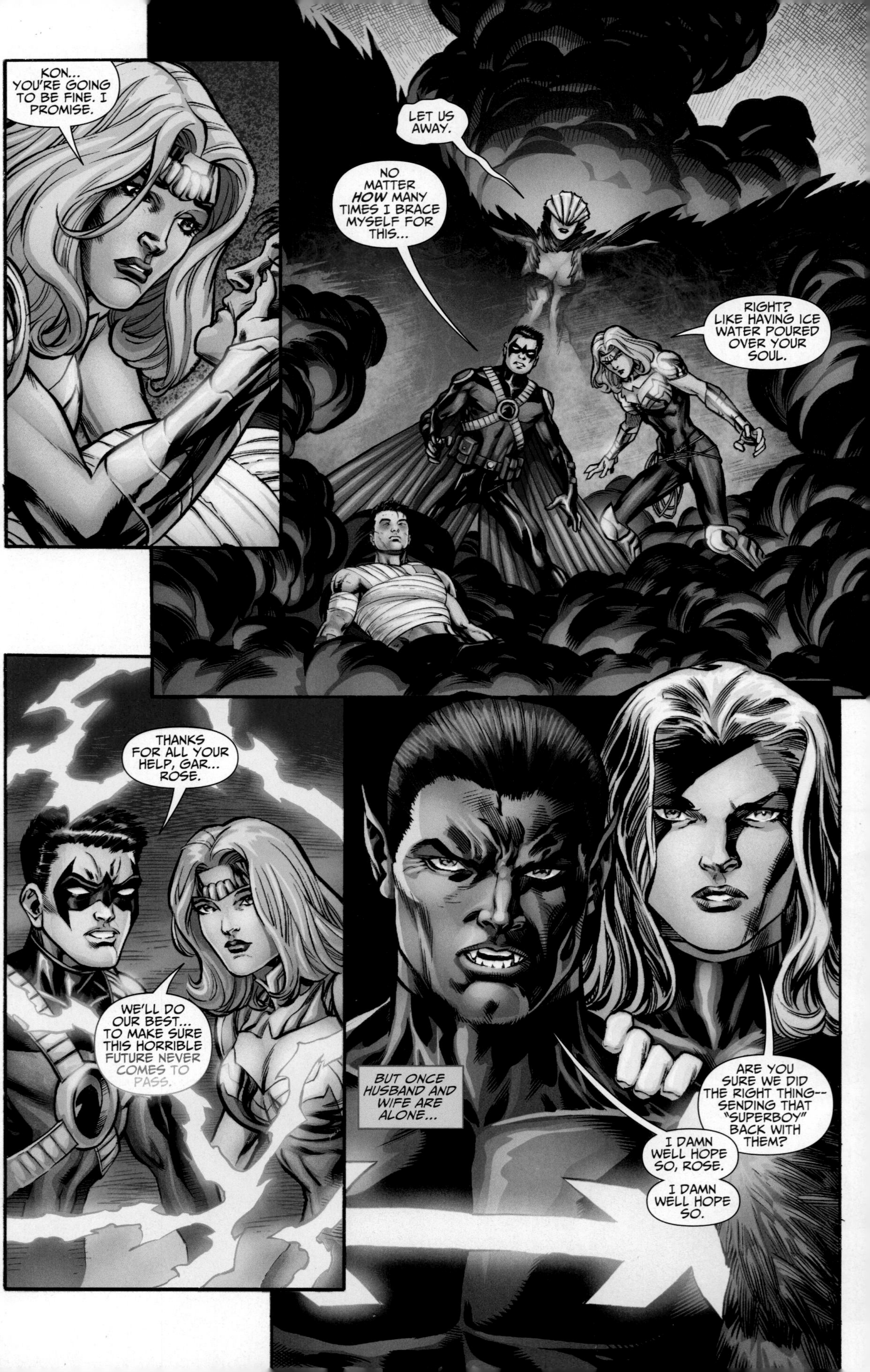
KON... YOU'RE GOING TO BE FINE. I PROMISE.
LET US AWAY.
NO MATTER HOW MANY TIMES I BRACE MYSELF FOR THIS...
RIGHT? LIKE HAVING ICE WATER POURED OVER YOUR SOUL.
THANKS FOR ALL YOUR HELP, GAR... ROSE.
WE'LL DO OUR BEST... TO MAKE SURE THIS HORRIBLE FUTURE NEVER COMES TO PASS.
BUT ONCE HUSBAND AND WIFE ARE ALONE...
ARE YOU SURE WE DID THE RIGHT THING--SENDING THAT "SUPERBOY" BACK WITH THEM?
I DAMN WELL HOPE SO, ROSE.
I DAMN WELL HOPE SO.

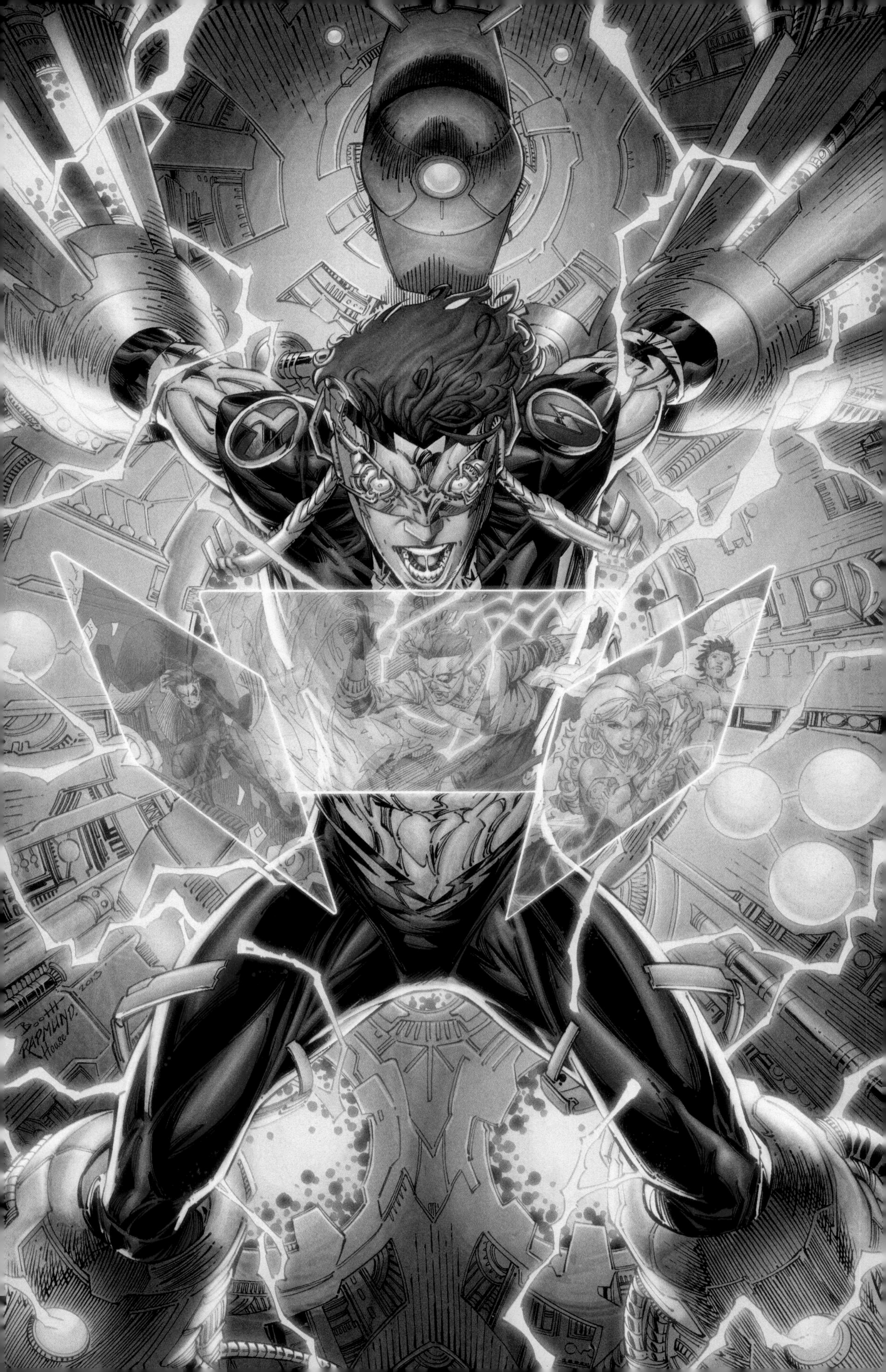
Booth
RAPMUND.
House
2013

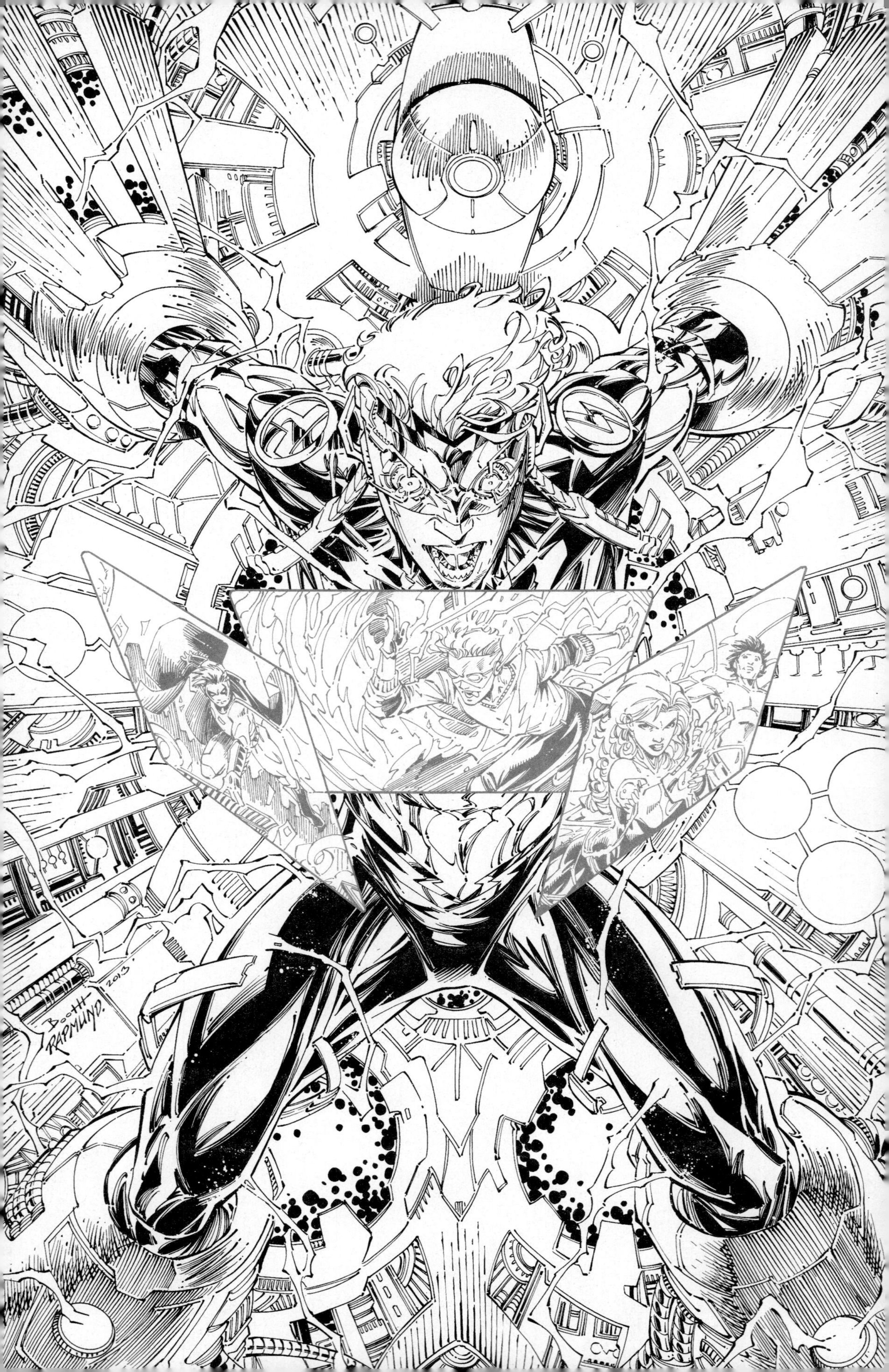
Booth
RAPMUND.
2013

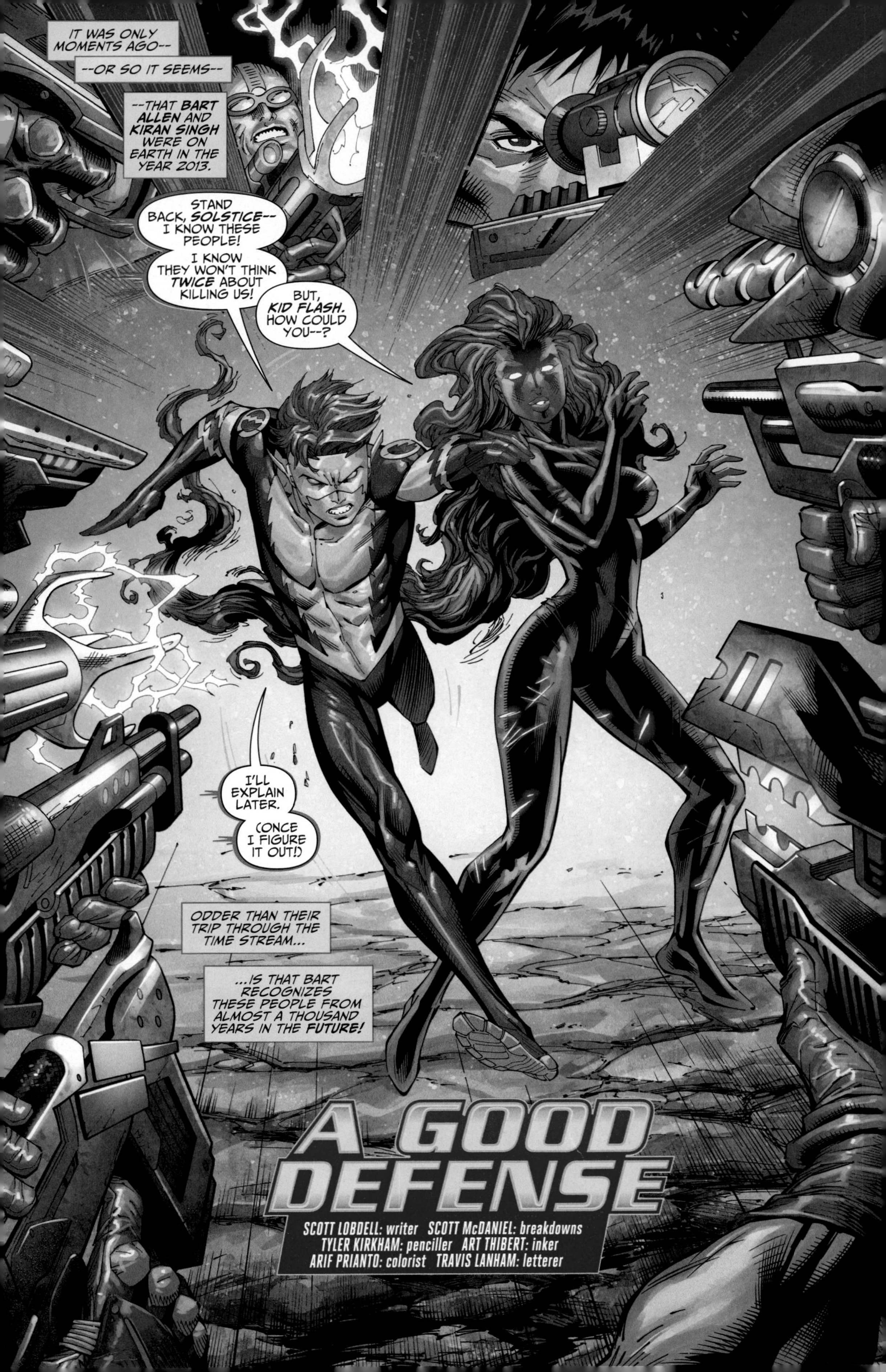
IT WAS ONLY MOMENTS AGO--
--OR SO IT SEEMS--
--THAT BART ALLEN AND KIRAN SINGH WERE ON EARTH IN THE YEAR 2013.
STAND BACK, SOLSTICE-- I KNOW THESE PEOPLE!
I KNOW THEY WON'T THINK TWICE ABOUT KILLING US!
BUT, KID FLASH. HOW COULD YOU--?
I'LL EXPLAIN LATER.
(ONCE I FIGURE IT OUT!)
ODDER THAN THEIR TRIP THROUGH THE TIME STREAM...
...IS THAT BART RECOGNIZES THESE PEOPLE FROM ALMOST A THOUSAND YEARS IN THE FUTURE!
A GOOD DEFENSE
SCOTT LOBDELL: writer SCOTT McDANIEL: breakdowns
TYLER KIRKHAM: penciller ART THIBERT: inker
ARIF PRIANTO: colorist TRAVIS LANHAM: letterer

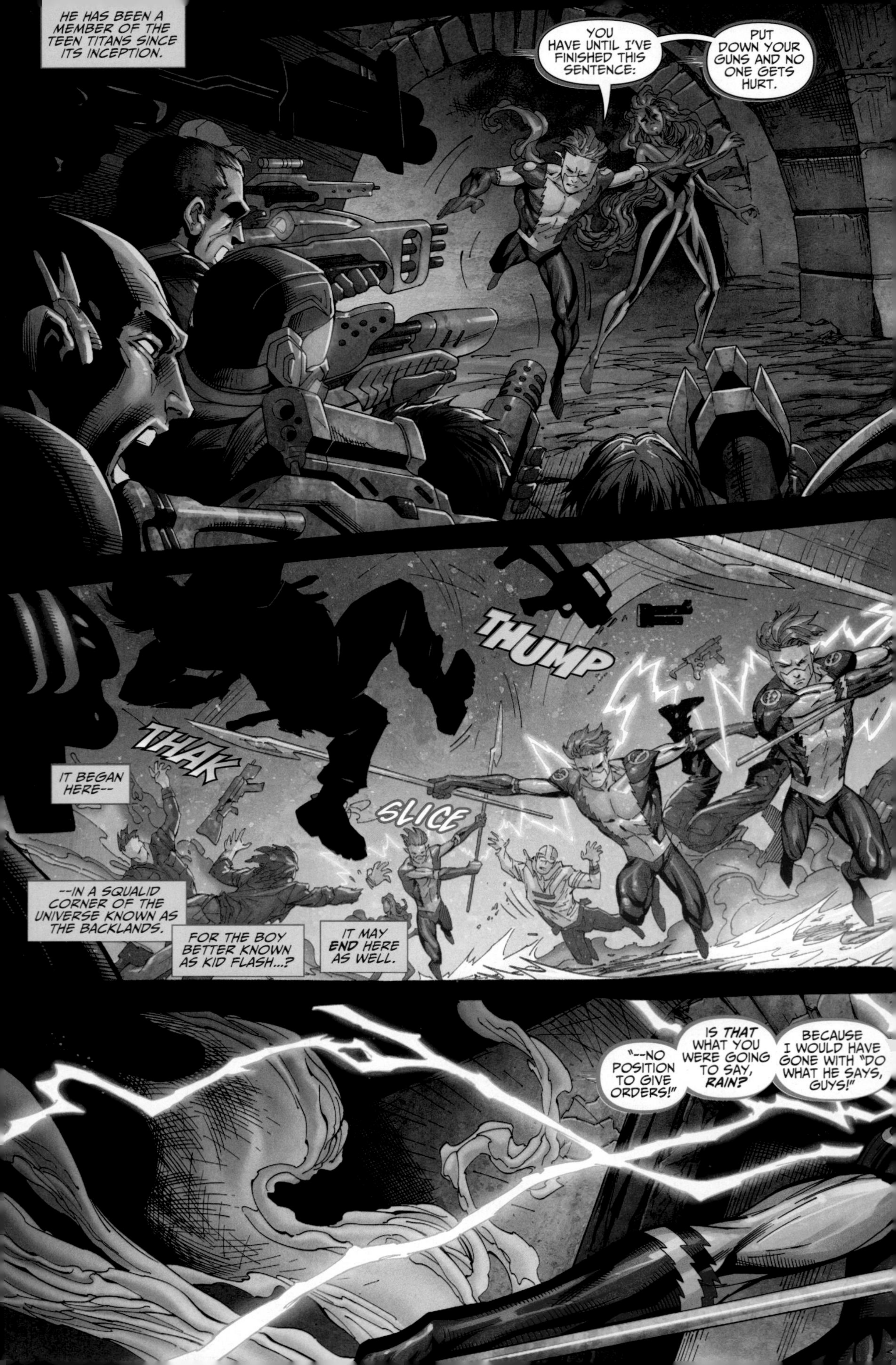
HE HAS BEEN A MEMBER OF THE TEEN TITANS SINCE ITS INCEPTION.
YOU HAVE UNTIL I'VE FINISHED THIS SENTENCE:
PUT DOWN YOUR GUNS AND NO ONE GETS HURT.
THUMP
THAK
IT BEGAN HERE--
SLICE
--IN A SQUALID CORNER OF THE UNIVERSE KNOWN AS THE BACKLANDS.
FOR THE BOY BETTER KNOWN AS KID FLASH...?
IT MAY END HERE AS WELL.
"--NO POSITION TO GIVE ORDERS!"
IS THAT WHAT YOU WERE GOING TO SAY, RAIN?
BECAUSE I WOULD HAVE GONE WITH "DO WHAT HE SAYS, GUYS!"

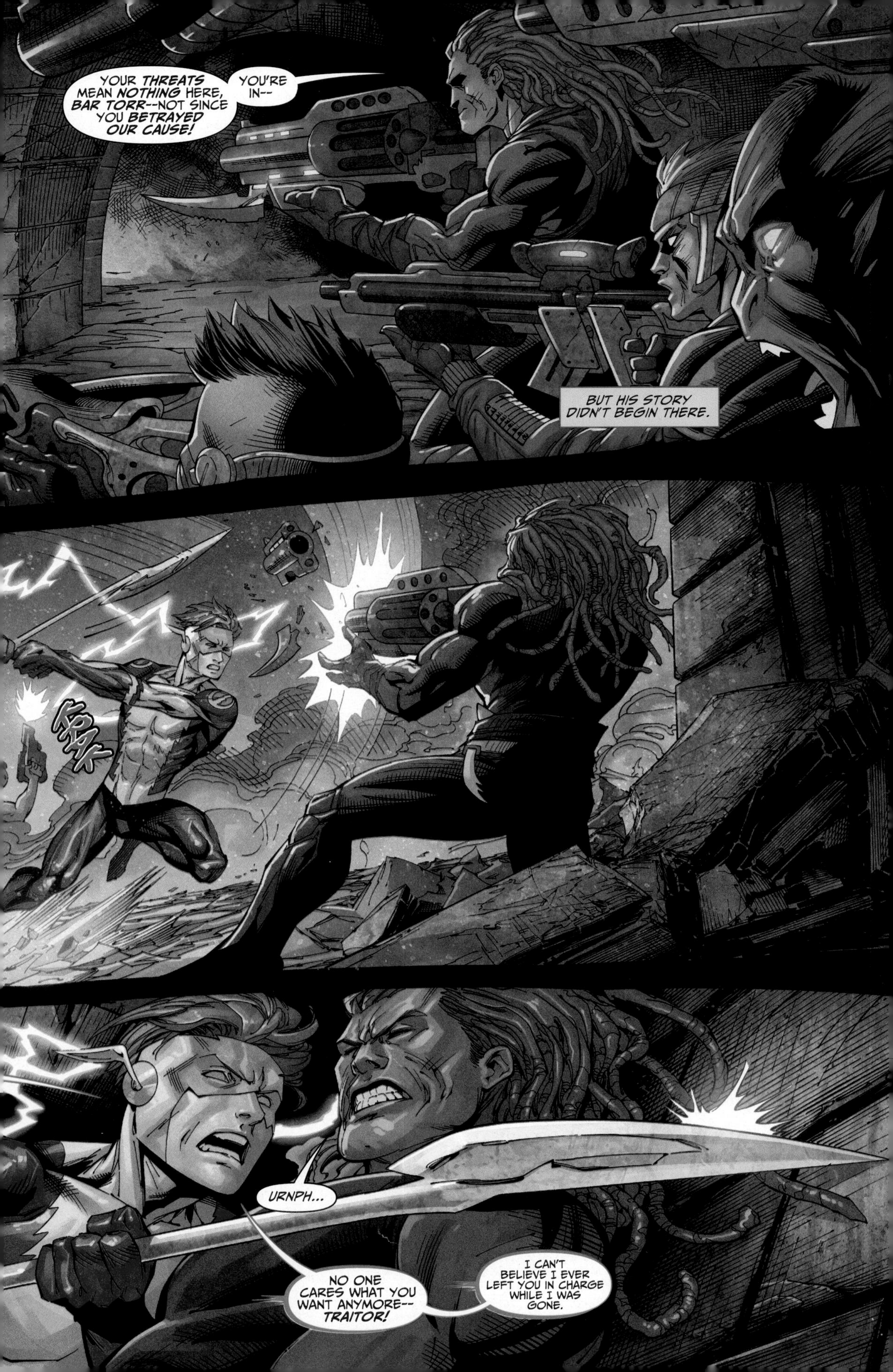
YOUR THREATS MEAN NOTHING HERE, BAR TORR--NOT SINCE YOU BETRAYED OUR CAUSE!
YOU'RE IN--
BUT HIS STORY DIDN'T BEGIN THERE.
KRAK
URNPH...
NO ONE CARES WHAT YOU WANT ANYMORE-- TRAITOR!
I CAN'T BELIEVE I EVER LEFT YOU IN CHARGE WHILE I WAS GONE.

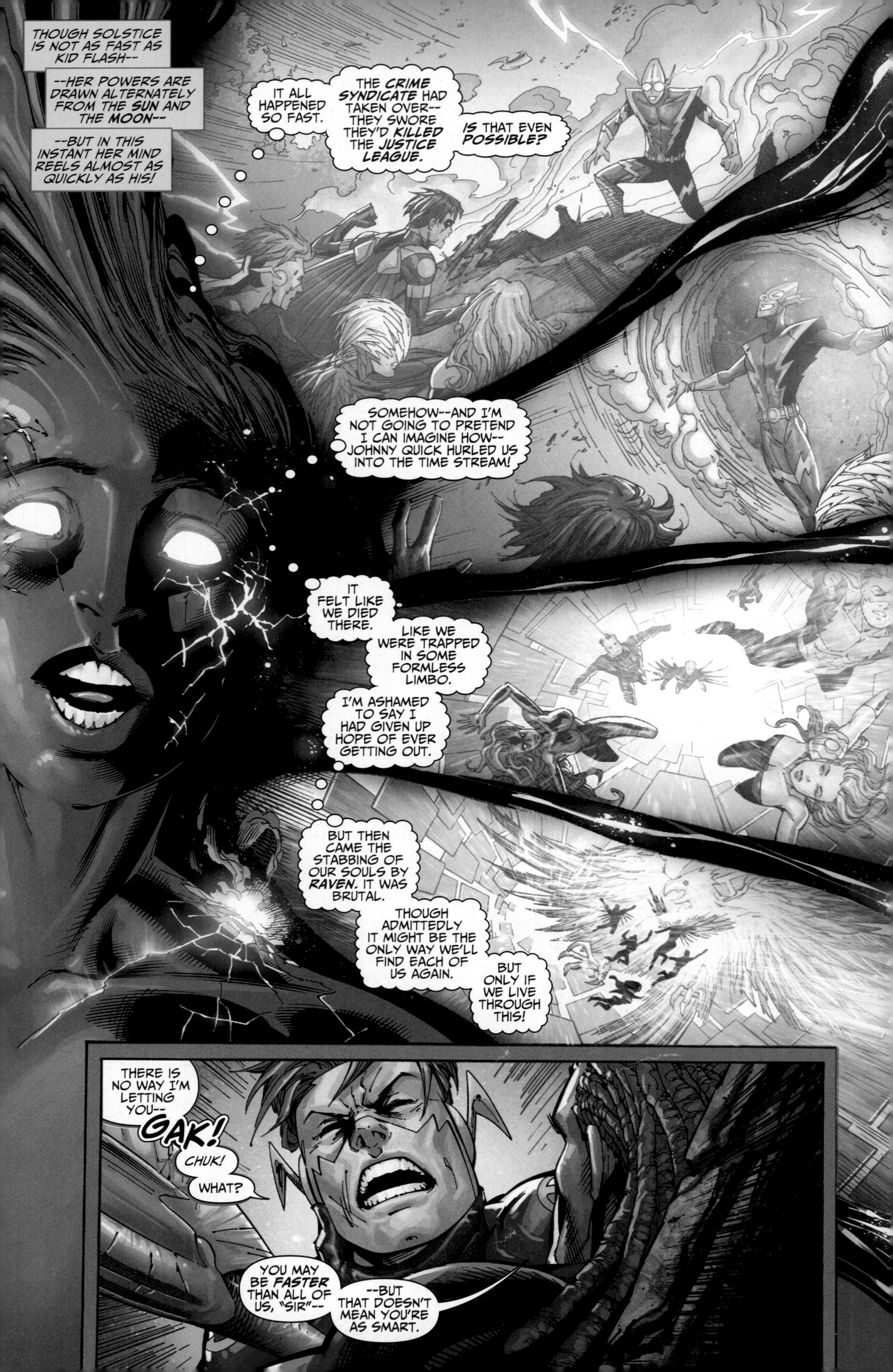

THOUGH SOLSTICE IS NOT AS FAST AS KID FLASH--
--HER POWERS ARE DRAWN ALTERNATELY FROM THE SUN AND THE MOON--
--BUT IN THIS INSTANT HER MIND REELS ALMOST AS QUICKLY AS HIS!
IT ALL HAPPENED SO FAST.
THE CRIME SYNDICATE HAD TAKEN OVER-- THEY SWORE THEY'D KILLED THE JUSTICE LEAGUE.
IS THAT EVEN POSSIBLE?
SOMEHOW--AND I'M NOT GOING TO PRETEND I CAN IMAGINE HOW-- JOHNNY QUICK HURLED US INTO THE TIME STREAM!
IT FELT LIKE WE DIED THERE.
LIKE WE WERE TRAPPED IN SOME FORMLESS LIMBO.
I'M ASHAMED TO SAY I HAD GIVEN UP HOPE OF EVER GETTING OUT.
BUT THEN CAME THE STABBING OF OUR SOULS BY RAVEN. IT WAS BRUTAL.
THOUGH ADMITTEDLY IT MIGHT BE THE ONLY WAY WE'LL FIND EACH OF US AGAIN.
BUT ONLY IF WE LIVE THROUGH THIS!
THERE IS NO WAY I'M LETTING YOU--
GAK!
CHUK!
WHAT?
YOU MAY BE FASTER THAN ALL OF US, "SIR"--
--BUT THAT DOESN'T MEAN YOU'RE AS SMART.

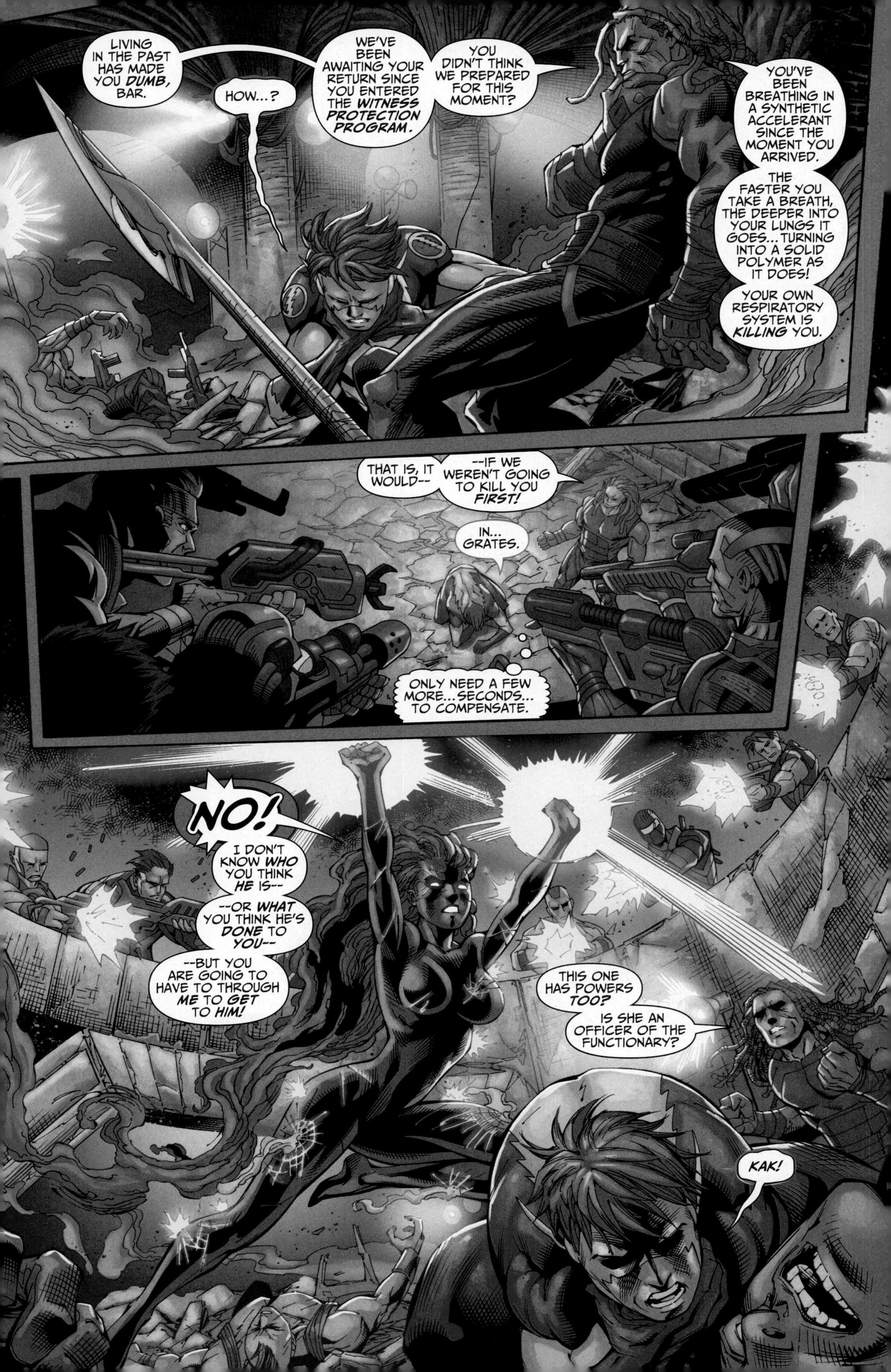
LIVING IN THE PAST HAS MADE YOU DUMB, BAR.
HOW...?
WE'VE BEEN AWAITING YOUR RETURN SINCE YOU ENTERED THE WITNESS PROTECTION PROGRAM.
YOU DIDN'T THINK WE PREPARED FOR THIS MOMENT?
YOU'VE BEEN BREATHING IN A SYNTHETIC ACCELERANT SINCE THE MOMENT YOU ARRIVED.
THE FASTER YOU TAKE A BREATH, THE DEEPER INTO YOUR LUNGS IT GOES...TURNING INTO A SOLID POLYMER AS IT DOES!
YOUR OWN RESPIRATORY SYSTEM IS KILLING YOU.
THAT IS, IT WOULD--
--IF WE WEREN'T GOING TO KILL YOU FIRST!
IN... GRATES.
ONLY NEED A FEW MORE...SECONDS... TO COMPENSATE.
NO!
I DON'T KNOW WHO YOU THINK HE IS--
--OR WHAT YOU THINK HE'S DONE TO YOU--
--BUT YOU ARE GOING TO HAVE TO THROUGH ME TO GET TO HIM!
THIS ONE HAS POWERS TOO?
IS SHE AN OFFICER OF THE FUNCTIONARY?
KAK!

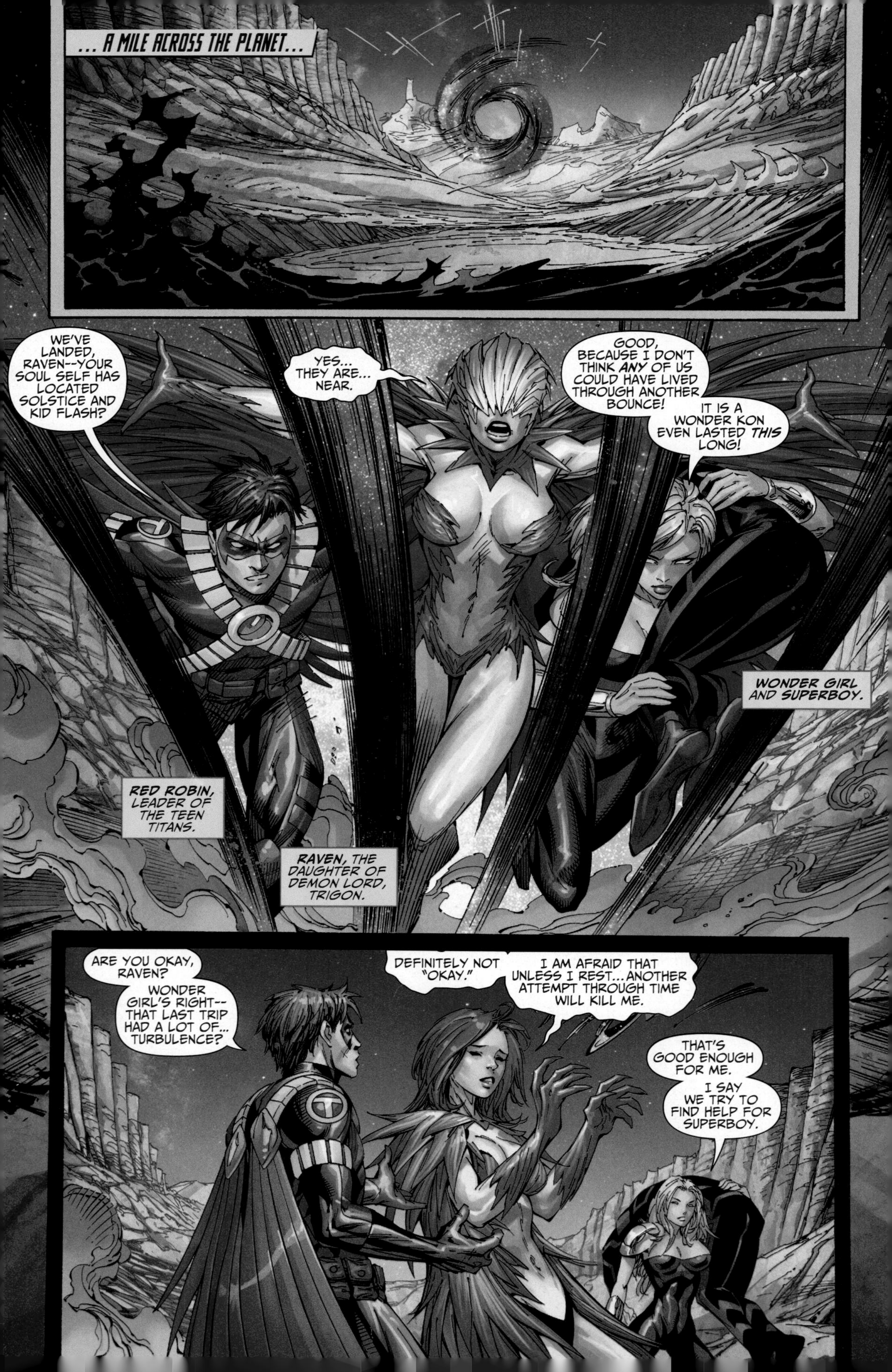
... A MILE ACROSS THE PLANET...
WE'VE LANDED, RAVEN--YOUR SOUL SELF HAS LOCATED SOLSTICE AND KID FLASH?
YES... THEY ARE... NEAR.
GOOD, BECAUSE I DON'T THINK ANY OF US COULD HAVE LIVED THROUGH ANOTHER BOUNCE!
IT IS A WONDER KON EVEN LASTED THIS LONG!
WONDER GIRL AND SUPERBOY.
RED ROBIN, LEADER OF THE TEEN TITANS.
RAVEN, THE DAUGHTER OF DEMON LORD, TRIGON.
ARE YOU OKAY, RAVEN?
WONDER GIRL'S RIGHT-- THAT LAST TRIP HAD A LOT OF... TURBULENCE?
DEFINITELY NOT "OKAY."
I AM AFRAID THAT UNLESS I REST... ANOTHER ATTEMPT THROUGH TIME WILL KILL ME.
THAT'S GOOD ENOUGH FOR ME.
I SAY WE TRY TO FIND HELP FOR SUPERBOY.

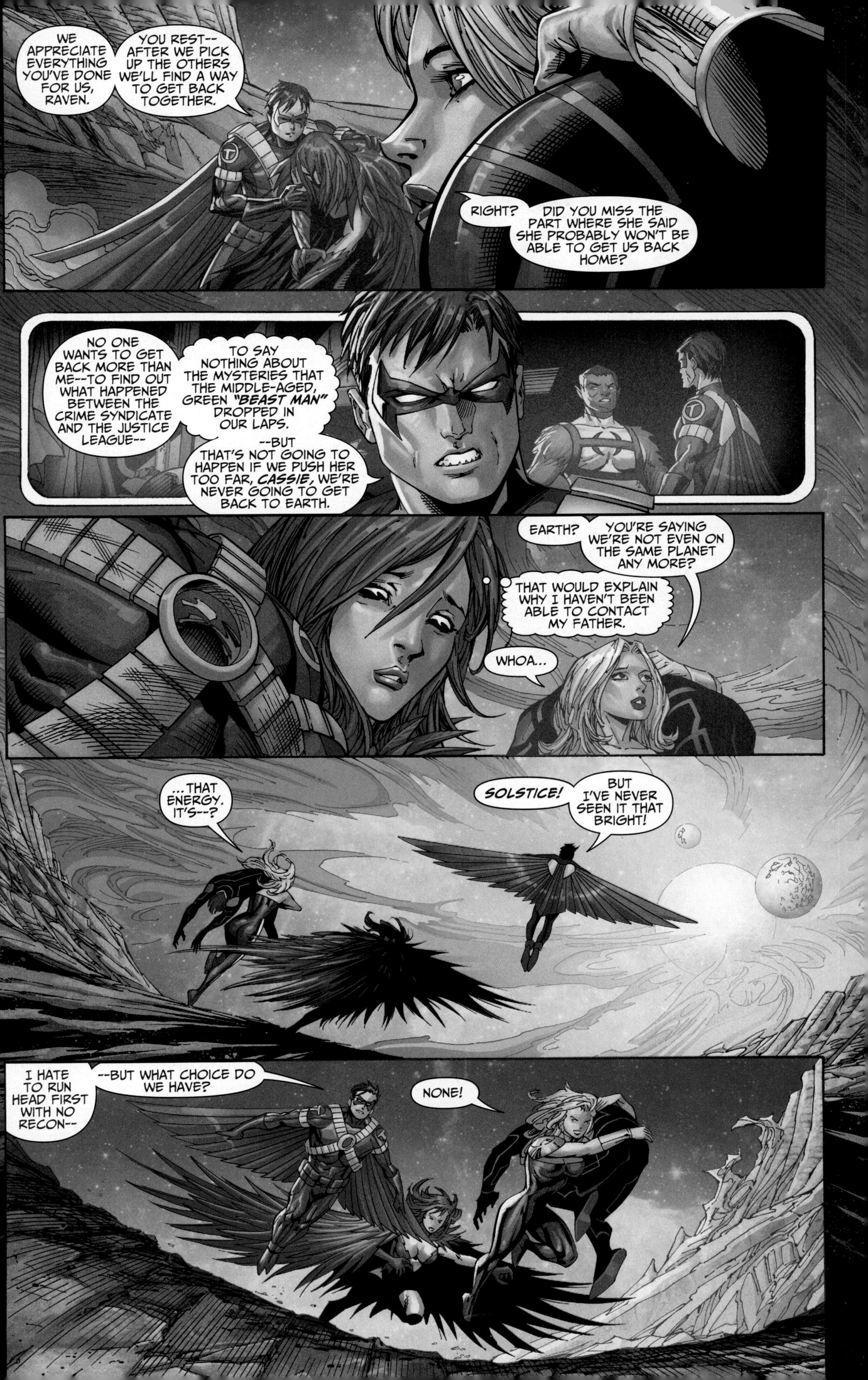
WE APPRECIATE EVERYTHING YOU'VE DONE FOR US, RAVEN.
YOU REST-- AFTER WE PICK UP THE OTHERS WE'LL FIND A WAY TO GET BACK TOGETHER.
RIGHT?
DID YOU MISS THE PART WHERE SHE SAID SHE PROBABLY WON'T BE ABLE TO GET US BACK HOME?
NO ONE WANTS TO GET BACK MORE THAN ME--TO FIND OUT WHAT HAPPENED BETWEEN THE CRIME SYNDICATE AND THE JUSTICE LEAGUE--
TO SAY NOTHING ABOUT THE MYSTERIES THAT THE MIDDLE-AGED, GREEN "BEAST MAN" DROPPED IN OUR LAPS.
--BUT THAT'S NOT GOING TO HAPPEN IF WE PUSH HER TOO FAR, CASSIE, WE'RE NEVER GOING TO GET BACK TO EARTH.
EARTH?
YOU'RE SAYING WE'RE NOT EVEN ON THE SAME PLANET ANY MORE?
THAT WOULD EXPLAIN WHY I HAVEN'T BEEN ABLE TO CONTACT MY FATHER.
WHOA...
...THAT ENERGY. IT'S--?
SOLSTICE!
BUT I'VE NEVER SEEN IT THAT BRIGHT!
I HATE TO RUN HEAD FIRST WITH NO RECON--
--BUT WHAT CHOICE DO WE HAVE?
NONE!

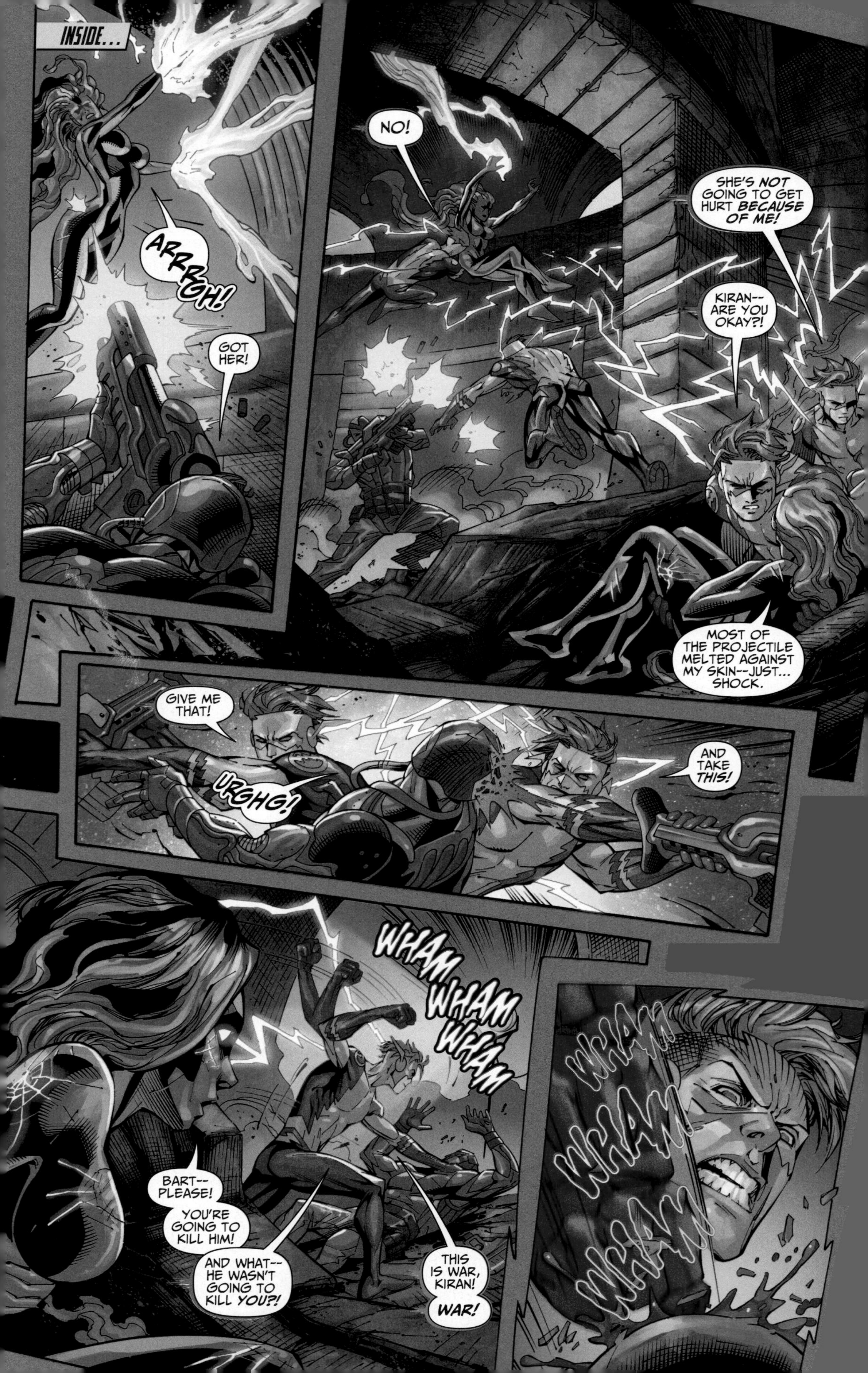
INSIDE...
ARRRGH!
GOT HER!
NO!
SHE'S NOT GOING TO GET HURT BECAUSE OF ME!
KIRAN-- ARE YOU OKAY?!
MOST OF THE PROJECTILE MELTED AGAINST MY SKIN--JUST... SHOCK.
GIVE ME THAT!
URGHG!
AND TAKE THIS!
WHAM WHAM WHAM
BART-- PLEASE!
YOU'RE GOING TO KILL HIM!
AND WHAT-- HE WASN'T GOING TO KILL YOU?!
THIS IS WAR, KIRAN!
WAR!
WHAM WHAM WHAM

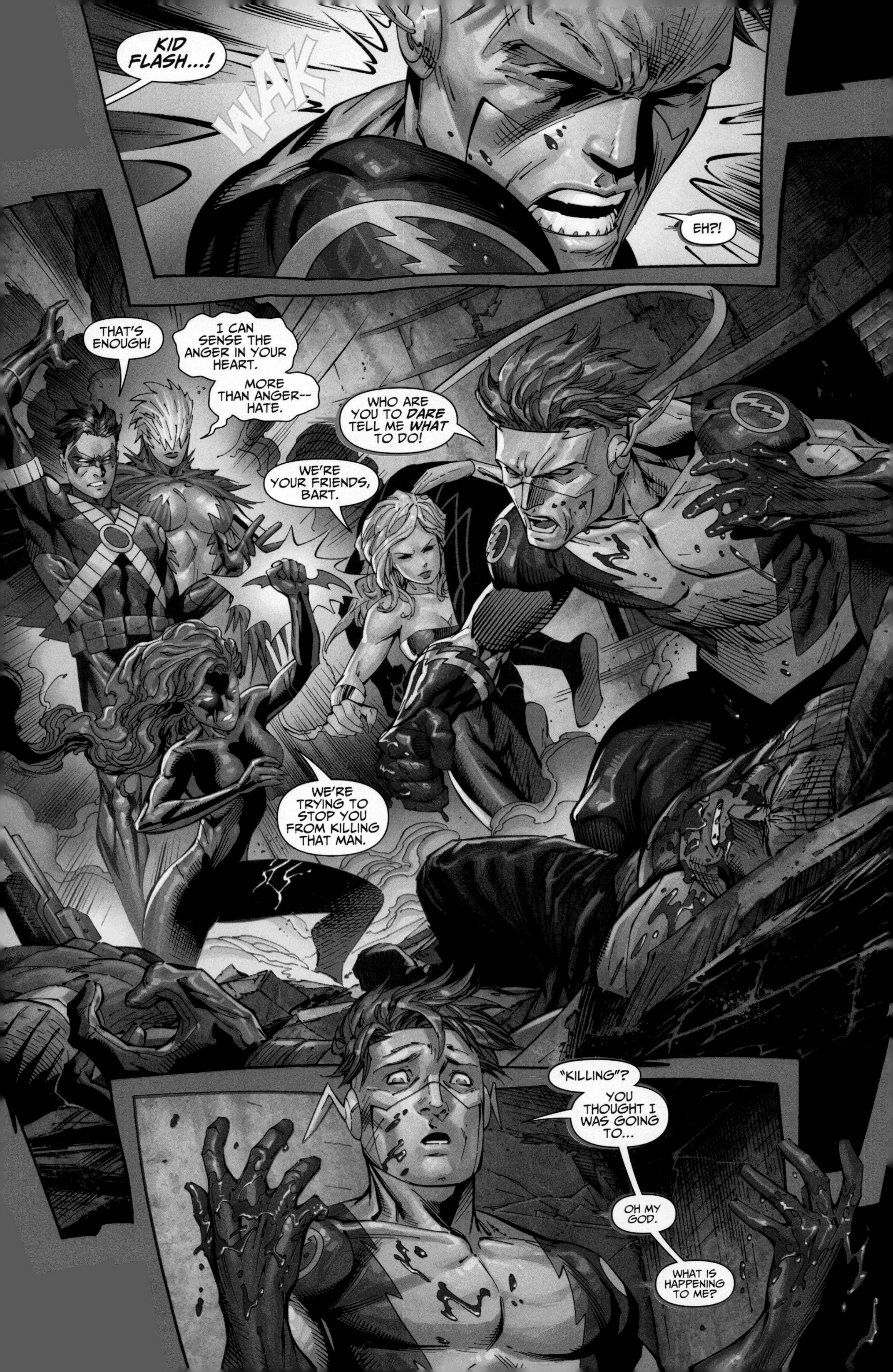
KID FLASH...!
WAK
EH?!
THAT'S ENOUGH!
I CAN SENSE THE ANGER IN YOUR HEART.
MORE THAN ANGER-- HATE.
WHO ARE YOU TO DARE TELL ME WHAT TO DO!
WE'RE YOUR FRIENDS, BART.
WE'RE TRYING TO STOP YOU FROM KILLING THAT MAN.
"KILLING"?
YOU THOUGHT I WAS GOING TO...
OH MY GOD.
WHAT IS HAPPENING TO ME?

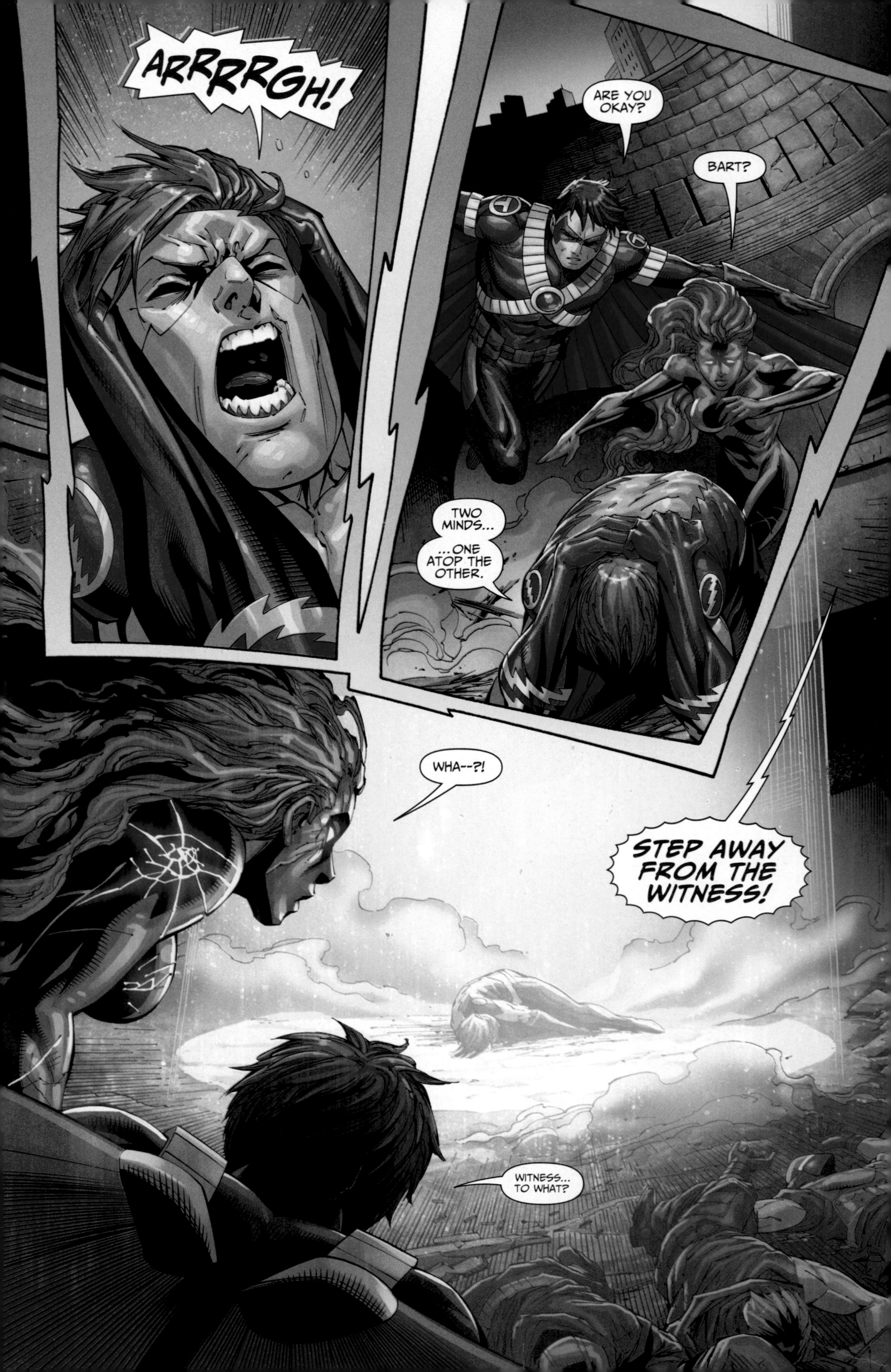
ARRRRGH!
ARE YOU OKAY?
BART?
TWO MINDS...
...ONE ATOP THE OTHER.
WHA--?!
STEP AWAY FROM THE WITNESS!
WITNESS... TO WHAT?

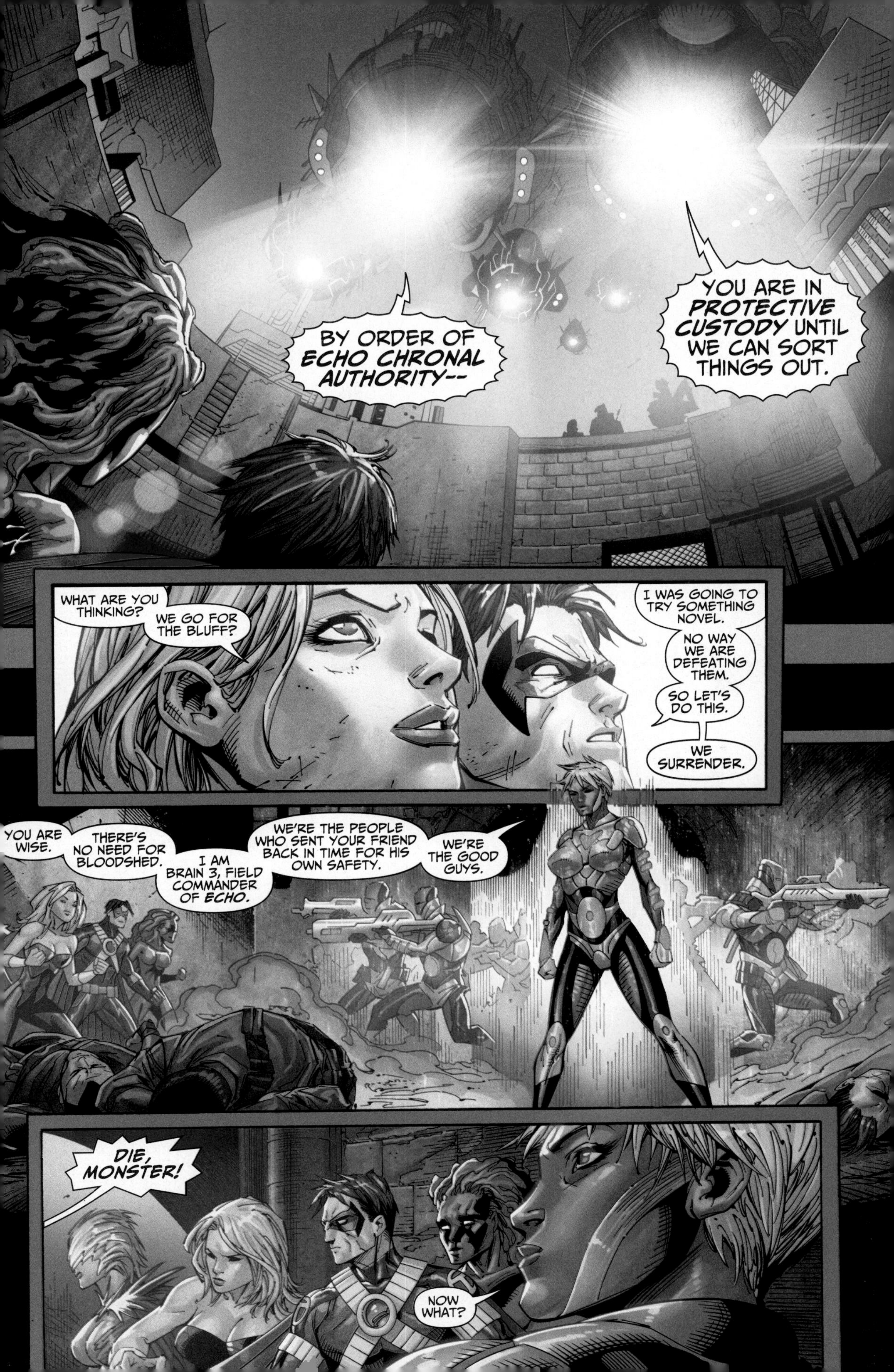
BY ORDER OF *ECHO CHRONAL AUTHORITY*--
YOU ARE IN *PROTECTIVE CUSTODY* UNTIL WE CAN SORT THINGS OUT.
WHAT ARE YOU THINKING?
WE GO FOR THE BLUFF?
I WAS GOING TO TRY SOMETHING NOVEL.
NO WAY WE ARE DEFEATING THEM.
SO LET'S DO THIS.
WE SURRENDER.
YOU ARE WISE.
THERE'S NO NEED FOR BLOODSHED.
I AM BRAIN 3, FIELD COMMANDER OF *ECHO*.
WE'RE THE PEOPLE WHO SENT YOUR FRIEND BACK IN TIME FOR HIS OWN SAFETY.
WE'RE THE GOOD GUYS.
DIE, MONSTER!
NOW WHAT?

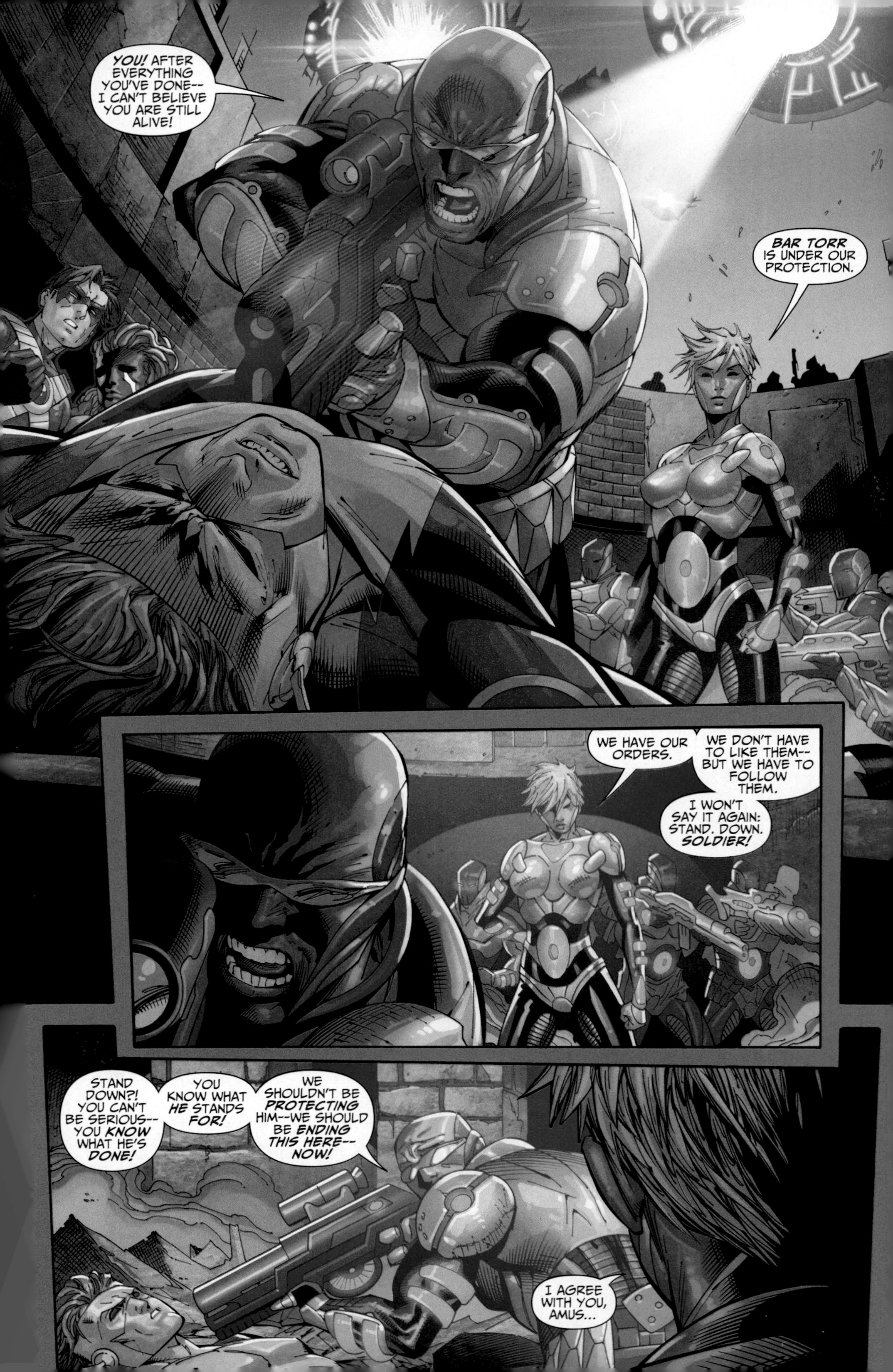
YOU! AFTER EVERYTHING YOU'VE DONE-- I CAN'T BELIEVE YOU ARE STILL ALIVE!
BAR TORR IS UNDER OUR PROTECTION.
WE HAVE OUR ORDERS.
WE DON'T HAVE TO LIKE THEM-- BUT WE HAVE TO FOLLOW THEM.
I WON'T SAY IT AGAIN: STAND. DOWN. SOLDIER!
STAND DOWN?! YOU CAN'T BE SERIOUS-- YOU KNOW WHAT HE'S DONE!
YOU KNOW WHAT HE STANDS FOR!
WE SHOULDN'T BE PROTECTING HIM--WE SHOULD BE ENDING THIS HERE-- NOW!
I AGREE WITH YOU, AMUS...

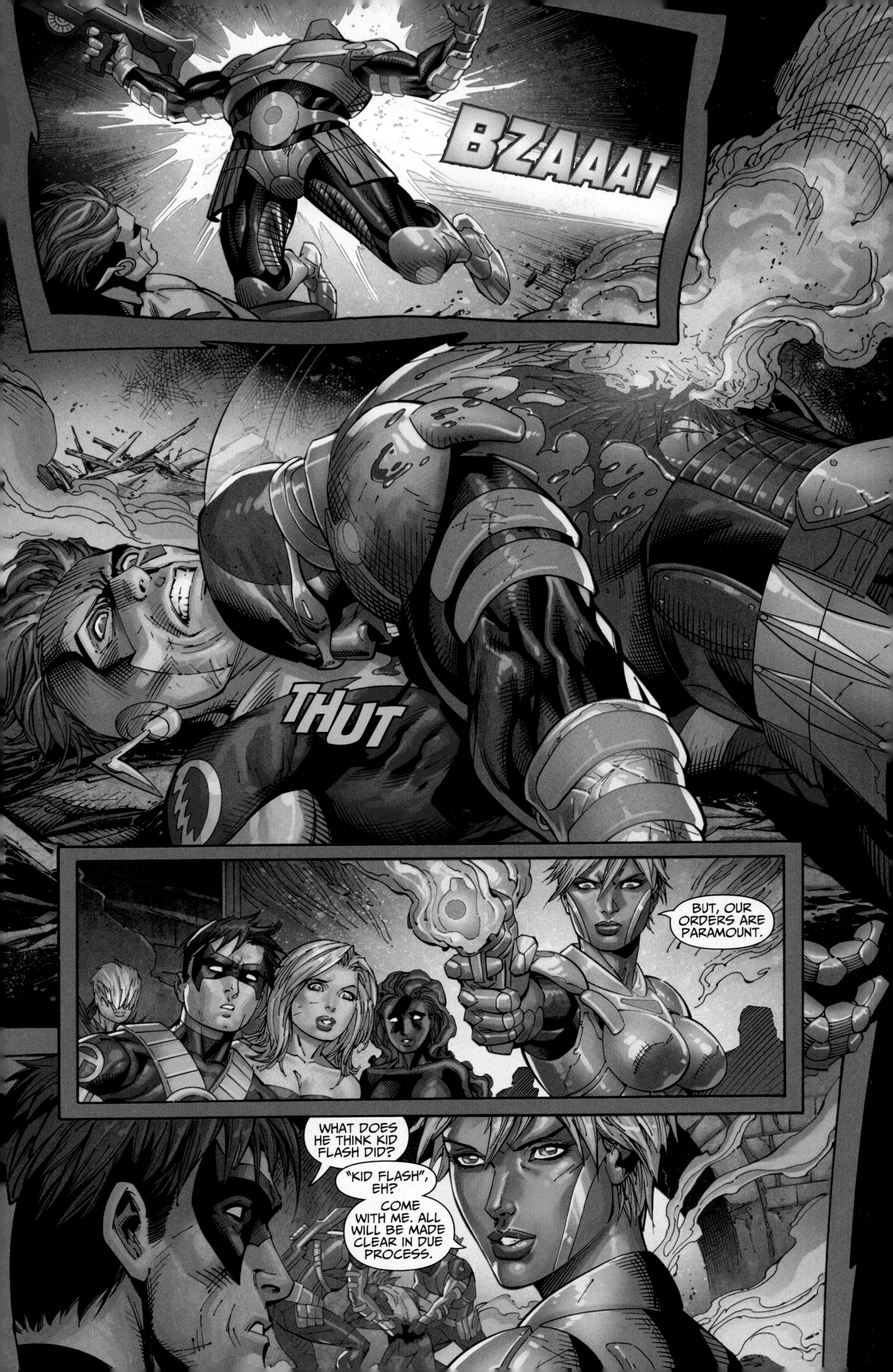
BZAAAT
THUT
BUT, OUR ORDERS ARE PARAMOUNT.
WHAT DOES HE THINK KID FLASH DID?
"KID FLASH", EH?
COME WITH ME. ALL WILL BE MADE CLEAR IN DUE PROCESS.

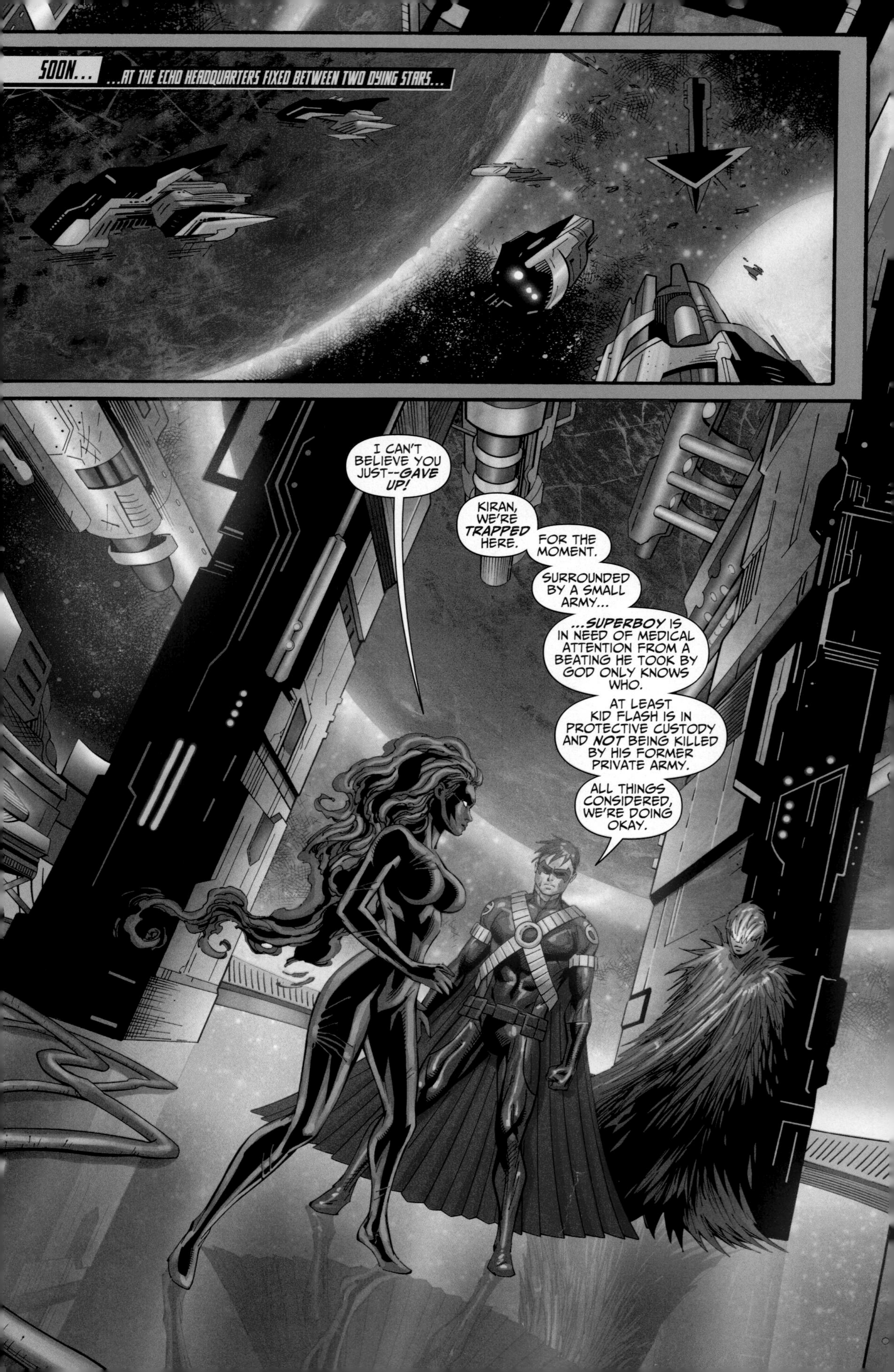
SOON...
...AT THE ECHO HEADQUARTERS FIXED BETWEEN TWO DYING STARS...
I CAN'T BELIEVE YOU JUST--GAVE UP!
KIRAN, WE'RE TRAPPED HERE.
FOR THE MOMENT.
SURROUNDED BY A SMALL ARMY...
...SUPERBOY IS IN NEED OF MEDICAL ATTENTION FROM A BEATING HE TOOK BY GOD ONLY KNOWS WHO.
AT LEAST KID FLASH IS IN PROTECTIVE CUSTODY AND NOT BEING KILLED BY HIS FORMER PRIVATE ARMY.
ALL THINGS CONSIDERED, WE'RE DOING OKAY.

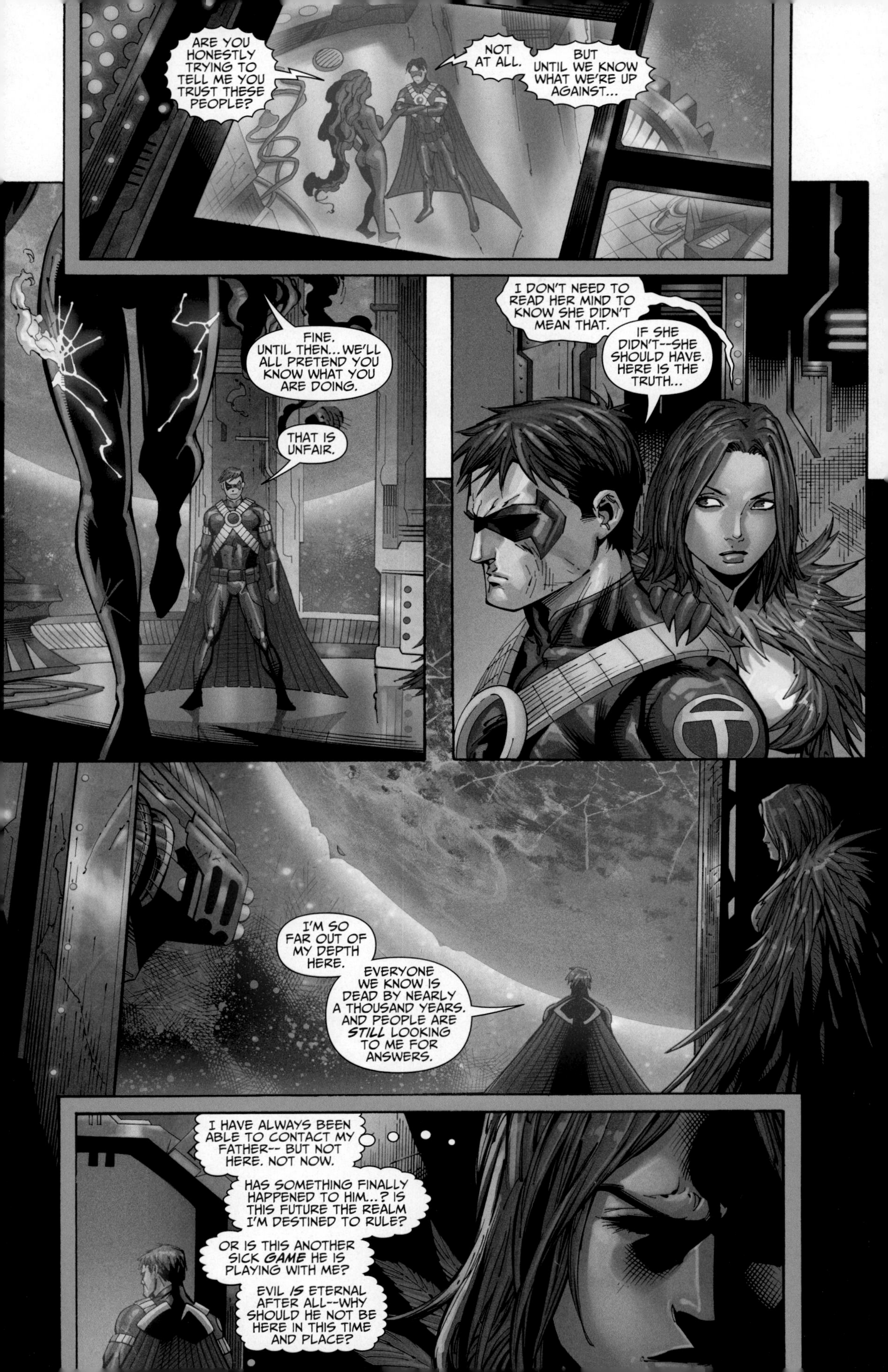

ARE YOU HONESTLY TRYING TO TELL ME YOU TRUST THESE PEOPLE?
NOT AT ALL.
BUT UNTIL WE KNOW WHAT WE'RE UP AGAINST...
FINE. UNTIL THEN... WE'LL ALL PRETEND YOU KNOW WHAT YOU ARE DOING.
THAT IS UNFAIR.
I DON'T NEED TO READ HER MIND TO KNOW SHE DIDN'T MEAN THAT.
IF SHE DIDN'T--SHE SHOULD HAVE. HERE IS THE TRUTH...
I'M SO FAR OUT OF MY DEPTH HERE.
EVERYONE WE KNOW IS DEAD BY NEARLY A THOUSAND YEARS. AND PEOPLE ARE STILL LOOKING TO ME FOR ANSWERS.
I HAVE ALWAYS BEEN ABLE TO CONTACT MY FATHER-- BUT NOT HERE. NOT NOW.
HAS SOMETHING FINALLY HAPPENED TO HIM...? IS THIS FUTURE THE REALM I'M DESTINED TO RULE?
OR IS THIS ANOTHER SICK GAME HE IS PLAYING WITH ME?
EVIL IS ETERNAL AFTER ALL--WHY SHOULD HE NOT BE HERE IN THIS TIME AND PLACE?

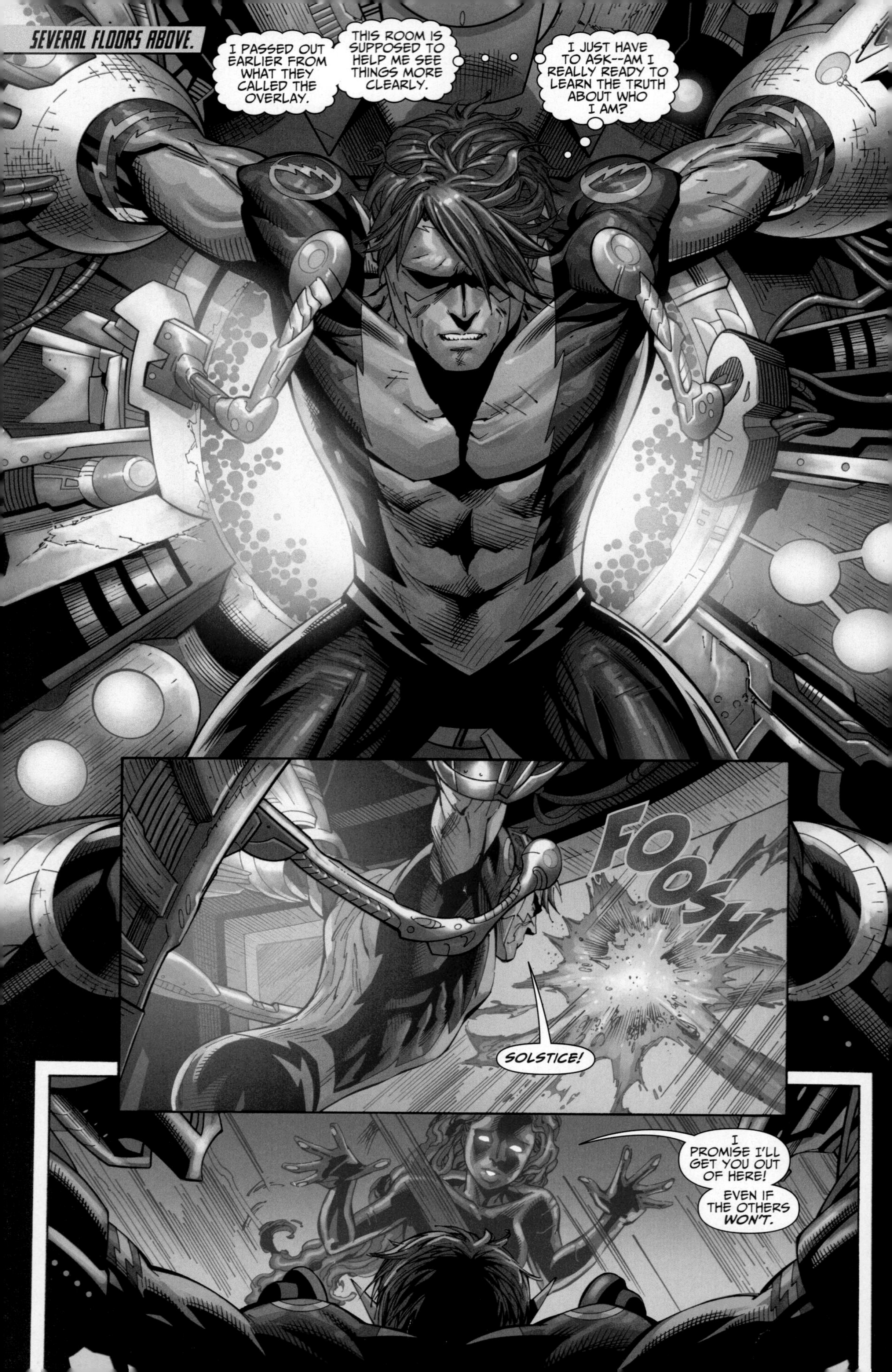
SEVERAL FLOORS ABOVE.
I PASSED OUT EARLIER FROM WHAT THEY CALLED THE OVERLAY.
THIS ROOM IS SUPPOSED TO HELP ME SEE THINGS MORE CLEARLY.
I JUST HAVE TO ASK--AM I REALLY READY TO LEARN THE TRUTH ABOUT WHO I AM?
FOOSH
SOLSTICE!
I PROMISE I'LL GET YOU OUT OF HERE!
EVEN IF THE OTHERS WON'T.

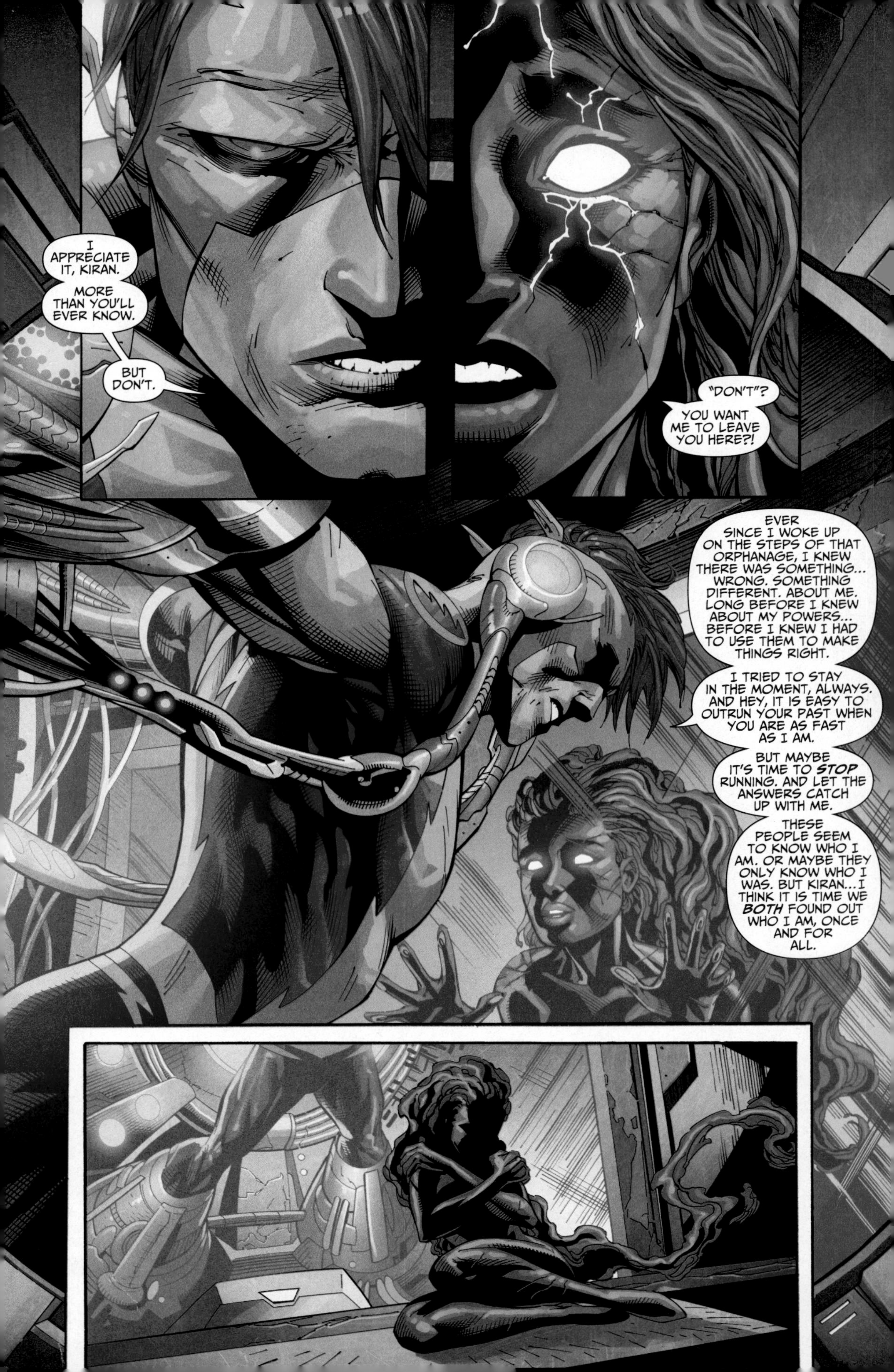
I APPRECIATE IT, KIRAN.
MORE THAN YOU'LL EVER KNOW.
BUT DON'T.
"DON'T"?
YOU WANT ME TO LEAVE YOU HERE?!
EVER SINCE I WOKE UP ON THE STEPS OF THAT ORPHANAGE, I KNEW THERE WAS SOMETHING... WRONG. SOMETHING DIFFERENT. ABOUT ME. LONG BEFORE I KNEW ABOUT MY POWERS... BEFORE I KNEW I HAD TO USE THEM TO MAKE THINGS RIGHT.
I TRIED TO STAY IN THE MOMENT, ALWAYS. AND HEY, IT IS EASY TO OUTRUN YOUR PAST WHEN YOU ARE AS FAST AS I AM.
BUT MAYBE IT'S TIME TO *STOP* RUNNING. AND LET THE ANSWERS CATCH UP WITH ME.
THESE PEOPLE SEEM TO KNOW WHO I AM. OR MAYBE THEY ONLY KNOW WHO I WAS. BUT KIRAN... I THINK IT IS TIME WE *BOTH* FOUND OUT WHO I AM, ONCE AND FOR ALL.

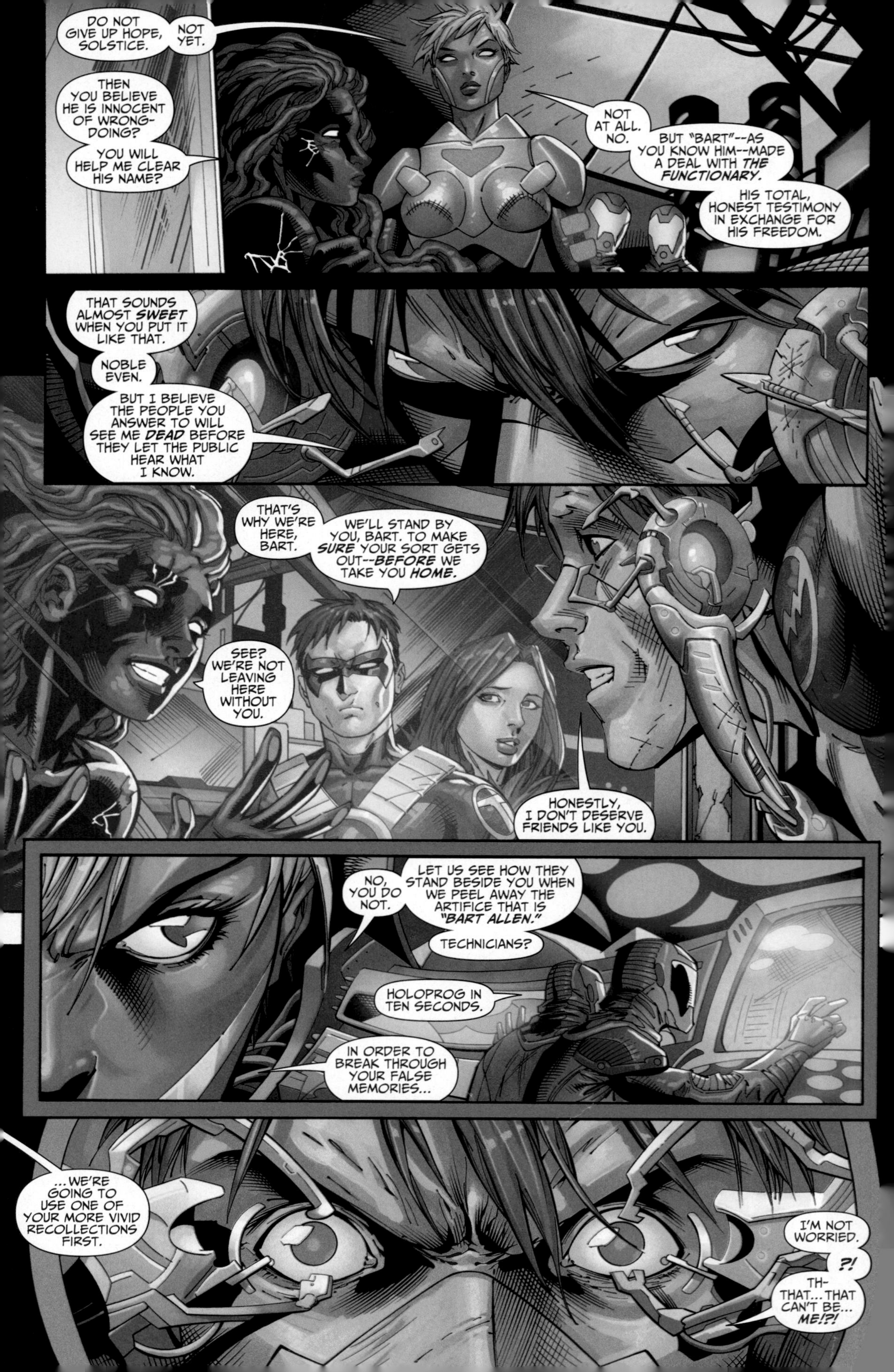
DO NOT GIVE UP HOPE, SOLSTICE.
NOT YET.
THEN YOU BELIEVE HE IS INNOCENT OF WRONG-DOING?
YOU WILL HELP ME CLEAR HIS NAME?
NOT AT ALL. NO.
BUT "BART"--AS YOU KNOW HIM--MADE A DEAL WITH *THE FUNCTIONARY.*
HIS TOTAL, HONEST TESTIMONY IN EXCHANGE FOR HIS FREEDOM.
THAT SOUNDS ALMOST **SWEET** WHEN YOU PUT IT LIKE THAT.
NOBLE EVEN.
BUT I BELIEVE THE PEOPLE YOU ANSWER TO WILL SEE ME **DEAD** BEFORE THEY LET THE PUBLIC HEAR WHAT I KNOW.
THAT'S WHY WE'RE HERE, BART.
WE'LL STAND BY YOU, BART. TO MAKE **SURE** YOUR SORT GETS OUT--**BEFORE** WE TAKE YOU **HOME.**
SEE? WE'RE NOT LEAVING HERE WITHOUT YOU.
HONESTLY, I DON'T DESERVE FRIENDS LIKE YOU.
NO, YOU DO NOT.
LET US SEE HOW THEY STAND BESIDE YOU WHEN WE PEEL AWAY THE ARTIFICE THAT IS *"BART ALLEN."*
TECHNICIANS?
HOLOPROG IN TEN SECONDS.
IN ORDER TO BREAK THROUGH YOUR FALSE MEMORIES...
...WE'RE GOING TO USE ONE OF YOUR MORE VIVID RECOLLECTIONS FIRST.
I'M NOT WORRIED.
?!
TH-THAT...THAT CAN'T BE... *ME!?!*

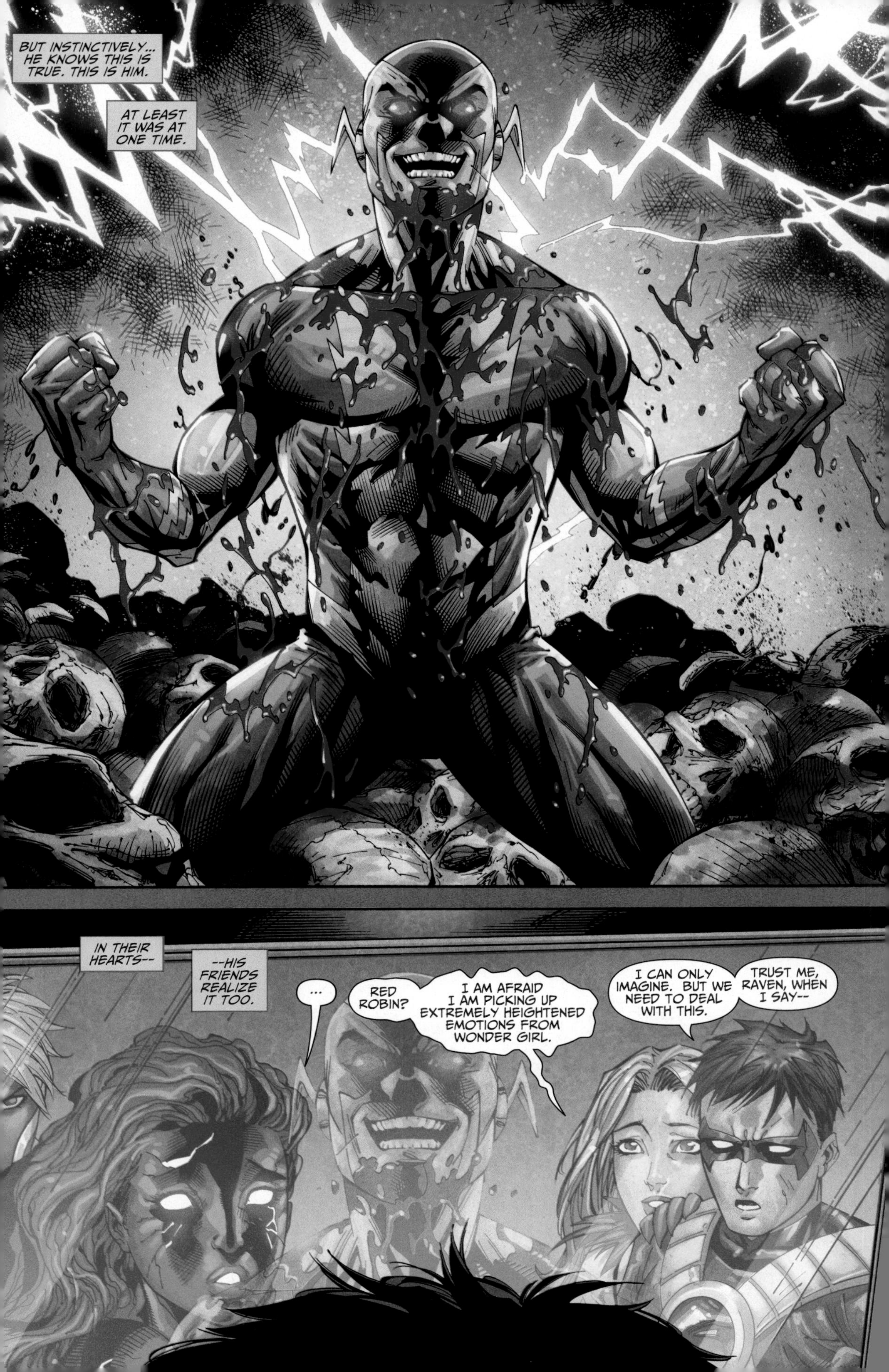
BUT INSTINCTIVELY... HE KNOWS THIS IS TRUE. THIS IS HIM.
AT LEAST IT WAS AT ONE TIME.
IN THEIR HEARTS--
--HIS FRIENDS REALIZE IT TOO.
...
RED ROBIN?
I AM AFRAID I AM PICKING UP EXTREMELY HEIGHTENED EMOTIONS FROM WONDER GIRL.
I CAN ONLY IMAGINE. BUT WE NEED TO DEAL WITH THIS.
TRUST ME, RAVEN, WHEN I SAY--

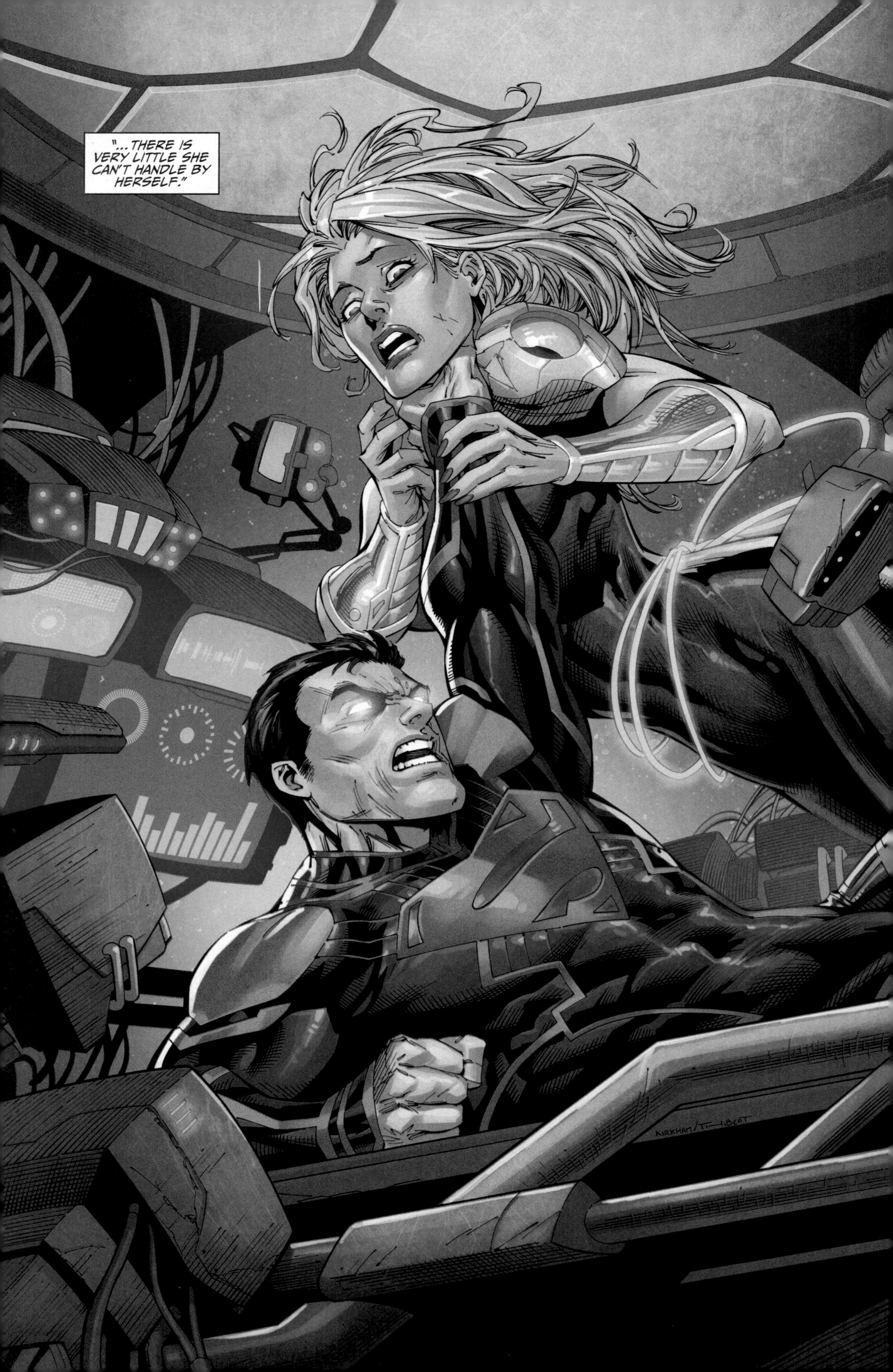
"...THERE IS VERY LITTLE SHE CAN'T HANDLE BY HERSELF."

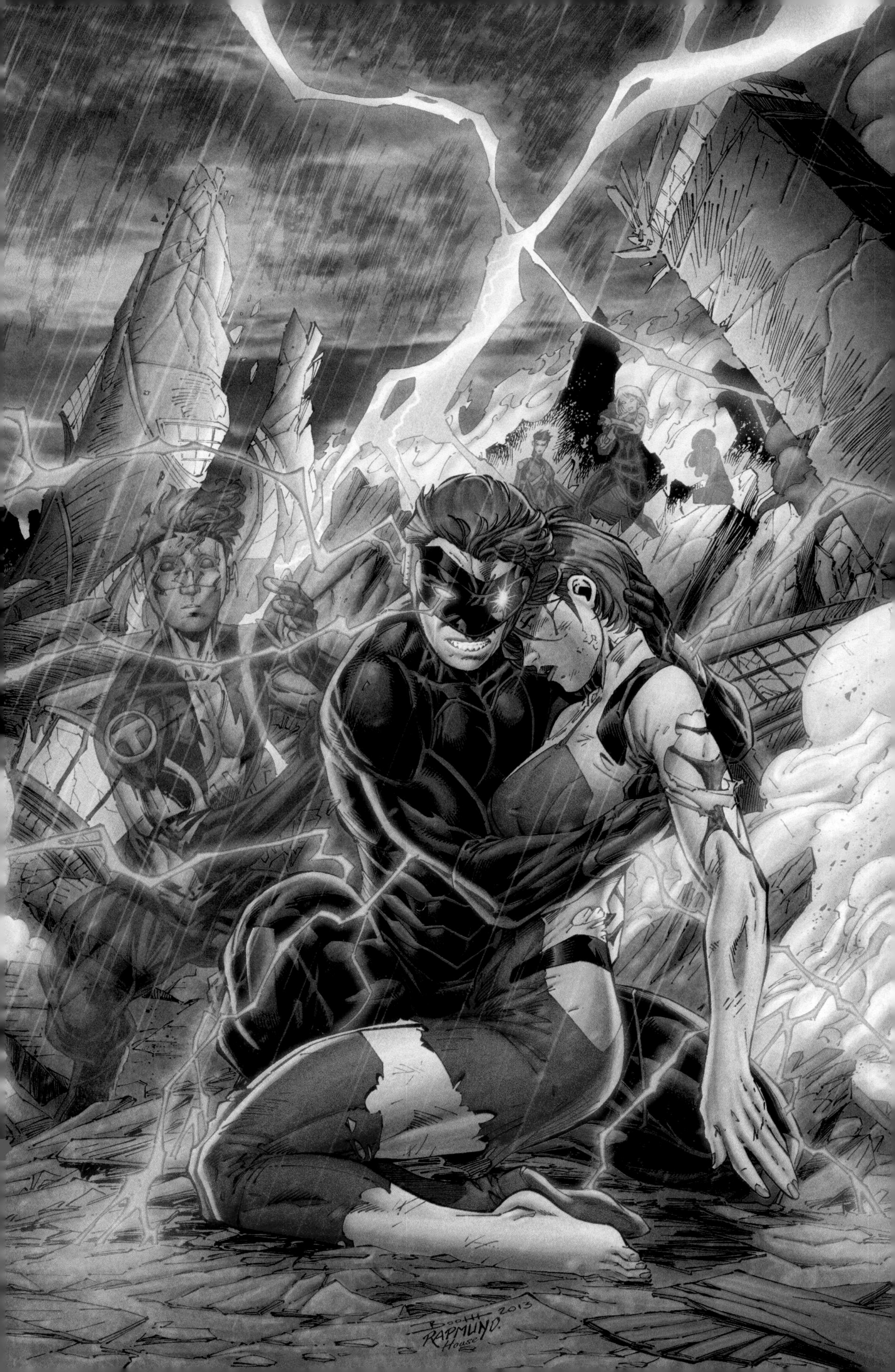
Booth 2013
RAPMUND.
House

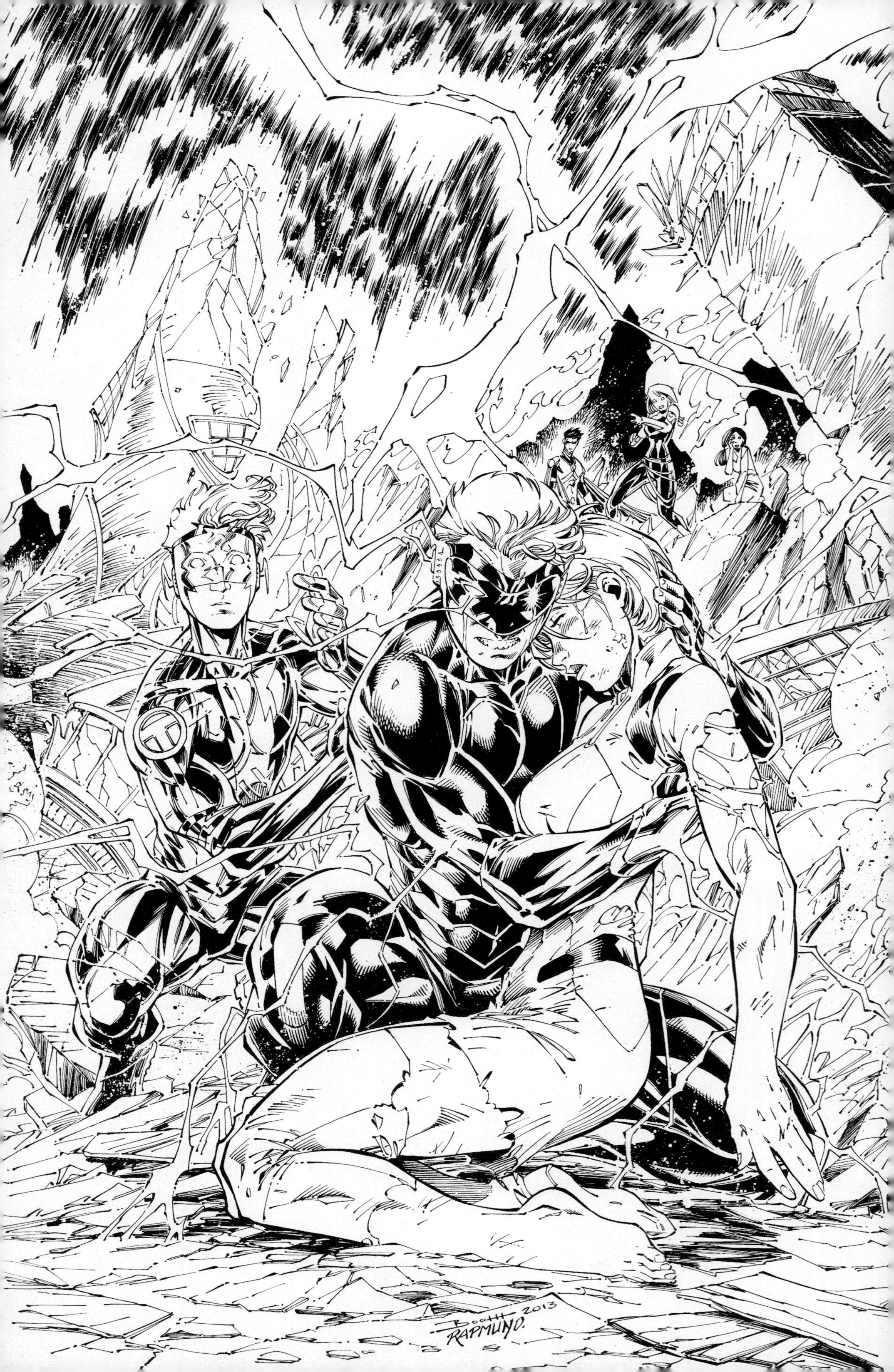
Booth 2013
RAPMUND.

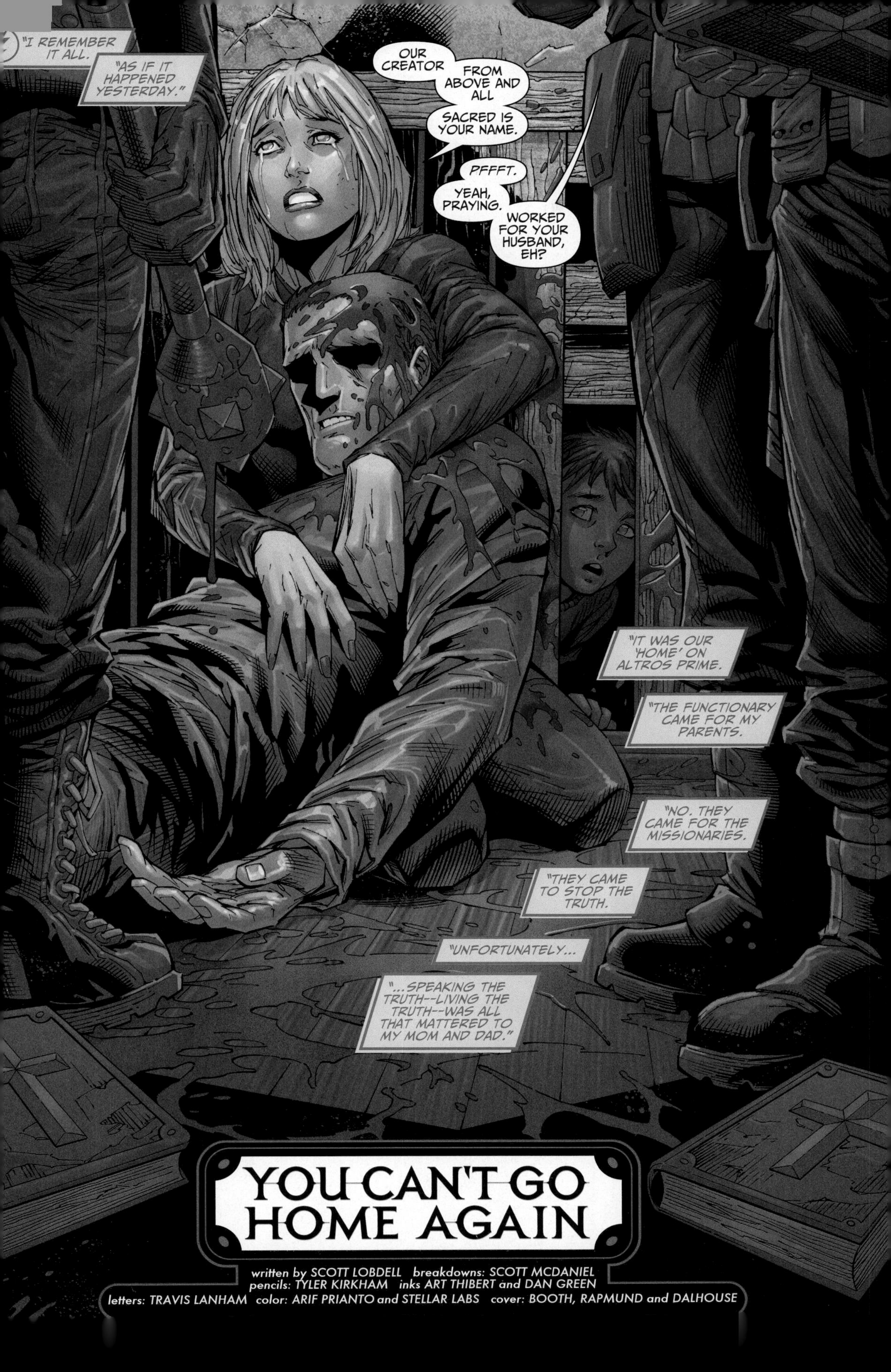

"I REMEMBER IT ALL.
"AS IF IT HAPPENED YESTERDAY."
OUR CREATOR
FROM ABOVE AND ALL
SACRED IS YOUR NAME.
PFFFT.
YEAH, PRAYING.
WORKED FOR YOUR HUSBAND, EH?
"IT WAS OUR 'HOME' ON ALTROS PRIME.
"THE FUNCTIONARY CAME FOR MY PARENTS.
"NO. THEY CAME FOR THE MISSIONARIES.
"THEY CAME TO STOP THE TRUTH.
"UNFORTUNATELY...
"...SPEAKING THE TRUTH--LIVING THE TRUTH--WAS ALL THAT MATTERED TO MY MOM AND DAD."
YOU CAN'T GO HOME AGAIN
written by SCOTT LOBDELL breakdowns: SCOTT MCDANIEL
pencils: TYLER KIRKHAM inks ART THIBERT and DAN GREEN
letters: TRAVIS LANHAM color: ARIF PRIANTO and STELLAR LABS cover: BOOTH, RAPMUND and DALHOUSE

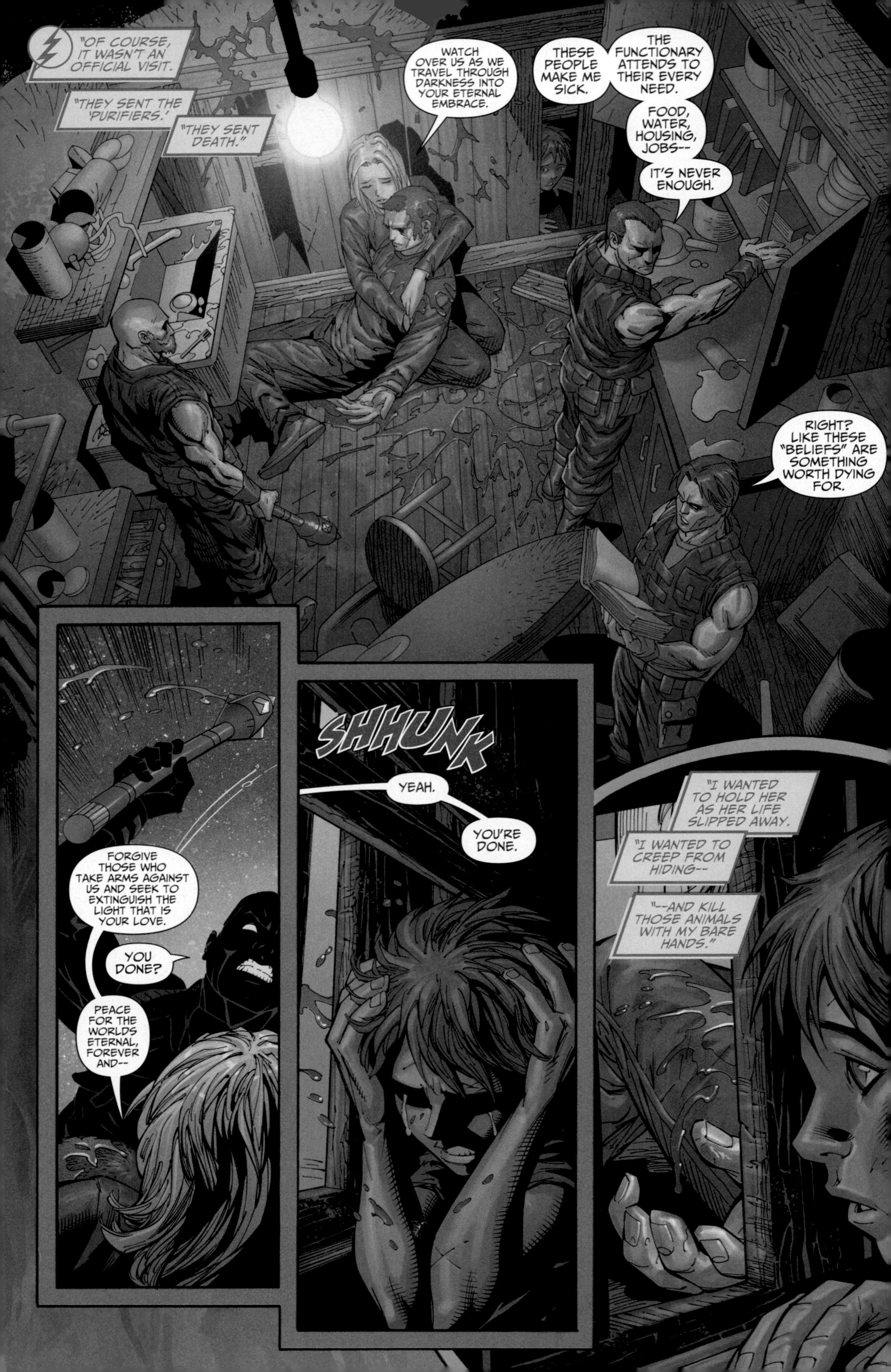
"OF COURSE, IT WASN'T AN OFFICIAL VISIT.
"THEY SENT THE 'PURIFIERS.'
"THEY SENT DEATH."
WATCH OVER US AS WE TRAVEL THROUGH DARKNESS INTO YOUR ETERNAL EMBRACE.
THESE PEOPLE MAKE ME SICK.
THE FUNCTIONARY ATTENDS TO THEIR EVERY NEED.
FOOD, WATER, HOUSING, JOBS--
IT'S NEVER ENOUGH.
RIGHT? LIKE THESE "BELIEFS" ARE SOMETHING WORTH DYING FOR.
FORGIVE THOSE WHO TAKE ARMS AGAINST US AND SEEK TO EXTINGUISH THE LIGHT THAT IS YOUR LOVE.
YOU DONE?
PEACE FOR THE WORLDS ETERNAL, FOREVER AND--
SHHUNK
YEAH.
YOU'RE DONE.
"I WANTED TO HOLD HER AS HER LIFE SLIPPED AWAY.
"I WANTED TO CREEP FROM HIDING--
"--AND KILL THOSE ANIMALS WITH MY BARE HANDS."

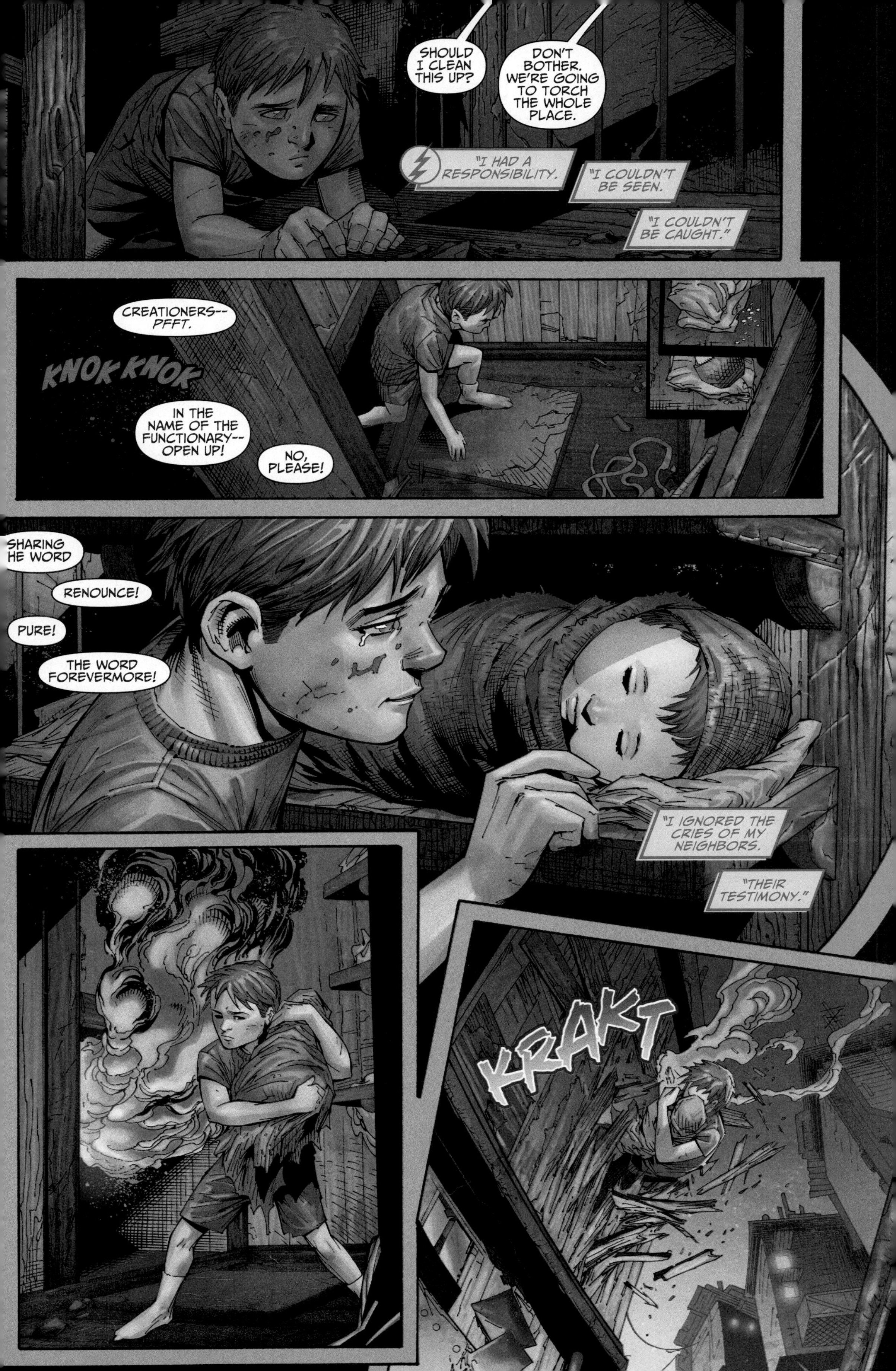
SHOULD I CLEAN THIS UP?
DON'T BOTHER. WE'RE GOING TO TORCH THE WHOLE PLACE.
"I HAD A RESPONSIBILITY.
"I COULDN'T BE SEEN.
"I COULDN'T BE CAUGHT."
CREATIONERS-- PFFT.
KNOK KNOK
IN THE NAME OF THE FUNCTIONARY-- OPEN UP!
NO, PLEASE!
SHARING HE WORD
RENOUNCE!
PURE!
THE WORD FOREVERMORE!
"I IGNORED THE CRIES OF MY NEIGHBORS.
"THEIR TESTIMONY."
KRAKT

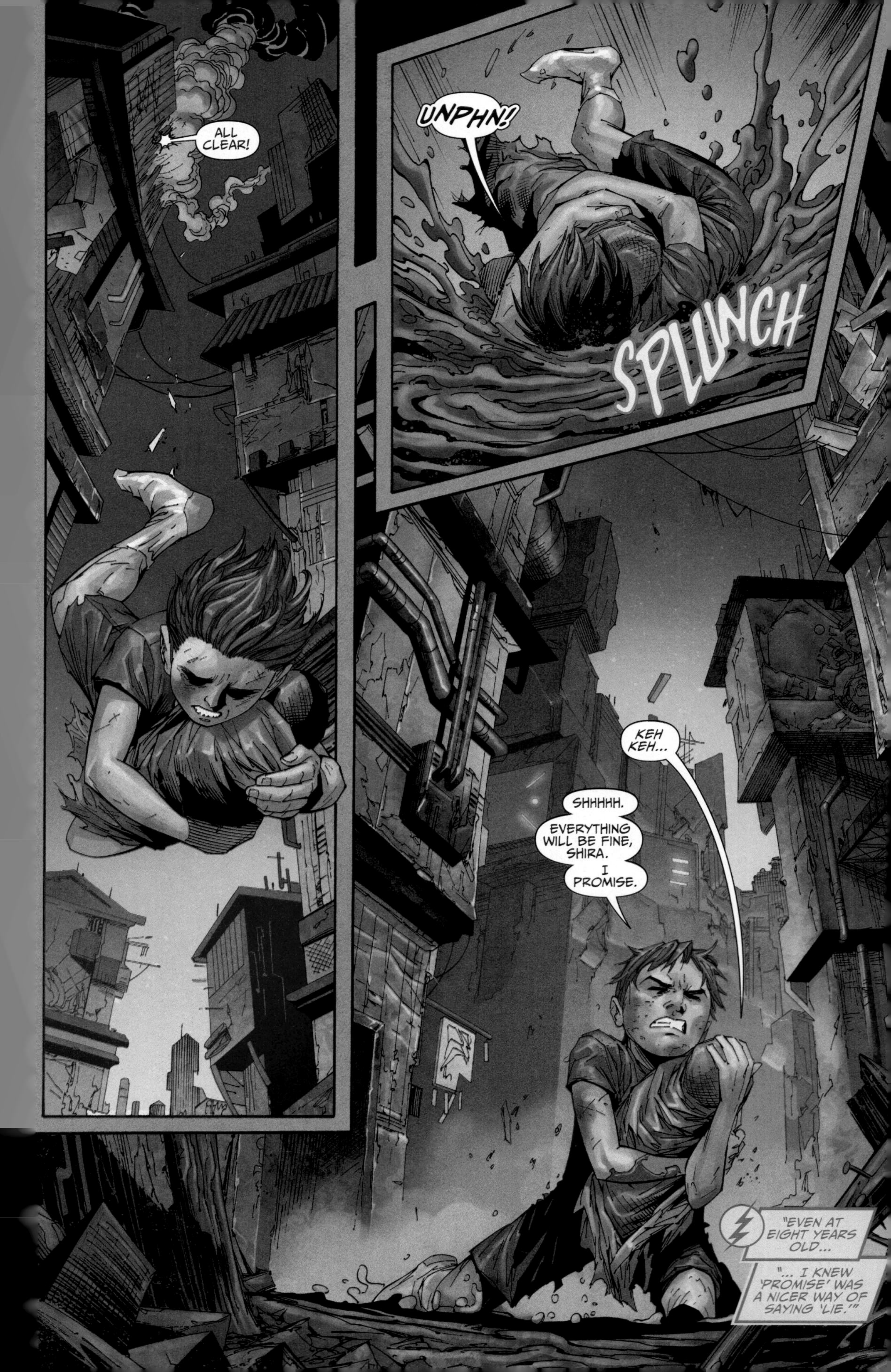
ALL CLEAR!
UNPHN!
SPLUNCH
KEH KEH...
SHHHHH.
EVERYTHING WILL BE FINE, SHIRA.
I PROMISE.
"EVEN AT EIGHT YEARS OLD...
"... I KNEW 'PROMISE' WAS A NICER WAY OF SAYING 'LIE.'"

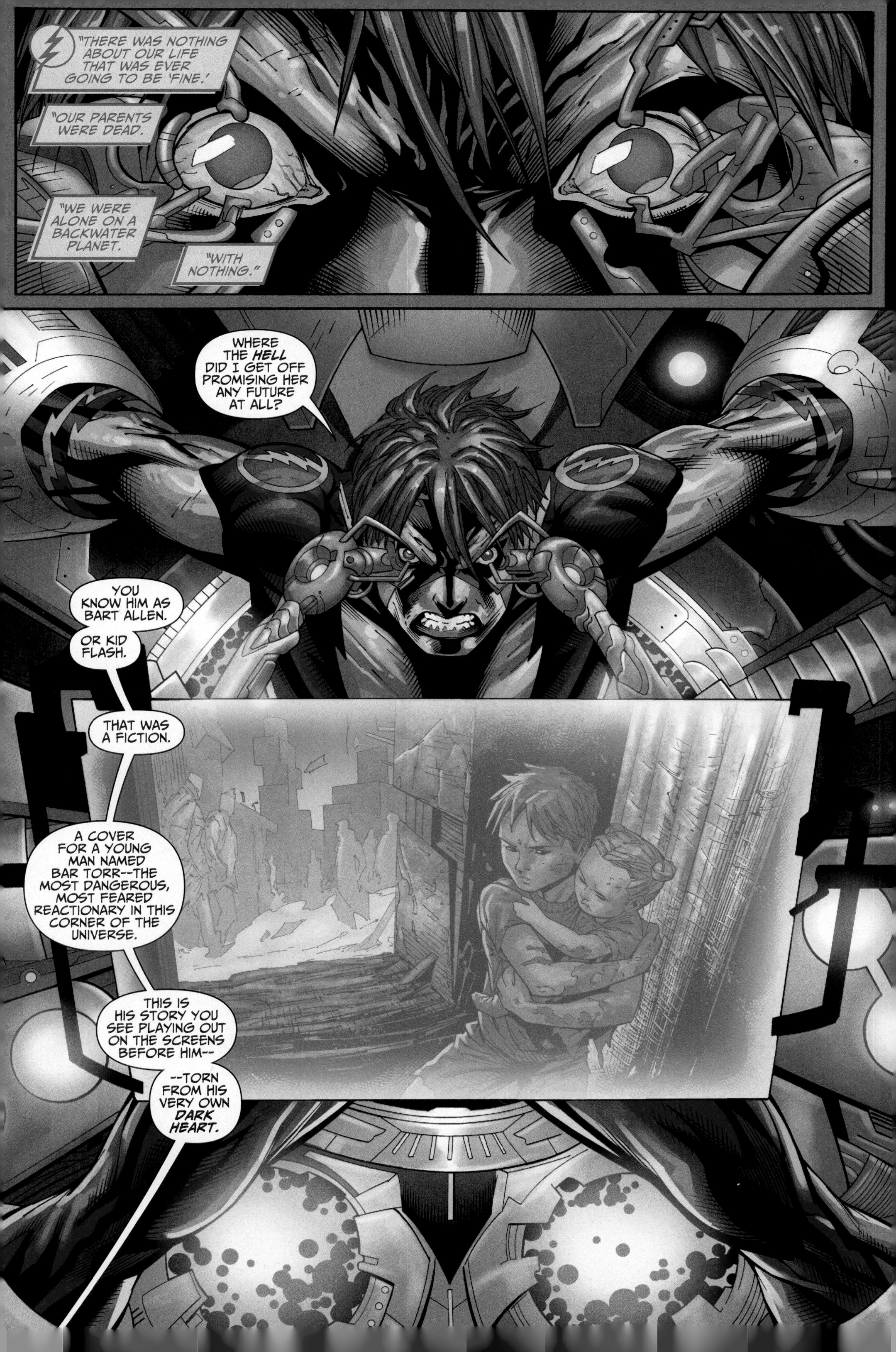
"THERE WAS NOTHING ABOUT OUR LIFE THAT WAS EVER GOING TO BE 'FINE.'
"OUR PARENTS WERE DEAD.
"WE WERE ALONE ON A BACKWATER PLANET.
"WITH NOTHING."
WHERE THE HELL DID I GET OFF PROMISING HER ANY FUTURE AT ALL?
YOU KNOW HIM AS BART ALLEN.
OR KID FLASH.
THAT WAS A FICTION.
A COVER FOR A YOUNG MAN NAMED BAR TORR--THE MOST DANGEROUS, MOST FEARED REACTIONARY IN THIS CORNER OF THE UNIVERSE.
THIS IS HIS STORY YOU SEE PLAYING OUT ON THE SCREENS BEFORE HIM--
--TORN FROM HIS VERY OWN DARK HEART.

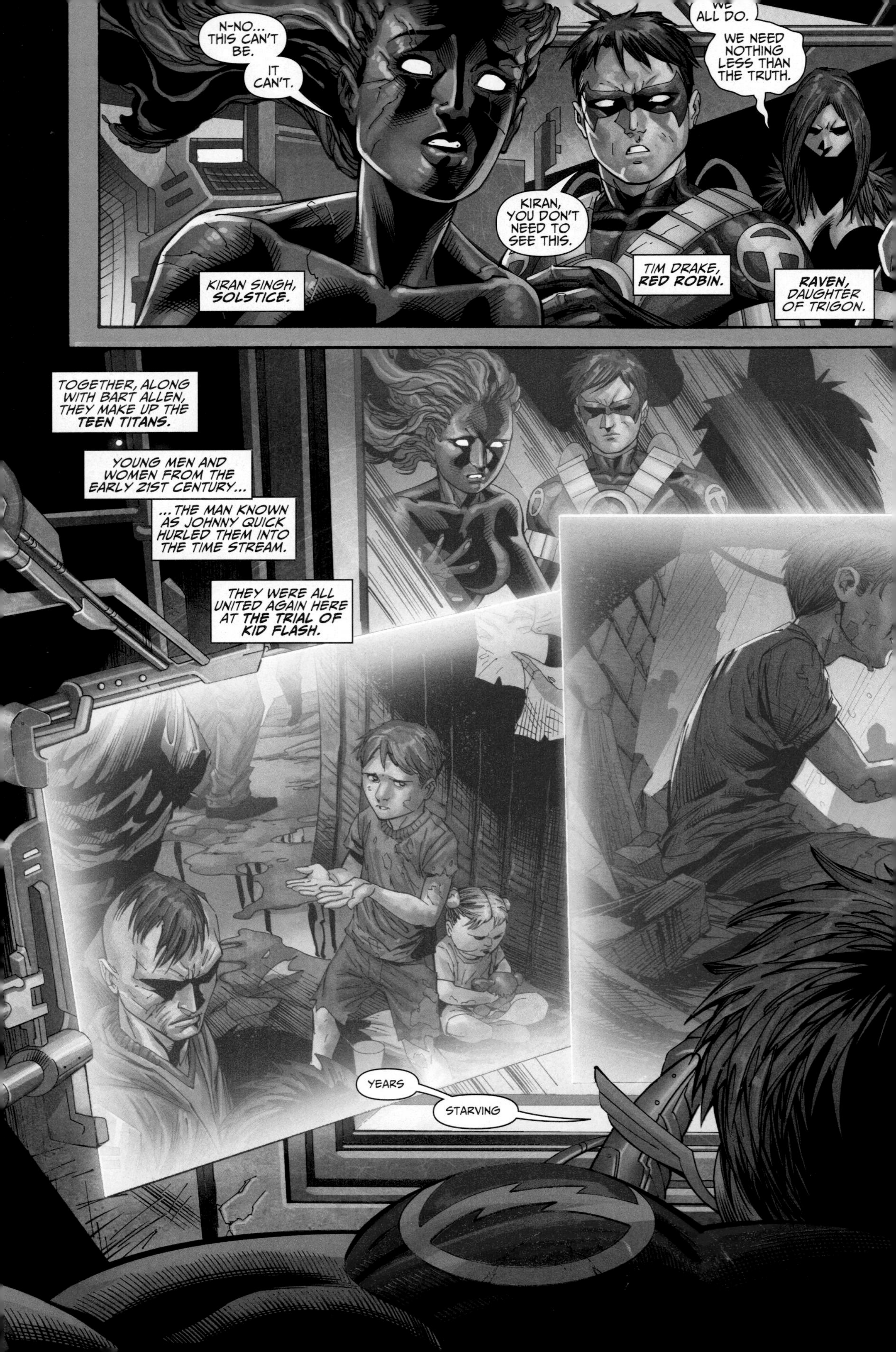
N-NO... THIS CAN'T BE.
IT CAN'T.
WE ALL DO.
WE NEED NOTHING LESS THAN THE TRUTH.
KIRAN, YOU DON'T NEED TO SEE THIS.
KIRAN SINGH, SOLSTICE.
TIM DRAKE, RED ROBIN.
RAVEN, DAUGHTER OF TRIGON.
TOGETHER, ALONG WITH BART ALLEN, THEY MAKE UP THE TEEN TITANS.
YOUNG MEN AND WOMEN FROM THE EARLY 21ST CENTURY...
...THE MAN KNOWN AS JOHNNY QUICK HURLED THEM INTO THE TIME STREAM.
THEY WERE ALL UNITED AGAIN HERE AT THE TRIAL OF KID FLASH.
YEARS
STARVING

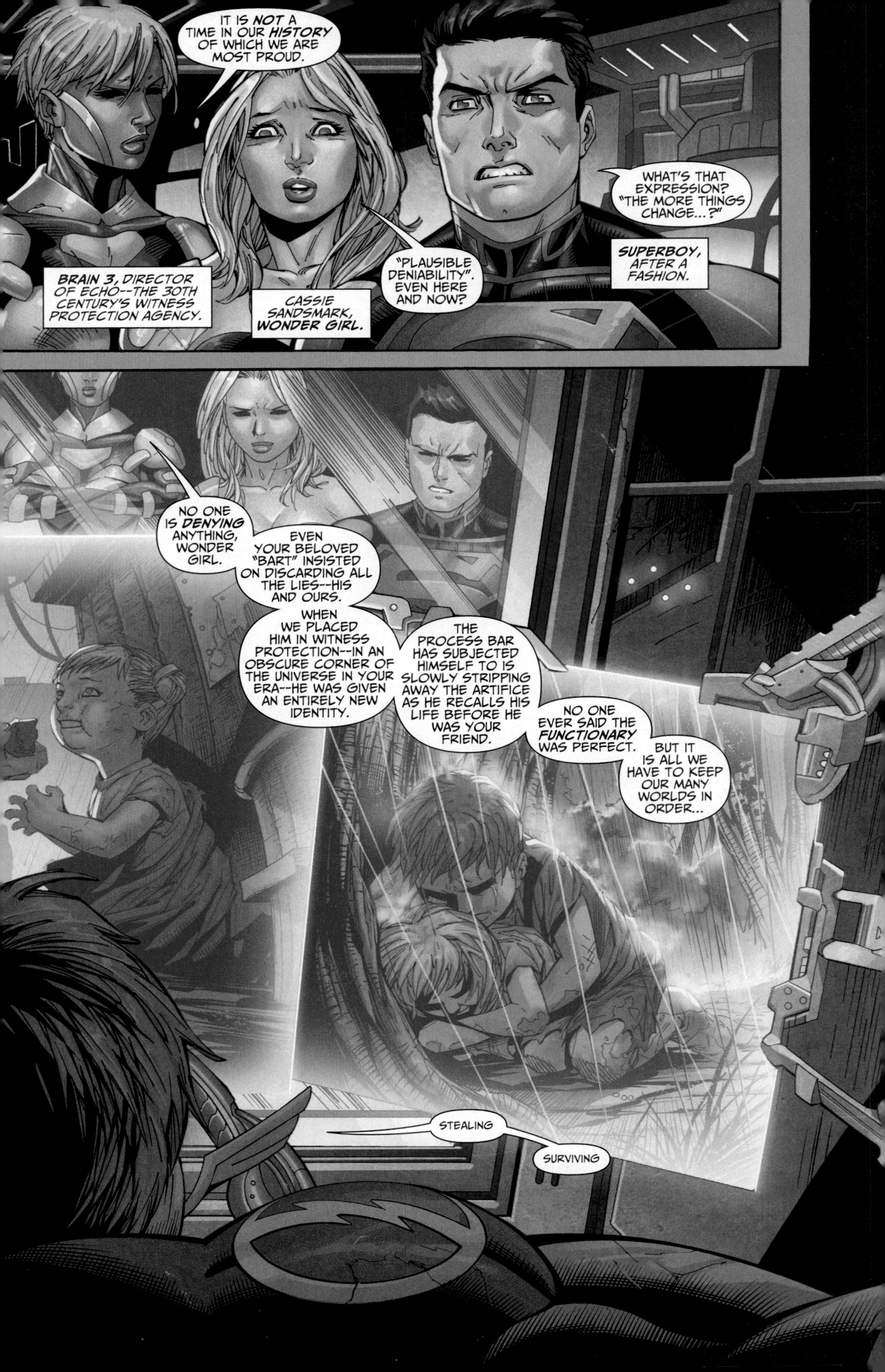

IT IS **NOT** A TIME IN OUR **HISTORY** OF WHICH WE ARE MOST PROUD.
WHAT'S THAT EXPRESSION? "THE MORE THINGS CHANGE...?"
BRAIN 3, DIRECTOR OF ECHO--THE 30TH CENTURY'S WITNESS PROTECTION AGENCY.
CASSIE SANDSMARK, **WONDER GIRL.**
"PLAUSIBLE DENIABILITY". EVEN HERE AND NOW?
SUPERBOY, AFTER A FASHION.
NO ONE IS **DENYING** ANYTHING, WONDER GIRL.
EVEN YOUR BELOVED "BART" INSISTED ON DISCARDING ALL THE LIES--HIS AND OURS.
WHEN WE PLACED HIM IN WITNESS PROTECTION--IN AN OBSCURE CORNER OF THE UNIVERSE IN YOUR ERA--HE WAS GIVEN AN ENTIRELY NEW IDENTITY.
THE PROCESS BAR HAS SUBJECTED HIMSELF TO IS SLOWLY STRIPPING AWAY THE ARTIFICE AS HE RECALLS HIS LIFE BEFORE HE WAS YOUR FRIEND.
NO ONE EVER SAID THE **FUNCTIONARY** WAS PERFECT.
BUT IT IS ALL WE HAVE TO KEEP OUR MANY WORLDS IN ORDER...
STEALING
SURVIVING

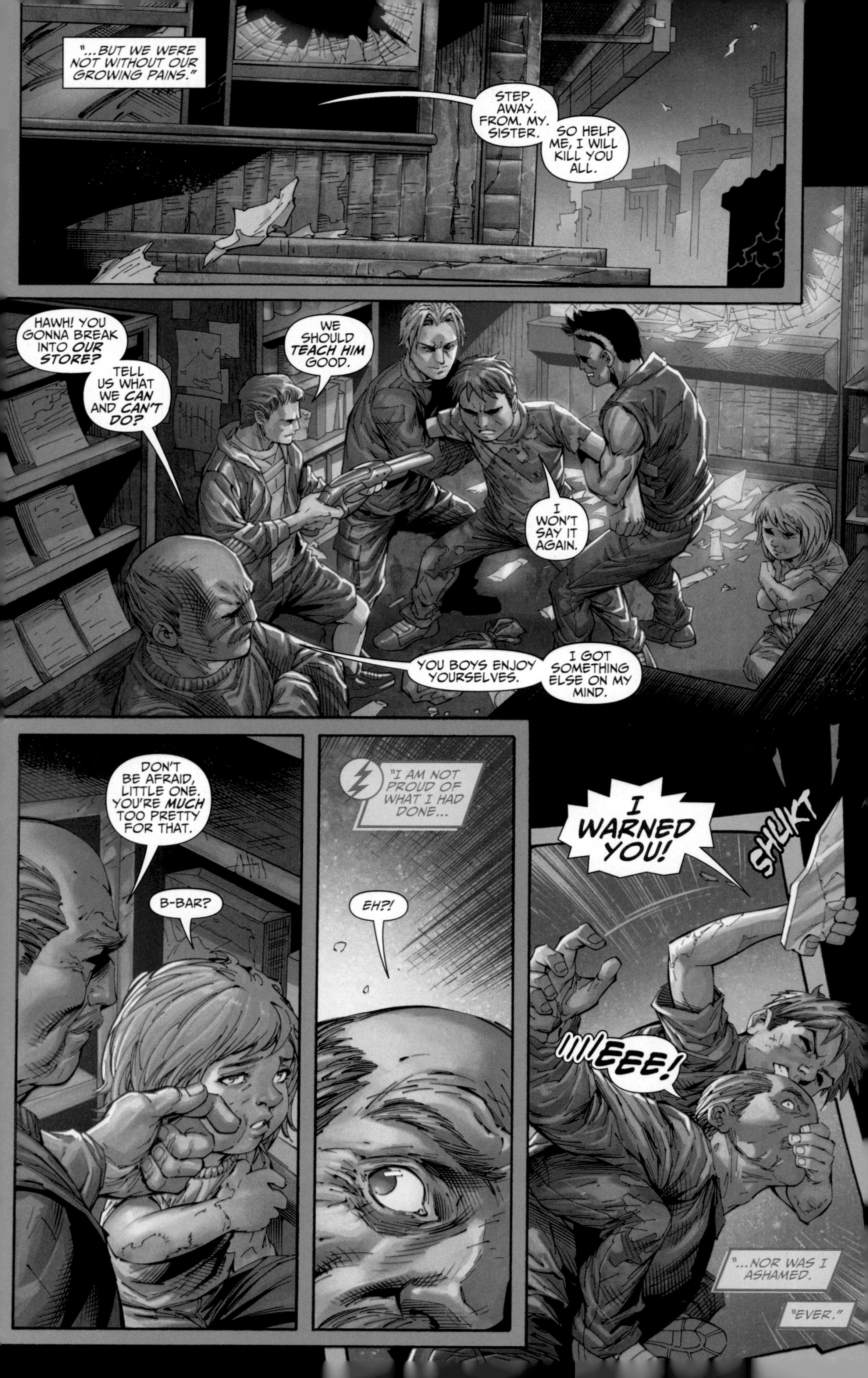
"...BUT WE WERE NOT WITHOUT OUR GROWING PAINS."
STEP. AWAY. FROM. MY. SISTER.
SO HELP ME, I WILL KILL YOU ALL.
HAWH! YOU GONNA BREAK INTO OUR STORE?
TELL US WHAT WE CAN AND CAN'T DO?
WE SHOULD TEACH HIM GOOD.
I WON'T SAY IT AGAIN.
YOU BOYS ENJOY YOURSELVES.
I GOT SOMETHING ELSE ON MY MIND.
DON'T BE AFRAID, LITTLE ONE. YOU'RE MUCH TOO PRETTY FOR THAT.
B-BAR?
"I AM NOT PROUD OF WHAT I HAD DONE...
EH?!
I WARNED YOU!
SHUKT
IIIIIEEEE!
"...NOR WAS I ASHAMED.
"EVER."

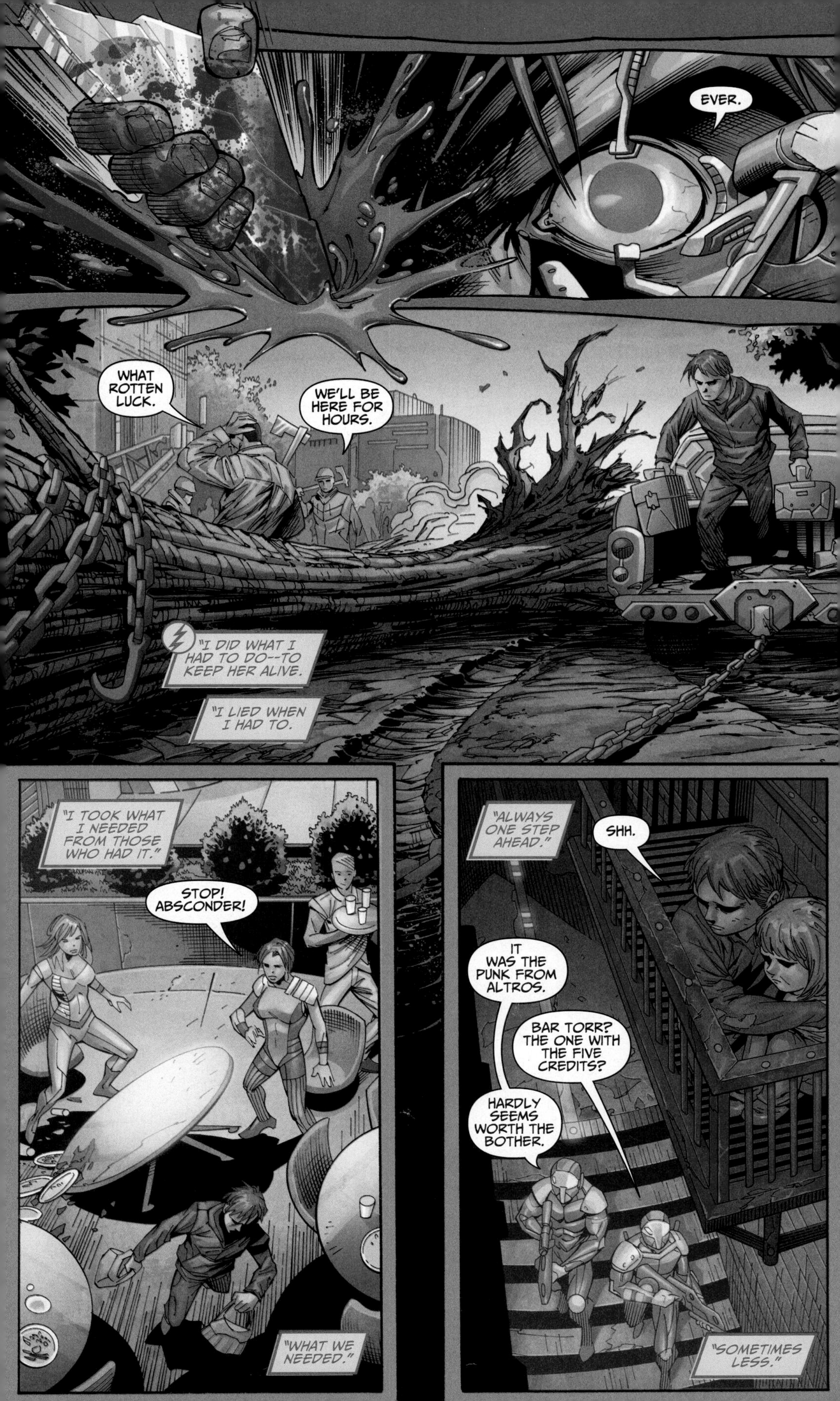
EVER.
WHAT ROTTEN LUCK.
WE'LL BE HERE FOR HOURS.
"I DID WHAT I HAD TO DO--TO KEEP HER ALIVE.
"I LIED WHEN I HAD TO.
"I TOOK WHAT I NEEDED FROM THOSE WHO HAD IT."
STOP! ABSCONDER!
"WHAT WE NEEDED."
"ALWAYS ONE STEP AHEAD."
SHH.
IT WAS THE PUNK FROM ALTROS.
BAR TORR? THE ONE WITH THE FIVE CREDITS?
HARDLY SEEMS WORTH THE BOTHER.
"SOMETIMES LESS."

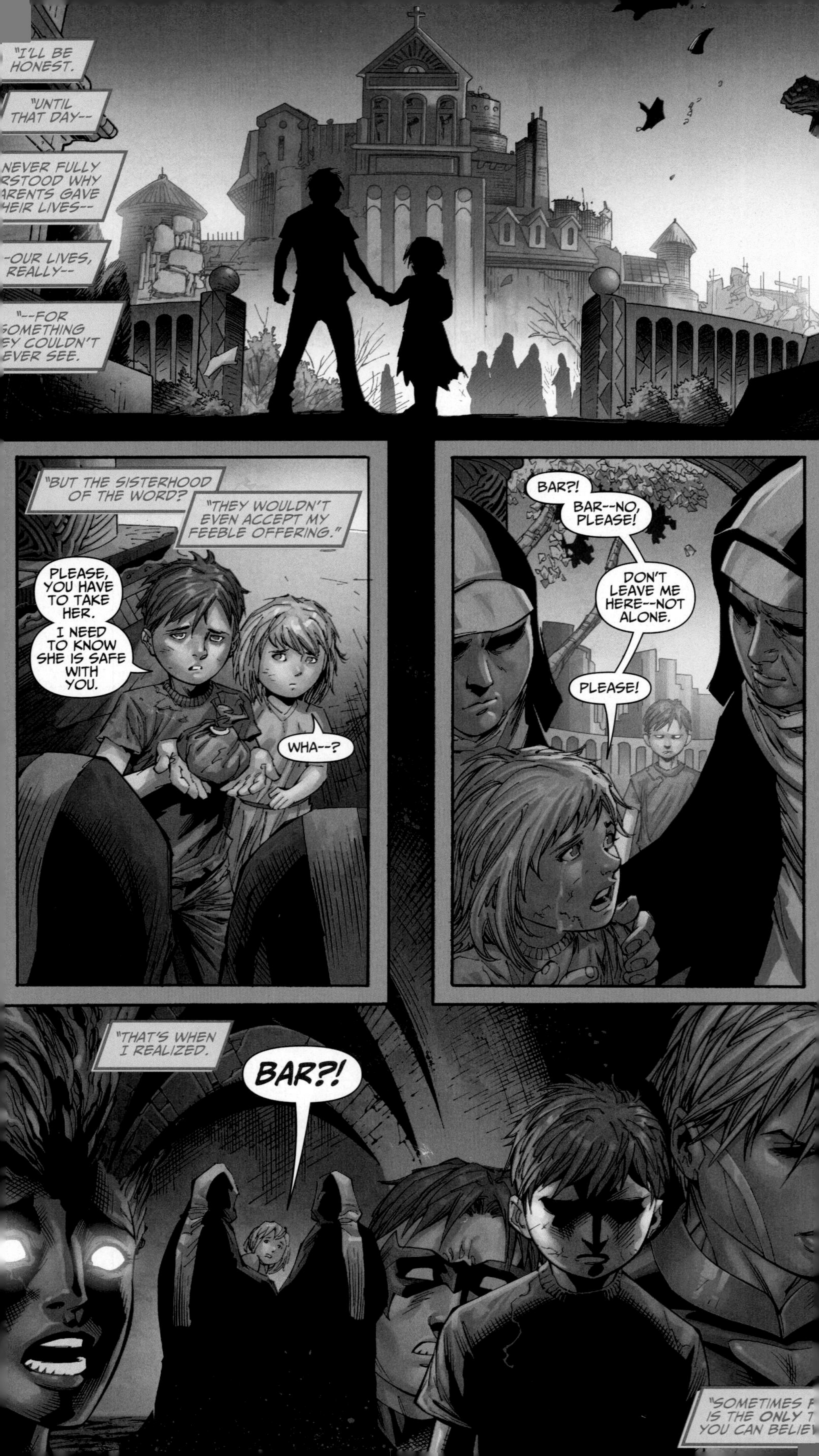
"I'LL BE HONEST.
"UNTIL THAT DAY--
NEVER FULLY RSTOOD WHY ARENTS GAVE HEIR LIVES--
-OUR LIVES, REALLY--
"--FOR SOMETHING EY COULDN'T EVER SEE.
"BUT THE SISTERHOOD OF THE WORD?
"THEY WOULDN'T EVEN ACCEPT MY FEEBLE OFFERING."
PLEASE, YOU HAVE TO TAKE HER.
I NEED TO KNOW SHE IS SAFE WITH YOU.
WHA--?
BAR?!
BAR--NO, PLEASE!
DON'T LEAVE ME HERE--NOT ALONE.
PLEASE!
"THAT'S WHEN I REALIZED.
BAR?!
"SOMETIMES
IS THE ONLY
YOU CAN BELIEV

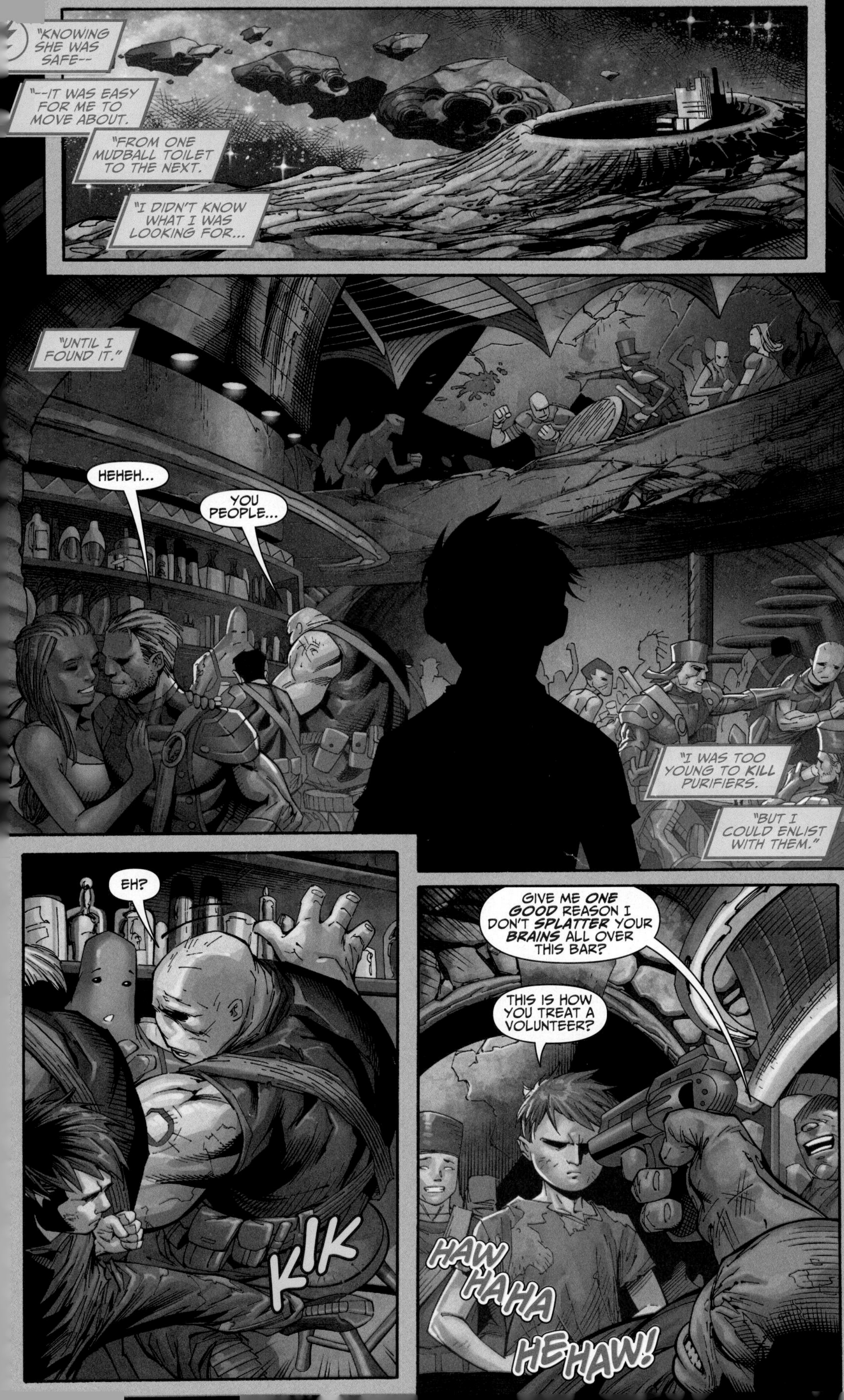

"KNOWING SHE WAS SAFE--
"--IT WAS EASY FOR ME TO MOVE ABOUT.
"FROM ONE MUDBALL TOILET TO THE NEXT.
"I DIDN'T KNOW WHAT I WAS LOOKING FOR...
"UNTIL I FOUND IT."
HEHEH...
YOU PEOPLE...
"I WAS TOO YOUNG TO KILL PURIFIERS.
"BUT I COULD ENLIST WITH THEM."
EH?
KIK
GIVE ME ONE GOOD REASON I DON'T SPLATTER YOUR BRAINS ALL OVER THIS BAR?
THIS IS HOW YOU TREAT A VOLUNTEER?
HAW HAHA HEHAW!

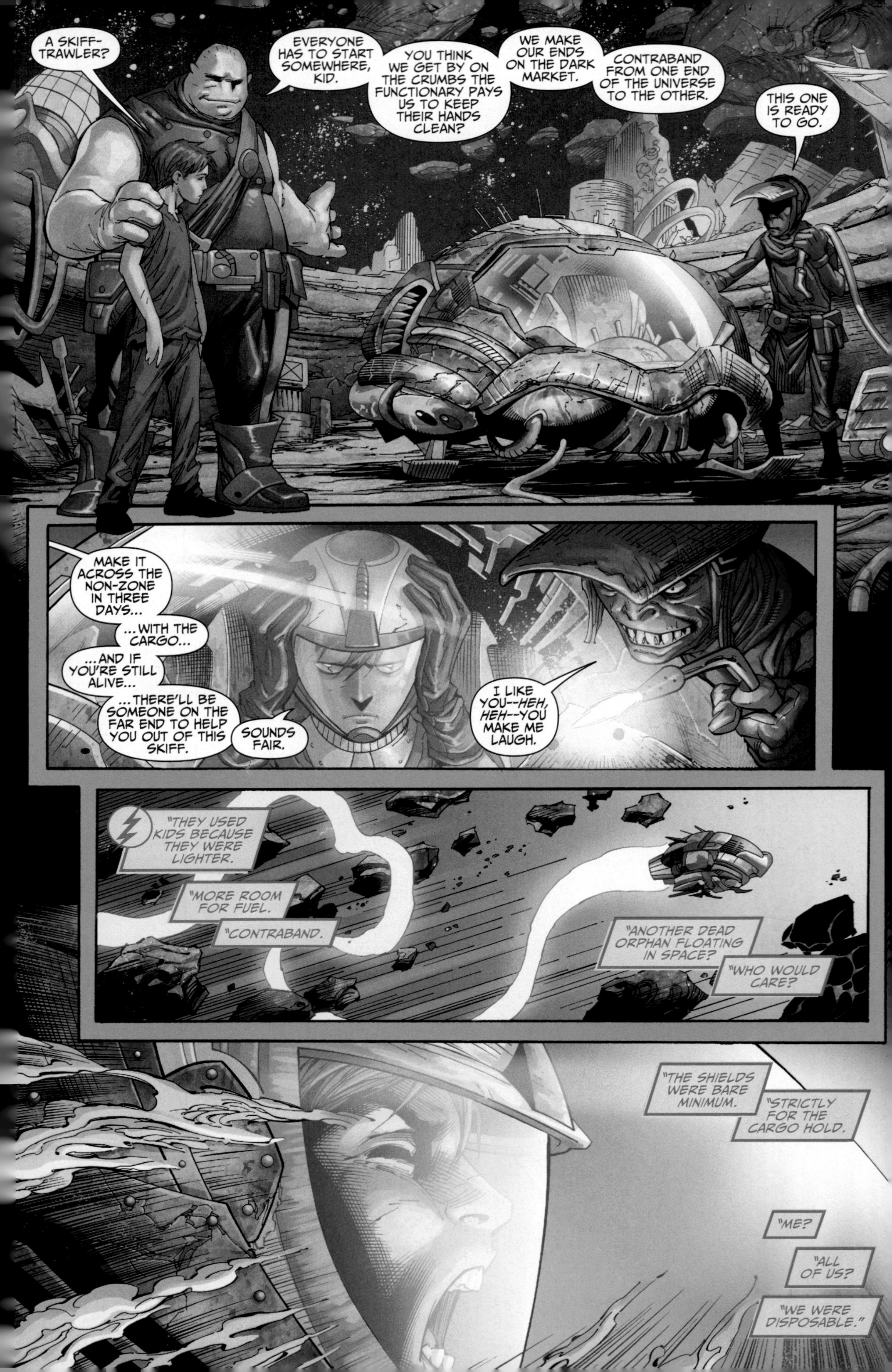
A SKIFF-TRAWLER?
EVERYONE HAS TO START SOMEWHERE, KID.
YOU THINK WE GET BY ON THE CRUMBS THE FUNCTIONARY PAYS US TO KEEP THEIR HANDS CLEAN?
WE MAKE OUR ENDS ON THE DARK MARKET.
CONTRABAND FROM ONE END OF THE UNIVERSE TO THE OTHER.
THIS ONE IS READY TO GO.
MAKE IT ACROSS THE NON-ZONE IN THREE DAYS...
...WITH THE CARGO...
...AND IF YOU'RE STILL ALIVE...
...THERE'LL BE SOMEONE ON THE FAR END TO HELP YOU OUT OF THIS SKIFF.
SOUNDS FAIR.
I LIKE YOU--*HEH, HEH*--YOU MAKE ME LAUGH.
"THEY USED KIDS BECAUSE THEY WERE LIGHTER.
"MORE ROOM FOR FUEL.
"CONTRABAND.
"ANOTHER DEAD ORPHAN FLOATING IN SPACE?
"WHO WOULD CARE?
"THE SHIELDS WERE BARE MINIMUM.
"STRICTLY FOR THE CARGO HOLD.
"ME?
"ALL OF US?
"WE WERE DISPOSABLE."

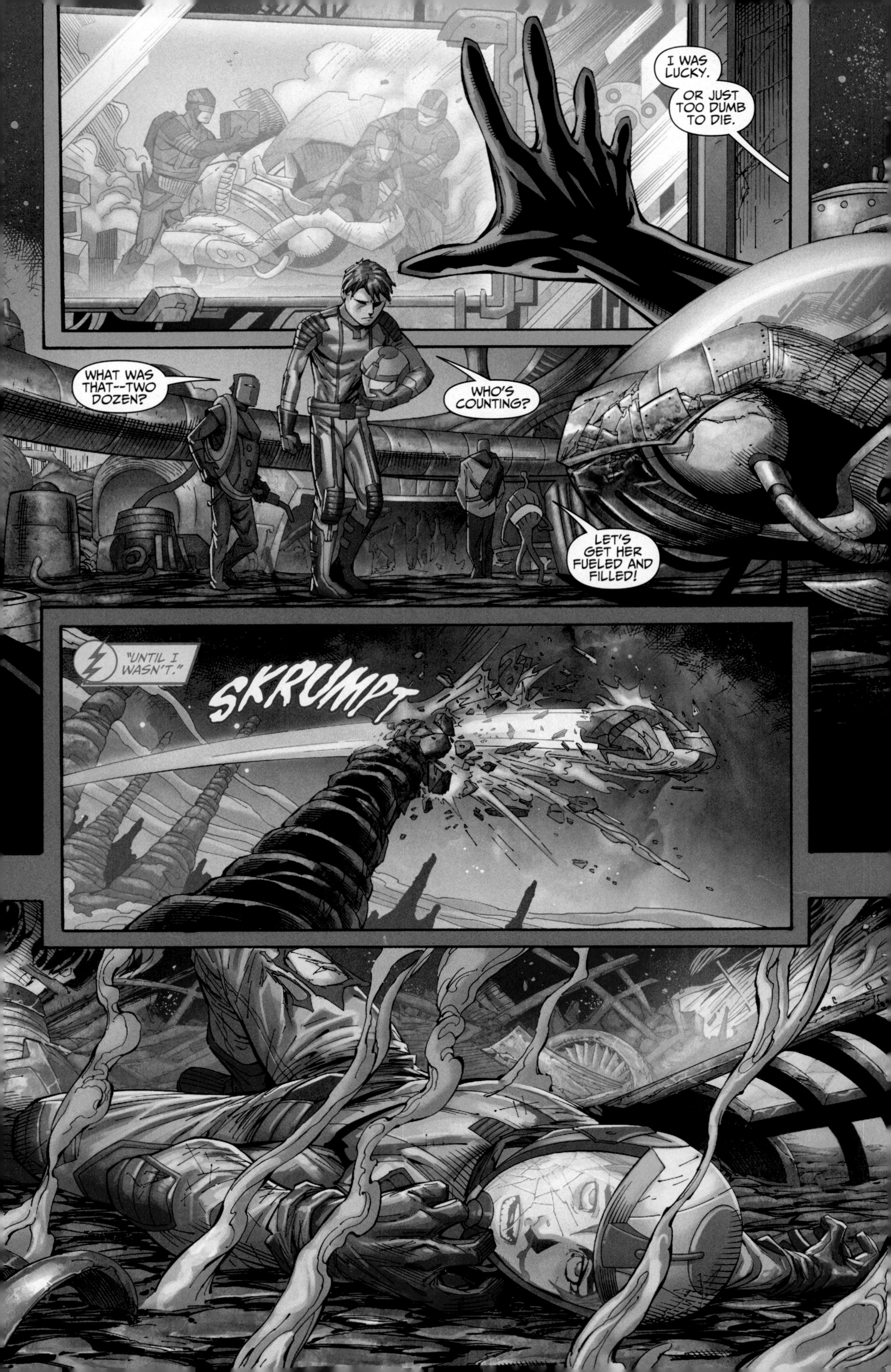

I WAS LUCKY.
OR JUST TOO DUMB TO DIE.
WHAT WAS THAT--TWO DOZEN?
WHO'S COUNTING?
LET'S GET HER FUELED AND FILLED!
"UNTIL I WASN'T."
SKRUMPT

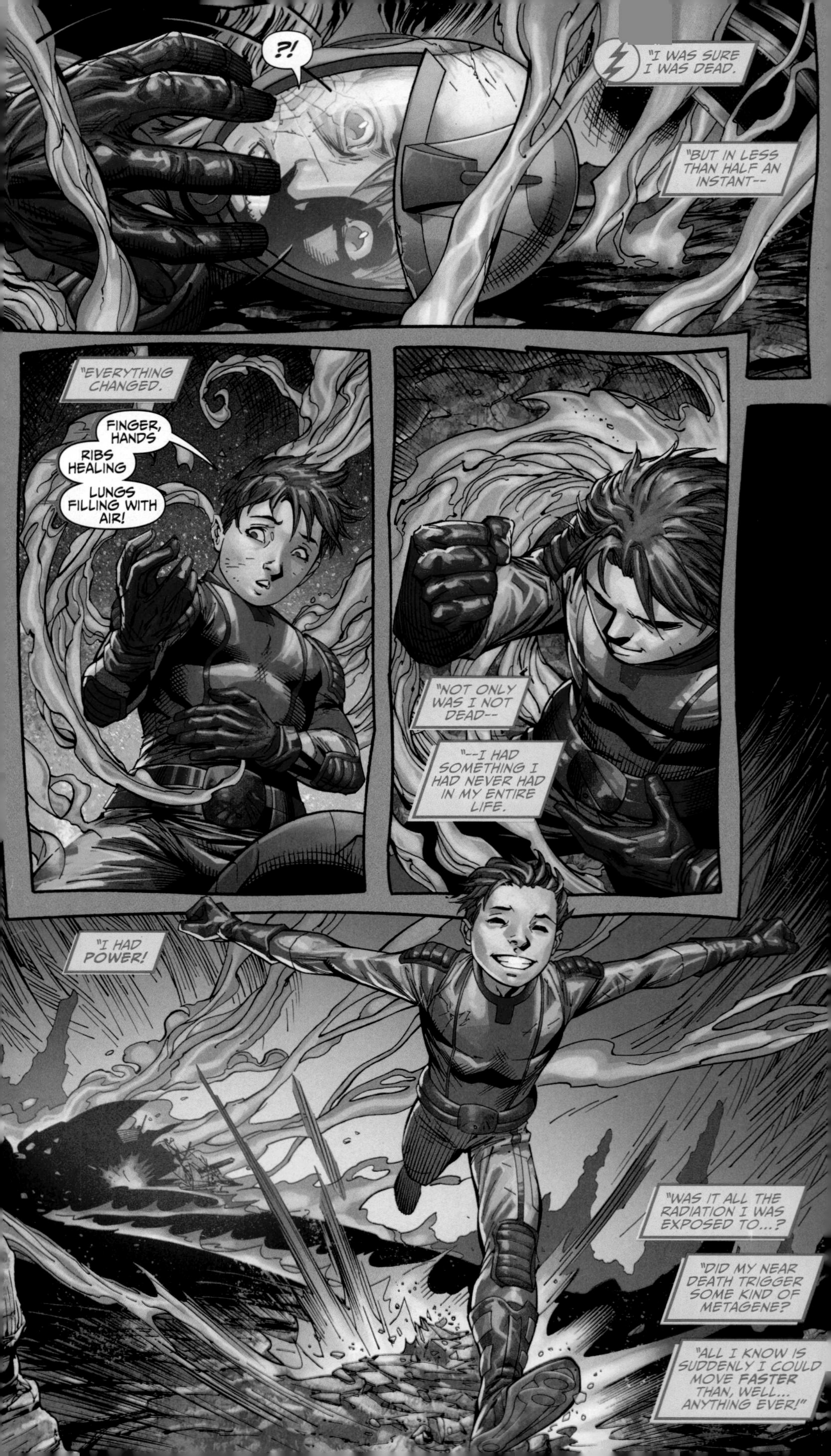
?!
"I WAS SURE I WAS DEAD.
"BUT IN LESS THAN HALF AN INSTANT--
"EVERYTHING CHANGED.
FINGER, HANDS
RIBS HEALING
LUNGS FILLING WITH AIR!
"NOT ONLY WAS I NOT DEAD--
"--I HAD SOMETHING I HAD NEVER HAD IN MY ENTIRE LIFE.
"I HAD POWER!
"WAS IT ALL THE RADIATION I WAS EXPOSED TO...?
"DID MY NEAR DEATH TRIGGER SOME KIND OF METAGENE?
"ALL I KNOW IS SUDDENLY I COULD MOVE FASTER THAN, WELL... ANYTHING EVER!"

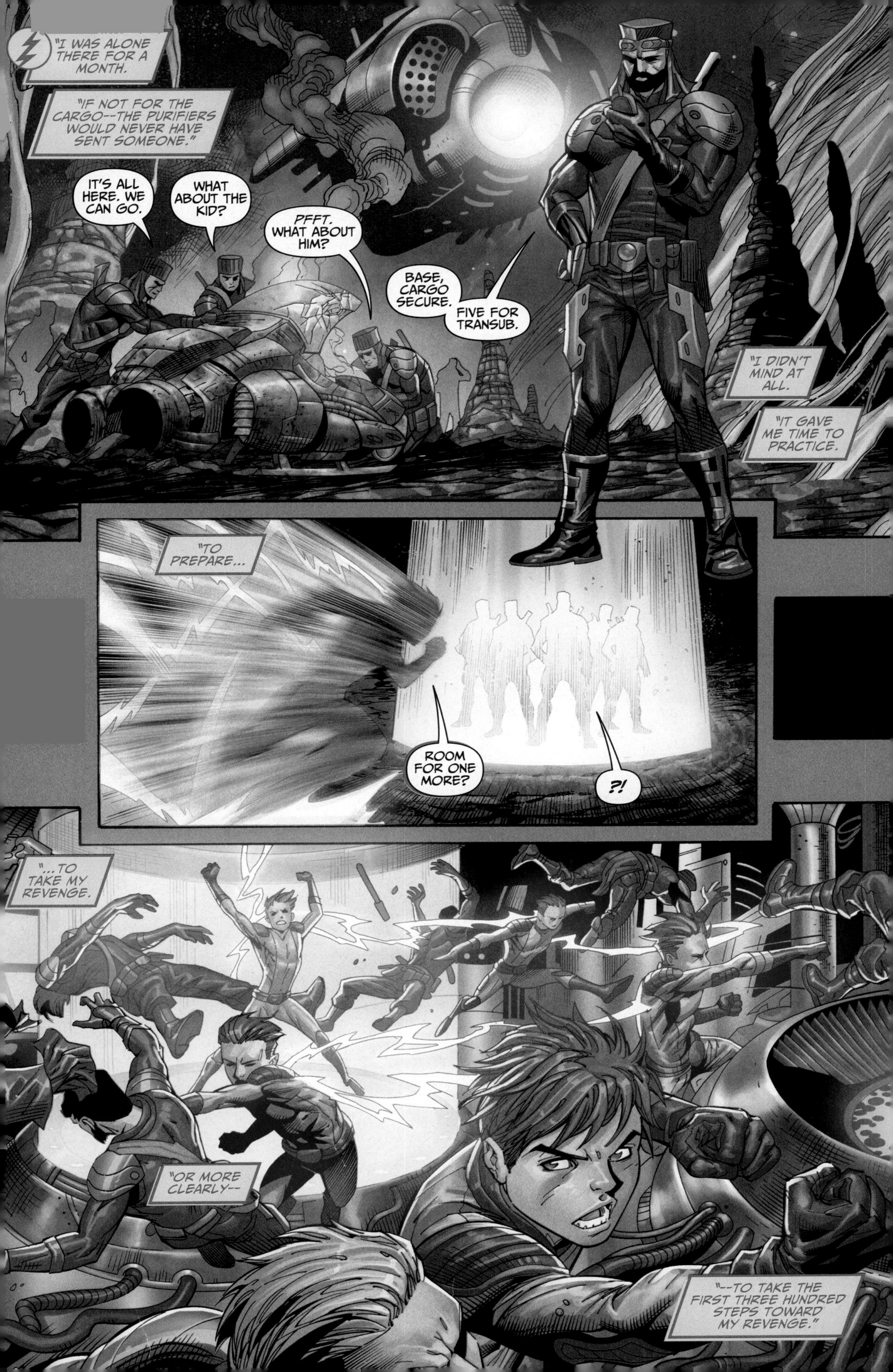
"I WAS ALONE THERE FOR A MONTH.
"IF NOT FOR THE CARGO--THE PURIFIERS WOULD NEVER HAVE SENT SOMEONE."
IT'S ALL HERE. WE CAN GO.
WHAT ABOUT THE KID?
PFFT. WHAT ABOUT HIM?
BASE, CARGO SECURE.
FIVE FOR TRANSUB.
"I DIDN'T MIND AT ALL.
"IT GAVE ME TIME TO PRACTICE.
"TO PREPARE...
ROOM FOR ONE MORE?
?!
"...TO TAKE MY REVENGE.
"OR MORE CLEARLY--
"--TO TAKE THE FIRST THREE HUNDRED STEPS TOWARD MY REVENGE."

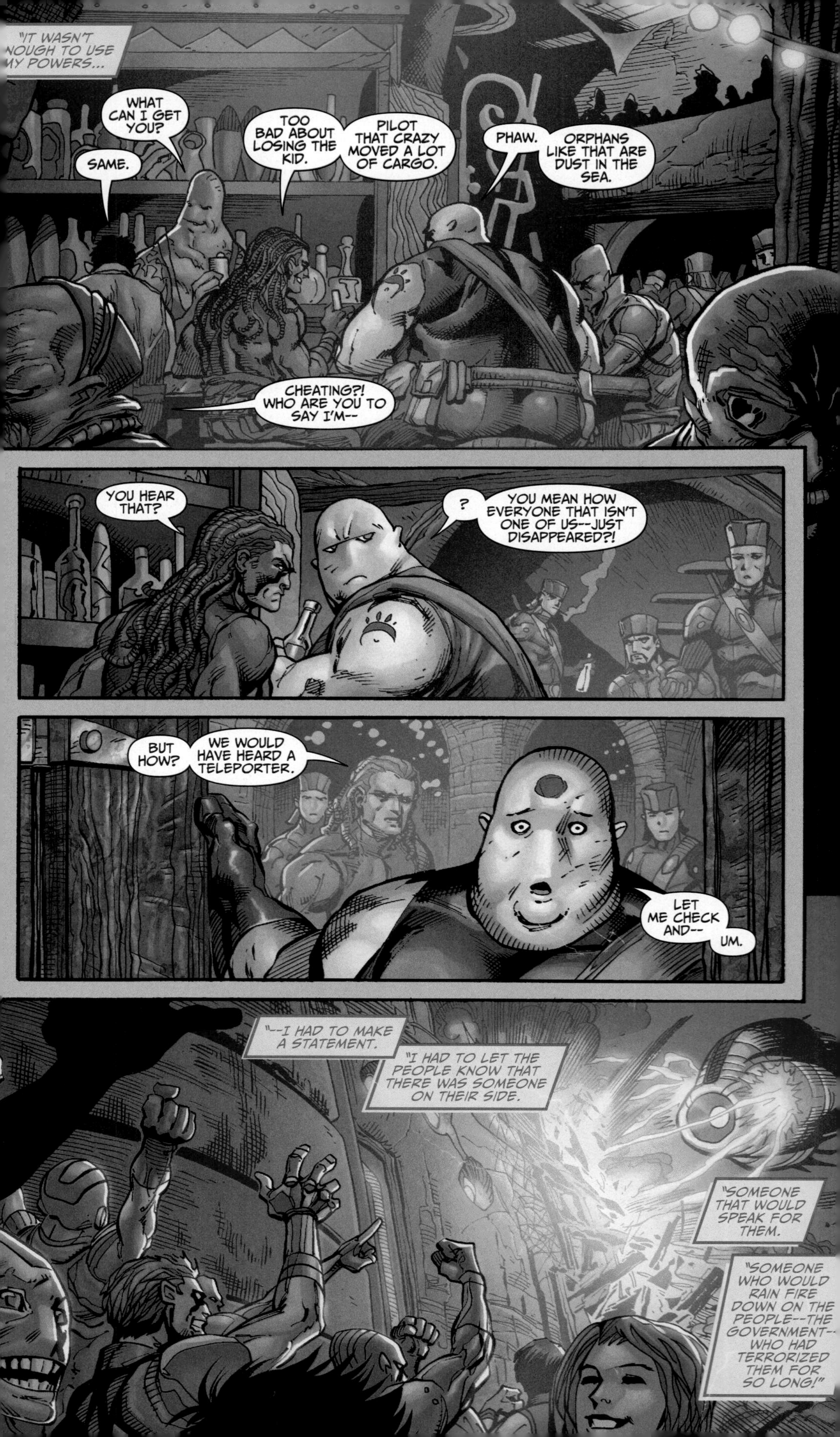
"IT WASN'T NOUGH TO USE MY POWERS...
WHAT CAN I GET YOU?
SAME.
TOO BAD ABOUT LOSING THE KID.
PILOT THAT CRAZY MOVED A LOT OF CARGO.
PHAW.
ORPHANS LIKE THAT ARE DUST IN THE SEA.
CHEATING?! WHO ARE YOU TO SAY I'M--
YOU HEAR THAT?
?
YOU MEAN HOW EVERYONE THAT ISN'T ONE OF US--JUST DISAPPEARED?!
BUT HOW?
WE WOULD HAVE HEARD A TELEPORTER.
LET ME CHECK AND--
UM.
"--I HAD TO MAKE A STATEMENT.
"I HAD TO LET THE PEOPLE KNOW THAT THERE WAS SOMEONE ON THEIR SIDE.
"SOMEONE THAT WOULD SPEAK FOR THEM.
"SOMEONE WHO WOULD RAIN FIRE DOWN ON THE PEOPLE--THE GOVERNMENT--WHO HAD TERRORIZED THEM FOR SO LONG!"

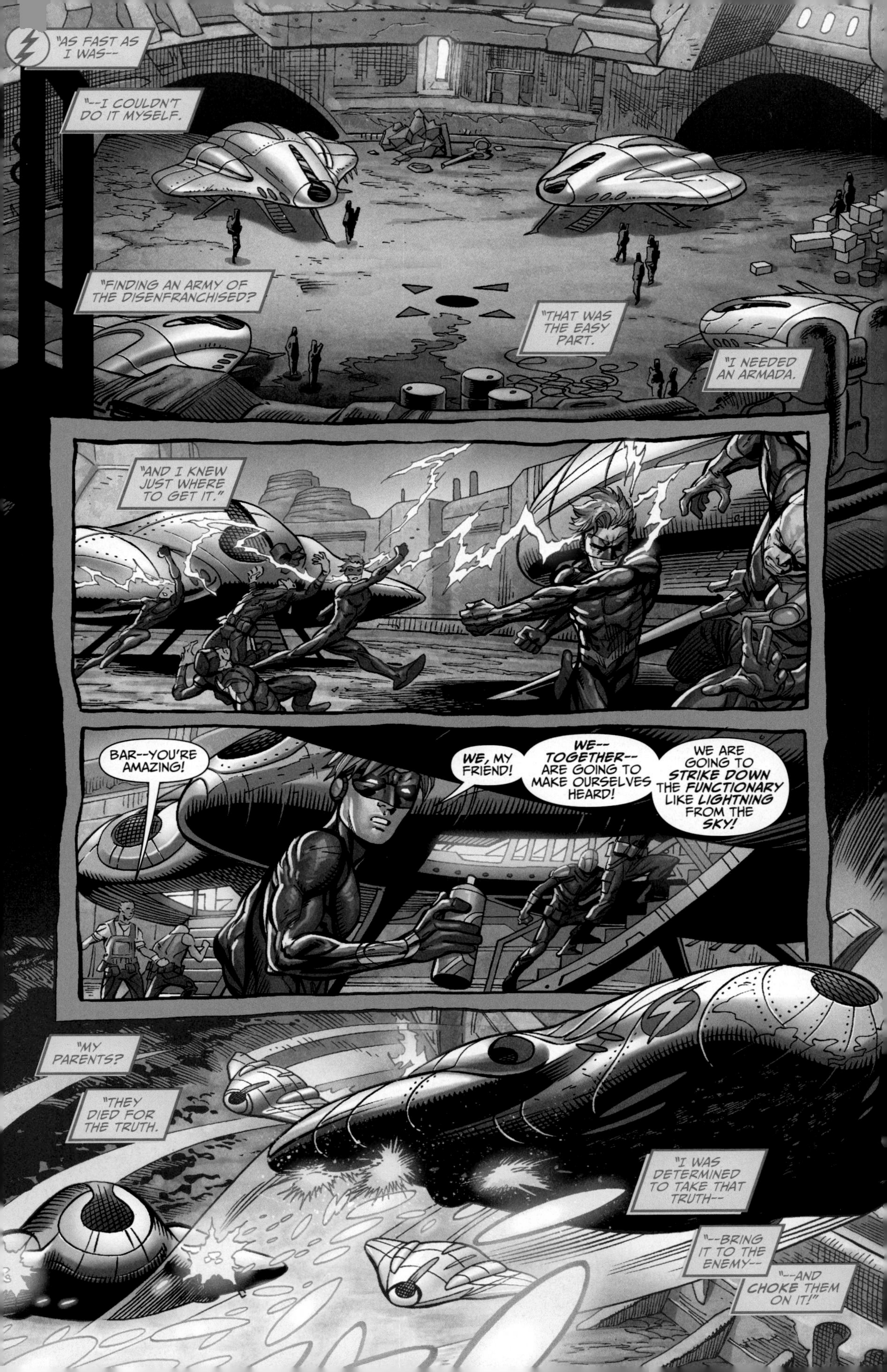
"AS FAST AS I WAS--
"--I COULDN'T DO IT MYSELF.
"FINDING AN ARMY OF THE DISENFRANCHISED?
"THAT WAS THE EASY PART.
"I NEEDED AN ARMADA.
"AND I KNEW JUST WHERE TO GET IT."
BAR--YOU'RE AMAZING!
WE, MY FRIEND!
WE--TOGETHER--ARE GOING TO MAKE OURSELVES HEARD!
WE ARE GOING TO STRIKE DOWN THE FUNCTIONARY LIKE LIGHTNING FROM THE SKY!
"MY PARENTS?
"THEY DIED FOR THE TRUTH.
"I WAS DETERMINED TO TAKE THAT TRUTH--
"--BRING IT TO THE ENEMY--
"--AND CHOKE THEM ON IT!"

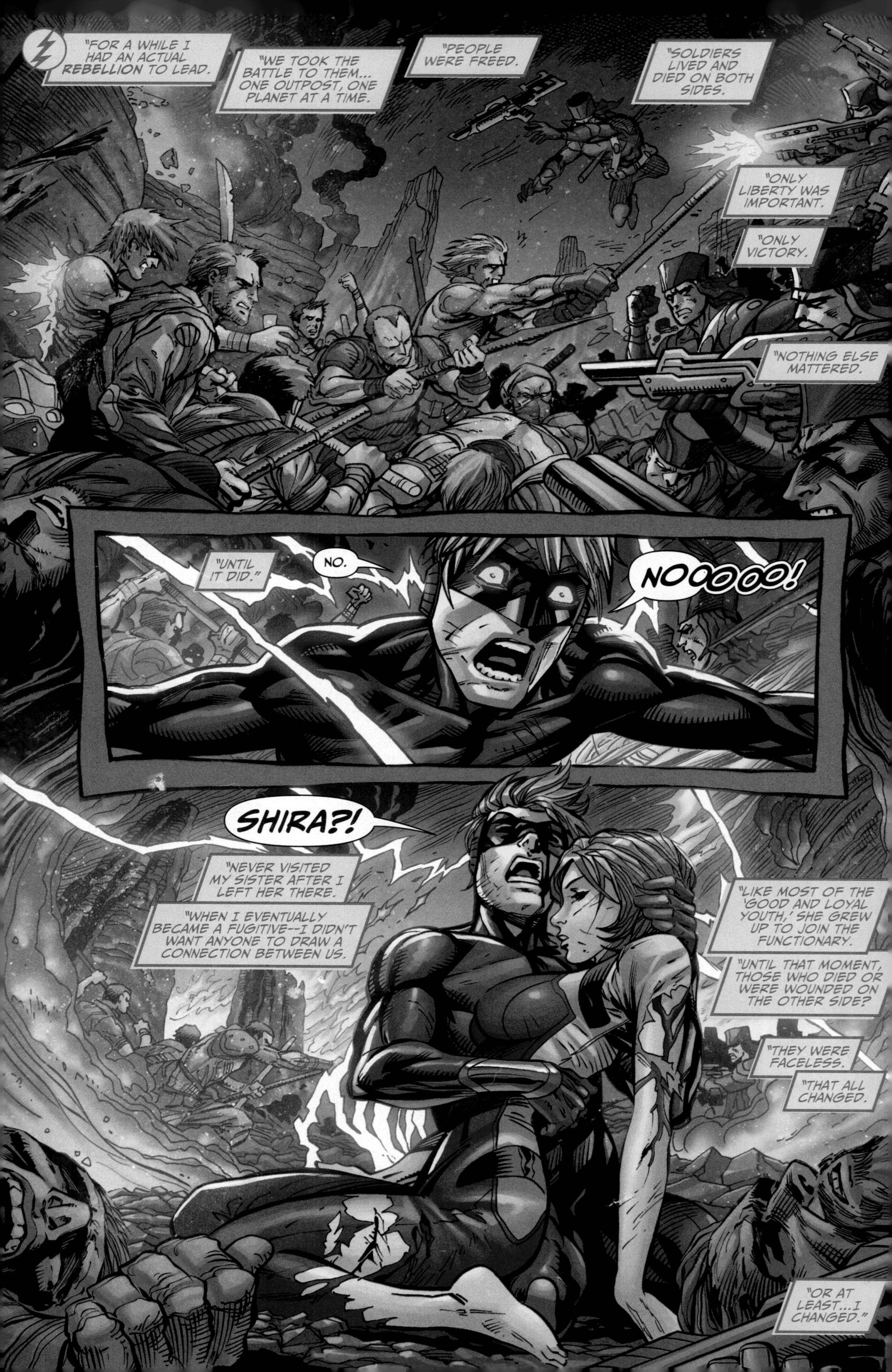
"FOR A WHILE I HAD AN ACTUAL REBELLION TO LEAD.
"WE TOOK THE BATTLE TO THEM... ONE OUTPOST, ONE PLANET AT A TIME.
"PEOPLE WERE FREED.
"SOLDIERS LIVED AND DIED ON BOTH SIDES.
"ONLY LIBERTY WAS IMPORTANT.
"ONLY VICTORY.
"NOTHING ELSE MATTERED.
"UNTIL IT DID."
NO.
NOOOOO!
SHIRA?!
"NEVER VISITED MY SISTER AFTER I LEFT HER THERE.
"WHEN I EVENTUALLY BECAME A FUGITIVE--I DIDN'T WANT ANYONE TO DRAW A CONNECTION BETWEEN US.
"LIKE MOST OF THE 'GOOD AND LOYAL YOUTH,' SHE GREW UP TO JOIN THE FUNCTIONARY.
"UNTIL THAT MOMENT, THOSE WHO DIED OR WERE WOUNDED ON THE OTHER SIDE?
"THEY WERE FACELESS.
"THAT ALL CHANGED.
"OR AT LEAST...I CHANGED."

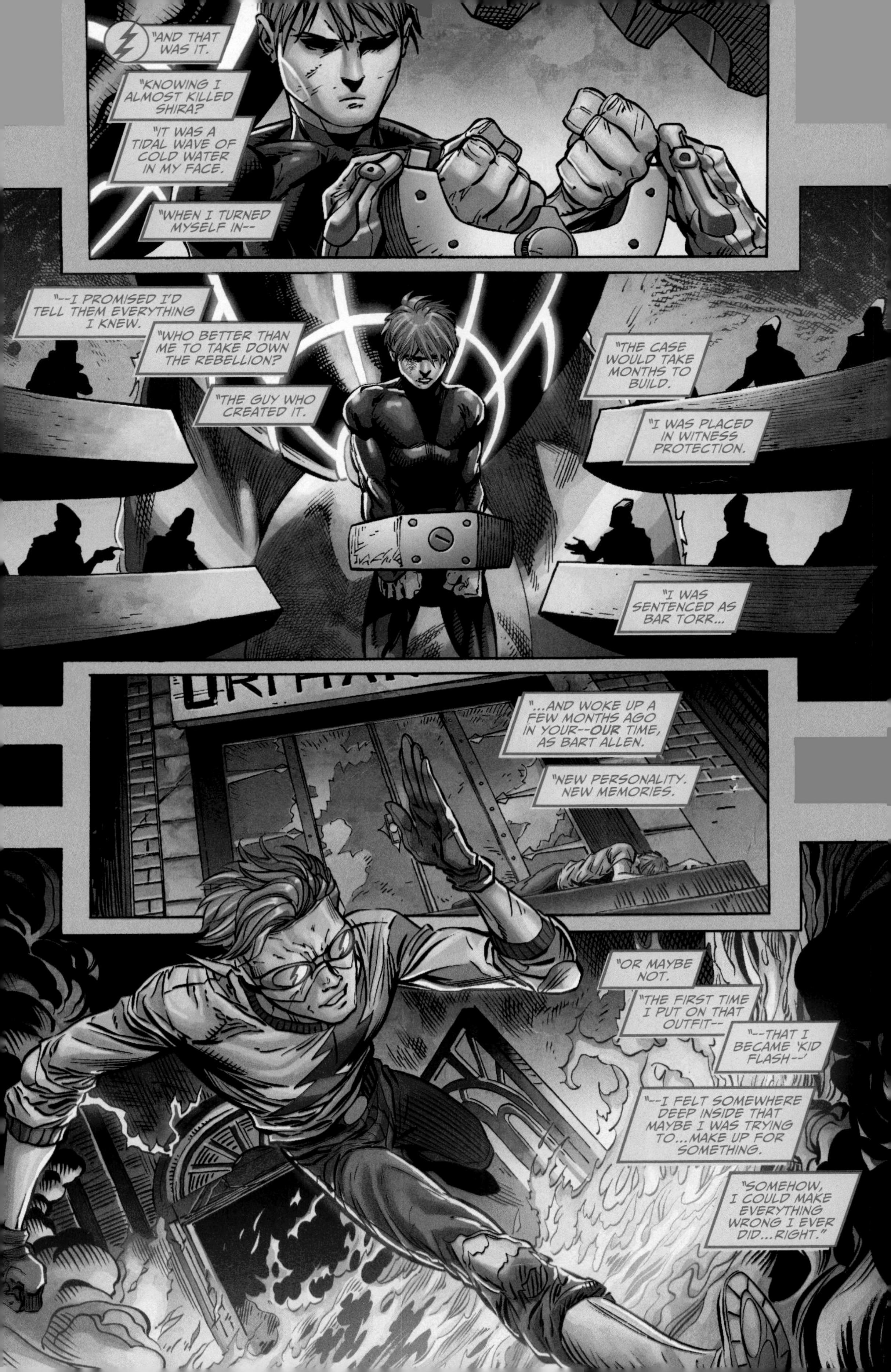
"AND THAT WAS IT.
"KNOWING I ALMOST KILLED SHIRA?
"IT WAS A TIDAL WAVE OF COLD WATER IN MY FACE.
"WHEN I TURNED MYSELF IN--
"--I PROMISED I'D TELL THEM EVERYTHING I KNEW.
"WHO BETTER THAN ME TO TAKE DOWN THE REBELLION?
"THE GUY WHO CREATED IT.
"THE CASE WOULD TAKE MONTHS TO BUILD.
"I WAS PLACED IN WITNESS PROTECTION.
"I WAS SENTENCED AS BAR TORR...
"...AND WOKE UP A FEW MONTHS AGO IN YOUR--OUR TIME, AS BART ALLEN.
"NEW PERSONALITY. NEW MEMORIES.
"OR MAYBE NOT.
"THE FIRST TIME I PUT ON THAT OUTFIT--
"--THAT I BECAME 'KID FLASH'--
"--I FELT SOMEWHERE DEEP INSIDE THAT MAYBE I WAS TRYING TO...MAKE UP FOR SOMETHING.
"SOMEHOW, I COULD MAKE EVERYTHING WRONG I EVER DID...RIGHT."

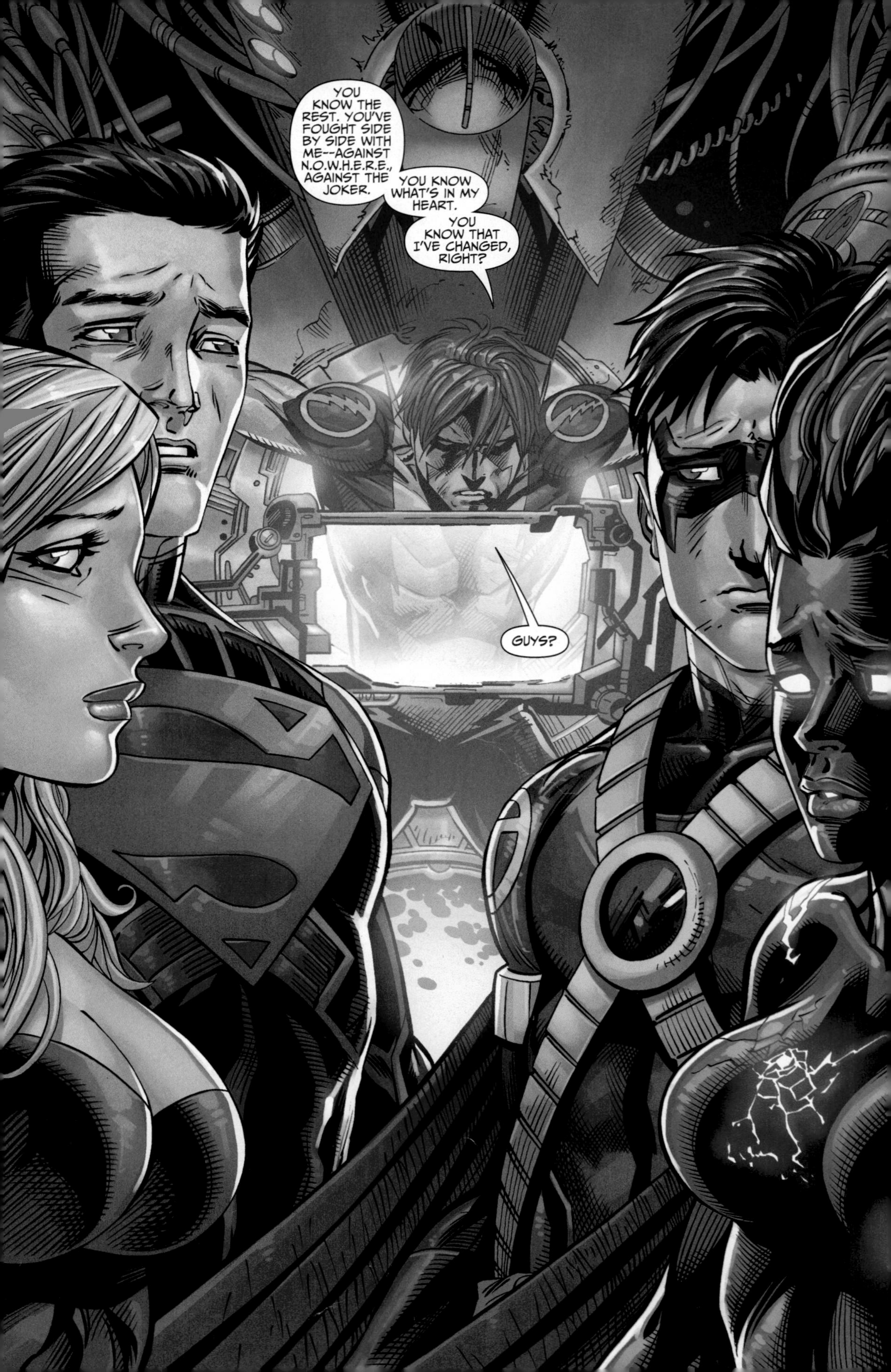
YOU KNOW THE REST. YOU'VE FOUGHT SIDE BY SIDE WITH ME--AGAINST N.O.W.H.E.R.E., AGAINST THE JOKER.
YOU KNOW WHAT'S IN MY HEART.
YOU KNOW THAT I'VE CHANGED, RIGHT?
GUYS?

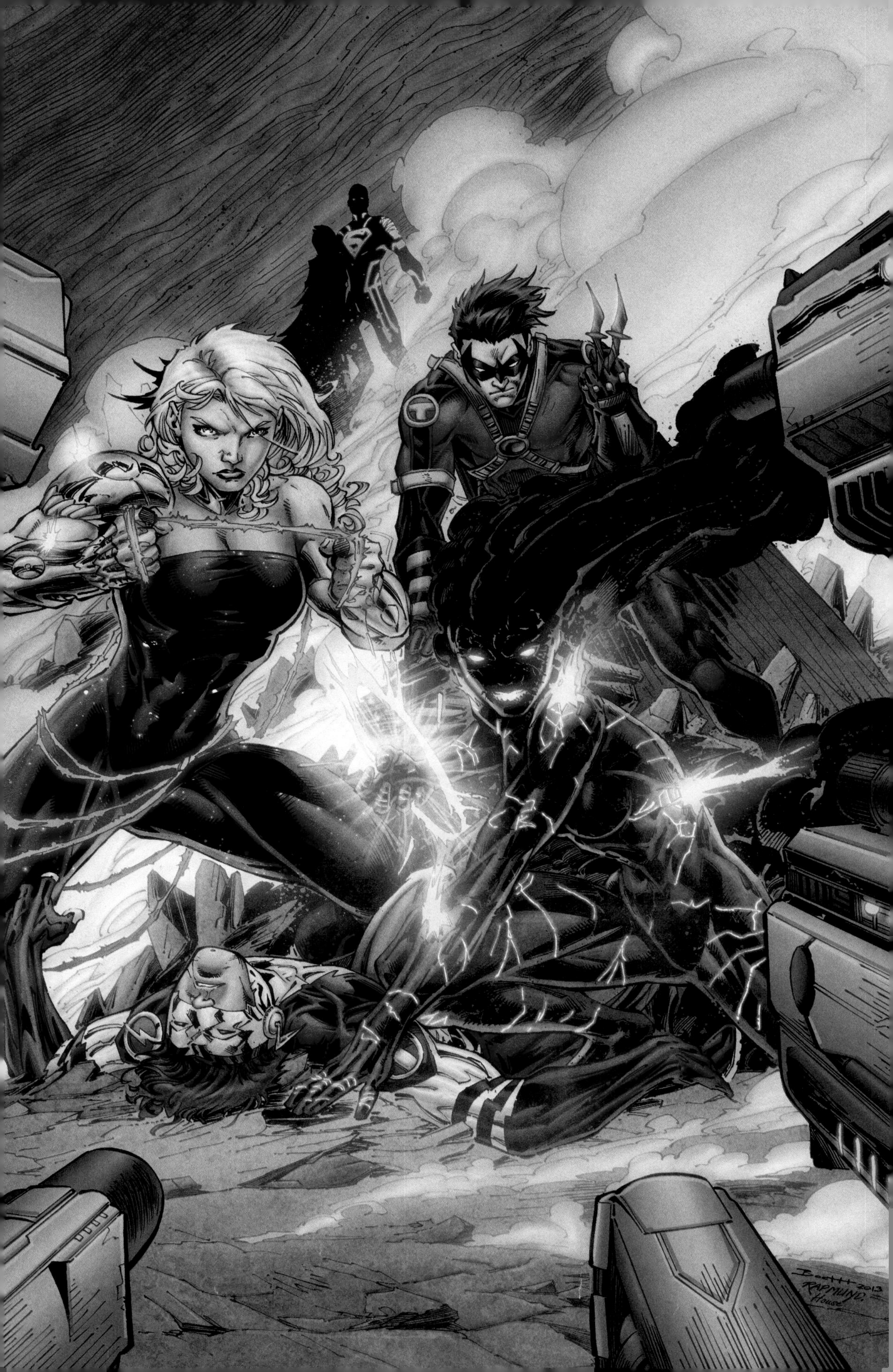
2013
RAPMUND.
House

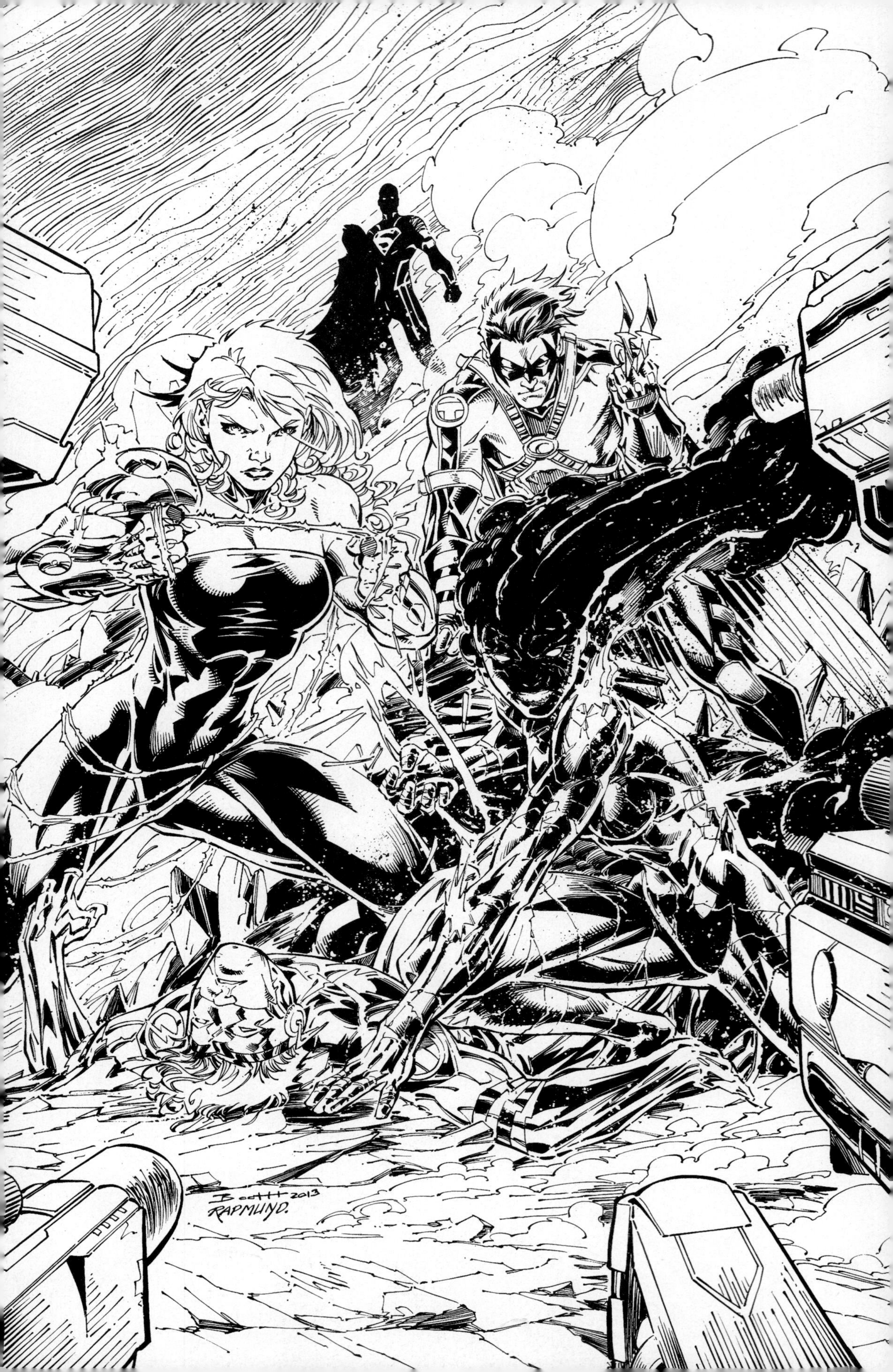
Boottt 2013
RAPMUND.

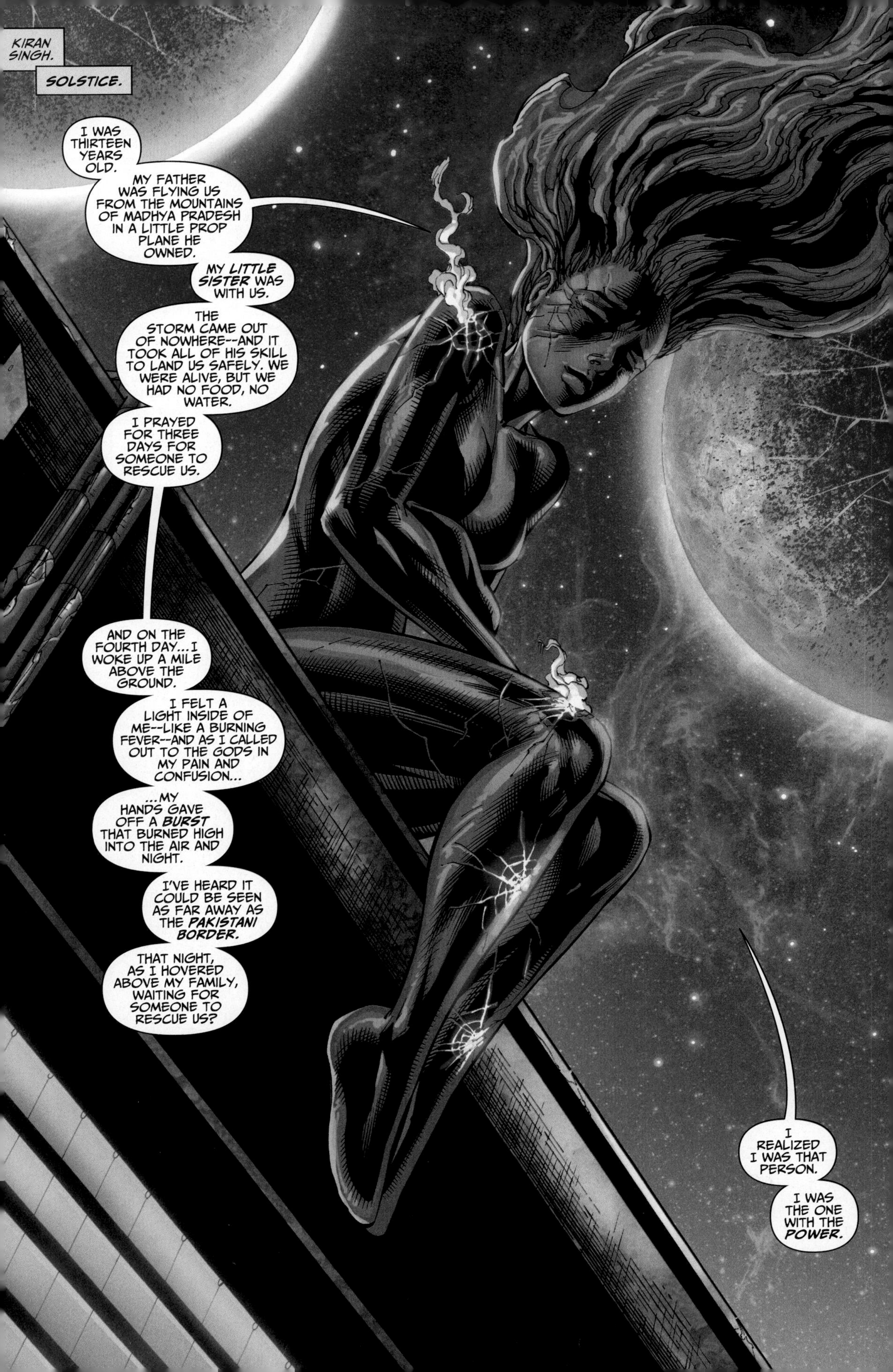
KIRAN SINGH.
SOLSTICE.
I WAS THIRTEEN YEARS OLD.
MY FATHER WAS FLYING US FROM THE MOUNTAINS OF MADHYA PRADESH IN A LITTLE PROP PLANE HE OWNED.
MY LITTLE SISTER WAS WITH US.
THE STORM CAME OUT OF NOWHERE--AND IT TOOK ALL OF HIS SKILL TO LAND US SAFELY. WE WERE ALIVE, BUT WE HAD NO FOOD, NO WATER.
I PRAYED FOR THREE DAYS FOR SOMEONE TO RESCUE US.
AND ON THE FOURTH DAY...I WOKE UP A MILE ABOVE THE GROUND.
I FELT A LIGHT INSIDE OF ME--LIKE A BURNING FEVER--AND AS I CALLED OUT TO THE GODS IN MY PAIN AND CONFUSION...
...MY HANDS GAVE OFF A BURST THAT BURNED HIGH INTO THE AIR AND NIGHT.
I'VE HEARD IT COULD BE SEEN AS FAR AWAY AS THE PAKISTANI BORDER.
THAT NIGHT, AS I HOVERED ABOVE MY FAMILY, WAITING FOR SOMEONE TO RESCUE US?
I REALIZED I WAS THAT PERSON.
I WAS THE ONE WITH THE POWER.

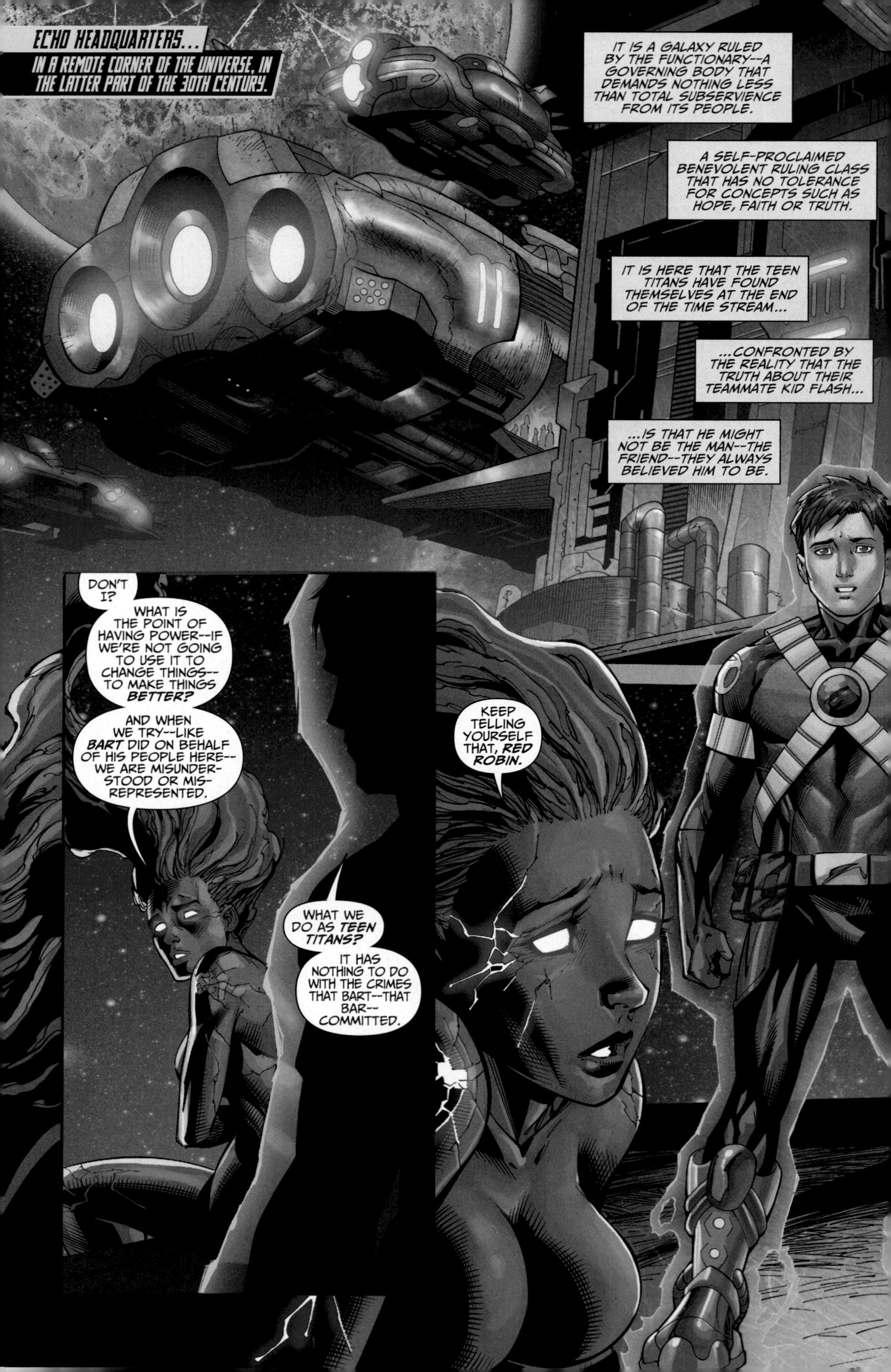
ECHO HEADQUARTERS...
IN A REMOTE CORNER OF THE UNIVERSE, IN THE LATTER PART OF THE 30TH CENTURY.
IT IS A GALAXY RULED BY THE FUNCTIONARY--A GOVERNING BODY THAT DEMANDS NOTHING LESS THAN TOTAL SUBSERVIENCE FROM ITS PEOPLE.
A SELF-PROCLAIMED BENEVOLENT RULING CLASS THAT HAS NO TOLERANCE FOR CONCEPTS SUCH AS HOPE, FAITH OR TRUTH.
IT IS HERE THAT THE TEEN TITANS HAVE FOUND THEMSELVES AT THE END OF THE TIME STREAM...
...CONFRONTED BY THE REALITY THAT THE TRUTH ABOUT THEIR TEAMMATE KID FLASH...
...IS THAT HE MIGHT NOT BE THE MAN--THE FRIEND--THEY ALWAYS BELIEVED HIM TO BE.
DON'T I?
WHAT IS THE POINT OF HAVING POWER--IF WE'RE NOT GOING TO USE IT TO CHANGE THINGS--TO MAKE THINGS BETTER?
AND WHEN WE TRY--LIKE BART DID ON BEHALF OF HIS PEOPLE HERE--WE ARE MISUNDERSTOOD OR MISREPRESENTED.
WHAT WE DO AS TEEN TITANS?
IT HAS NOTHING TO DO WITH THE CRIMES THAT BART--THAT BAR--COMMITTED.
KEEP TELLING YOURSELF THAT, RED ROBIN.

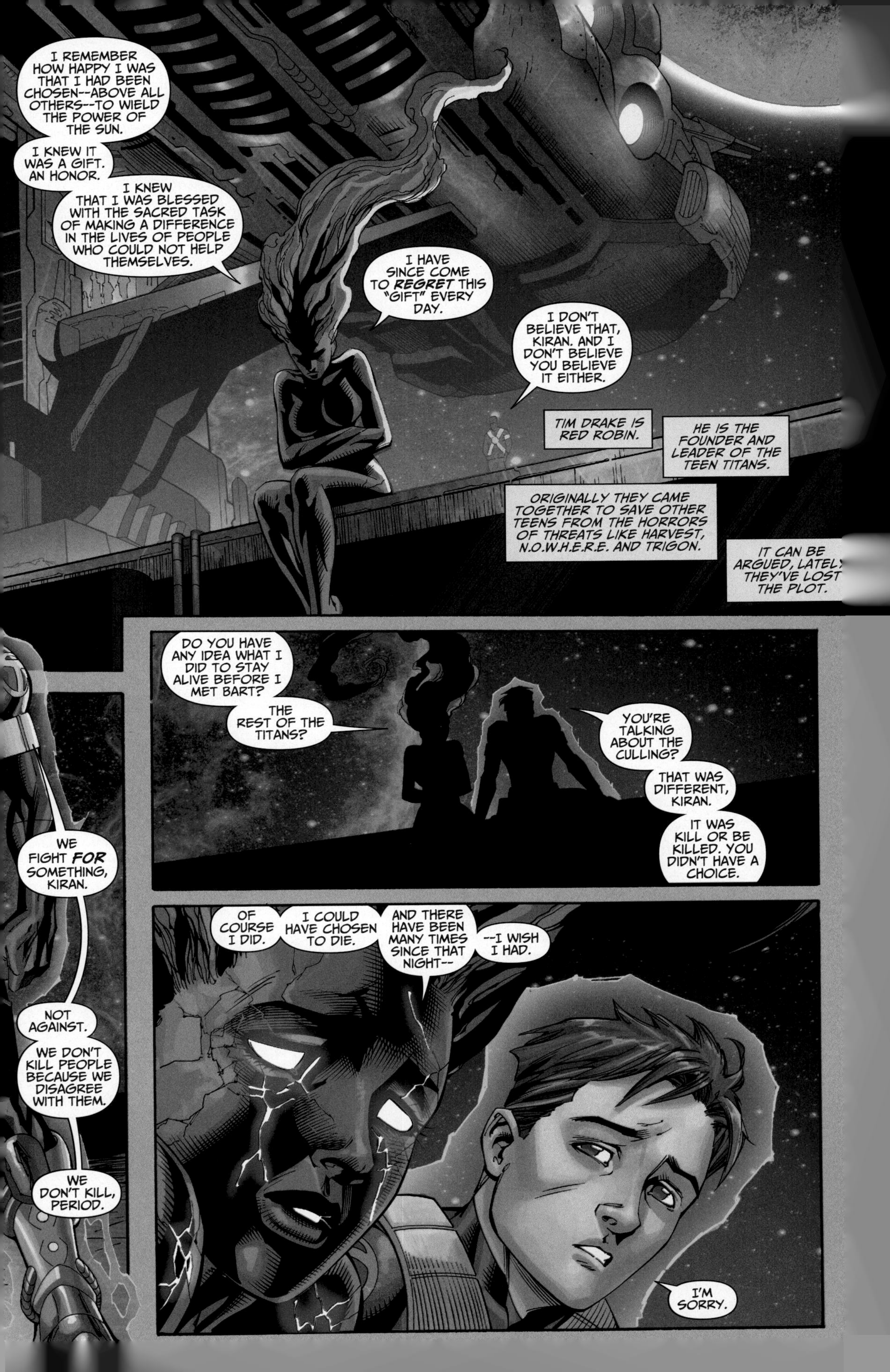

I REMEMBER HOW HAPPY I WAS THAT I HAD BEEN CHOSEN--ABOVE ALL OTHERS--TO WIELD THE POWER OF THE SUN.
I KNEW IT WAS A GIFT. AN HONOR.
I KNEW THAT I WAS BLESSED WITH THE SACRED TASK OF MAKING A DIFFERENCE IN THE LIVES OF PEOPLE WHO COULD NOT HELP THEMSELVES.
I HAVE SINCE COME TO REGRET THIS "GIFT" EVERY DAY.
I DON'T BELIEVE THAT, KIRAN. AND I DON'T BELIEVE YOU BELIEVE IT EITHER.
TIM DRAKE IS RED ROBIN.
HE IS THE FOUNDER AND LEADER OF THE TEEN TITANS.
ORIGINALLY THEY CAME TOGETHER TO SAVE OTHER TEENS FROM THE HORRORS OF THREATS LIKE HARVEST, N.O.W.H.E.R.E. AND TRIGON.
IT CAN BE ARGUED, LATELY THEY'VE LOST THE PLOT.
DO YOU HAVE ANY IDEA WHAT I DID TO STAY ALIVE BEFORE I MET BART?
THE REST OF THE TITANS?
YOU'RE TALKING ABOUT THE CULLING?
THAT WAS DIFFERENT, KIRAN.
IT WAS KILL OR BE KILLED. YOU DIDN'T HAVE A CHOICE.
WE FIGHT FOR SOMETHING, KIRAN.
NOT AGAINST.
WE DON'T KILL PEOPLE BECAUSE WE DISAGREE WITH THEM.
WE DON'T KILL, PERIOD.
OF COURSE I DID.
I COULD HAVE CHOSEN TO DIE.
AND THERE HAVE BEEN MANY TIMES SINCE THAT NIGHT--
--I WISH I HAD.
I'M SORRY.

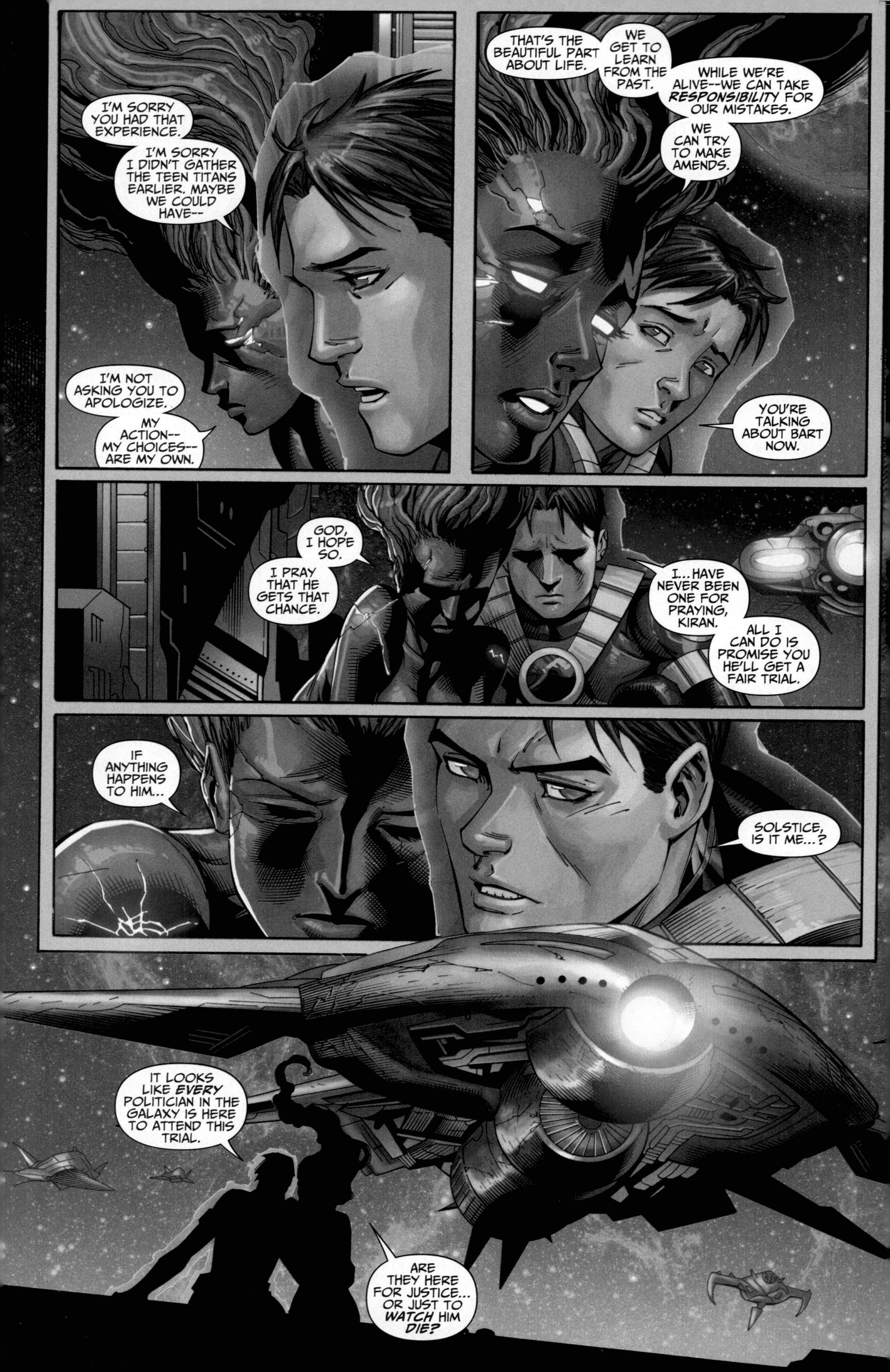
I'M SORRY YOU HAD THAT EXPERIENCE.
I'M SORRY I DIDN'T GATHER THE TEEN TITANS EARLIER. MAYBE WE COULD HAVE--
I'M NOT ASKING YOU TO APOLOGIZE.
MY ACTION-- MY CHOICES-- ARE MY OWN.
THAT'S THE BEAUTIFUL PART ABOUT LIFE.
WE GET TO LEARN FROM THE PAST.
WHILE WE'RE ALIVE--WE CAN TAKE RESPONSIBILITY FOR OUR MISTAKES.
WE CAN TRY TO MAKE AMENDS.
YOU'RE TALKING ABOUT BART NOW.
GOD, I HOPE SO.
I PRAY THAT HE GETS THAT CHANCE.
I...HAVE NEVER BEEN ONE FOR PRAYING, KIRAN.
ALL I CAN DO IS PROMISE YOU HE'LL GET A FAIR TRIAL.
IF ANYTHING HAPPENS TO HIM...
SOLSTICE, IS IT ME...?
IT LOOKS LIKE EVERY POLITICIAN IN THE GALAXY IS HERE TO ATTEND THIS TRIAL.
ARE THEY HERE FOR JUSTICE... OR JUST TO WATCH HIM DIE?

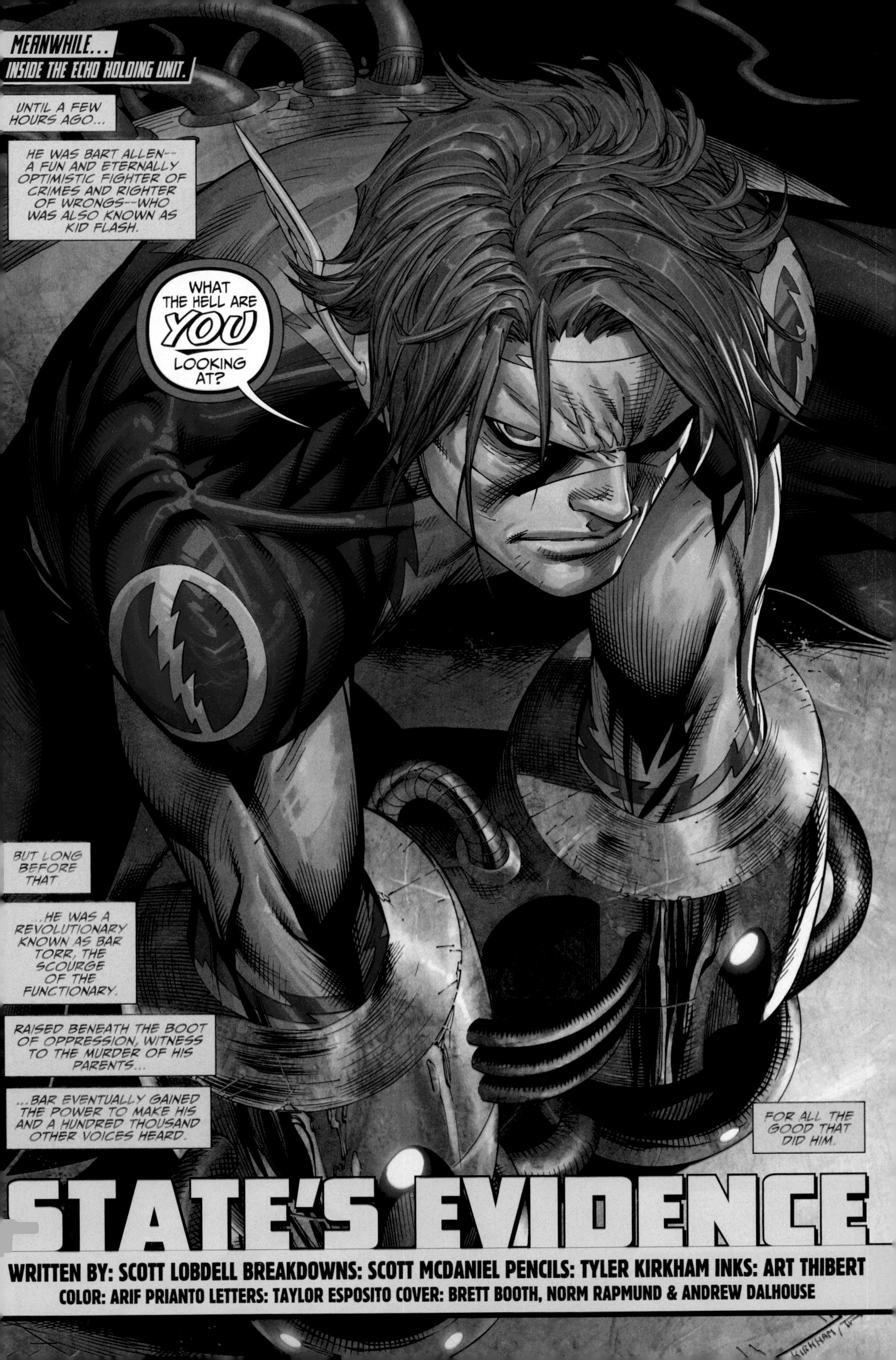
MEANWHILE...
INSIDE THE ECHO HOLDING UNIT.
UNTIL A FEW HOURS AGO...
HE WAS BART ALLEN--A FUN AND ETERNALLY OPTIMISTIC FIGHTER OF CRIMES AND RIGHTER OF WRONGS--WHO WAS ALSO KNOWN AS KID FLASH.
WHAT THE HELL ARE YOU LOOKING AT?
BUT LONG BEFORE THAT
...HE WAS A REVOLUTIONARY KNOWN AS BAR TORR, THE SCOURGE OF THE FUNCTIONARY.
RAISED BENEATH THE BOOT OF OPPRESSION, WITNESS TO THE MURDER OF HIS PARENTS...
...BAR EVENTUALLY GAINED THE POWER TO MAKE HIS AND A HUNDRED THOUSAND OTHER VOICES HEARD.
FOR ALL THE GOOD THAT DID HIM.
STATE'S EVIDENCE
WRITTEN BY: SCOTT LOBDELL BREAKDOWNS: SCOTT MCDANIEL PENCILS: TYLER KIRKHAM INKS: ART THIBERT
COLOR: ARIF PRIANTO LETTERS: TAYLOR ESPOSITO COVER: BRETT BOOTH, NORM RAPMUND & ANDREW DALHOUSE

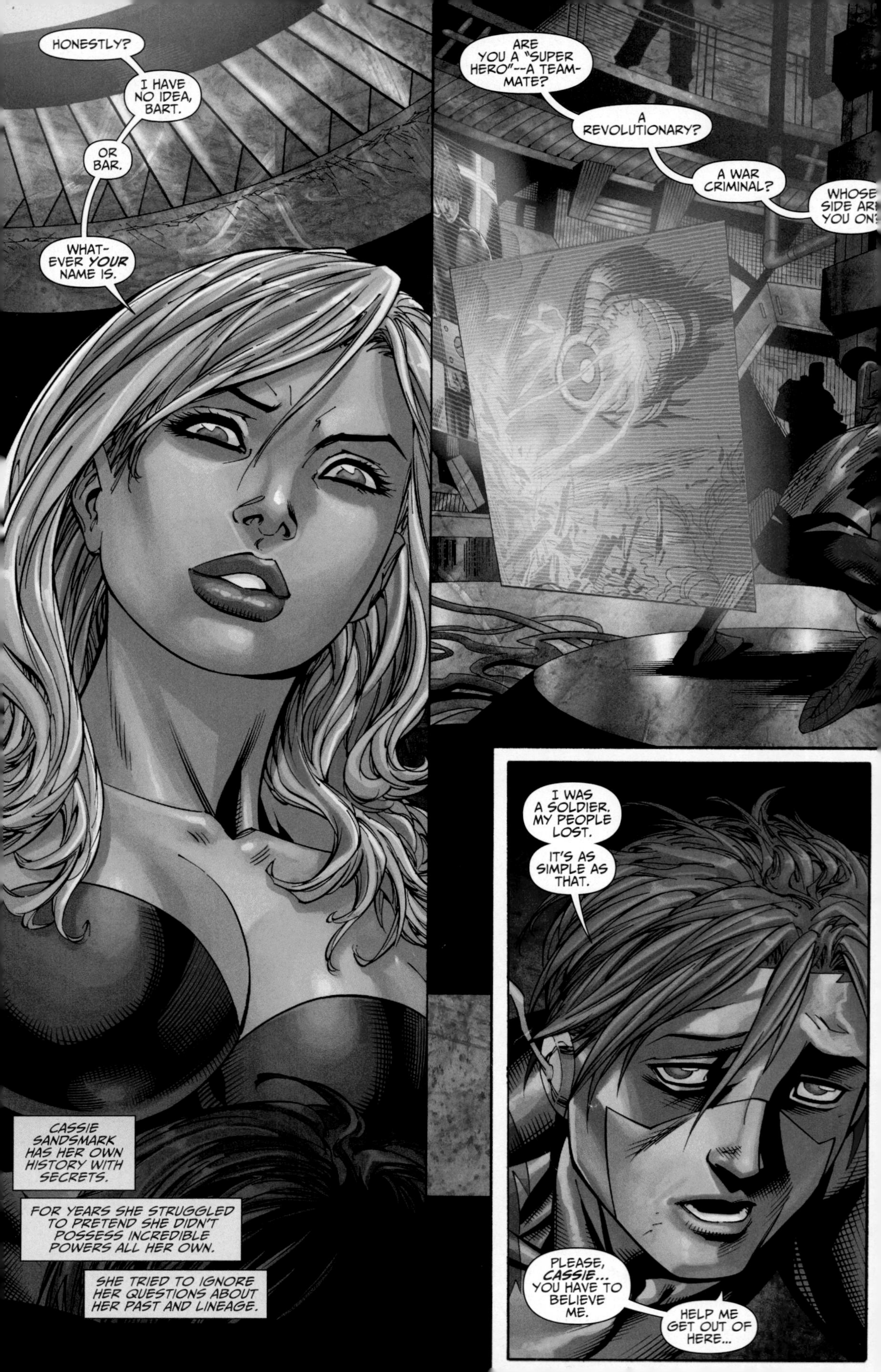
HONESTLY?
I HAVE NO IDEA, BART.
OR BAR.
WHAT-EVER YOUR NAME IS.
ARE YOU A "SUPER HERO"--A TEAM-MATE?
A REVOLUTIONARY?
A WAR CRIMINAL?
CASSIE SANDSMARK HAS HER OWN HISTORY WITH SECRETS.
FOR YEARS SHE STRUGGLED TO PRETEND SHE DIDN'T POSSESS INCREDIBLE POWERS ALL HER OWN.
SHE TRIED TO IGNORE HER QUESTIONS ABOUT HER PAST AND LINEAGE.
I WAS A SOLDIER. MY PEOPLE LOST.
IT'S AS SIMPLE AS THAT.
PLEASE, CASSIE... YOU HAVE TO BELIEVE ME.
HELP ME GET OUT OF HERE...

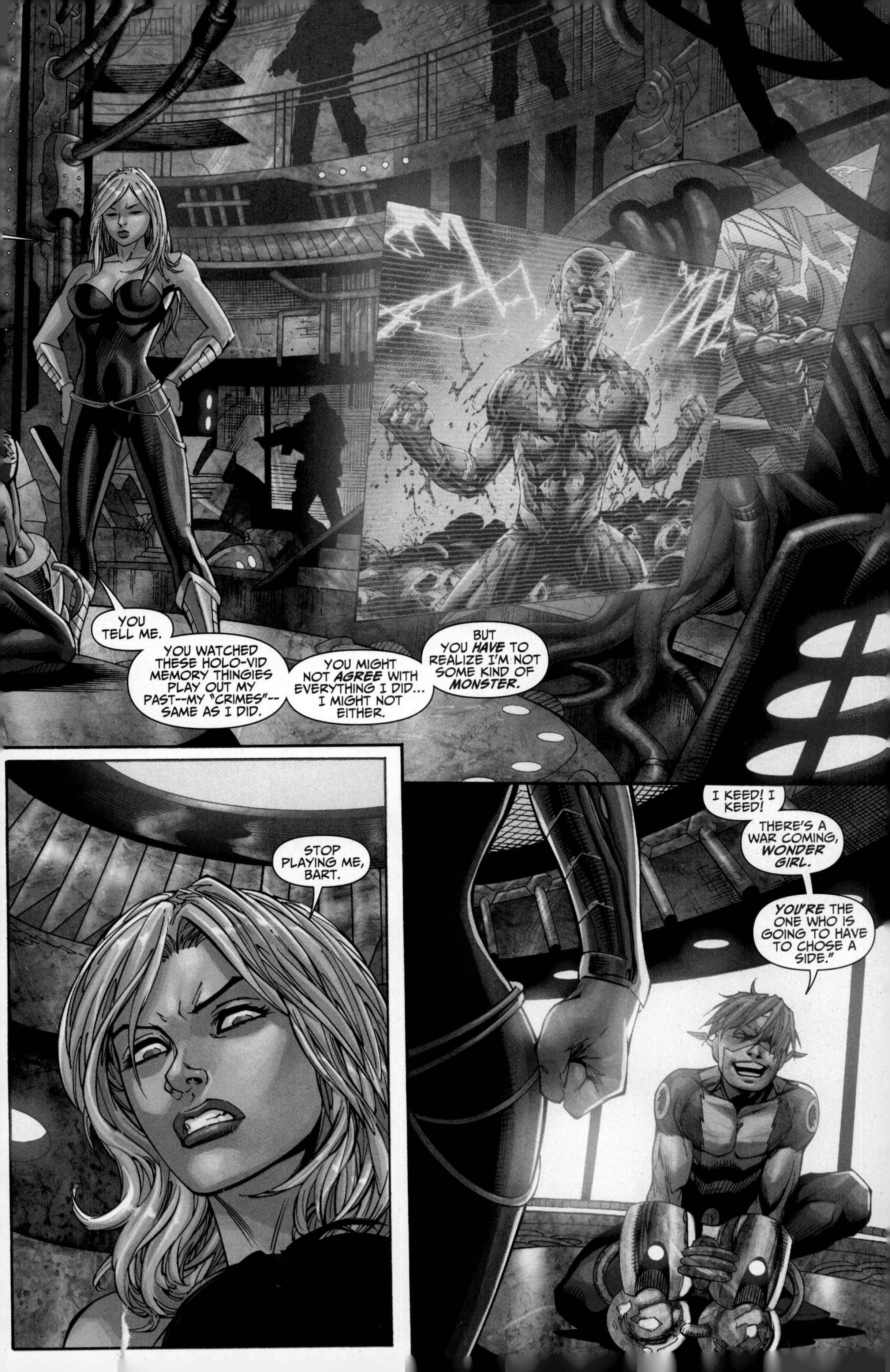
YOU TELL ME.
YOU WATCHED THESE HOLO-VID MEMORY THINGIES PLAY OUT MY PAST--MY "CRIMES"--SAME AS I DID.
YOU MIGHT NOT AGREE WITH EVERYTHING I DID... I MIGHT NOT EITHER.
BUT YOU HAVE TO REALIZE I'M NOT SOME KIND OF MONSTER.
STOP PLAYING ME, BART.
I KEED! I KEED!
THERE'S A WAR COMING, WONDER GIRL.
YOU'RE THE ONE WHO IS GOING TO HAVE TO CHOSE A SIDE."

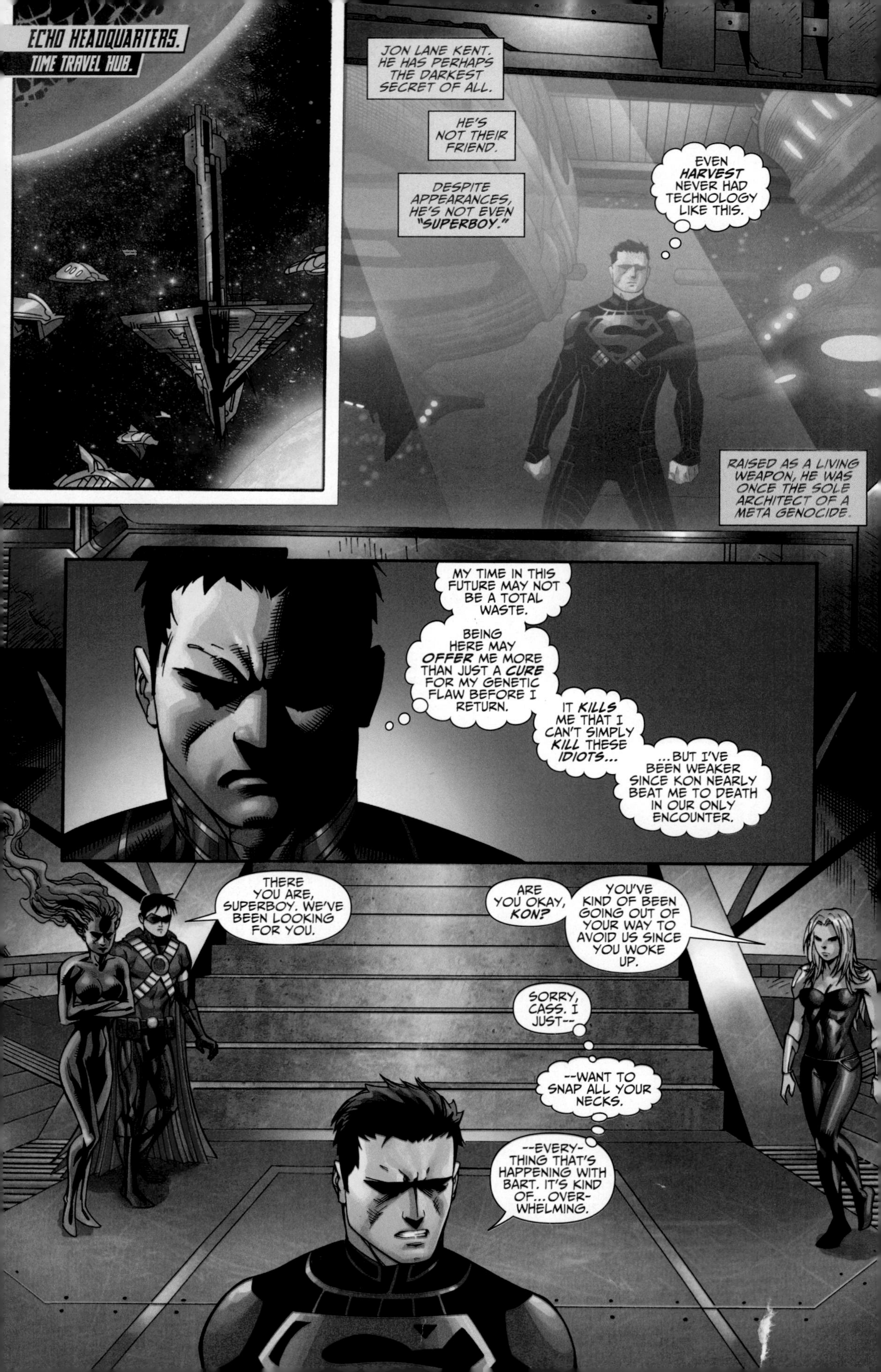
ECHO HEADQUARTERS.
TIME TRAVEL HUB.
JON LANE KENT. HE HAS PERHAPS THE DARKEST SECRET OF ALL.
HE'S NOT THEIR FRIEND.
DESPITE APPEARANCES, HE'S NOT EVEN "SUPERBOY."
EVEN HARVEST NEVER HAD TECHNOLOGY LIKE THIS.
RAISED AS A LIVING WEAPON, HE WAS ONCE THE SOLE ARCHITECT OF A META GENOCIDE.
MY TIME IN THIS FUTURE MAY NOT BE A TOTAL WASTE.
BEING HERE MAY OFFER ME MORE THAN JUST A CURE FOR MY GENETIC FLAW BEFORE I RETURN.
IT KILLS ME THAT I CAN'T SIMPLY KILL THESE IDIOTS...
...BUT I'VE BEEN WEAKER SINCE KON NEARLY BEAT ME TO DEATH IN OUR ONLY ENCOUNTER.
THERE YOU ARE, SUPERBOY. WE'VE BEEN LOOKING FOR YOU.
ARE YOU OKAY, KON?
YOU'VE KIND OF BEEN GOING OUT OF YOUR WAY TO AVOID US SINCE YOU WOKE UP.
SORRY, CASS. I JUST--
--WANT TO SNAP ALL YOUR NECKS.
--EVERY-THING THAT'S HAPPENING WITH BART. IT'S KIND OF...OVER-WHELMING.

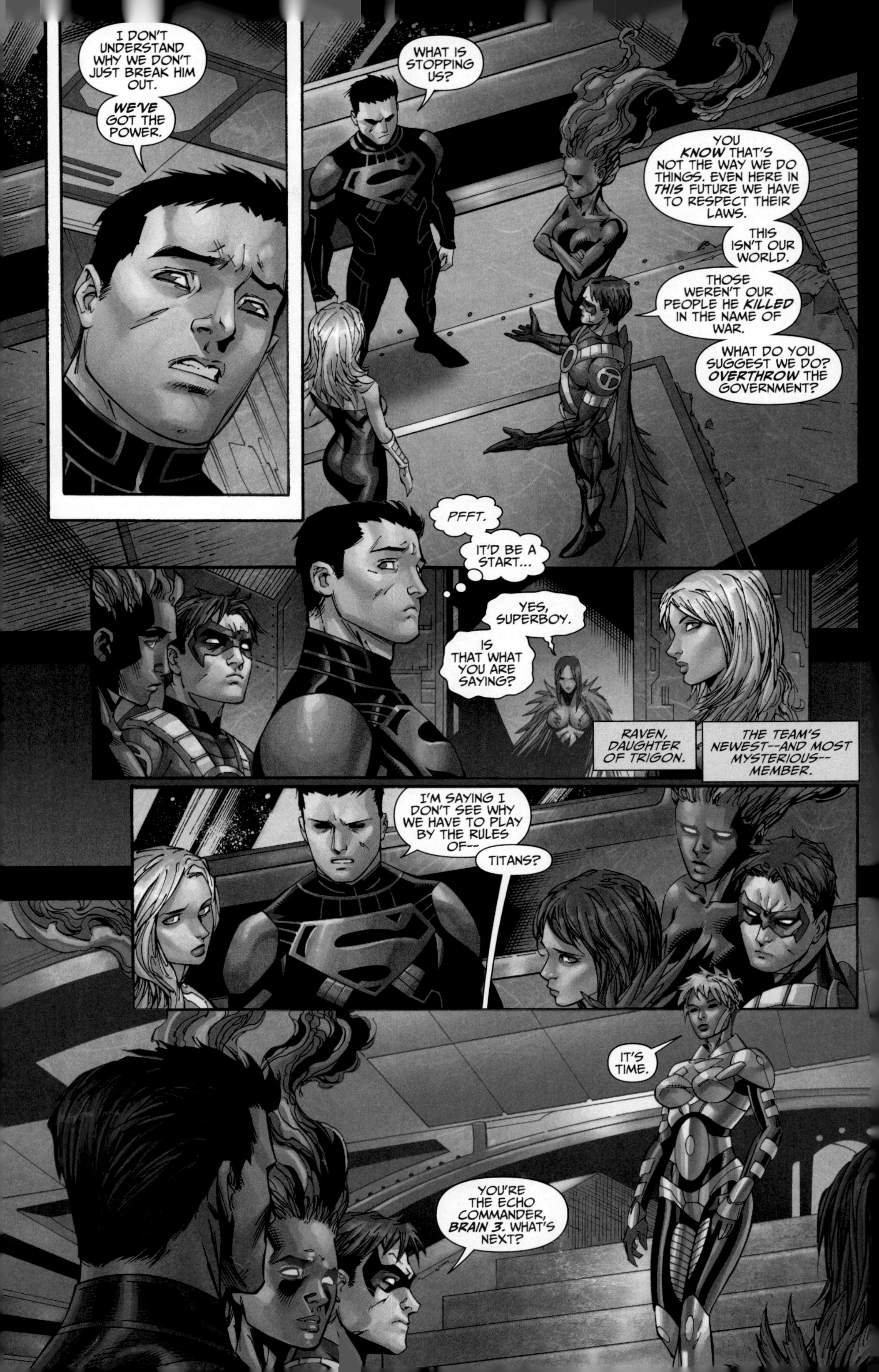
I DON'T UNDERSTAND WHY WE DON'T JUST BREAK HIM OUT.
WE'VE GOT THE POWER.
WHAT IS STOPPING US?
YOU *KNOW* THAT'S NOT THE WAY WE DO THINGS. EVEN HERE IN *THIS* FUTURE WE HAVE TO RESPECT THEIR LAWS.
THIS ISN'T OUR WORLD.
THOSE WEREN'T OUR PEOPLE HE *KILLED* IN THE NAME OF WAR.
WHAT DO YOU SUGGEST WE DO? *OVERTHROW* THE GOVERNMENT?
PFFT.
IT'D BE A START...
YES, SUPERBOY.
IS THAT WHAT YOU ARE SAYING?
RAVEN, DAUGHTER OF TRIGON.
THE TEAM'S NEWEST--AND MOST MYSTERIOUS--MEMBER.
I'M SAYING I DON'T SEE WHY WE HAVE TO PLAY BY THE RULES OF--
TITANS?
IT'S TIME.
YOU'RE THE ECHO COMMANDER, *BRAIN 3*. WHAT'S NEXT?

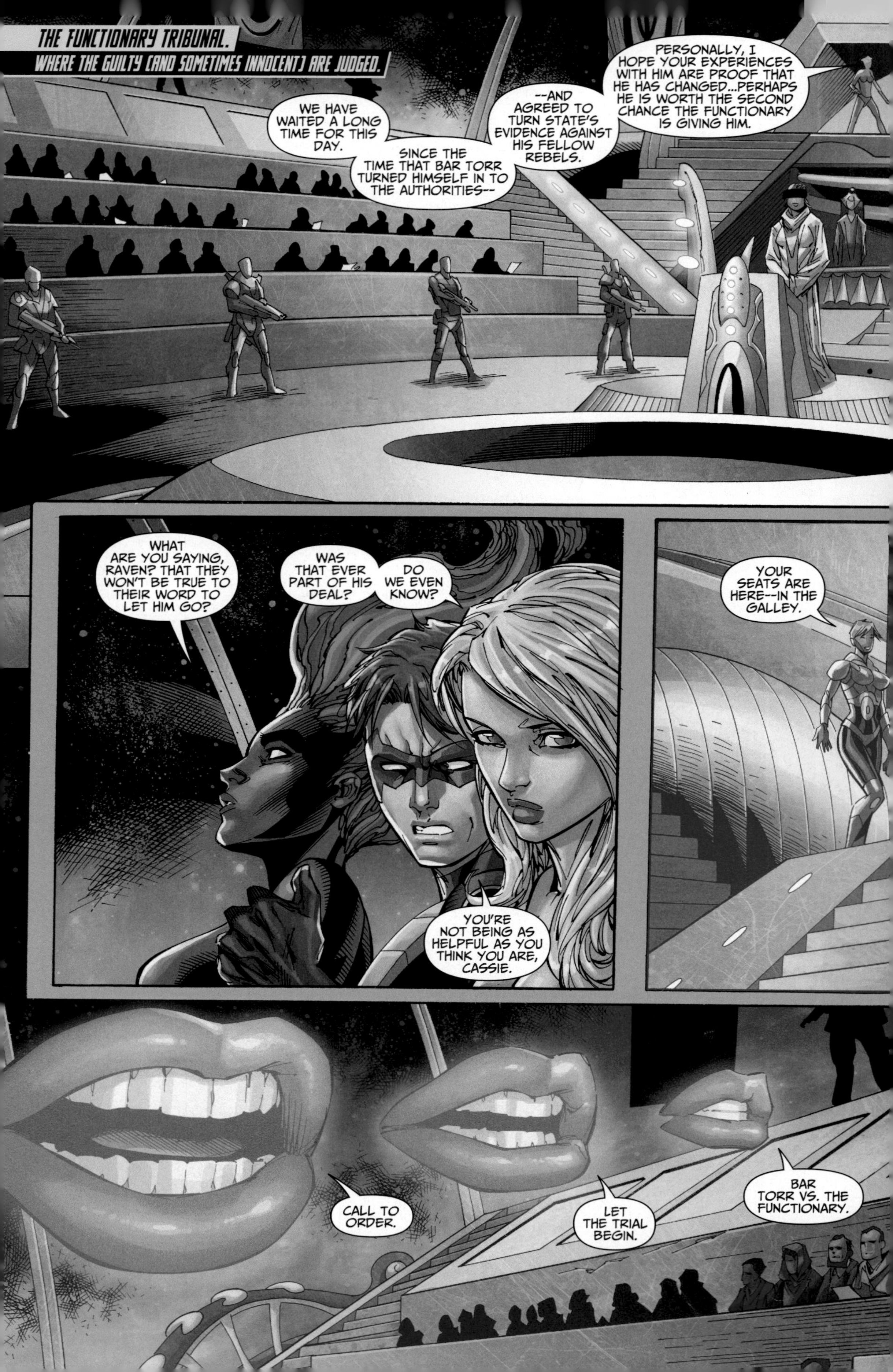
THE FUNCTIONARY TRIBUNAL.
WHERE THE GUILTY (AND SOMETIMES INNOCENT) ARE JUDGED.
WE HAVE WAITED A LONG TIME FOR THIS DAY.
SINCE THE TIME THAT BAR TORR TURNED HIMSELF IN TO THE AUTHORITIES--
--AND AGREED TO TURN STATE'S EVIDENCE AGAINST HIS FELLOW REBELS.
PERSONALLY, I HOPE YOUR EXPERIENCES WITH HIM ARE PROOF THAT HE HAS CHANGED...PERHAPS HE IS WORTH THE SECOND CHANCE THE FUNCTIONARY IS GIVING HIM.
WHAT ARE YOU SAYING, RAVEN? THAT THEY WON'T BE TRUE TO THEIR WORD TO LET HIM GO?
WAS THAT EVER PART OF HIS DEAL?
DO WE EVEN KNOW?
YOU'RE NOT BEING AS HELPFUL AS YOU THINK YOU ARE, CASSIE.
YOUR SEATS ARE HERE--IN THE GALLEY.
CALL TO ORDER.
LET THE TRIAL BEGIN.
BAR TORR VS. THE FUNCTIONARY.

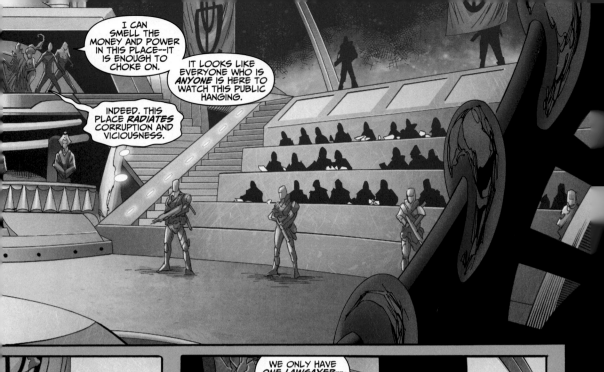

I CAN SMELL THE MONEY AND POWER IN THIS PLACE--IT IS ENOUGH TO CHOKE ON.

IT LOOKS LIKE EVERYONE WHO IS *ANYONE* IS HERE TO WATCH THIS PUBLIC HANGING.

INDEED. THIS PLACE *RADIATES* CORRUPTION AND VICIOUSNESS.

IS THERE A JURY? WHERE ARE THE LAWYERS?

WE ONLY HAVE *ONE LAWSAYER*-- BECAUSE WE ONLY HAVE ONE LAW.

THAT SOUNDS DEPRESSINGLY LIKE MESSAGE BOARDS ON THE INTERNET: ONLY GROUP THINK NEED APPLY.

"INTERNET"? IS THAT YOUR GOVERNING BODY?

THEY'D LIKE TO BE. BUT MERCI-FULLY, NO.

NOT TOO BIASED.

WHY DO I THINK THIS IS NOT GOING TO TAKE LONG?

RIGHT?

THINGS AREN'T ALWAYS AS THEY APPEAR TO BE...

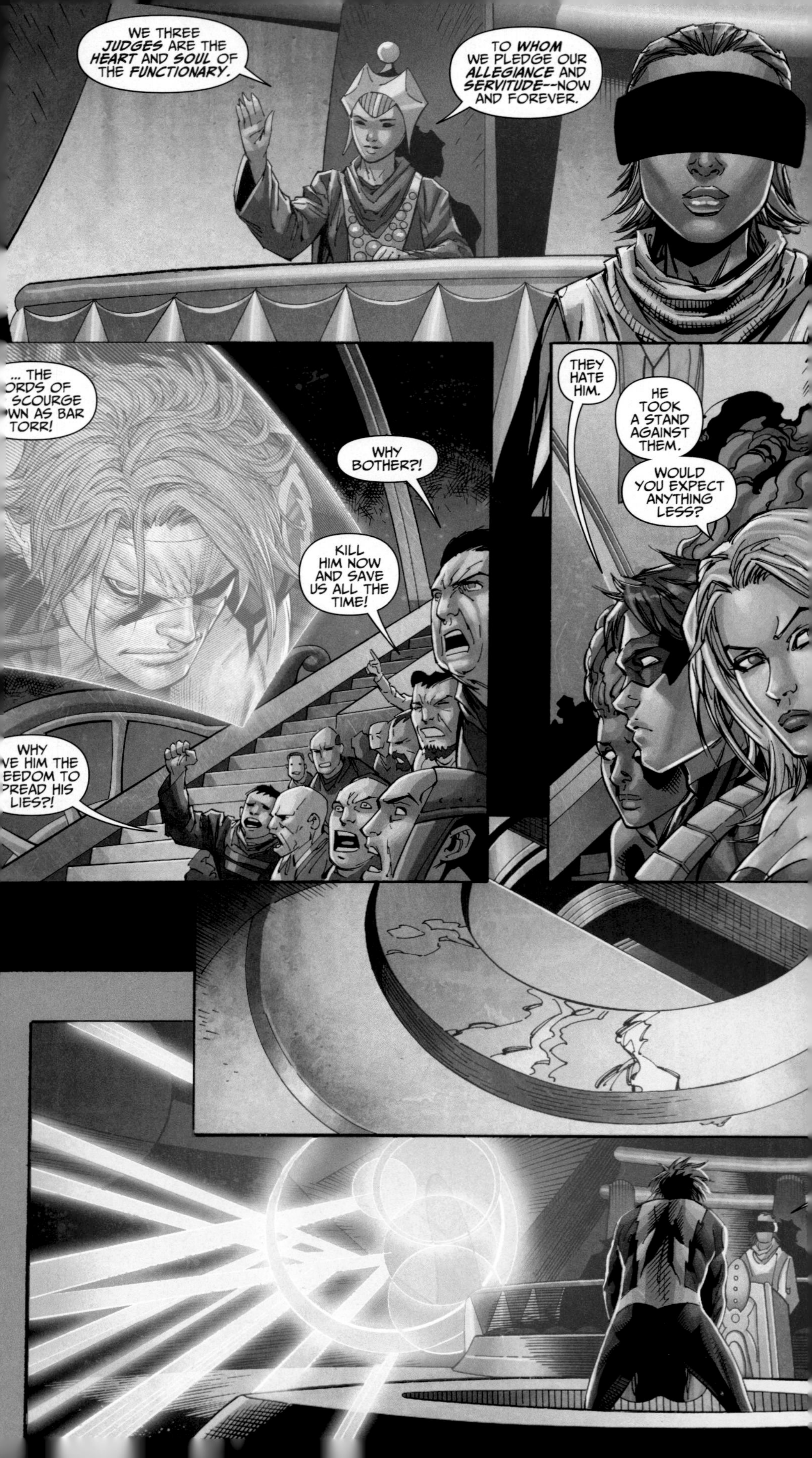
WE THREE JUDGES ARE THE HEART AND SOUL OF THE FUNCTIONARY.
TO WHOM WE PLEDGE OUR ALLEGIANCE AND SERVITUDE--NOW AND FOREVER.
... THE ORDS OF SCOURGE WN AS BAR TORR!
WHY BOTHER?!
KILL HIM NOW AND SAVE US ALL THE TIME!
WHY VE HIM THE EEDOM TO PREAD HIS LIES?!
THEY HATE HIM.
HE TOOK A STAND AGAINST THEM.
WOULD YOU EXPECT ANYTHING LESS?

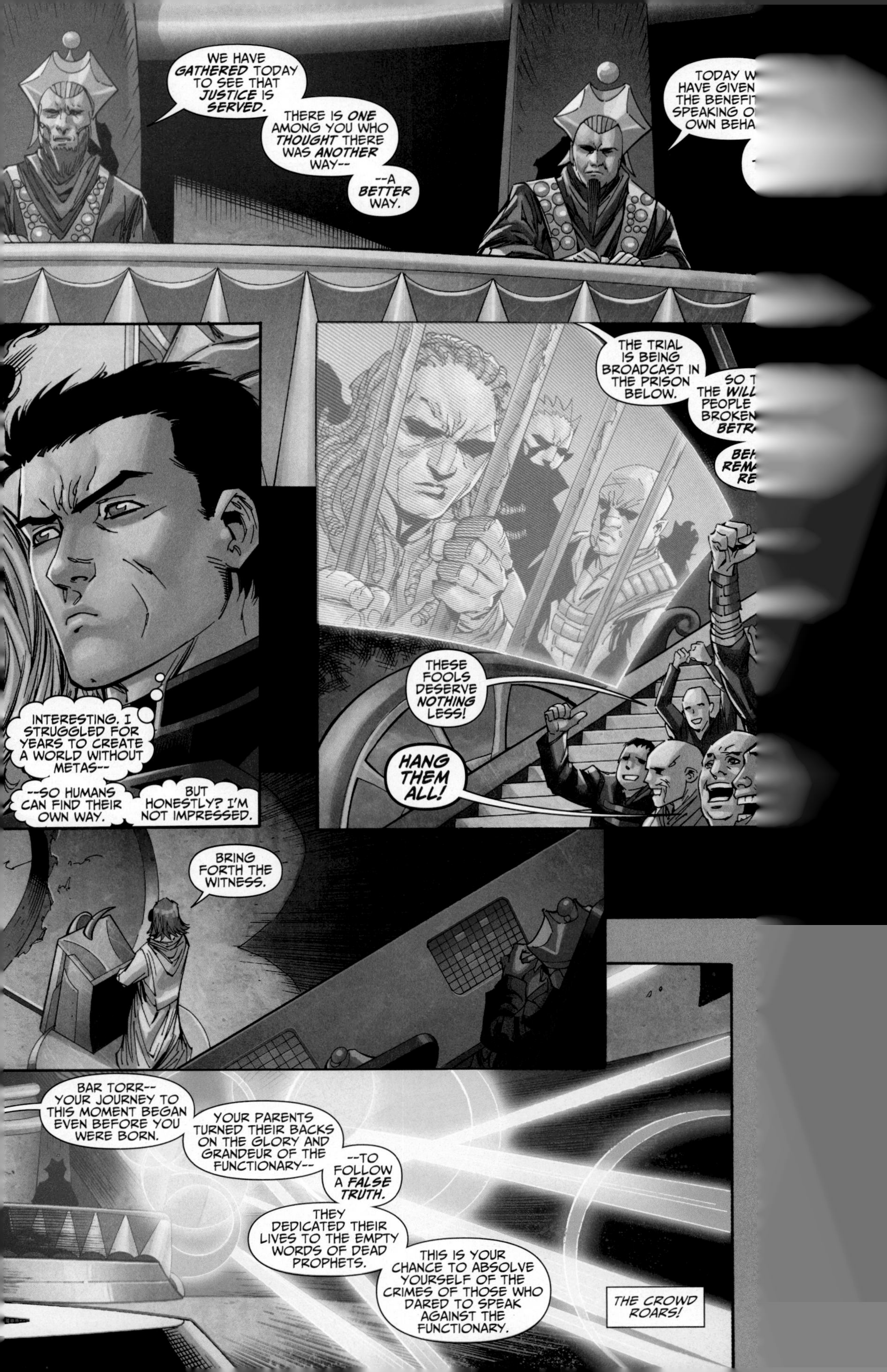

WE HAVE GATHERED TODAY TO SEE THAT JUSTICE IS SERVED.
THERE IS ONE AMONG YOU WHO THOUGHT THERE WAS ANOTHER WAY--
--A BETTER WAY.
THE TRIAL IS BEING BROADCAST IN THE PRISON BELOW.
INTERESTING. I STRUGGLED FOR YEARS TO CREATE A WORLD WITHOUT METAS--
--SO HUMANS CAN FIND THEIR OWN WAY.
BUT HONESTLY? I'M NOT IMPRESSED.
THESE FOOLS DESERVE NOTHING LESS!
HANG THEM ALL!
BRING FORTH THE WITNESS.
BAR TORR--YOUR JOURNEY TO THIS MOMENT BEGAN EVEN BEFORE YOU WERE BORN.
YOUR PARENTS TURNED THEIR BACKS ON THE GLORY AND GRANDEUR OF THE FUNCTIONARY--
--TO FOLLOW A FALSE TRUTH.
THEY DEDICATED THEIR LIVES TO THE EMPTY WORDS OF DEAD PROPHETS.
THIS IS YOUR CHANCE TO ABSOLVE YOURSELF OF THE CRIMES OF THOSE WHO DARED TO SPEAK AGAINST THE FUNCTIONARY.
THE CROWD ROARS!

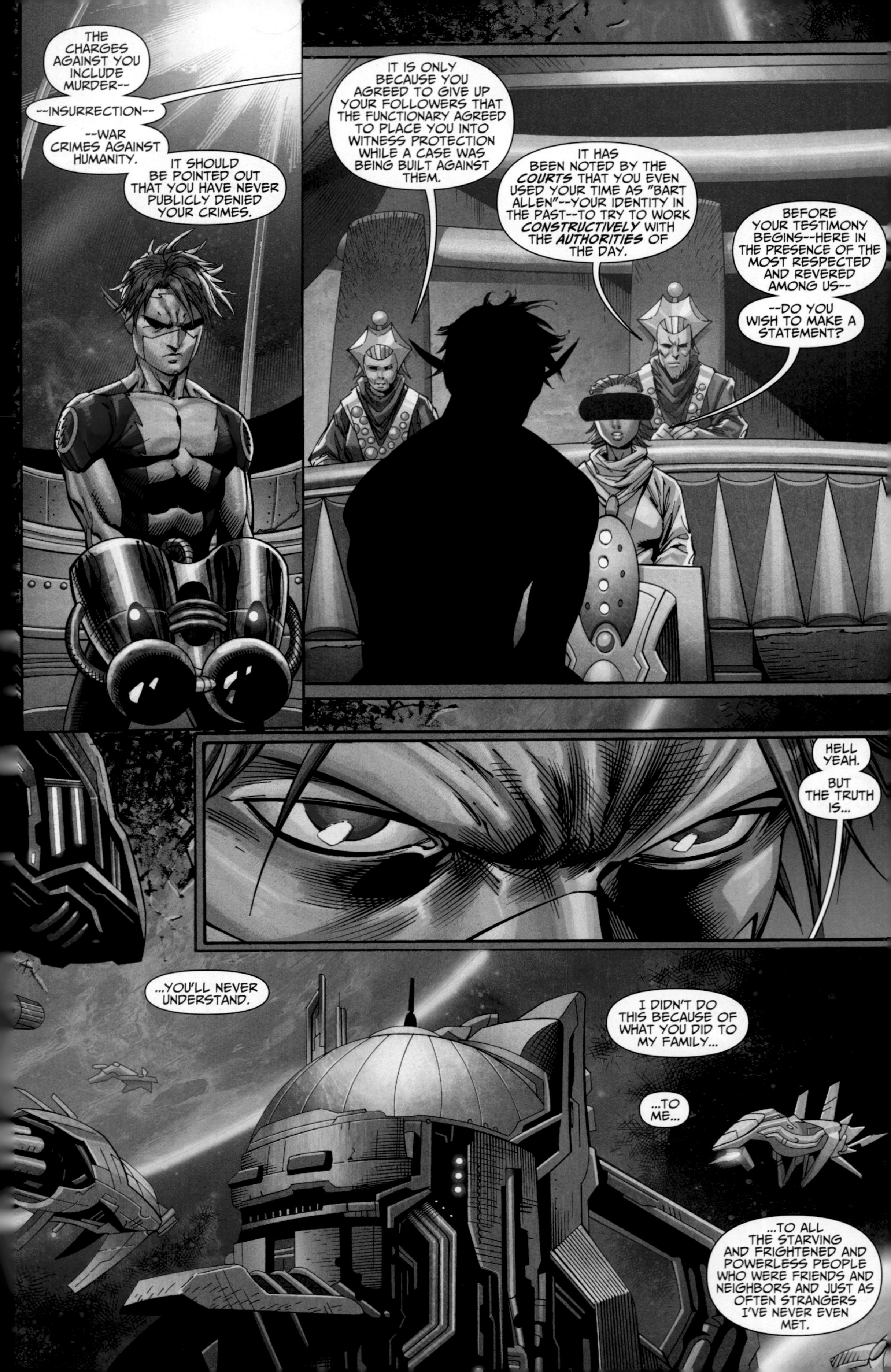
THE CHARGES AGAINST YOU INCLUDE MURDER--
--INSURRECTION--
--WAR CRIMES AGAINST HUMANITY.
IT SHOULD BE POINTED OUT THAT YOU HAVE NEVER PUBLICLY DENIED YOUR CRIMES.
IT IS ONLY BECAUSE YOU AGREED TO GIVE UP YOUR FOLLOWERS THAT THE FUNCTIONARY AGREED TO PLACE YOU INTO WITNESS PROTECTION WHILE A CASE WAS BEING BUILT AGAINST THEM.
IT HAS BEEN NOTED BY THE COURTS THAT YOU EVEN USED YOUR TIME AS "BART ALLEN"--YOUR IDENTITY IN THE PAST--TO TRY TO WORK CONSTRUCTIVELY WITH THE AUTHORITIES OF THE DAY.
BEFORE YOUR TESTIMONY BEGINS--HERE IN THE PRESENCE OF THE MOST RESPECTED AND REVERED AMONG US--
--DO YOU WISH TO MAKE A STATEMENT?
HELL YEAH.
BUT THE TRUTH IS...
...YOU'LL NEVER UNDERSTAND.
I DIDN'T DO THIS BECAUSE OF WHAT YOU DID TO MY FAMILY...
...TO ME...
...TO ALL THE STARVING AND FRIGHTENED AND POWERLESS PEOPLE WHO WERE FRIENDS AND NEIGHBORS AND JUST AS OFTEN STRANGERS I'VE NEVER EVEN MET.

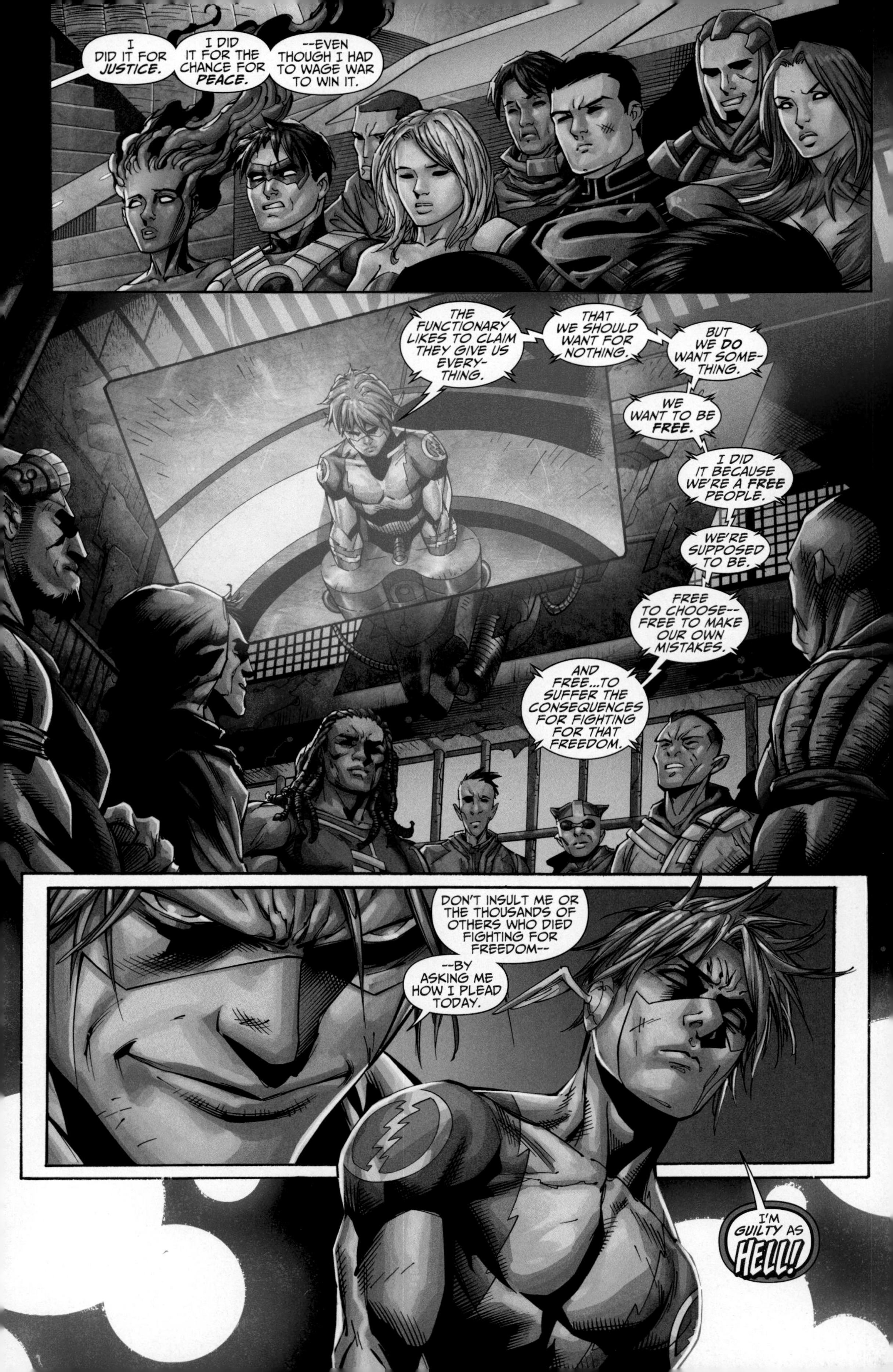
I DID IT FOR JUSTICE.
I DID IT FOR THE CHANCE FOR PEACE.
--EVEN THOUGH I HAD TO WAGE WAR TO WIN IT.
THE FUNCTIONARY LIKES TO CLAIM THEY GIVE US EVERYTHING.
THAT WE SHOULD WANT FOR NOTHING.
BUT WE DO WANT SOMETHING.
WE WANT TO BE FREE.
I DID IT BECAUSE WE'RE A FREE PEOPLE.
WE'RE SUPPOSED TO BE.
FREE TO CHOOSE--FREE TO MAKE OUR OWN MISTAKES.
AND FREE...TO SUFFER THE CONSEQUENCES FOR FIGHTING FOR THAT FREEDOM.
DON'T INSULT ME OR THE THOUSANDS OF OTHERS WHO DIED FIGHTING FOR FREEDOM--
--BY ASKING ME HOW I PLEAD TODAY.
I'M GUILTY AS HELL!!

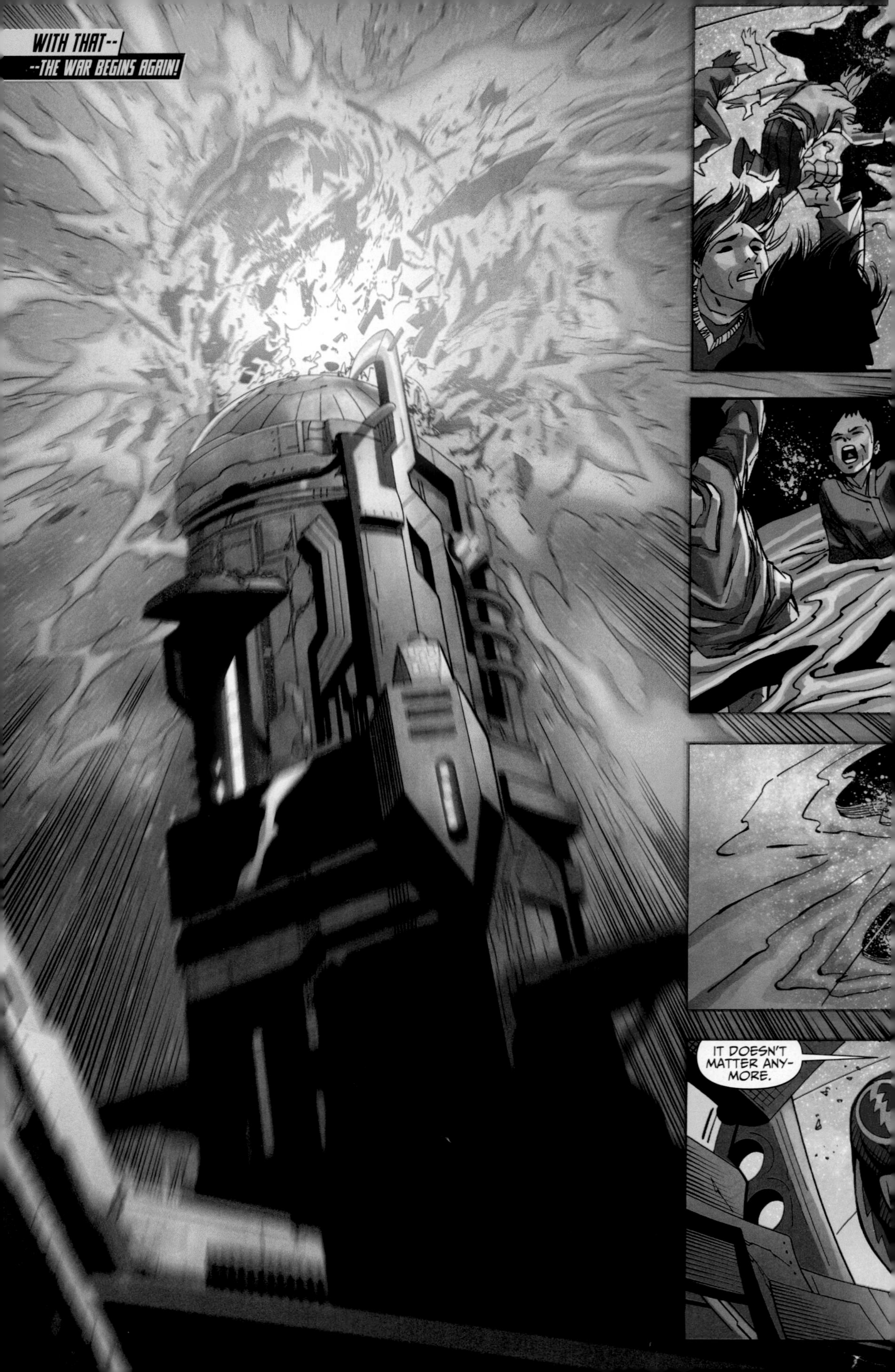
WITH THAT--
--THE WAR BEGINS AGAIN!
IT DOESN'T MATTER ANY-MORE.

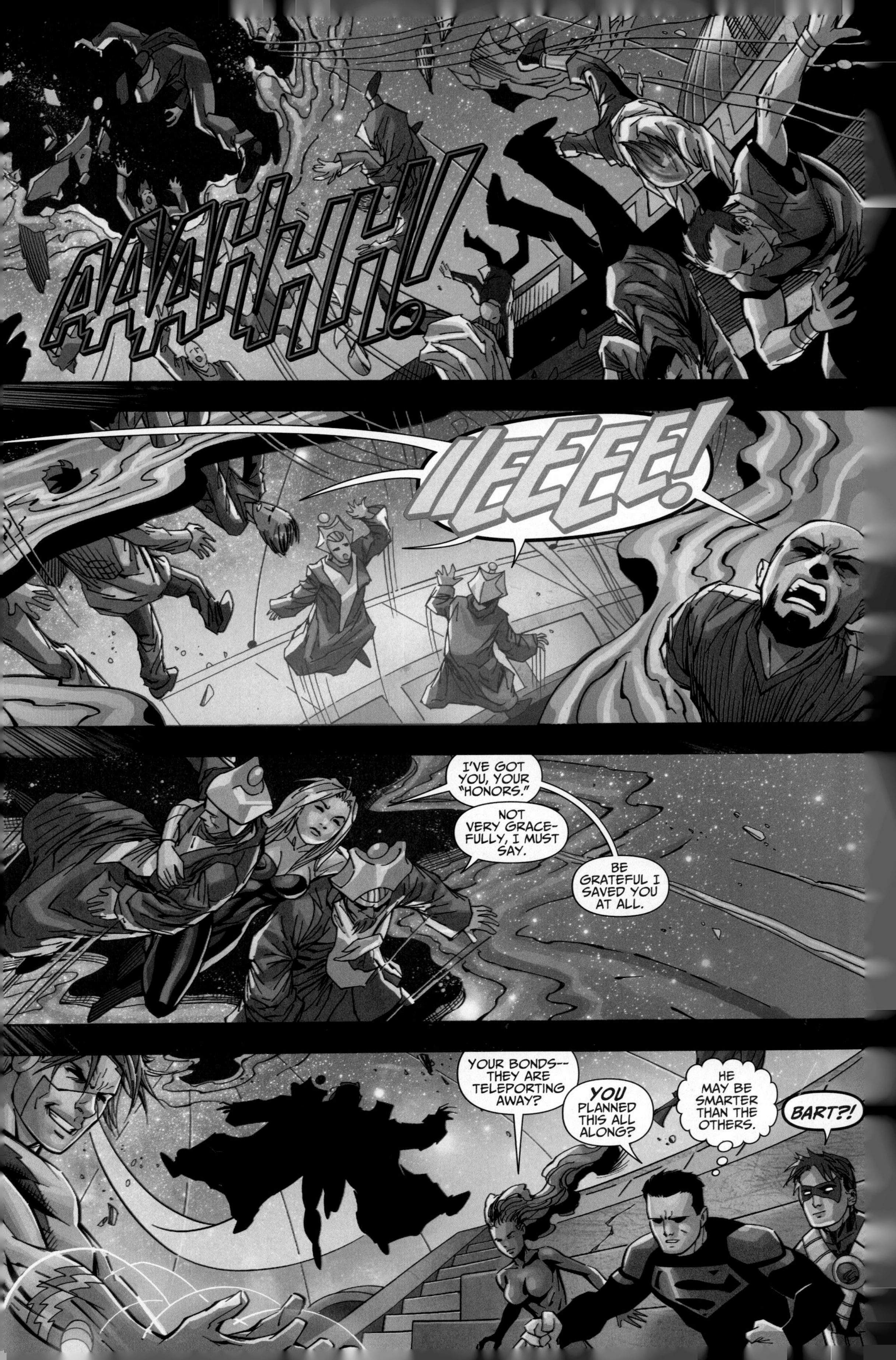
AAAHHH!!
IIEEEEE!
I'VE GOT YOU, YOUR "HONORS."
NOT VERY GRACEFULLY, I MUST SAY.
BE GRATEFUL I SAVED YOU AT ALL.
YOUR BONDS-- THEY ARE TELEPORTING AWAY?
YOU PLANNED THIS ALL ALONG?
HE MAY BE SMARTER THAN THE OTHERS.
BART?!

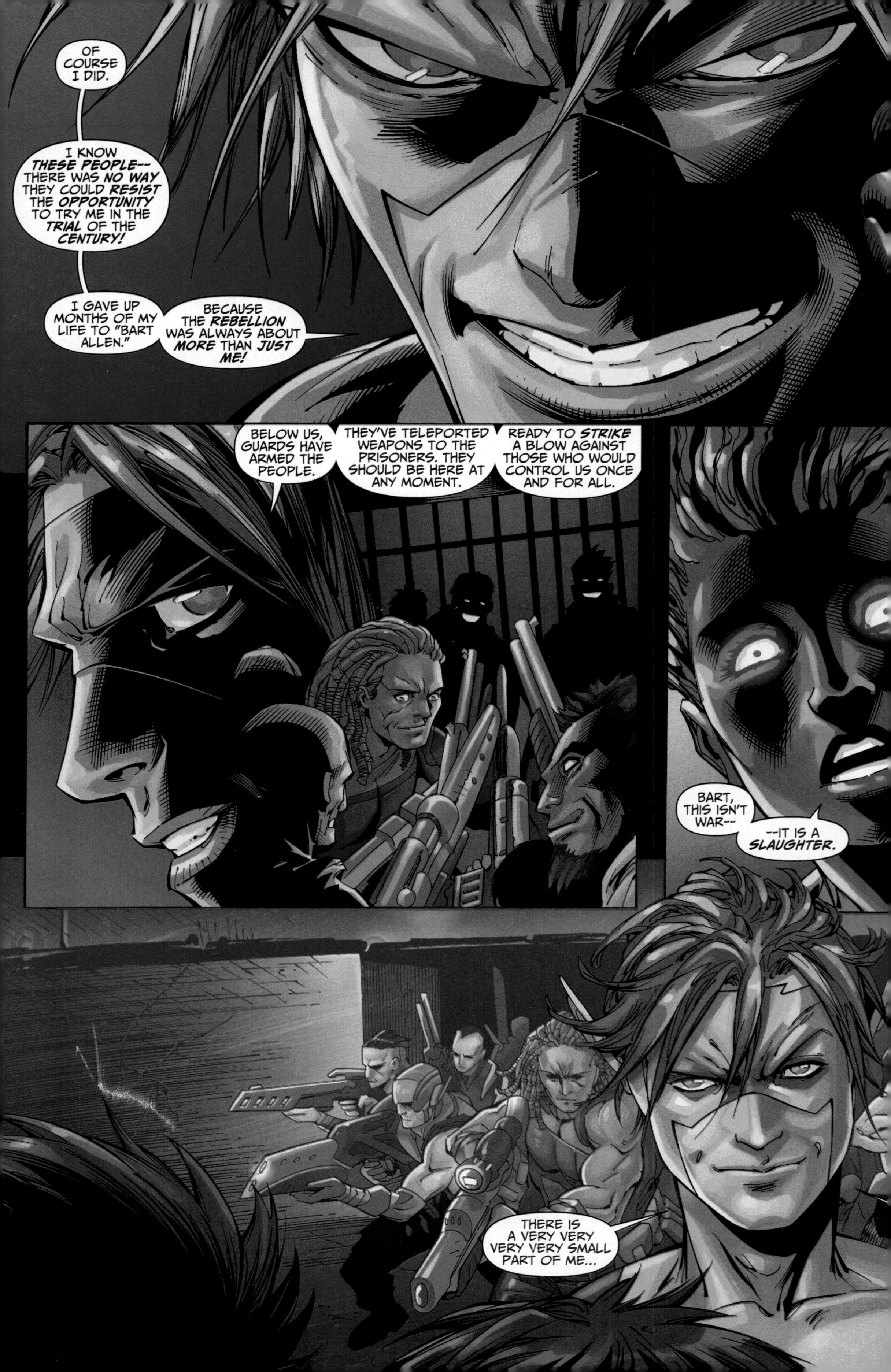
OF COURSE I DID.
I KNOW THESE PEOPLE-- THERE WAS NO WAY THEY COULD RESIST THE OPPORTUNITY TO TRY ME IN THE TRIAL OF THE CENTURY!
I GAVE UP MONTHS OF MY LIFE TO "BART ALLEN."
BECAUSE THE REBELLION WAS ALWAYS ABOUT MORE THAN JUST ME!
BELOW US, GUARDS HAVE ARMED THE PEOPLE.
THEY'VE TELEPORTED WEAPONS TO THE PRISONERS. THEY SHOULD BE HERE AT ANY MOMENT.
READY TO STRIKE A BLOW AGAINST THOSE WHO WOULD CONTROL US ONCE AND FOR ALL.
BART, THIS ISN'T WAR--
--IT IS A SLAUGHTER.
THERE IS A VERY VERY VERY VERY SMALL PART OF ME...

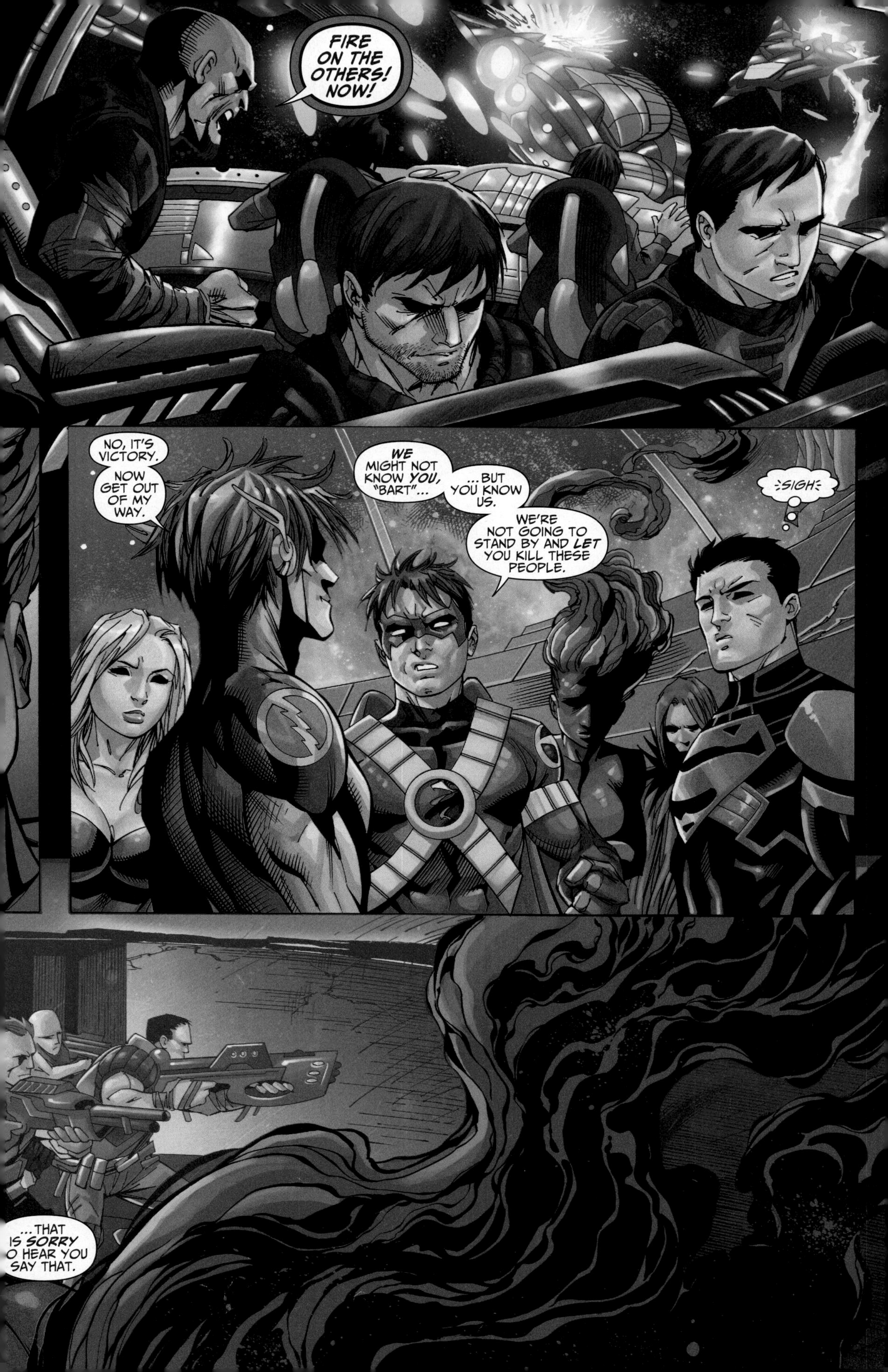
FIRE ON THE OTHERS! NOW!
NO, IT'S VICTORY. NOW GET OUT OF MY WAY.
WE MIGHT NOT KNOW YOU, "BART"...
...BUT YOU KNOW US.
WE'RE NOT GOING TO STAND BY AND LET YOU KILL THESE PEOPLE.
SIGH
...THAT IS SORRY O HEAR YOU SAY THAT.

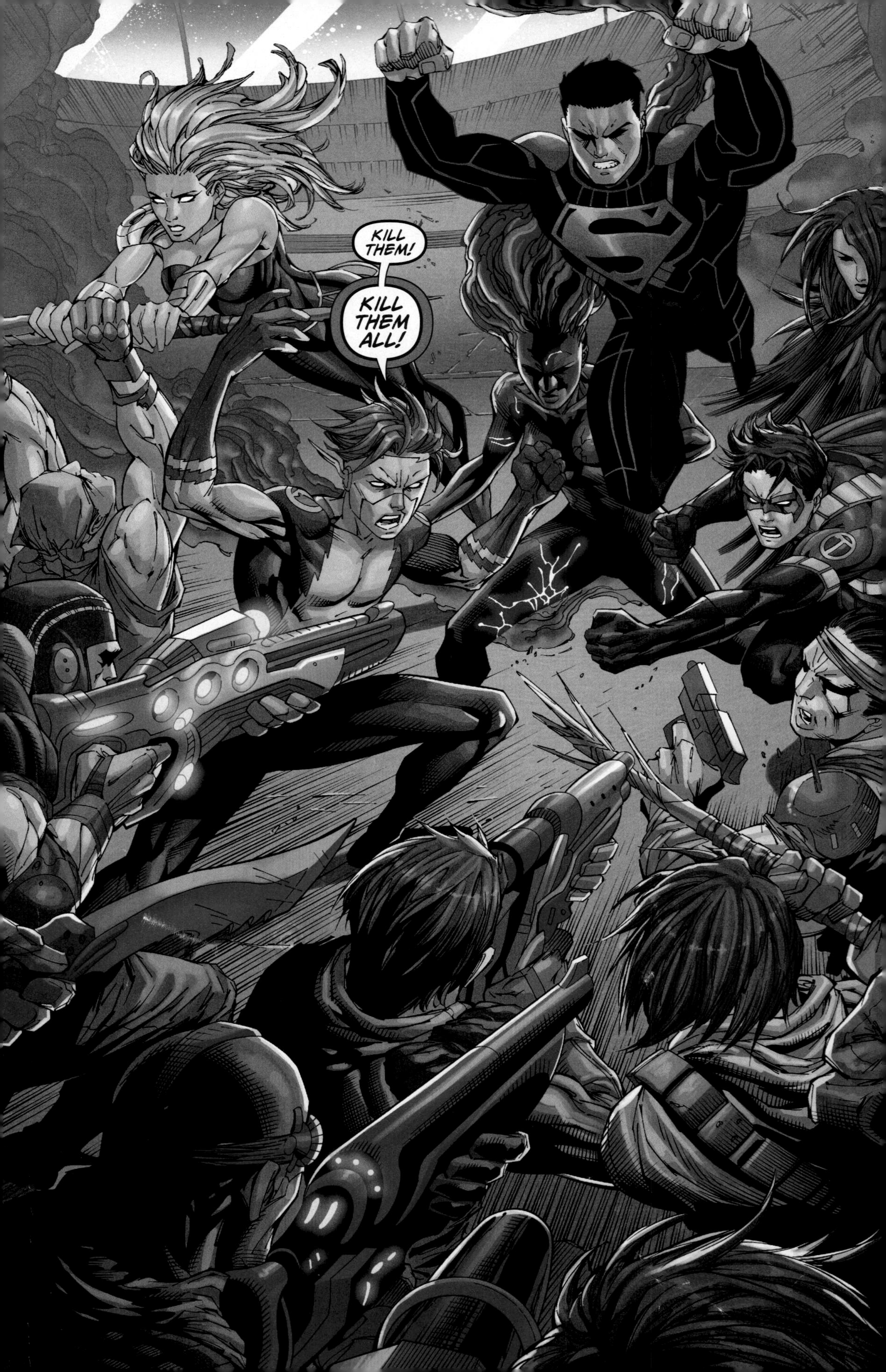
KILL THEM!
KILL THEM ALL!

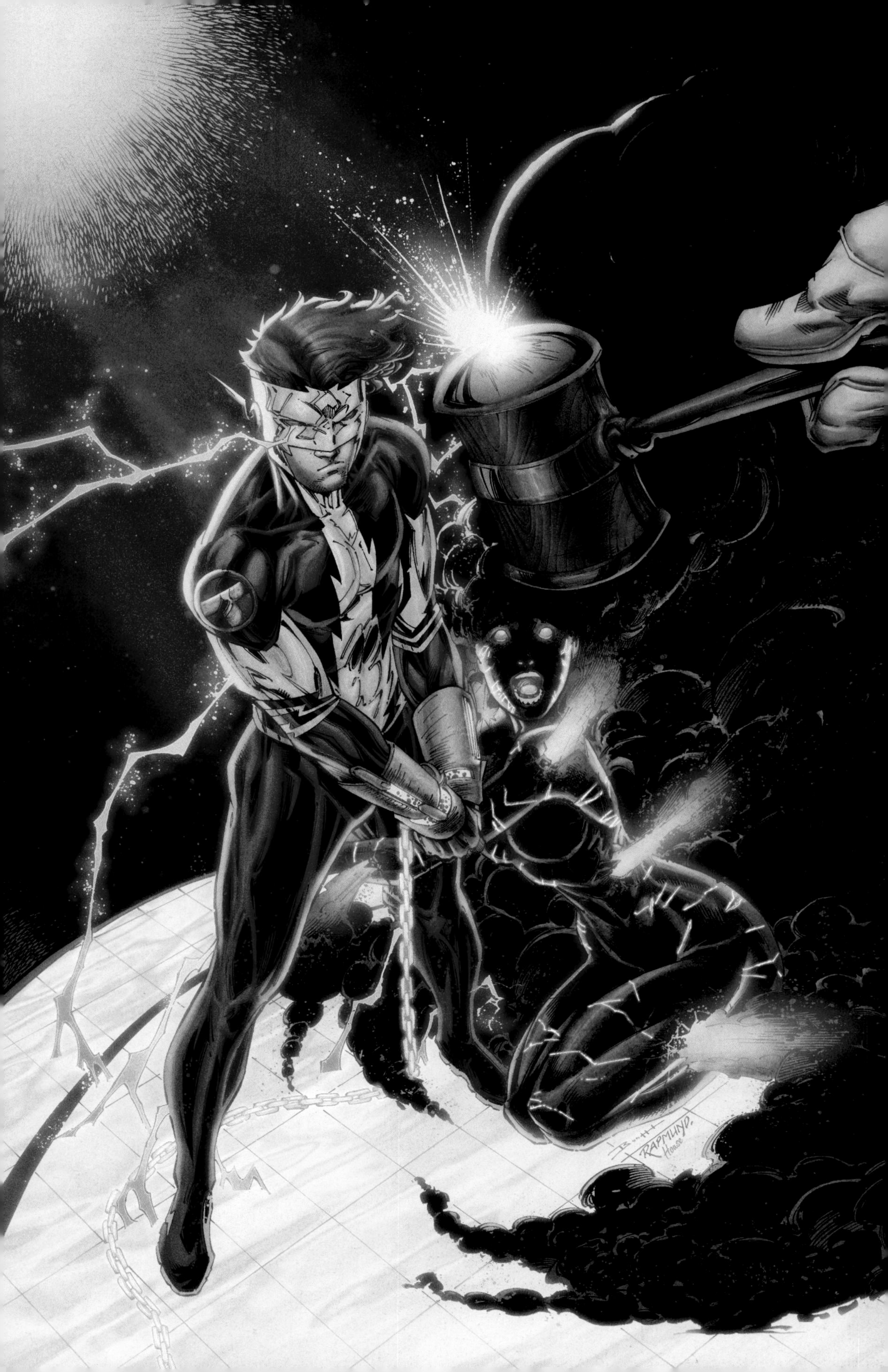
RAPMUND.

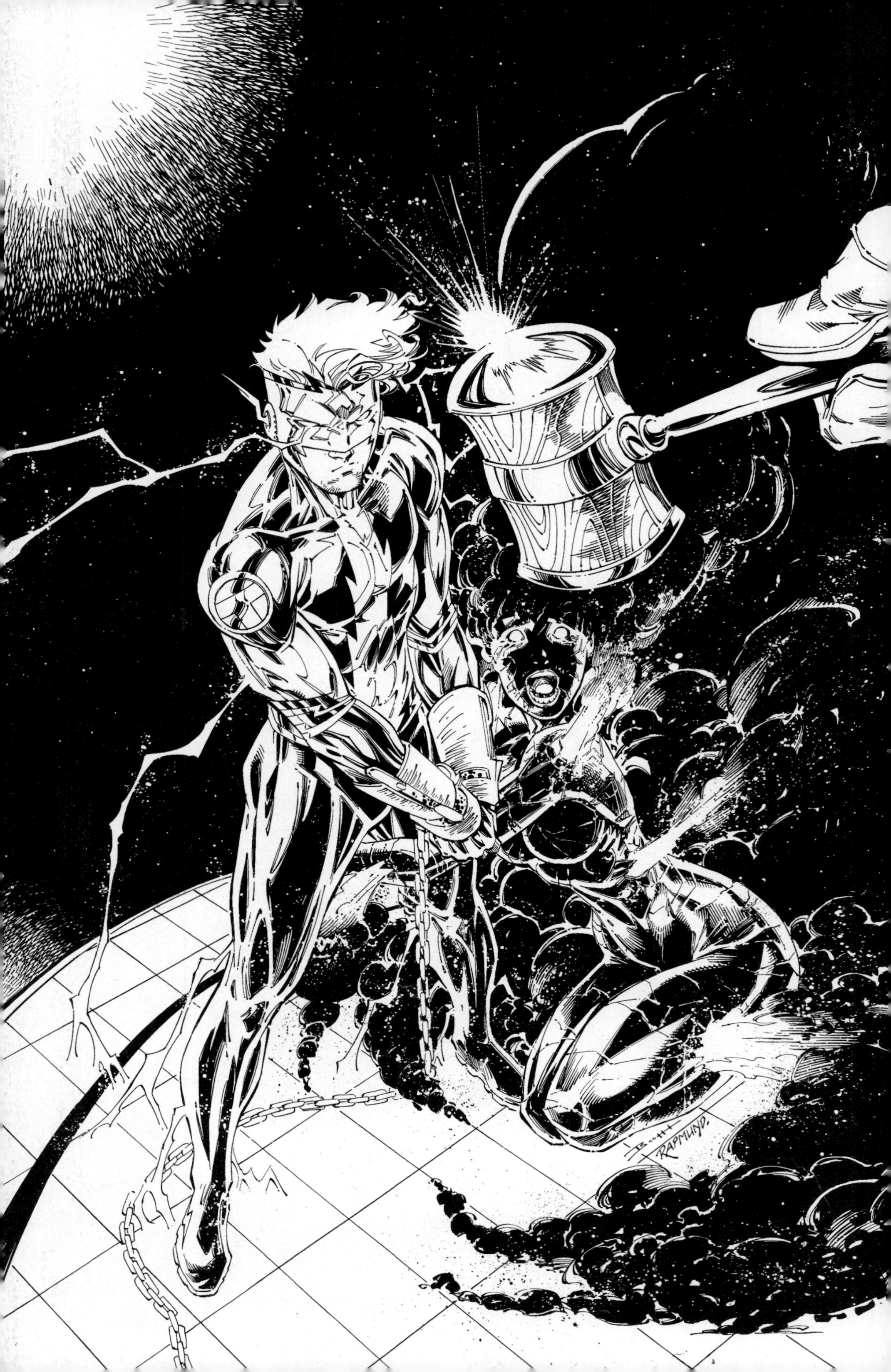
RAPMUND.

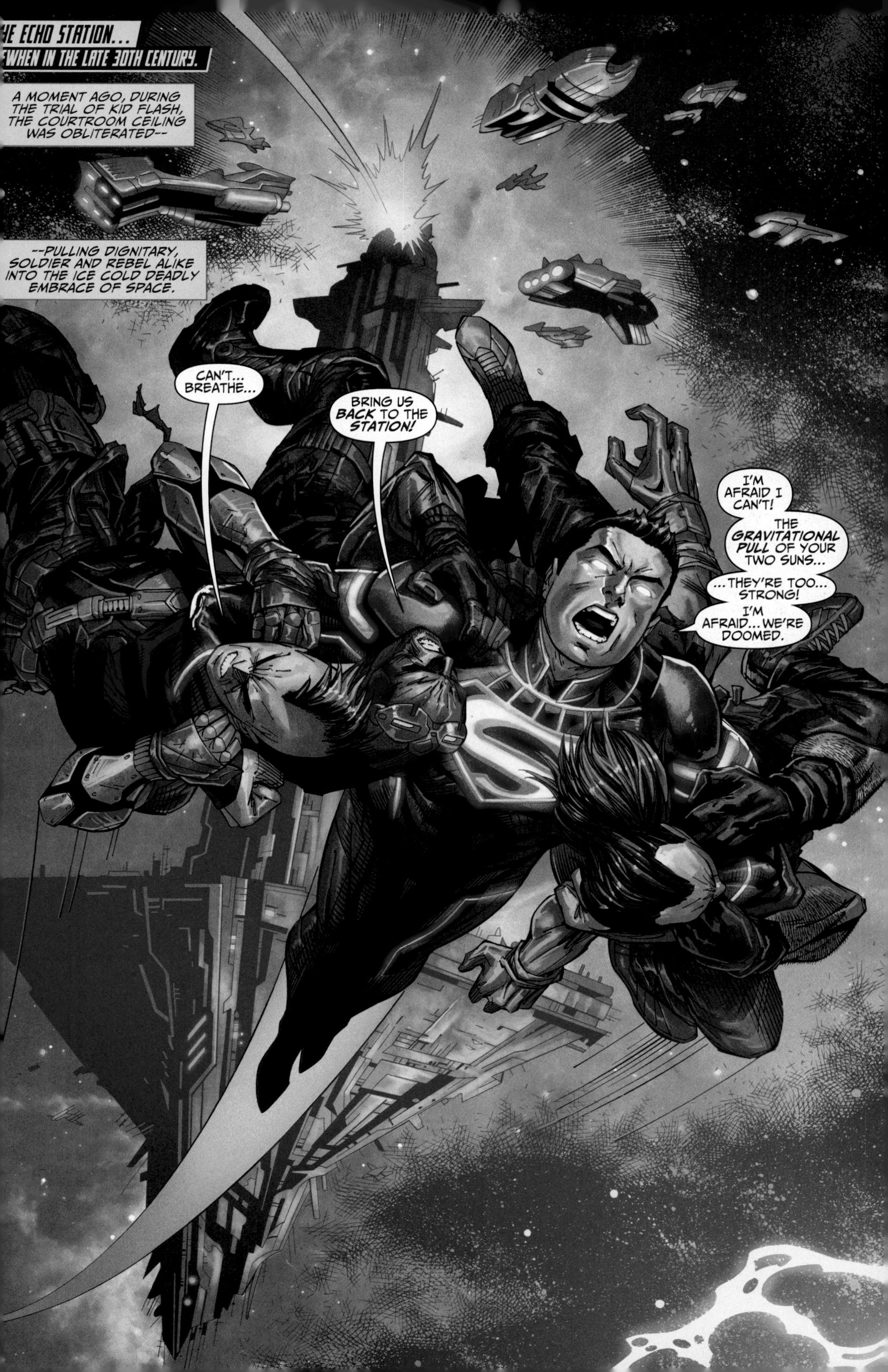
HE ECHO STATION...
WHEN IN THE LATE 30TH CENTURY.
A MOMENT AGO, DURING THE TRIAL OF KID FLASH, THE COURTROOM CEILING WAS OBLITERATED--
--PULLING DIGNITARY, SOLDIER AND REBEL ALIKE INTO THE ICE COLD DEADLY EMBRACE OF SPACE.
CAN'T... BREATHE...
BRING US BACK TO THE STATION!
I'M AFRAID I CAN'T!
THE GRAVITATIONAL PULL OF YOUR TWO SUNS...
...THEY'RE TOO... STRONG!
I'M AFRAID... WE'RE DOOMED.

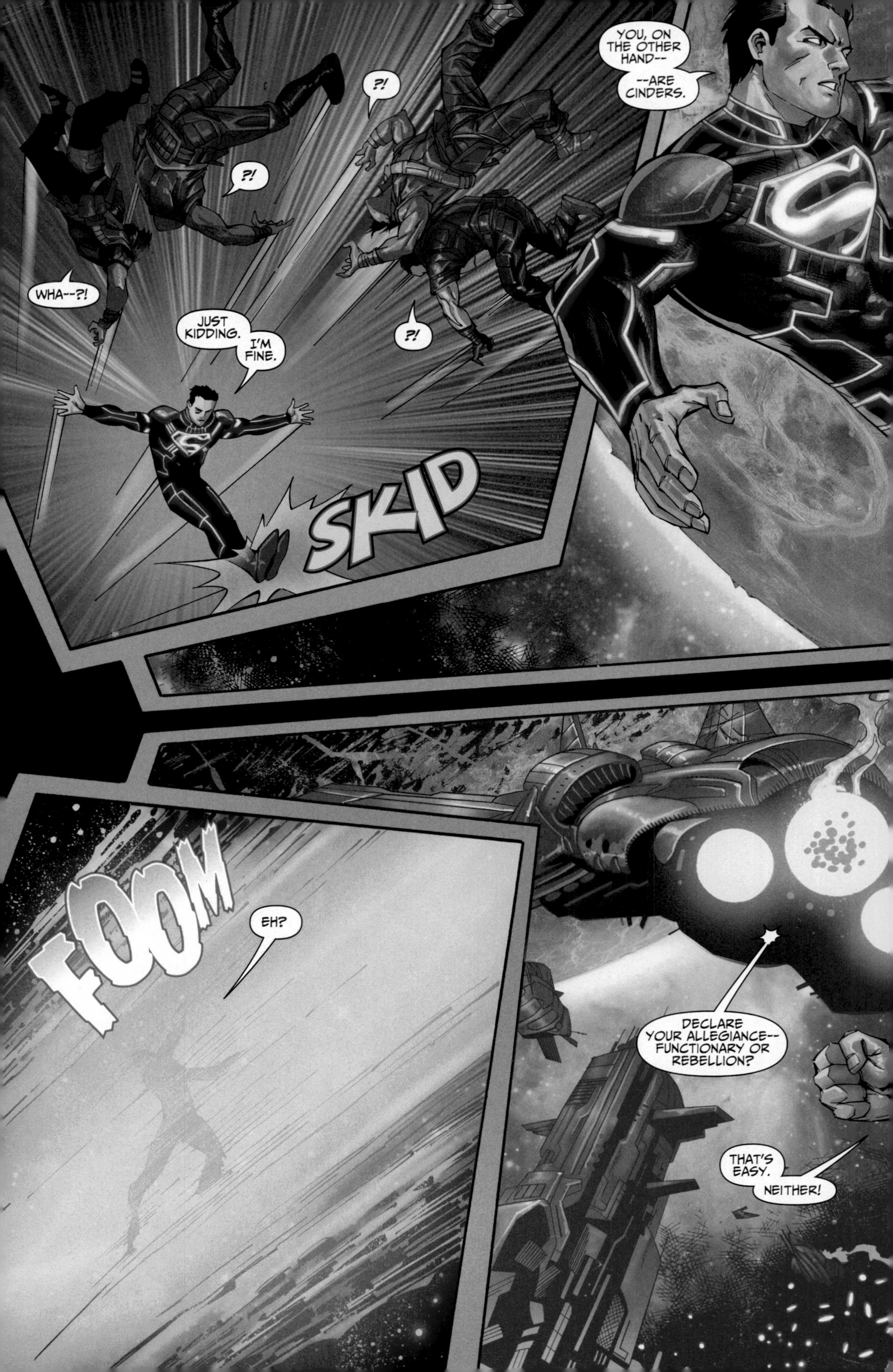
?!
?!
WHA--?!
?!
JUST KIDDING.
I'M FINE.
SKID
YOU, ON THE OTHER HAND--
--ARE CINDERS.
FOOM
EH?
DECLARE YOUR ALLEGIANCE-- FUNCTIONARY OR REBELLION?
THAT'S EASY.
NEITHER!

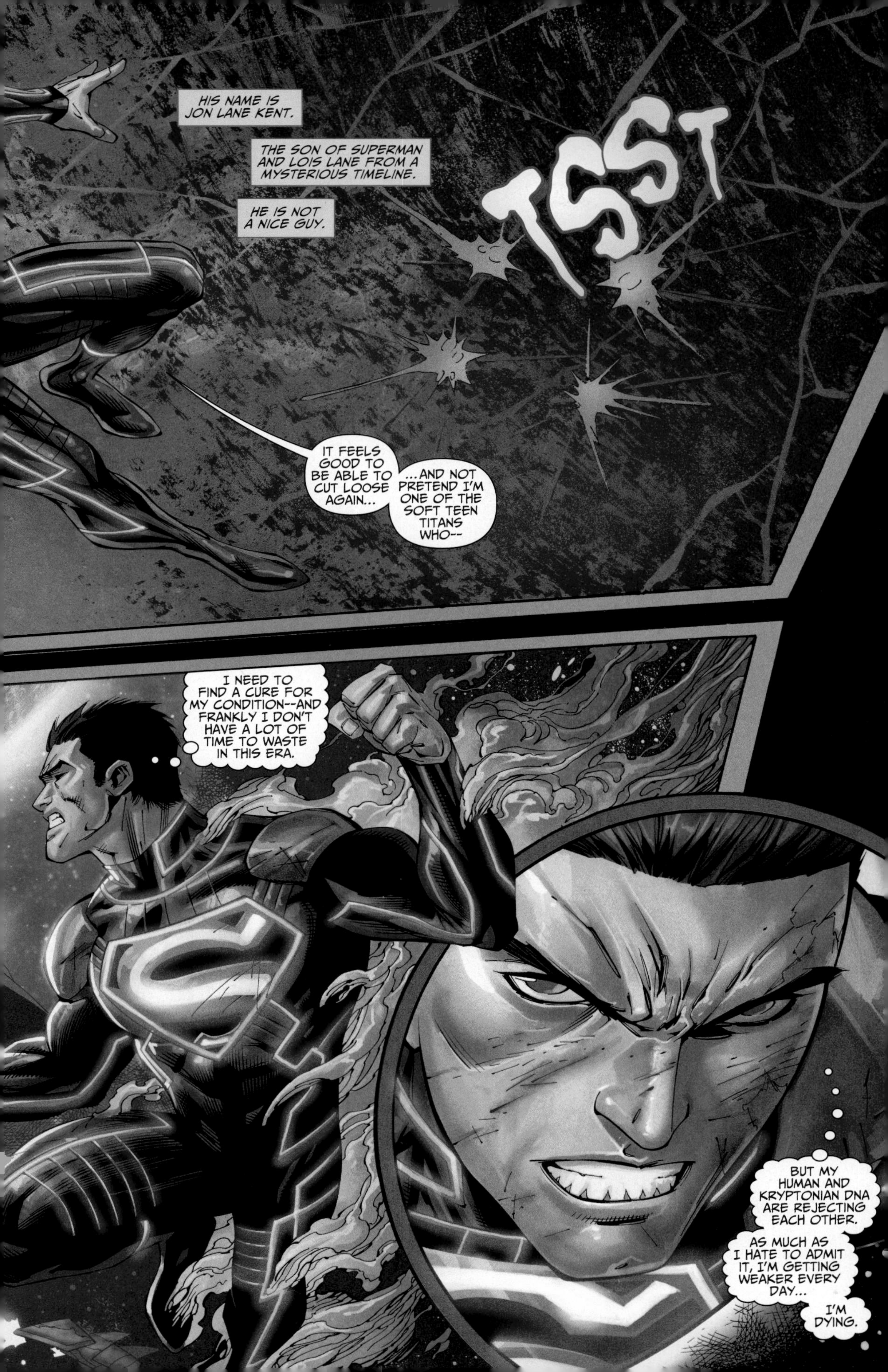
HIS NAME IS JON LANE KENT.
THE SON OF SUPERMAN AND LOIS LANE FROM A MYSTERIOUS TIMELINE.
HE IS NOT A NICE GUY.
TSST
IT FEELS GOOD TO BE ABLE TO CUT LOOSE AGAIN...
...AND NOT PRETEND I'M ONE OF THE SOFT TEEN TITANS WHO--
I NEED TO FIND A CURE FOR MY CONDITION--AND FRANKLY I DON'T HAVE A LOT OF TIME TO WASTE IN THIS ERA.
BUT MY HUMAN AND KRYPTONIAN DNA ARE REJECTING EACH OTHER.
AS MUCH AS I HATE TO ADMIT IT, I'M GETTING WEAKER EVERY DAY...
I'M DYING.

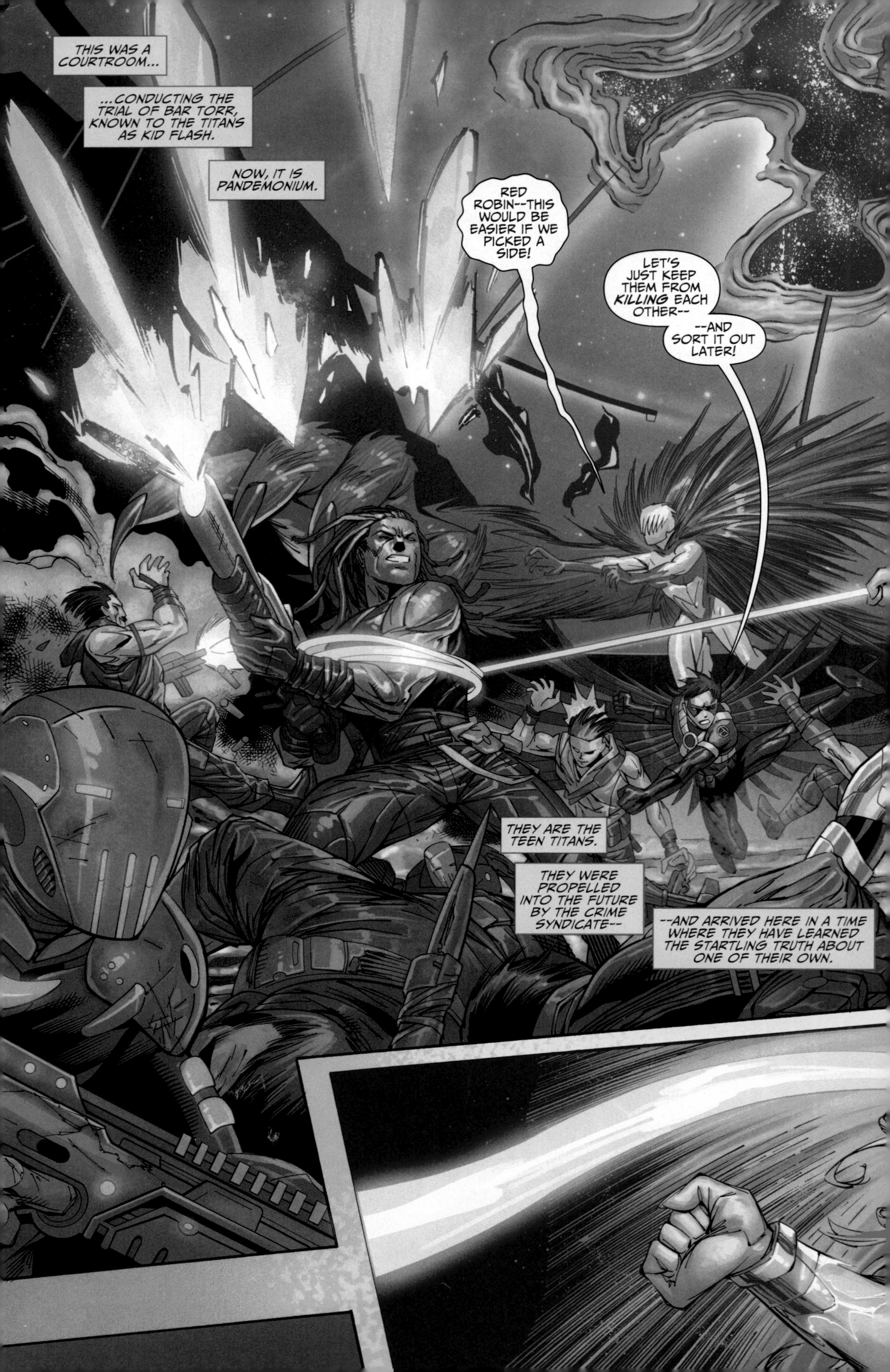
THIS WAS A COURTROOM...
...CONDUCTING THE TRIAL OF BAR TORR, KNOWN TO THE TITANS AS KID FLASH.
NOW, IT IS PANDEMONIUM.
RED ROBIN--THIS WOULD BE EASIER IF WE PICKED A SIDE!
LET'S JUST KEEP THEM FROM KILLING EACH OTHER--
--AND SORT IT OUT LATER!
THEY ARE THE TEEN TITANS.
THEY WERE PROPELLED INTO THE FUTURE BY THE CRIME SYNDICATE--
--AND ARRIVED HERE IN A TIME WHERE THEY HAVE LEARNED THE STARTLING TRUTH ABOUT ONE OF THEIR OWN.

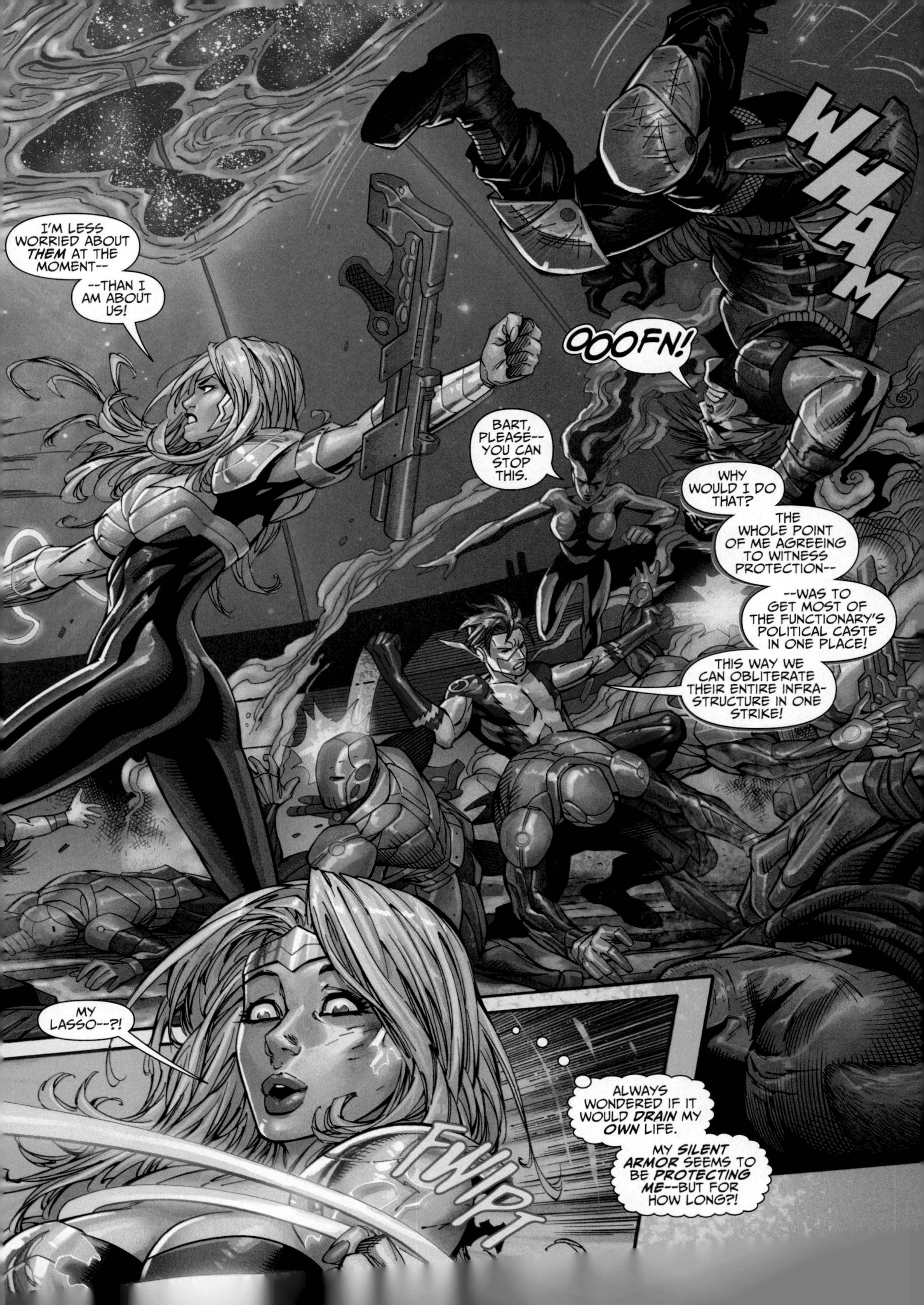
I'M LESS WORRIED ABOUT THEM AT THE MOMENT--
--THAN I AM ABOUT US!
WHAM
OOOFN!
BART, PLEASE--YOU CAN STOP THIS.
WHY WOULD I DO THAT?
THE WHOLE POINT OF ME AGREEING TO WITNESS PROTECTION--
--WAS TO GET MOST OF THE FUNCTIONARY'S POLITICAL CASTE IN ONE PLACE!
THIS WAY WE CAN OBLITERATE THEIR ENTIRE INFRA-STRUCTURE IN ONE STRIKE!
MY LASSO--?!
ALWAYS WONDERED IF IT WOULD DRAIN MY OWN LIFE.
MY SILENT ARMOR SEEMS TO BE PROTECTING ME--BUT FOR HOW LONG?!
FWIPT

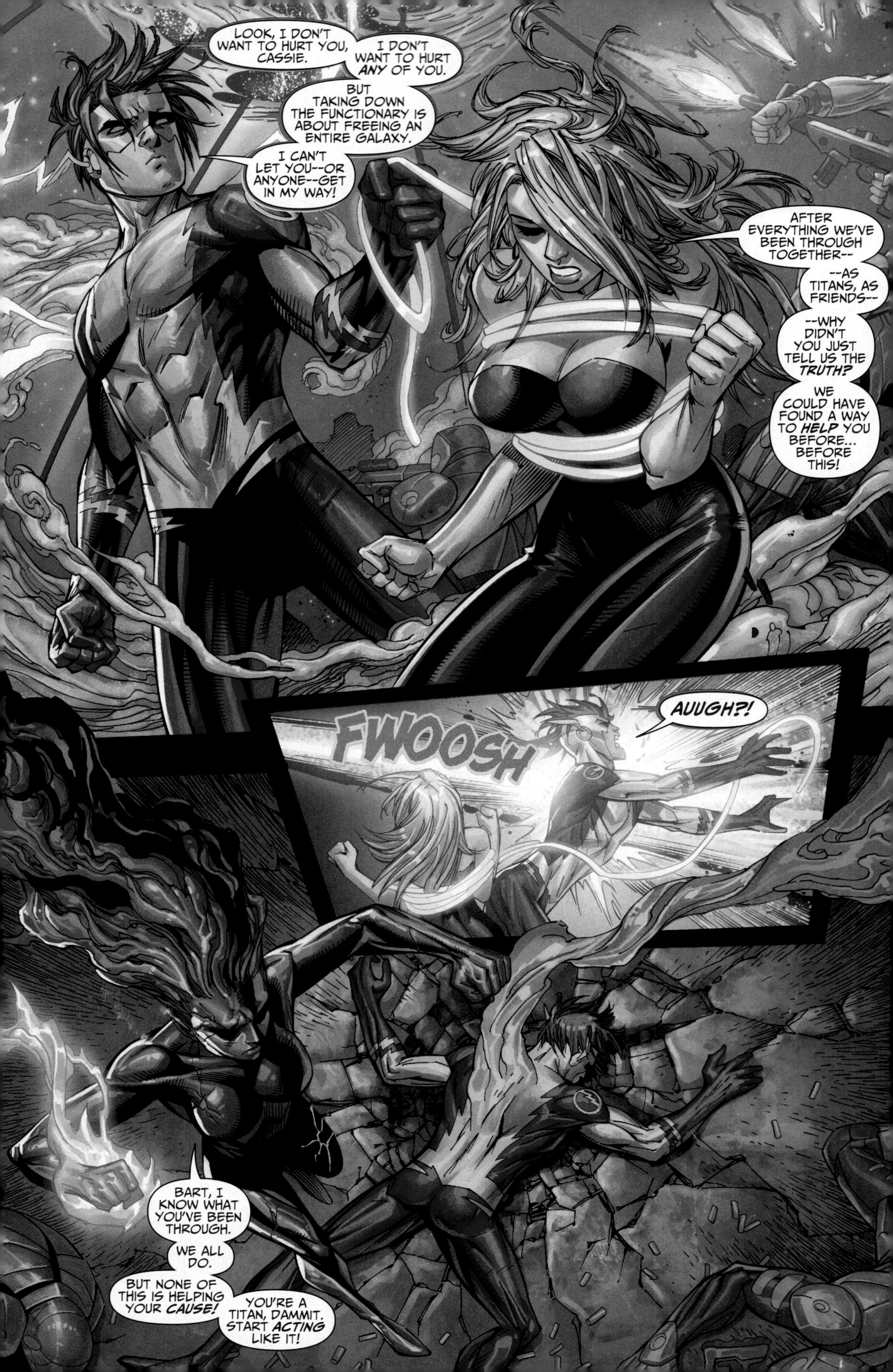
LOOK, I DON'T WANT TO HURT YOU, CASSIE.
I DON'T WANT TO HURT *ANY* OF YOU.
BUT TAKING DOWN THE FUNCTIONARY IS ABOUT FREEING AN ENTIRE GALAXY.
I CAN'T LET YOU--OR ANYONE--GET IN MY WAY!
AFTER EVERYTHING WE'VE BEEN THROUGH TOGETHER--
--AS TITANS, AS FRIENDS--
--WHY DIDN'T YOU JUST TELL US THE *TRUTH?*
WE COULD HAVE FOUND A WAY TO *HELP* YOU BEFORE... BEFORE THIS!
FWOOSH
AUUGH?!
BART, I KNOW WHAT YOU'VE BEEN THROUGH.
WE ALL DO.
BUT NONE OF THIS IS HELPING YOUR *CAUSE!*
YOU'RE A TITAN, DAMMIT. START *ACTING* LIKE IT!

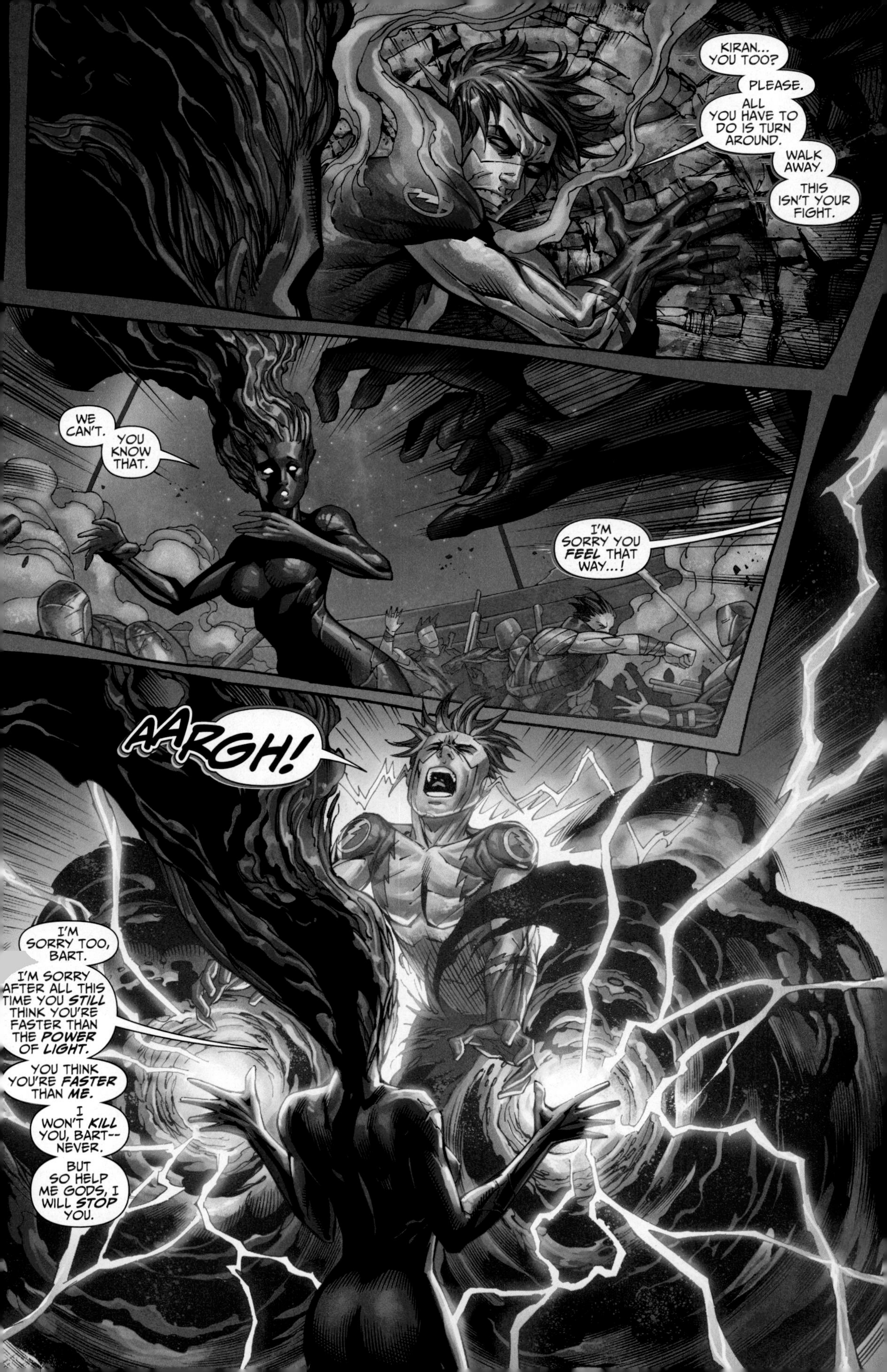
KIRAN... YOU TOO?
PLEASE.
ALL YOU HAVE TO DO IS TURN AROUND.
WALK AWAY.
THIS ISN'T YOUR FIGHT.
WE CAN'T.
YOU KNOW THAT.
I'M SORRY YOU FEEL THAT WAY...!
AARGH!
I'M SORRY TOO, BART.
I'M SORRY AFTER ALL THIS TIME YOU STILL THINK YOU'RE FASTER THAN THE POWER OF LIGHT.
YOU THINK YOU'RE FASTER THAN ME.
I WON'T KILL YOU, BART-- NEVER.
BUT SO HELP ME GODS, I WILL STOP YOU.

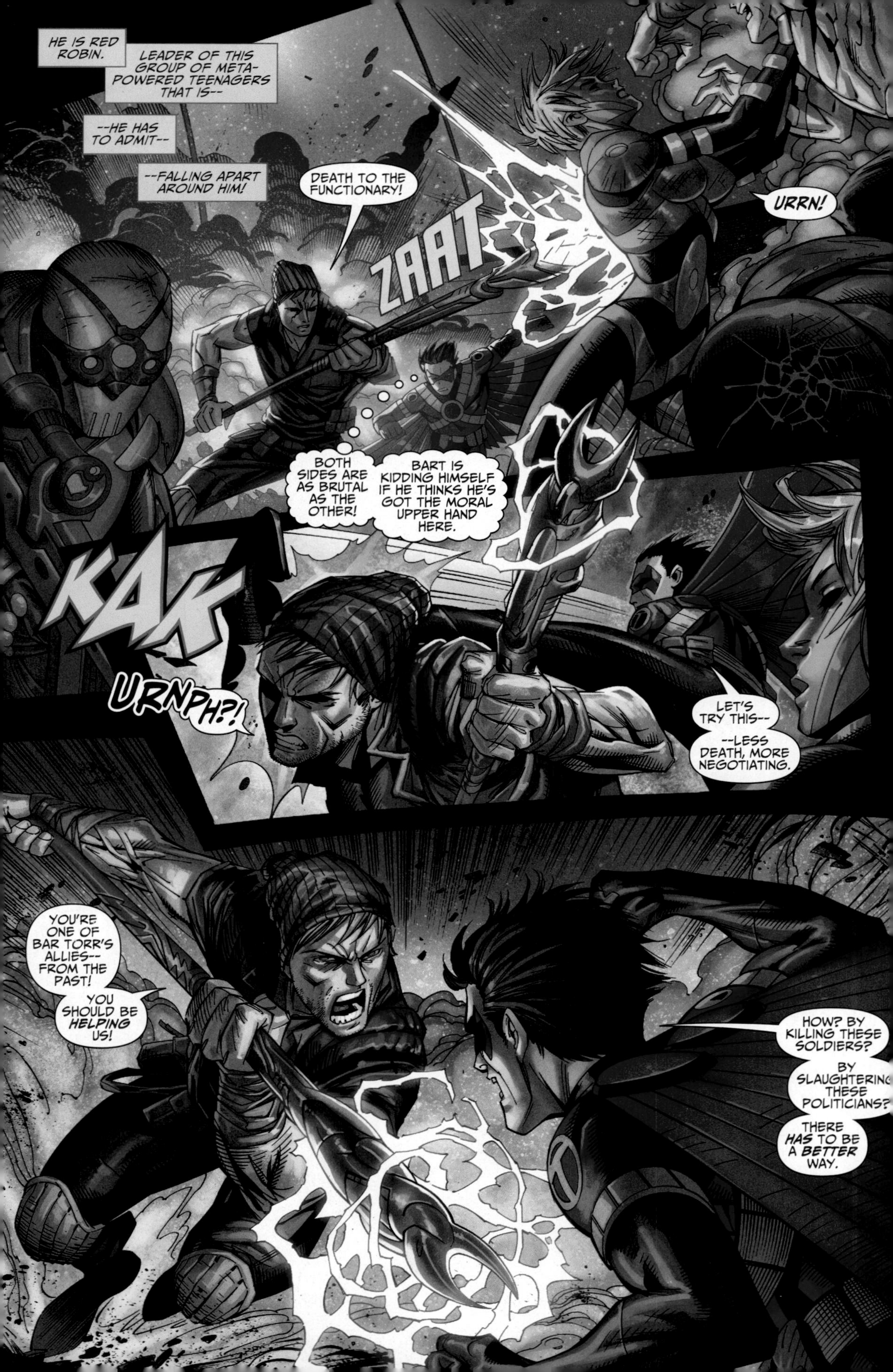
HE IS RED ROBIN.
LEADER OF THIS GROUP OF META-POWERED TEENAGERS THAT IS--
--HE HAS TO ADMIT--
--FALLING APART AROUND HIM!
DEATH TO THE FUNCTIONARY!
ZAAT
URRN!
BOTH SIDES ARE AS BRUTAL AS THE OTHER!
BART IS KIDDING HIMSELF IF HE THINKS HE'S GOT THE MORAL UPPER HAND HERE.
KAK
URNPH?!
LET'S TRY THIS--
--LESS DEATH, MORE NEGOTIATING.
YOU'RE ONE OF BAR TORR'S ALLIES--FROM THE PAST!
YOU SHOULD BE HELPING US!
HOW? BY KILLING THESE SOLDIERS?
BY SLAUGHTERING THESE POLITICIANS?
THERE HAS TO BE A BETTER WAY.

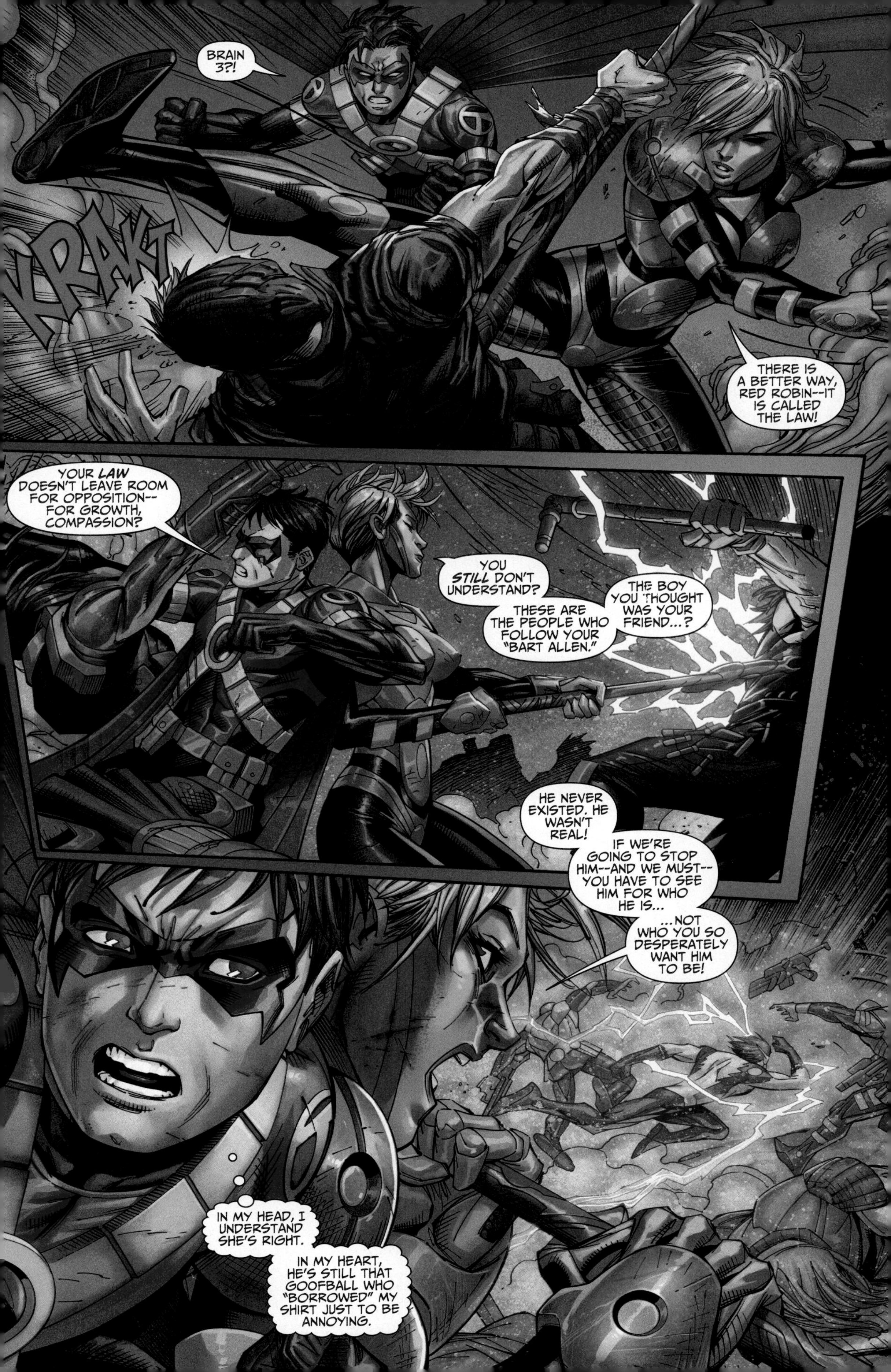
BRAIN 3?!
KRAK!
THERE IS A BETTER WAY, RED ROBIN--IT IS CALLED THE LAW!
YOUR LAW DOESN'T LEAVE ROOM FOR OPPOSITION--FOR GROWTH, COMPASSION?
YOU STILL DON'T UNDERSTAND?
THESE ARE THE PEOPLE WHO FOLLOW YOUR "BART ALLEN."
THE BOY YOU THOUGHT WAS YOUR FRIEND...?
HE NEVER EXISTED. HE WASN'T REAL!
IF WE'RE GOING TO STOP HIM--AND WE MUST--YOU HAVE TO SEE HIM FOR WHO HE IS...
...NOT WHO YOU SO DESPERATELY WANT HIM TO BE!
IN MY HEAD, I UNDERSTAND SHE'S RIGHT.
IN MY HEART, HE'S STILL THAT GOOFBALL WHO "BORROWED" MY SHIRT JUST TO BE ANNOYING.

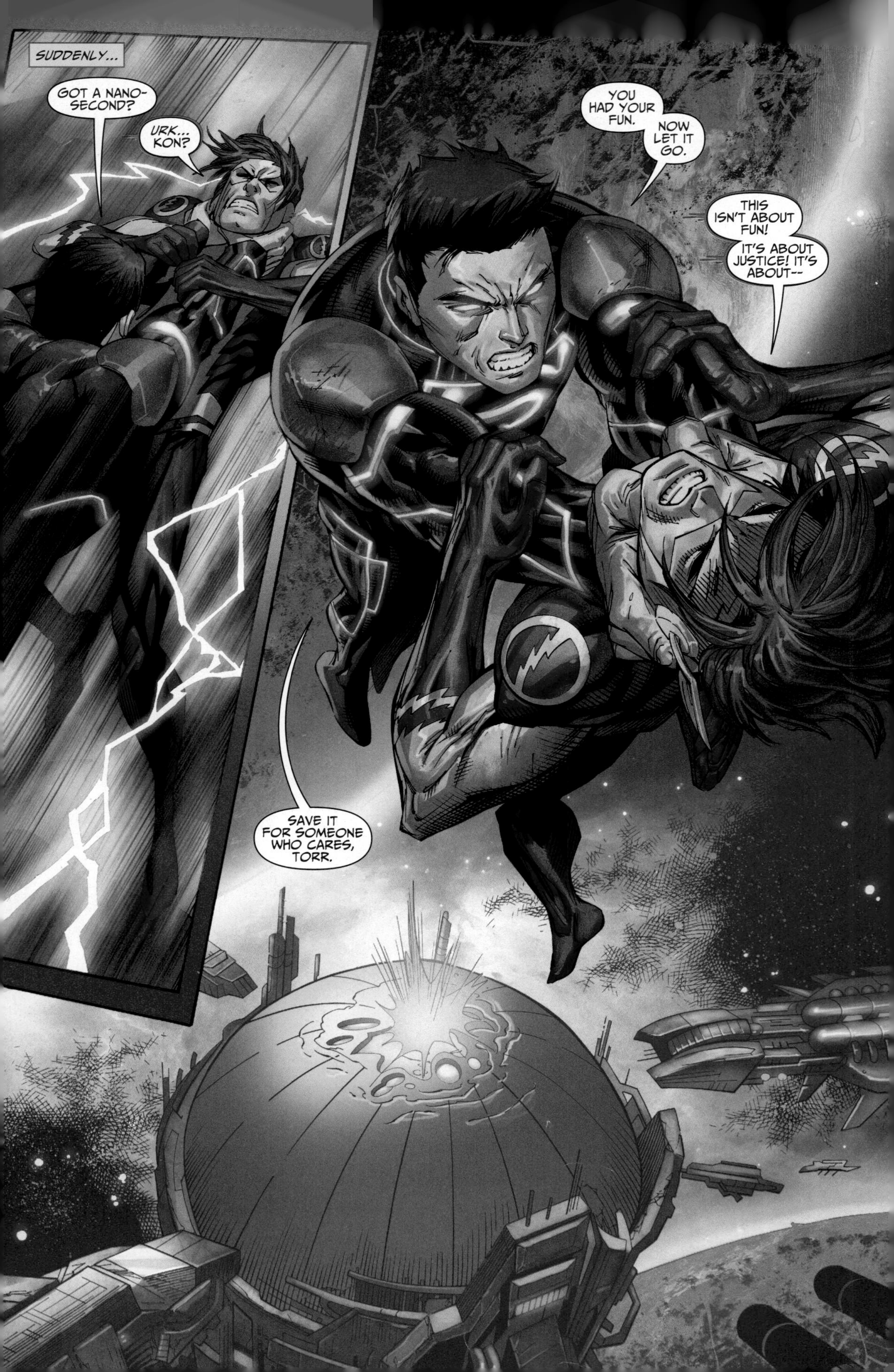
SUDDENLY...
GOT A NANO-SECOND?
URK... KON?
YOU HAD YOUR FUN.
NOW LET IT GO.
THIS ISN'T ABOUT FUN!
IT'S ABOUT JUSTICE! IT'S ABOUT--
SAVE IT FOR SOMEONE WHO CARES, TORR.

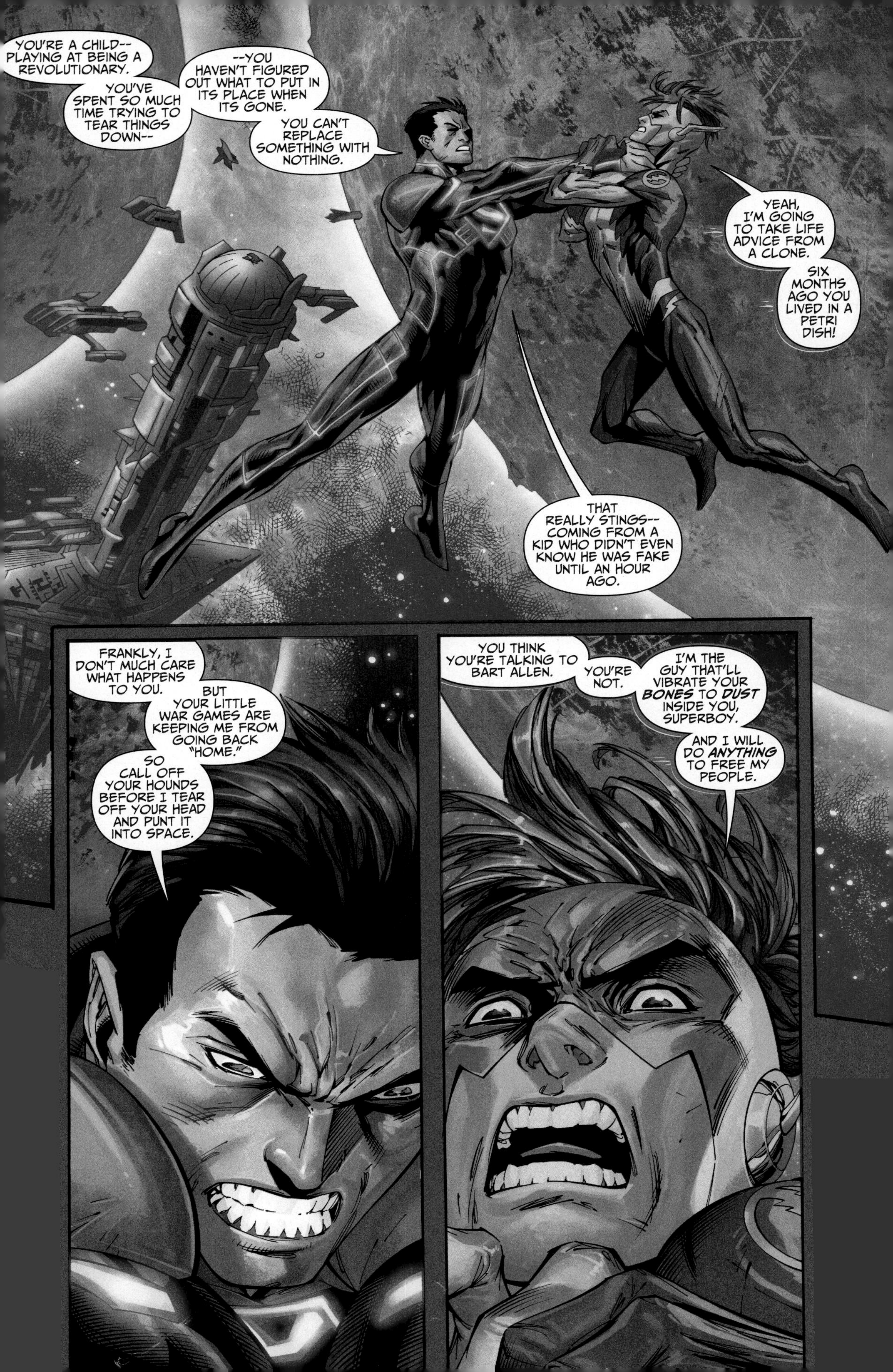

YOU'RE A CHILD--PLAYING AT BEING A REVOLUTIONARY.
YOU'VE SPENT SO MUCH TIME TRYING TO TEAR THINGS DOWN--
--YOU HAVEN'T FIGURED OUT WHAT TO PUT IN ITS PLACE WHEN ITS GONE.
YOU CAN'T REPLACE SOMETHING WITH NOTHING.
YEAH, I'M GOING TO TAKE LIFE ADVICE FROM A CLONE.
SIX MONTHS AGO YOU LIVED IN A PETRI DISH!
THAT REALLY STINGS--COMING FROM A KID WHO DIDN'T EVEN KNOW HE WAS FAKE UNTIL AN HOUR AGO.
FRANKLY, I DON'T MUCH CARE WHAT HAPPENS TO YOU.
BUT YOUR LITTLE WAR GAMES ARE KEEPING ME FROM GOING BACK "HOME."
SO CALL OFF YOUR HOUNDS BEFORE I TEAR OFF YOUR HEAD AND PUNT IT INTO SPACE.
YOU THINK YOU'RE TALKING TO BART ALLEN.
YOU'RE NOT.
I'M THE GUY THAT'LL VIBRATE YOUR ***BONES*** TO ***DUST*** INSIDE YOU, SUPERBOY.
AND I WILL DO ***ANYTHING*** TO FREE MY PEOPLE.

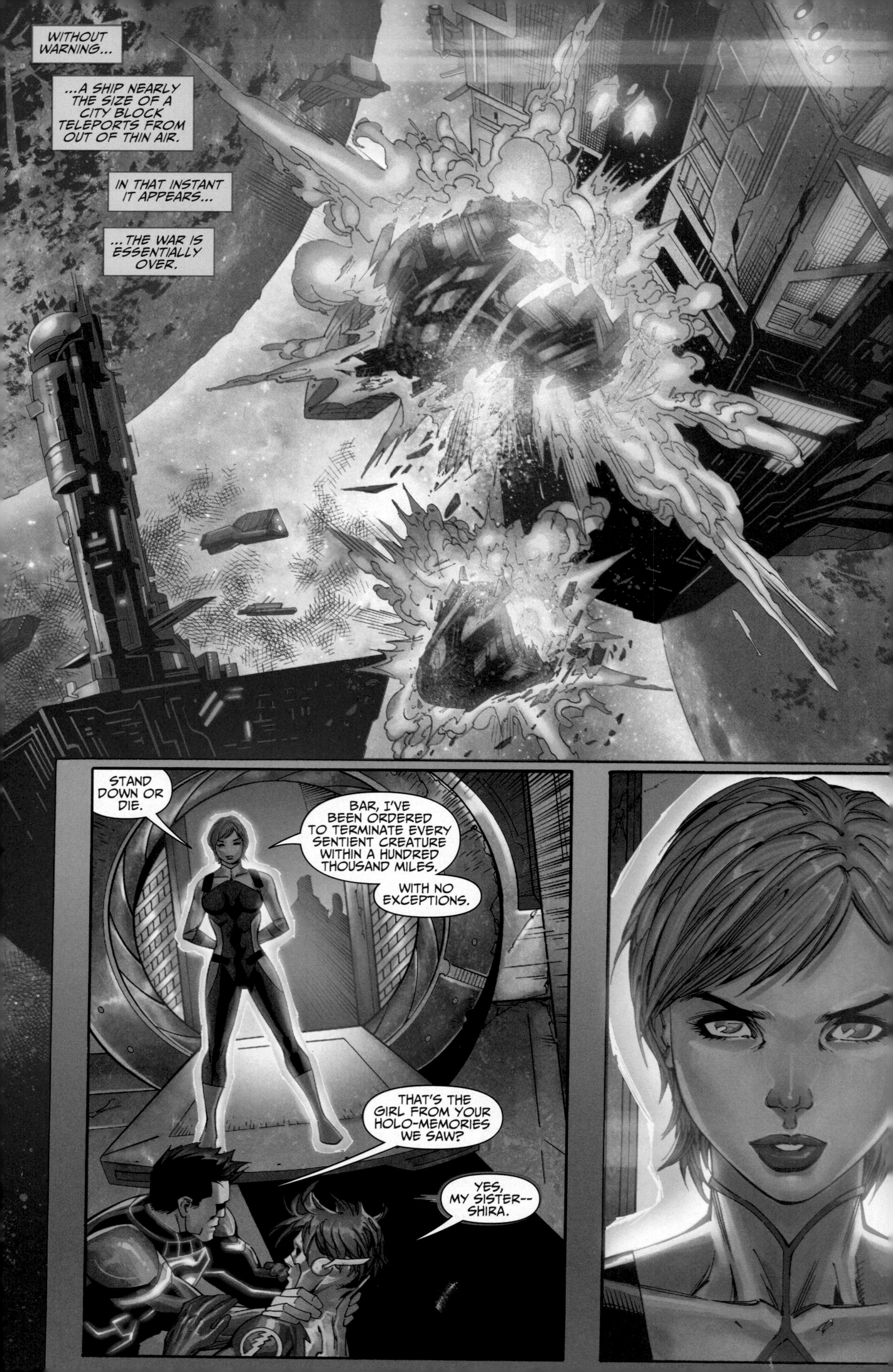
WITHOUT WARNING...
...A SHIP NEARLY THE SIZE OF A CITY BLOCK TELEPORTS FROM OUT OF THIN AIR.
IN THAT INSTANT IT APPEARS...
...THE WAR IS ESSENTIALLY OVER.
STAND DOWN OR DIE.
BAR, I'VE BEEN ORDERED TO TERMINATE EVERY SENTIENT CREATURE WITHIN A HUNDRED THOUSAND MILES.
WITH NO EXCEPTIONS.
THAT'S THE GIRL FROM YOUR HOLO-MEMORIES WE SAW?
YES, MY SISTER-- SHIRA.

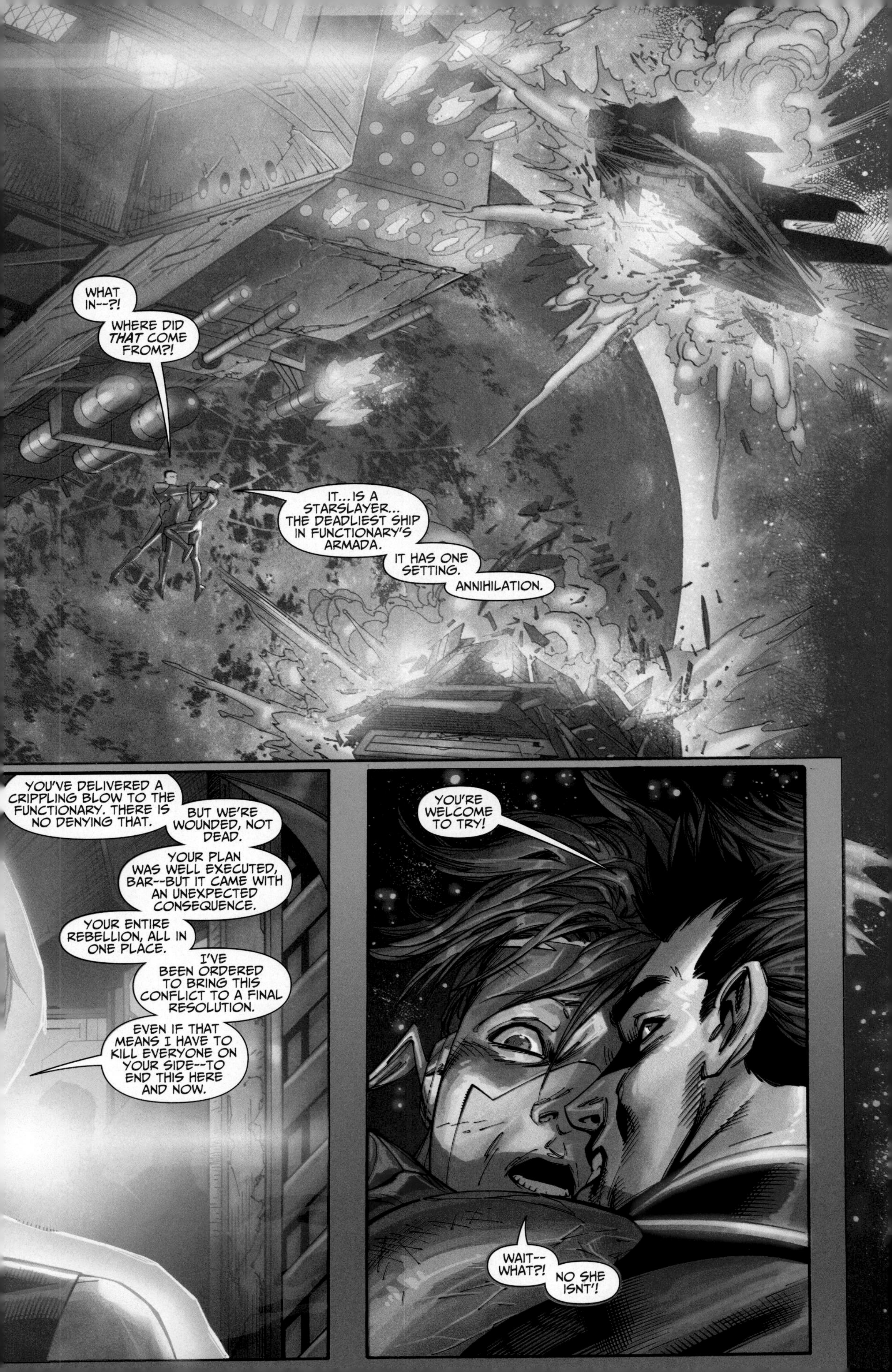
WHAT IN--?!
WHERE DID THAT COME FROM?!
IT...IS A STARSLAYER... THE DEADLIEST SHIP IN FUNCTIONARY'S ARMADA.
IT HAS ONE SETTING.
ANNIHILATION.
YOU'VE DELIVERED A CRIPPLING BLOW TO THE FUNCTIONARY. THERE IS NO DENYING THAT.
BUT WE'RE WOUNDED, NOT DEAD.
YOUR PLAN WAS WELL EXECUTED, BAR--BUT IT CAME WITH AN UNEXPECTED CONSEQUENCE.
YOUR ENTIRE REBELLION, ALL IN ONE PLACE.
I'VE BEEN ORDERED TO BRING THIS CONFLICT TO A FINAL RESOLUTION.
EVEN IF THAT MEANS I HAVE TO KILL EVERYONE ON YOUR SIDE--TO END THIS HERE AND NOW.
YOU'RE WELCOME TO TRY!
WAIT-- WHAT?!
NO SHE ISNT'!

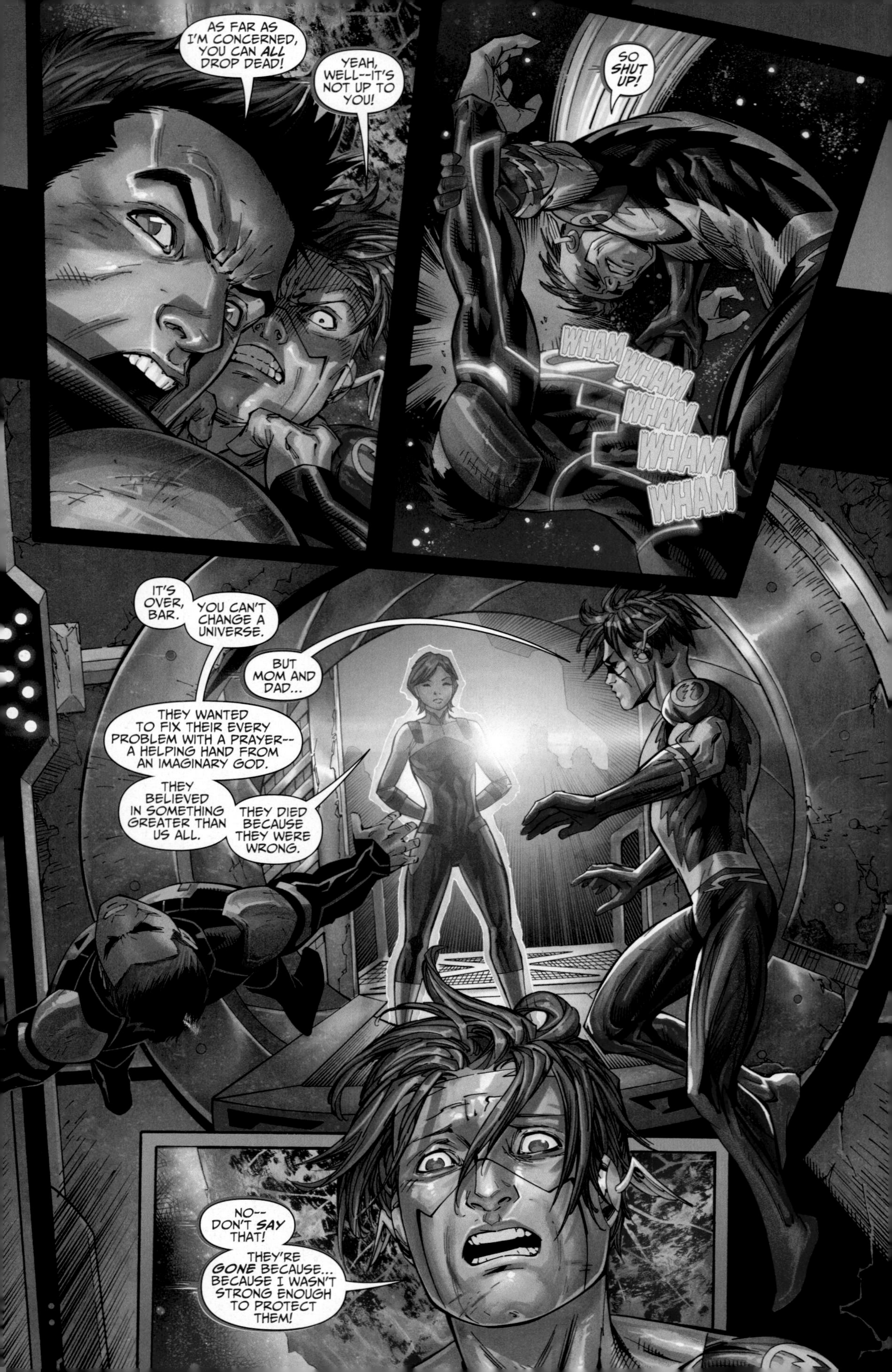

AS FAR AS I'M CONCERNED, YOU CAN ALL DROP DEAD!
YEAH, WELL--IT'S NOT UP TO YOU!
SO SHUT UP!
WHAM WHAM WHAM WHAM WHAM
IT'S OVER, BAR.
YOU CAN'T CHANGE A UNIVERSE.
BUT MOM AND DAD...
THEY WANTED TO FIX THEIR EVERY PROBLEM WITH A PRAYER--A HELPING HAND FROM AN IMAGINARY GOD.
THEY BELIEVED IN SOMETHING GREATER THAN US ALL.
THEY DIED BECAUSE THEY WERE WRONG.
NO--DON'T SAY THAT!
THEY'RE GONE BECAUSE... BECAUSE I WASN'T STRONG ENOUGH TO PROTECT THEM!

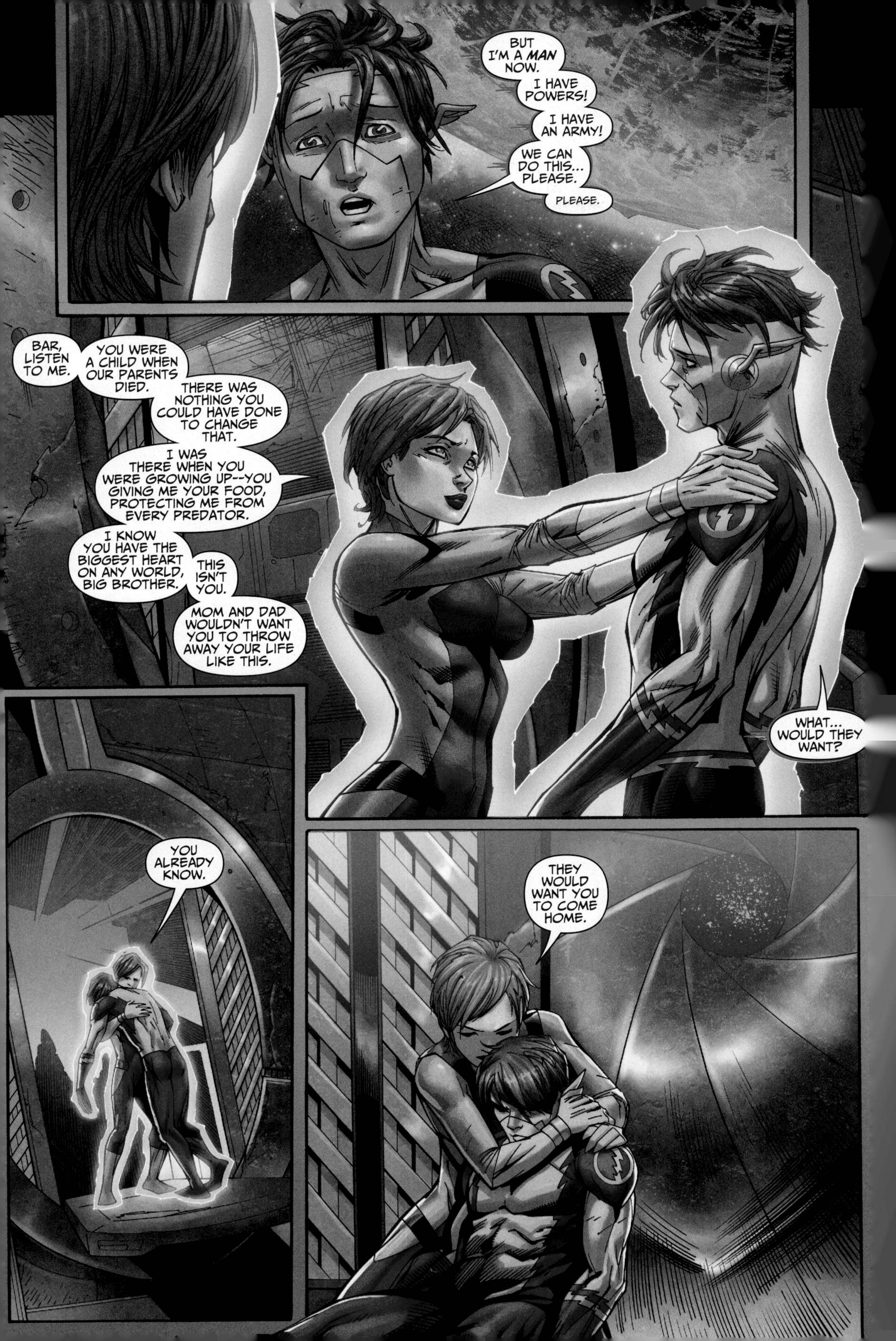

BUT I'M A MAN NOW.
I HAVE POWERS!
I HAVE AN ARMY!
WE CAN DO THIS... PLEASE.
PLEASE.
BAR, LISTEN TO ME.
YOU WERE A CHILD WHEN OUR PARENTS DIED.
THERE WAS NOTHING YOU COULD HAVE DONE TO CHANGE THAT.
I WAS THERE WHEN YOU WERE GROWING UP--YOU GIVING ME YOUR FOOD, PROTECTING ME FROM EVERY PREDATOR.
I KNOW YOU HAVE THE BIGGEST HEART ON ANY WORLD, BIG BROTHER.
THIS ISN'T YOU.
MOM AND DAD WOULDN'T WANT YOU TO THROW AWAY YOUR LIFE LIKE THIS.
WHAT... WOULD THEY WANT?
YOU ALREADY KNOW.
THEY WOULD WANT YOU TO COME HOME.

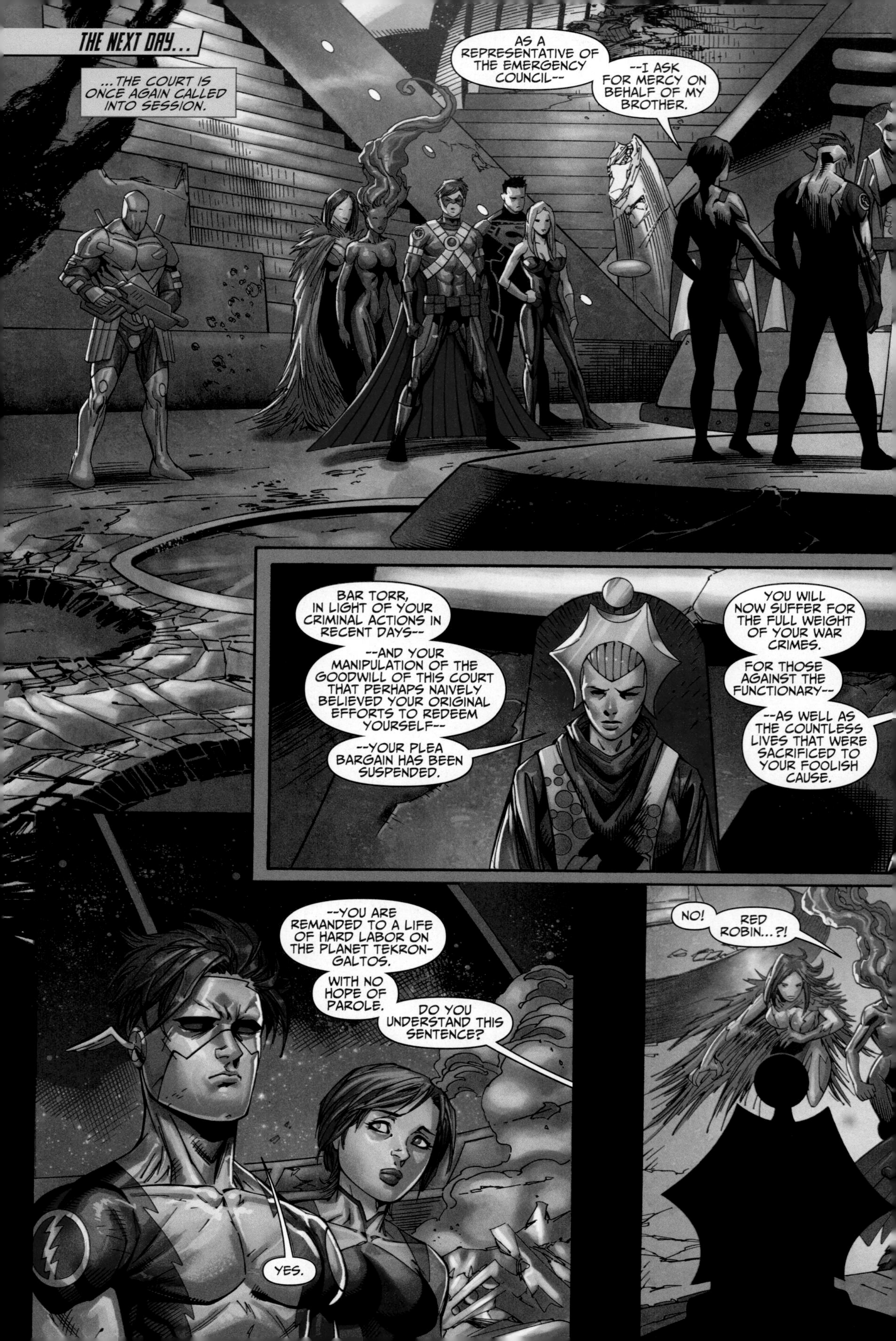
THE NEXT DAY...
...THE COURT IS ONCE AGAIN CALLED INTO SESSION.
AS A REPRESENTATIVE OF THE EMERGENCY COUNCIL--
--I ASK FOR MERCY ON BEHALF OF MY BROTHER.
BAR TORR, IN LIGHT OF YOUR CRIMINAL ACTIONS IN RECENT DAYS--
--AND YOUR MANIPULATION OF THE GOODWILL OF THIS COURT THAT PERHAPS NAIVELY BELIEVED YOUR ORIGINAL EFFORTS TO REDEEM YOURSELF--
--YOUR PLEA BARGAIN HAS BEEN SUSPENDED.
YOU WILL NOW SUFFER FOR THE FULL WEIGHT OF YOUR WAR CRIMES.
FOR THOSE AGAINST THE FUNCTIONARY--
--AS WELL AS THE COUNTLESS LIVES THAT WERE SACRIFICED TO YOUR FOOLISH CAUSE.
--YOU ARE REMANDED TO A LIFE OF HARD LABOR ON THE PLANET TEKRON-GALTOS.
WITH NO HOPE OF PAROLE.
DO YOU UNDERSTAND THIS SENTENCE?
YES.
NO!
RED ROBIN...?!

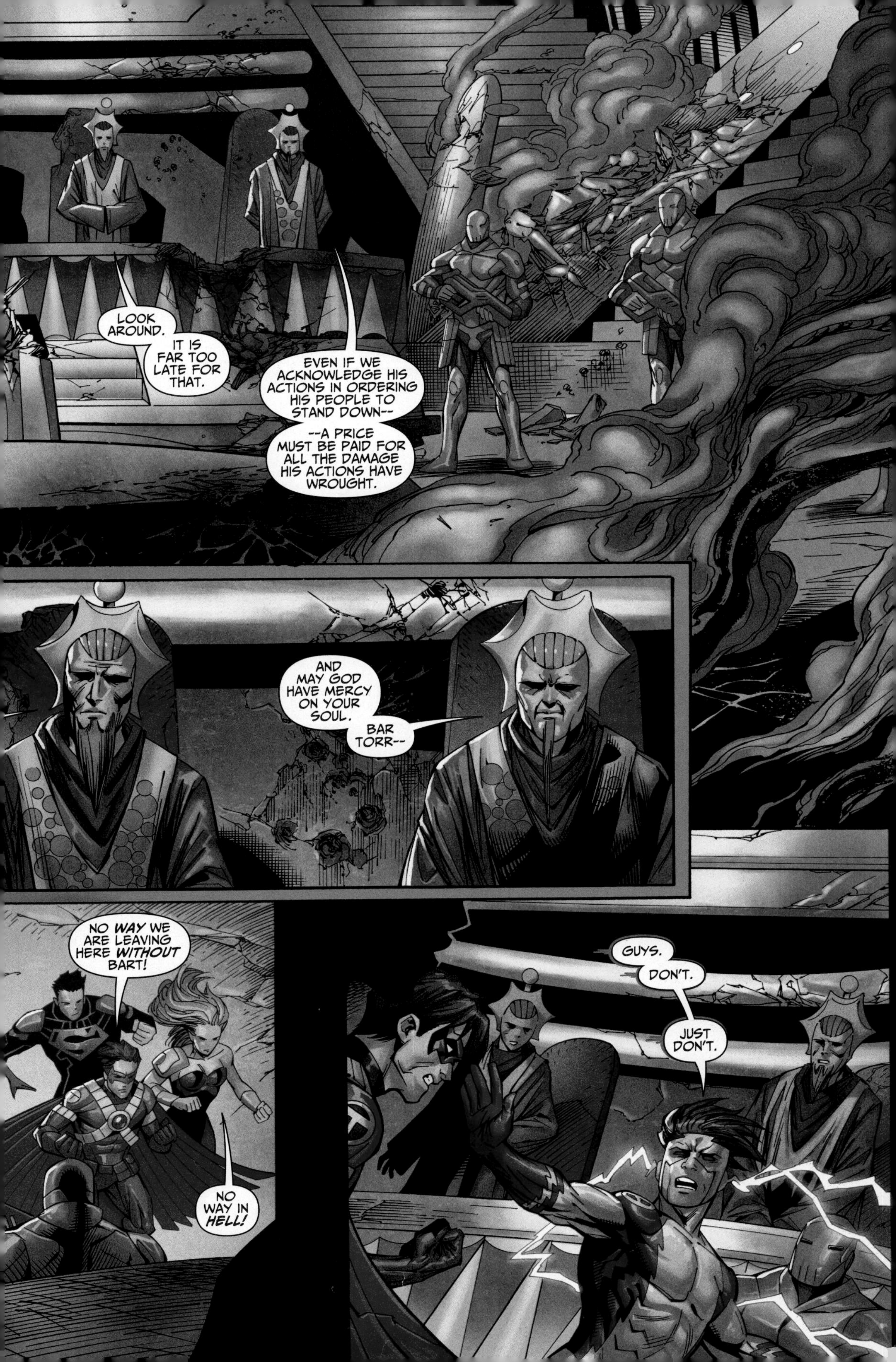

LOOK AROUND.
IT IS FAR TOO LATE FOR THAT.
EVEN IF WE ACKNOWLEDGE HIS ACTIONS IN ORDERING HIS PEOPLE TO STAND DOWN--
--A PRICE MUST BE PAID FOR ALL THE DAMAGE HIS ACTIONS HAVE WROUGHT.
AND MAY GOD HAVE MERCY ON YOUR SOUL.
BAR TORR--
NO WAY WE ARE LEAVING HERE WITHOUT BART!
NO WAY IN HELL!
GUYS.
DON'T.
JUST DON'T.

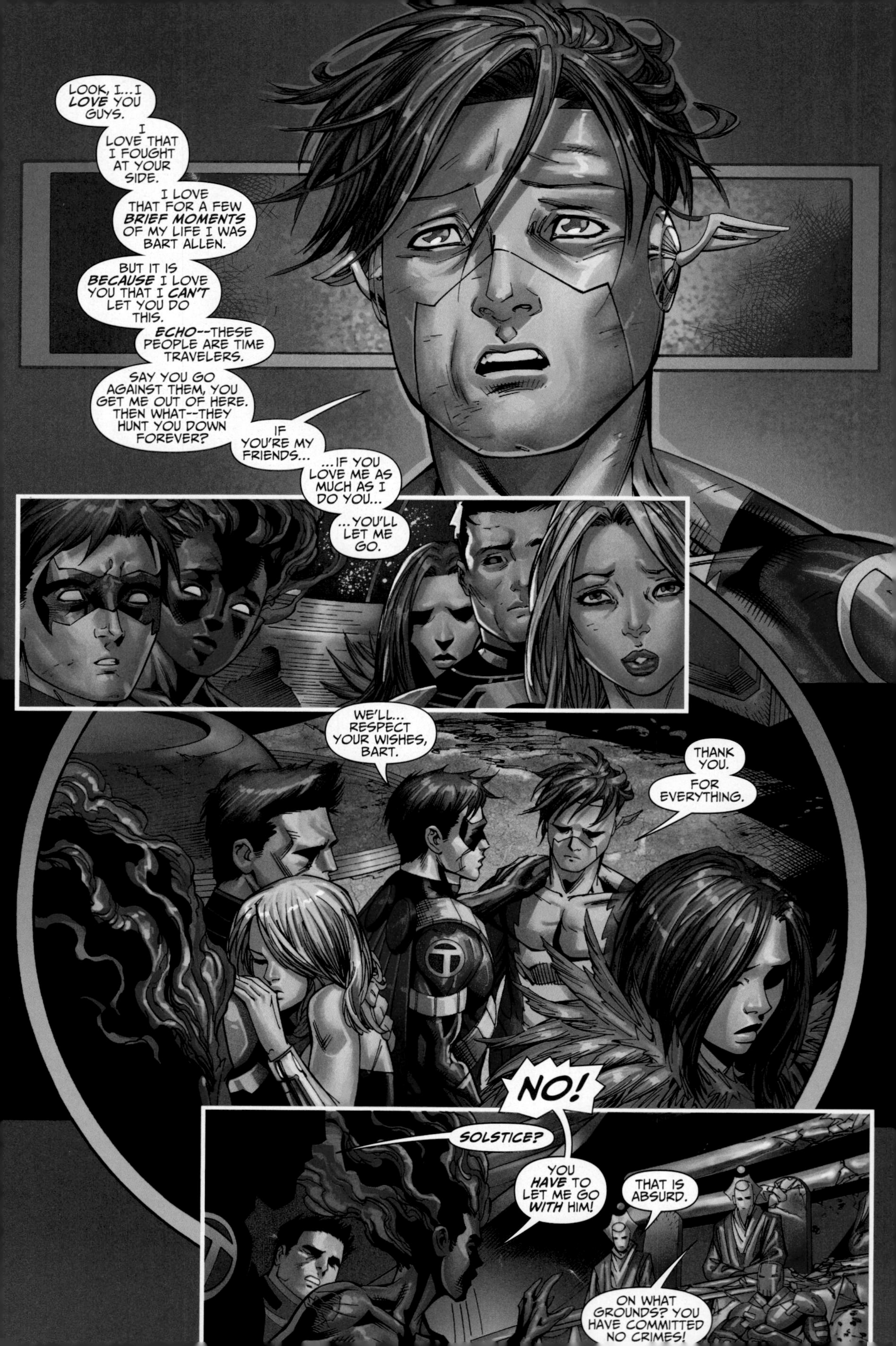
LOOK, I...I LOVE YOU GUYS.
I LOVE THAT I FOUGHT AT YOUR SIDE.
I LOVE THAT FOR A FEW BRIEF MOMENTS OF MY LIFE I WAS BART ALLEN.
BUT IT IS BECAUSE I LOVE YOU THAT I CAN'T LET YOU DO THIS.
ECHO--THESE PEOPLE ARE TIME TRAVELERS.
SAY YOU GO AGAINST THEM, YOU GET ME OUT OF HERE. THEN WHAT--THEY HUNT YOU DOWN FOREVER?
IF YOU'RE MY FRIENDS...
...IF YOU LOVE ME AS MUCH AS I DO YOU...
...YOU'LL LET ME GO.
WE'LL... RESPECT YOUR WISHES, BART.
THANK YOU.
FOR EVERYTHING.
NO!
SOLSTICE?
YOU HAVE TO LET ME GO WITH HIM!
THAT IS ABSURD.
ON WHAT GROUNDS? YOU HAVE COMMITTED NO CRIMES!

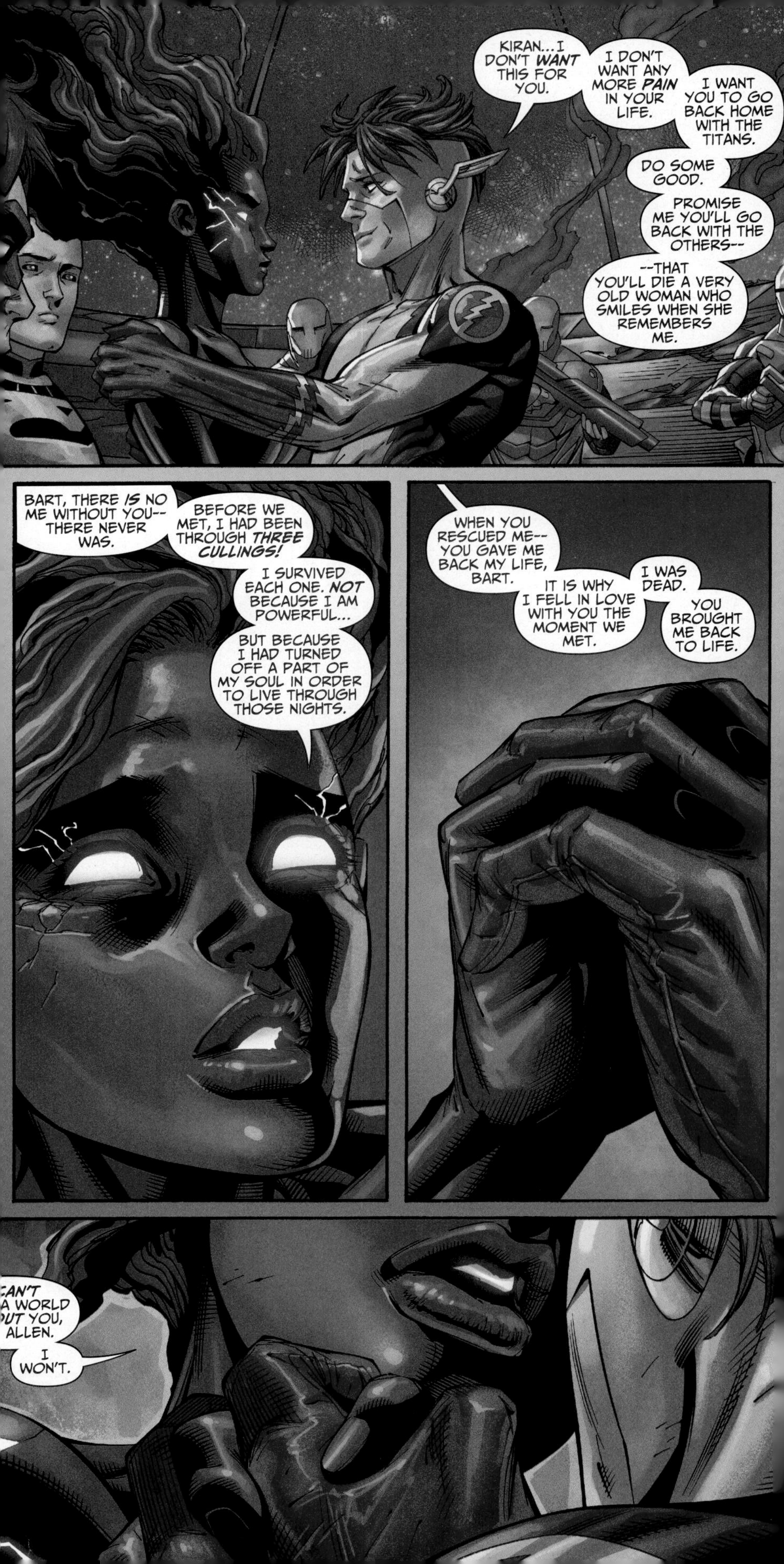
KIRAN... I DON'T *WANT* THIS FOR YOU.
I DON'T WANT ANY MORE *PAIN* IN YOUR LIFE.
I WANT YOU TO GO BACK HOME WITH THE TITANS.
DO SOME GOOD.
PROMISE ME YOU'LL GO BACK WITH THE OTHERS--
--THAT YOU'LL DIE A VERY OLD WOMAN WHO SMILES WHEN SHE REMEMBERS ME.
BART, THERE *IS* NO ME WITHOUT YOU--THERE NEVER WAS.
BEFORE WE MET, I HAD BEEN THROUGH *THREE CULLINGS!*
I SURVIVED EACH ONE. *NOT* BECAUSE I AM POWERFUL...
BUT BECAUSE I HAD TURNED OFF A PART OF MY SOUL IN ORDER TO LIVE THROUGH THOSE NIGHTS.
WHEN YOU RESCUED ME--YOU GAVE ME BACK MY LIFE, BART.
IT IS WHY I FELL IN LOVE WITH YOU THE MOMENT WE MET.
I WAS DEAD.
YOU BROUGHT ME BACK TO LIFE.
CAN'T A WORLD *OUT* YOU, ALLEN.
I WON'T.

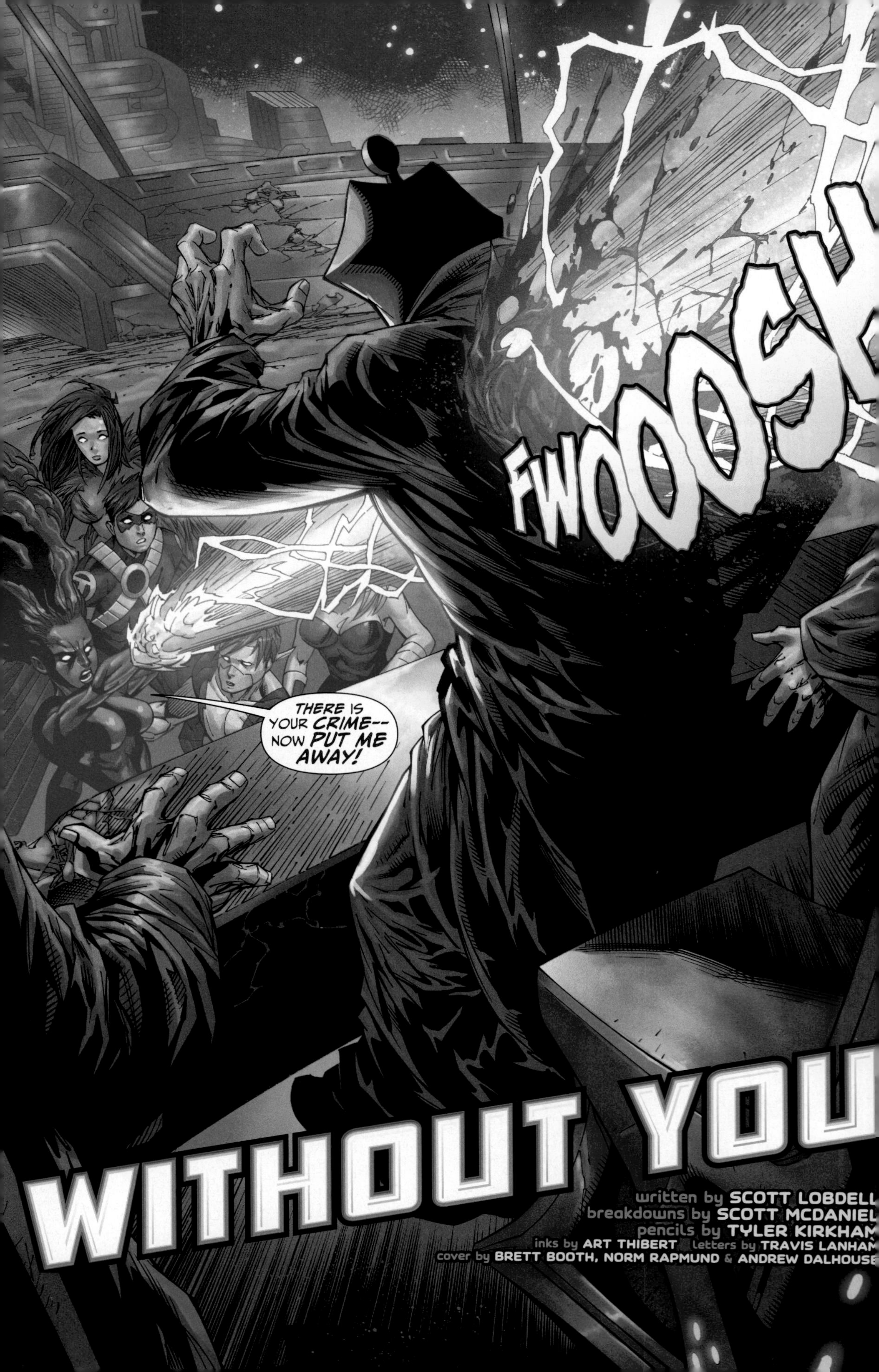
FWOOOSH
THERE IS YOUR CRIME-- NOW PUT ME AWAY!
WITHOUT YOU
written by SCOTT LOBDELL
breakdowns by SCOTT MCDANIEL
pencils by TYLER KIRKHAM
inks by ART THIBERT letters by TRAVIS LANHAM
cover by BRETT BOOTH, NORM RAPMUND & ANDREW DALHOUSE

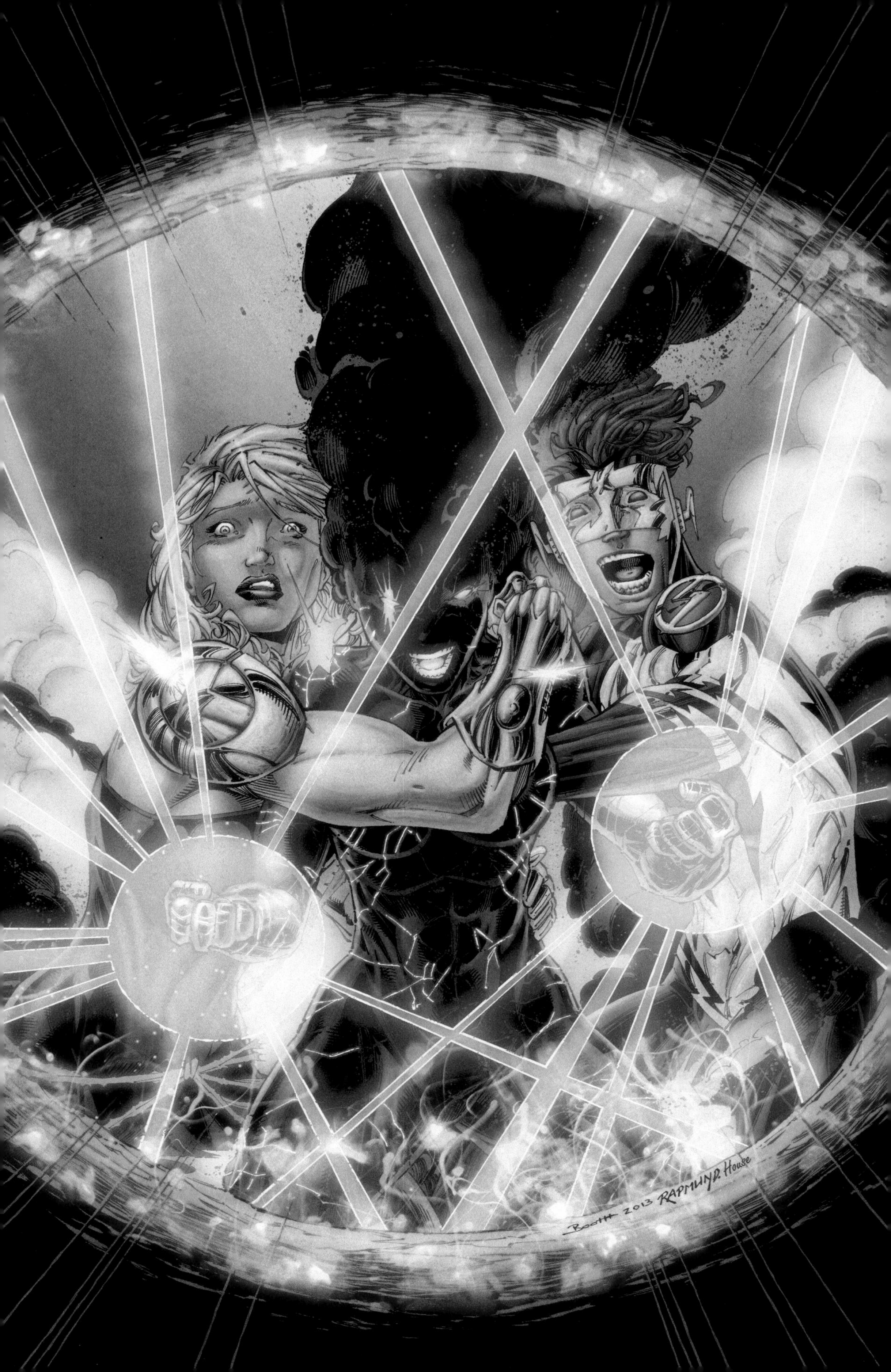
BOOTH 2013 RAPMUND House

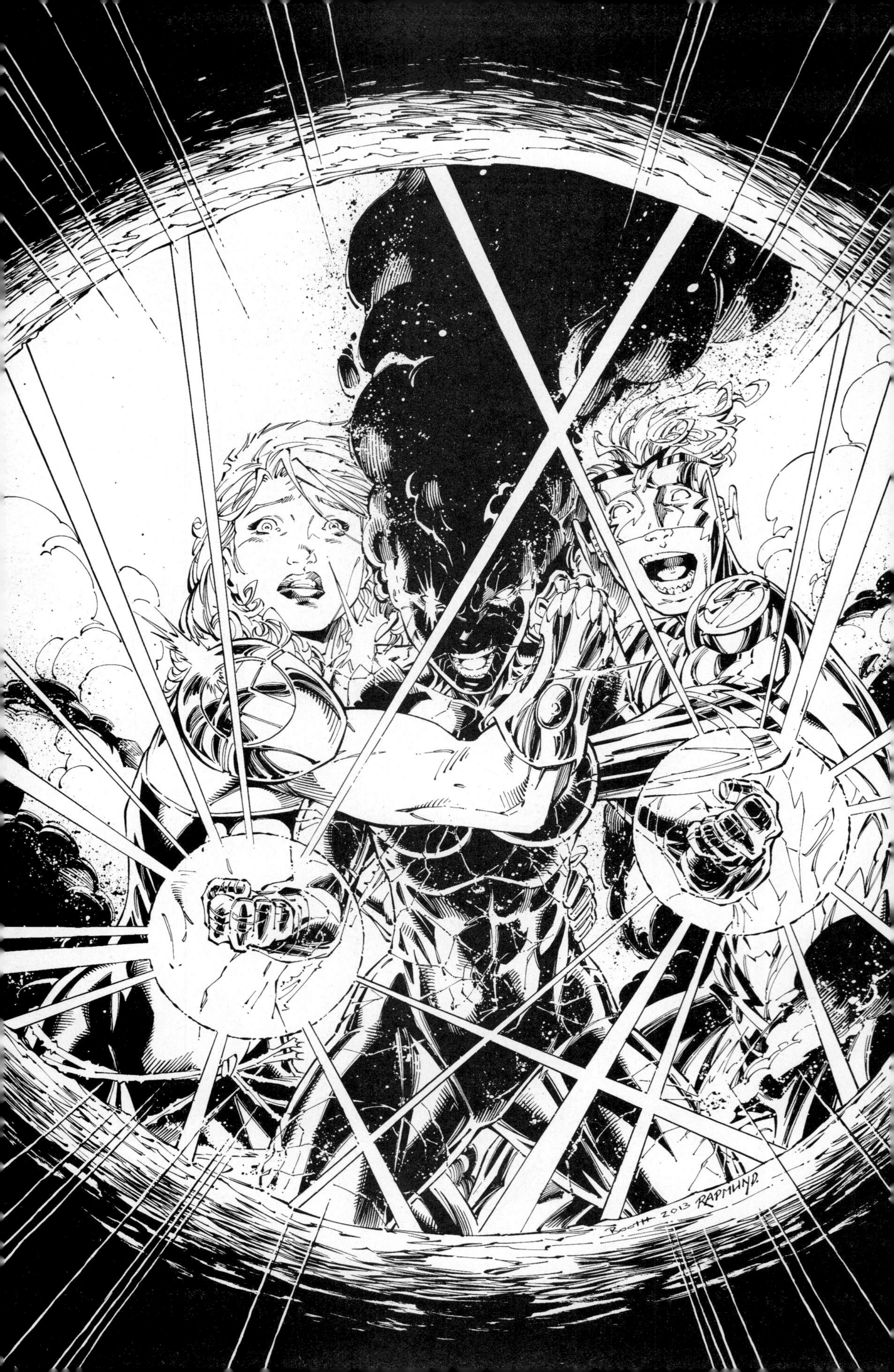
BOOTH 2013 RAPMUND.

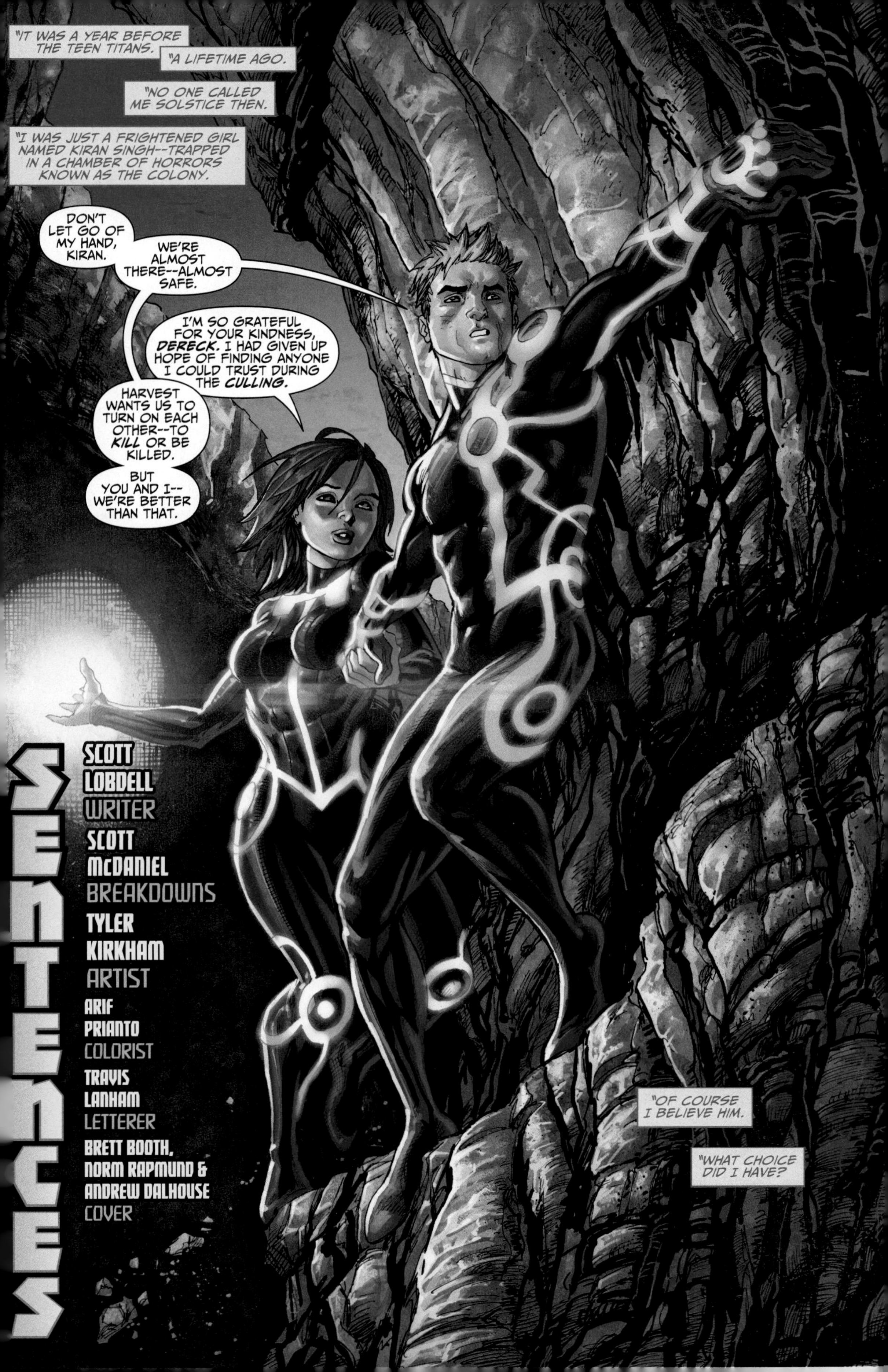
"IT WAS A YEAR BEFORE THE TEEN TITANS.
"A LIFETIME AGO.
"NO ONE CALLED ME SOLSTICE THEN.
"I WAS JUST A FRIGHTENED GIRL NAMED KIRAN SINGH--TRAPPED IN A CHAMBER OF HORRORS KNOWN AS THE COLONY.
DON'T LET GO OF MY HAND, KIRAN.
WE'RE ALMOST THERE--ALMOST SAFE.
I'M SO GRATEFUL FOR YOUR KINDNESS, DERECK. I HAD GIVEN UP HOPE OF FINDING ANYONE I COULD TRUST DURING THE CULLING.
HARVEST WANTS US TO TURN ON EACH OTHER--TO KILL OR BE KILLED.
BUT YOU AND I--WE'RE BETTER THAN THAT.
SENTENCES
SCOTT LOBDELL WRITER
SCOTT McDANIEL BREAKDOWNS
TYLER KIRKHAM ARTIST
ARIF PRIANTO COLORIST
TRAVIS LANHAM LETTERER
BRETT BOOTH, NORM RAPMUND & ANDREW DALHOUSE COVER
"OF COURSE I BELIEVE HIM.
"WHAT CHOICE DID I HAVE?

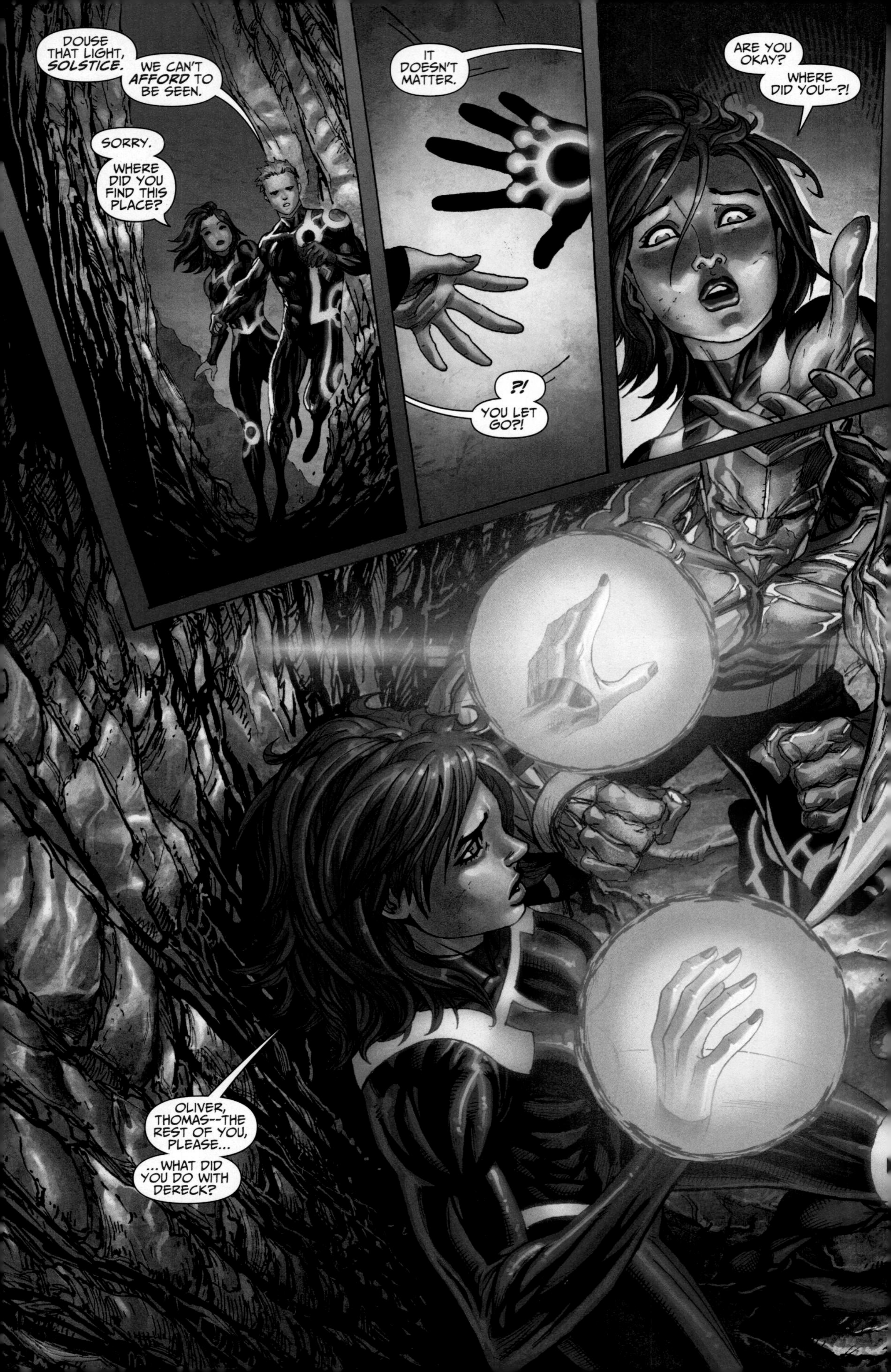
DOUSE THAT LIGHT, SOLSTICE.
WE CAN'T AFFORD TO BE SEEN.
SORRY.
WHERE DID YOU FIND THIS PLACE?
IT DOESN'T MATTER.
?!
YOU LET GO?!
ARE YOU OKAY?
WHERE DID YOU--?!
OLIVER, THOMAS--THE REST OF YOU, PLEASE...
...WHAT DID YOU DO WITH DERECK?

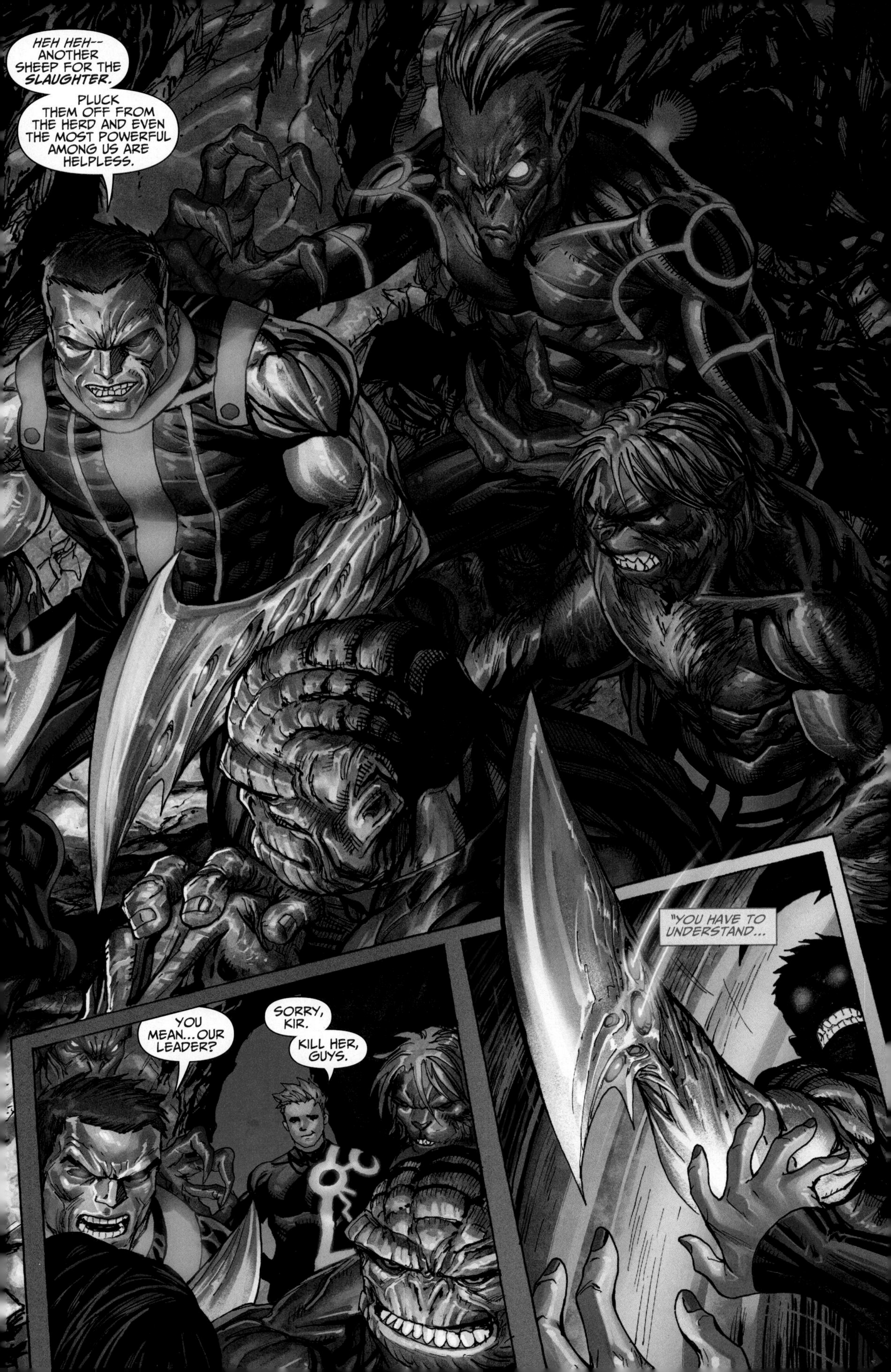
HEH HEH-- ANOTHER SHEEP FOR THE *SLAUGHTER.*
PLUCK THEM OFF FROM THE HERD AND EVEN THE MOST POWERFUL AMONG US ARE HELPLESS.
"YOU HAVE TO UNDERSTAND...
YOU MEAN...OUR LEADER?
SORRY, KIR.
KILL HER, GUYS.

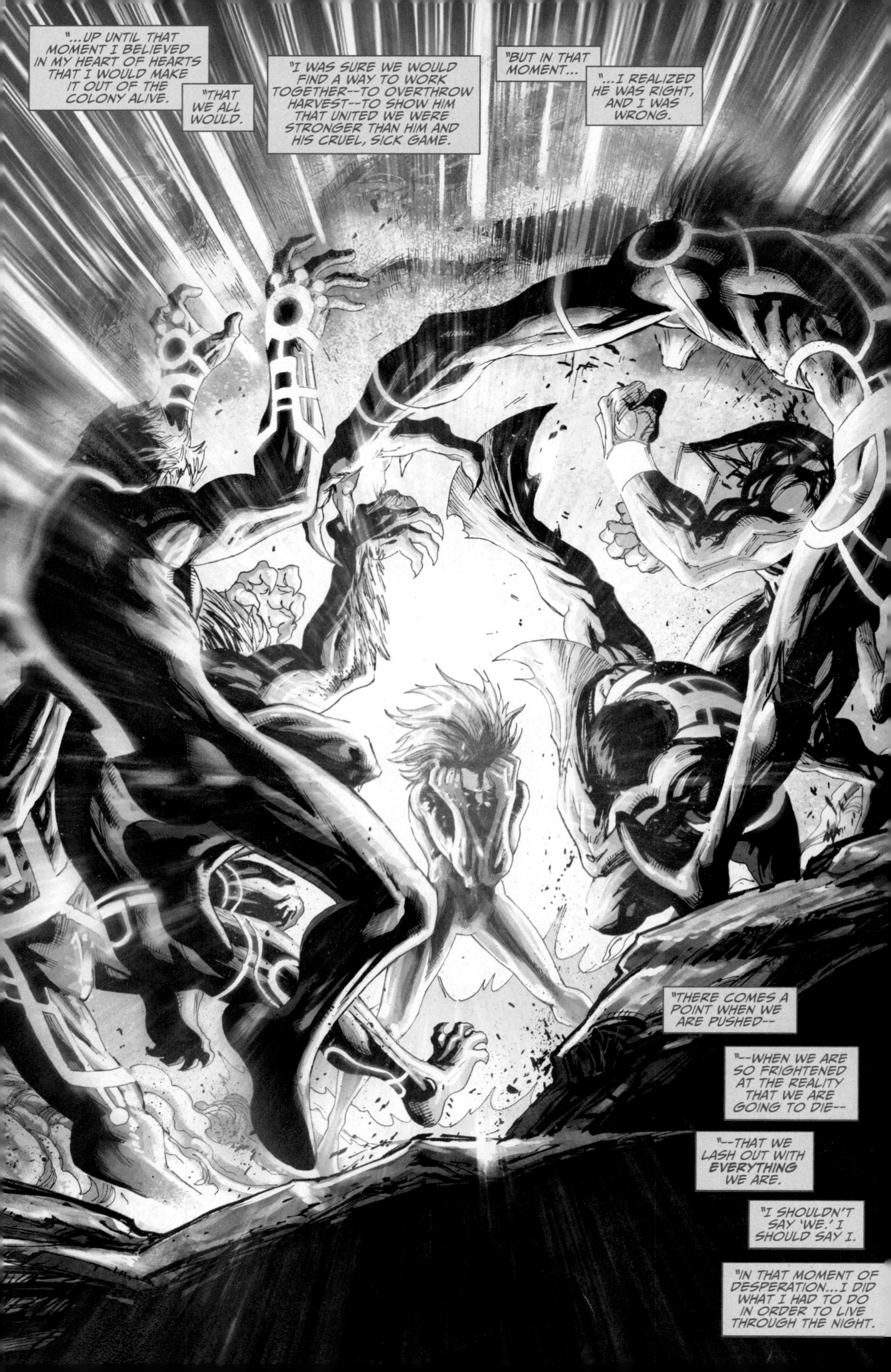
"...UP UNTIL THAT MOMENT I BELIEVED IN MY HEART OF HEARTS THAT I WOULD MAKE IT OUT OF THE COLONY ALIVE.
"THAT WE ALL WOULD.
"I WAS SURE WE WOULD FIND A WAY TO WORK TOGETHER--TO OVERTHROW HARVEST--TO SHOW HIM THAT UNITED WE WERE STRONGER THAN HIM AND HIS CRUEL, SICK GAME.
"BUT IN THAT MOMENT...
"...I REALIZED HE WAS RIGHT, AND I WAS WRONG.
"THERE COMES A POINT WHEN WE ARE PUSHED--
"--WHEN WE ARE SO FRIGHTENED AT THE REALITY THAT WE ARE GOING TO DIE--
"--THAT WE LASH OUT WITH EVERYTHING WE ARE.
"I SHOULDN'T SAY 'WE.' I SHOULD SAY I.
"IN THAT MOMENT OF DESPERATION...I DID WHAT I HAD TO DO IN ORDER TO LIVE THROUGH THE NIGHT.

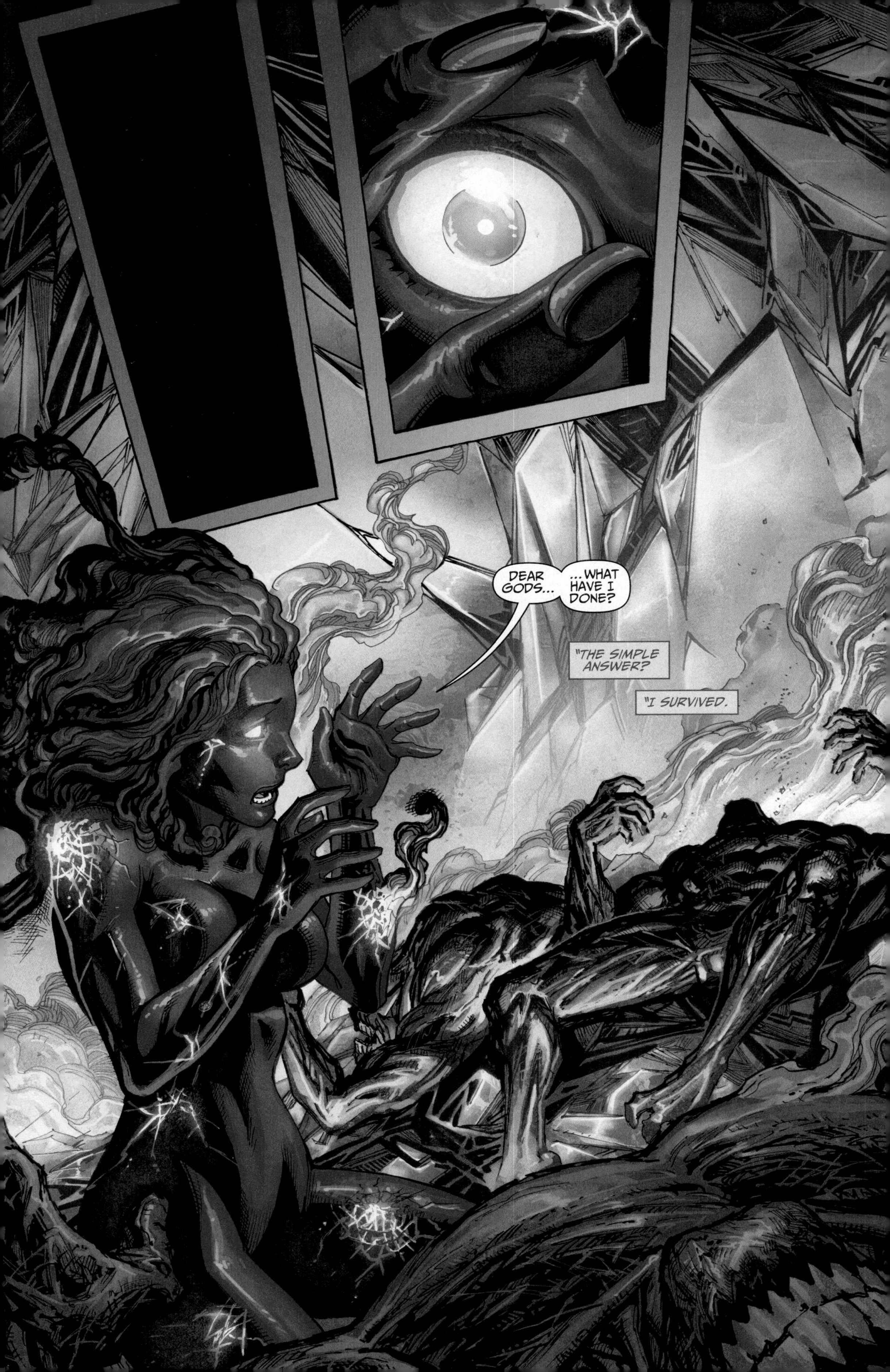

DEAR GODS...
...WHAT HAVE I DONE?
"THE SIMPLE ANSWER?
"I SURVIVED.

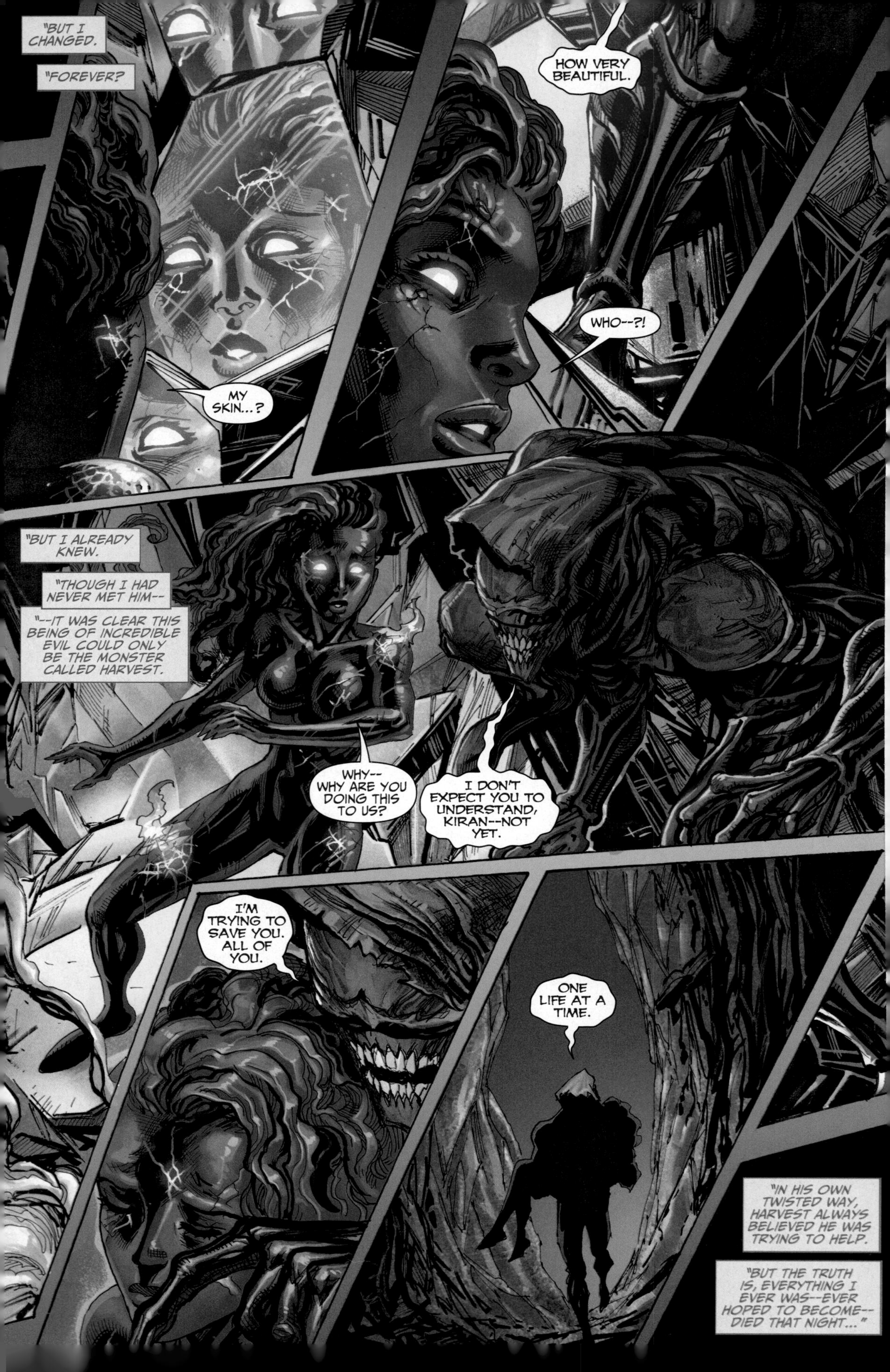
"BUT I CHANGED.
"FOREVER?
MY SKIN...?
HOW VERY BEAUTIFUL.
WHO--?!
"BUT I ALREADY KNEW.
"THOUGH I HAD NEVER MET HIM--
"--IT WAS CLEAR THIS BEING OF INCREDIBLE EVIL COULD ONLY BE THE MONSTER CALLED HARVEST.
WHY-- WHY ARE YOU DOING THIS TO US?
I DON'T EXPECT YOU TO UNDERSTAND, KIRAN--NOT YET.
I'M TRYING TO SAVE YOU. ALL OF YOU.
ONE LIFE AT A TIME.
"IN HIS OWN TWISTED WAY, HARVEST ALWAYS BELIEVED HE WAS TRYING TO HELP.
"BUT THE TRUTH IS, EVERYTHING I EVER WAS--EVER HOPED TO BECOME--DIED THAT NIGHT..."

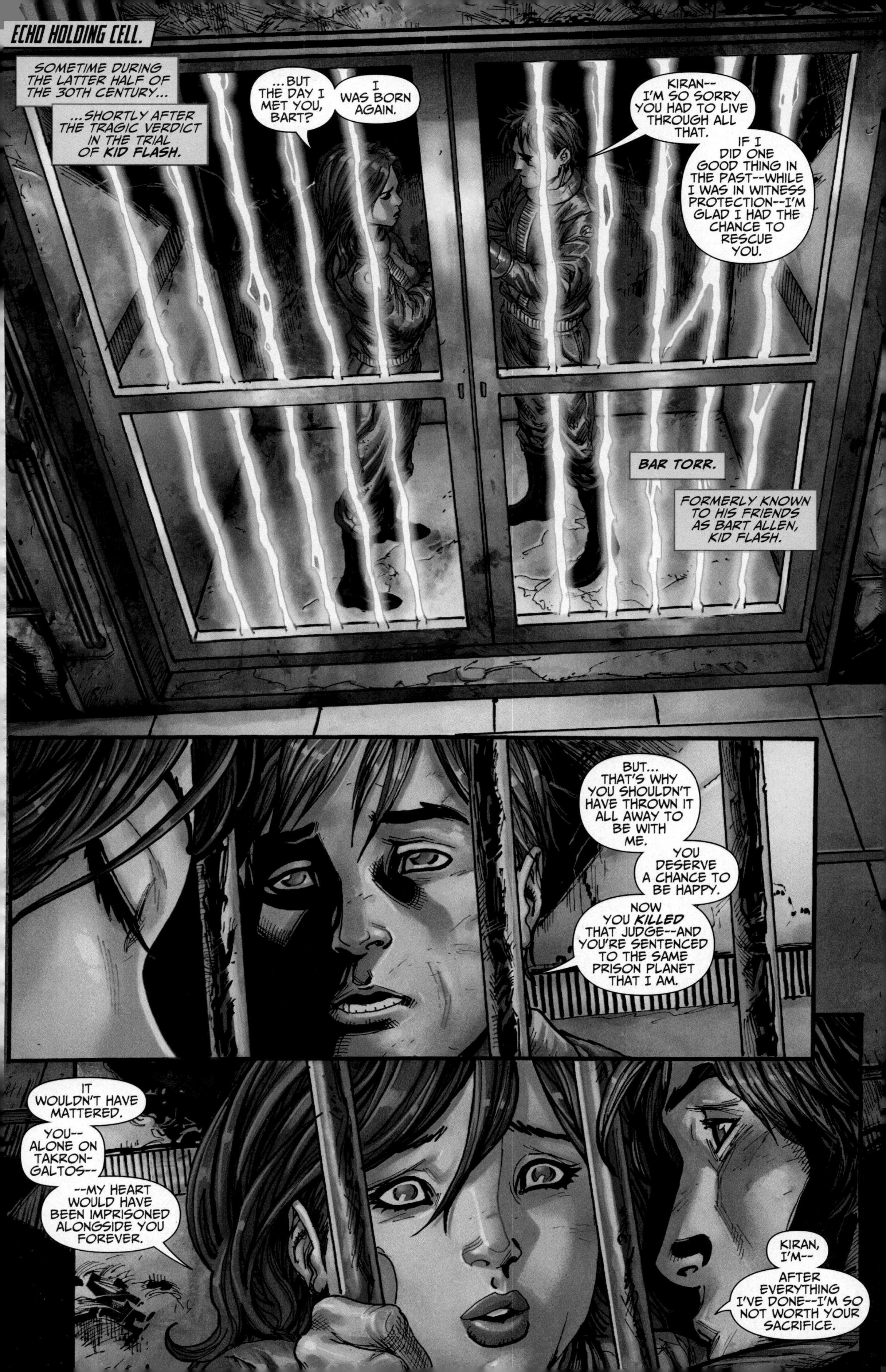
ECHO HOLDING CELL.
SOMETIME DURING THE LATTER HALF OF THE 30TH CENTURY...
...SHORTLY AFTER THE TRAGIC VERDICT IN THE TRIAL OF KID FLASH.
...BUT THE DAY I MET YOU, BART?
I WAS BORN AGAIN.
KIRAN-- I'M SO SORRY YOU HAD TO LIVE THROUGH ALL THAT.
IF I DID ONE GOOD THING IN THE PAST--WHILE I WAS IN WITNESS PROTECTION--I'M GLAD I HAD THE CHANCE TO RESCUE YOU.
BAR TORR.
FORMERLY KNOWN TO HIS FRIENDS AS BART ALLEN, KID FLASH.
BUT... THAT'S WHY YOU SHOULDN'T HAVE THROWN IT ALL AWAY TO BE WITH ME.
YOU DESERVE A CHANCE TO BE HAPPY.
NOW YOU KILLED THAT JUDGE--AND YOU'RE SENTENCED TO THE SAME PRISON PLANET THAT I AM.
IT WOULDN'T HAVE MATTERED.
YOU-- ALONE ON TAKRON-GALTOS--
--MY HEART WOULD HAVE BEEN IMPRISONED ALONGSIDE YOU FOREVER.
KIRAN, I'M--
AFTER EVERYTHING I'VE DONE--I'M SO NOT WORTH YOUR SACRIFICE.

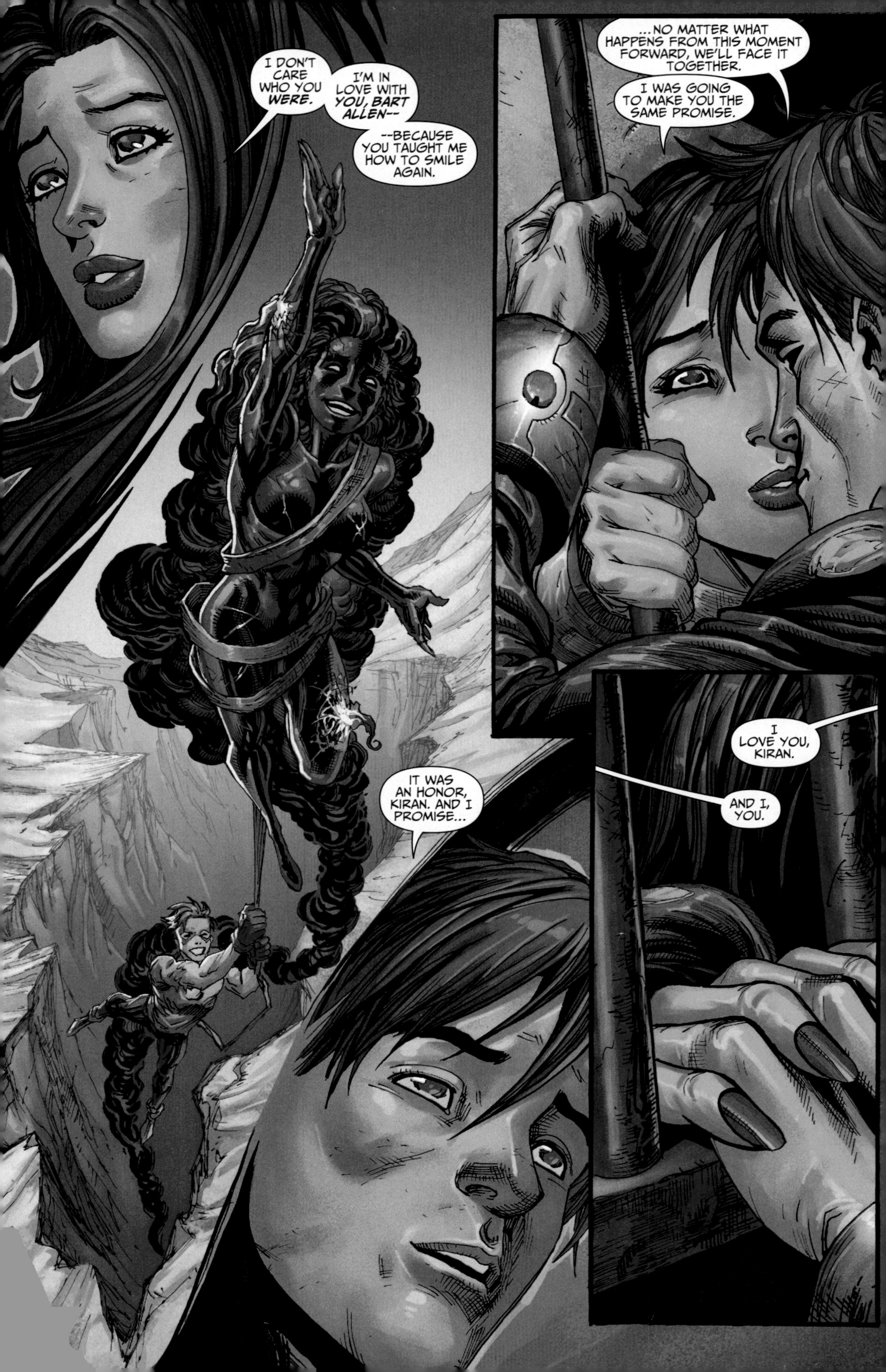
I DON'T CARE WHO YOU *WERE*.
I'M IN LOVE WITH *YOU, BART ALLEN*--
--BECAUSE YOU TAUGHT ME HOW TO SMILE AGAIN.
IT WAS AN HONOR, KIRAN. AND I PROMISE...
...NO MATTER WHAT HAPPENS FROM THIS MOMENT FORWARD, WE'LL FACE IT TOGETHER.
I WAS GOING TO MAKE YOU THE SAME PROMISE.
I LOVE YOU, KIRAN.
AND I, YOU.

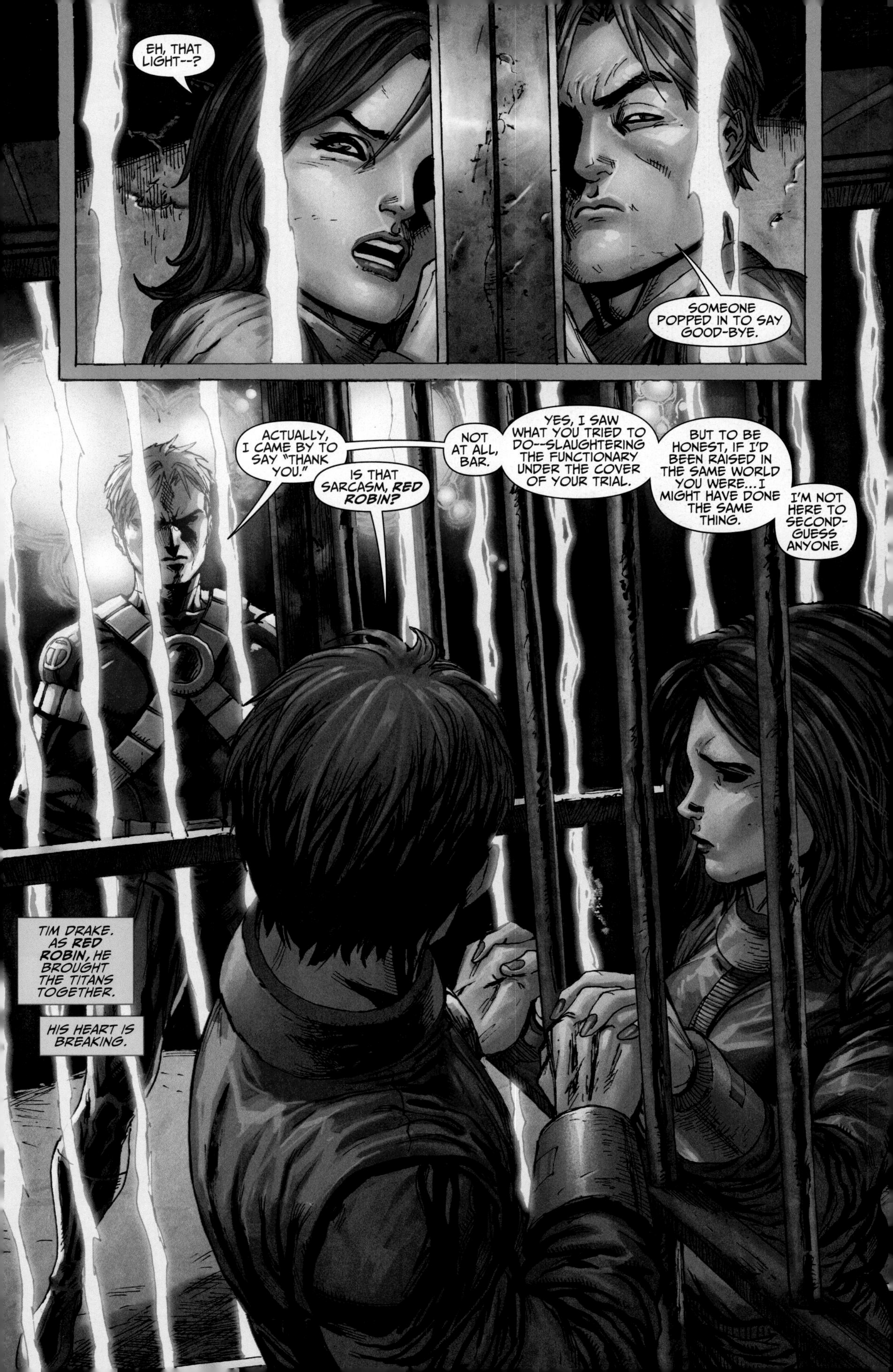
EH, THAT LIGHT--?
SOMEONE POPPED IN TO SAY GOOD-BYE.
ACTUALLY, I CAME BY TO SAY "THANK YOU."
IS THAT SARCASM, RED ROBIN?
NOT AT ALL, BAR.
YES, I SAW WHAT YOU TRIED TO DO--SLAUGHTERING THE FUNCTIONARY UNDER THE COVER OF YOUR TRIAL.
BUT TO BE HONEST, IF I'D BEEN RAISED IN THE SAME WORLD YOU WERE... I MIGHT HAVE DONE THE SAME THING.
I'M NOT HERE TO SECOND-GUESS ANYONE.
TIM DRAKE. AS RED ROBIN, HE BROUGHT THE TITANS TOGETHER.
HIS HEART IS BREAKING.

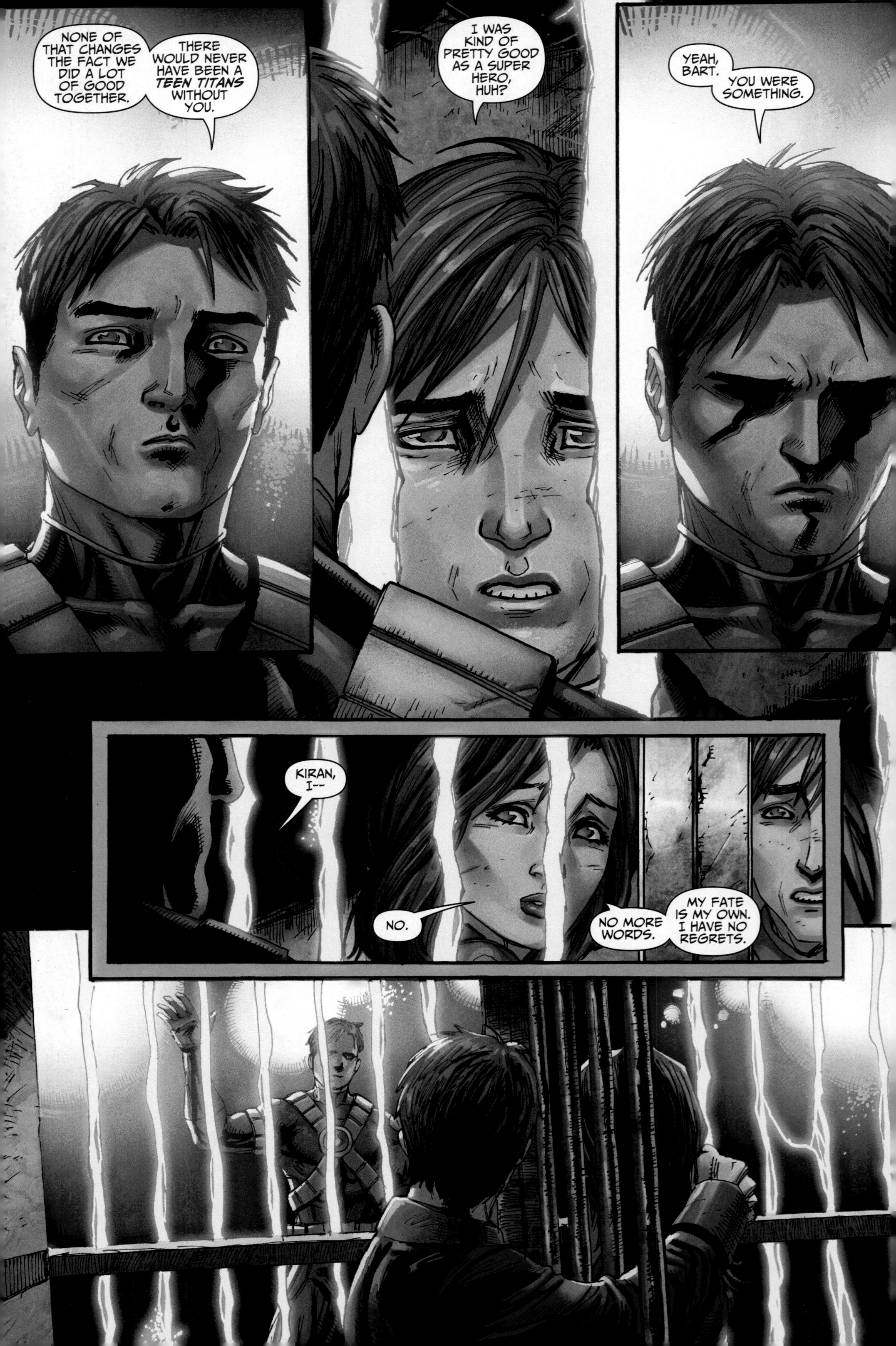

NONE OF THAT CHANGES THE FACT WE DID A LOT OF GOOD TOGETHER.
THERE WOULD NEVER HAVE BEEN A *TEEN TITANS* WITHOUT YOU.
I WAS KIND OF PRETTY GOOD AS A SUPER HERO, HUH?
YEAH, BART.
YOU WERE SOMETHING.
KIRAN, I--
NO.
NO MORE WORDS.
MY FATE IS MY OWN. I HAVE NO REGRETS.

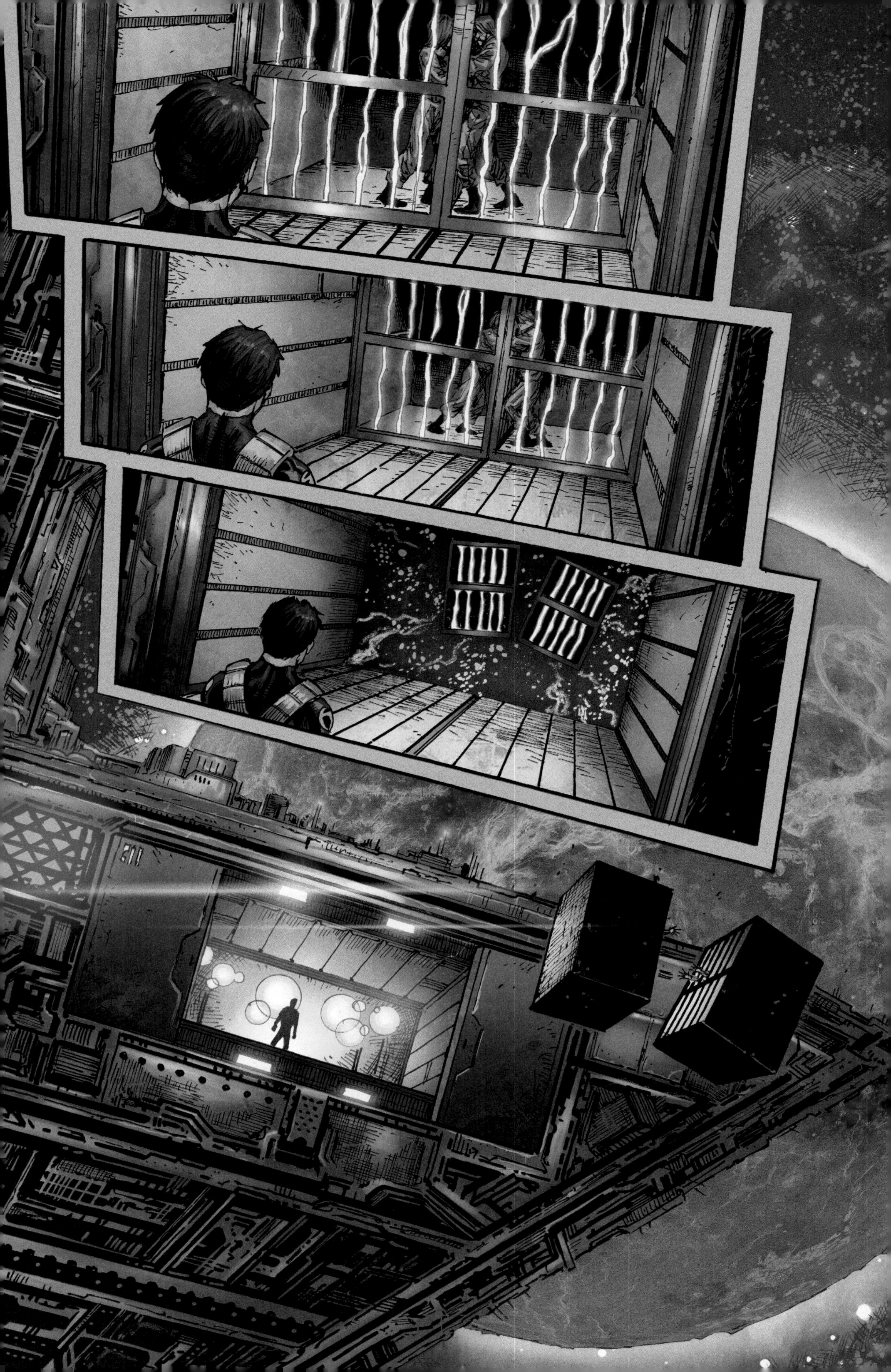

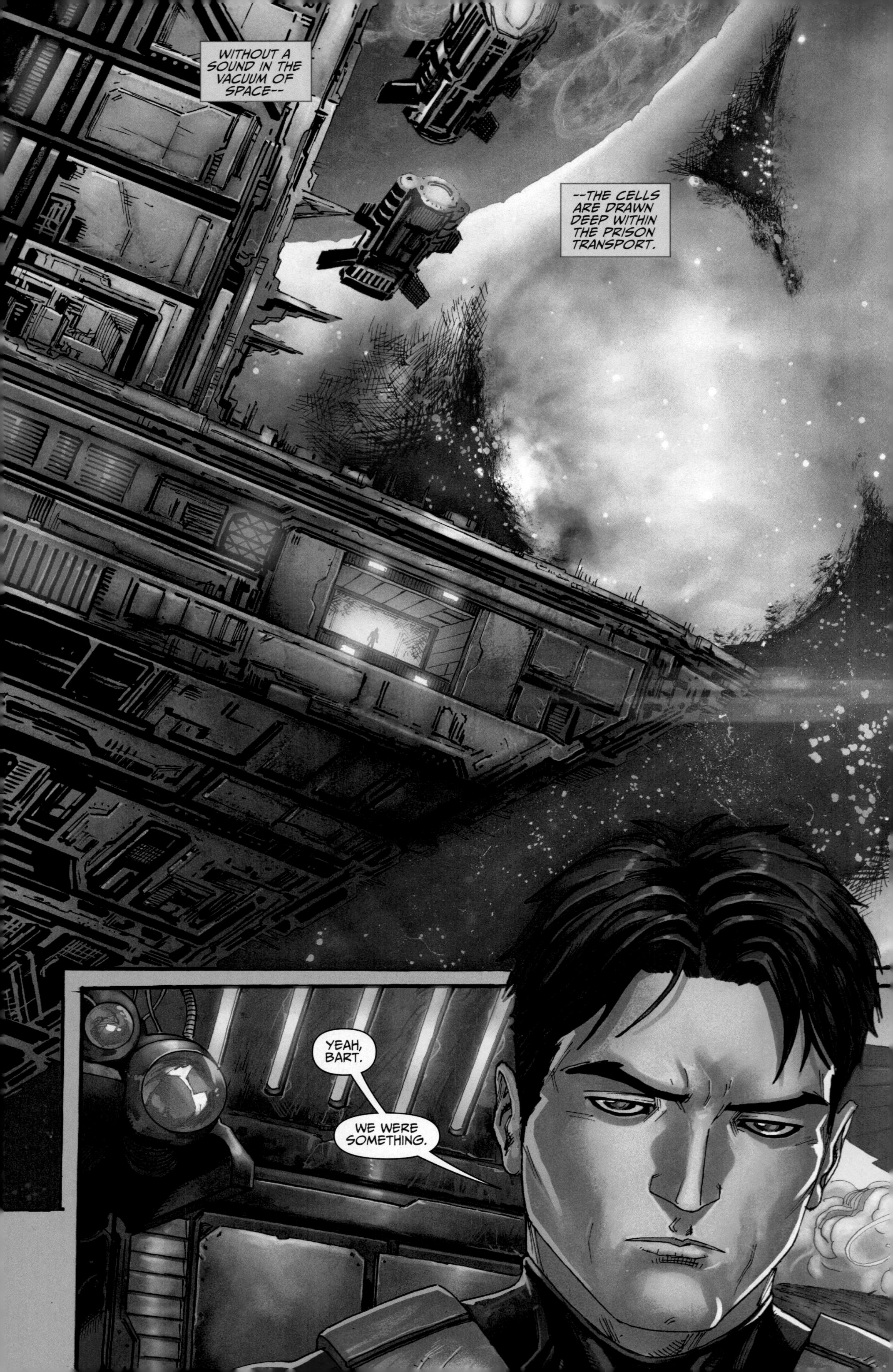
WITHOUT A SOUND IN THE VACUUM OF SPACE--
--THE CELLS ARE DRAWN DEEP WITHIN THE PRISON TRANSPORT.
YEAH, BART.
WE WERE SOMETHING.

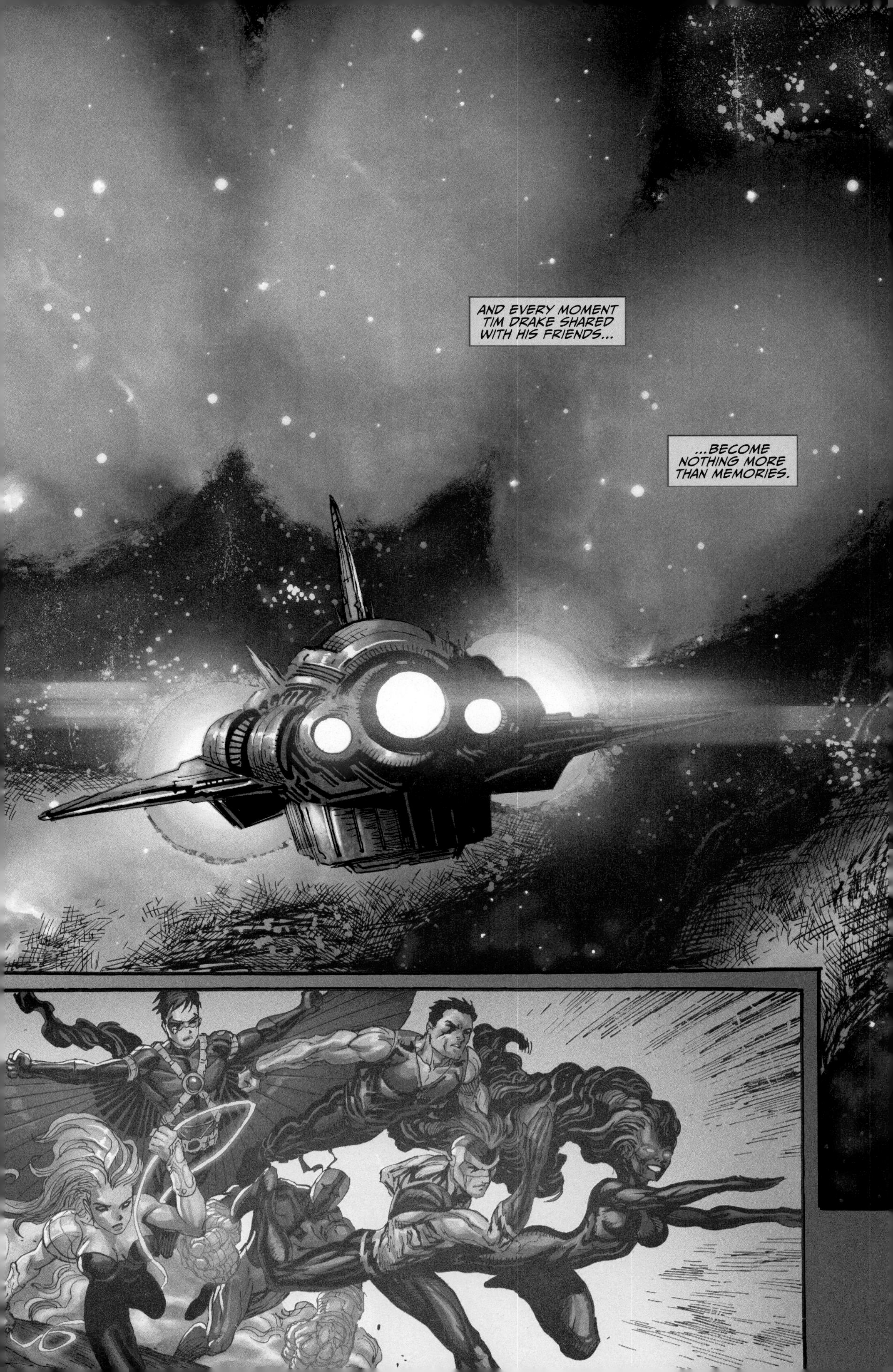
AND EVERY MOMENT TIM DRAKE SHARED WITH HIS FRIENDS...
...BECOME NOTHING MORE THAN MEMORIES.

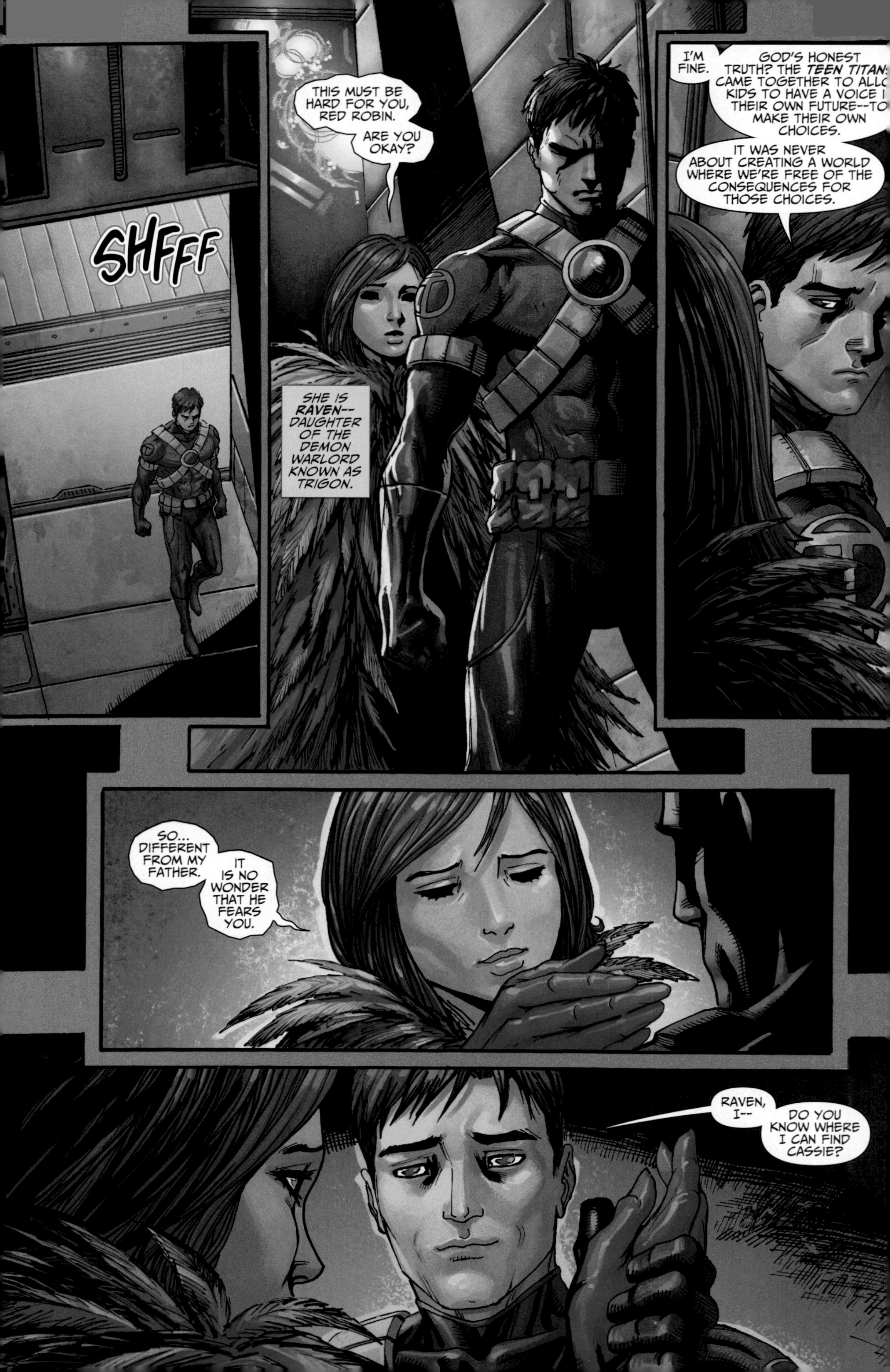
SHFFF
THIS MUST BE HARD FOR YOU, RED ROBIN.
ARE YOU OKAY?
SHE IS RAVEN--DAUGHTER OF THE DEMON WARLORD KNOWN AS TRIGON.
I'M FINE.
GOD'S HONEST TRUTH? THE TEEN TITAN CAME TOGETHER TO ALLO KIDS TO HAVE A VOICE I THEIR OWN FUTURE--TO MAKE THEIR OWN CHOICES.
IT WAS NEVER ABOUT CREATING A WORLD WHERE WE'RE FREE OF THE CONSEQUENCES FOR THOSE CHOICES.
SO... DIFFERENT FROM MY FATHER.
IT IS NO WONDER THAT HE FEARS YOU.
RAVEN, I--
DO YOU KNOW WHERE I CAN FIND CASSIE?

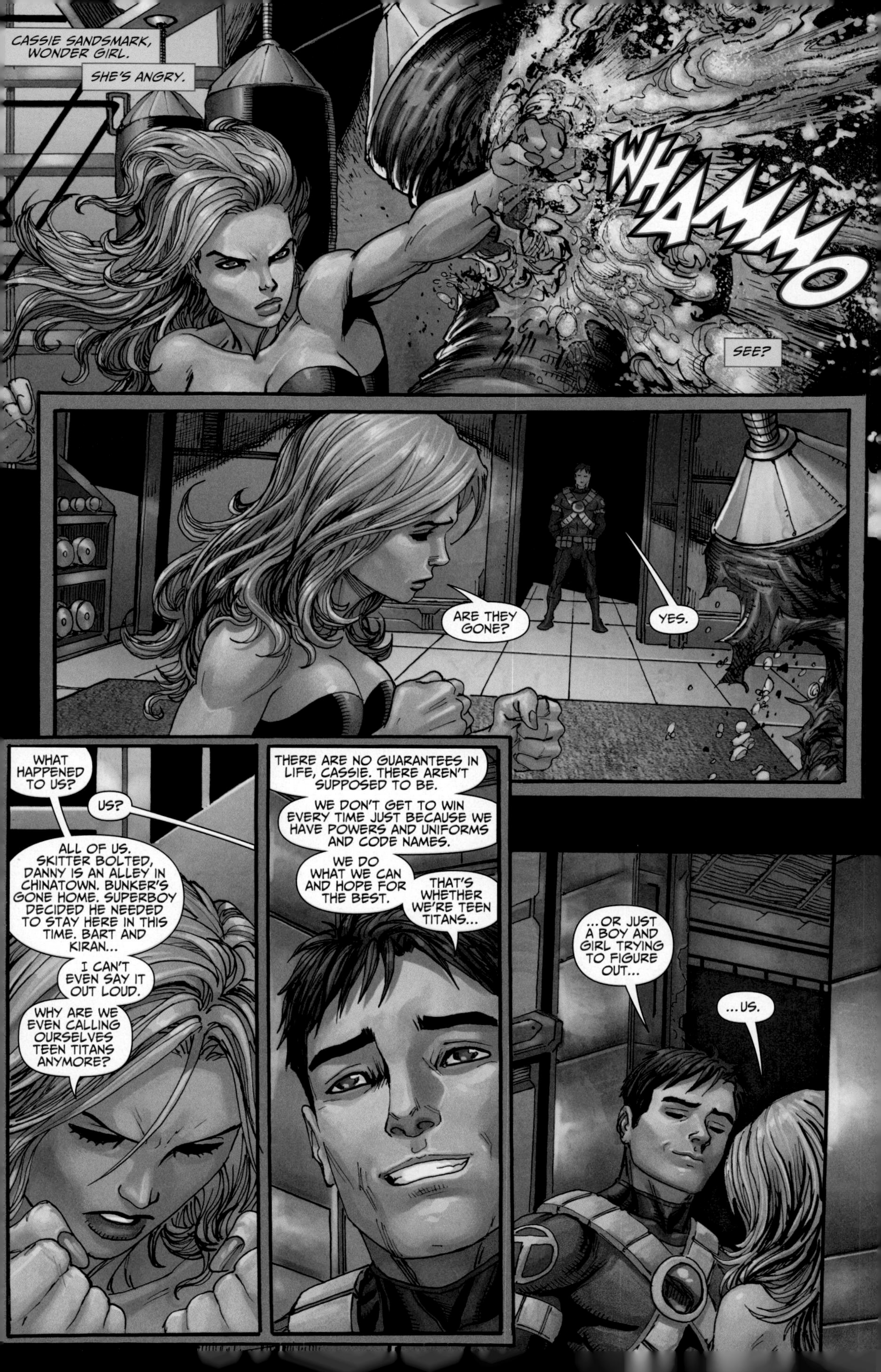
CASSIE SANDSMARK, WONDER GIRL.
SHE'S ANGRY.
WHAMMO
SEE?
ARE THEY GONE?
YES.
WHAT HAPPENED TO US?
US?
ALL OF US. SKITTER BOLTED, DANNY IS AN ALLEY IN CHINATOWN. BUNKER'S GONE HOME. SUPERBOY DECIDED HE NEEDED TO STAY HERE IN THIS TIME. BART AND KIRAN...
I CAN'T EVEN SAY IT OUT LOUD.
WHY ARE WE EVEN CALLING OURSELVES TEEN TITANS ANYMORE?
THERE ARE NO GUARANTEES IN LIFE, CASSIE. THERE AREN'T SUPPOSED TO BE.
WE DON'T GET TO WIN EVERY TIME JUST BECAUSE WE HAVE POWERS AND UNIFORMS AND CODE NAMES.
WE DO WHAT WE CAN AND HOPE FOR THE BEST.
THAT'S WHETHER WE'RE TEEN TITANS...
...OR JUST A BOY AND GIRL TRYING TO FIGURE OUT...
...US.

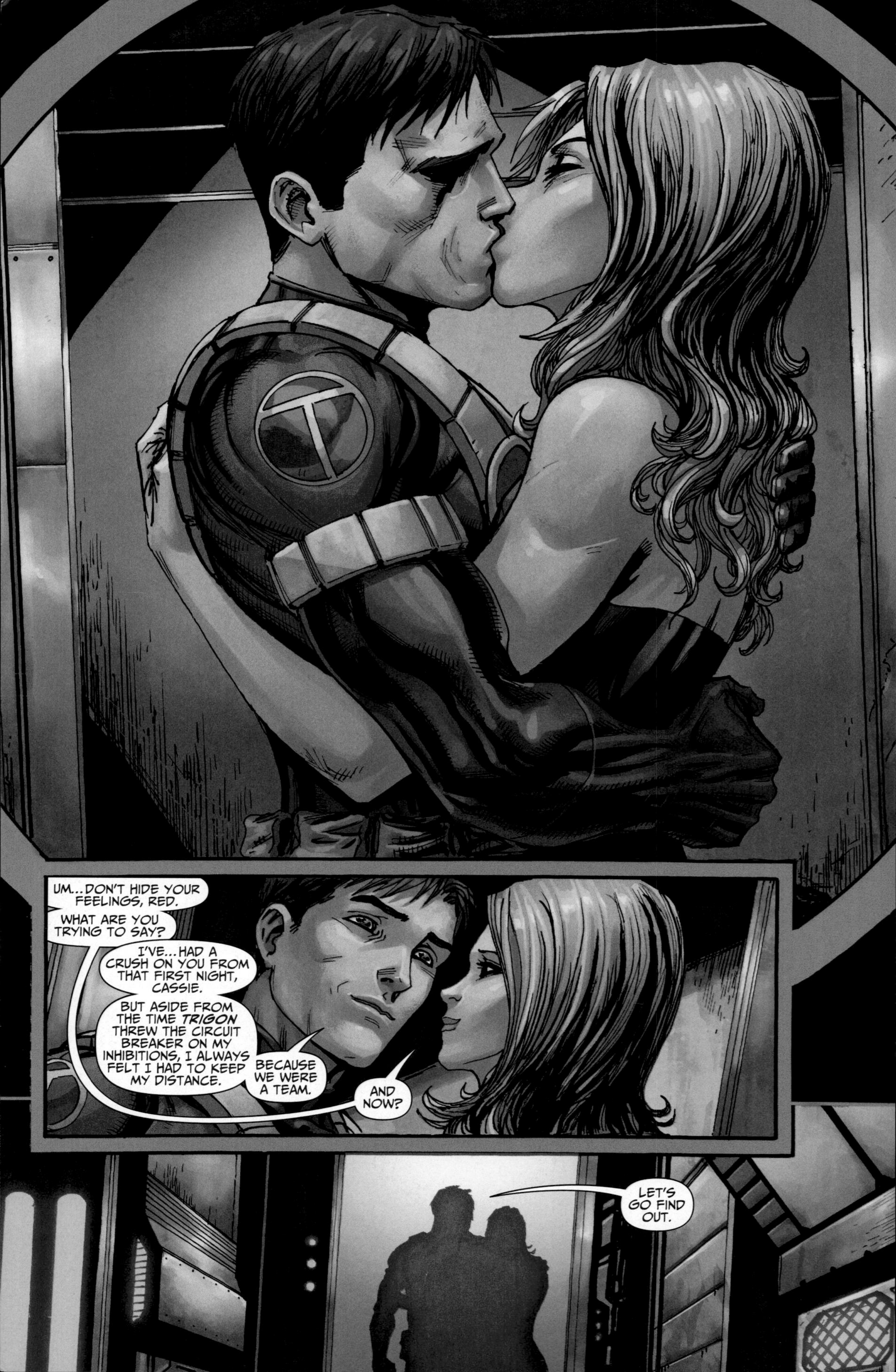
UM...DON'T HIDE YOUR FEELINGS, RED.
WHAT ARE YOU TRYING TO SAY?
I'VE...HAD A CRUSH ON YOU FROM THAT FIRST NIGHT, CASSIE.
BUT ASIDE FROM THE TIME TRIGON THREW THE CIRCUIT BREAKER ON MY INHIBITIONS, I ALWAYS FELT I HAD TO KEEP MY DISTANCE.
BECAUSE WE WERE A TEAM.
AND NOW?
LET'S GO FIND OUT.

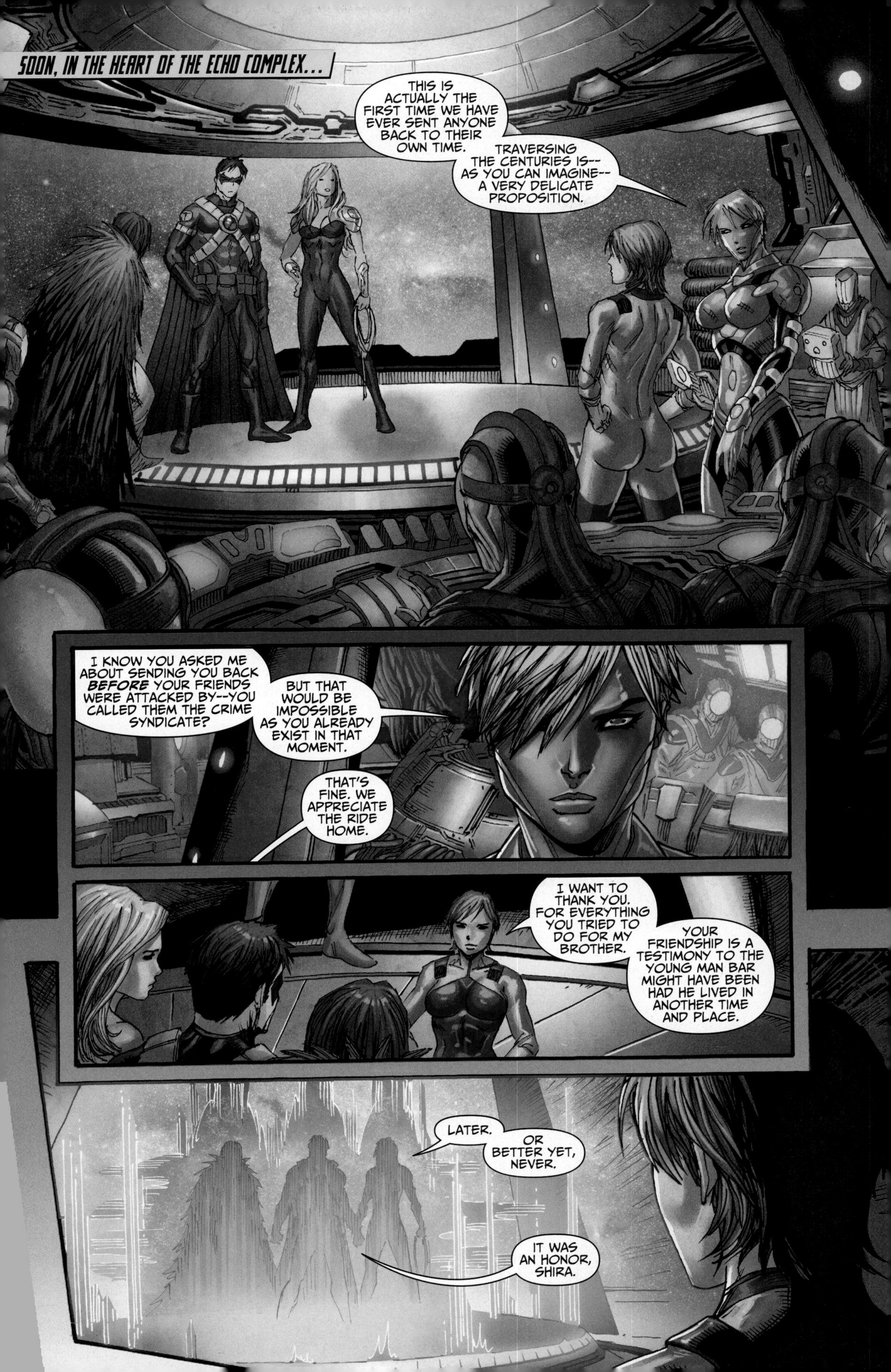
SOON, IN THE HEART OF THE ECHO COMPLEX...
THIS IS ACTUALLY THE FIRST TIME WE HAVE EVER SENT ANYONE BACK TO THEIR OWN TIME.
TRAVERSING THE CENTURIES IS-- AS YOU CAN IMAGINE-- A VERY DELICATE PROPOSITION.
I KNOW YOU ASKED ME ABOUT SENDING YOU BACK BEFORE YOUR FRIENDS WERE ATTACKED BY--YOU CALLED THEM THE CRIME SYNDICATE?
BUT THAT WOULD BE IMPOSSIBLE AS YOU ALREADY EXIST IN THAT MOMENT.
THAT'S FINE. WE APPRECIATE THE RIDE HOME.
I WANT TO THANK YOU. FOR EVERYTHING YOU TRIED TO DO FOR MY BROTHER.
YOUR FRIENDSHIP IS A TESTIMONY TO THE YOUNG MAN BAR MIGHT HAVE BEEN HAD HE LIVED IN ANOTHER TIME AND PLACE.
LATER.
OR BETTER YET, NEVER.
IT WAS AN HONOR, SHIRA.

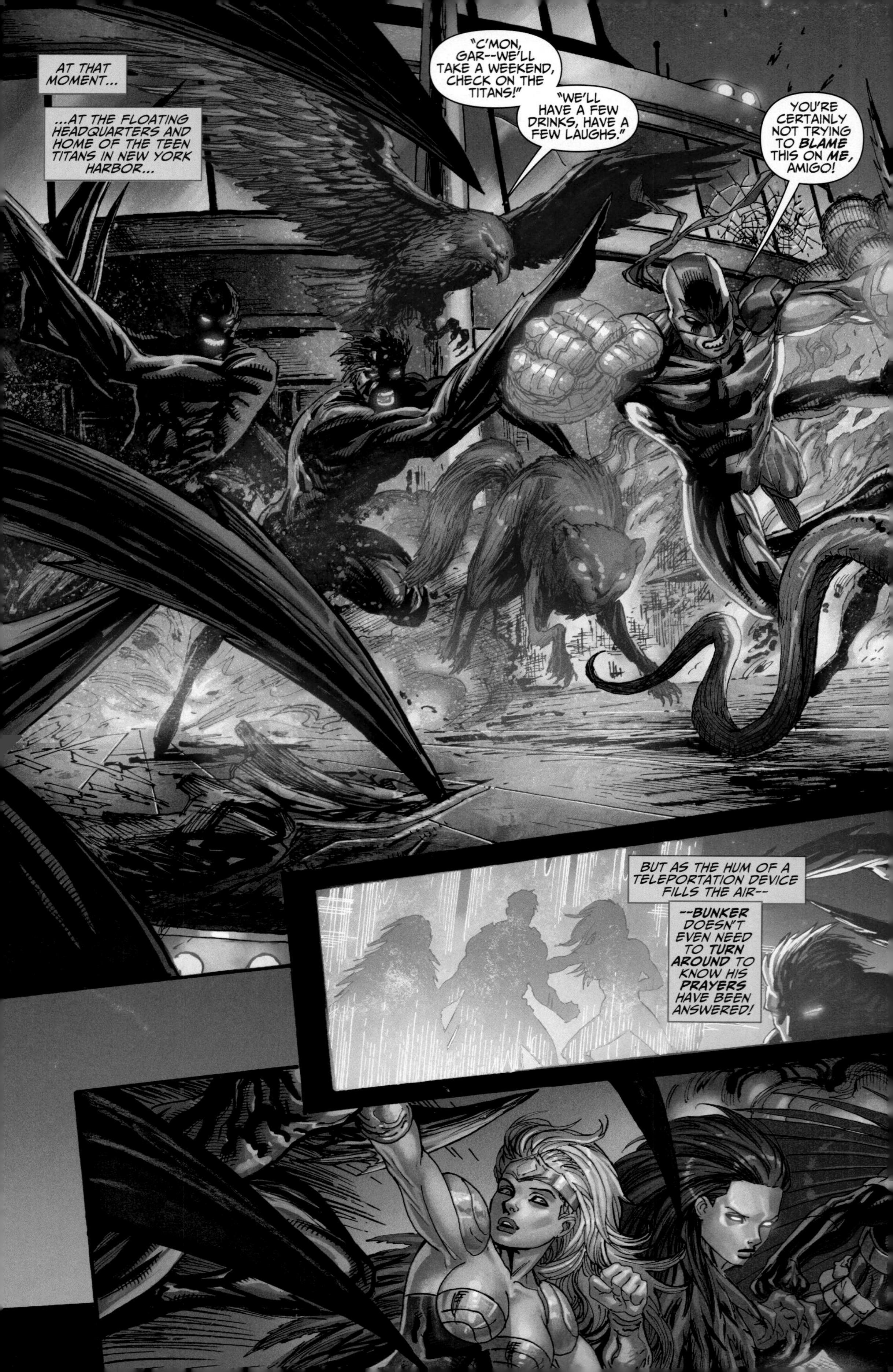
AT THAT MOMENT...
...AT THE FLOATING HEADQUARTERS AND HOME OF THE TEEN TITANS IN NEW YORK HARBOR...
"C'MON, GAR--WE'LL TAKE A WEEKEND, CHECK ON THE TITANS!"
"WE'LL HAVE A FEW DRINKS, HAVE A FEW LAUGHS."
YOU'RE CERTAINLY NOT TRYING TO BLAME THIS ON ME, AMIGO!
BUT AS THE HUM OF A TELEPORTATION DEVICE FILLS THE AIR--
--BUNKER DOESN'T EVEN NEED TO TURN AROUND TO KNOW HIS PRAYERS HAVE BEEN ANSWERED!

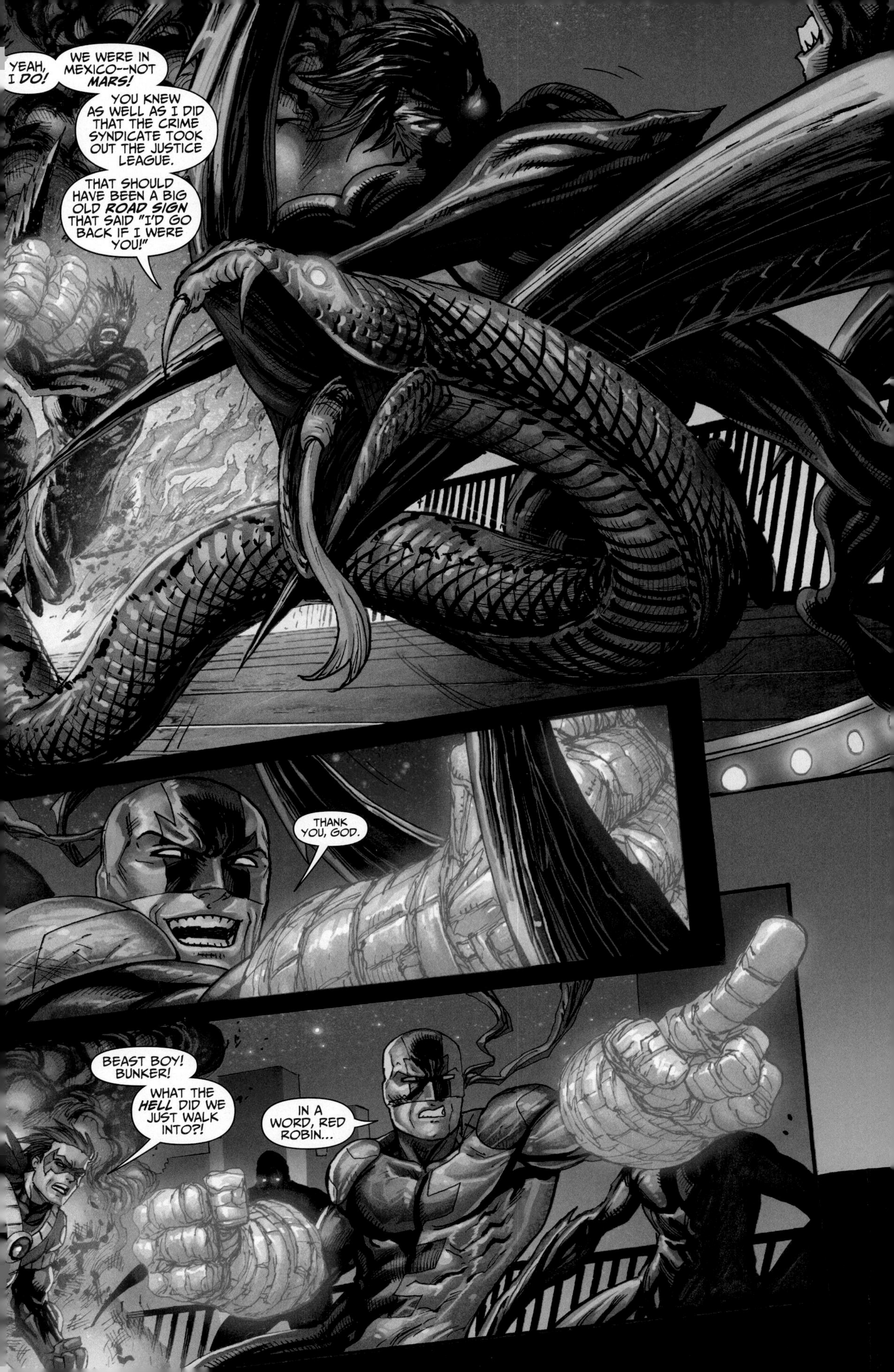
YEAH, I DO!
WE WERE IN MEXICO--NOT MARS!
YOU KNEW AS WELL AS I DID THAT THE CRIME SYNDICATE TOOK OUT THE JUSTICE LEAGUE.
THAT SHOULD HAVE BEEN A BIG OLD ROAD SIGN THAT SAID "I'D GO BACK IF I WERE YOU!"
THANK YOU, GOD.
BEAST BOY! BUNKER!
WHAT THE HELL DID WE JUST WALK INTO?!
IN A WORD, RED ROBIN...

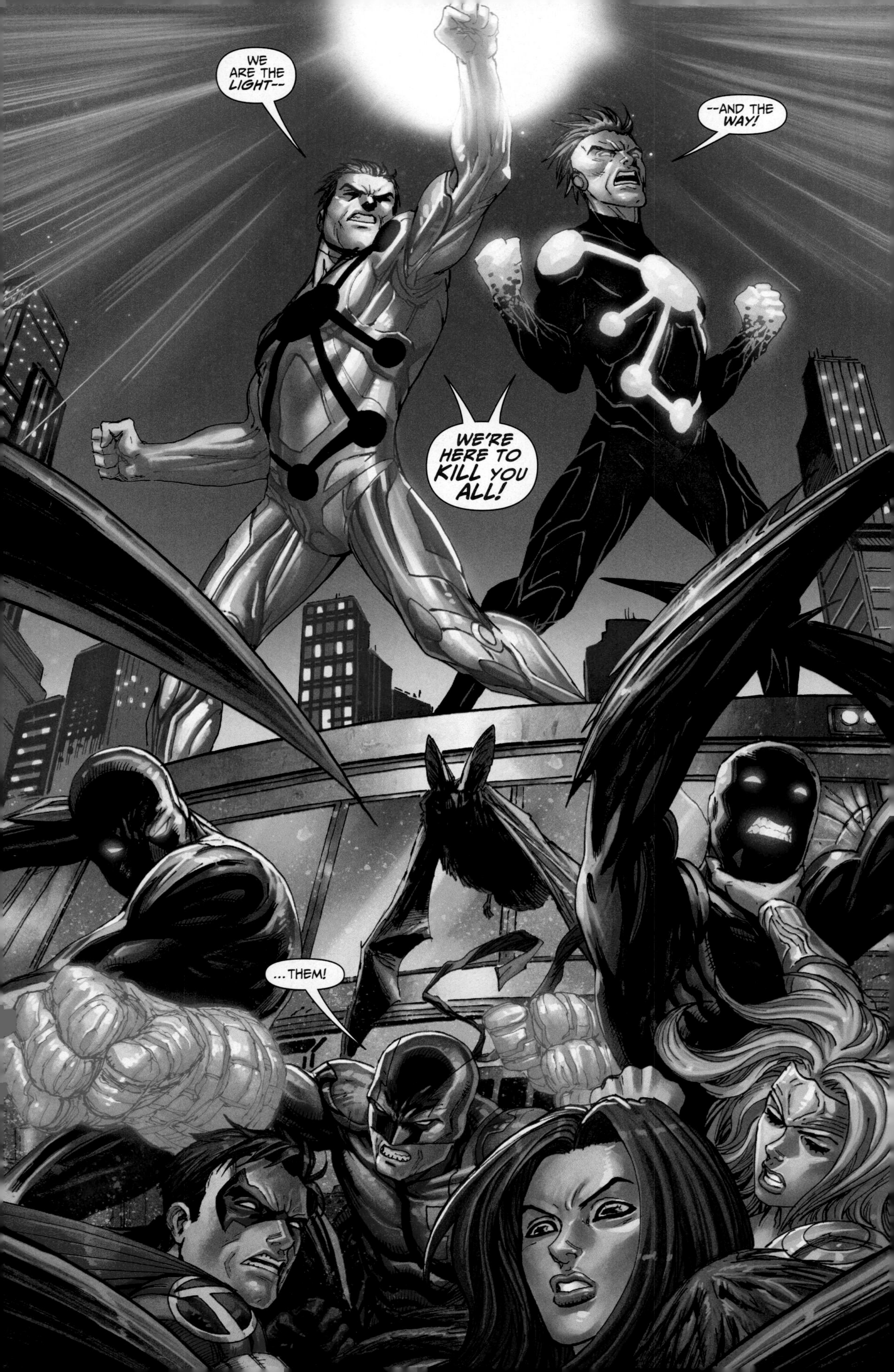
WE ARE THE LIGHT--
--AND THE WAY!
WE'RE HERE TO KILL YOU ALL!
...THEM!

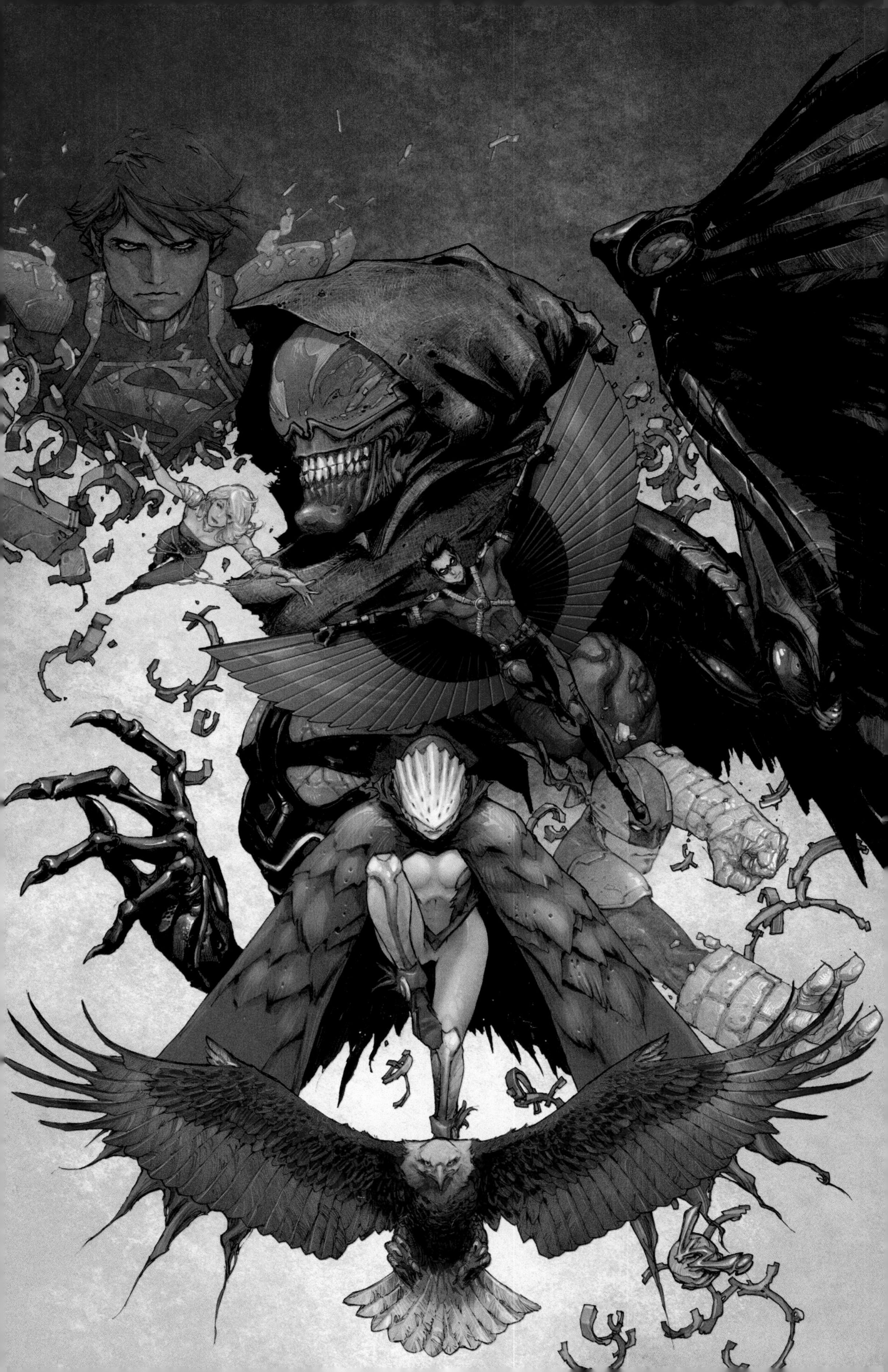

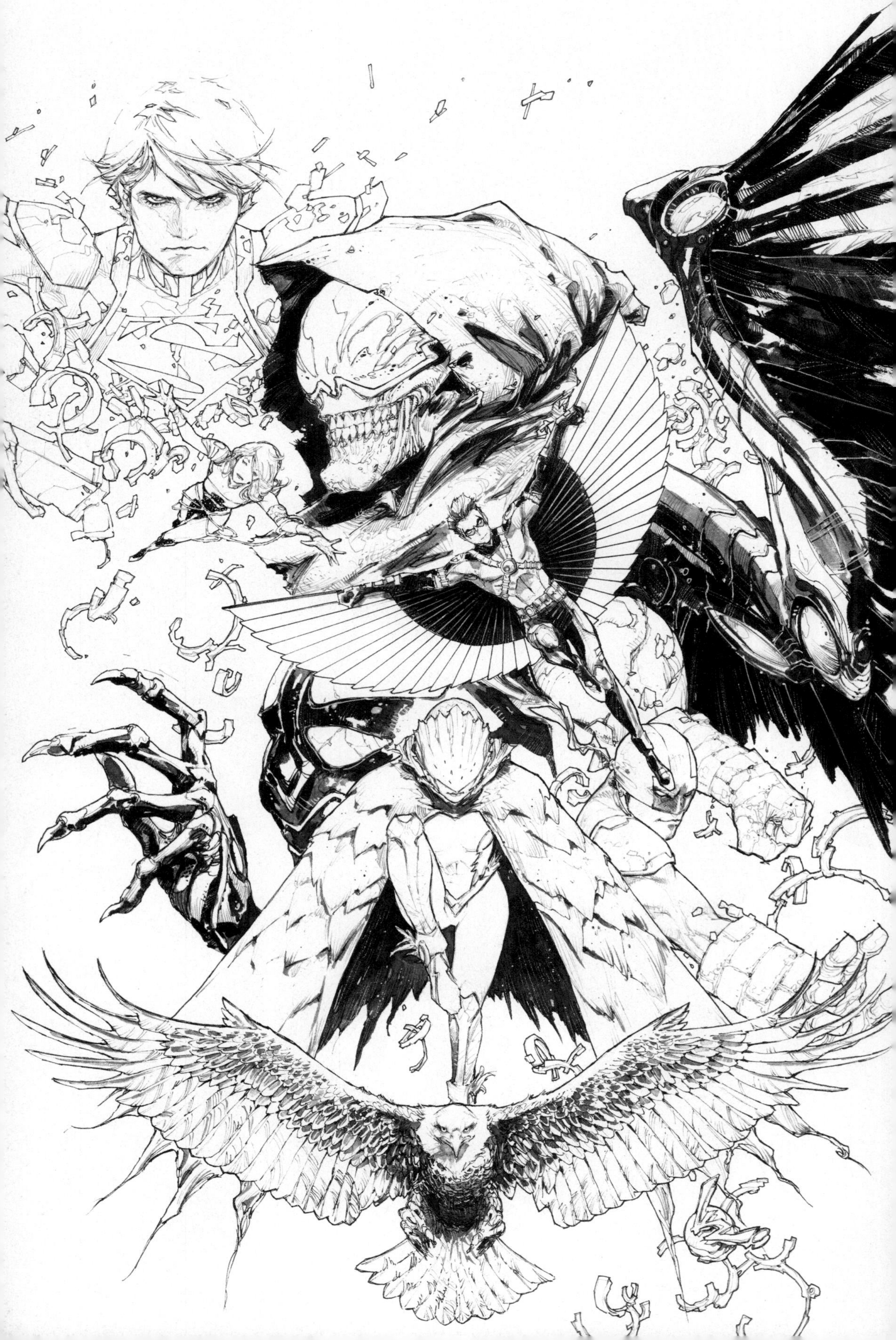

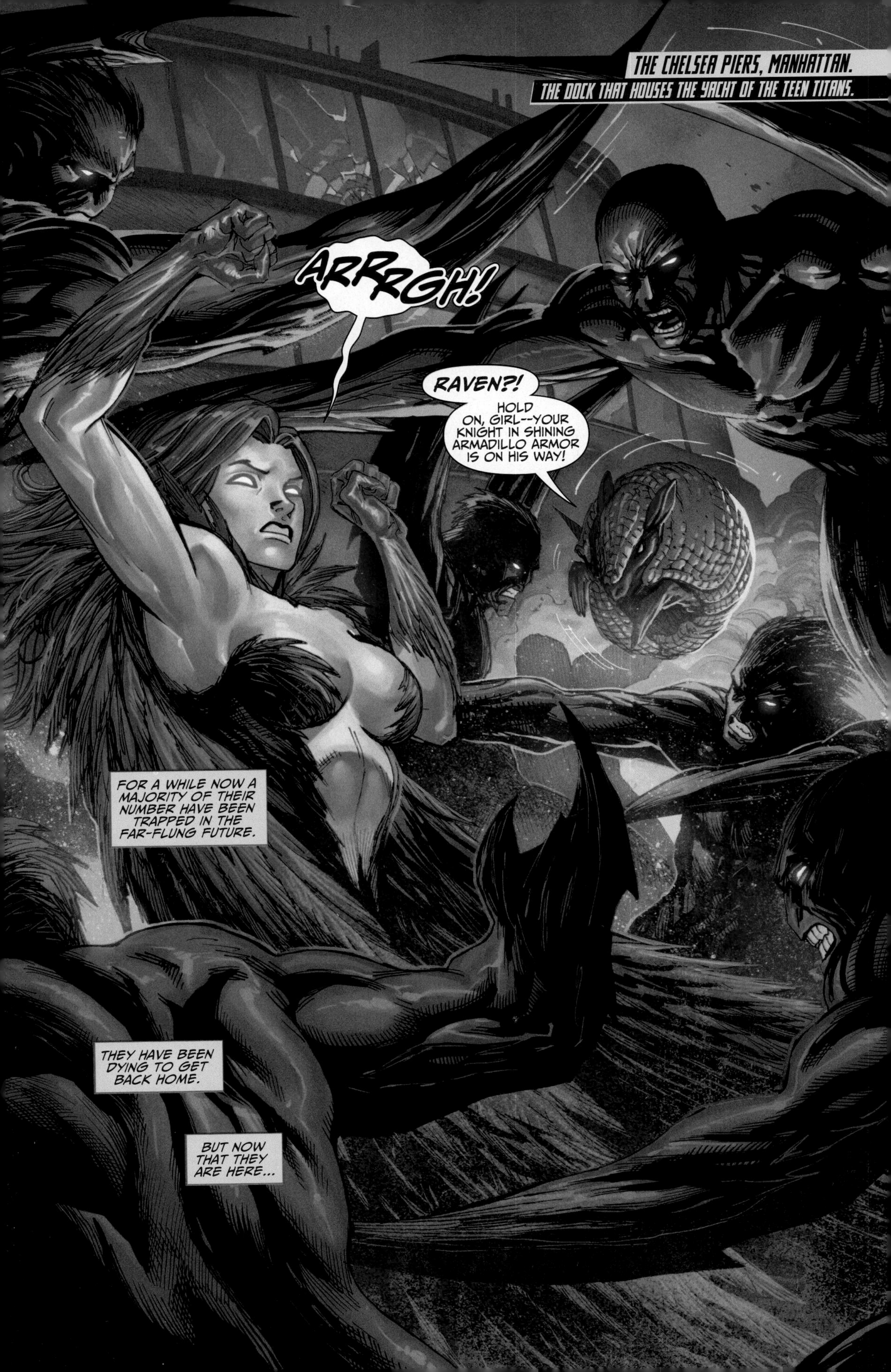
THE CHELSEA PIERS, MANHATTAN.
THE DOCK THAT HOUSES THE YACHT OF THE TEEN TITANS.
ARRRGH!
RAVEN?!
HOLD ON, GIRL--YOUR KNIGHT IN SHINING ARMADILLO ARMOR IS ON HIS WAY!
FOR A WHILE NOW A MAJORITY OF THEIR NUMBER HAVE BEEN TRAPPED IN THE FAR-FLUNG FUTURE.
THEY HAVE BEEN DYING TO GET BACK HOME.
BUT NOW THAT THEY ARE HERE...

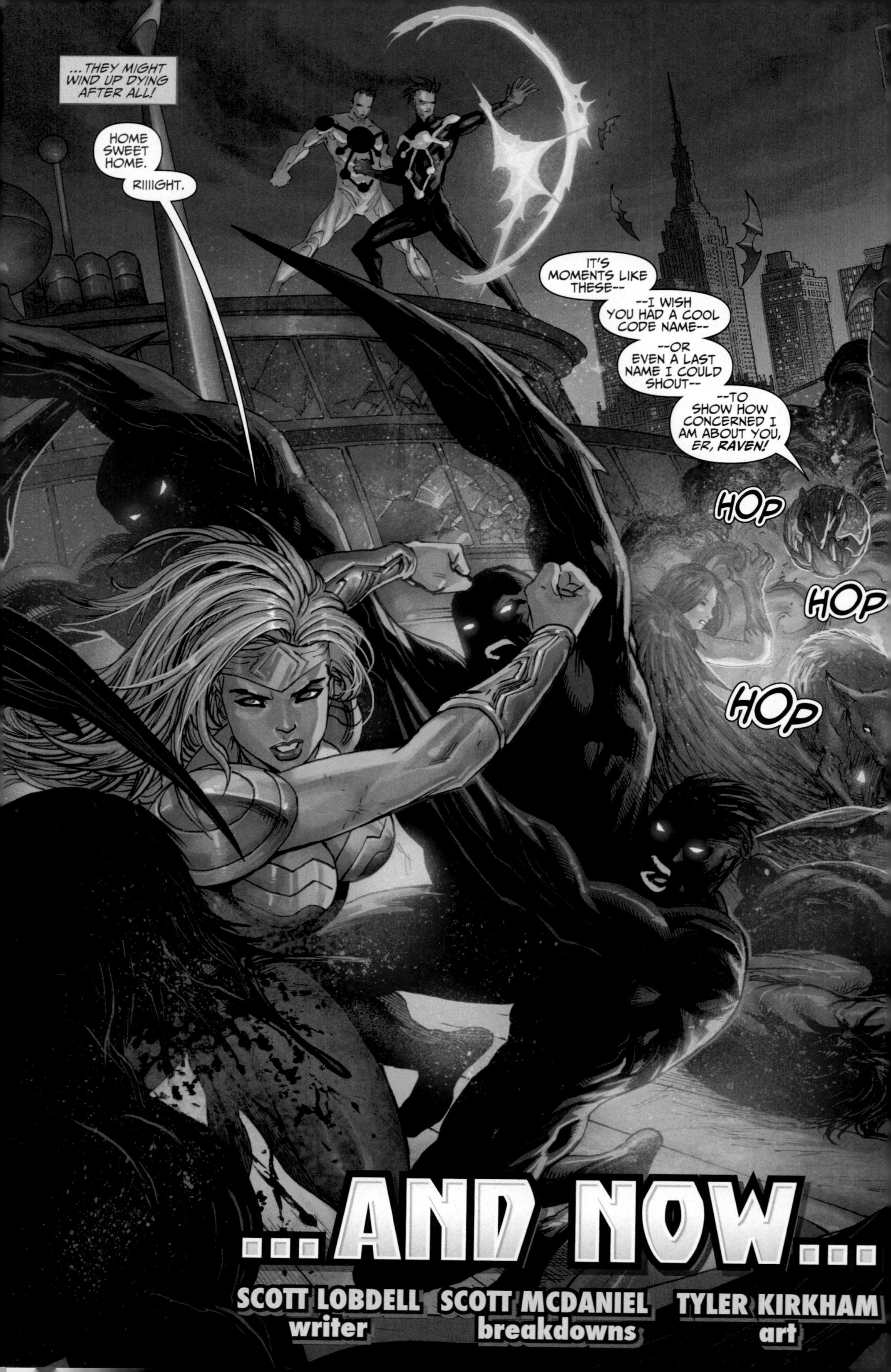
...THEY MIGHT WIND UP DYING AFTER ALL!
HOME SWEET HOME.
RIIIIGHT.
IT'S MOMENTS LIKE THESE--
--I WISH YOU HAD A COOL CODE NAME--
--OR EVEN A LAST NAME I COULD SHOUT--
--TO SHOW HOW CONCERNED I AM ABOUT YOU, ER, RAVEN!
HOP
HOP
HOP
...AND NOW...
SCOTT LOBDELL writer
SCOTT MCDANIEL breakdowns
TYLER KIRKHAM art

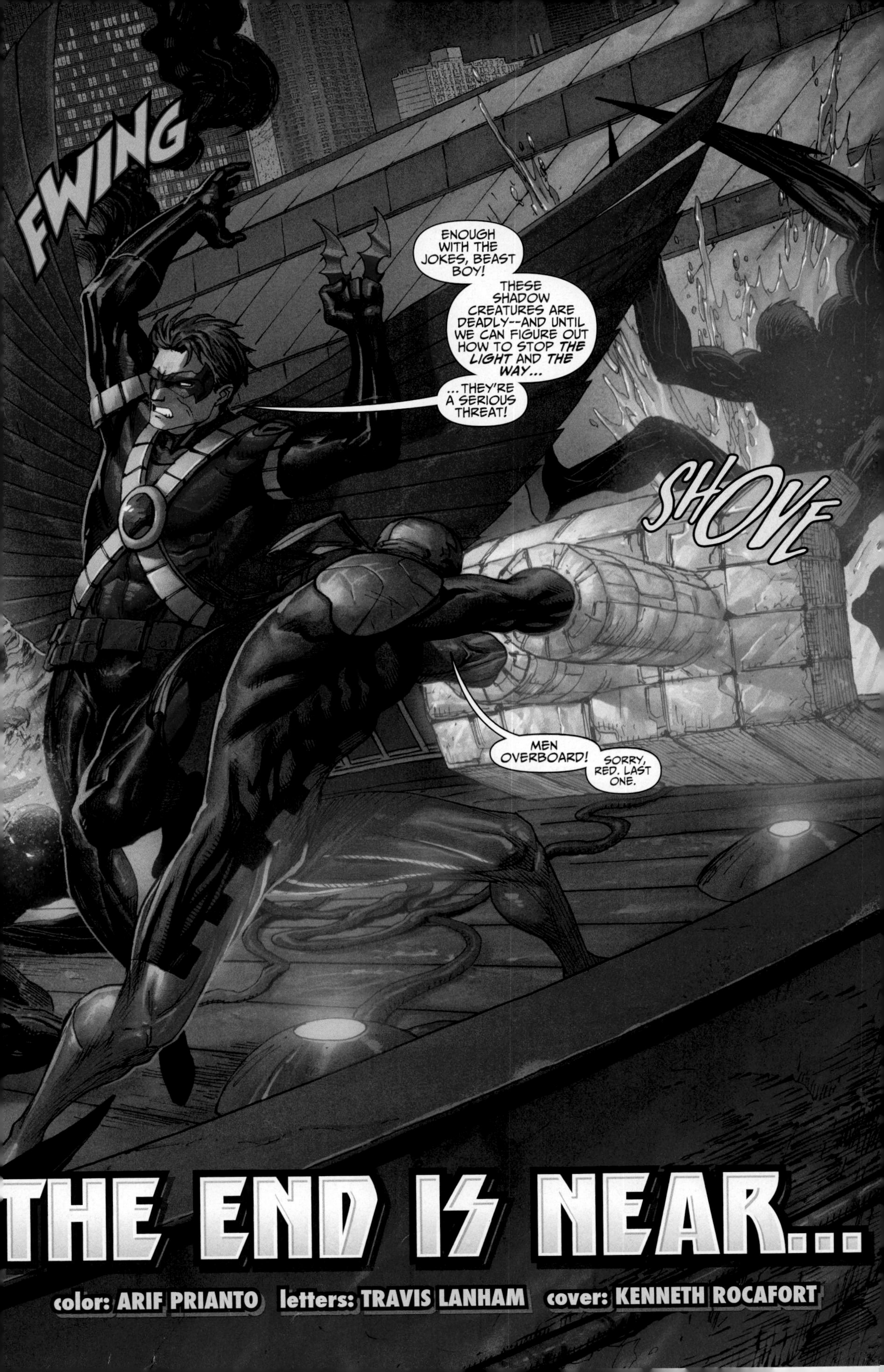
FWING
ENOUGH WITH THE JOKES, BEAST BOY!
THESE SHADOW CREATURES ARE DEADLY--AND UNTIL WE CAN FIGURE OUT HOW TO STOP THE LIGHT AND THE WAY...
...THEY'RE A SERIOUS THREAT!
SHOVE
MEN OVERBOARD!
SORRY, RED. LAST ONE.
THE END IS NEAR...
color: ARIF PRIANTO letters: TRAVIS LANHAM cover: KENNETH ROCAFORT

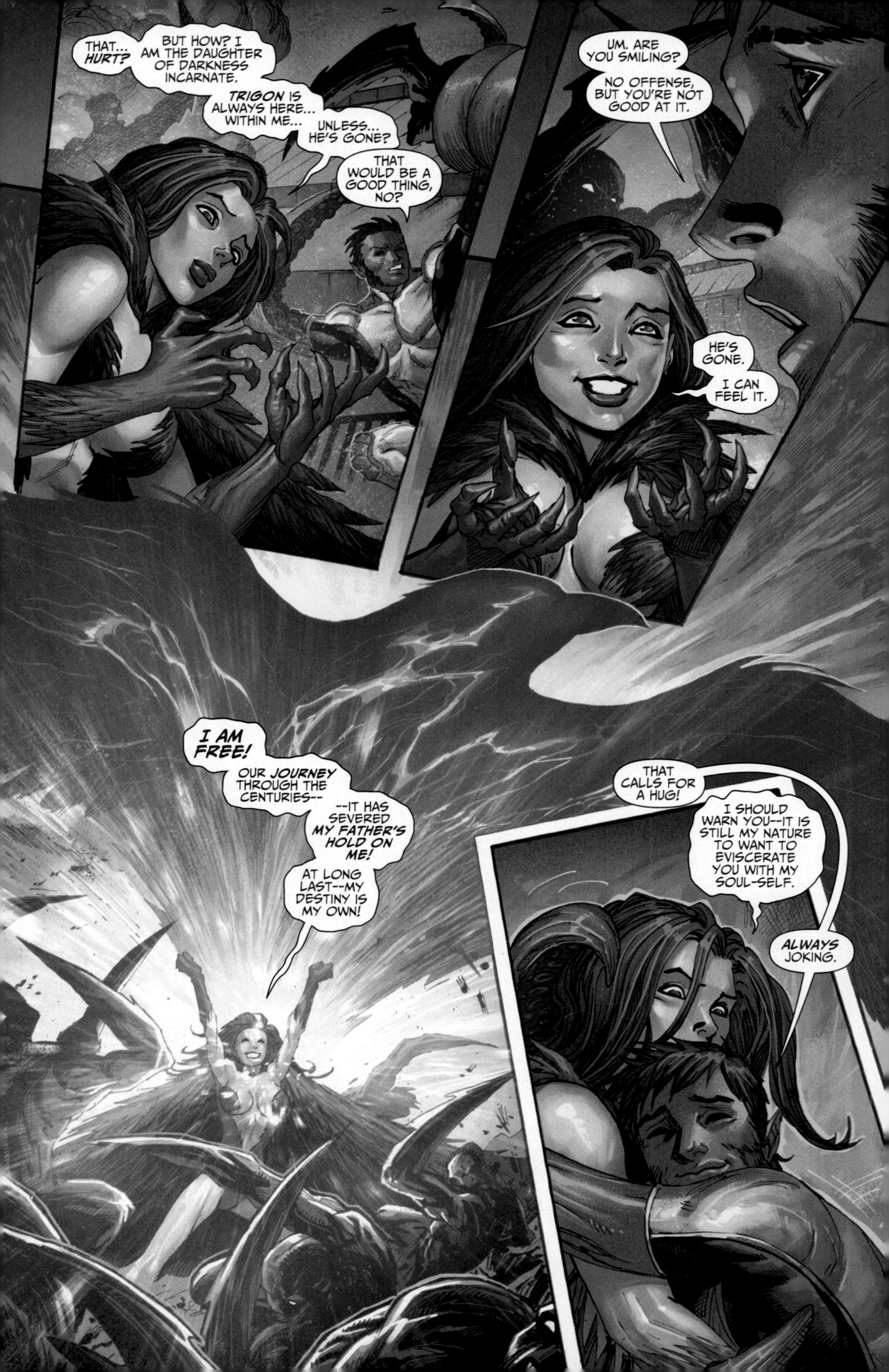
THAT... HURT?
BUT HOW? I AM THE DAUGHTER OF DARKNESS INCARNATE.
TRIGON IS ALWAYS HERE... WITHIN ME...
UNLESS... HE'S GONE?
THAT WOULD BE A GOOD THING, NO?
UM. ARE YOU SMILING?
NO OFFENSE, BUT YOU'RE NOT GOOD AT IT.
HE'S GONE.
I CAN FEEL IT.
I AM FREE!
OUR JOURNEY THROUGH THE CENTURIES--
--IT HAS SEVERED MY FATHER'S HOLD ON ME!
AT LONG LAST--MY DESTINY IS MY OWN!
THAT CALLS FOR A HUG!
I SHOULD WARN YOU--IT IS STILL MY NATURE TO WANT TO EVISCERATE YOU WITH MY SOUL-SELF.
ALWAYS JOKING.

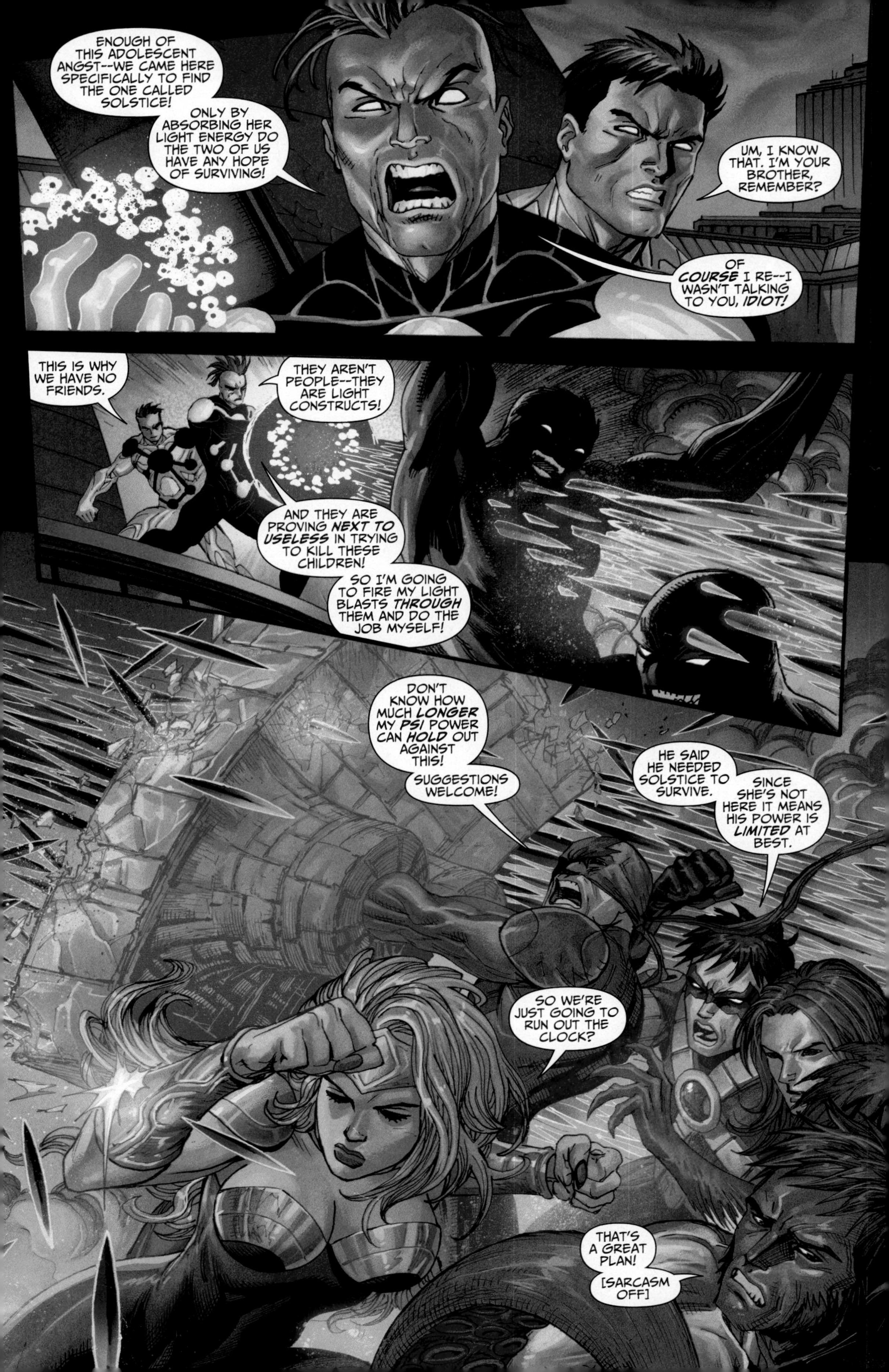
ENOUGH OF THIS ADOLESCENT ANGST--WE CAME HERE SPECIFICALLY TO FIND THE ONE CALLED SOLSTICE!
ONLY BY ABSORBING HER LIGHT ENERGY DO THE TWO OF US HAVE ANY HOPE OF SURVIVING!
UM, I KNOW THAT. I'M YOUR BROTHER, REMEMBER?
OF COURSE I RE--I WASN'T TALKING TO YOU, IDIOT!
THIS IS WHY WE HAVE NO FRIENDS.
THEY AREN'T PEOPLE--THEY ARE LIGHT CONSTRUCTS!
AND THEY ARE PROVING NEXT TO USELESS IN TRYING TO KILL THESE CHILDREN!
SO I'M GOING TO FIRE MY LIGHT BLASTS THROUGH THEM AND DO THE JOB MYSELF!
DON'T KNOW HOW MUCH LONGER MY PSI POWER CAN HOLD OUT AGAINST THIS!
SUGGESTIONS WELCOME!
HE SAID HE NEEDED SOLSTICE TO SURVIVE.
SINCE SHE'S NOT HERE IT MEANS HIS POWER IS LIMITED AT BEST.
SO WE'RE JUST GOING TO RUN OUT THE CLOCK?
THAT'S A GREAT PLAN!
[SARCASM OFF]

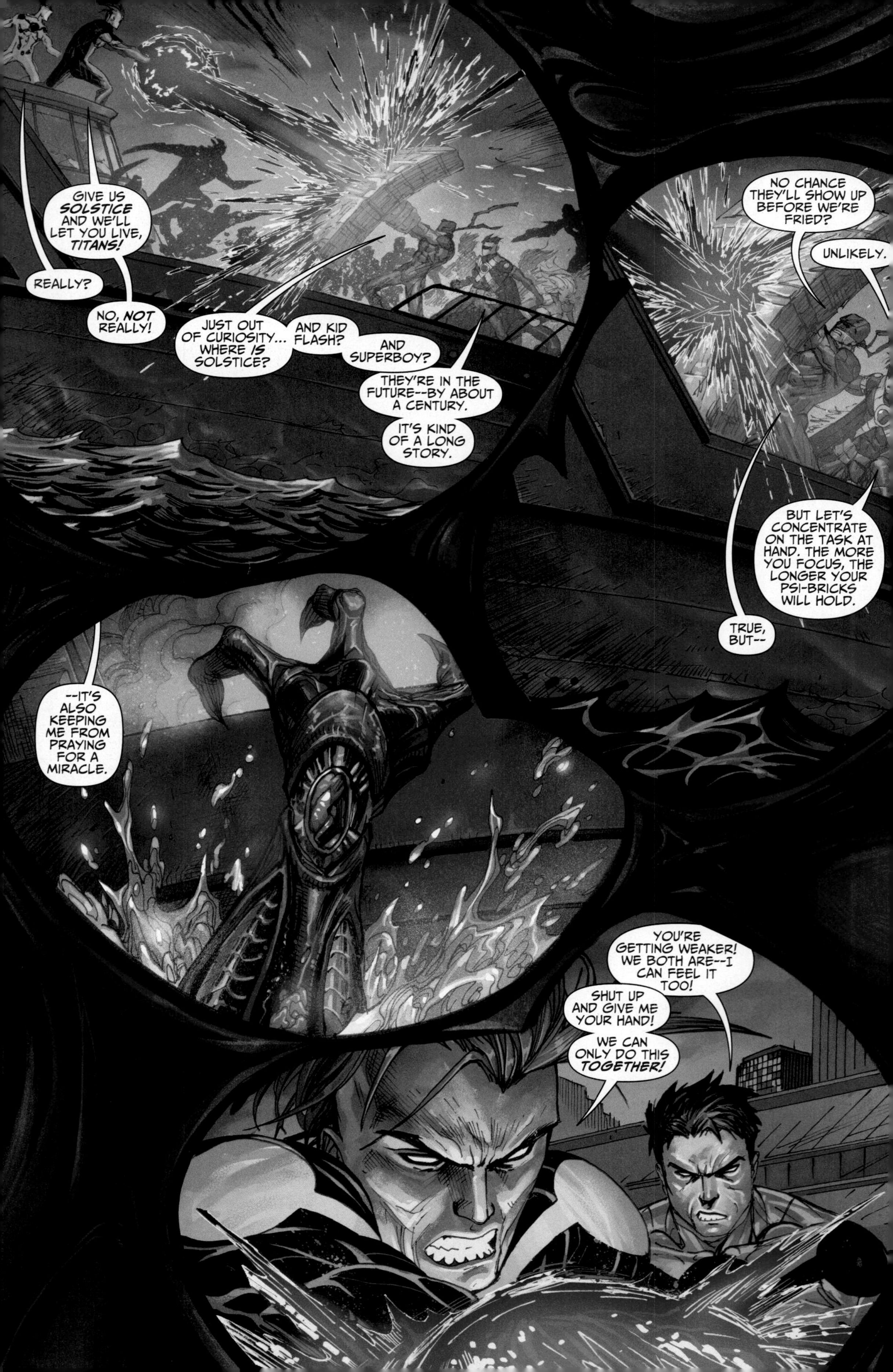

GIVE US SOLSTICE AND WE'LL LET YOU LIVE, TITANS!
REALLY?
NO, NOT REALLY!
JUST OUT OF CURIOSITY... WHERE IS SOLSTICE?
AND KID FLASH?
AND SUPERBOY?
THEY'RE IN THE FUTURE--BY ABOUT A CENTURY.
IT'S KIND OF A LONG STORY.
NO CHANCE THEY'LL SHOW UP BEFORE WE'RE FRIED?
UNLIKELY.
BUT LET'S CONCENTRATE ON THE TASK AT HAND. THE MORE YOU FOCUS, THE LONGER YOUR PSI-BRICKS WILL HOLD.
TRUE, BUT--
--IT'S ALSO KEEPING ME FROM PRAYING FOR A MIRACLE.
YOU'RE GETTING WEAKER! WE BOTH ARE--I CAN FEEL IT TOO!
SHUT UP AND GIVE ME YOUR HAND!
WE CAN ONLY DO THIS TOGETHER!

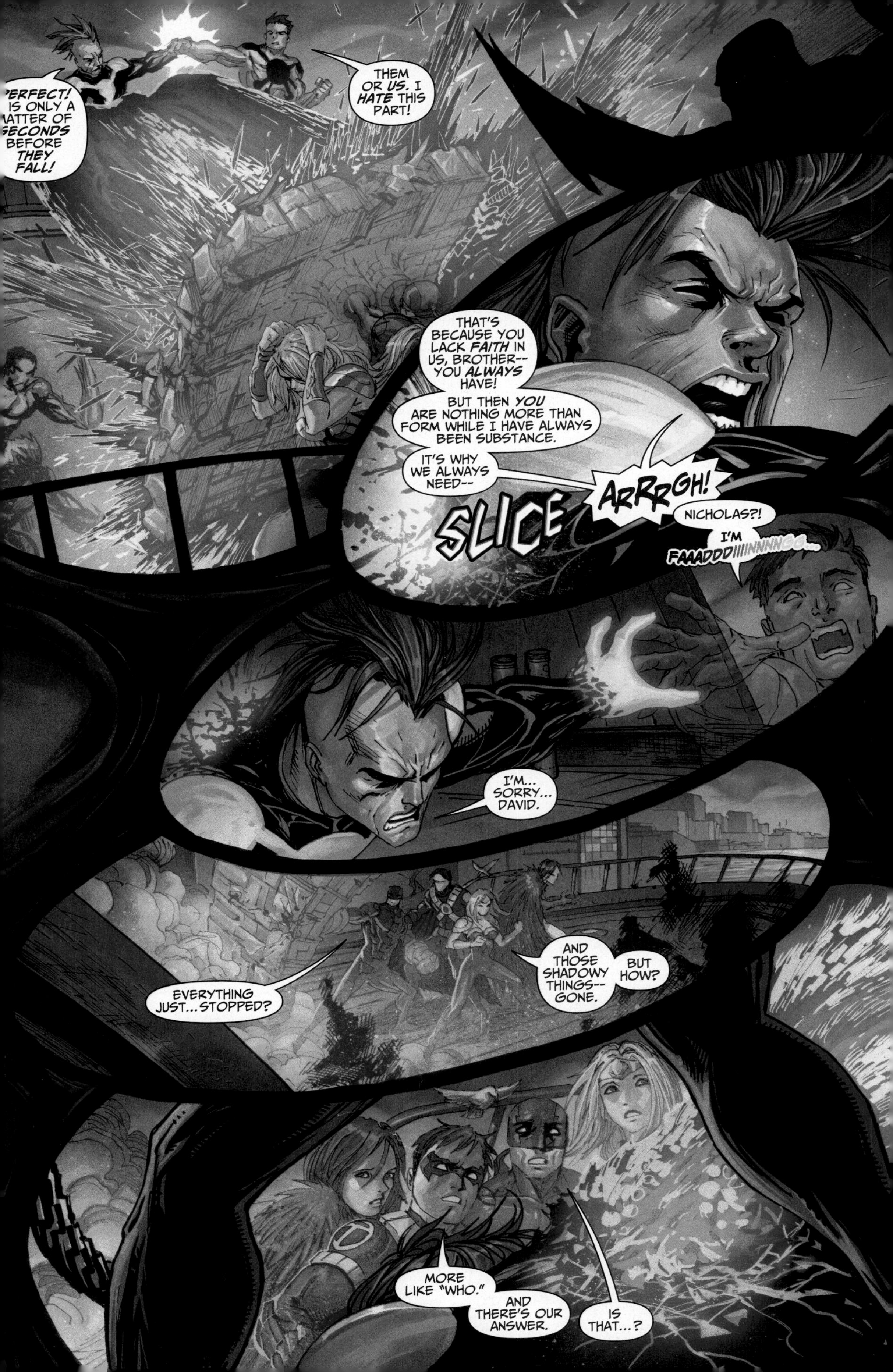
PERFECT! IS ONLY A MATTER OF SECONDS BEFORE THEY FALL!
THEM OR US. I HATE THIS PART!
THAT'S BECAUSE YOU LACK FAITH IN US, BROTHER-- YOU ALWAYS HAVE!
BUT THEN YOU ARE NOTHING MORE THAN FORM WHILE I HAVE ALWAYS BEEN SUBSTANCE.
IT'S WHY WE ALWAYS NEED--
SLICE
ARRRGH!
NICHOLAS?!
I'M FAAADDDIIIINNNNGG...
I'M... SORRY... DAVID.
EVERYTHING JUST...STOPPED?
AND THOSE SHADOWY THINGS-- GONE.
BUT HOW?
MORE LIKE "WHO."
AND THERE'S OUR ANSWER.
IS THAT...?

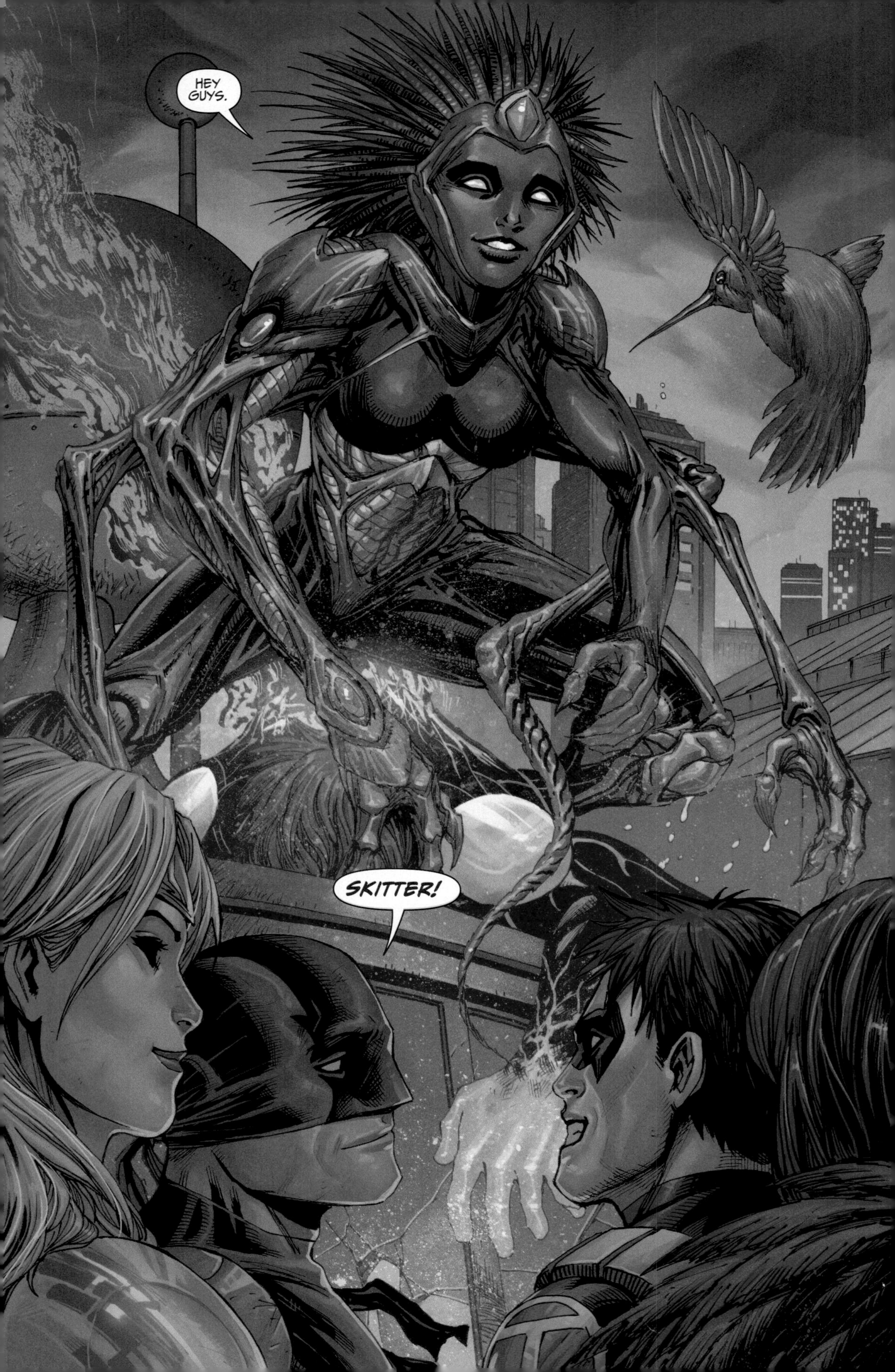
HEY GUYS.
SKITTER!

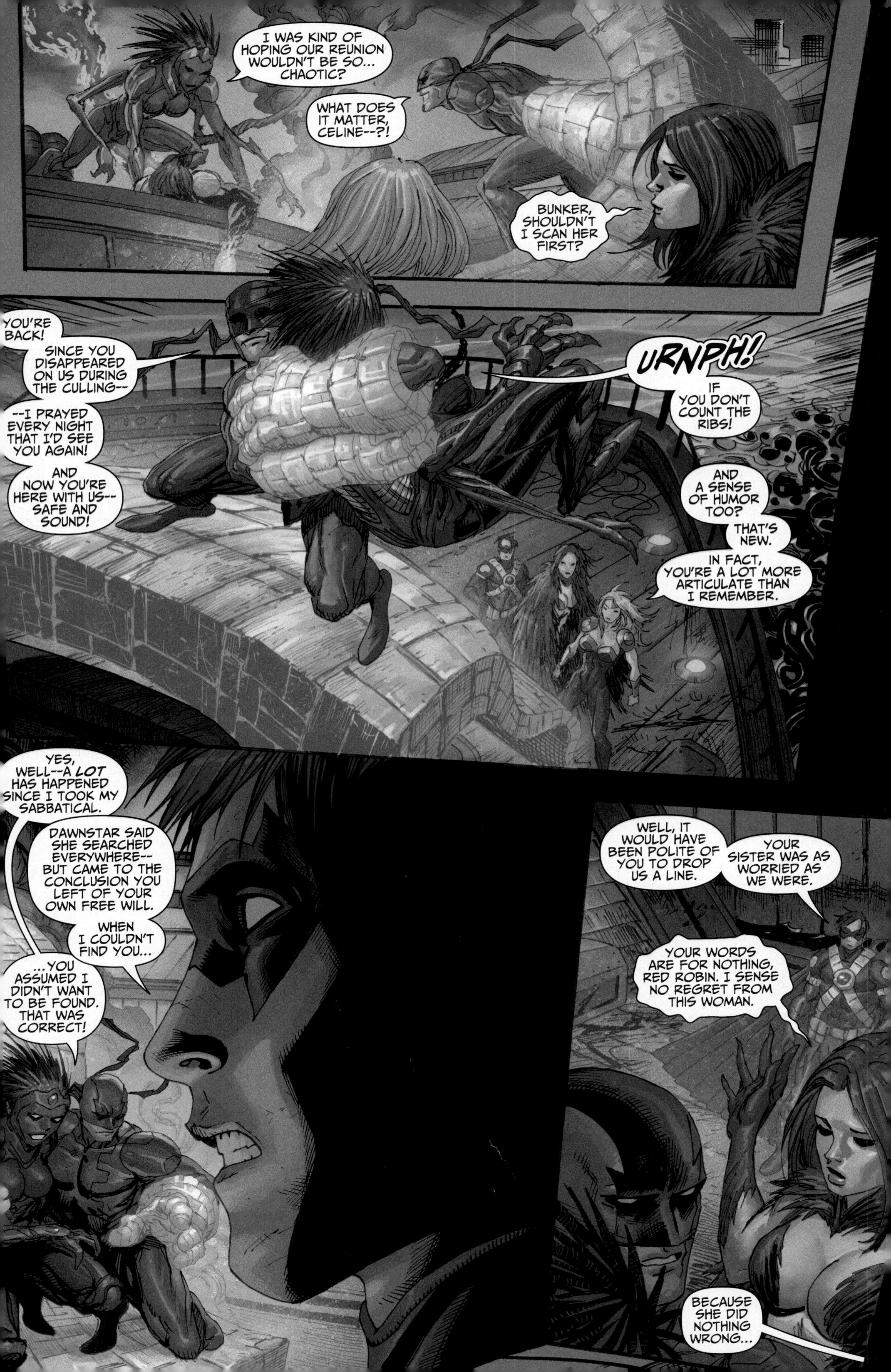
I WAS KIND OF HOPING OUR REUNION WOULDN'T BE SO... CHAOTIC?
WHAT DOES IT MATTER, CELINE--?!
BUNKER, SHOULDN'T I SCAN HER FIRST?
YOU'RE BACK!
SINCE YOU DISAPPEARED ON US DURING THE CULLING--
--I PRAYED EVERY NIGHT THAT I'D SEE YOU AGAIN!
AND NOW YOU'RE HERE WITH US--SAFE AND SOUND!
URNPH!
IF YOU DON'T COUNT THE RIBS!
AND A SENSE OF HUMOR TOO?
THAT'S NEW.
IN FACT, YOU'RE A LOT MORE ARTICULATE THAN I REMEMBER.
YES, WELL--A *LOT* HAS HAPPENED SINCE I TOOK MY SABBATICAL.
DAWNSTAR SAID SHE SEARCHED EVERYWHERE--BUT CAME TO THE CONCLUSION YOU LEFT OF YOUR OWN FREE WILL.
WHEN I COULDN'T FIND YOU...
...YOU ASSUMED I DIDN'T WANT TO BE FOUND. THAT WAS CORRECT!
WELL, IT WOULD HAVE BEEN POLITE OF YOU TO DROP US A LINE.
YOUR SISTER WAS AS WORRIED AS WE WERE.
YOUR WORDS ARE FOR NOTHING, RED ROBIN. I SENSE NO REGRET FROM THIS WOMAN.
BECAUSE SHE DID NOTHING WRONG...

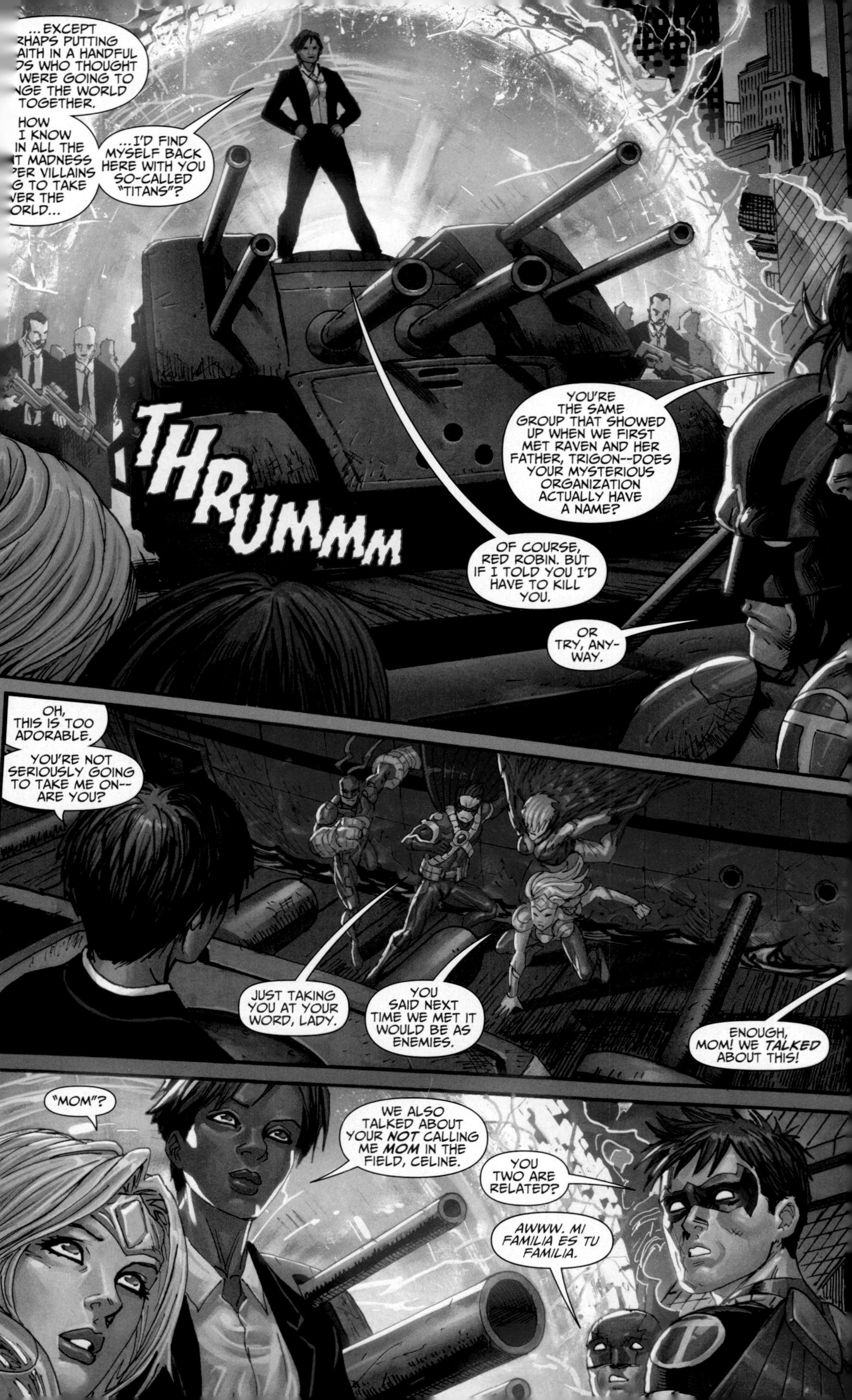
...EXCEPT
RHAPS PUTTING
AITH IN A HANDFUL
DS WHO THOUGHT
WERE GOING TO
NGE THE WORLD
TOGETHER.
HOW
I KNOW
IN ALL THE
T MADNESS
PER VILLAINS
G TO TAKE
VER THE
ORLD...
...I'D FIND MYSELF BACK HERE WITH YOU SO-CALLED "TITANS"?
THRUMMM
YOU'RE THE SAME GROUP THAT SHOWED UP WHEN WE FIRST MET RAVEN AND HER FATHER, TRIGON--DOES YOUR MYSTERIOUS ORGANIZATION ACTUALLY HAVE A NAME?
OF COURSE, RED ROBIN. BUT IF I TOLD YOU I'D HAVE TO KILL YOU.
OR TRY, ANY-WAY.
OH, THIS IS TOO ADORABLE.
YOU'RE NOT SERIOUSLY GOING TO TAKE ME ON--ARE YOU?
JUST TAKING YOU AT YOUR WORD, LADY.
YOU SAID NEXT TIME WE MET IT WOULD BE AS ENEMIES.
ENOUGH, MOM! WE TALKED ABOUT THIS!
"MOM"?
WE ALSO TALKED ABOUT YOUR NOT CALLING ME MOM IN THE FIELD, CELINE.
YOU TWO ARE RELATED?
AWWW. MI FAMILIA ES TU FAMILIA.

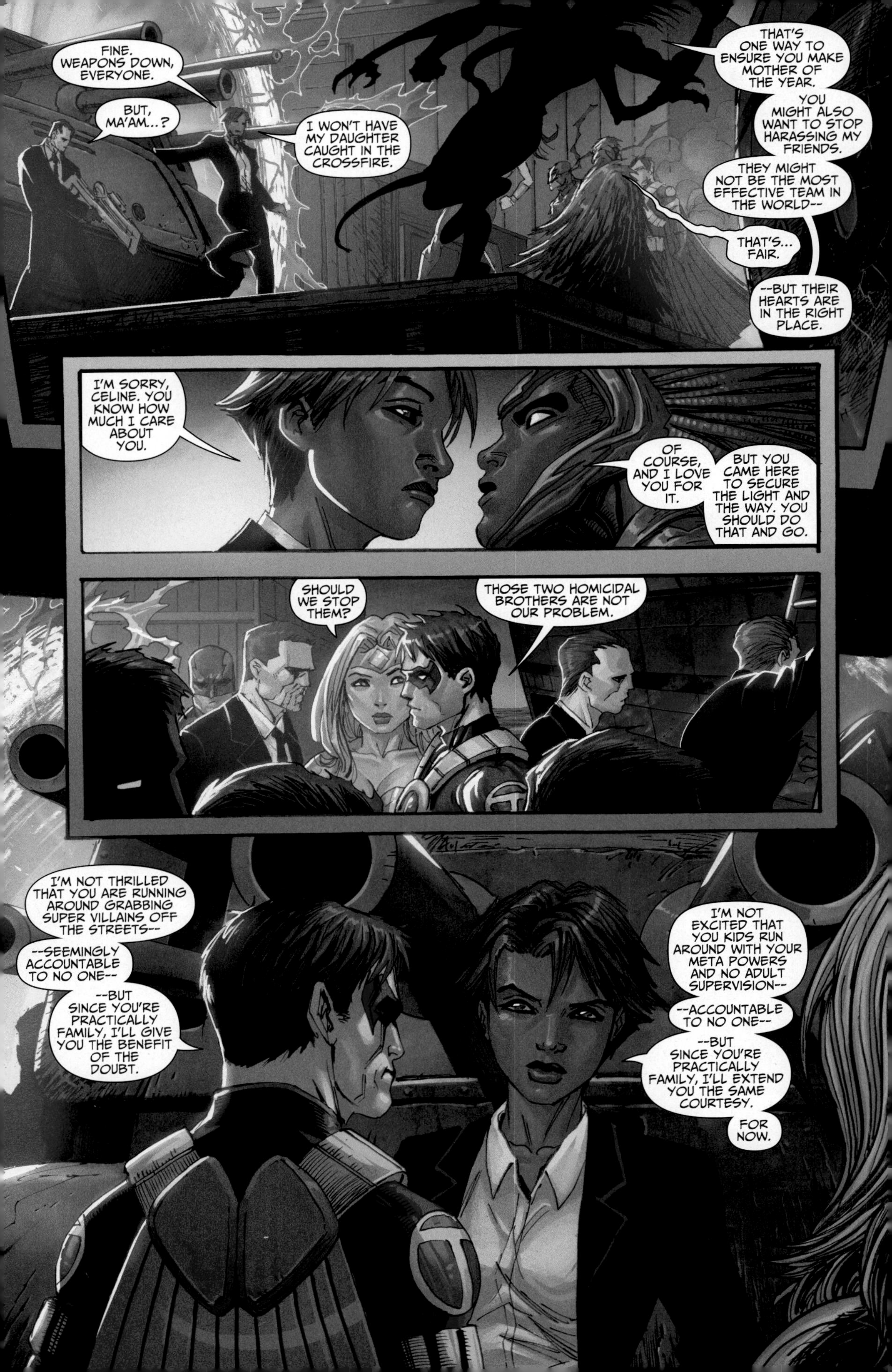
FINE. WEAPONS DOWN, EVERYONE.
BUT, MA'AM...?
I WON'T HAVE MY DAUGHTER CAUGHT IN THE CROSSFIRE.
THAT'S ONE WAY TO ENSURE YOU MAKE MOTHER OF THE YEAR.
YOU MIGHT ALSO WANT TO STOP HARASSING MY FRIENDS.
THEY MIGHT NOT BE THE MOST EFFECTIVE TEAM IN THE WORLD--
THAT'S... FAIR.
--BUT THEIR HEARTS ARE IN THE RIGHT PLACE.
I'M SORRY, CELINE. YOU KNOW HOW MUCH I CARE ABOUT YOU.
OF COURSE, AND I LOVE YOU FOR IT.
BUT YOU CAME HERE TO SECURE THE LIGHT AND THE WAY. YOU SHOULD DO THAT AND GO.
SHOULD WE STOP THEM?
THOSE TWO HOMICIDAL BROTHERS ARE NOT OUR PROBLEM.
I'M NOT THRILLED THAT YOU ARE RUNNING AROUND GRABBING SUPER VILLAINS OFF THE STREETS--
--SEEMINGLY ACCOUNTABLE TO NO ONE--
--BUT SINCE YOU'RE PRACTICALLY FAMILY, I'LL GIVE YOU THE BENEFIT OF THE DOUBT.
I'M NOT EXCITED THAT YOU KIDS RUN AROUND WITH YOUR META POWERS AND NO ADULT SUPERVISION--
--ACCOUNTABLE TO NO ONE--
--BUT SINCE YOU'RE PRACTICALLY FAMILY, I'LL EXTEND YOU THE SAME COURTESY.
FOR NOW.

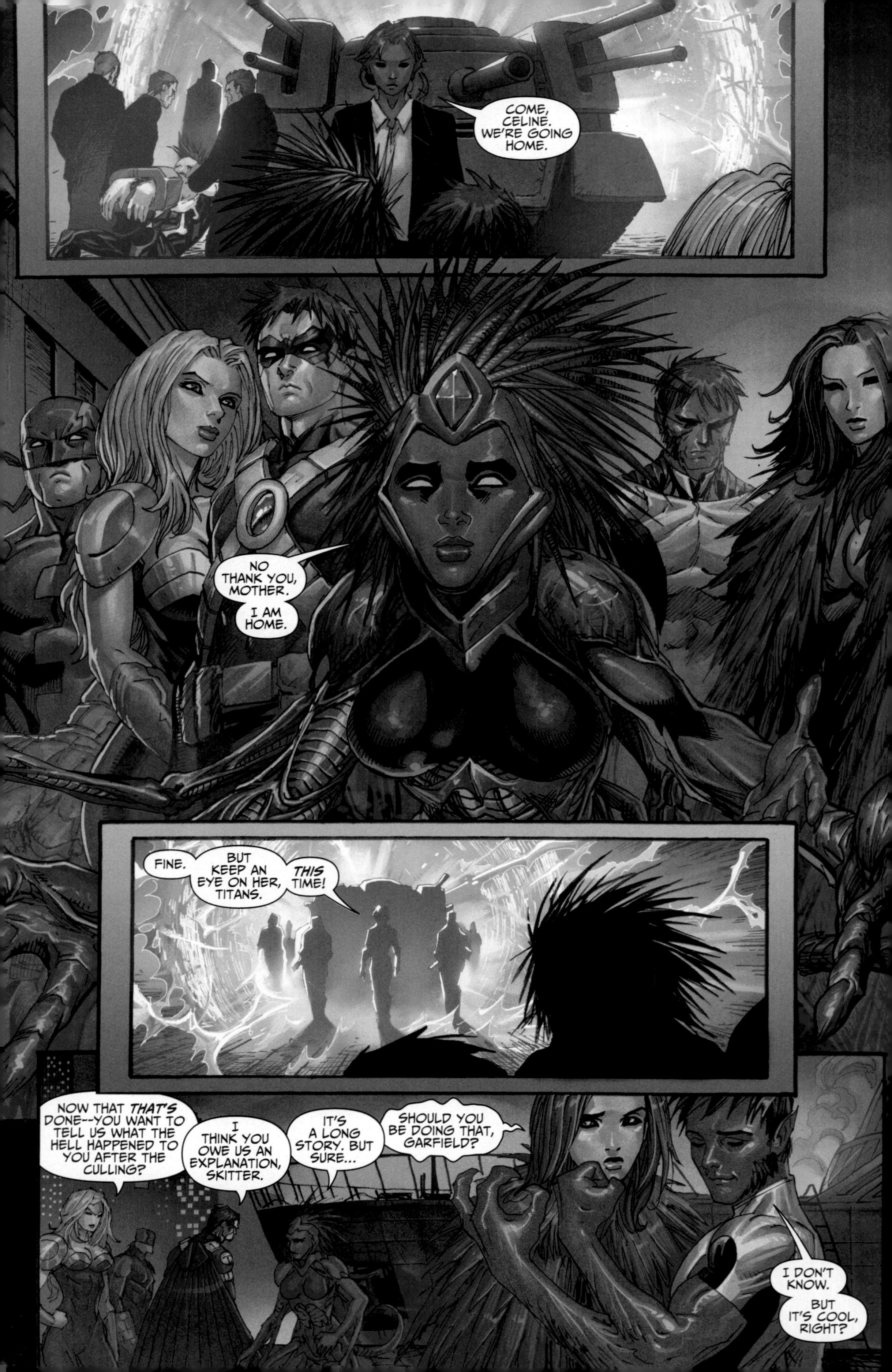
COME, CELINE. WE'RE GOING HOME.
NO THANK YOU, MOTHER.
I AM HOME.
FINE.
BUT KEEP AN EYE ON HER, TITANS.
THIS TIME!
NOW THAT THAT'S DONE--YOU WANT TO TELL US WHAT THE HELL HAPPENED TO YOU AFTER THE CULLING?
I THINK YOU OWE US AN EXPLANATION, SKITTER.
IT'S A LONG STORY. BUT SURE...
SHOULD YOU BE DOING THAT, GARFIELD?
I DON'T KNOW.
BUT IT'S COOL, RIGHT?

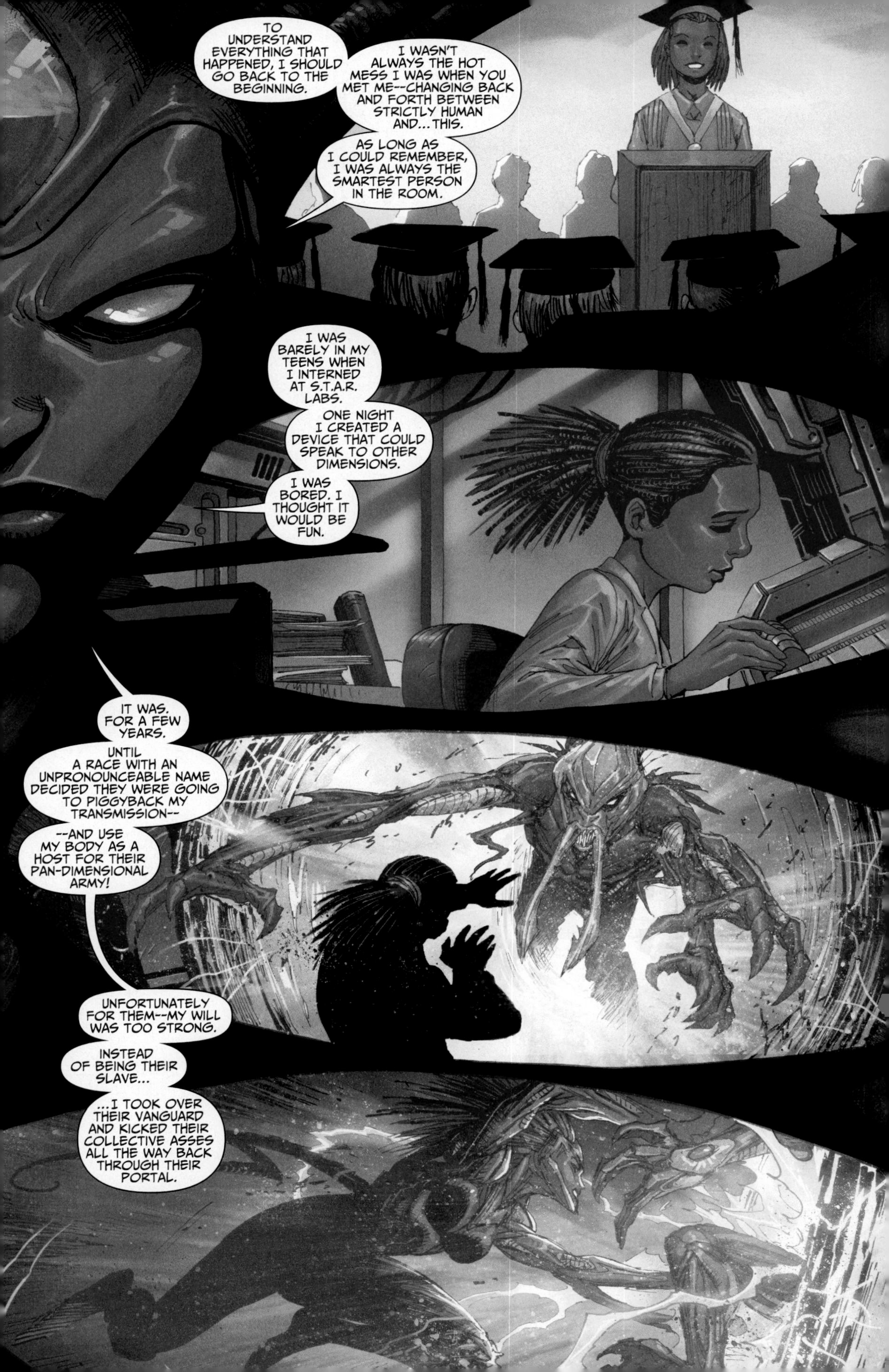
TO UNDERSTAND EVERYTHING THAT HAPPENED, I SHOULD GO BACK TO THE BEGINNING.
I WASN'T ALWAYS THE HOT MESS I WAS WHEN YOU MET ME--CHANGING BACK AND FORTH BETWEEN STRICTLY HUMAN AND... THIS.
AS LONG AS I COULD REMEMBER, I WAS ALWAYS THE SMARTEST PERSON IN THE ROOM.
I WAS BARELY IN MY TEENS WHEN I INTERNED AT S.T.A.R. LABS.
ONE NIGHT I CREATED A DEVICE THAT COULD SPEAK TO OTHER DIMENSIONS.
I WAS BORED. I THOUGHT IT WOULD BE FUN.
IT WAS. FOR A FEW YEARS.
UNTIL A RACE WITH AN UNPRONOUNCEABLE NAME DECIDED THEY WERE GOING TO PIGGYBACK MY TRANSMISSION--
--AND USE MY BODY AS A HOST FOR THEIR PAN-DIMENSIONAL ARMY!
UNFORTUNATELY FOR THEM--MY WILL WAS TOO STRONG.
INSTEAD OF BEING THEIR SLAVE...
...I TOOK OVER THEIR VANGUARD AND KICKED THEIR COLLECTIVE ASSES ALL THE WAY BACK THROUGH THEIR PORTAL.

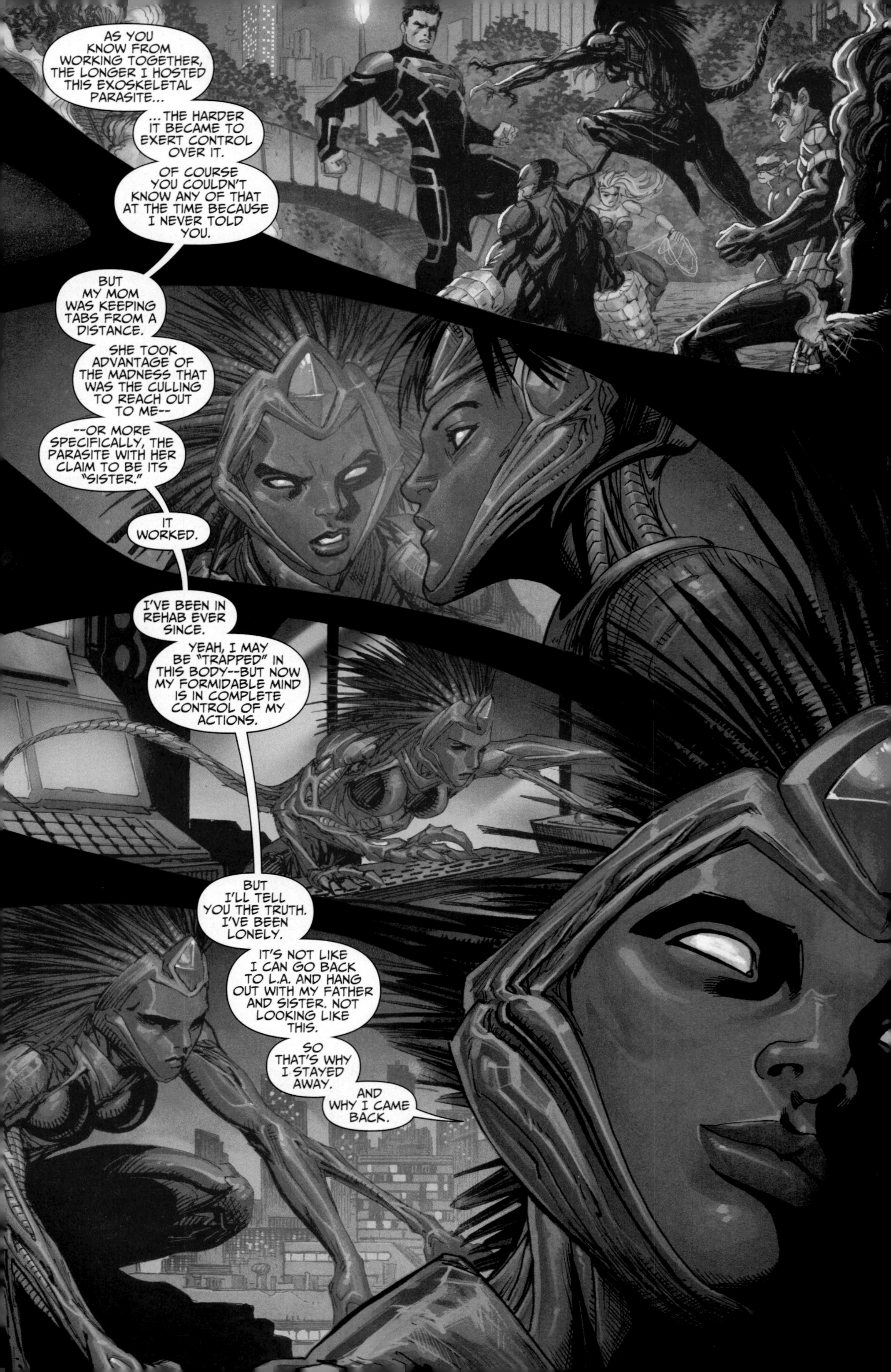
AS YOU KNOW FROM WORKING TOGETHER, THE LONGER I HOSTED THIS EXOSKELETAL PARASITE...
...THE HARDER IT BECAME TO EXERT CONTROL OVER IT.
OF COURSE YOU COULDN'T KNOW ANY OF THAT AT THE TIME BECAUSE I NEVER TOLD YOU.
BUT MY MOM WAS KEEPING TABS FROM A DISTANCE.
SHE TOOK ADVANTAGE OF THE MADNESS THAT WAS THE CULLING TO REACH OUT TO ME--
--OR MORE SPECIFICALLY, THE PARASITE WITH HER CLAIM TO BE ITS "SISTER."
IT WORKED.
I'VE BEEN IN REHAB EVER SINCE.
YEAH, I MAY BE "TRAPPED" IN THIS BODY--BUT NOW MY FORMIDABLE MIND IS IN COMPLETE CONTROL OF MY ACTIONS.
BUT I'LL TELL YOU THE TRUTH. I'VE BEEN LONELY.
IT'S NOT LIKE I CAN GO BACK TO L.A. AND HANG OUT WITH MY FATHER AND SISTER. NOT LOOKING LIKE THIS.
SO THAT'S WHY I STAYED AWAY.
AND WHY I CAME BACK.

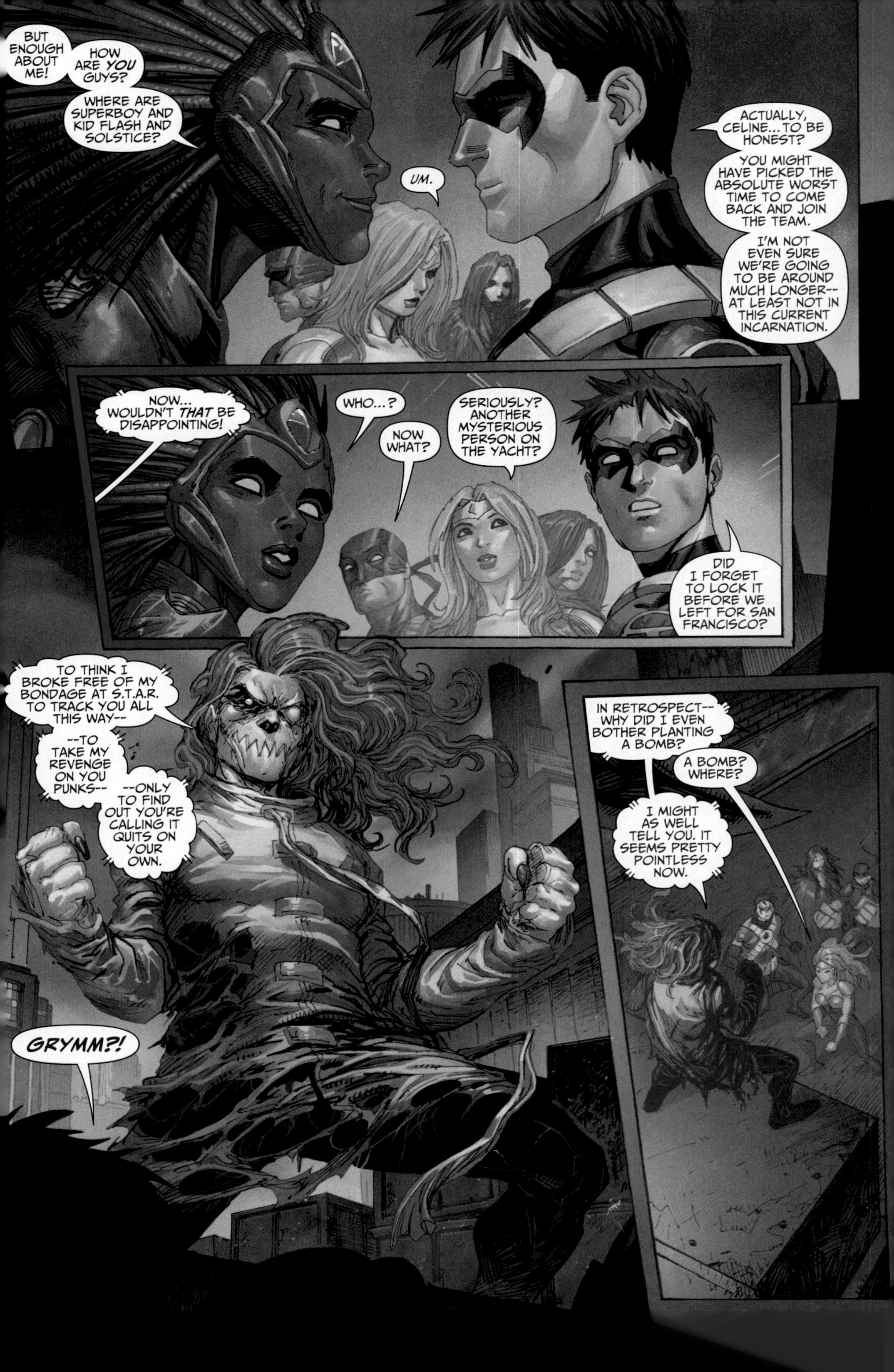
BUT ENOUGH ABOUT ME!
HOW ARE *YOU* GUYS?
WHERE ARE SUPERBOY AND KID FLASH AND SOLSTICE?
UM.
ACTUALLY, CELINE...TO BE HONEST?
YOU MIGHT HAVE PICKED THE ABSOLUTE WORST TIME TO COME BACK AND JOIN THE TEAM.
I'M NOT EVEN SURE WE'RE GOING TO BE AROUND MUCH LONGER--AT LEAST NOT IN THIS CURRENT INCARNATION.
NOW... WOULDN'T *THAT* BE DISAPPOINTING!
WHO...?
NOW WHAT?
SERIOUSLY? ANOTHER MYSTERIOUS PERSON ON THE YACHT?
DID I FORGET TO LOCK IT BEFORE WE LEFT FOR SAN FRANCISCO?
TO THINK I BROKE FREE OF MY BONDAGE AT S.T.A.R. TO TRACK YOU ALL THIS WAY--
--TO TAKE MY REVENGE ON YOU PUNKS--
--ONLY TO FIND OUT YOU'RE CALLING IT QUITS ON YOUR OWN.
GRYMM?!
IN RETROSPECT--WHY DID I EVEN BOTHER PLANTING A BOMB?
A BOMB? WHERE?
I MIGHT AS WELL TELL YOU. IT SEEMS PRETTY POINTLESS NOW.

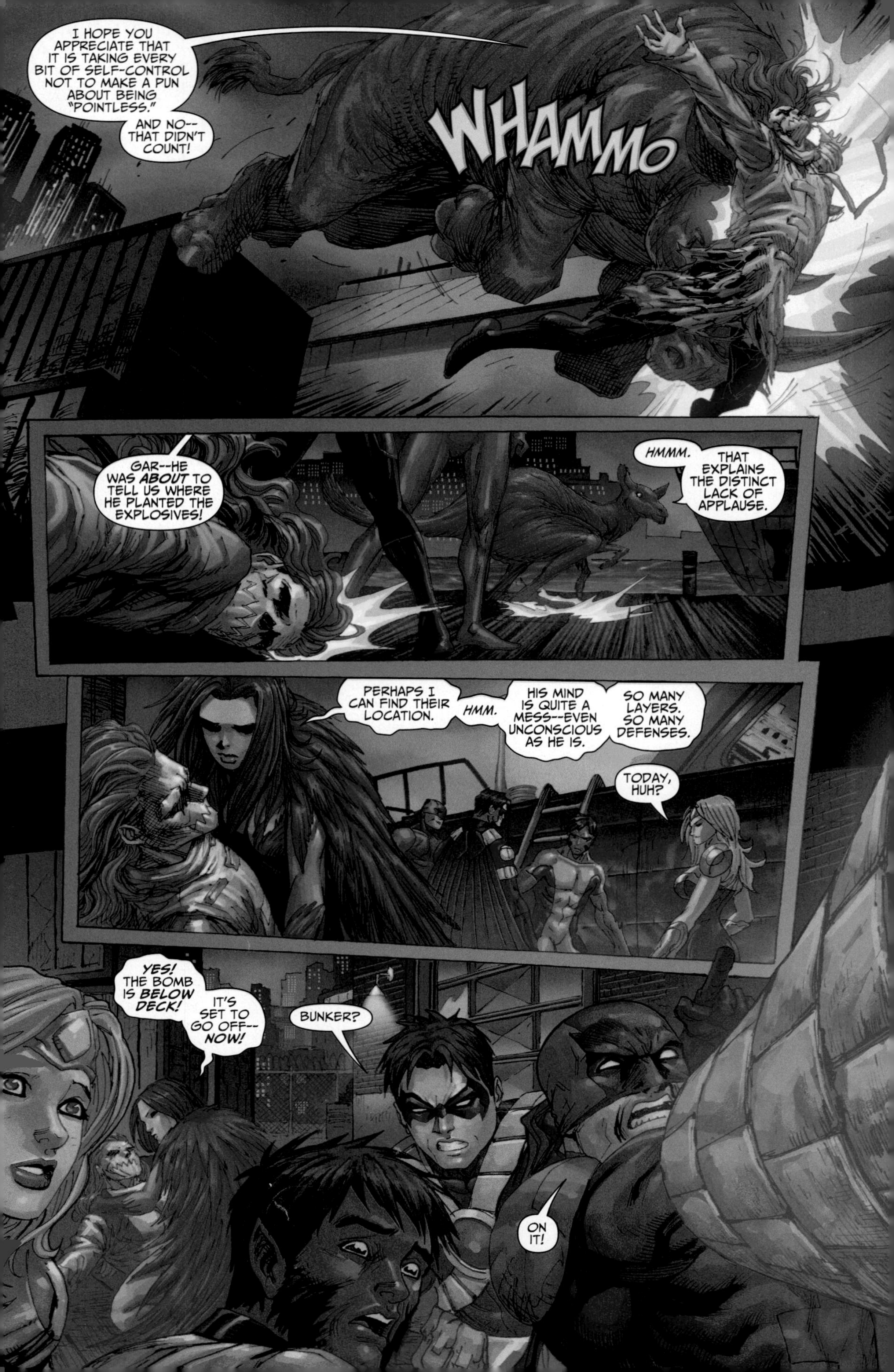
I HOPE YOU APPRECIATE THAT IT IS TAKING EVERY BIT OF SELF-CONTROL NOT TO MAKE A PUN ABOUT BEING "POINTLESS."
AND NO-- THAT DIDN'T COUNT!
WHAMMO
GAR--HE WAS ABOUT TO TELL US WHERE HE PLANTED THE EXPLOSIVES!
HMMM.
THAT EXPLAINS THE DISTINCT LACK OF APPLAUSE.
PERHAPS I CAN FIND THEIR LOCATION.
HMM.
HIS MIND IS QUITE A MESS--EVEN UNCONSCIOUS AS HE IS.
SO MANY LAYERS. SO MANY DEFENSES.
TODAY, HUH?
YES! THE BOMB IS BELOW DECK!
IT'S SET TO GO OFF-- NOW!
BUNKER?
ON IT!

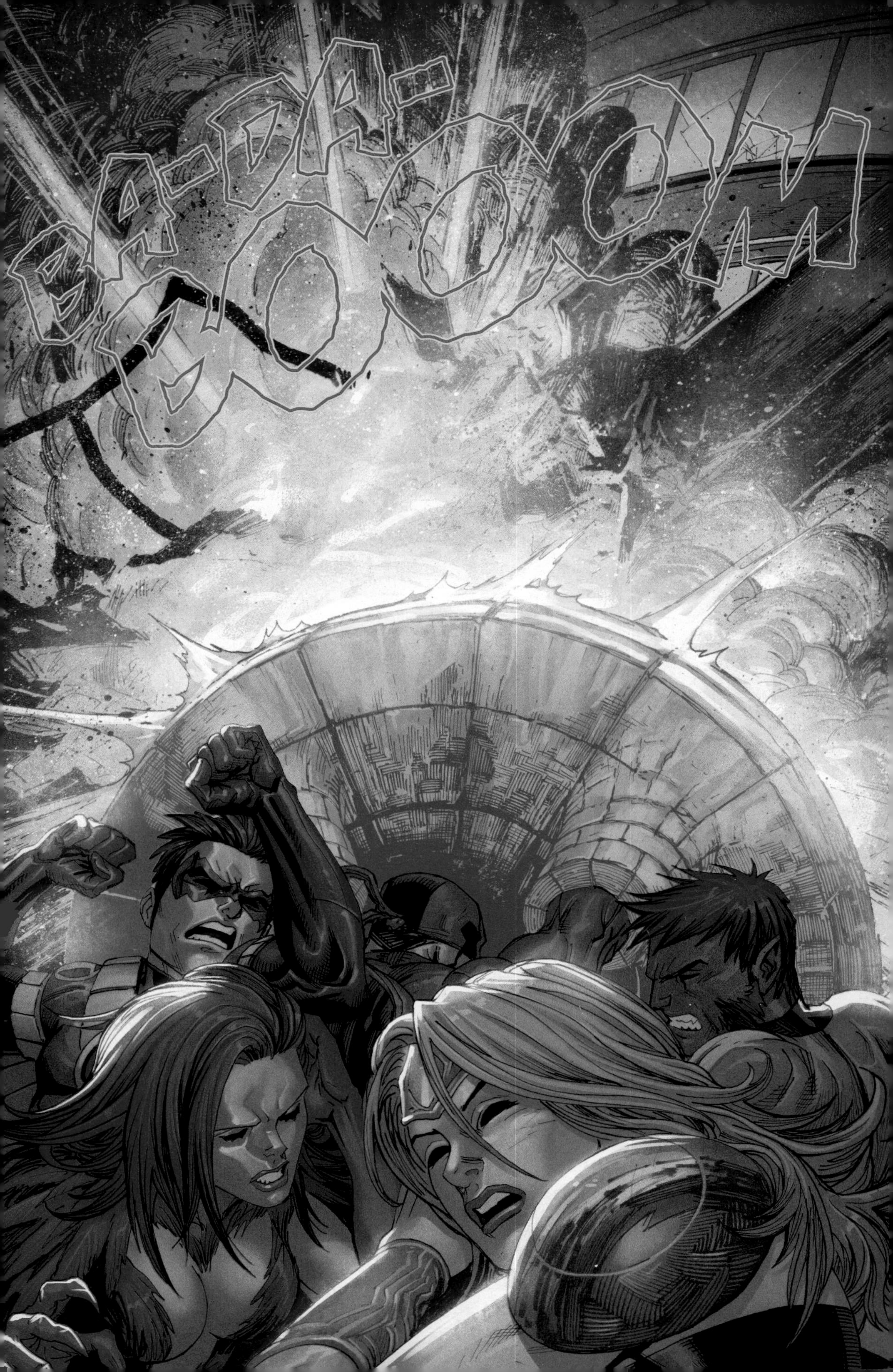
BA-DA-BOOOM

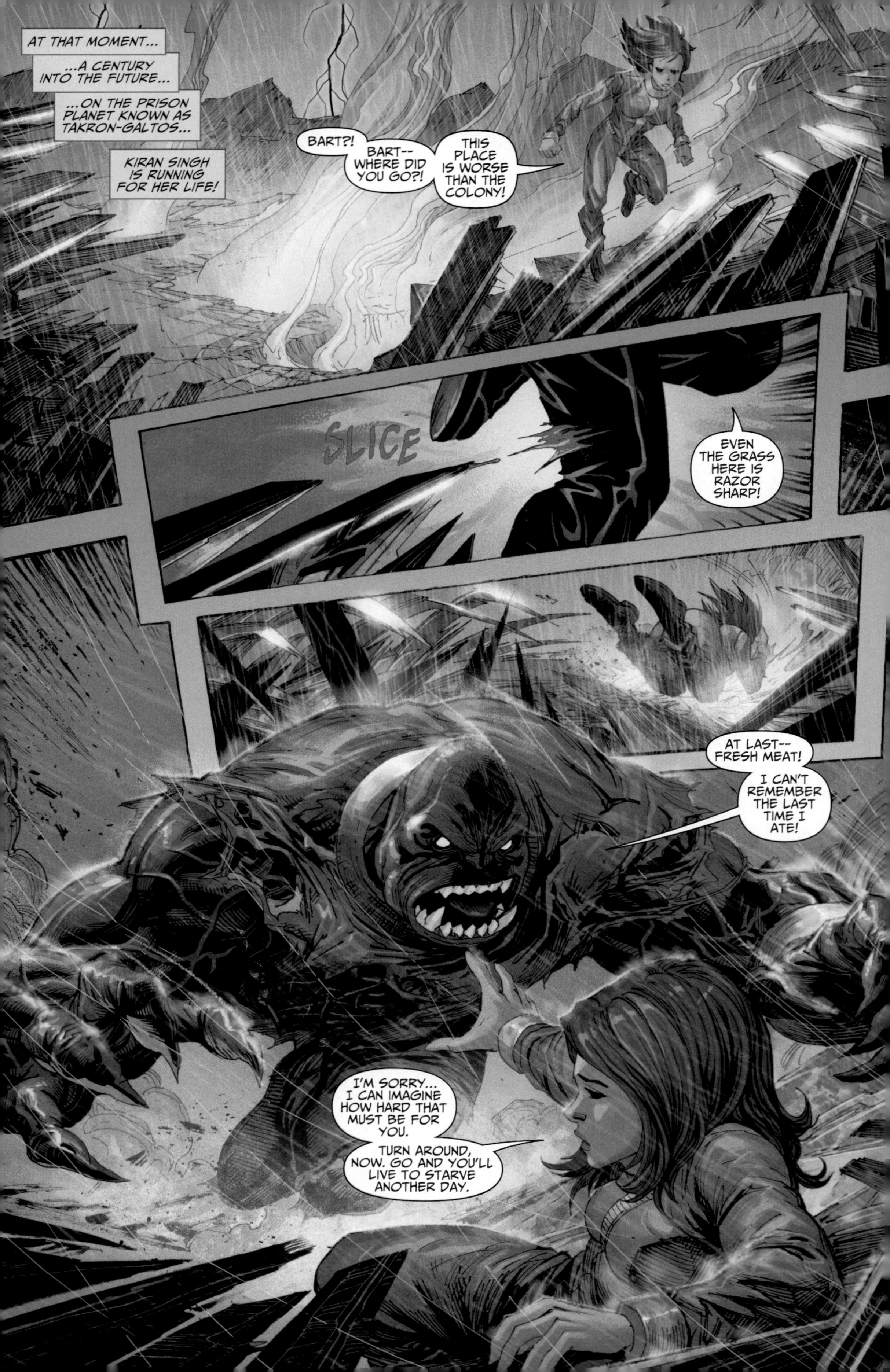
AT THAT MOMENT...
...A CENTURY INTO THE FUTURE...
...ON THE PRISON PLANET KNOWN AS TAKRON-GALTOS...
KIRAN SINGH IS RUNNING FOR HER LIFE!
BART?!
BART-- WHERE DID YOU GO?!
THIS PLACE IS WORSE THAN THE COLONY!
SLICE
EVEN THE GRASS HERE IS RAZOR SHARP!
AT LAST-- FRESH MEAT!
I CAN'T REMEMBER THE LAST TIME I ATE!
I'M SORRY... I CAN IMAGINE HOW HARD THAT MUST BE FOR YOU.
TURN AROUND, NOW. GO AND YOU'LL LIVE TO STARVE ANOTHER DAY.

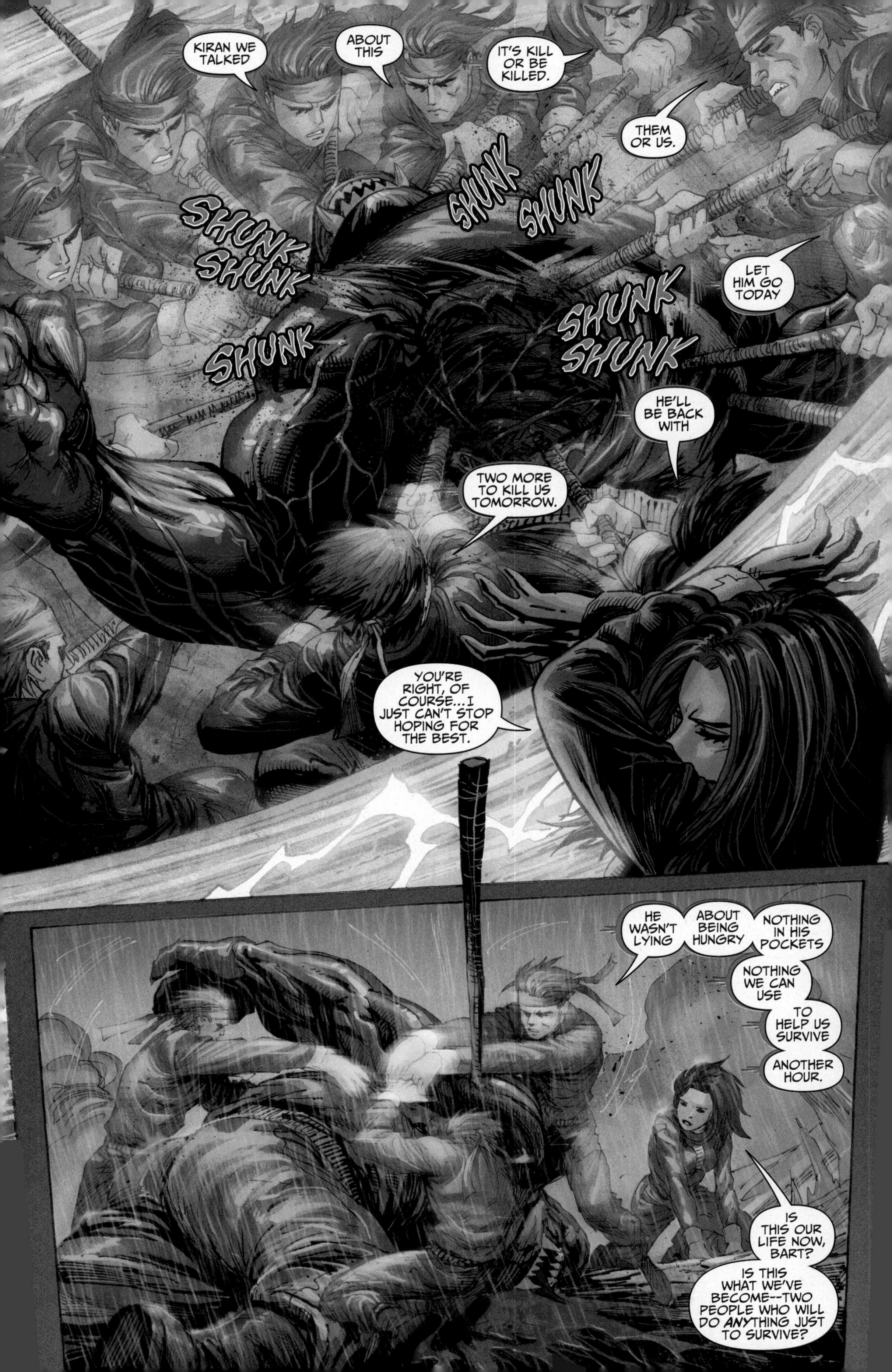
KIRAN WE TALKED
ABOUT THIS
IT'S KILL OR BE KILLED.
THEM OR US.
SHUNK SHUNK SHUNK
SHUNK SHUNK
SHUNK
SHUNK SHUNK
LET HIM GO TODAY
HE'LL BE BACK WITH
TWO MORE TO KILL US TOMORROW.
YOU'RE RIGHT, OF COURSE...I JUST CAN'T STOP HOPING FOR THE BEST.
HE WASN'T LYING
ABOUT BEING HUNGRY
NOTHING IN HIS POCKETS
NOTHING WE CAN USE
TO HELP US SURVIVE
ANOTHER HOUR.
IS THIS OUR LIFE NOW, BART?
IS THIS WHAT WE'VE BECOME--TWO PEOPLE WHO WILL DO *ANY*THING JUST TO SURVIVE?

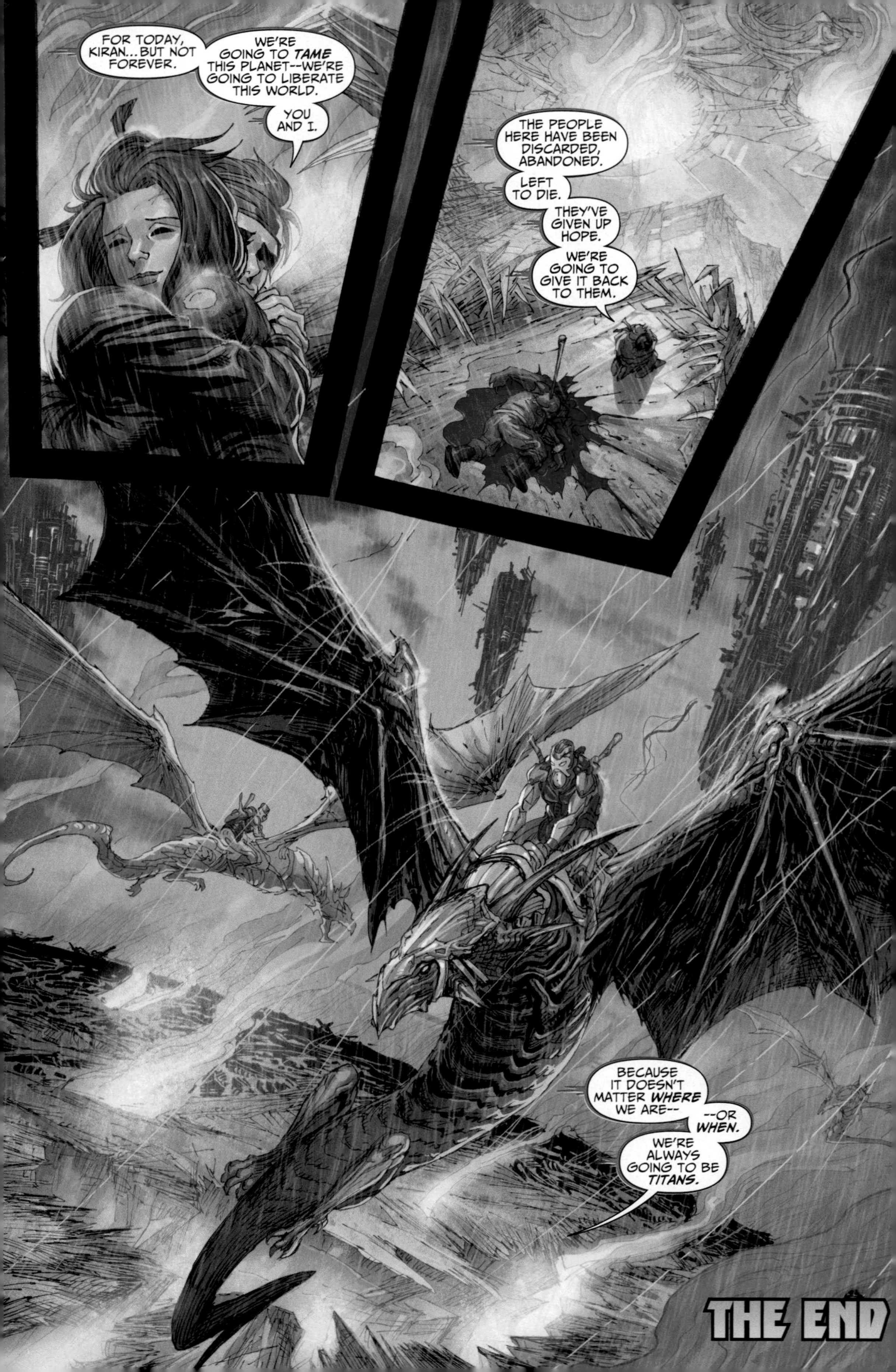
FOR TODAY, KIRAN...BUT NOT FOREVER.
WE'RE GOING TO *TAME* THIS PLANET--WE'RE GOING TO LIBERATE THIS WORLD.
YOU AND I.
THE PEOPLE HERE HAVE BEEN DISCARDED, ABANDONED.
LEFT TO DIE.
THEY'VE GIVEN UP HOPE.
WE'RE GOING TO GIVE IT BACK TO THEM.
BECAUSE IT DOESN'T MATTER *WHERE* WE ARE--
--OR *WHEN.*
WE'RE ALWAYS GOING TO BE *TITANS.*
THE END

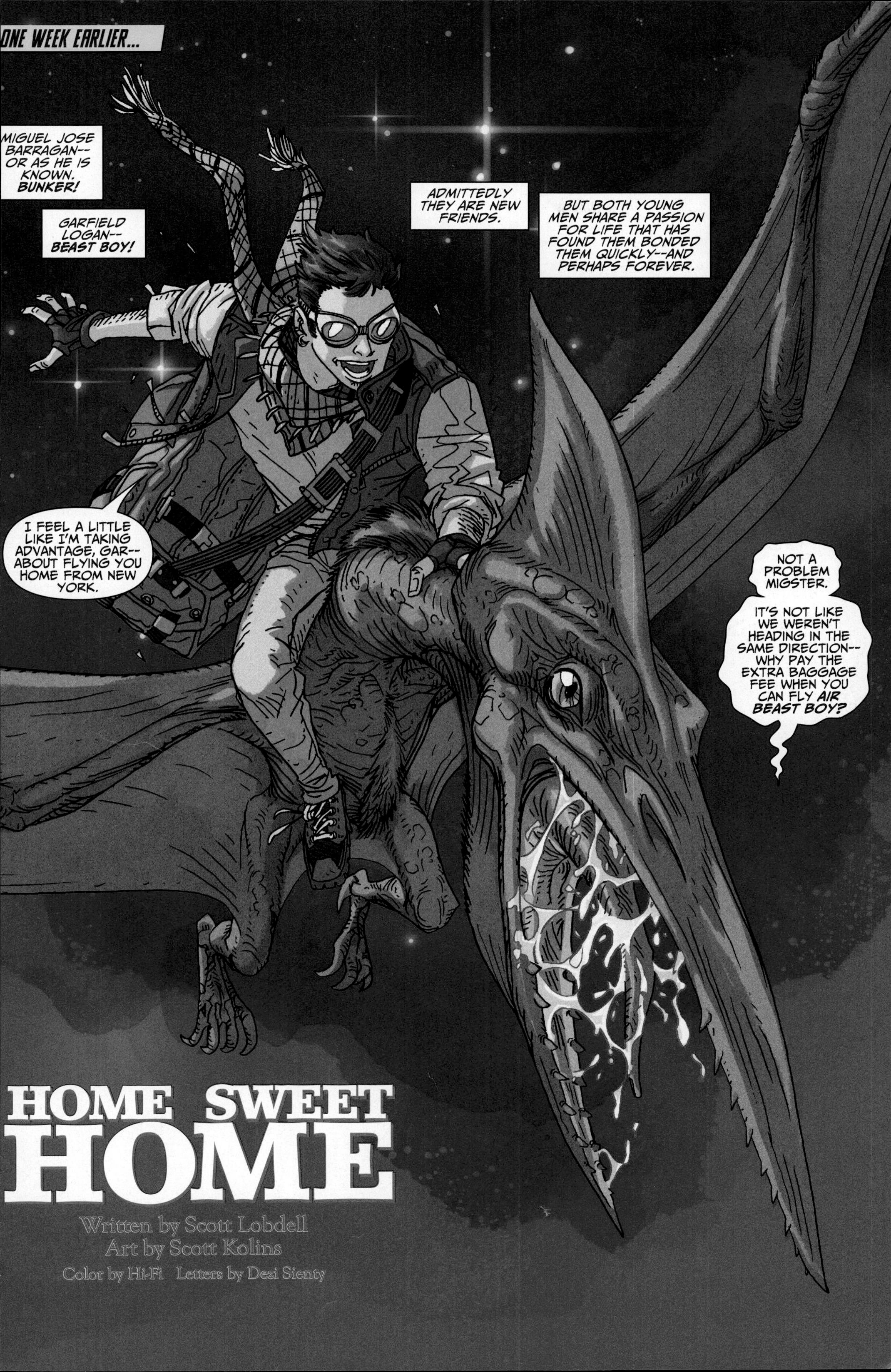
ONE WEEK EARLIER...
MIGUEL JOSE BARRAGAN-- OR AS HE IS KNOWN, BUNKER!
GARFIELD LOGAN-- BEAST BOY!
ADMITTEDLY THEY ARE NEW FRIENDS.
BUT BOTH YOUNG MEN SHARE A PASSION FOR LIFE THAT HAS FOUND THEM BONDED THEM QUICKLY--AND PERHAPS FOREVER.
I FEEL A LITTLE LIKE I'M TAKING ADVANTAGE, GAR-- ABOUT FLYING YOU HOME FROM NEW YORK.
NOT A PROBLEM MIGSTER.
IT'S NOT LIKE WE WEREN'T HEADING IN THE SAME DIRECTION-- WHY PAY THE EXTRA BAGGAGE FEE WHEN YOU CAN FLY AIR BEAST BOY?
HOME SWEET HOME
Written by Scott Lobdell
Art by Scott Kolins
Color by Hi-Fi Letters by Dezi Sienty

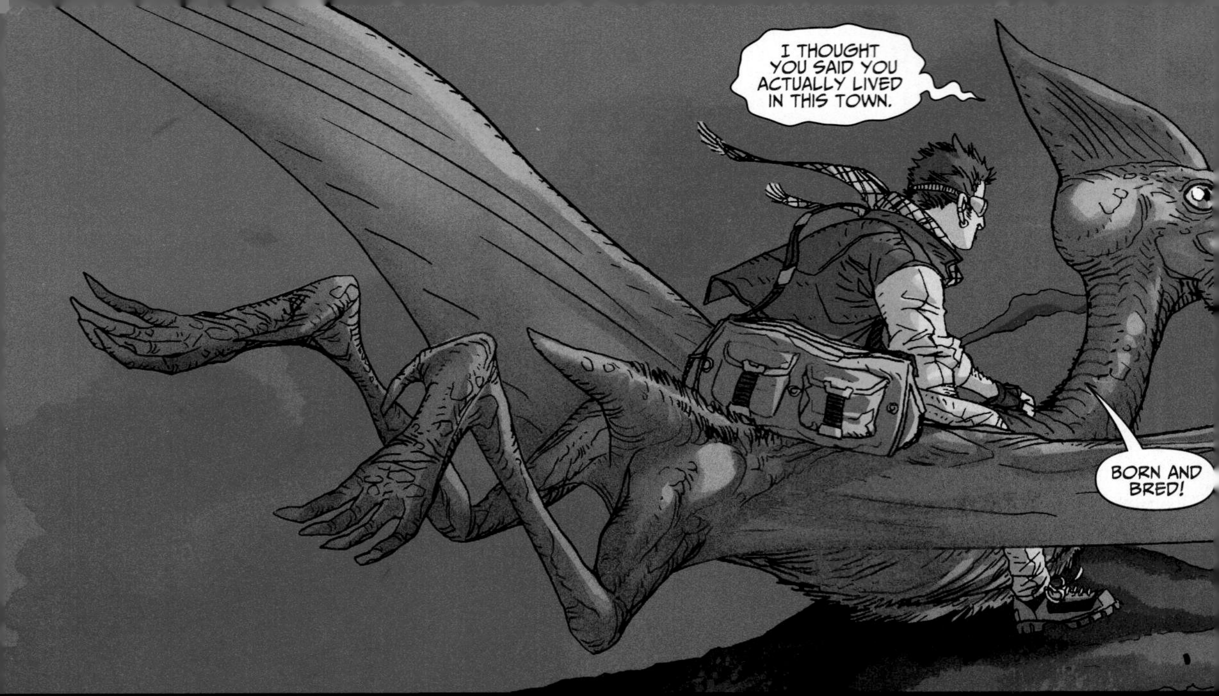
I THOUGHT YOU SAID YOU ACTUALLY LIVED IN THIS TOWN.
BORN AND BRED!

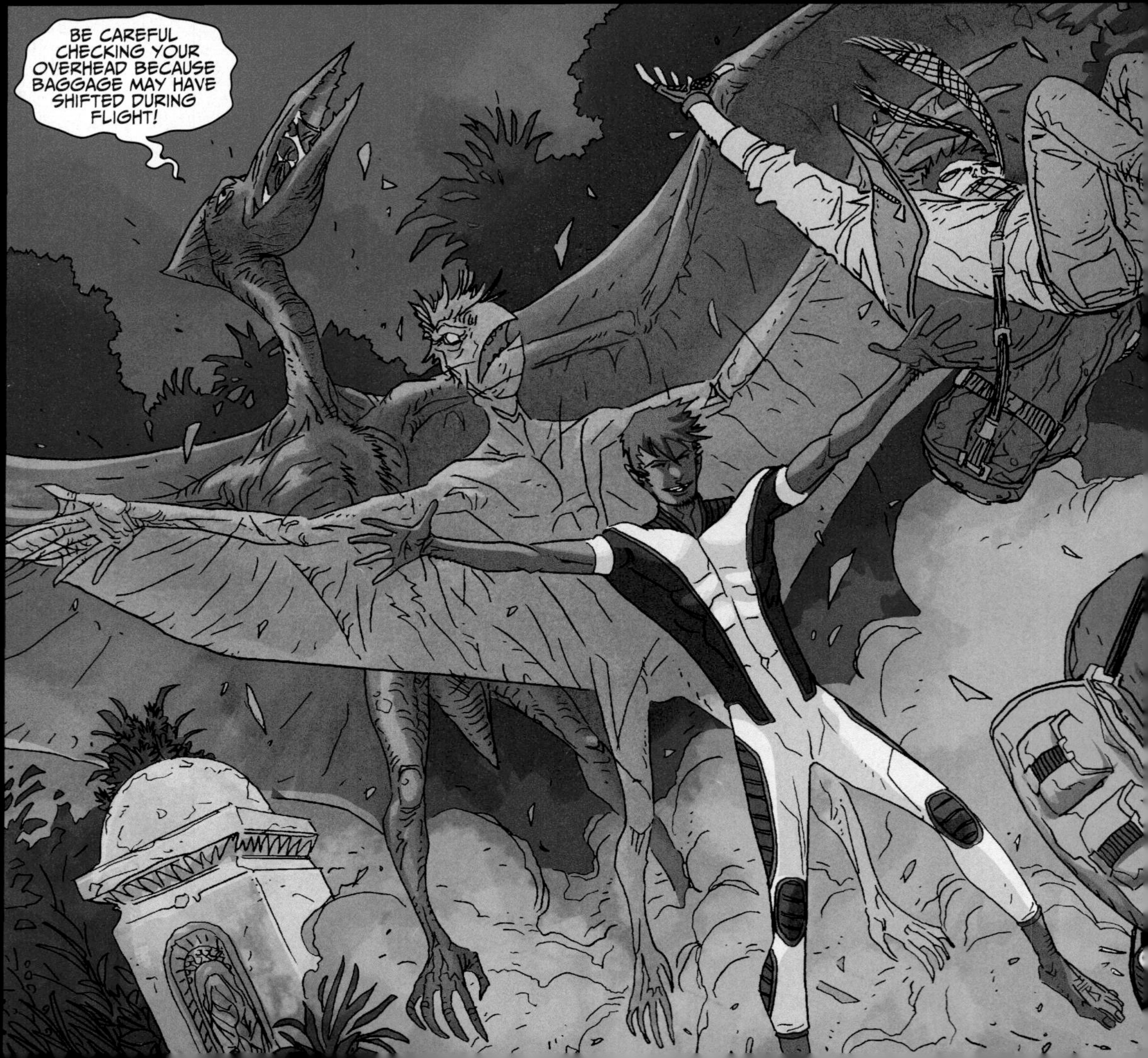
BE CAREFUL CHECKING YOUR OVERHEAD BECAUSE BAGGAGE MAY HAVE SHIFTED DURING FLIGHT!

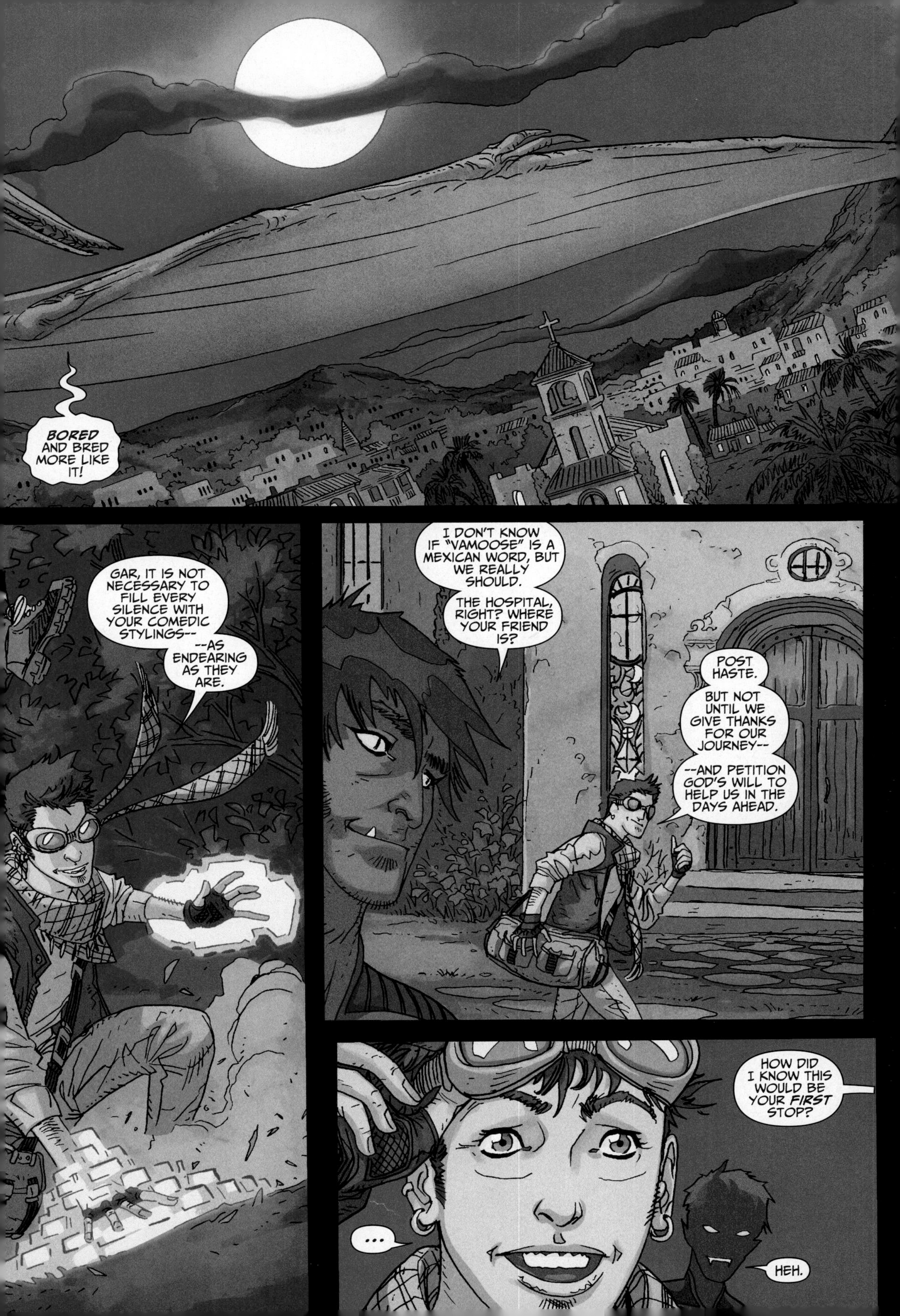
BORED AND BRED MORE LIKE IT!
GAR, IT IS NOT NECESSARY TO FILL EVERY SILENCE WITH YOUR COMEDIC STYLINGS--
--AS ENDEARING AS THEY ARE.
I DON'T KNOW IF "VAMOOSE" IS A MEXICAN WORD, BUT WE REALLY SHOULD.
THE HOSPITAL, RIGHT? WHERE YOUR FRIEND IS?
POST HASTE.
BUT NOT UNTIL WE GIVE THANKS FOR OUR JOURNEY--
--AND PETITION GOD'S WILL TO HELP US IN THE DAYS AHEAD.
HOW DID I KNOW THIS WOULD BE YOUR FIRST STOP?
...
HEH.

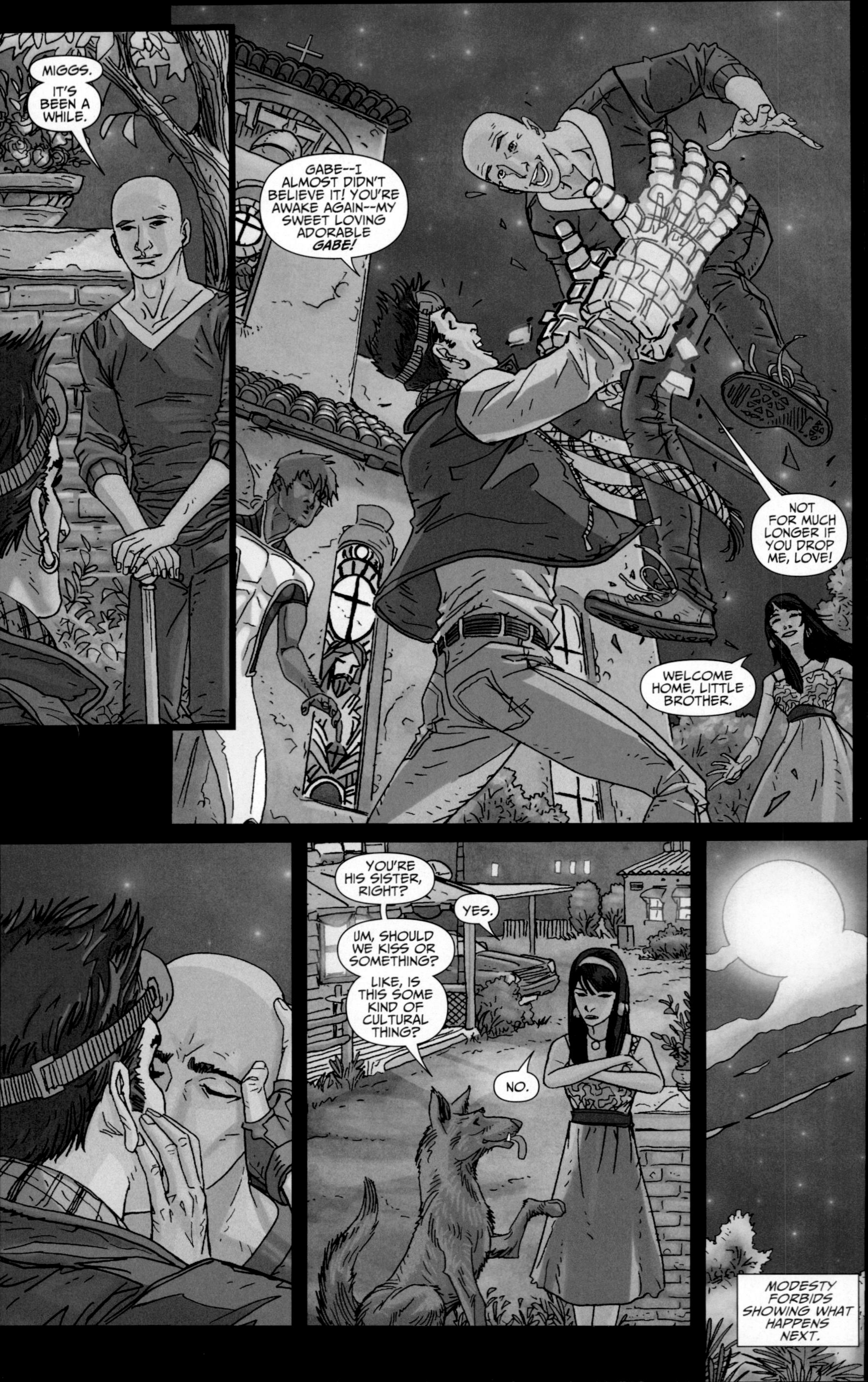
MIGGS. IT'S BEEN A WHILE.
GABE--I ALMOST DIDN'T BELIEVE IT! YOU'RE AWAKE AGAIN--MY SWEET LOVING ADORABLE *GABE!*
NOT FOR MUCH LONGER IF YOU DROP ME, LOVE!
WELCOME HOME, LITTLE BROTHER.
YOU'RE HIS SISTER, RIGHT?
YES.
UM, SHOULD WE KISS OR SOMETHING?
LIKE, IS THIS SOME KIND OF CULTURAL THING?
NO.
MODESTY FORBIDS SHOWING WHAT HAPPENS NEXT.

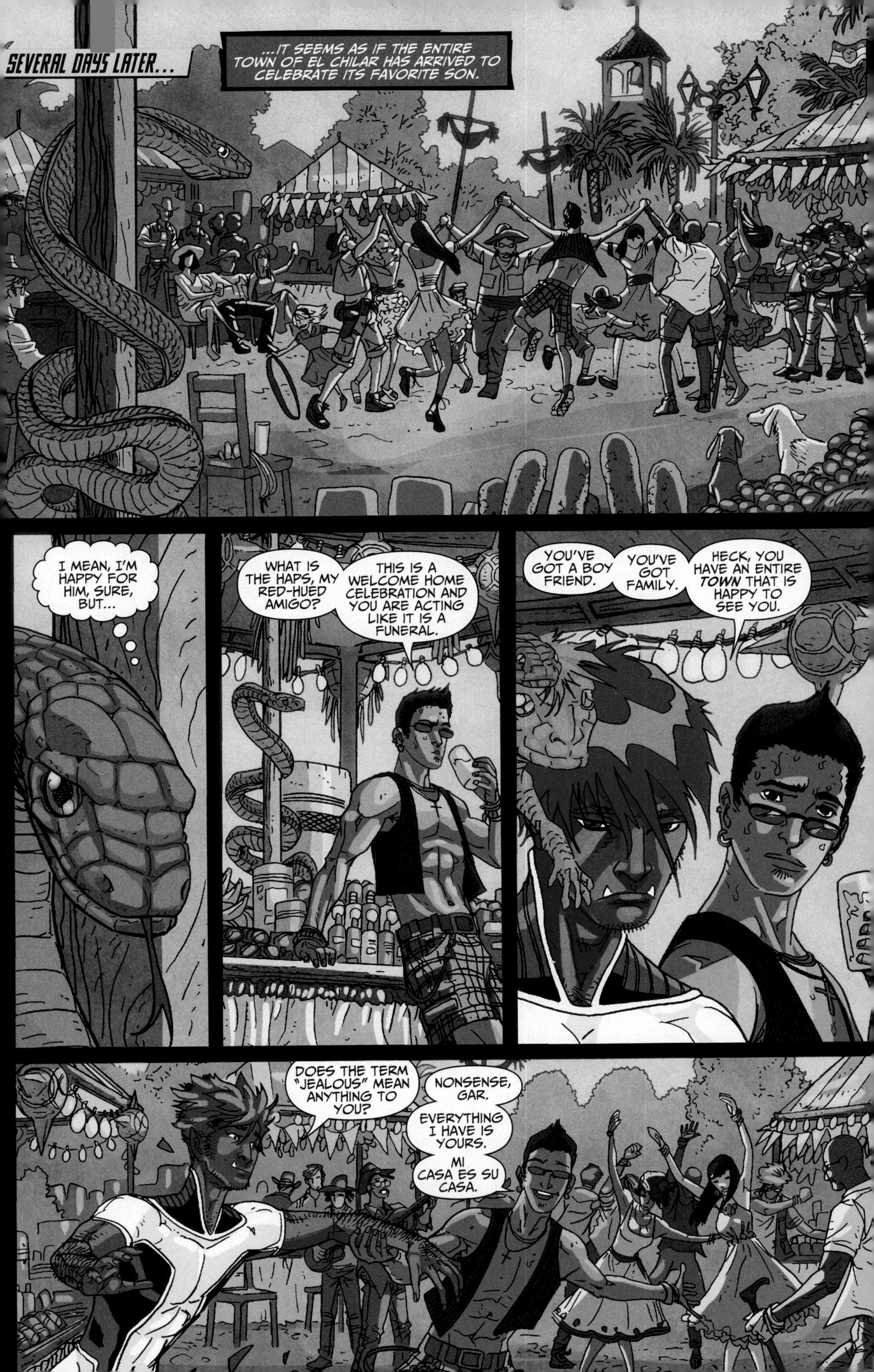

SEVERAL DAYS LATER...
...IT SEEMS AS IF THE ENTIRE TOWN OF EL CHILAR HAS ARRIVED TO CELEBRATE ITS FAVORITE SON.
I MEAN, I'M HAPPY FOR HIM, SURE, BUT...
WHAT IS THE HAPS, MY RED-HUED AMIGO?
THIS IS A WELCOME HOME CELEBRATION AND YOU ARE ACTING LIKE IT IS A FUNERAL.
YOU'VE GOT A BOY FRIEND.
YOU'VE GOT FAMILY.
HECK, YOU HAVE AN ENTIRE TOWN THAT IS HAPPY TO SEE YOU.
DOES THE TERM "JEALOUS" MEAN ANYTHING TO YOU?
NONSENSE, GAR.
EVERYTHING I HAVE IS YOURS.
MI CASA ES SU CASA.

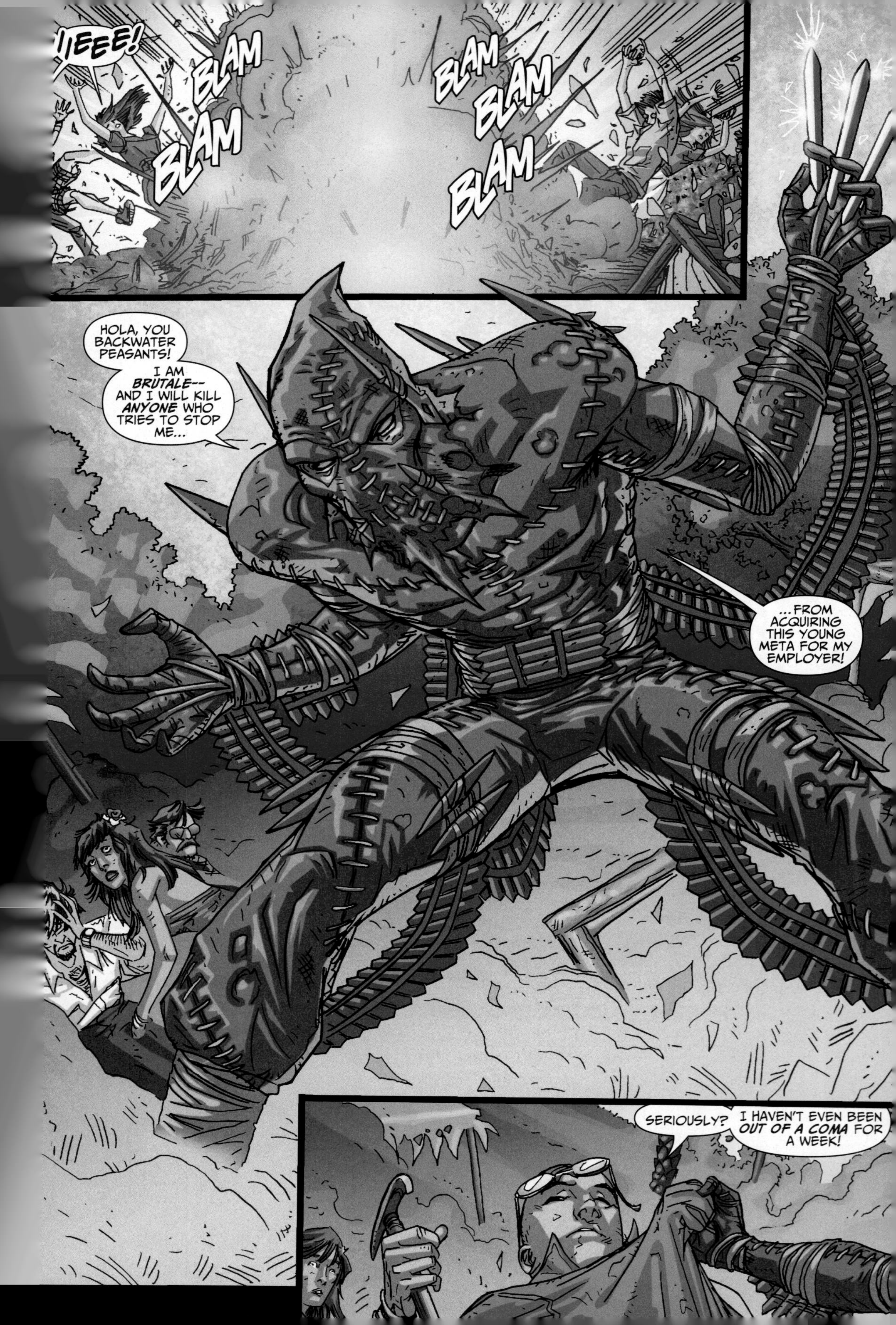
!!EEEE!
BLAM
BLAM
BLAM
BLAM
BLAM
HOLA, YOU BACKWATER PEASANTS!
I AM *BRUTALE*-- AND I WILL KILL *ANYONE* WHO TRIES TO STOP ME...
...FROM ACQUIRING THIS YOUNG META FOR MY EMPLOYER!
SERIOUSLY?
I HAVEN'T EVEN BEEN *OUT OF A COMA* FOR A WEEK!

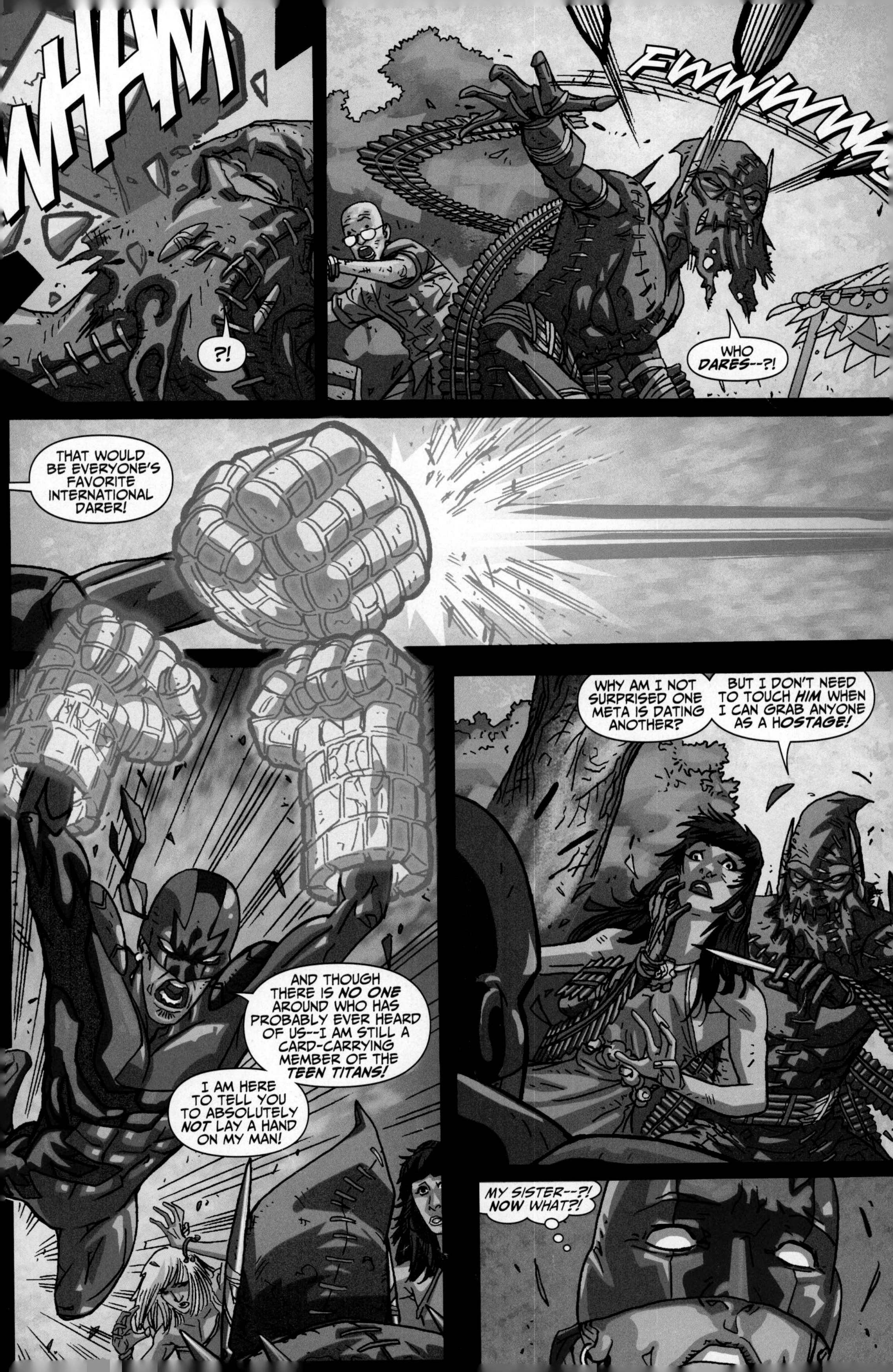
WHAM
?!
FWWWWWW
WHO DARES--?!
THAT WOULD BE EVERYONE'S FAVORITE INTERNATIONAL DARER!
AND THOUGH THERE IS NO ONE AROUND WHO HAS PROBABLY EVER HEARD OF US--I AM STILL A CARD-CARRYING MEMBER OF THE TEEN TITANS!
I AM HERE TO TELL YOU TO ABSOLUTELY NOT LAY A HAND ON MY MAN!
WHY AM I NOT SURPRISED ONE META IS DATING ANOTHER?
BUT I DON'T NEED TO TOUCH HIM WHEN I CAN GRAB ANYONE AS A HOSTAGE!
MY SISTER--?! NOW WHAT?!

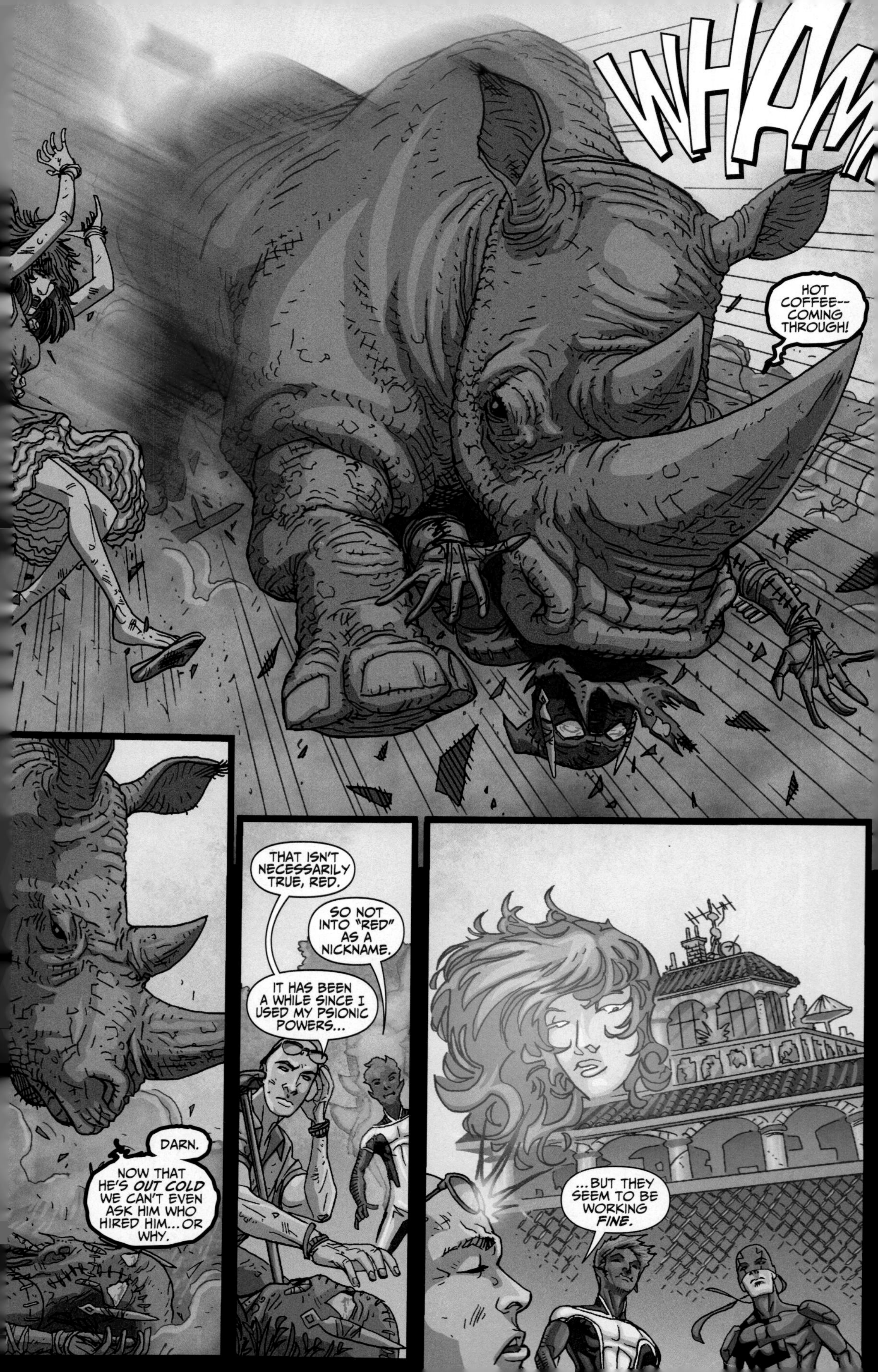

WHAM
HOT COFFEE-- COMING THROUGH!
DARN.
NOW THAT HE'S OUT COLD WE CAN'T EVEN ASK HIM WHO HIRED HIM...OR WHY.
THAT ISN'T NECESSARILY TRUE, RED.
SO NOT INTO "RED" AS A NICKNAME.
IT HAS BEEN A WHILE SINCE I USED MY PSIONIC POWERS...
...BUT THEY SEEM TO BE WORKING FINE.

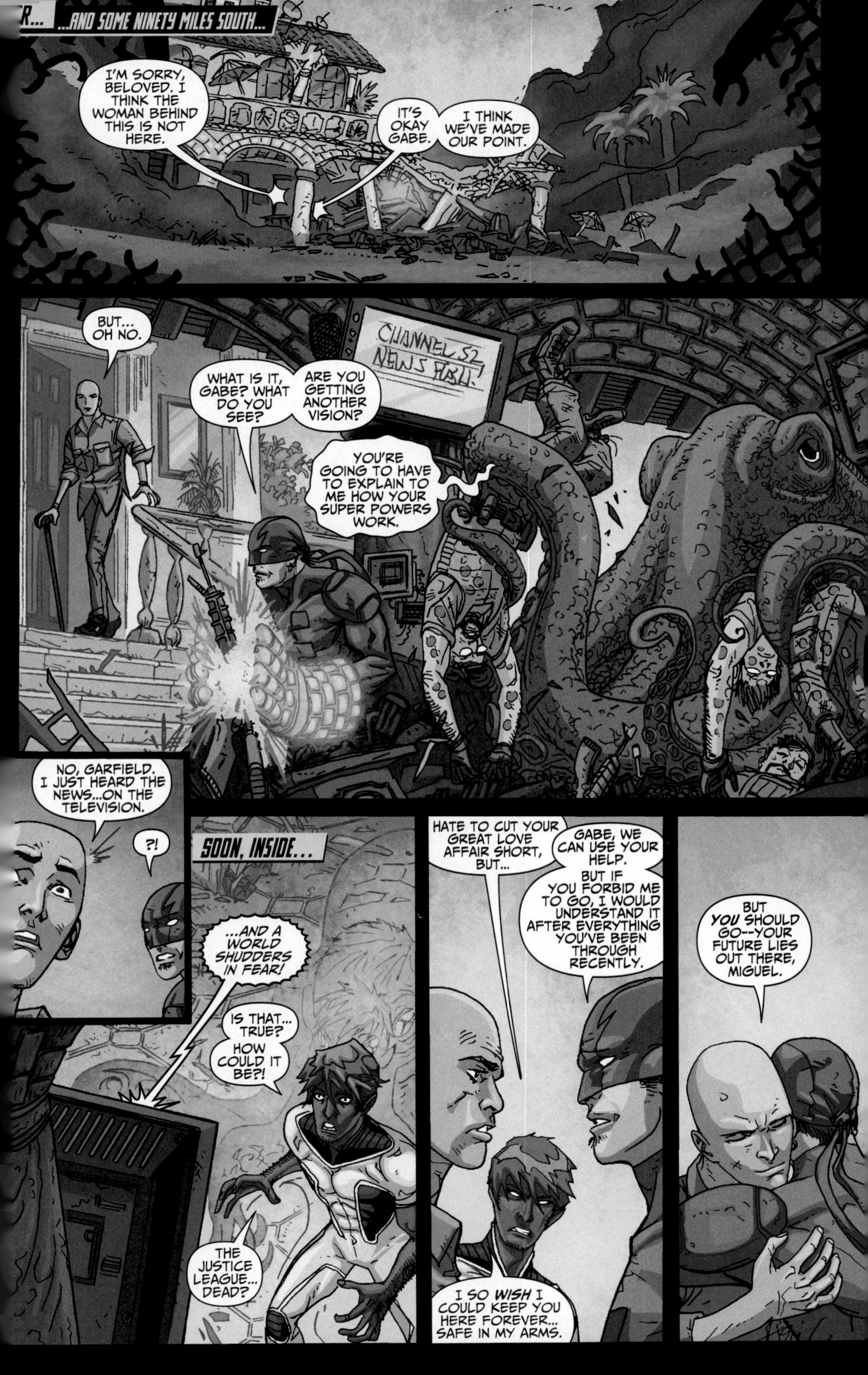

...AND SOME NINETY MILES SOUTH...
I'M SORRY, BELOVED. I THINK THE WOMAN BEHIND THIS IS NOT HERE.
IT'S OKAY GABE.
I THINK WE'VE MADE OUR POINT.
BUT... OH NO.
WHAT IS IT, GABE? WHAT DO YOU SEE?
ARE YOU GETTING ANOTHER VISION?
YOU'RE GOING TO HAVE TO EXPLAIN TO ME HOW YOUR SUPER POWERS WORK.
NO, GARFIELD. I JUST HEARD THE NEWS...ON THE TELEVISION.
?!
SOON, INSIDE...
...AND A WORLD SHUDDERS IN FEAR!
IS THAT... TRUE? HOW COULD IT BE?!
THE JUSTICE LEAGUE... DEAD?
HATE TO CUT YOUR GREAT LOVE AFFAIR SHORT, BUT...
GABE, WE CAN USE YOUR HELP.
BUT IF YOU FORBID ME TO GO, I WOULD UNDERSTAND IT AFTER EVERYTHING YOU'VE BEEN THROUGH RECENTLY.
I SO WISH I COULD KEEP YOU HERE FOREVER... SAFE IN MY ARMS.
BUT YOU SHOULD GO--YOUR FUTURE LIES OUT THERE, MIGUEL.

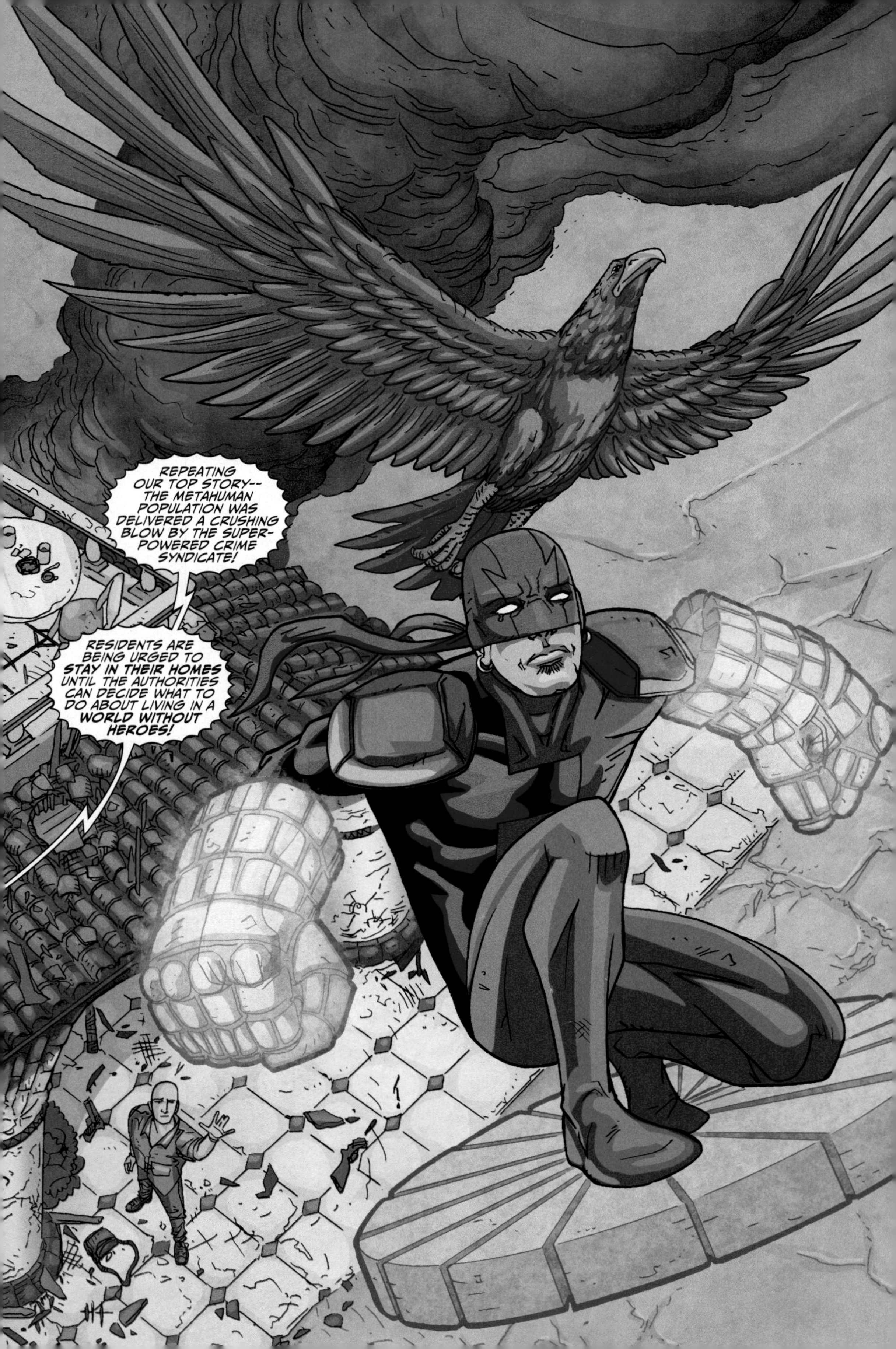
REPEATING OUR TOP STORY-- THE METAHUMAN POPULATION WAS DELIVERED A CRUSHING BLOW BY THE SUPER-POWERED CRIME SYNDICATE!
RESIDENTS ARE BEING URGED TO STAY IN THEIR HOMES UNTIL THE AUTHORITIES CAN DECIDE WHAT TO DO ABOUT LIVING IN A WORLD WITHOUT HEROES!

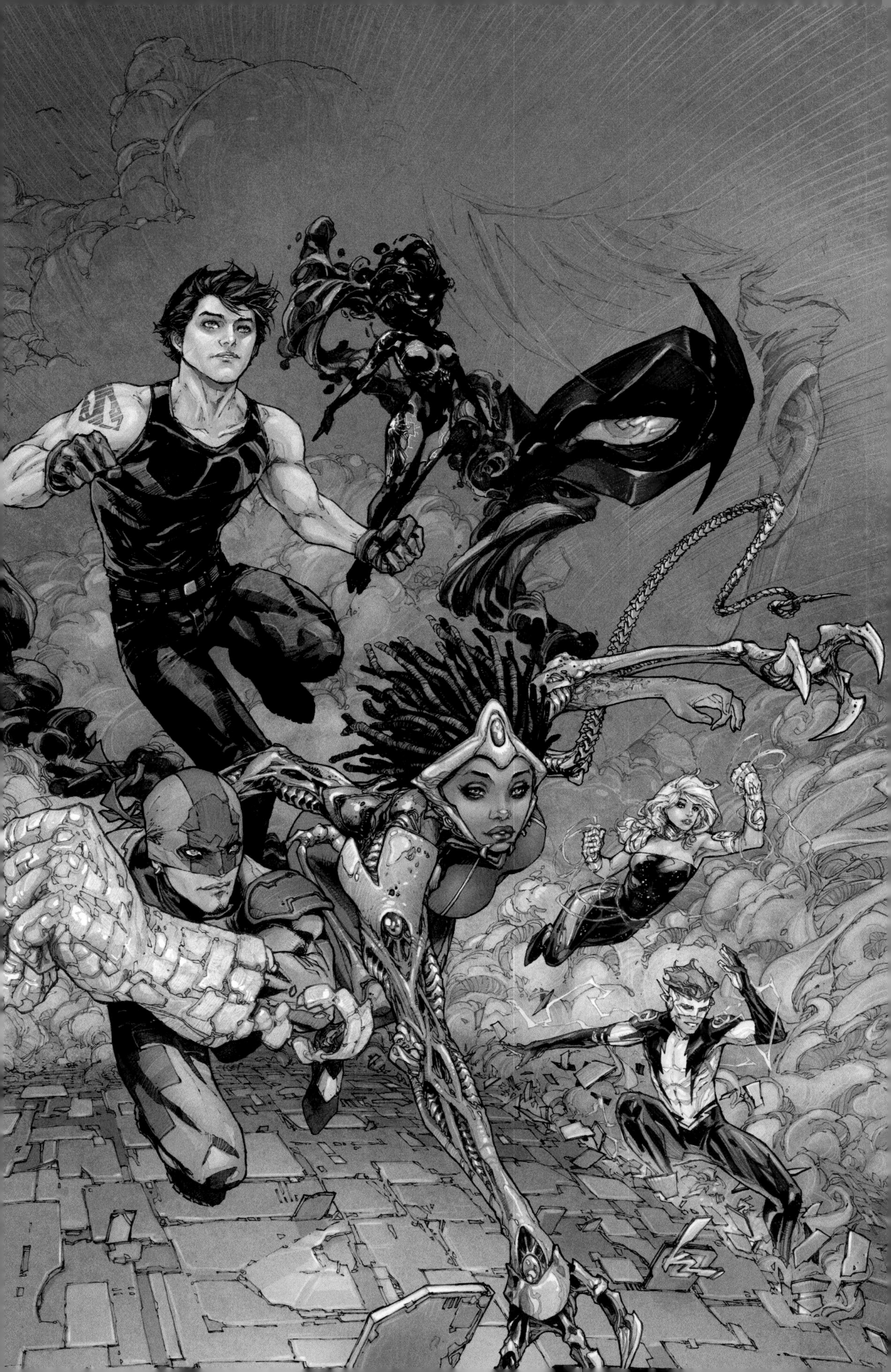

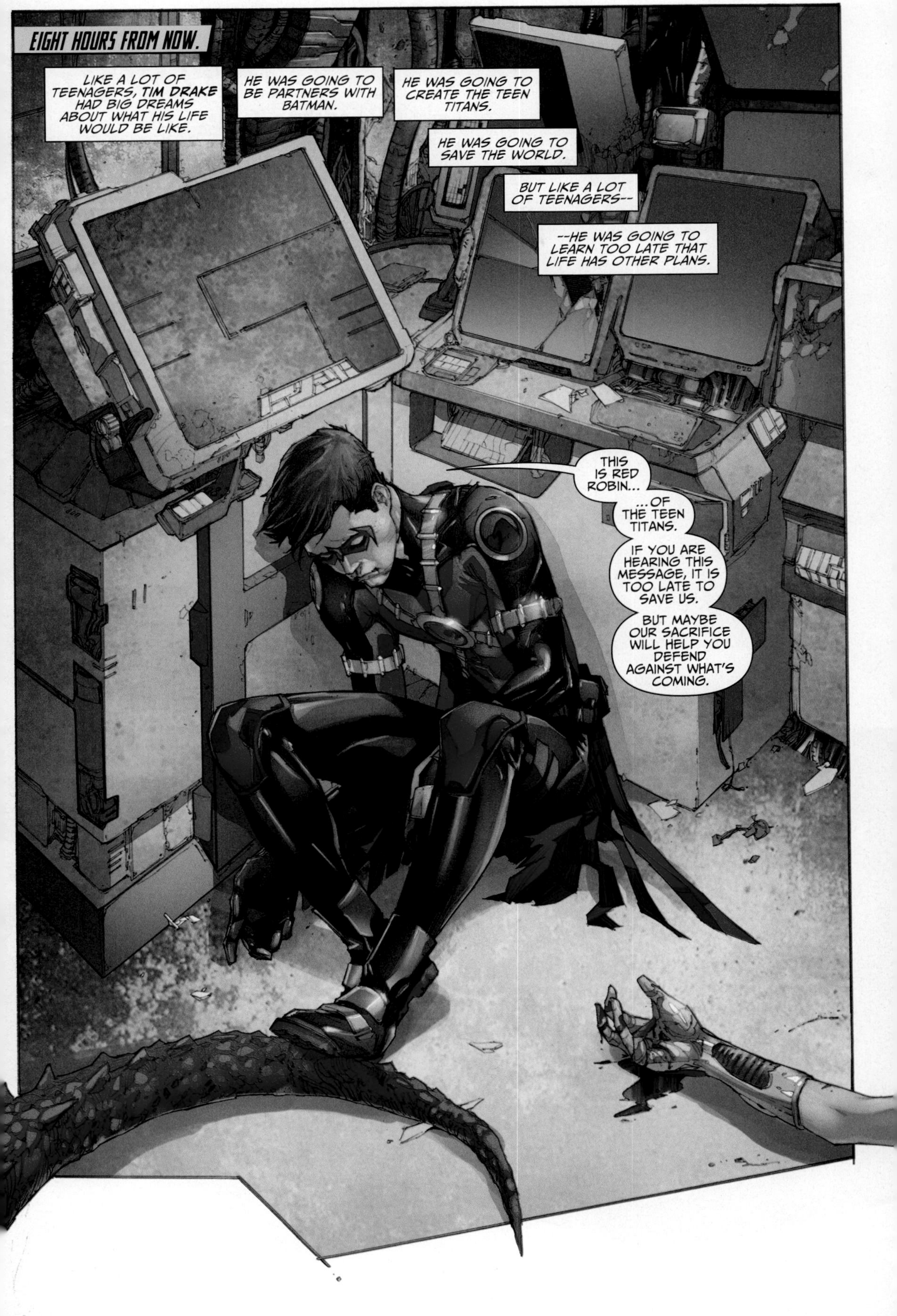
EIGHT HOURS FROM NOW.
LIKE A LOT OF TEENAGERS, TIM DRAKE HAD BIG DREAMS ABOUT WHAT HIS LIFE WOULD BE LIKE.
HE WAS GOING TO BE PARTNERS WITH BATMAN.
HE WAS GOING TO CREATE THE TEEN TITANS.
HE WAS GOING TO SAVE THE WORLD.
BUT LIKE A LOT OF TEENAGERS--
--HE WAS GOING TO LEARN TOO LATE THAT LIFE HAS OTHER PLANS.
THIS IS RED ROBIN...
...OF THE TEEN TITANS.
IF YOU ARE HEARING THIS MESSAGE, IT IS TOO LATE TO SAVE US.
BUT MAYBE OUR SACRIFICE WILL HELP YOU DEFEND AGAINST WHAT'S COMING.

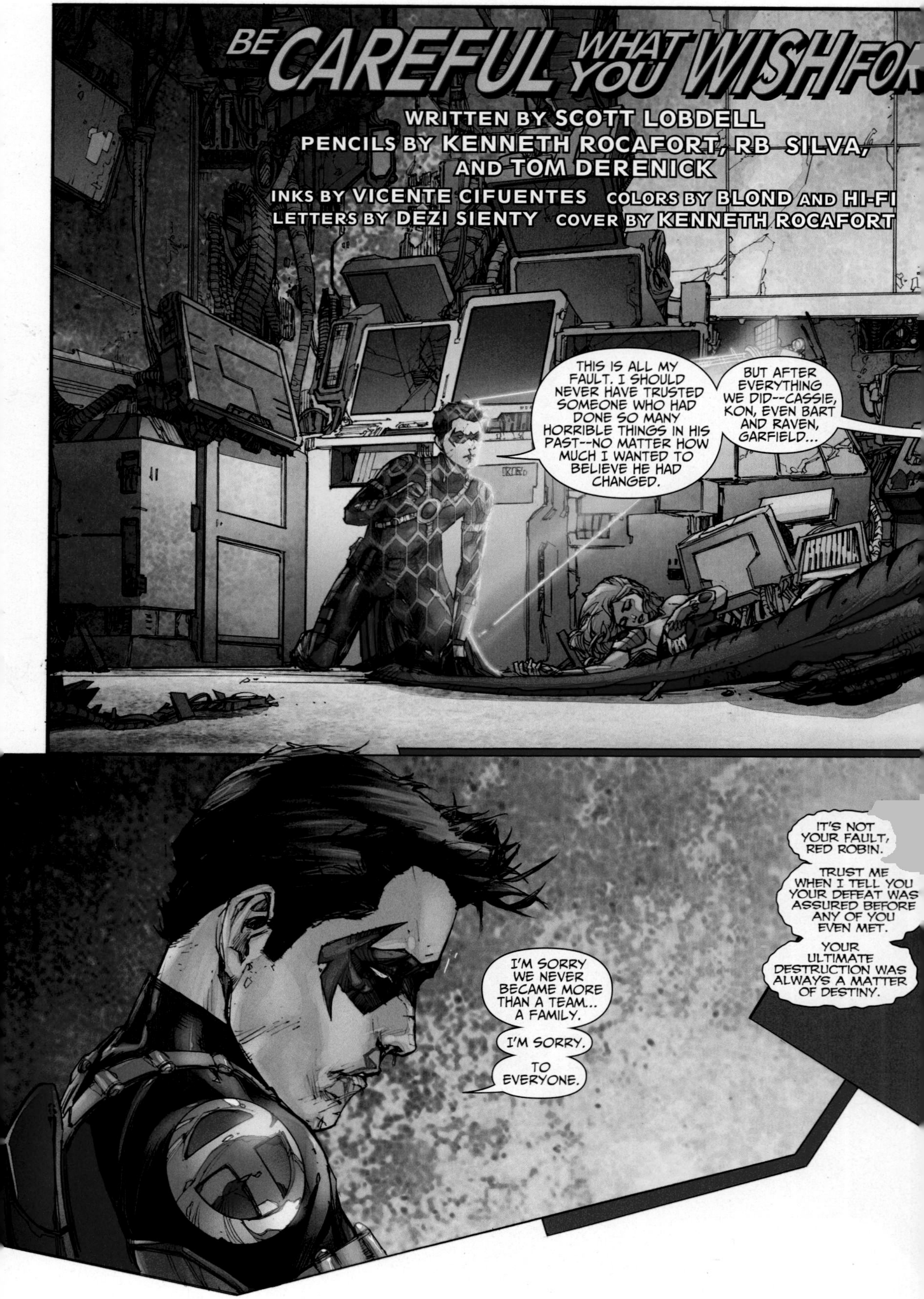
BE CAREFUL WHAT YOU WISH FOR
WRITTEN BY SCOTT LOBDELL
PENCILS BY KENNETH ROCAFORT, RB SILVA, AND TOM DERENICK
INKS BY VICENTE CIFUENTES COLORS BY BLOND AND HI-FI
LETTERS BY DEZI SIENTY COVER BY KENNETH ROCAFORT
THIS IS ALL MY FAULT. I SHOULD NEVER HAVE TRUSTED SOMEONE WHO HAD DONE SO MANY HORRIBLE THINGS IN HIS PAST--NO MATTER HOW MUCH I WANTED TO BELIEVE HE HAD CHANGED.
BUT AFTER EVERYTHING WE DID--CASSIE, KON, EVEN BART AND RAVEN, GARFIELD...
I'M SORRY WE NEVER BECAME MORE THAN A TEAM... A FAMILY.
I'M SORRY.
TO EVERYONE.
IT'S NOT YOUR FAULT, RED ROBIN.
TRUST ME WHEN I TELL YOU YOUR DEFEAT WAS ASSURED BEFORE ANY OF YOU EVEN MET.
YOUR ULTIMATE DESTRUCTION WAS ALWAYS A MATTER OF DESTINY.

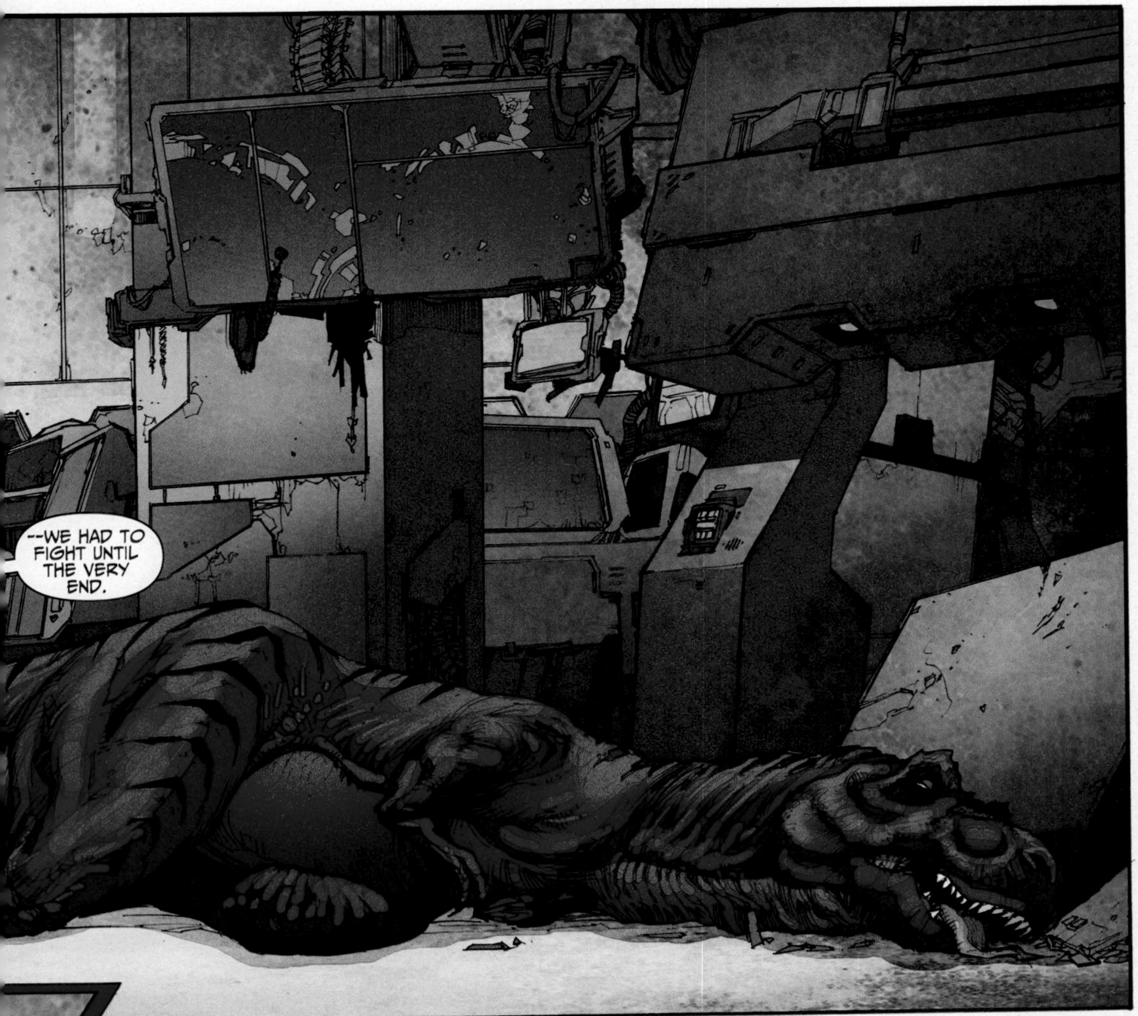
--WE HAD TO FIGHT UNTIL THE VERY END.

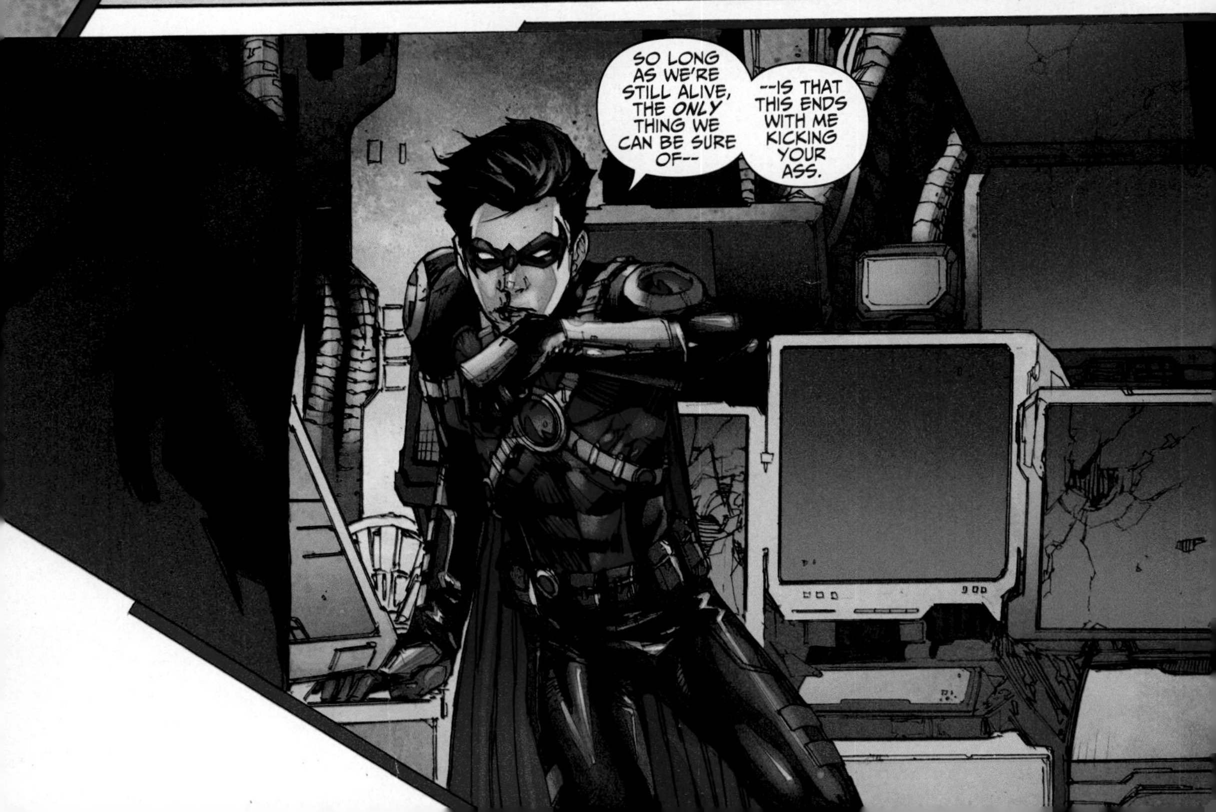
SO LONG AS WE'RE STILL ALIVE, THE *ONLY* THING WE CAN BE SURE OF--
--IS THAT THIS ENDS WITH ME KICKING YOUR ASS.

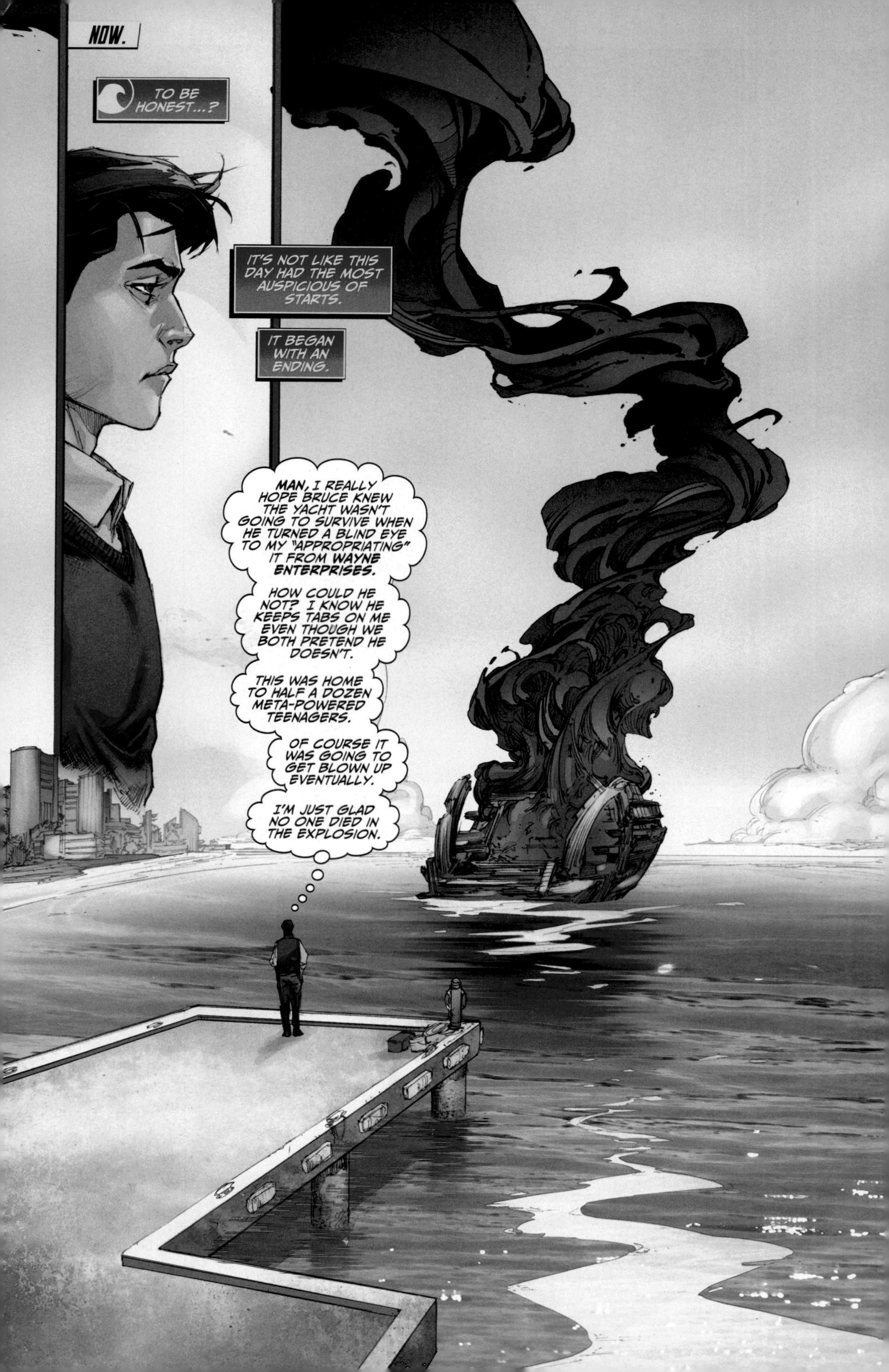
NOW.
TO BE HONEST...?
IT'S NOT LIKE THIS DAY HAD THE MOST AUSPICIOUS OF STARTS.
IT BEGAN WITH AN ENDING.
MAN, I REALLY HOPE BRUCE KNEW THE YACHT WASN'T GOING TO SURVIVE WHEN HE TURNED A BLIND EYE TO MY "APPROPRIATING" IT FROM WAYNE ENTERPRISES.
HOW COULD HE NOT? I KNOW HE KEEPS TABS ON ME EVEN THOUGH WE BOTH PRETEND HE DOESN'T.
THIS WAS HOME TO HALF A DOZEN META-POWERED TEENAGERS.
OF COURSE IT WAS GOING TO GET BLOWN UP EVENTUALLY.
I'M JUST GLAD NO ONE DIED IN THE EXPLOSION.

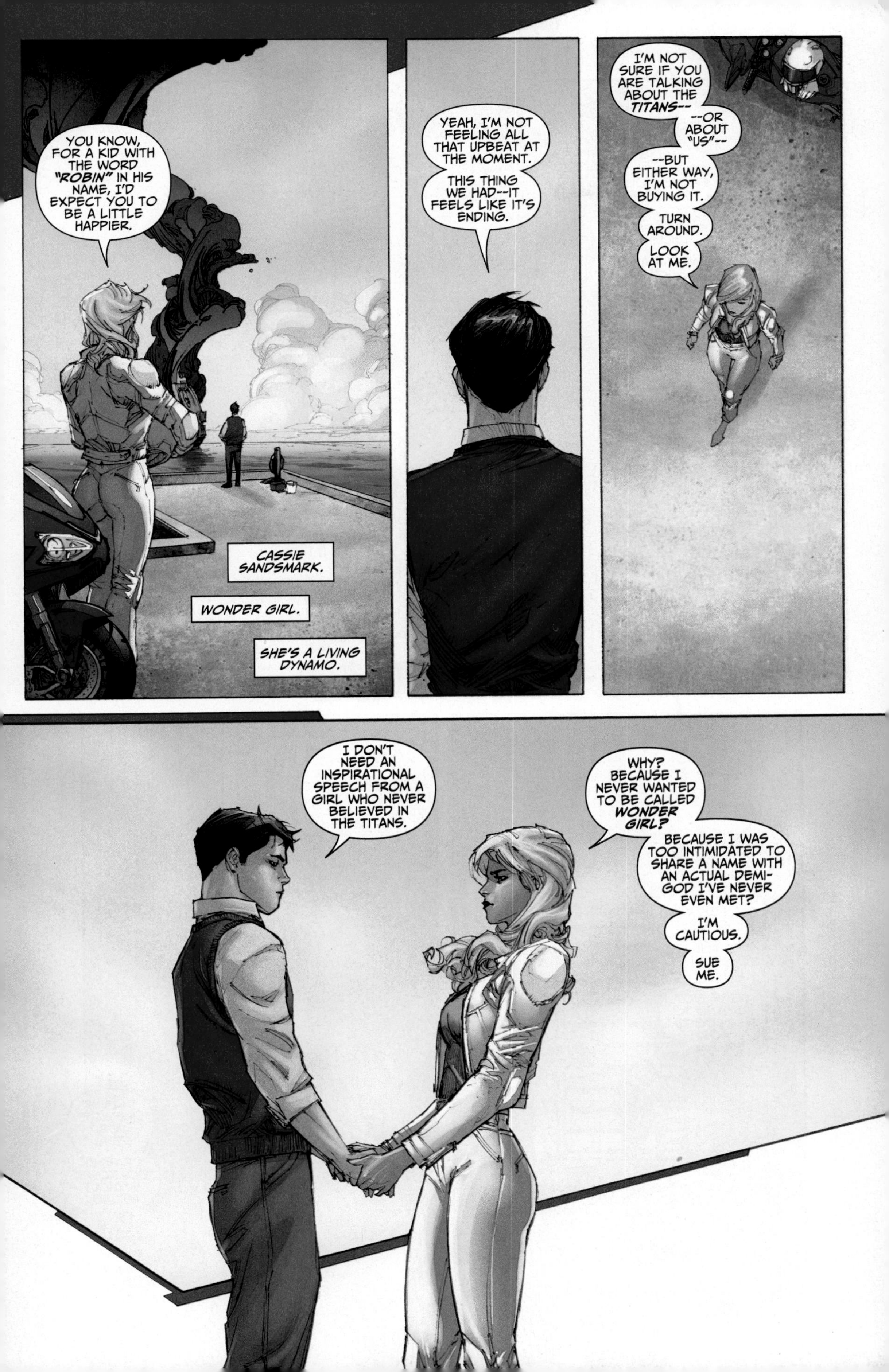
YOU KNOW, FOR A KID WITH THE WORD "ROBIN" IN HIS NAME, I'D EXPECT YOU TO BE A LITTLE HAPPIER.
CASSIE SANDSMARK.
WONDER GIRL.
SHE'S A LIVING DYNAMO.
YEAH, I'M NOT FEELING ALL THAT UPBEAT AT THE MOMENT.
THIS THING WE HAD--IT FEELS LIKE IT'S ENDING.
I'M NOT SURE IF YOU ARE TALKING ABOUT THE TITANS--
--OR ABOUT "US"--
--BUT EITHER WAY, I'M NOT BUYING IT.
TURN AROUND.
LOOK AT ME.
I DON'T NEED AN INSPIRATIONAL SPEECH FROM A GIRL WHO NEVER BELIEVED IN THE TITANS.
WHY? BECAUSE I NEVER WANTED TO BE CALLED WONDER GIRL?
BECAUSE I WAS TOO INTIMIDATED TO SHARE A NAME WITH AN ACTUAL DEMI-GOD I'VE NEVER EVEN MET?
I'M CAUTIOUS.
SUE ME.

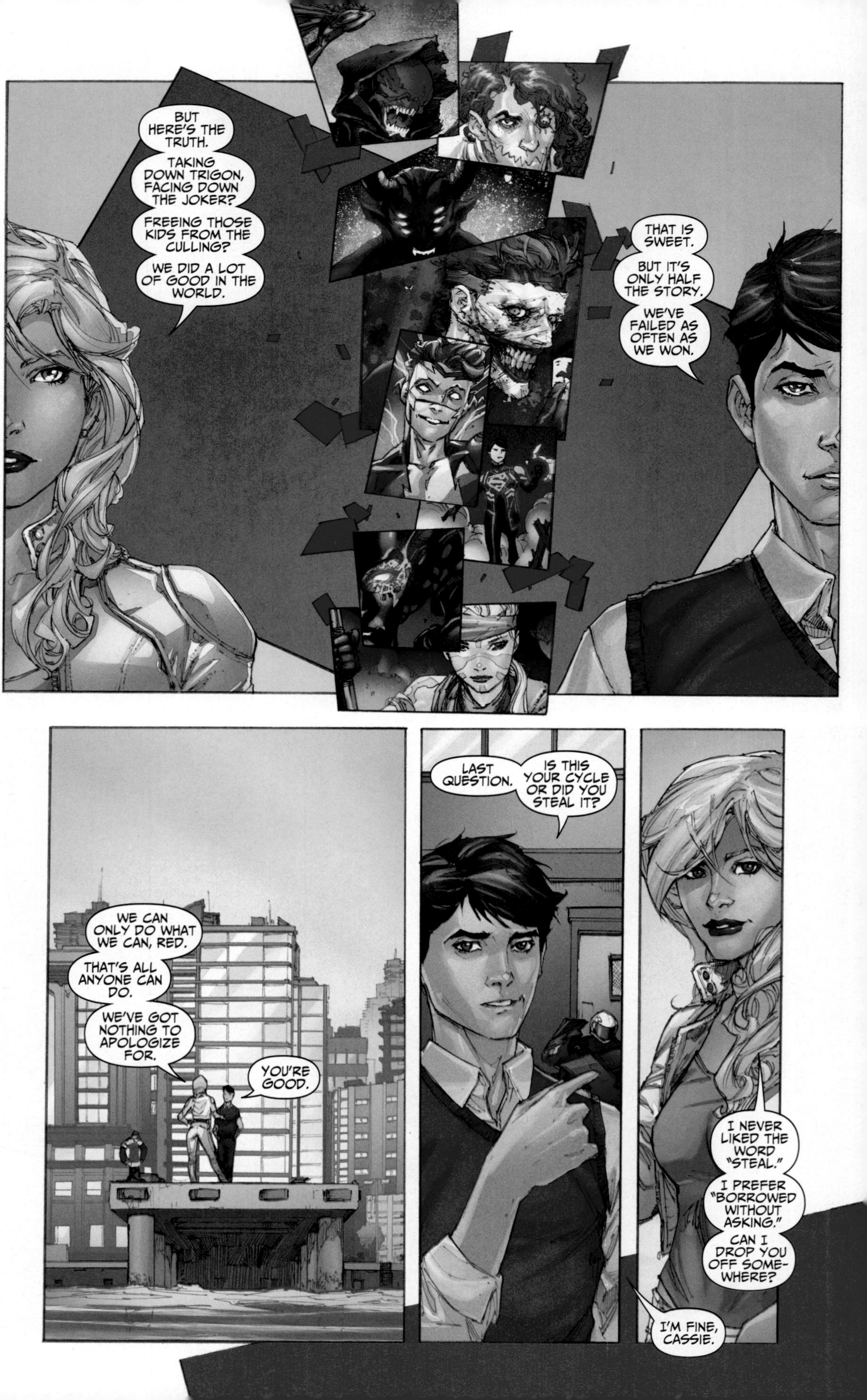
BUT HERE'S THE TRUTH.
TAKING DOWN TRIGON, FACING DOWN THE JOKER?
FREEING THOSE KIDS FROM THE CULLING?
WE DID A LOT OF GOOD IN THE WORLD.
THAT IS SWEET.
BUT IT'S ONLY HALF THE STORY.
WE'VE FAILED AS OFTEN AS WE WON.
WE CAN ONLY DO WHAT WE CAN, RED.
THAT'S ALL ANYONE CAN DO.
WE'VE GOT NOTHING TO APOLOGIZE FOR.
YOU'RE GOOD.
LAST QUESTION.
IS THIS YOUR CYCLE OR DID YOU STEAL IT?
I NEVER LIKED THE WORD "STEAL."
I PREFER "BORROWED WITHOUT ASKING."
CAN I DROP YOU OFF SOME-WHERE?
I'M FINE, CASSIE.

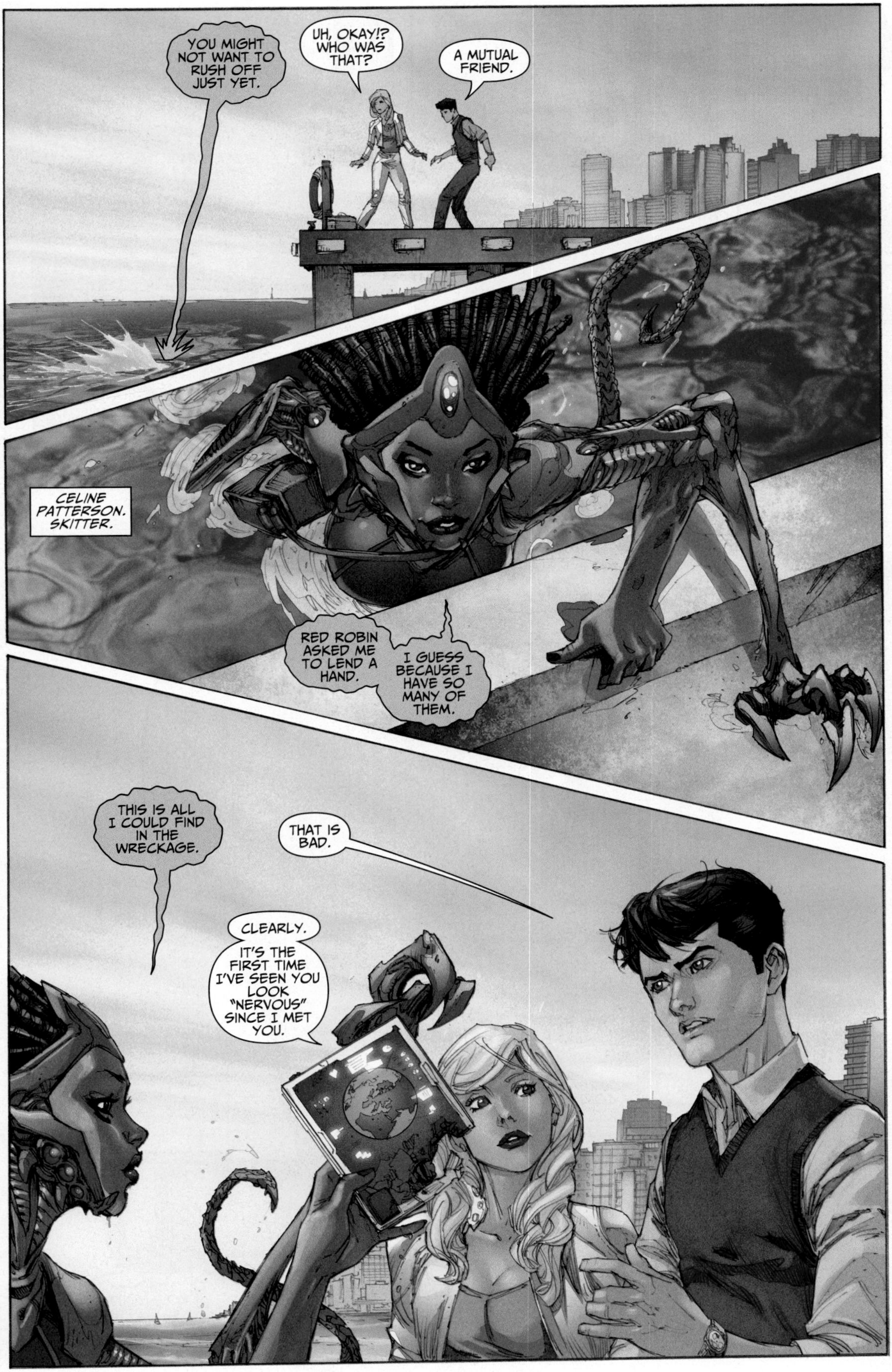
YOU MIGHT NOT WANT TO RUSH OFF JUST YET.
UH, OKAY!? WHO WAS THAT?
A MUTUAL FRIEND.
CELINE PATTERSON. SKITTER.
RED ROBIN ASKED ME TO LEND A HAND.
I GUESS BECAUSE I HAVE SO MANY OF THEM.
THIS IS ALL I COULD FIND IN THE WRECKAGE.
THAT IS BAD.
CLEARLY.
IT'S THE FIRST TIME I'VE SEEN YOU LOOK "NERVOUS" SINCE I MET YOU.

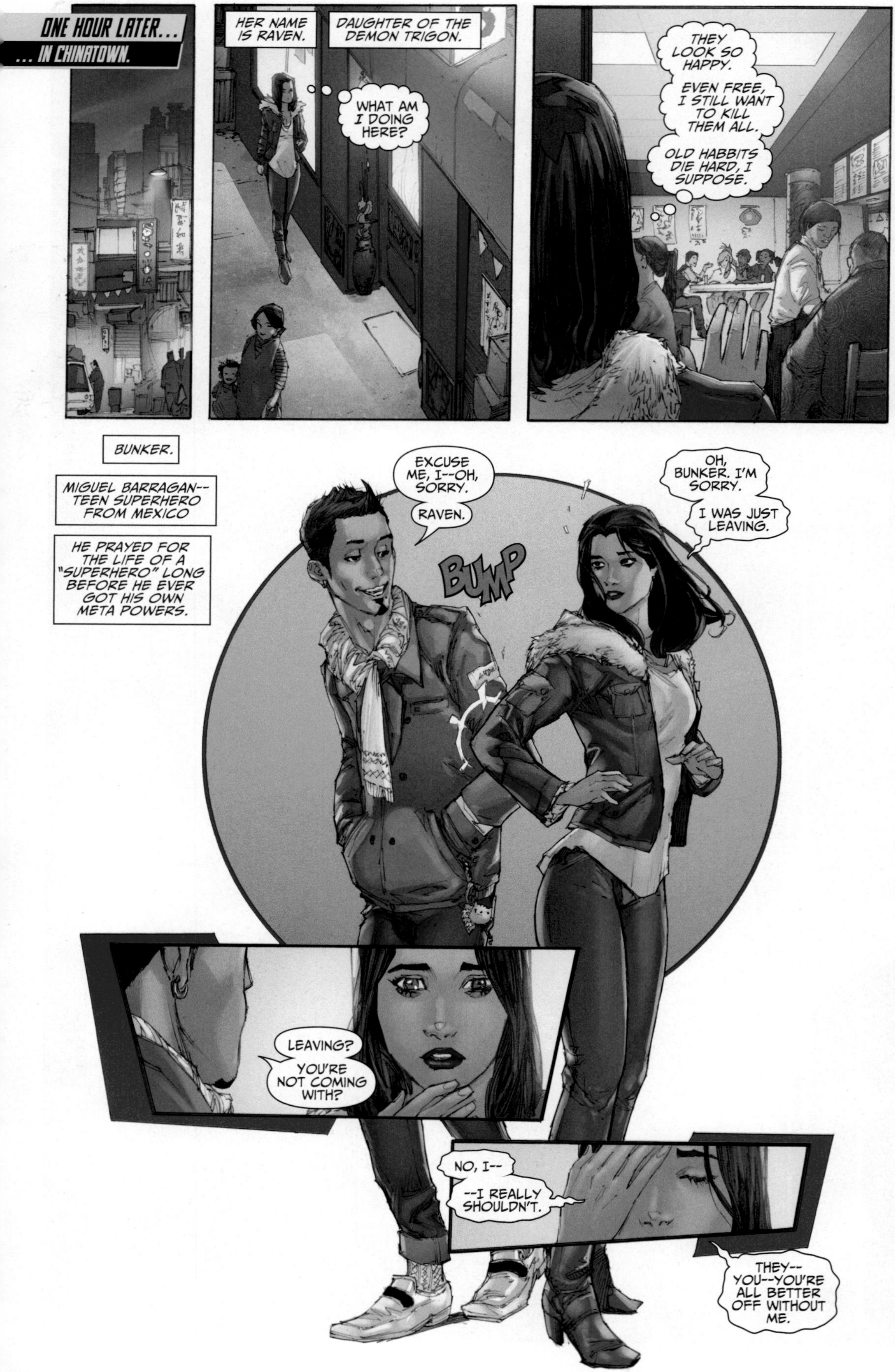
ONE HOUR LATER...
... IN CHINATOWN.
HER NAME IS RAVEN.
DAUGHTER OF THE DEMON TRIGON.
WHAT AM I DOING HERE?
THEY LOOK SO HAPPY.
EVEN FREE, I STILL WANT TO KILL THEM ALL.
OLD HABBITS DIE HARD, I SUPPOSE.
BUNKER.
MIGUEL BARRAGAN-- TEEN SUPERHERO FROM MEXICO
HE PRAYED FOR THE LIFE OF A "SUPERHERO" LONG BEFORE HE EVER GOT HIS OWN META POWERS.
EXCUSE ME, I--OH, SORRY.
RAVEN.
BUMP
OH, BUNKER. I'M SORRY.
I WAS JUST LEAVING.
LEAVING?
YOU'RE NOT COMING WITH?
NO, I--
--I REALLY SHOULDN'T.
THEY-- YOU--YOU'RE ALL BETTER OFF WITHOUT ME.

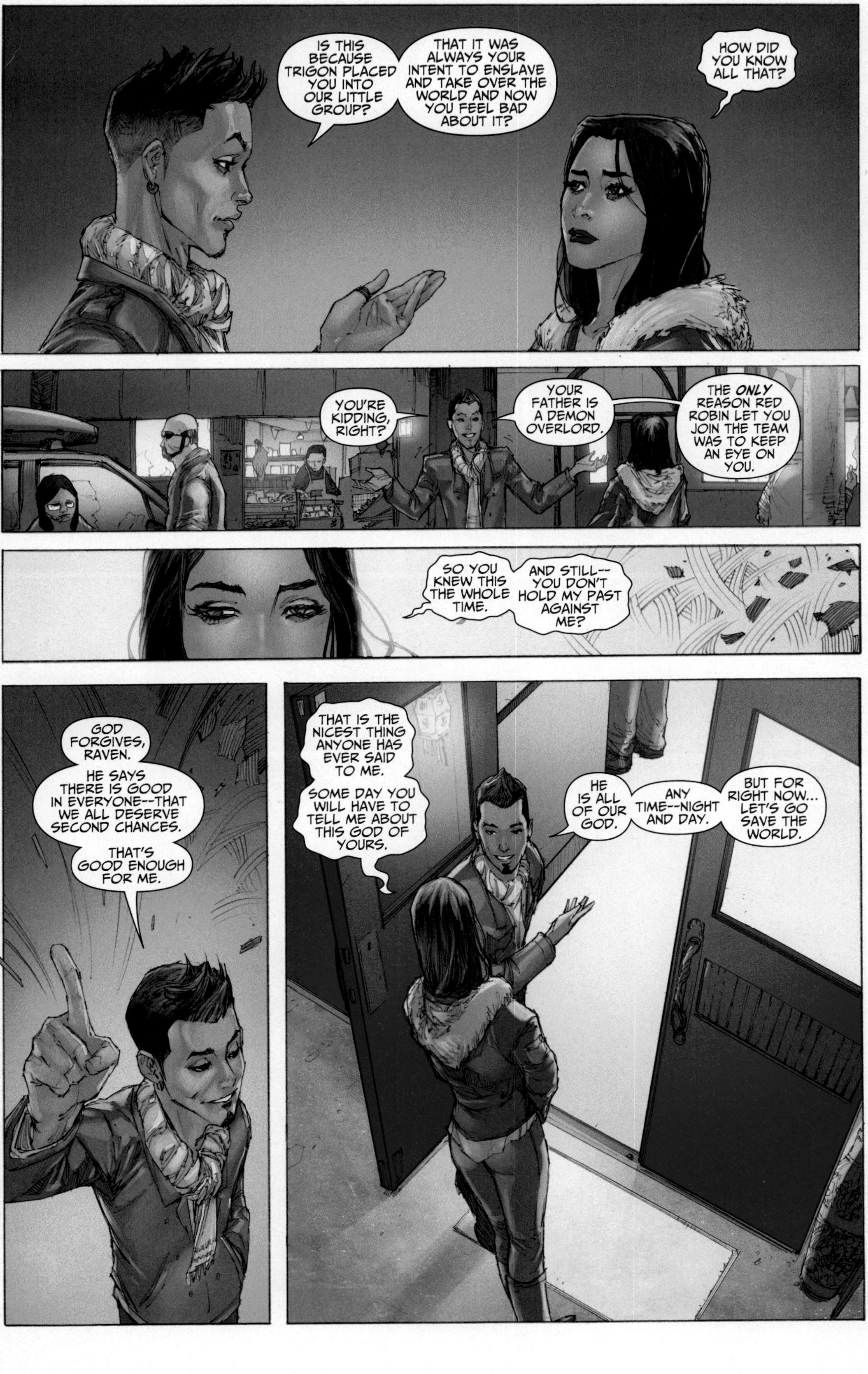
IS THIS BECAUSE TRIGON PLACED YOU INTO OUR LITTLE GROUP?
THAT IT WAS ALWAYS YOUR INTENT TO ENSLAVE AND TAKE OVER THE WORLD AND NOW YOU FEEL BAD ABOUT IT?
HOW DID YOU KNOW ALL THAT?
YOU'RE KIDDING, RIGHT?
YOUR FATHER IS A DEMON OVERLORD.
THE *ONLY* REASON RED ROBIN LET YOU JOIN THE TEAM WAS TO KEEP AN EYE ON YOU.
SO YOU KNEW THIS THE WHOLE TIME.
AND STILL--YOU DON'T HOLD MY PAST AGAINST ME?
GOD FORGIVES, RAVEN.
HE SAYS THERE IS GOOD IN EVERYONE--THAT WE ALL DESERVE SECOND CHANCES.
THAT'S GOOD ENOUGH FOR ME.
THAT IS THE NICEST THING ANYONE HAS EVER SAID TO ME.
SOME DAY YOU WILL HAVE TO TELL ME ABOUT THIS GOD OF YOURS.
HE IS ALL OF OUR GOD.
ANY TIME--NIGHT AND DAY.
BUT FOR RIGHT NOW... LET'S GO SAVE THE WORLD.

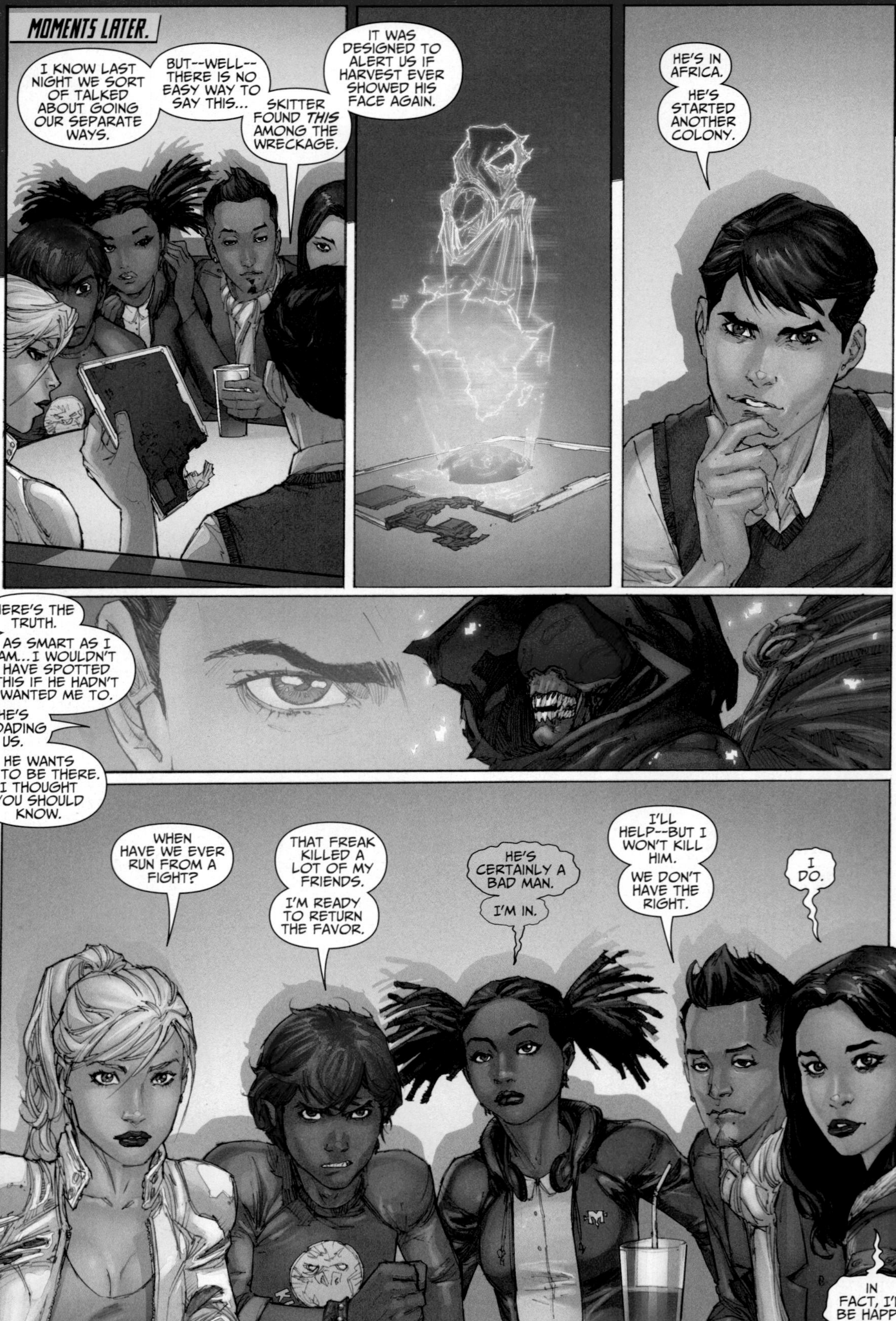
MOMENTS LATER.
I KNOW LAST NIGHT WE SORT OF TALKED ABOUT GOING OUR SEPARATE WAYS.
BUT--WELL-- THERE IS NO EASY WAY TO SAY THIS...
SKITTER FOUND THIS AMONG THE WRECKAGE.
IT WAS DESIGNED TO ALERT US IF HARVEST EVER SHOWED HIS FACE AGAIN.
HE'S IN AFRICA.
HE'S STARTED ANOTHER COLONY.
HERE'S THE TRUTH.
AS SMART AS I AM...I WOULDN'T HAVE SPOTTED THIS IF HE HADN'T WANTED ME TO.
HE'S GOADING US.
HE WANTS US TO BE THERE. I THOUGHT YOU SHOULD KNOW.
WHEN HAVE WE EVER RUN FROM A FIGHT?
THAT FREAK KILLED A LOT OF MY FRIENDS.
I'M READY TO RETURN THE FAVOR.
HE'S CERTAINLY A BAD MAN.
I'M IN.
I'LL HELP--BUT I WON'T KILL HIM.
WE DON'T HAVE THE RIGHT.
I DO.
IN FACT, I'D BE HAPPY TO.

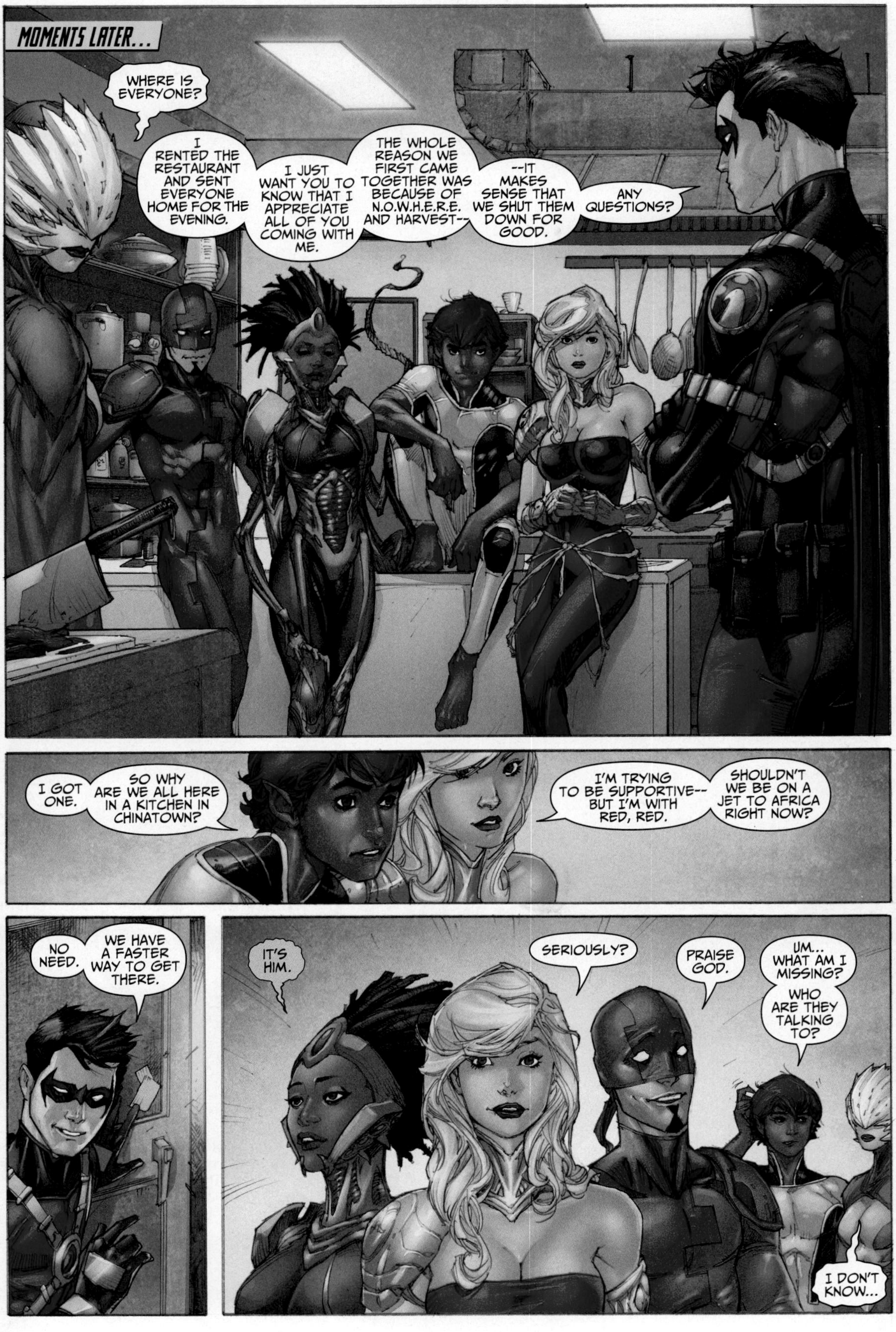
MOMENTS LATER...
WHERE IS EVERYONE?
I RENTED THE RESTAURANT AND SENT EVERYONE HOME FOR THE EVENING.
I JUST WANT YOU TO KNOW THAT I APPRECIATE ALL OF YOU COMING WITH ME.
THE WHOLE REASON WE FIRST CAME TOGETHER WAS BECAUSE OF N.O.W.H.E.R.E. AND HARVEST--
--IT MAKES SENSE THAT WE SHUT THEM DOWN FOR GOOD.
ANY QUESTIONS?
I GOT ONE.
SO WHY ARE WE ALL HERE IN A KITCHEN IN CHINATOWN?
I'M TRYING TO BE SUPPORTIVE-- BUT I'M WITH RED, RED.
SHOULDN'T WE BE ON A JET TO AFRICA RIGHT NOW?
NO NEED.
WE HAVE A FASTER WAY TO GET THERE.
IT'S HIM.
SERIOUSLY?
PRAISE GOD.
UM... WHAT AM I MISSING?
WHO ARE THEY TALKING TO?
I DON'T KNOW...

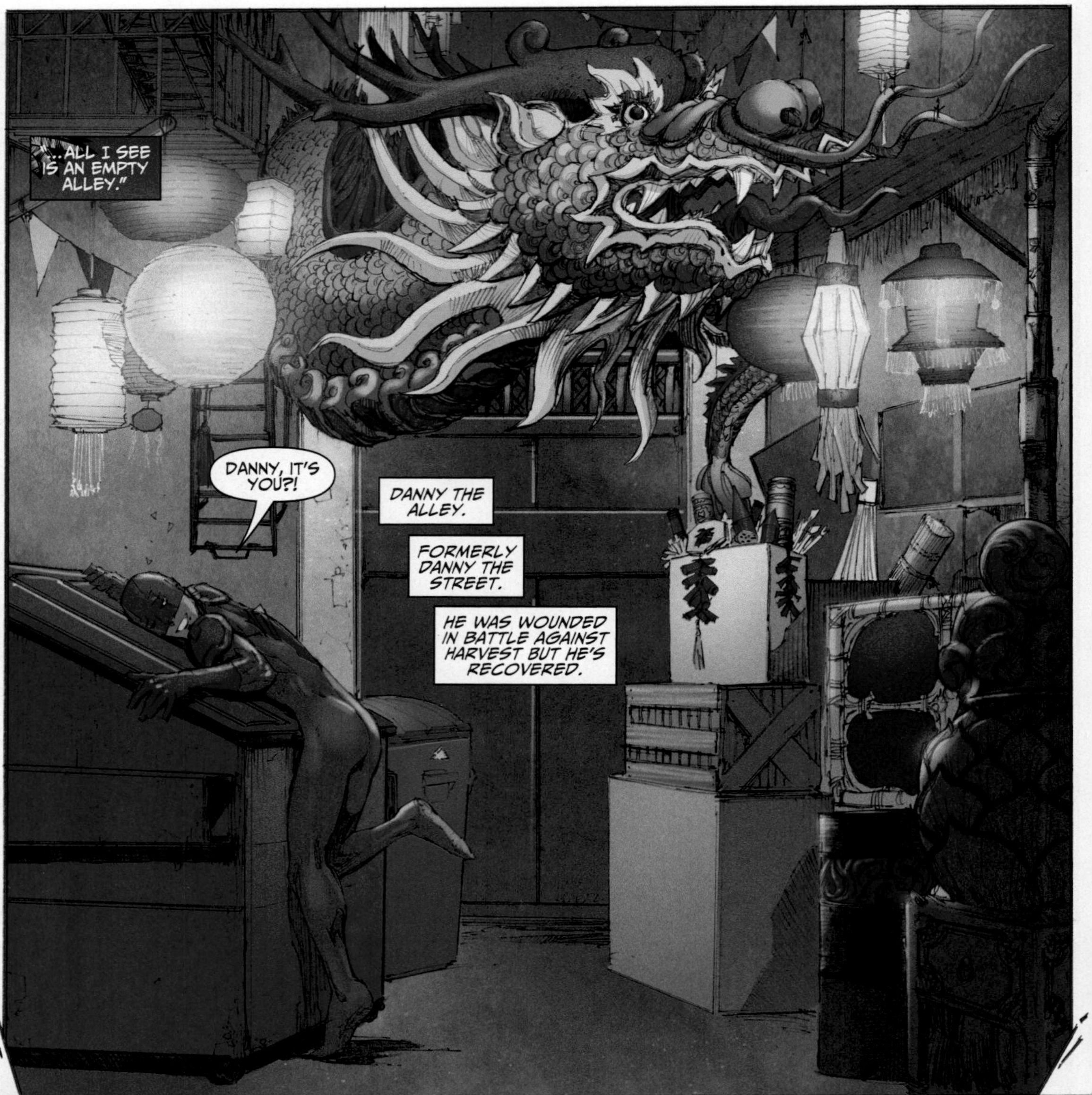
"...ALL I SEE IS AN EMPTY ALLEY."
DANNY, IT'S YOU?!
DANNY THE ALLEY.
FORMERLY DANNY THE STREET.
HE WAS WOUNDED IN BATTLE AGAINST HARVEST BUT HE'S RECOVERED.

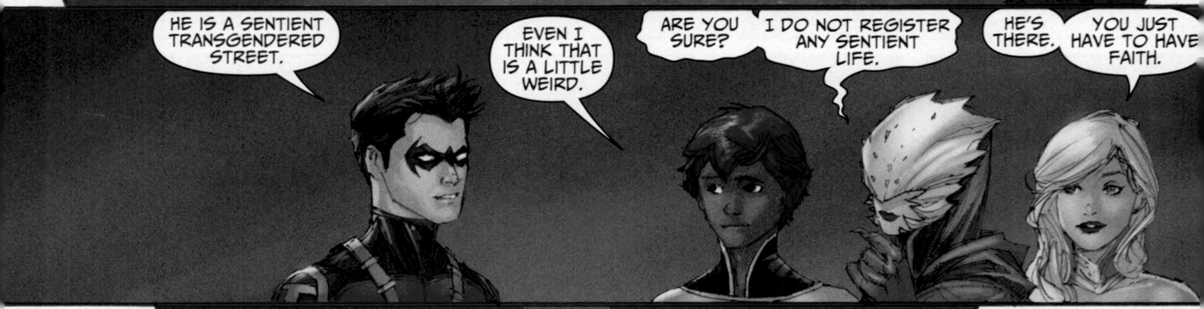
HE IS A SENTIENT TRANSGENDERED STREET.
EVEN I THINK THAT IS A LITTLE WEIRD.
ARE YOU SURE?
I DO NOT REGISTER ANY SENTIENT LIFE.
HE'S THERE.
YOU JUST HAVE TO HAVE FAITH.

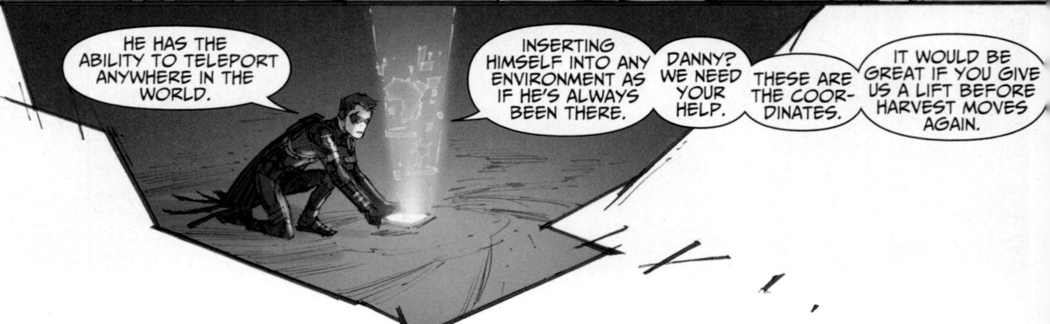
HE HAS THE ABILITY TO TELEPORT ANYWHERE IN THE WORLD.
INSERTING HIMSELF INTO ANY ENVIRONMENT AS IF HE'S ALWAYS BEEN THERE.
DANNY? WE NEED YOUR HELP.
THESE ARE THE COOR-DINATES.
IT WOULD BE GREAT IF YOU GIVE US A LIFT BEFORE HARVEST MOVES AGAIN.

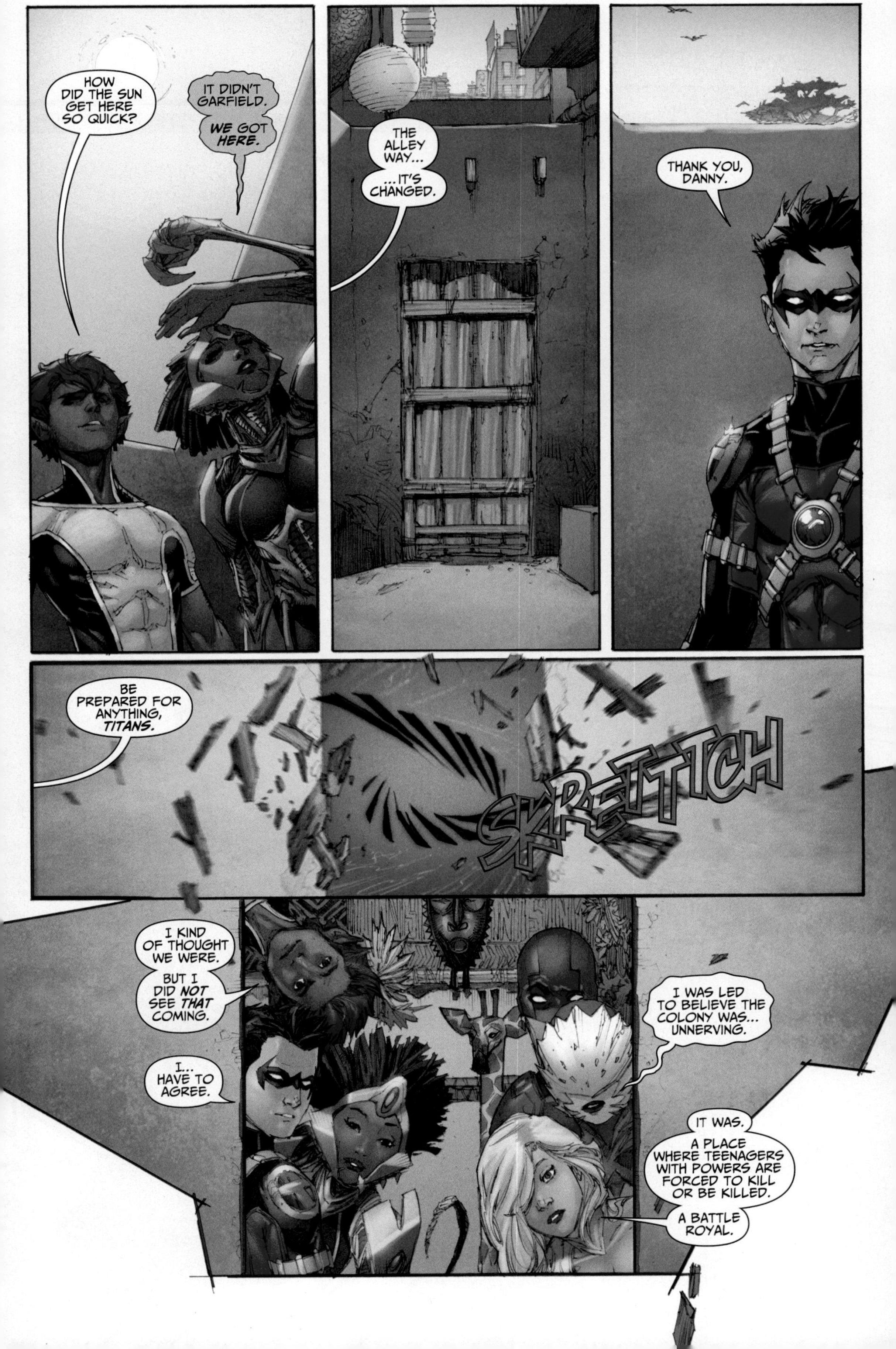
HOW DID THE SUN GET HERE SO QUICK?
IT DIDN'T GARFIELD.
WE GOT HERE.
THE ALLEY WAY...
...IT'S CHANGED.
THANK YOU, DANNY.
BE PREPARED FOR ANYTHING, TITANS.
SKRETTTCH
I KIND OF THOUGHT WE WERE.
BUT I DID NOT SEE THAT COMING.
I... HAVE TO AGREE.
I WAS LED TO BELIEVE THE COLONY WAS... UNNERVING.
IT WAS.
A PLACE WHERE TEENAGERS WITH POWERS ARE FORCED TO KILL OR BE KILLED.
A BATTLE ROYAL.

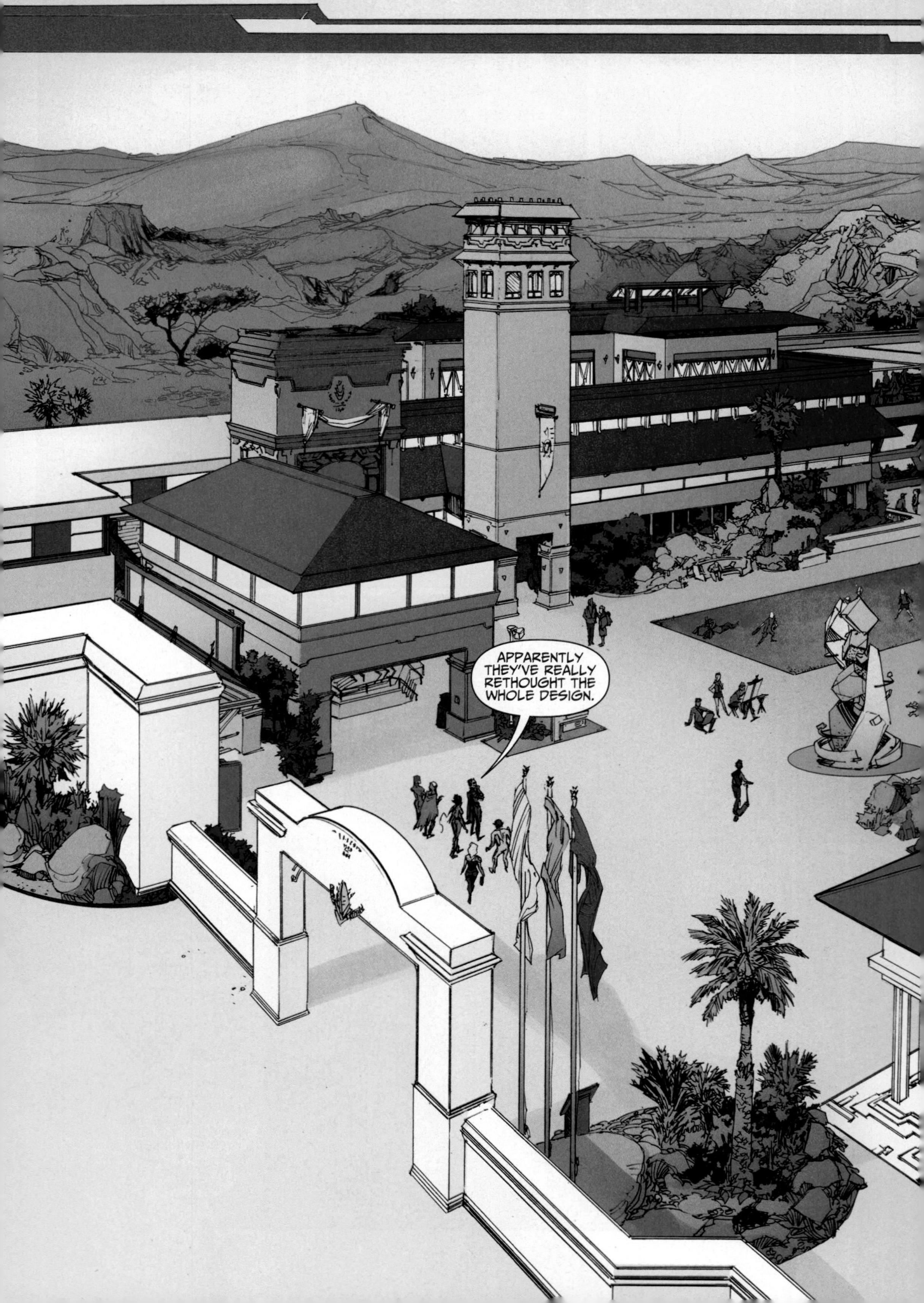
APPARENTLY THEY'VE REALLY RETHOUGHT THE WHOLE DESIGN.

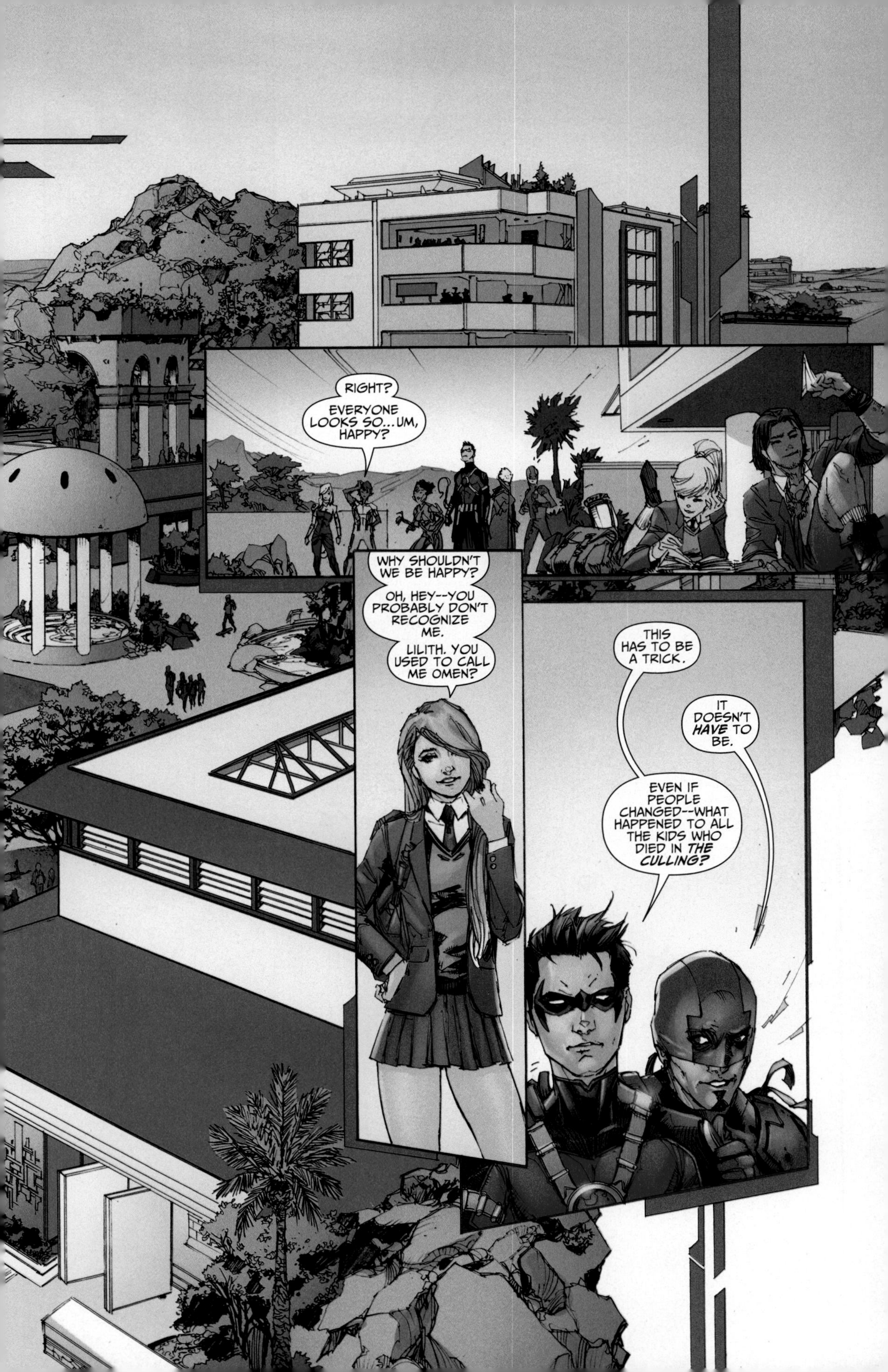
RIGHT?
EVERYONE LOOKS SO...UM, HAPPY?
WHY SHOULDN'T WE BE HAPPY?
OH, HEY--YOU PROBABLY DON'T RECOGNIZE ME.
LILITH. YOU USED TO CALL ME OMEN?
THIS HAS TO BE A TRICK.
IT DOESN'T *HAVE* TO BE.
EVEN IF PEOPLE CHANGED--WHAT HAPPENED TO ALL THE KIDS WHO DIED IN *THE CULLING?*

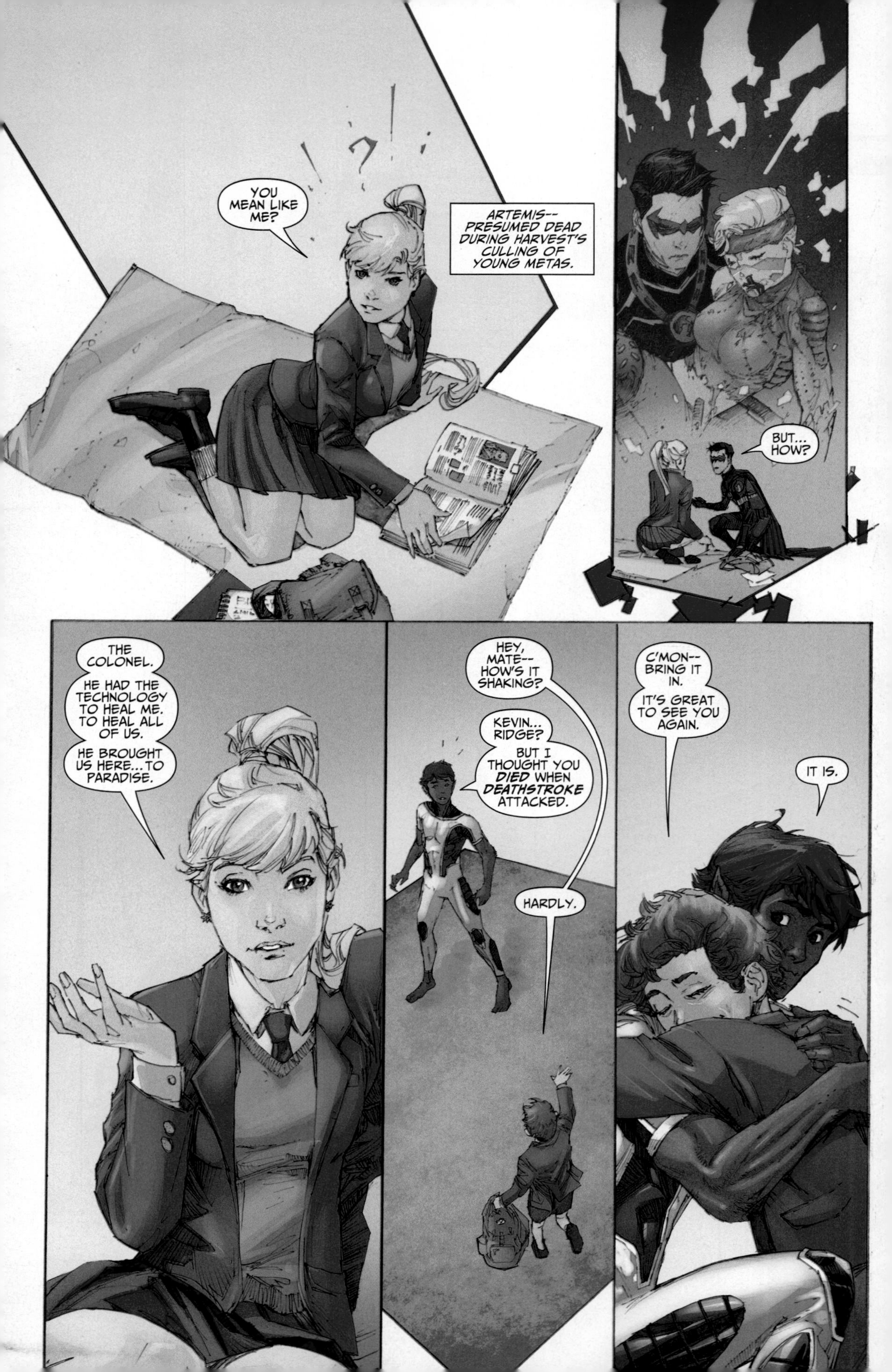
?!
YOU MEAN LIKE ME?
ARTEMIS-- PRESUMED DEAD DURING HARVEST'S CULLING OF YOUNG METAS.
BUT... HOW?
THE COLONEL.
HE HAD THE TECHNOLOGY TO HEAL ME. TO HEAL ALL OF US.
HE BROUGHT US HERE...TO PARADISE.
HEY, MATE-- HOW'S IT SHAKING?
KEVIN... RIDGE?
BUT I THOUGHT YOU DIED WHEN DEATHSTROKE ATTACKED.
HARDLY.
C'MON-- BRING IT IN.
IT'S GREAT TO SEE YOU AGAIN.
IT IS.

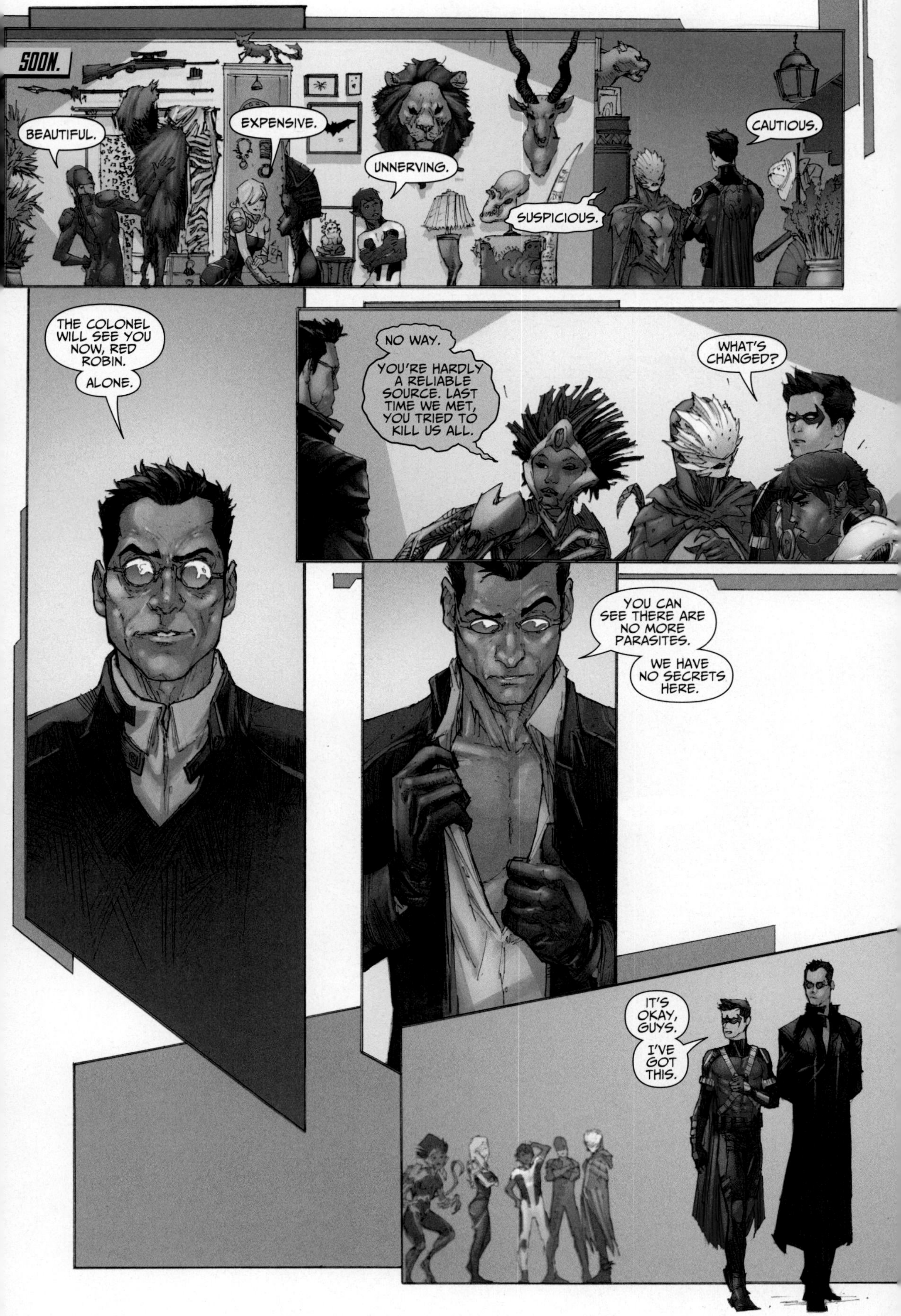
SOON.
BEAUTIFUL.
EXPENSIVE.
UNNERVING.
SUSPICIOUS.
CAUTIOUS.
THE COLONEL WILL SEE YOU NOW, RED ROBIN.
ALONE.
NO WAY.
YOU'RE HARDLY A RELIABLE SOURCE. LAST TIME WE MET, YOU TRIED TO KILL US ALL.
WHAT'S CHANGED?
YOU CAN SEE THERE ARE NO MORE PARASITES.
WE HAVE NO SECRETS HERE.
IT'S OKAY, GUYS.
I'VE GOT THIS.

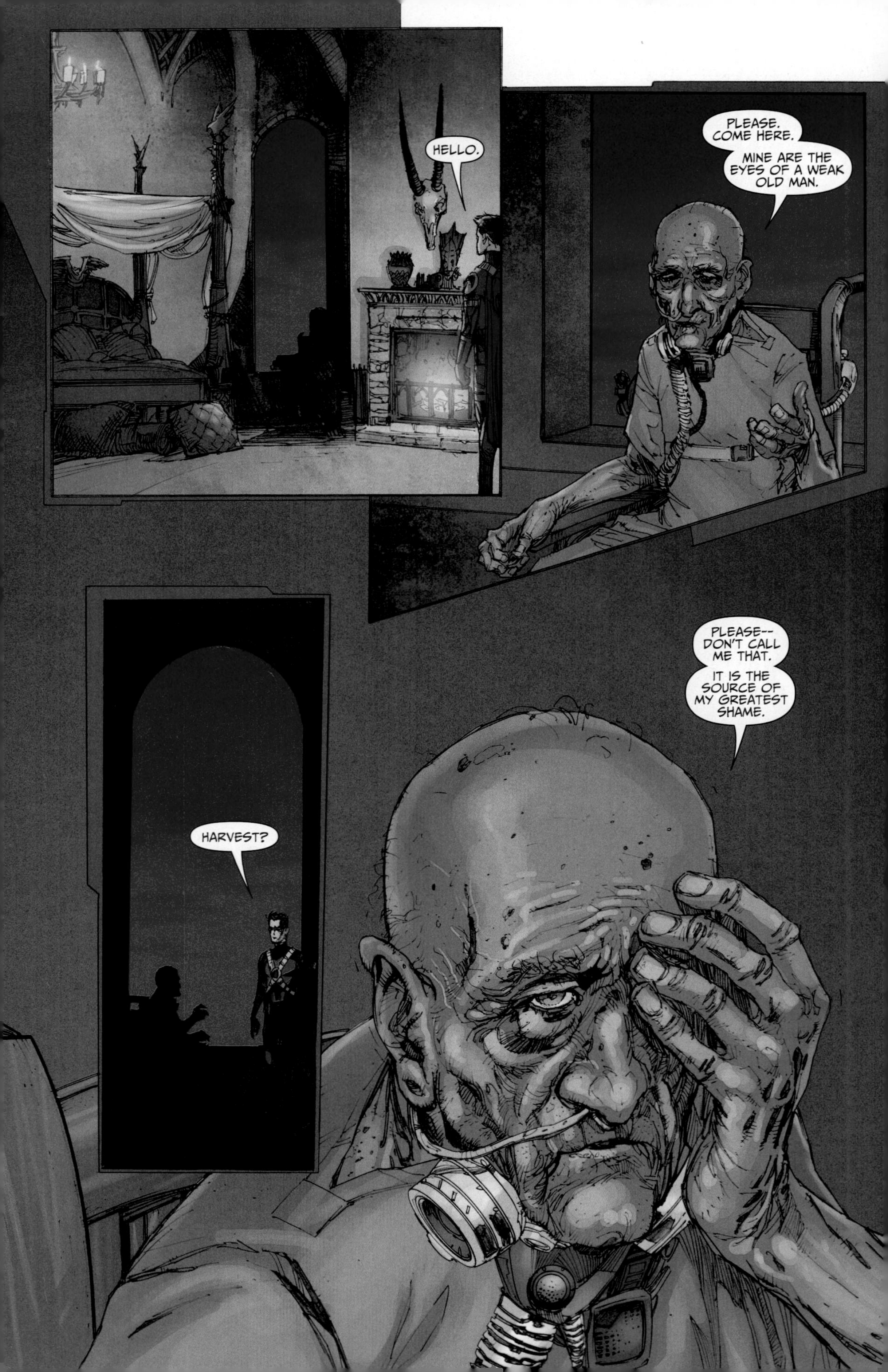
HELLO.
PLEASE. COME HERE.
MINE ARE THE EYES OF A WEAK OLD MAN.
HARVEST?
PLEASE-- DON'T CALL ME THAT.
IT IS THE SOURCE OF MY GREATEST SHAME.

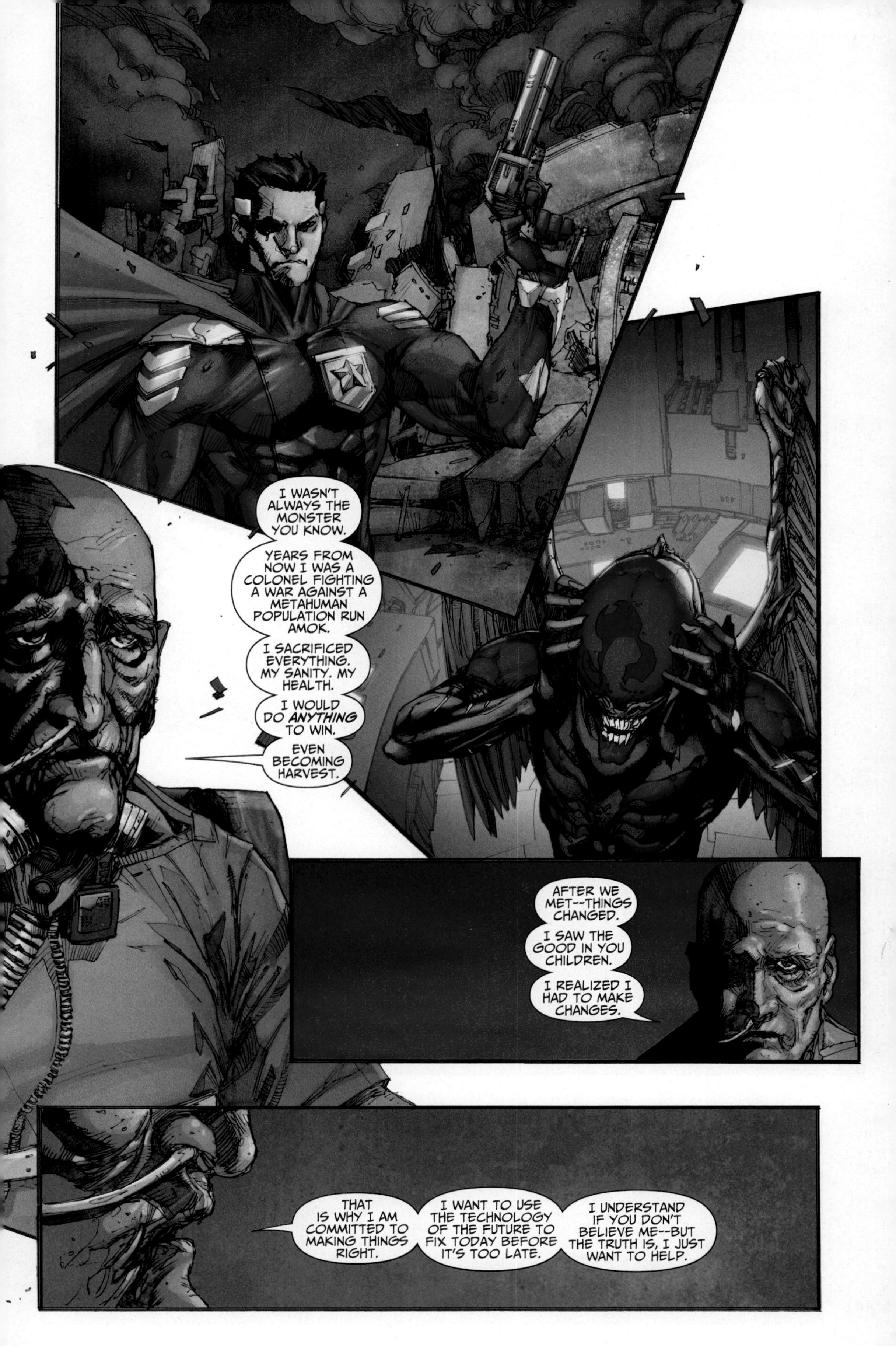
I WASN'T ALWAYS THE MONSTER YOU KNOW.
YEARS FROM NOW I WAS A COLONEL FIGHTING A WAR AGAINST A METAHUMAN POPULATION RUN AMOK.
I SACRIFICED EVERYTHING. MY SANITY. MY HEALTH.
I WOULD DO ***ANYTHING*** TO WIN.
EVEN BECOMING HARVEST.
AFTER WE MET--THINGS CHANGED.
I SAW THE GOOD IN YOU CHILDREN.
I REALIZED I HAD TO MAKE CHANGES.
THAT IS WHY I AM COMMITTED TO MAKING THINGS RIGHT.
I WANT TO USE THE TECHNOLOGY OF THE FUTURE TO FIX TODAY BEFORE IT'S TOO LATE.
I UNDERSTAND IF YOU DON'T BELIEVE ME--BUT THE TRUTH IS, I JUST WANT TO HELP.

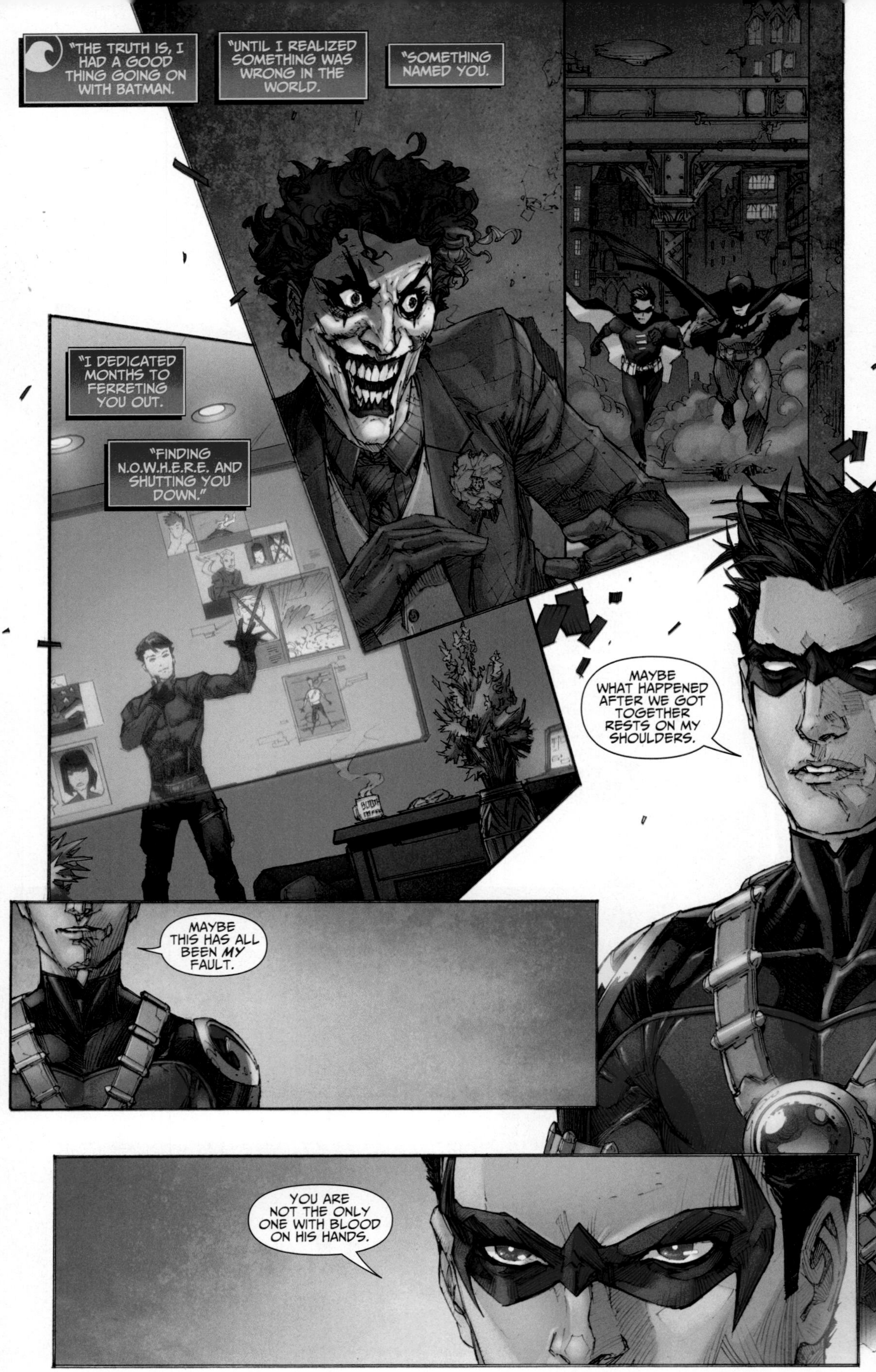
"THE TRUTH IS, I HAD A GOOD THING GOING ON WITH BATMAN.
"UNTIL I REALIZED SOMETHING WAS WRONG IN THE WORLD.
"SOMETHING NAMED YOU.
"I DEDICATED MONTHS TO FERRETING YOU OUT.
"FINDING N.O.W.H.E.R.E. AND SHUTTING YOU DOWN."
MAYBE WHAT HAPPENED AFTER WE GOT TOGETHER RESTS ON MY SHOULDERS.
MAYBE THIS HAS ALL BEEN *MY* FAULT.
YOU ARE NOT THE ONLY ONE WITH BLOOD ON HIS HANDS.

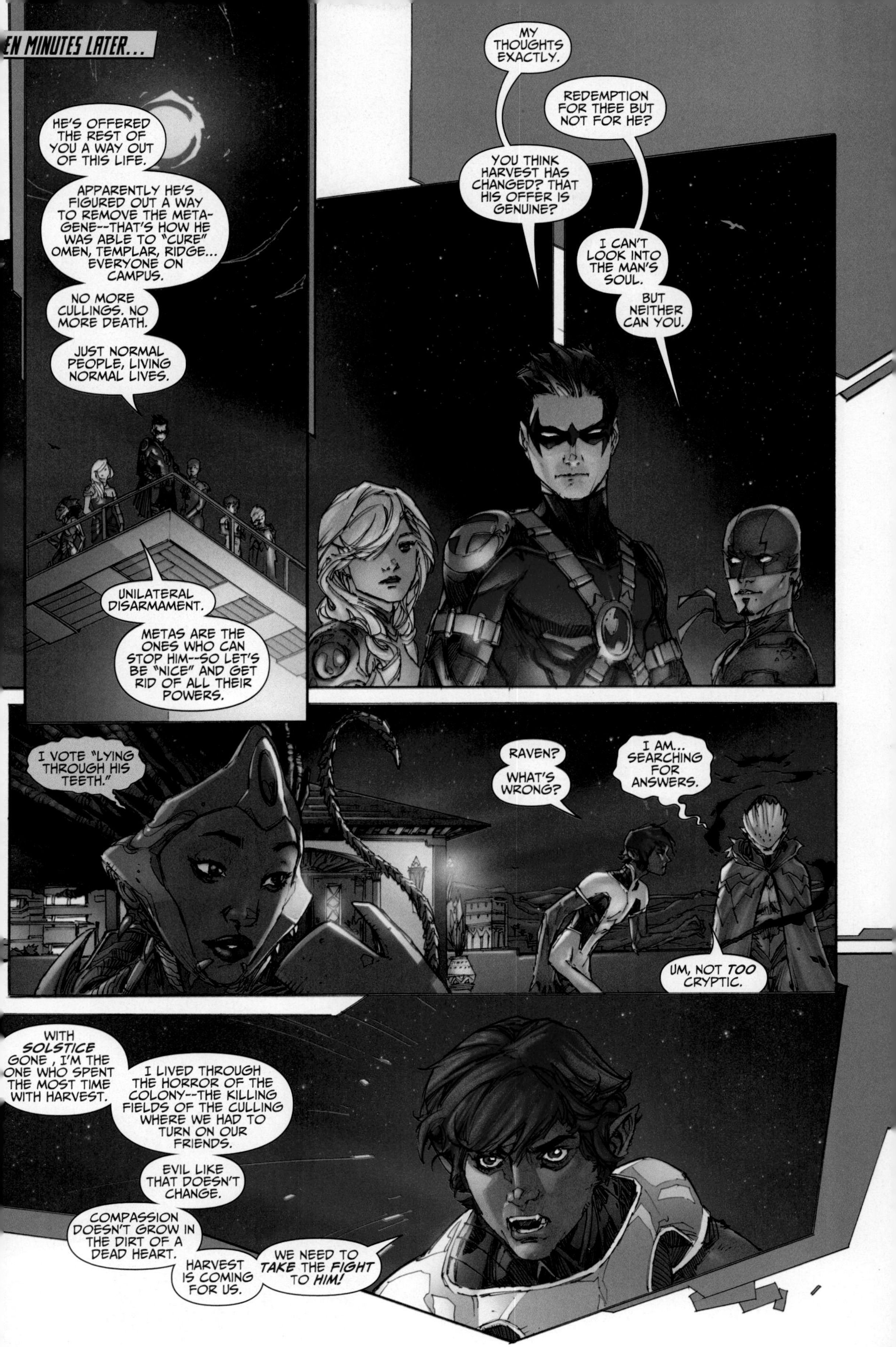
EN MINUTES LATER...
HE'S OFFERED THE REST OF YOU A WAY OUT OF THIS LIFE.
APPARENTLY HE'S FIGURED OUT A WAY TO REMOVE THE META-GENE--THAT'S HOW HE WAS ABLE TO "CURE" OMEN, TEMPLAR, RIDGE... EVERYONE ON CAMPUS.
NO MORE CULLINGS. NO MORE DEATH.
JUST NORMAL PEOPLE, LIVING NORMAL LIVES.
UNILATERAL DISARMAMENT.
METAS ARE THE ONES WHO CAN STOP HIM--SO LET'S BE "NICE" AND GET RID OF ALL THEIR POWERS.
MY THOUGHTS EXACTLY.
YOU THINK HARVEST HAS CHANGED? THAT HIS OFFER IS GENUINE?
REDEMPTION FOR THEE BUT NOT FOR HE?
I CAN'T LOOK INTO THE MAN'S SOUL.
BUT NEITHER CAN YOU.
I VOTE "LYING THROUGH HIS TEETH."
RAVEN?
WHAT'S WRONG?
I AM... SEARCHING FOR ANSWERS.
UM, NOT TOO CRYPTIC.
WITH SOLSTICE GONE, I'M THE ONE WHO SPENT THE MOST TIME WITH HARVEST.
I LIVED THROUGH THE HORROR OF THE COLONY--THE KILLING FIELDS OF THE CULLING WHERE WE HAD TO TURN ON OUR FRIENDS.
EVIL LIKE THAT DOESN'T CHANGE.
COMPASSION DOESN'T GROW IN THE DIRT OF A DEAD HEART.
HARVEST IS COMING FOR US.
WE NEED TO TAKE THE FIGHT TO HIM!

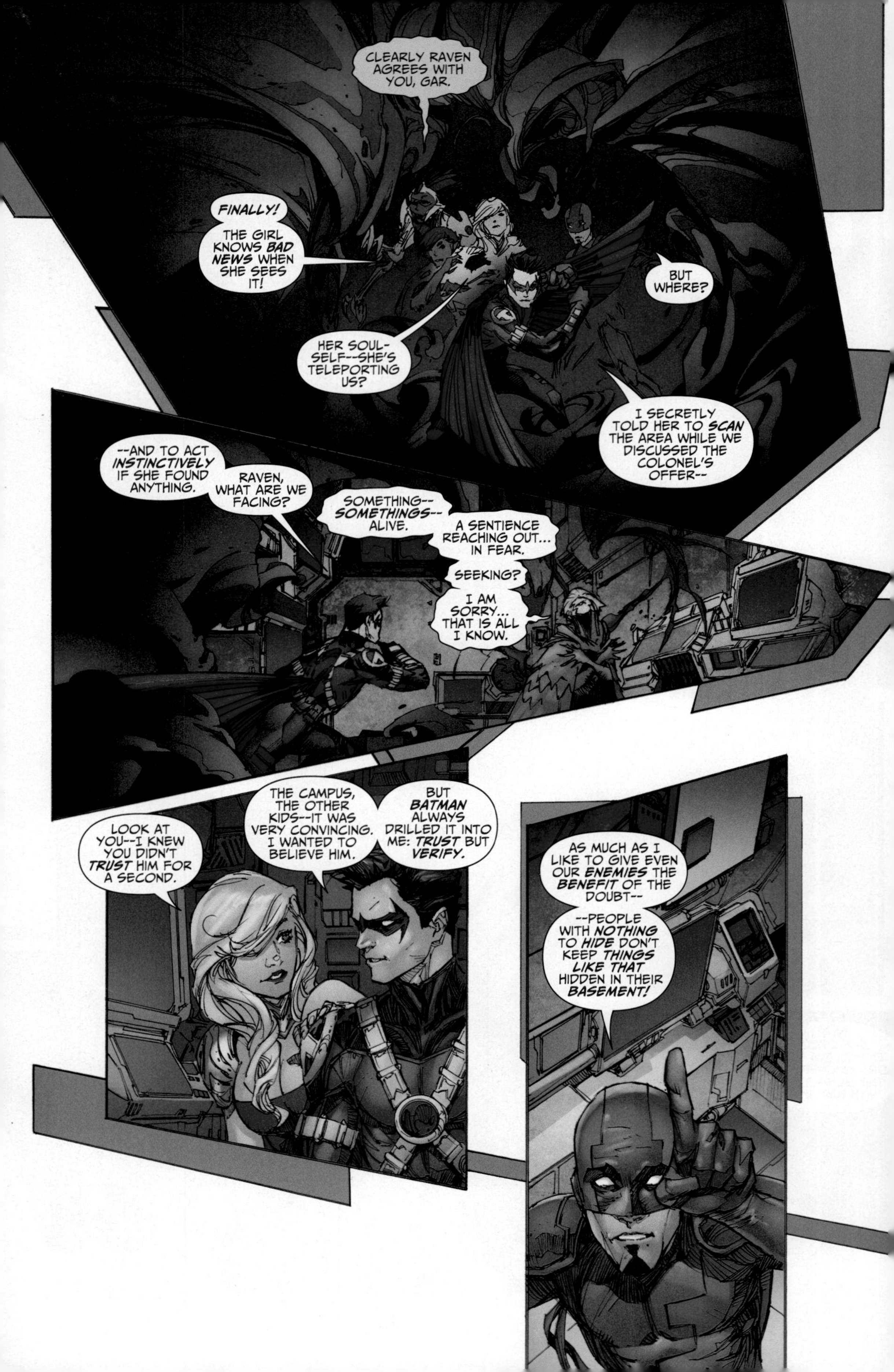
CLEARLY RAVEN AGREES WITH YOU, GAR.
FINALLY!
THE GIRL KNOWS BAD NEWS WHEN SHE SEES IT!
HER SOUL-SELF--SHE'S TELEPORTING US?
BUT WHERE?
I SECRETLY TOLD HER TO SCAN THE AREA WHILE WE DISCUSSED THE COLONEL'S OFFER--
--AND TO ACT INSTINCTIVELY IF SHE FOUND ANYTHING.
RAVEN, WHAT ARE WE FACING?
SOMETHING-- SOMETHINGS-- ALIVE.
A SENTIENCE REACHING OUT... IN FEAR.
SEEKING?
I AM SORRY... THAT IS ALL I KNOW.
LOOK AT YOU--I KNEW YOU DIDN'T TRUST HIM FOR A SECOND.
THE CAMPUS, THE OTHER KIDS--IT WAS VERY CONVINCING. I WANTED TO BELIEVE HIM.
BUT BATMAN ALWAYS DRILLED IT INTO ME: TRUST BUT VERIFY.
AS MUCH AS I LIKE TO GIVE EVEN OUR ENEMIES THE BENEFIT OF THE DOUBT--
--PEOPLE WITH NOTHING TO HIDE DON'T KEEP THINGS LIKE THAT HIDDEN IN THEIR BASEMENT!

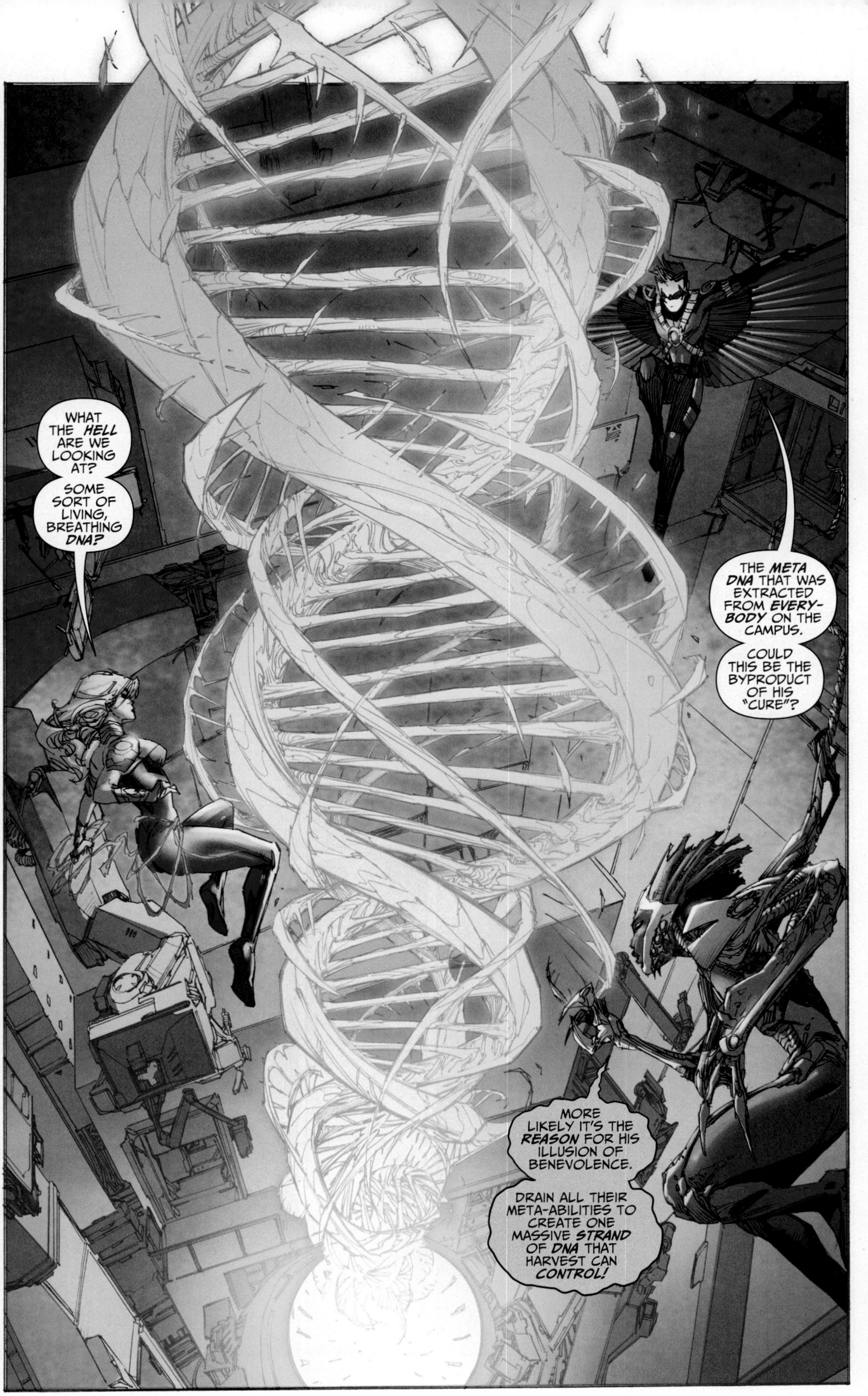

WHAT THE *HELL* ARE WE LOOKING AT?
SOME SORT OF LIVING, BREATHING *DNA?*
THE *META DNA* THAT WAS EXTRACTED FROM *EVERY-BODY* ON THE CAMPUS.
COULD THIS BE THE BYPRODUCT OF HIS "CURE"?
MORE LIKELY IT'S THE *REASON* FOR HIS ILLUSION OF BENEVOLENCE.
DRAIN ALL THEIR META-ABILITIES TO CREATE ONE MASSIVE *STRAND* OF *DNA* THAT HARVEST CAN *CONTROL!*

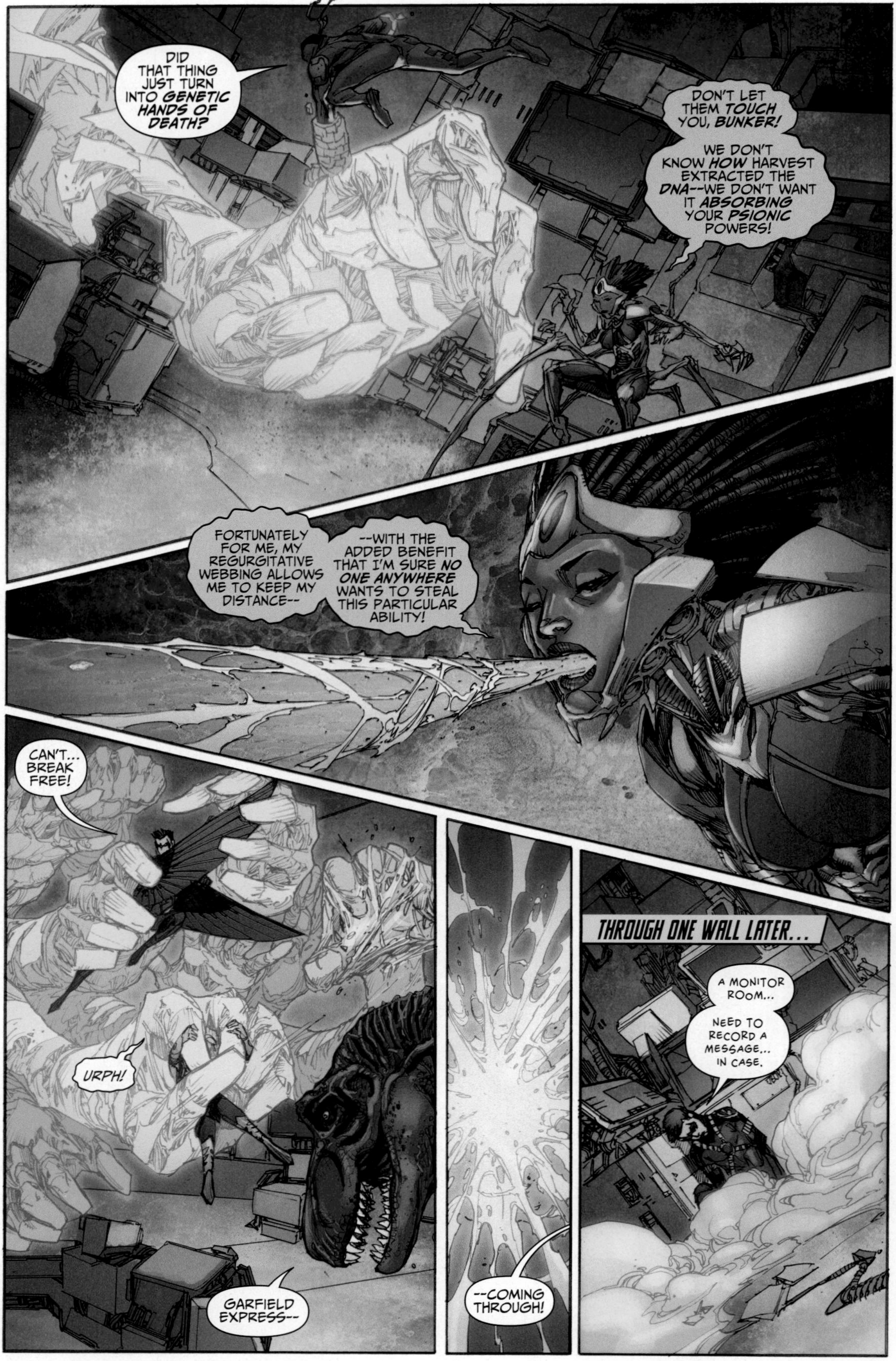
DID THAT THING JUST TURN INTO GENETIC HANDS OF DEATH?
DON'T LET THEM TOUCH YOU, BUNKER!
WE DON'T KNOW HOW HARVEST EXTRACTED THE DNA--WE DON'T WANT IT ABSORBING YOUR PSIONIC POWERS!
FORTUNATELY FOR ME, MY REGURGITATIVE WEBBING ALLOWS ME TO KEEP MY DISTANCE--
--WITH THE ADDED BENEFIT THAT I'M SURE NO ONE ANYWHERE WANTS TO STEAL THIS PARTICULAR ABILITY!
CAN'T... BREAK FREE!
URPH!
GARFIELD EXPRESS--
--COMING THROUGH!
THROUGH ONE WALL LATER...
A MONITOR ROOM...
NEED TO RECORD A MESSAGE... IN CASE.

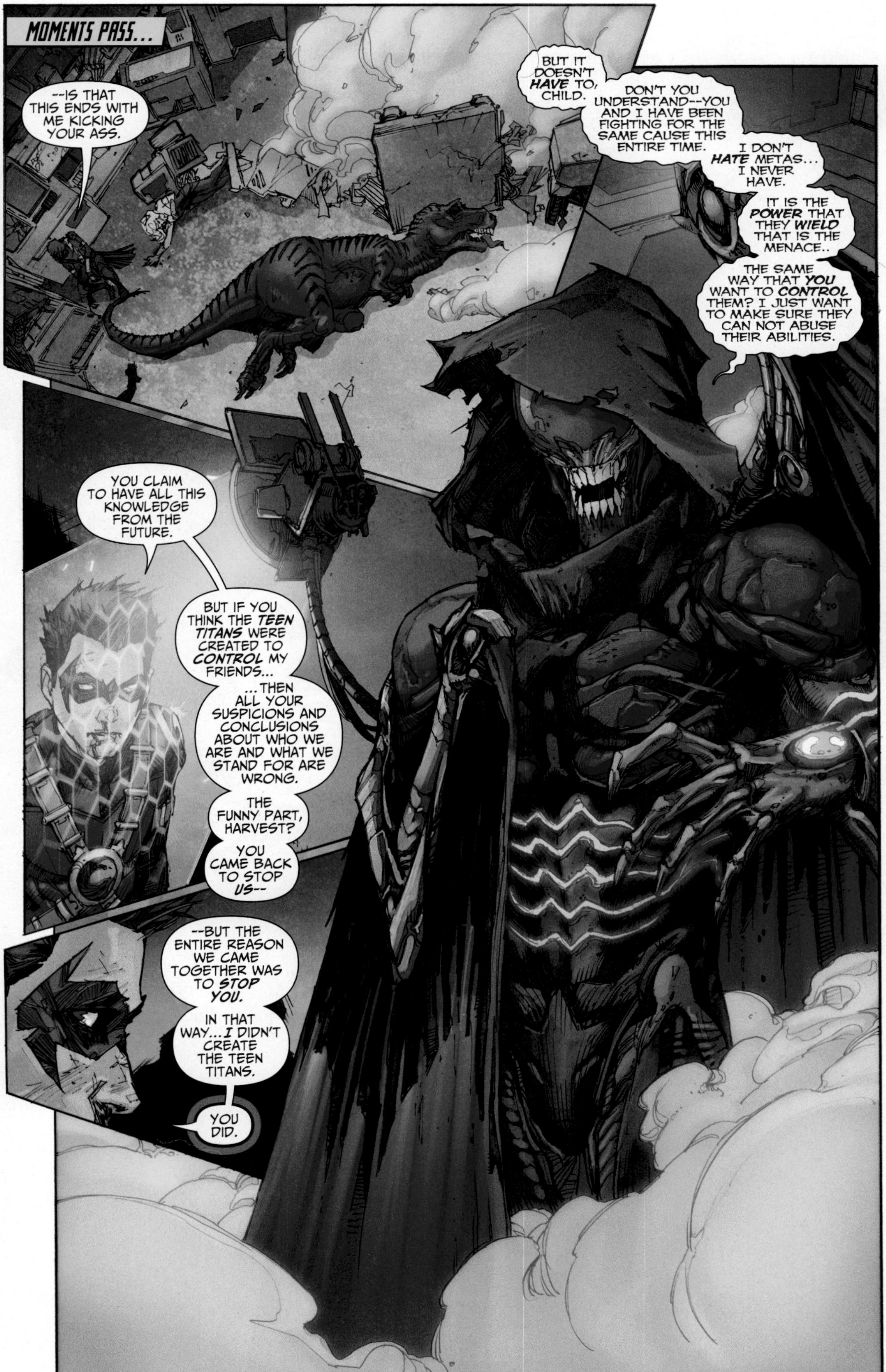
MOMENTS PASS...
--IS THAT THIS ENDS WITH ME KICKING YOUR ASS.
BUT IT DOESN'T HAVE TO, CHILD.
DON'T YOU UNDERSTAND--YOU AND I HAVE BEEN FIGHTING FOR THE SAME CAUSE THIS ENTIRE TIME.
I DON'T HATE METAS... I NEVER HAVE.
IT IS THE POWER THAT THEY WIELD THAT IS THE MENACE..
THE SAME WAY THAT YOU WANT TO CONTROL THEM? I JUST WANT TO MAKE SURE THEY CAN NOT ABUSE THEIR ABILITIES.
YOU CLAIM TO HAVE ALL THIS KNOWLEDGE FROM THE FUTURE.
BUT IF YOU THINK THE TEEN TITANS WERE CREATED TO CONTROL MY FRIENDS...
...THEN ALL YOUR SUSPICIONS AND CONCLUSIONS ABOUT WHO WE ARE AND WHAT WE STAND FOR ARE WRONG.
THE FUNNY PART, HARVEST?
YOU CAME BACK TO STOP US--
--BUT THE ENTIRE REASON WE CAME TOGETHER WAS TO STOP YOU.
IN THAT WAY...I DIDN'T CREATE THE TEEN TITANS.
YOU DID.

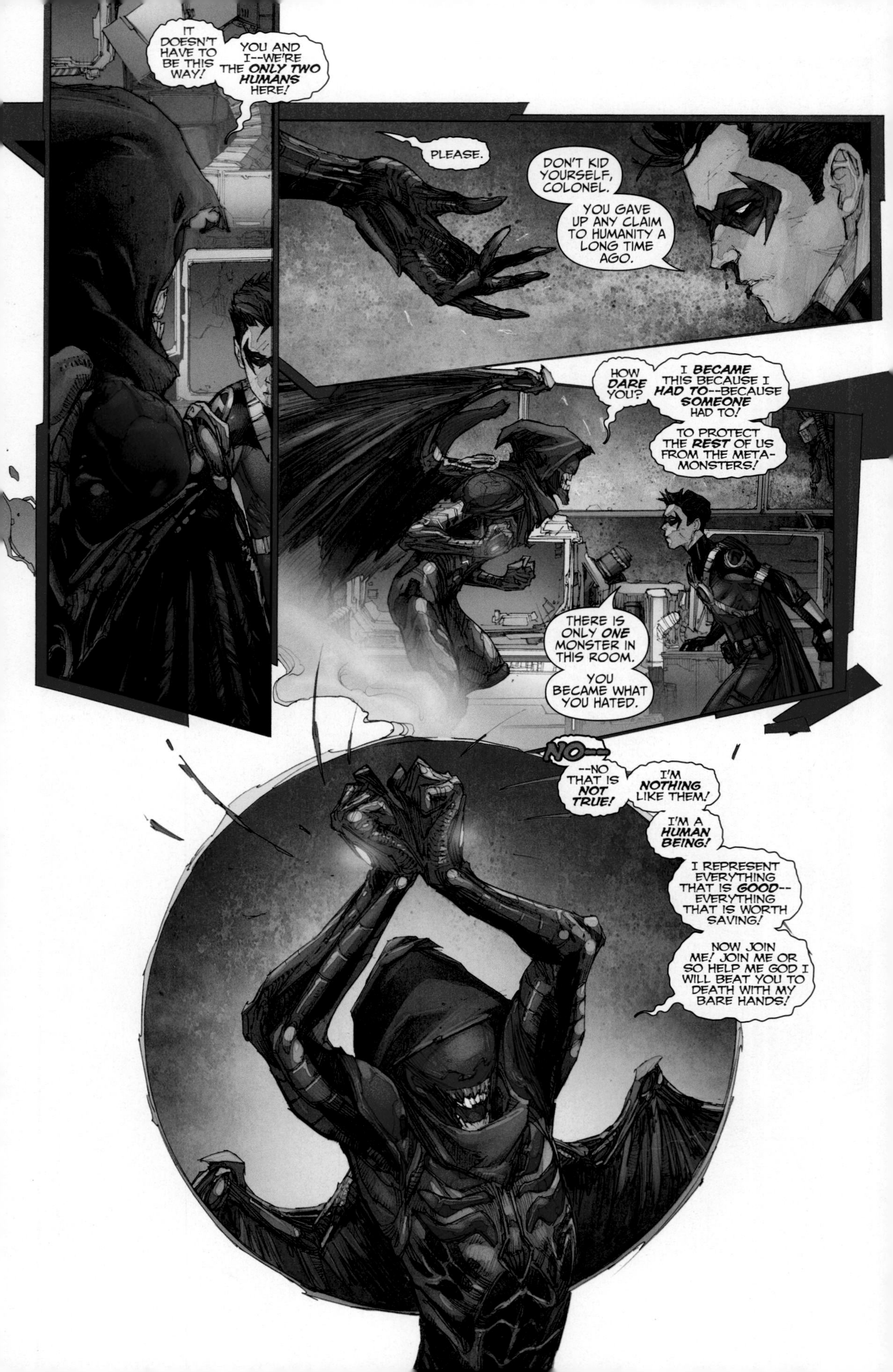
IT DOESN'T HAVE TO BE THIS WAY!
YOU AND I--WE'RE THE ONLY TWO HUMANS HERE!
PLEASE.
DON'T KID YOURSELF, COLONEL.
YOU GAVE UP ANY CLAIM TO HUMANITY A LONG TIME AGO.
HOW DARE YOU?
I BECAME THIS BECAUSE I HAD TO--BECAUSE SOMEONE HAD TO!
TO PROTECT THE REST OF US FROM THE META-MONSTERS!
THERE IS ONLY ONE MONSTER IN THIS ROOM.
YOU BECAME WHAT YOU HATED.
NO--
--NO THAT IS NOT TRUE!
I'M NOTHING LIKE THEM!
I'M A HUMAN BEING!
I REPRESENT EVERYTHING THAT IS GOOD--EVERYTHING THAT IS WORTH SAVING!
NOW JOIN ME! JOIN ME OR SO HELP ME GOD I WILL BEAT YOU TO DEATH WITH MY BARE HANDS!

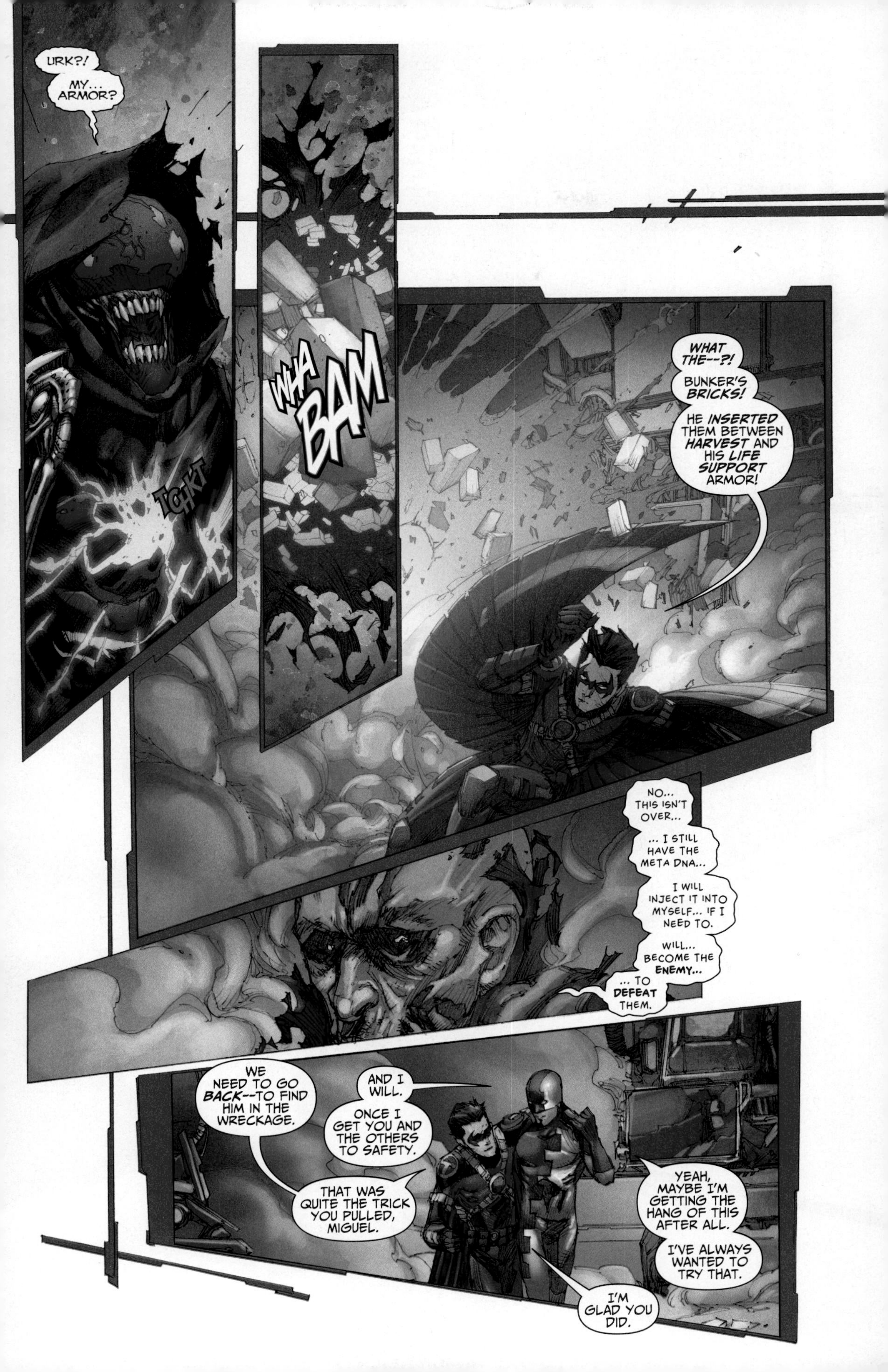
URK?!
MY... ARMOR?
TCHKT
WHA BAM
WHAT THE--?!
BUNKER'S BRICKS!
HE INSERTED THEM BETWEEN HARVEST AND HIS LIFE SUPPORT ARMOR!
NO... THIS ISN'T OVER...
... I STILL HAVE THE META DNA...
I WILL INJECT IT INTO MYSELF... IF I NEED TO.
WILL... BECOME THE ENEMY...
... TO DEFEAT THEM.
WE NEED TO GO BACK--TO FIND HIM IN THE WRECKAGE.
AND I WILL.
ONCE I GET YOU AND THE OTHERS TO SAFETY.
THAT WAS QUITE THE TRICK YOU PULLED, MIGUEL.
YEAH, MAYBE I'M GETTING THE HANG OF THIS AFTER ALL.
I'VE ALWAYS WANTED TO TRY THAT.
I'M GLAD YOU DID.

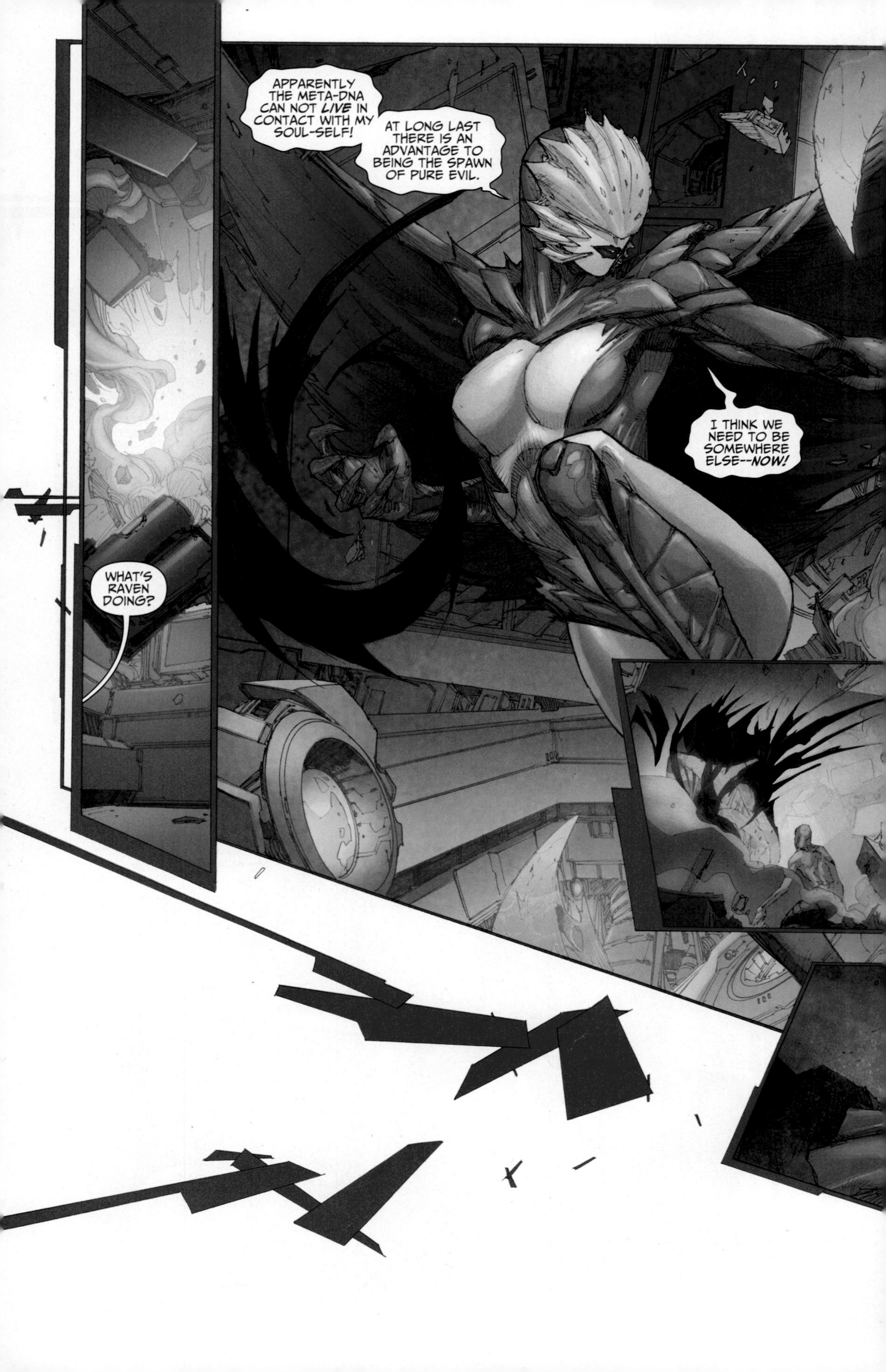
APPARENTLY THE META-DNA CAN NOT LIVE IN CONTACT WITH MY SOUL-SELF!
AT LONG LAST THERE IS AN ADVANTAGE TO BEING THE SPAWN OF PURE EVIL.
WHAT'S RAVEN DOING?
I THINK WE NEED TO BE SOMEWHERE ELSE--NOW!

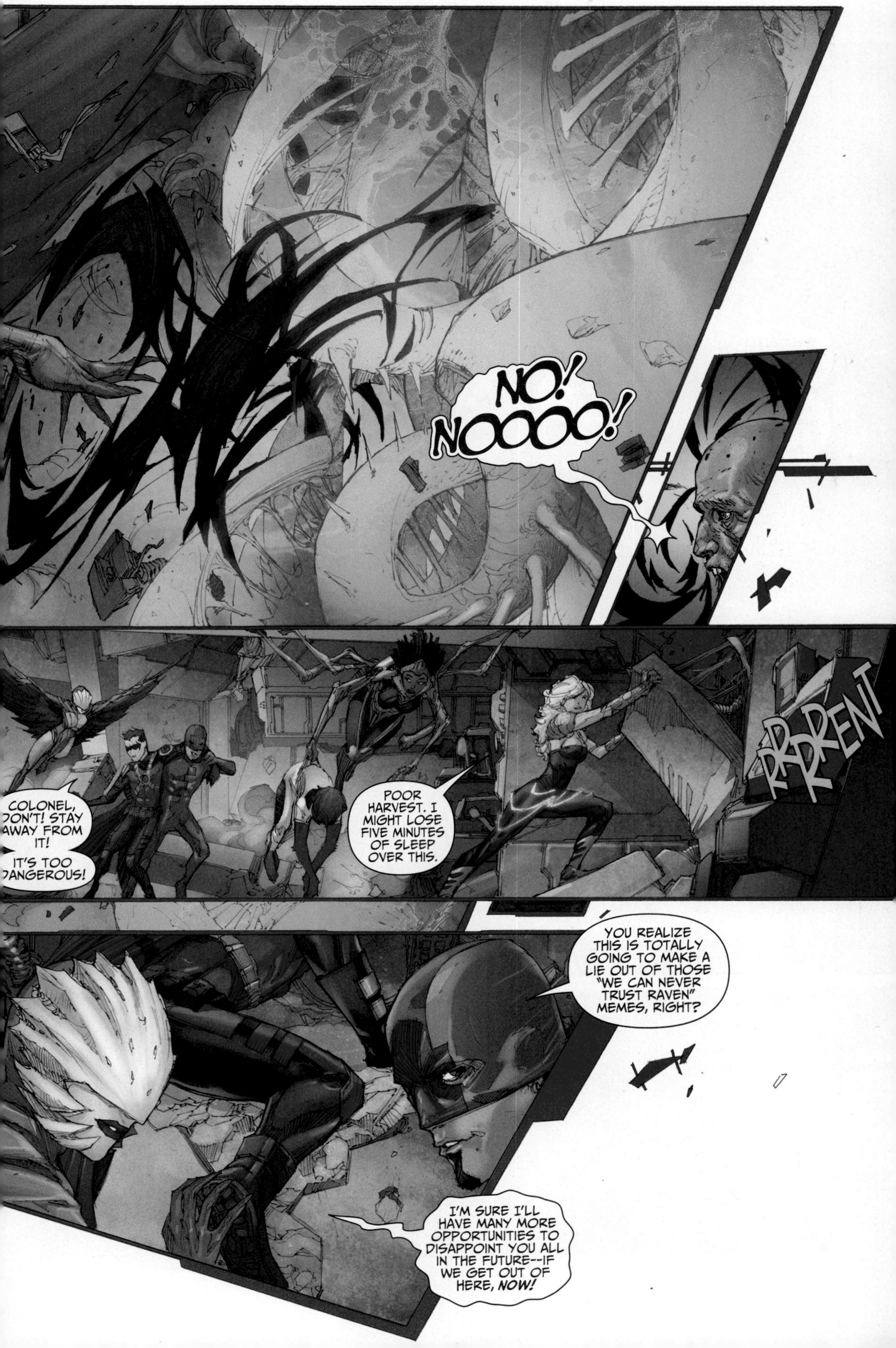
NO! NOOOO!
RRRRENT
COLONEL, DON'T! STAY AWAY FROM IT!
IT'S TOO DANGEROUS!
POOR HARVEST. I MIGHT LOSE FIVE MINUTES OF SLEEP OVER THIS.
YOU REALIZE THIS IS TOTALLY GOING TO MAKE A LIE OUT OF THOSE "WE CAN NEVER TRUST RAVEN" MEMES, RIGHT?
I'M SURE I'LL HAVE MANY MORE OPPORTUNITIES TO DISAPPOINT YOU ALL IN THE FUTURE--IF WE GET OUT OF HERE, NOW!

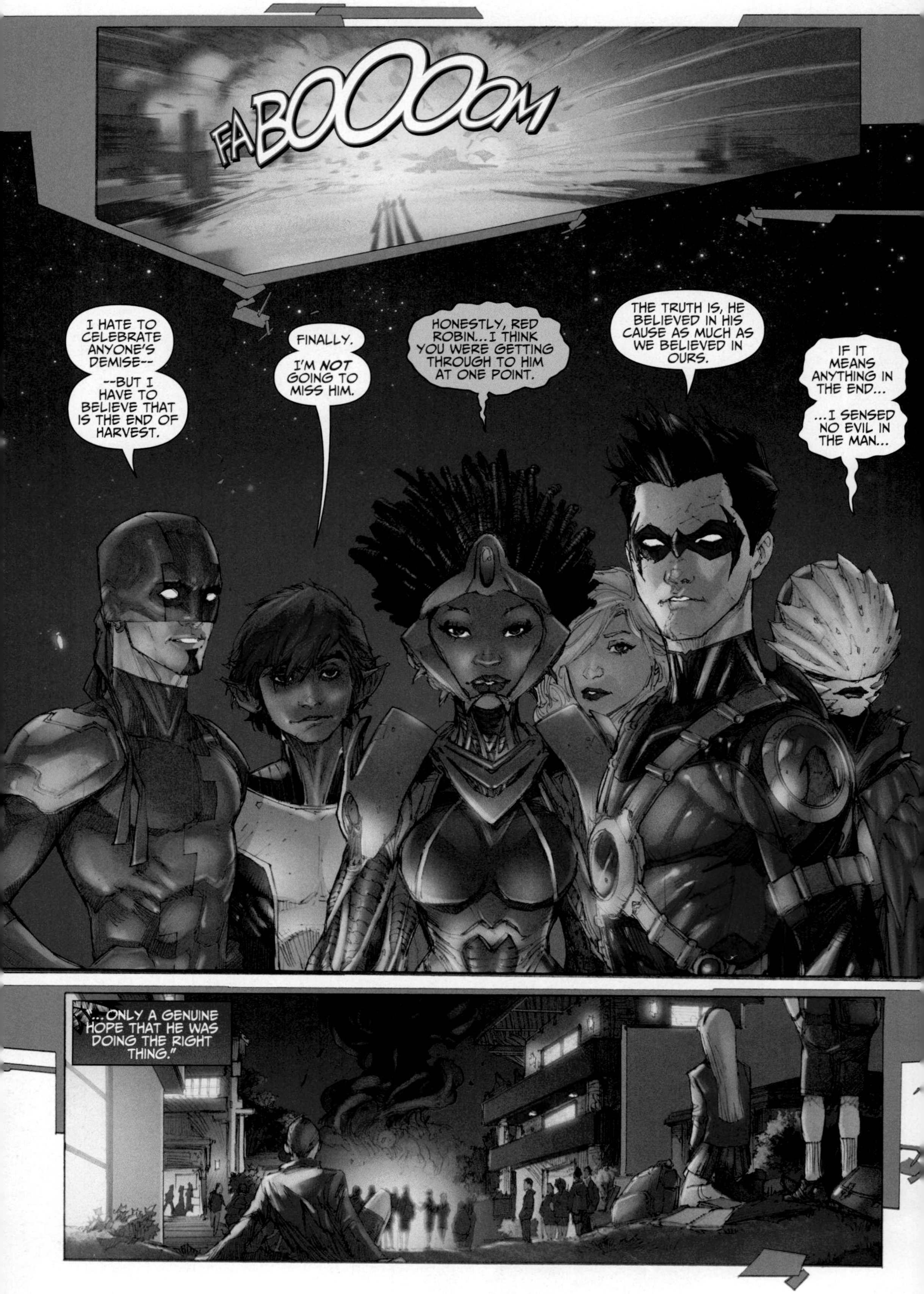
FABOOOOOM
I HATE TO CELEBRATE ANYONE'S DEMISE--
--BUT I HAVE TO BELIEVE THAT IS THE END OF HARVEST.
FINALLY.
I'M NOT GOING TO MISS HIM.
HONESTLY, RED ROBIN...I THINK YOU WERE GETTING THROUGH TO HIM AT ONE POINT.
THE TRUTH IS, HE BELIEVED IN HIS CAUSE AS MUCH AS WE BELIEVED IN OURS.
IF IT MEANS ANYTHING IN THE END...
...I SENSED NO EVIL IN THE MAN...
"...ONLY A GENUINE HOPE THAT HE WAS DOING THE RIGHT THING."

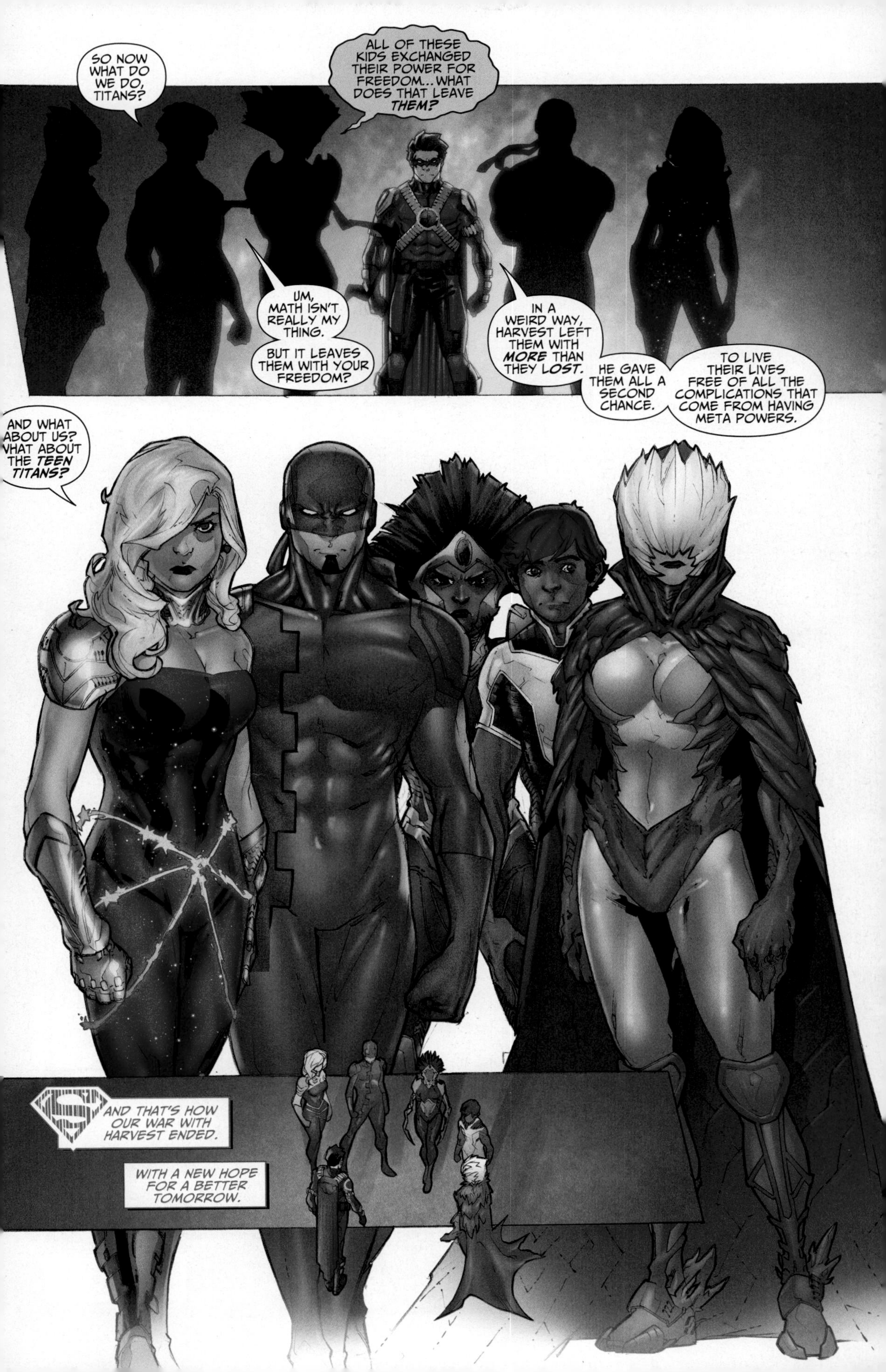

SO NOW WHAT DO WE DO, TITANS?
ALL OF THESE KIDS EXCHANGED THEIR POWER FOR FREEDOM... WHAT DOES THAT LEAVE *THEM?*
UM, MATH ISN'T REALLY MY THING.
BUT IT LEAVES THEM WITH YOUR FREEDOM?
IN A WEIRD WAY, HARVEST LEFT THEM WITH *MORE* THAN THEY *LOST.*
HE GAVE THEM ALL A SECOND CHANCE.
TO LIVE THEIR LIVES FREE OF ALL THE COMPLICATIONS THAT COME FROM HAVING META POWERS.
AND WHAT ABOUT US? WHAT ABOUT THE *TEEN TITANS?*
AND THAT'S HOW OUR WAR WITH HARVEST ENDED.
WITH A NEW HOPE FOR A BETTER TOMORROW.

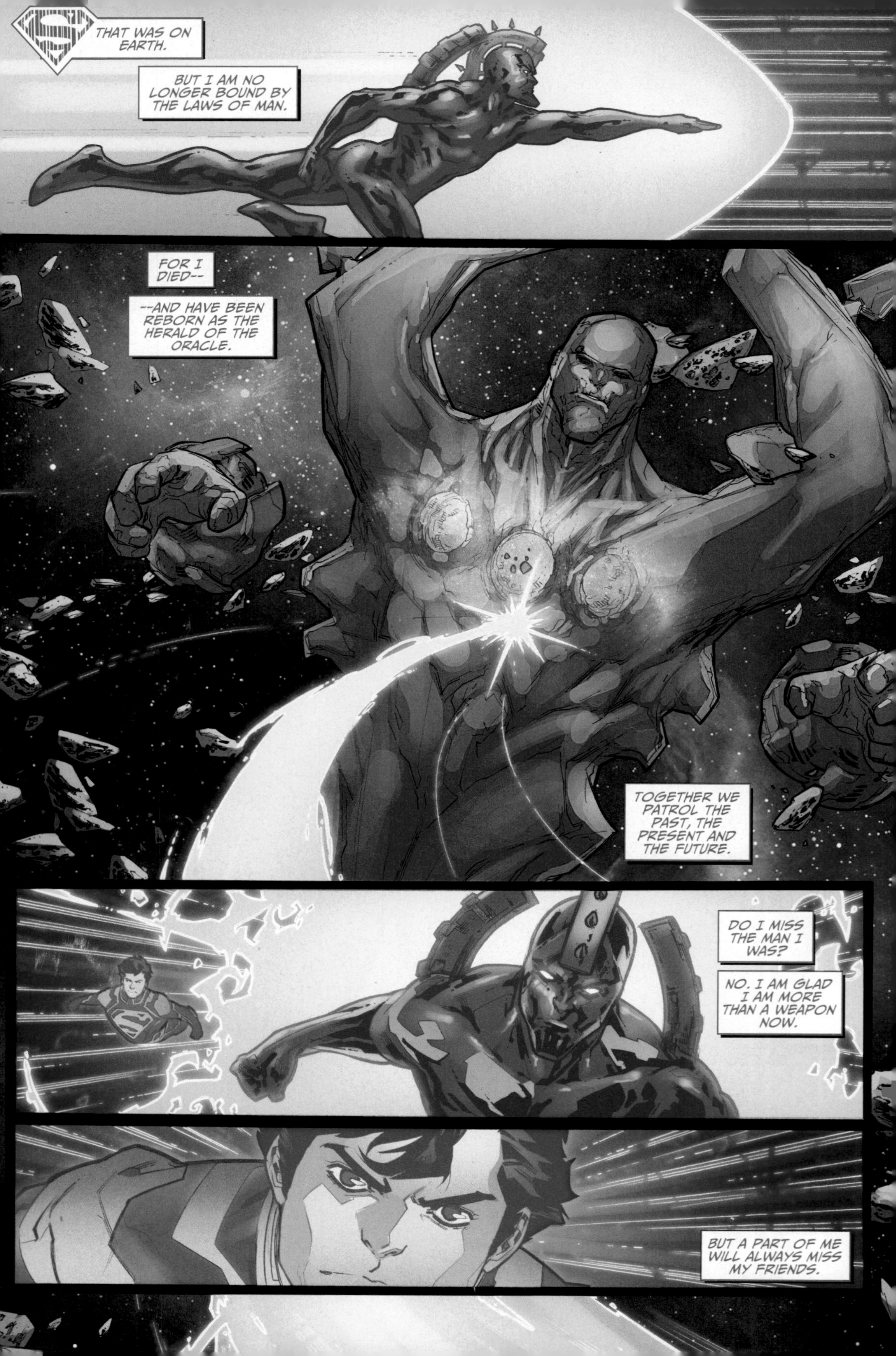
THAT WAS ON EARTH.
BUT I AM NO LONGER BOUND BY THE LAWS OF MAN.
FOR I DIED--
--AND HAVE BEEN REBORN AS THE HERALD OF THE ORACLE.
TOGETHER WE PATROL THE PAST, THE PRESENT AND THE FUTURE.
DO I MISS THE MAN I WAS?
NO. I AM GLAD I AM MORE THAN A WEAPON NOW.
BUT A PART OF ME WILL ALWAYS MISS MY FRIENDS.

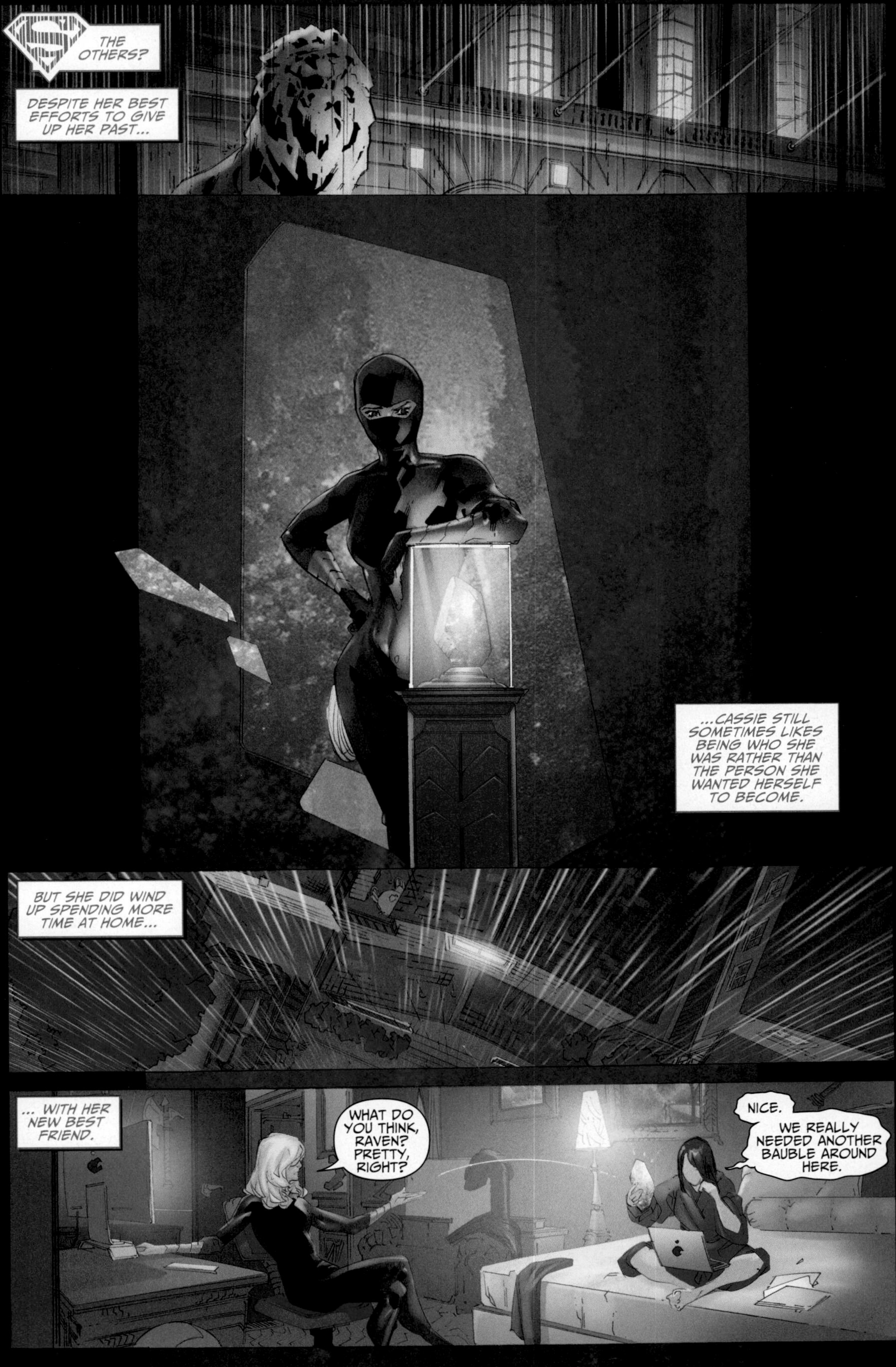
THE OTHERS?
DESPITE HER BEST EFFORTS TO GIVE UP HER PAST...
...CASSIE STILL SOMETIMES LIKES BEING WHO SHE WAS RATHER THAN THE PERSON SHE WANTED HERSELF TO BECOME.
BUT SHE DID WIND UP SPENDING MORE TIME AT HOME...
... WITH HER NEW BEST FRIEND.
WHAT DO YOU THINK, RAVEN? PRETTY, RIGHT?
NICE.
WE REALLY NEEDED ANOTHER BAUBLE AROUND HERE.

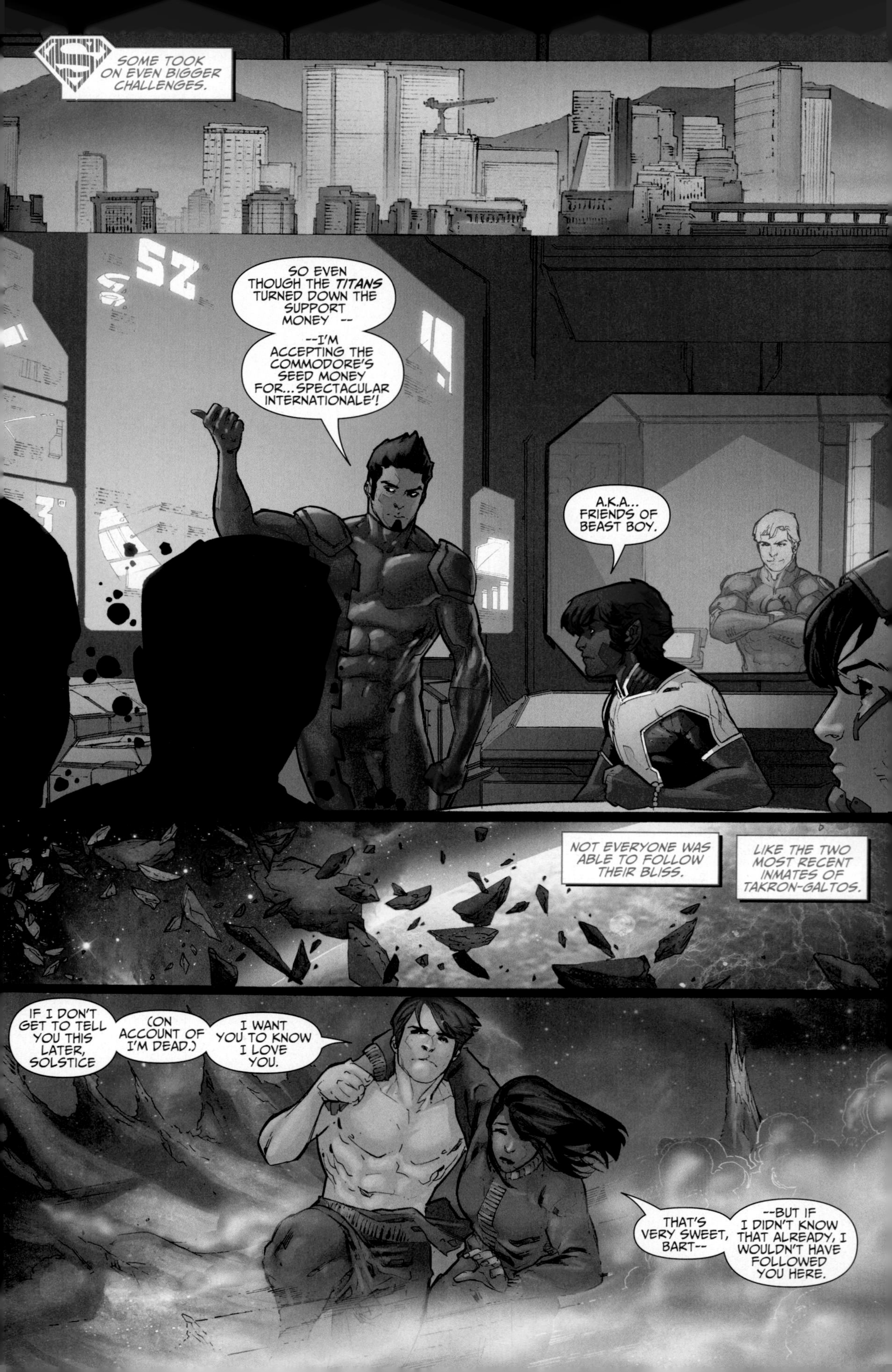
SOME TOOK ON EVEN BIGGER CHALLENGES.
SO EVEN THOUGH THE TITANS TURNED DOWN THE SUPPORT MONEY --
--I'M ACCEPTING THE COMMODORE'S SEED MONEY FOR...SPECTACULAR INTERNATIONALE'!
A.K.A... FRIENDS OF BEAST BOY.
NOT EVERYONE WAS ABLE TO FOLLOW THEIR BLISS.
LIKE THE TWO MOST RECENT INMATES OF TAKRON-GALTOS.
IF I DON'T GET TO TELL YOU THIS LATER, SOLSTICE
(ON ACCOUNT OF I'M DEAD.)
I WANT YOU TO KNOW I LOVE YOU.
THAT'S VERY SWEET, BART--
--BUT IF I DIDN'T KNOW THAT ALREADY, I WOULDN'T HAVE FOLLOWED YOU HERE.

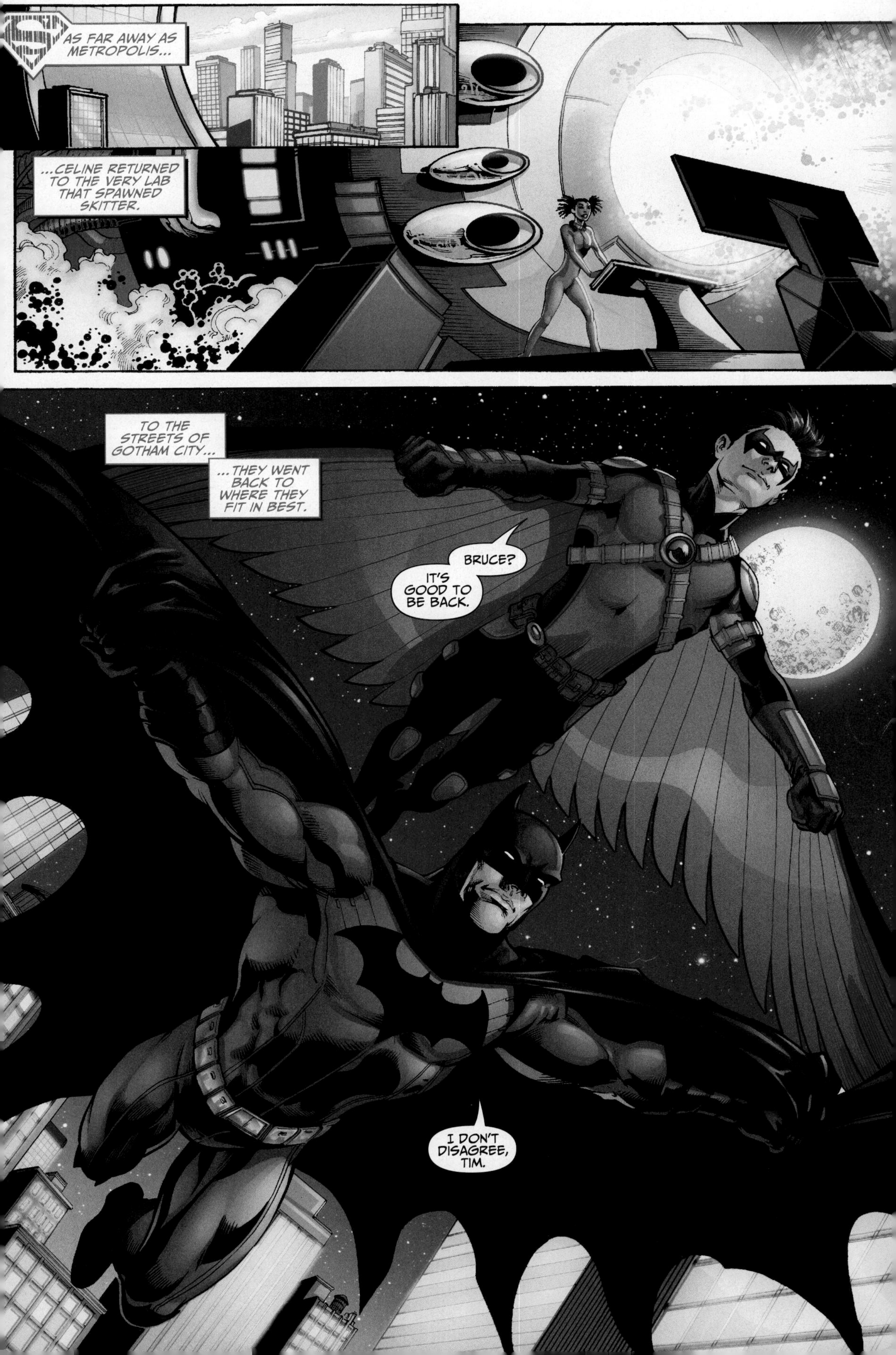
AS FAR AWAY AS METROPOLIS...
...CELINE RETURNED TO THE VERY LAB THAT SPAWNED SKITTER.
TO THE STREETS OF GOTHAM CITY...
...THEY WENT BACK TO WHERE THEY FIT IN BEST.
BRUCE?
IT'S GOOD TO BE BACK.
I DON'T DISAGREE, TIM.

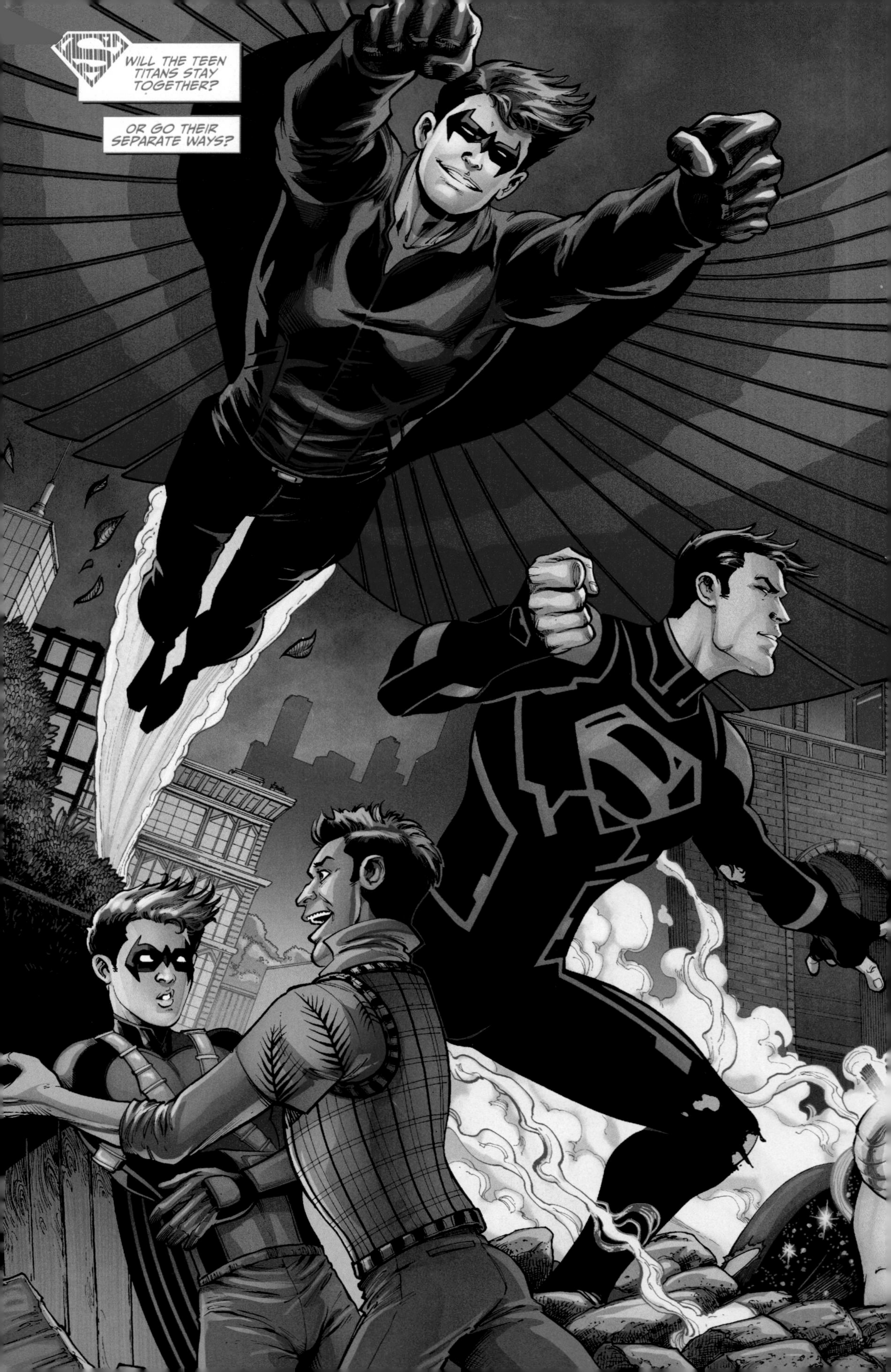
WILL THE TEEN TITANS STAY TOGETHER?
OR GO THEIR SEPARATE WAYS?

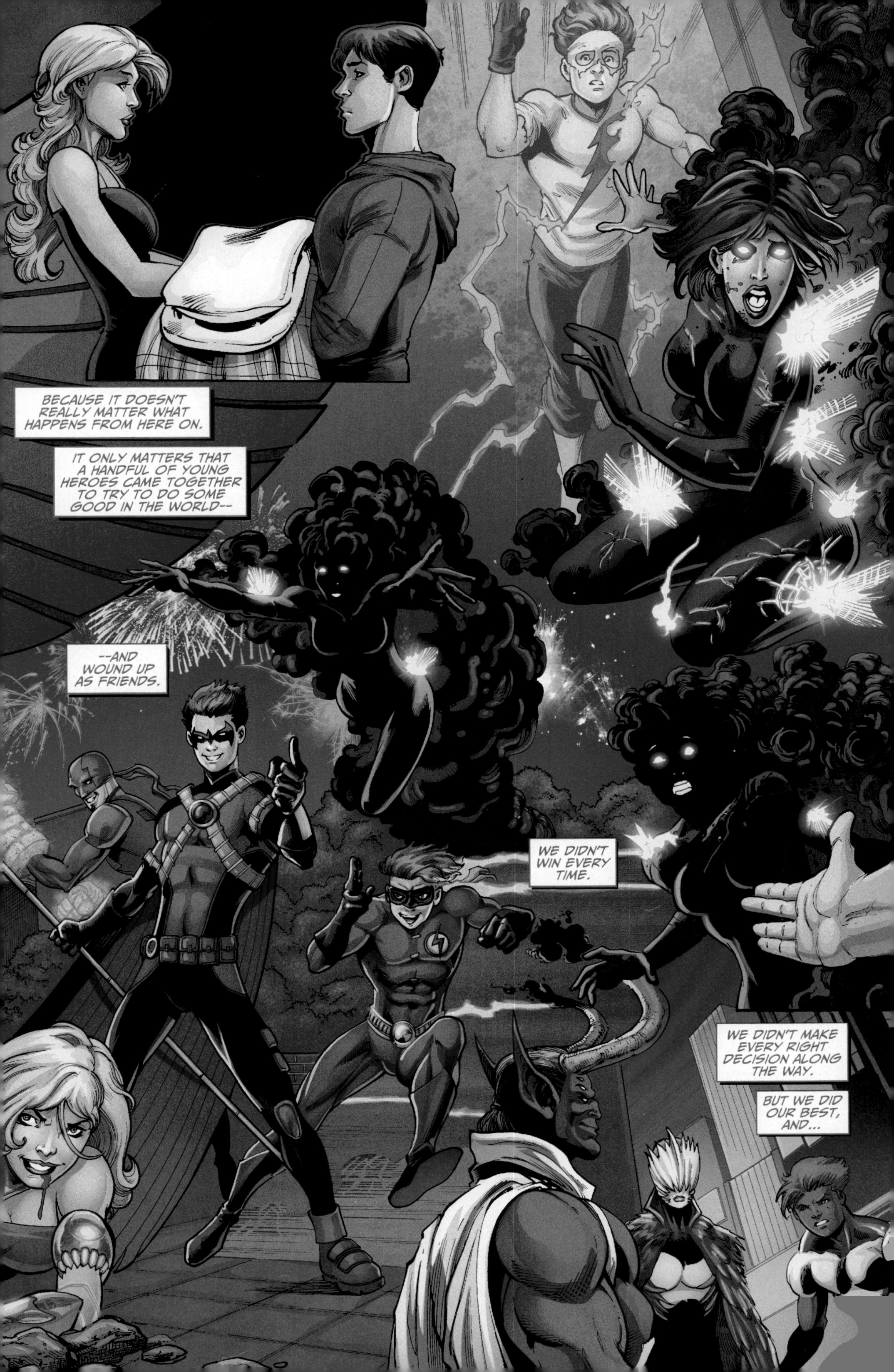
BECAUSE IT DOESN'T REALLY MATTER WHAT HAPPENS FROM HERE ON.
IT ONLY MATTERS THAT A HANDFUL OF YOUNG HEROES CAME TOGETHER TO TRY TO DO SOME GOOD IN THE WORLD--
--AND WOUND UP AS FRIENDS.
WE DIDN'T WIN EVERY TIME.
WE DIDN'T MAKE EVERY RIGHT DECISION ALONG THE WAY.
BUT WE DID OUR BEST, AND...

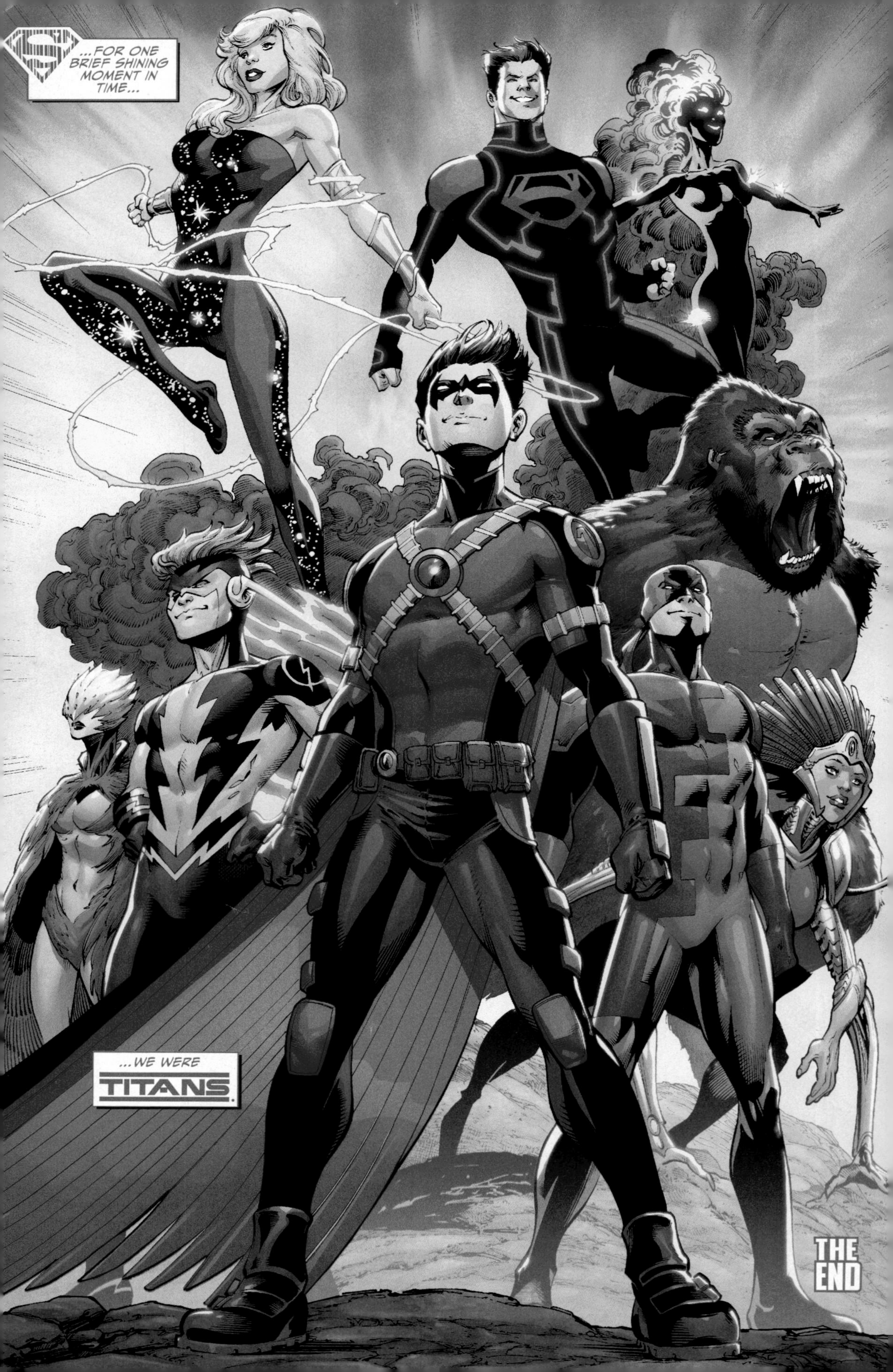
...FOR ONE BRIEF SHINING MOMENT IN TIME...
...WE WERE
TITANS.
THE END

VARIANT COVER GALLERY

TEEN TITANS #27
SCRIBBLENAUTS variant by Jon Katz after George Perez

TEEN TITANS #28 VARIANT
by Jason Pearson

TEEN TITANS #29
Robot Chicken variant by RC Stoodios, LLC

TEEN TITANS #30
MAD variant by Roberto Parada

TEEN TITANS UNUSED VARIANT
by Michael and Laura Allred

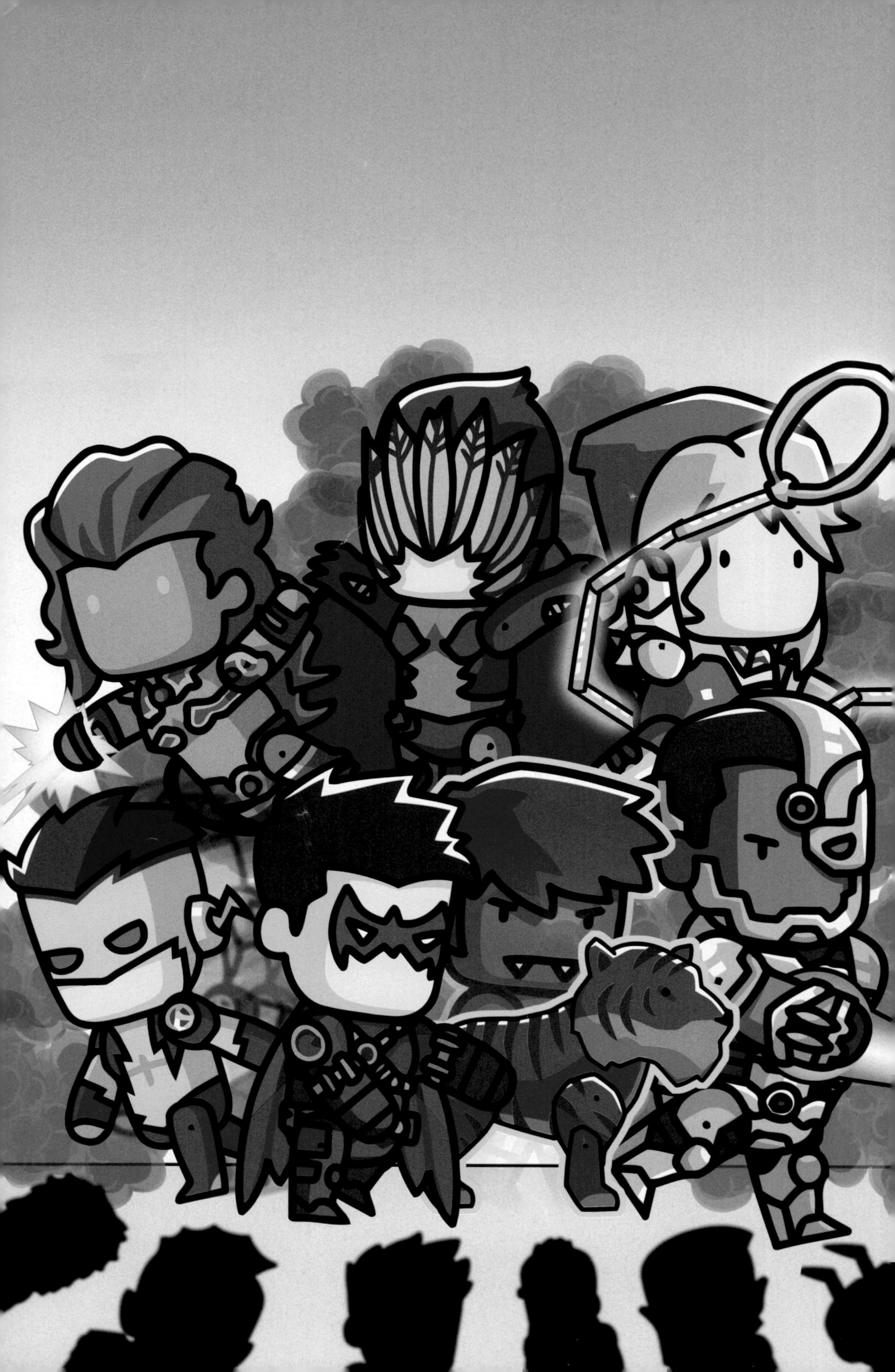

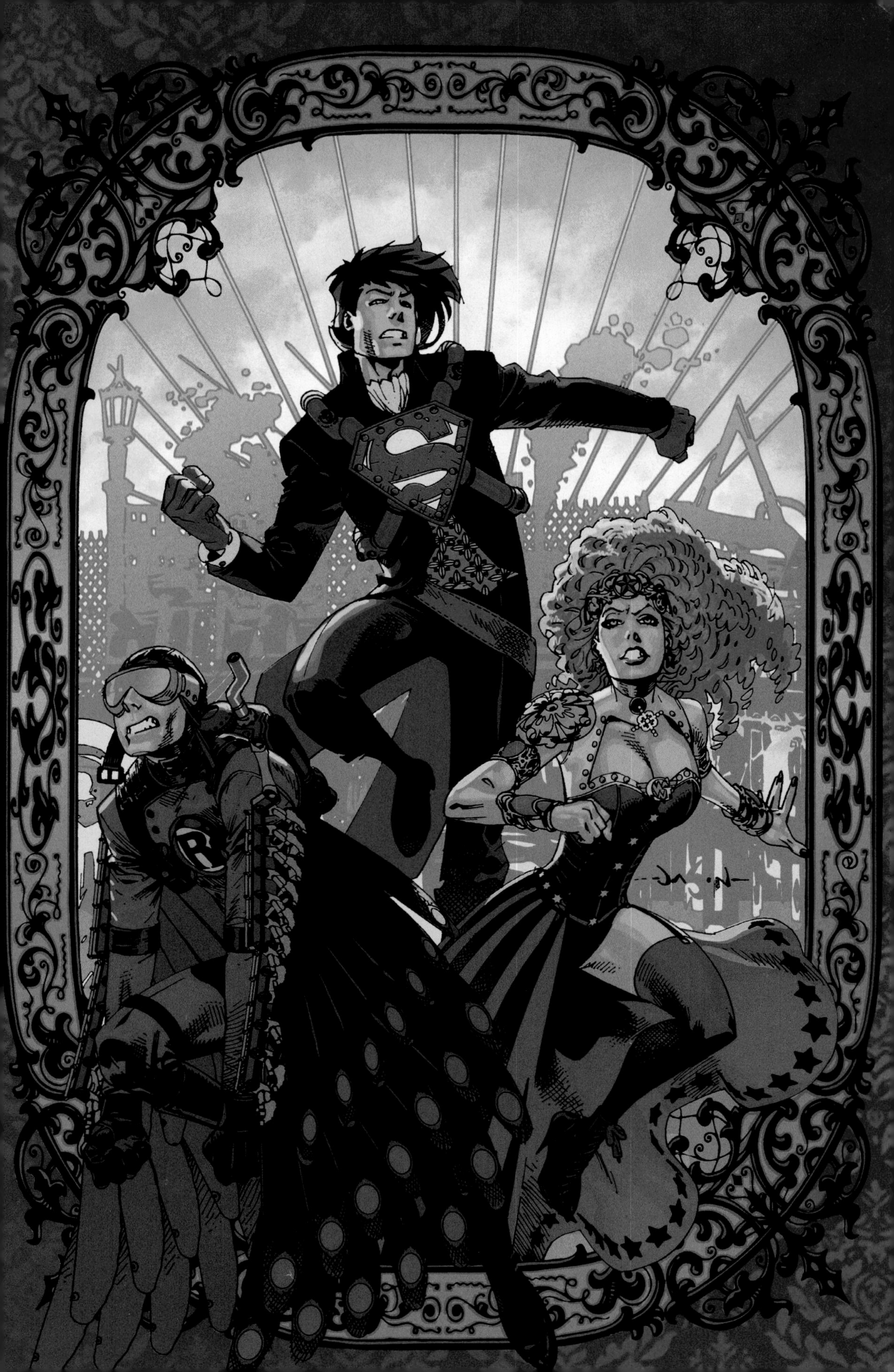

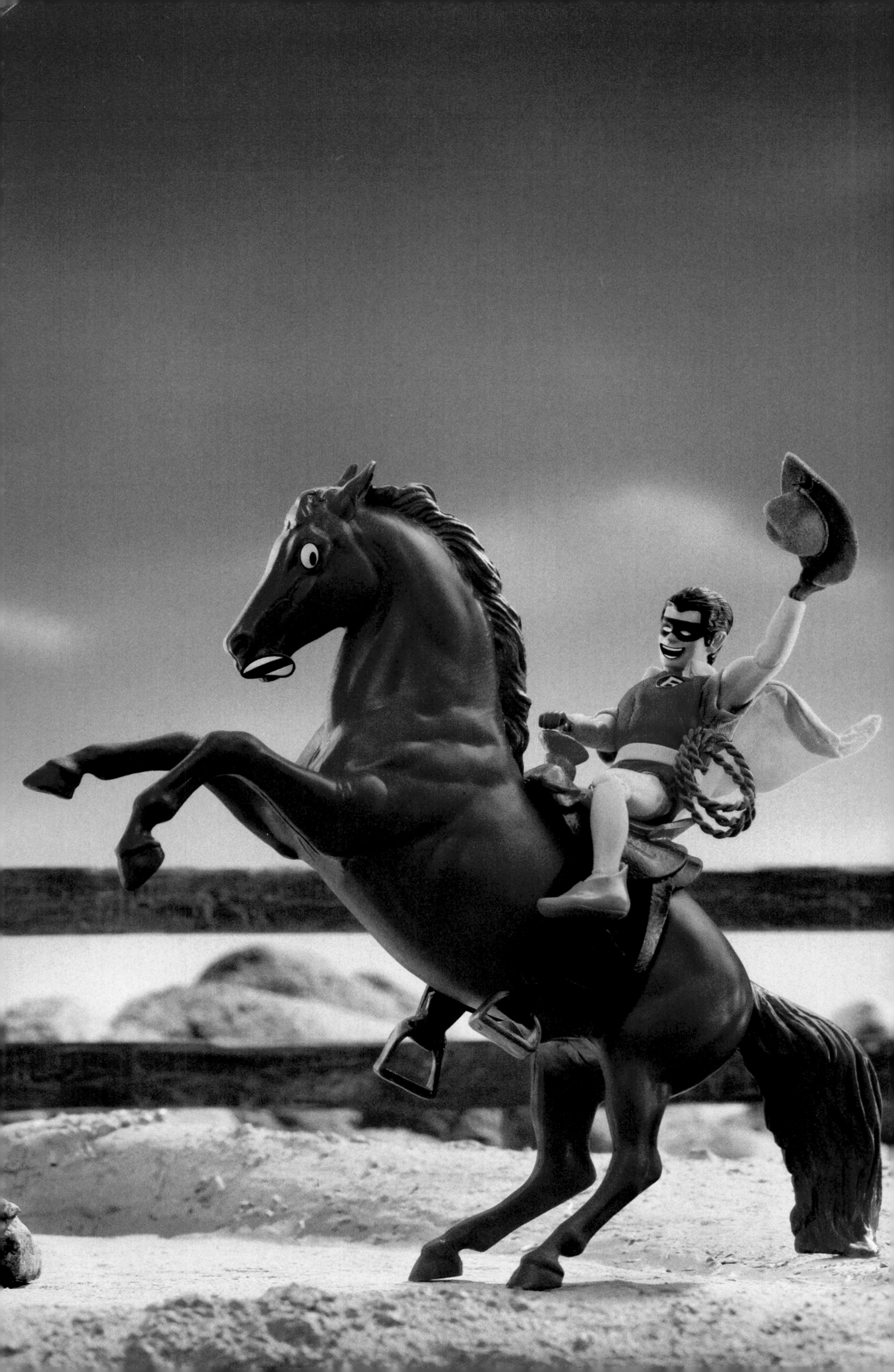

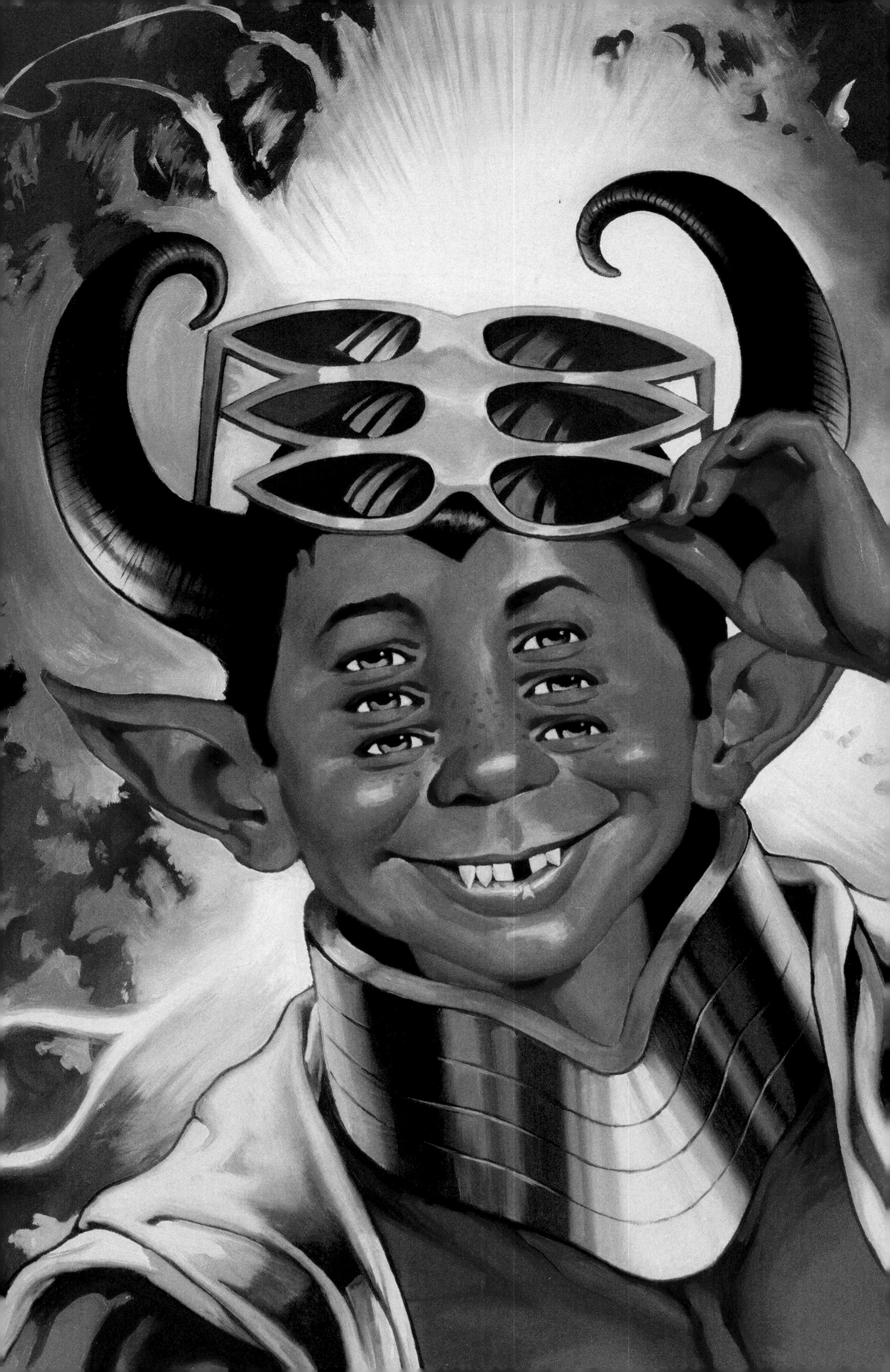

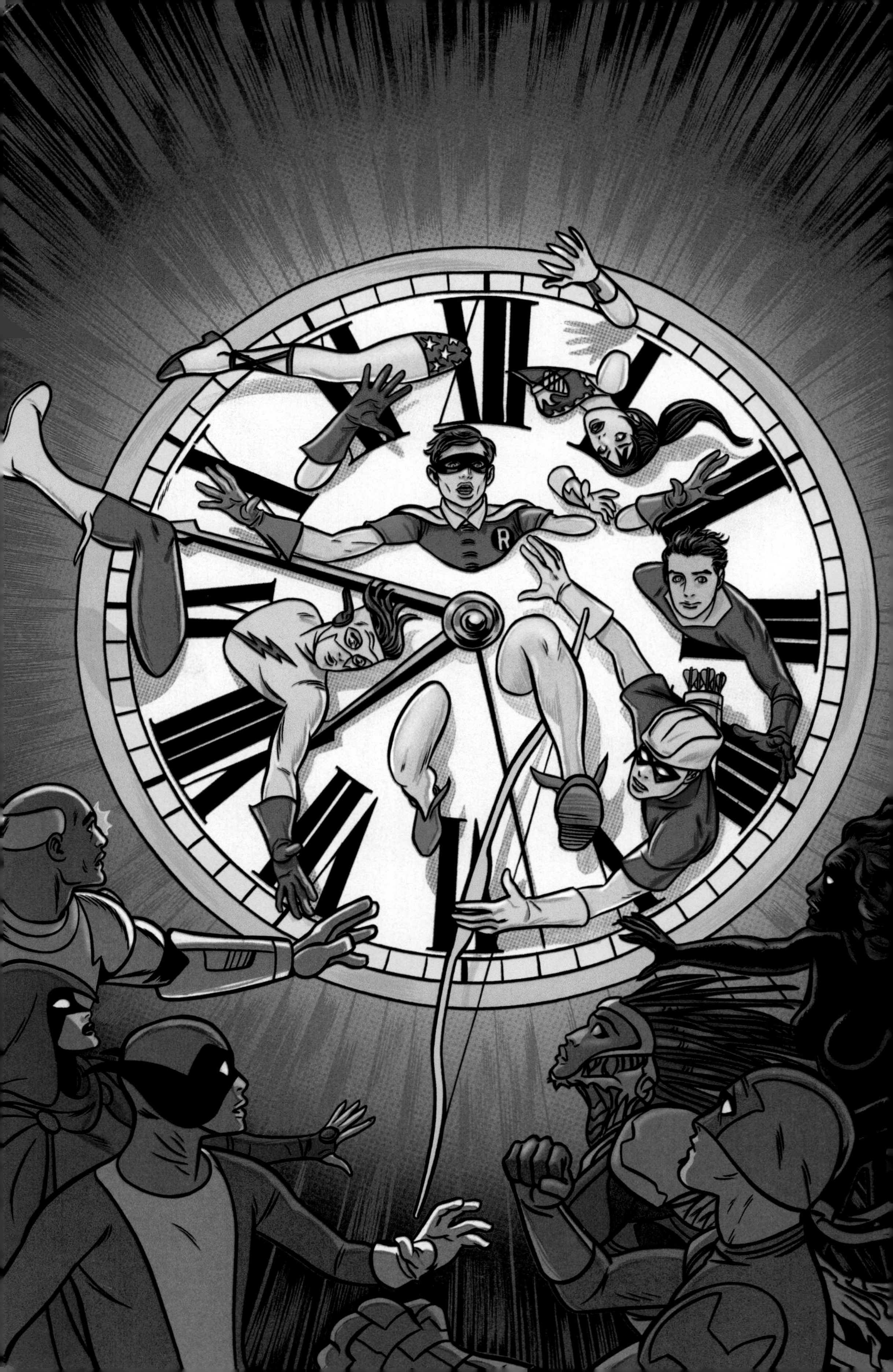

START AT THE BEGINNING!

TEEN TITANS
VOLUME 1: IT'S OUR RIGHT TO FIGHT

**TEEN TITANS
VOL. 2: THE CULLING**

**TEEN TITANS VOL. 3:
DEATH OF THE FAMILY**

**THE CULLING: RISE OF
THE RAVAGERS**

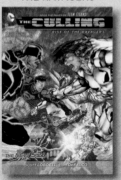

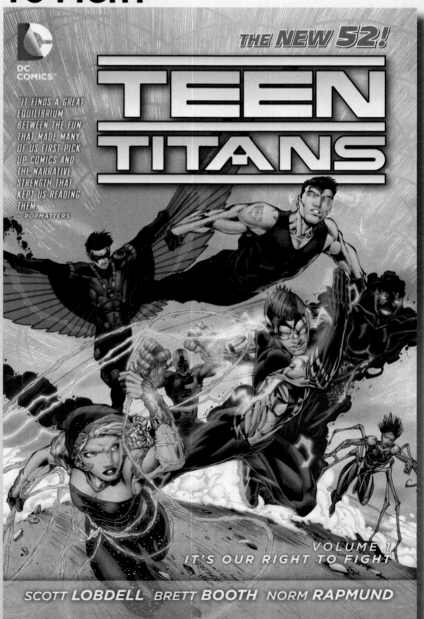

"Flash fans should breathe a sigh of relief that the character is 100% in the right hands."—MTV GEEK

START AT THE BEGINNING!

THE FLASH
VOLUME 1: MOVE FORWARD

THE FLASH VOL. 2: ROGUES REVOLUTION

THE FLASH VOL. 3: GORILLA WARFARE

JUSTICE LEAGUE VOL. 1: ORIGIN

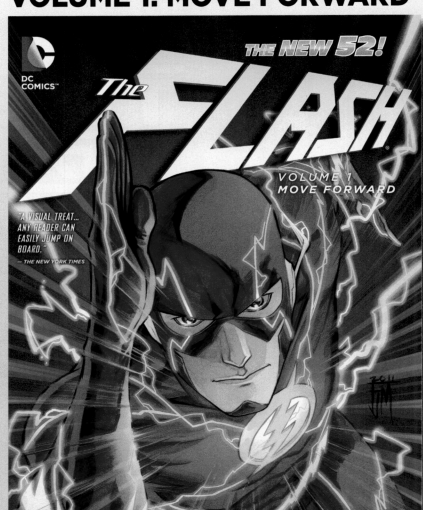

FRANCIS **MANAPUL**   BRIAN **BUCCELLATO**

"It's fresh air. I like this all-too-human Superman, and I think a lot of you will, too."
—SCRIPPS HOWARD NEWS SERVICE

START AT THE BEGINNING!

SUPERMAN: ACTION COMICS VOLUME 1: SUPERMAN AND THE MEN OF STEEL

SUPERMAN VOLUME 1: WHAT PRICE TOMORROW?

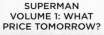

SUPERGIRL VOLUME 1: THE LAST DAUGHTER OF KRYPTON

SUPERBOY VOLUME 1: INCUBATION

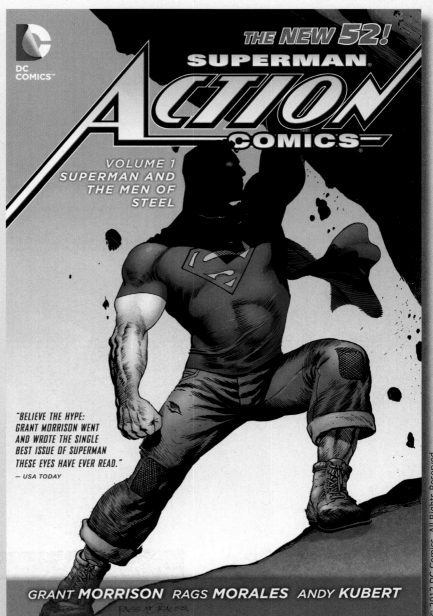

"BELIEVE THE HYPE: GRANT MORRISON WENT AND WROTE THE SINGLE BEST ISSUE OF SUPERMAN THESE EYES HAVE EVER READ."
— USA TODAY

GRANT **MORRISON**   RAGS **MORALES**   ANDY **KUBERT**